Under the Spell of Freedom

Under the Spell of Freedom

Theory of Religion after Hegel and Nietzsche

HANS JOAS

Translated by
ALEX SKINNER

OXFORD
UNIVERSITY PRESS

Oxford University Press is a department of the University of Oxford. It furthers the University's objective of excellence in research, scholarship, and education by publishing worldwide. Oxford is a registered trade mark of Oxford University Press in the UK and certain other countries.

Published in the United States of America by Oxford University Press
198 Madison Avenue, New York, NY 10016, United States of America.

© Oxford University Press 2024

All rights reserved. No part of this publication may be reproduced, stored in a retrieval system, or transmitted, in any form or by any means, without the prior permission in writing of Oxford University Press, or as expressly permitted by law, by license, or under terms agreed with the appropriate reproduction rights organization. Inquiries concerning reproduction outside the scope of the above should be sent to the Rights Department, Oxford University Press, at the address above.

You must not circulate this work in any other form
and you must impose this same condition on any acquirer.

CIP data is on file at the Library of Congress

ISBN 978-0-19-764215-3

DOI: 10.1093/oso/9780197642153.001.0001

Printed by Integrated Books International, United States of America

For my own part, I doubt whether a man can ever support at the same time complete religious independence and entire public freedom. And I am inclined to think, that if faith be wanting in him, he must serve; and if he be free, he must believe.

Alexis de Tocqueville[1]

Contents

Preface ix

Introduction: Hegel's Philosophy of Freedom and a Blind Spot in Present-Day Hegelianism 1

PART I. A NEW UNDERSTANDING OF RELIGION IN THE EARLY TWENTIETH CENTURY

1. Introductory Remarks 21
2. The Independence of Religion: Ernst Troeltsch 40
3. Secular Sacredness: Rudolf Otto 52
4. Self-Evidence or Sense of Self-Evidence?: Max Scheler 69

PART II. SECULARIZATION AND THE MODERN HISTORY OF FREEDOM

1. Introductory Remarks 87
2. The Sacralization of Democracy: John Dewey 99
3. Post-totalitarian Christianity: Alfred Döblin's Religious Dialogues 115
4. The Contingency of Secularization: Reinhart Koselleck's Theory of History 132
5. The Secular Option, Its Rise and Consequences: Charles Taylor 147

PART III. THE SEARCH FOR A DIFFERENT KIND OF FREEDOM

1. Introductory Remarks — 163
2. A German Idea of Freedom?: Cassirer and Troeltsch between Germany and the West — 173
3. Indebted Freedom: Paul Tillich — 196
4. Sieve of Norms and Holy Scripture, Theonomy, and Freedom: Paul Ricœur — 215
5. Communicative Freedom and Theology of Liberation: Wolfgang Huber — 226

PART IV. THE PROJECT OF A HISTORICAL SOCIOLOGY OF RELIGION

1. Introductory Remarks — 241
2. Religion Is More Than Culture: H. Richard Niebuhr — 256
3. Christianity and the Dangers of Self-Sacralization: Werner Stark — 277
4. More Weberian Than Weber?: David Martin — 299
5. Religious Evolution and Symbolic Realism: Robert Bellah — 316
6. Religion and Globalization: José Casanova — 330

Conclusion: Global History of Religion and Moral Universalism — 344

A Note on the Text — 363
Notes — 365
Bibliography — 435
Name Index — 473
Subject Index — 479

Preface

How do the history of religion and the history of political freedom relate to one another? The range of answers to be found within philosophy, the social sciences, and among the general public is vast and defies easy summation. For many, Hegel's grandiose philosophy-of-history synthesis, which presents us with a teleological development leading to Christianity and through it to political freedom, is still a vital source of orientation, however much it may have been revised in the detail. Even those who build on Hegel in Marxian ways tend to retain key components of this synthesis. For others, Nietzsche's strident critique of Christianity and his rejection of the modern liberal-democratic political order, again despite reservations of various kinds, are crucial to their own thinking.

For many years I have sought to formulate an alternative to these modes of thought. In addition to my engagement with American pragmatism, as the philosophical basis of such an alternative, and my books on a general theory of action, the genesis of values, the history of human rights, the history of religion, and war and violence, I have always been on the lookout for more "friends in history" (as the great Confucian philosopher Mencius put it), that is, thinkers of past and present whose writings are an enduring source of inspiration and provide important points of departure for the kind of alternative to Hegel and Nietzsche I have in mind.

The origins of the present book lie in the idea of bringing together the portraits, as I have drawn them over time in scattered writings, of these important twentieth-century and present-day thinkers and scholars who have contributed to the theory of religion, while adding a number of others as well. To avoid giving an impression of randomness, this must involve more than just lining these thinkers up in a row; I seek to show that here we can identify a tradition in its own right. It is in fact clear that these various intellectual approaches not only feature many parallels but also numerous influences and cross-references. In the introduction to this book and in the lead-ins to its four major parts, I tease out the thread—perhaps difficult to discern at first glance—that runs through these different accounts.

The result of these efforts is something halfway between a monograph and a collection of articles. If I may be permitted a literary analogy, we might say that this book is neither a novel nor a mere collection of stories, but rather a novella cycle, though one intended to paint a coherent overall picture.

While there are undoubtedly advantages to this approach, it does come at a certain cost. One of the pros, as I see it, is that what I grapple with here are not pre-schematized arguments corralled into a fictitious system, but individual intellectual "totalities," together with their historical embeddedness and specific genesis. Apart from anything else, this "holistic" view seems to me well suited to underlining the vitality of these ideas in their specific forms and within their particular intellectual constellations. It may also be a straightforward practical advantage that, as a result, the chapters can be read individually; there is no need to read them in the exact order in which I have arranged them here.

It must be acknowledged, however, that this approach also imposes certain limitations. The most important is that my scattered allusions to an alternative historical narrative are nowhere neatly summarized, not even when I look ahead in the concluding part. This is the task of a future project, for which my books on the "power of the sacred," the emergence of moral universalism in the so-called Axial Age, and the history of human rights provide the foundation stones. Another disadvantage is that while I examine thinkers and scholars who considered it important that they were neither Hegelians nor Nietzscheans, I do not provide an adequate account of Hegel and Nietzsche in all their own complexity. It is not my goal to add yet another title to the vast interpretative literature on these two thinkers. Instead, I seek to present alternatives to them.

The opportunities and risks entailed in this approach are intertwined. Some will doubt the value of engaging with forgotten or little-known authors, especially since they often worked within the disciplines of theology and sociology, which are at present perceived as sinking ships. Others will sense that in the writings of, for example, Ernst Troeltsch and Paul Tillich, H. Richard Niebuhr and Paul Ricœur, David Martin and Robert Bellah— as well as Charles Taylor, whose work drew heavily on Hegel—we can discern insights that diverge from or go beyond a renewed Hegelianism (or Nietzscheanism). Furthermore, these thinkers influenced each other in notable ways, and their academic careers were often interlinked, reinforcing the impression that it might be justifiable to refer to a concealed tradition here. This can be swiftly illustrated with reference to Paul Tillich, who described himself as a student of Ernst Troeltsch. Appointed to a post at Frankfurt University in 1928, there he saw himself as the intellectual successor to Max Scheler. He was also strongly influenced by Ernst Cassirer and Rudolf Otto. When Tillich emigrated from Germany to the United States soon after the Nazis took power, H. Richard Niebuhr, who had already translated one of Tillich's books into English, did much to help him in his new home. Later, at Harvard, Tillich became one of Robert Bellah's most important academic teachers. Tillich's successor in his chair at the University of Chicago was Paul Ricœur, who also drew intellectual inspiration from him.

It would be wholly inadequate to think solely in terms of a liberal-Protestant tradition in this regard; not all of the Protestant thinkers considered here would feel comfortable with this designation, and it would fail to account for their similarities with non-Protestant authors. Even more important than the interdenominational character of this intellectual development is its interdisciplinary character. To do justice to it, I use the term "theory of religion" in analogy to the increasingly common "social theory." The institutional locus of social theory and theory of religion is not a single discipline, not even philosophy or theology. It is precisely at the points of overlap between various disciplines that the developments with which I am concerned in this book have occurred. If this intuition gives rise to new lines of argument, the book's goal will have been achieved.

In the main, I express my appreciation for suggestions and help in the relevant individual chapters. At this point, though, I would like to thank Torsten Meireis (Berlin) for the opportunity to present certain parts of my manuscript for discussion in his advanced seminar. His comments and those of other participants were particularly useful when it came to reworking the introduction. Meanwhile, and this is worthy of special emphasis, a number of colleagues and friends took on the task of reading the entire manuscript. To them I owe a special debt of gratitude. The same three individuals also provided me with outstanding support to the benefit of the original German version of my book *The Power of the Sacred* in 2017. Due to the terrible pandemic that affected us all during the final phase of work on the present book, I was unable to listen to their feedback on my first draft in face-to-face meetings. Philosopher Matthias Jung (Koblenz) and sociologist Wolfgang Knöbl (Hamburg) helped me a great deal through their written critiques. Berlin-based theologian (and former Protestant bishop) Wolfgang Huber and I, meanwhile, were unwilling to forgo a spoken exchange. I will never forget our telephone conversation, conducted in quick succession over the course of three calls and lasting more than eight hours in total, which entailed a blend of substantive debate and thorough work on the text itself.

My work has been generously supported by the Porticus Foundation since 2014 and, since January 1, 2016, by a Max Planck Research Prize, for both of which I am extremely grateful. Thanks are also due to my research assistant Jan Philipp Hahn for his committed and attentive support; to Eva Gilmer, head of the scholarly books program at Suhrkamp Verlag, for encouraging comments and outstanding copyediting; and to Christian Scherer for once again, as so often in the past, making a signal contribution through his superb proofreading and compilation of the index. Finally, as ever, a huge thank-you to my wife, Heidrun, for her intellectual companionship and life-sustaining presence.

Introduction: Hegel's Philosophy of Freedom and a Blind Spot in Present-Day Hegelianism

This book deals with some of the most important figures in the theory of religion of the twentieth and early twenty-first centuries. Their selection is not based on an antecedent yardstick that might permit us to judge who does or does not deserve to be described as "important." Instead, my decision to explore the work of a given thinker was made in light of an exploratory survey of intellectual history and the history of scholarship. It was guided by my sense that each of the authors I consider is a leading light who excites current interest when it comes to the questions arising at the intersection of sociology, theology, philosophy, and history (when they grapple with religion in their different ways)—questions explored within these disciplines or in the field of religious studies.

The term "selection" actually sounds too voluntaristic to convey the picture that emerges from this survey. In no way do I seek to achieve encyclopedic completeness, nor do I strive to strike a balance between the confessions or between believers and advocates of secular worldviews. Representatives of religions other than Christianity are absent entirely. Since—as will become apparent—overcoming Eurocentric perspectives is one of the strongest motives underlying the present book, I myself view the lack of non-Western thinkers, Christian or otherwise, as reflecting the most significant limitation to my present state of knowledge. The fact—vital to mention in today's world—that all the chapters are devoted to male thinkers is, to the best of my knowledge and belief, not due to conscious or unconscious bias in my selection, but to history itself, which cannot be retrospectively corrected. Still, the introductions to the four major parts of the book make reference to other relevant thinkers, with whom I have dealt in detail elsewhere or whose work awaits in-depth exploration.

With regard to the theory of religion, I have already alluded to the existence of areas of overlap between different disciplines, a zone of intersection that merits special attention. Once again, this is not a matter of a subjective decision or an abstract preference for interdisciplinarity, as if this were bound to be more effective than a strictly disciplinary approach. Instead, I am guided by the substantive thesis that it has become impossible to discuss religion and the history of religion other than in connection with the normative demands and history of political freedom; after a world-historical phase of increasing globalization whose future trajectories are now a matter of uncertainty, this discussion must be undertaken within a global framework, one not limited to a particular country, continent, civilization, or religious community. This connection between discourses on religion and freedom is signaled in the book's title. Since the eighteenth century, I would assert, the dialogue on faith has, explicitly or implicitly, come under the "spell of freedom."

I borrow an expression here that appears in the ambitious blueprint for a theory of justice presented a few years ago by philosopher Axel Honneth.[1] This schema essentially sets out to revive and update ideas first developed in substantial form in Hegel's philosophy of law. Right at the start of the first main section of Honneth's book we read that it has now become almost impossible to articulate any one of the values of modernity without declaring it merely an ancillary facet of the idea of individual autonomy: "As if by magical attraction, all modern ethical ideals have been placed under the spell of freedom; sometimes they infuse this idea with greater depth or add new accents, but they never manage to posit an independent, stand-alone alternative."[2]

In a footnote to this passage, Honneth refers to an argument put forward by Canadian philosopher Charles Taylor that supposedly points in the same direction. This is somewhat perplexing: if we look up the relevant passage,[3] Taylor by no means states that the value of freedom has attained indubitable hegemony amid the competition of values, effectively bringing such competition to an end. Instead, Taylor is seeking to characterize modernity by positing an inherently pluralist and differentiated, by no means contradiction-free "package" of value orientations. This, Taylor contends, compels individuals to strike a balance between the values that coexist within this package despite appearing to be mutually exclusive. According to Taylor, then, what is hegemonic is not a specific value, not even that of freedom, but rather "a sense of self defined by the powers of disengaged reason as well as of the creative imagination." We moderns are all implicated "in the characteristically modern understandings of freedom and dignity and rights, in the ideals of self-fulfilment and expression, and in the demands of universal benevolence and justice."[4] By no means are we dealing here with mere shadows cast by the ideal of freedom.

Even so, Taylor would presumably not deny that the ideal of freedom is an important component of the "package" of modern values and that all questions of orientation have come under the spell of this complex of values that includes freedom.

The gap between Honneth and Taylor on this point has not gone unnoticed in the critical debate on Honneth's theory of justice. In a particularly astute contribution, Christoph Halbig goes so far as to state that Taylor drew "exactly the opposite conclusion" as Honneth.[5] But even more important than this observation is Halbig's distinction between three possible readings of the "spell" thesis. In line with my earlier remarks, he states that the primacy of the value of freedom could be meant in a normative sense. In other words, should there, for example, be a conflict between the values of self-determination and equality, we must always opt for freedom in the shape of self-determination. However, he goes on, this primacy might also be envisaged as explanatory, such that "the value of human subjects lies in their capacity for self-determination,"[6] though this by no means arises from self-evident moral intuitions. Finally, according to Halbig, this primacy may even be understood ontologically and semantically. This is what must be meant whenever it is stated that all other values of modernity can now only be understood within the framework of the ideal of freedom, as its semantic components, which in principle rules out a genuine conflict between freedom and other values.

This critic's demonstration of the ambiguity of his spell thesis gave Honneth a chance to clarify things, of which he availed himself in a reply. Here he emphasizes that, in line with the goals of a theory of justice, he is not really concerned with the range of values that individuals regard as guiding their lives, but only with the value "that can be generalized or . . . that falls within the realm of an 'overlapping consensus,' so that conclusions can then be drawn about the social or institutional preconditions for a realization of freedom that is equally possible for everyone."[7] This clarification may, of course, be viewed as a retreat to the quasi-orthodox position of a liberal theory of justice, as it appears in John Rawls's epoch-making oeuvre.[8] The primacy of freedom would then be limited to the idea of an institutional guarantee of "spheres of freedom" that "are equally in the interest of all of us, the members of modern societies, regardless of our particular goals of self-realization."[9] On this premise, the primacy of freedom would pertain only in the sense of a concept of justice conceived in light of the question of how to ensure equal freedom. This, however, would render Honneth's Hegelian ambitions incomprehensible.

The confusing argumentational situation arising from Honneth's contribution thus defies such simple resolution, which would also fail to do justice to his goal of envisaging different versions of freedom and interpreting value conflicts in the public realm as disputes over the correct understanding of freedom. This becomes all the clearer if we include the historical dimension, which is not at all necessary in a justice theory à la Rawls but is indispensable in Hegel. Honneth the Hegelian explicitly adopts a "teleological perspective" in this regard, which he even describes as an "inevitable element of modernity's self-understanding."[10] Hence, for Honneth, the triumph of the ideal of freedom in "Western Modernity" should not be imagined as a merely contingent and, in principle, reversible product of historical developments, but as a process of asserting universal normative validity. But here the ambiguity of the spell thesis resurfaces. Empirically, we obviously cannot rule out a reversal of the achievements of the history of freedom—as burned indelibly into our memory by the history of the "Third Reich"—and Honneth himself would have no need to pen polemics against "cognitive barbarization" if he considered such a reversal an empirical impossibility.

From the standpoint of those who share a value, there is in fact something inevitable about a teleology that is not meant empirically but purely in a normative sense,[11] but this has no empirical explanatory power. And a "semantic" thesis, according to which it would simply make no sense to allow a greater pluralism of values, even at the level of a normative theory of society, than Rawls and Honneth do, cannot be justified by the rapid embrace of a teleology.[12] Halbig articulates more sharply still the concern that a narrow focus on the value of freedom might lead to an "impoverishment of moral patterns of reasoning" and to a substantive distortion of alternatives[13]— a consequence that Honneth surely did not intend. But this is in fact the consequence—as it would appear at this point—if claims are made on the basis of Hegel that are underpinned in the latter's work by metaphysical background assumptions that Honneth expressly rejects and that virtually no one still seriously espouses. It is the assumption of a "spirit" gradually realizing itself over the course of world history, an assumption very few would now find persuasive, that facilitates a teleological history of freedom and religion.

The starting point of my reflections so far is the thesis that the discourse on religion, too, had come under the spell of freedom by the eighteenth century at the latest. This thesis is ultimately independent of whether it is put forward within the framework of value pluralism or assumes a monistic value of freedom; although this distinction will crop up time and again, it is not decisive in the present context. It is easy to illustrate what the foregrounding (however understood) of freedom in this field can mean. In the associated discussions, religious faith is either decried as an obstacle to political freedom, as a means of maintaining inequality and oppression, or conversely, at least in the form of Christianity or the Judeo-Christian tradition, is defended as crucial to facilitating political freedom. Religious experience itself is perceived by some as one of the most intense experiences of freedom human beings can have and by others as a gross form of heteronomy, the readiness to submit to imaginary powers of fate. One and the same religious tradition can, it is argued, undergird freedom at the level of doctrine, but as a lived practice it may impede individual freedom—for example, through a blinkered morality. Conversely, a religion whose doctrine is inimical to demands for political freedom may prove a source of strength and freedom for people if its religious practice enables certain experiences. In line with this, the ambiguity of the concept of freedom and its status within a broader philosophy and social theory find reflection in a variety of ways in the theory of religion, if it resides under the spell of freedom.

The same goes for the question of how to assess historically the relationship between faith and political freedom. Here, too, the most varied range of views compete in a way that hampers a clear overview.[14] Some hope for guidance from the grandest synthesis of the history of religion and history of freedom that Western thought has produced—namely Hegel's philosophy of history, along with contemporary thinkers' attempts to revise and update it. As understandable as this is and however obvious a step it may seem to return to Hegel after the loss of credibility suffered by Marxism and particularly its view of religion, I believe it to be a mistake. In fact, as I argue in this book, Hegel's synthesis itself has proven a dead end for the theory of religion. This synthesis must be questioned in fundamental ways and overcome if we are to resolve the problems arising for religion "under the spell of freedom." This I seek to do in the different parts of this book and by building on thinkers who have recognized the Hegelian cul-de-sac as such. The main task of this introduction is to adumbrate the key ways in which I undertake to do this. But let us first return briefly to Honneth's theory of justice from this perspective. This is necessary because it enables us to counter, in exemplary fashion, the impression that one can safely dispense with the theory of religion in present-day social philosophy and social theory.

The aforementioned philosophical reservations have found interesting parallels and supplements in sociological and theological debates. Through a sociological lens, Wolfgang Knöbl in particular has assailed Honneth's Hegelian-teleological line of argument for repeatedly sliding from the "normative reconstruction" of past developments into statements that ascribe to ideas themselves, and especially the idea of freedom, a history-shaping power so strong that the latter's ultimate victory seems inexorable.[15] For Knöbl, this is an extreme version of the evolutionist optimism found in the social scientific modernization theory of the 1950s and 1960s, one that supposedly provides a philosophical rationale for an even more extreme optimism about the future. Honneth has responded by limiting his theory's causal claims more clearly than his book does.[16] One of the criticisms made in theological quarters, meanwhile, is of some importance in the present context. In the introduction to his own reflections on the prospect of religious forms that can protect the present-day individual from the alienation induced by programs of self-optimization, Protestant theologian Rolf Schieder simply draws attention to the astonishing fact that "Axel Honneth's 'outline of a democratic morality' [part of the title of the original German version of the book] takes no account either of education or religion as institutions of the reproduction of that morality—and certainly not in light of their mutual interweaving."[17] This, Schieder contends, is all the more remarkable given that Honneth's book ends with a call for a transnational public sphere that has after all for centuries been prefigured in the "world religions" and the universities.

Honneth's response to Schieder's friendly exhortation to plug these obvious gaps in a future volume can only be described as astonishing. He fully admits to having overlooked "entirely the importance of public education to a democratic morality,"[18] attributing "this major omission" to a "slavish orientation toward Hegel's work"; he then criticizes Hegel and highlights his own attempts to improve on him. Yet he fails completely to respond to the other criticism, namely that he had not addressed the topic of religion at all.

Elsewhere in his reply he makes only very indirect and fleeting mention of cultural stimuli that may arise from religion, or of church-based communities as a form of intermediary organization alongside associations and cultural institutions.[19] Perhaps more important is his somewhat cryptic statement that he had omitted a planned section of concluding observations because then "an entire chapter on the present-day formation of the 'absolute spirit' [might have been] necessary":[20] in Hegel, of course, this is the systematic locus of the philosophy of religion. We can also read this remark as an expression of respect for the magnitude of the unfinished business involved. But the fact is that this important social-theoretical attempt to bring Hegel up to date not only fails to address the topic of religion but tacitly effaces the hinge points where Hegel's philosophy of law is bound up with his philosophy of religion and his understanding of religion and history.

It seems to me that the importance of this observation goes well beyond the identification of a thematic lacuna in the work of a single author. The tendency to leave Hegel shorn of his ideas on religion appears in the work of other contemporary Left Hegelians as well. Most important and prominent in this regard is American philosopher Robert Pippin, whose oeuvre has updated the most varied elements of Hegel's work, from aesthetics to logic, and who—unlike Honneth—also sees a possibility of rescuing Hegel's metaphysical premises through an ingenious reinterpretation of his logic.[21] But even his writings are devoid of references to Hegel and religion or Hegel and Christianity. Pippin's conception of Hegel is so secularized that he seems to feel no need to reexamine his thought in light of the theory of religion or critique of religion. This is all the more striking, not to say stunning, given that it was precisely Hegel's philosophy of religion in light of which "the dispute over the systematic validity of his philosophy as a whole was most fiercely fought out," while their attitude to this systematic validity was "the litmus test for the early Hegel critics and apologists."[22]

For Right Hegelians among political philosophers and Protestant theologians, the nexus of Hegel's philosophy of law and the state on the one hand and his justification of the Christian religion's claim to absoluteness on the other remained crucial—up to and including the idea of the state as an "earthly God"[23] and the future dispensability of the church as an organization of believers different from the state.[24] For early Left Hegelians, meanwhile, Hegel's Christianity formed the major contrast with their own ideas. This they highlighted in critiques of religion and the kind of militant atheist propaganda present in the work of Ludwig Feuerbach, the young Karl Marx, and others, a form of thinking that has made a profound historical impact.

Evidently, today's Left Hegelians do not identify with these ideas and are keen to avoid being perceived in their vicinity. But this does not mean that they have sought to identify just how their predecessors' criticism of religion differs from Hegel in order to steer expressly in a different, perhaps less critical direction. They pass over this point in silence, unwilling to endorse either the critique of religion espoused by the Left Hegelians or the Protestant deification of the state typical of the Right Hegelians who—after Hegel's death, when, in the discipline of philosophy, Hegelians "became as rare as hen's teeth and easily came across as rather comical figures"[25]—maintained his legacy within theology. This is entirely understandable, but it is unproductive in that they have failed to translate it into an explicit revision of Hegel. To be blunt, we might wonder whether, for them, a secularized conception of Hegel is simply a prerequisite for any full-blooded appropriation of his work.

Of course, criticism of individual Hegelians does not amount to a complete picture of present-day scholarship on Hegel and his understanding of religion. My concern here is not with assessing the specialist literature but with systematic contemporary theoretical schemas resting on Hegel's shoulders. Here we do find studies—particularly those by Charles Taylor and Michael Theunissen—that truly take Hegel's Christianity seriously.[26] But their work too is devoid of any explicit revision of those of Hegel's assumptions that led to the deification of the state or atheist propaganda among his students. I insist on this point not because I wish to restitute a more Christian Hegel as a major source of theoretical inspiration. On the contrary, I seek to show that the Hegelian route is a dead end in the theory of religion. Rather than continuing along either side of this dead end, what we have to do is depart from it entirely; we need to back up to the point where the wrong turn was taken.

Such a reversal faces tremendous obstacles. It is not only the enormous prestige of Hegel and the whole of German classical philosophy that makes all such attempts appear foolhardy—at least in Germany. One would also have to revise every account that ascribes to nineteenth-century German intellectual history an internal inevitability, which comes across as a systematic conceptual consequence, far beyond cultural peculiarities. Typical of this tendency is Karl Löwith's brilliant book *From Hegel to Nietzsche*.[27] Löwith was neither a Hegelian nor a Nietzschean, and in his book he emphasizes not the continuity of but a "revolutionary rupture" within German intellectual history. Yet he still paints a picture that is entirely informed by Germany and that makes Nietzsche's struggle against every form of latent Christianity and against every half-hearted defense of Christian morality—in the wake of the convulsions that had shaken the Christian faith—appear as the completion of a development begun by Hegel.

When it comes to Christianity, Löwith's tone is rather melancholy. He is certainly not militantly negative as in Marxism nor does he hysterically celebrate the overcoming of Christianity as a form of liberation in the manner of the Nietzscheans. Nevertheless, his account has been understood—in the words of Reinhart Koselleck—as a declaration that "there could be no way back, neither back to Christianity, for example in defiance of the new German paganism, nor back to Judaism, from which he saw himself as emancipated, nor even back to classical new humanism, to 'Goethe.'"[28] This interpretation is understandable, since Löwith did not contrast the real history of hegemonic thinkers "from Hegel to Nietzsche" with an alternative history, from "Schleiermacher to Troeltsch," for example. But this reading is also foreshortened: in the little-noticed final paragraph of his great book, Löwith hints, however vaguely, at an alternative:

> Since Hegel, and particularly through the work of Marx and Kierkegaard, the Christianity of the bourgeois-Christian world has come to an end. This does not mean that a faith which once conquered the world perishes with its last secular manifestations. For how should the Christian pilgrimage *in hoc saeculo* ever become homeless in the land where it has never been at home?[29]

For Löwith, then, no return to Christianity in the form it assumed in the bourgeois world of Germany or Europe does not mean it has no future at all. And no return to Hegel's Christianity does not mean the faith can only be justified in the form it took in Hegel's philosophy. Nor does it imply that Christianity loses all justification if this philosophy is over and done with or if its exponents are no longer interested in Hegel's version of the faith.

Löwith's historical reconstruction is by no means the only one to exaggerate the inner logic of German intellectual history. It finds parallels in Marxist and Enlightenment-minded reconstructions that analyze German thought from the vantage point of the emergence of Nazism and its prehistory.[30] The monumental work on the history of philosophy recently produced by Jürgen Habermas also suffers from its presupposition that the decisive crossroads lies between Hume and Kant. As Habermas sees it, the former gives rise only to a reductionist naturalism, while all that can emerge from the latter are forms of a philosophy of morality and history that can at most be understood as heirs to Christianity but not as articulations of it.[31]

So, is anyone wishing to free themselves from this predicament on a hiding to nothing? Are we faced here with a quixotism, with the inability to grasp that something has died out and will not be coming back? For my part, such self-doubt would be stronger if the "exploratory survey of intellectual history and the history of scholarship" to which I referred at the start of the introduction did not provide a wealth of starting points for the development of an alternative to Hegel's narrative of the history of religion and the history of political freedom. I will be providing a detailed account of these starting points in the various chapters of this book. In advance of these in-depth treatments, I now put forward a set of simplified theses to highlight only the most important differences from Hegel, though not in the form of detailed interpretations of him. At the end of the day, what matters at this point is not whether Hegel thought this or that or whether he expressed different ideas in other parts of his oeuvre. More important are the assertions that have taken on a life of their own vis-à-vis their originator, that have, as such, become influential and amenable to discussion.[32] Still, these assertions are expressed in their classic form in his writings, however far the later cultural-Protestant historical narrative may have moved away from him.[33]

Hegel's influential mode of thought is most accessible not in the short final part of his *Elements of the Philosophy of Right* (§§ 341–360), the most important relevant passage in the writings he himself had published, but in the lectures on the philosophy of world history that he held every other year at the University of Berlin, from the winter semester of 1822–1823 until shortly before his death in 1831, in other words a total of five times, which have come down to us in the shape of various transcripts and the publications based on them.[34]

Following detailed reflections on the possible "methods of treating history," these lectures set out the main elements of Hegel's philosophical conceptions of "spirit" and its realization in history along with his ideas on the course of world history, before elucidating empirically (after a fashion) the geographical foundations of world history. The main part provides a more detailed account of the "Oriental," Greek, Roman, and Germanic worlds in four lengthy sections. Crucially, these different cultural "worlds" are not simply juxtaposed, examined to identify possible mutual influences and scrutinized with respect to their developmental potential. Instead, they are arranged into a value-based hierarchical order, for which Hegel goes so far as to deploy the metaphor of ages in the life of humankind. These worlds he views as stages in a single world-historical process, one through which an idea inherent in the history of humankind is gradually realized. This idea is that of "freedom." Hegel thus interprets history as a whole as the history of the self-realization of the spirit, as the history of the advancing self-knowledge of divine reason.

As easy as it is to find Hegelian articulations of this basic idea, and as common as these may be in philosophical circles, from a certain distance it is far from easy to state exactly what this means. At present, the easiest term to use is "self-realization," as it expresses an ideal that is extremely influential today, a specifically "expressive" conception of freedom.[35] On closer reflection, a strange paradox quickly becomes apparent in this term, because it is quite unclear what constitutes this self before it is realized, that is, what sort of reality we might ascribe to the unrealized self. But this conceptual problem has not stopped the triumphal march of the ideal of self-realization in "Western" culture and beyond. Yet what is meant here is only ever the self-realization of individuals, or collectives in a few cases, but not that of the "spirit."

Hegel himself seems to have been the first to use the term "self-realization" philosophically,[36] and the term "spirit" is of course central to his mature thinking. But only later thinkers, writing in Hegel's wake, worked with the notion of the "self-realization of the spirit."[37] What is already hard to grasp with respect to individuals is all the more mysterious when applied to this "spirit." In the course of his oeuvre, Hegel relied more and more on this concept, which was supposed to enable him to move beyond the mere contrasting of ideal and reality. If ideals are themselves a product of historical developments, it was vital to include this fact self-reflectively in every observation on history and morality. This opened up the prospect of conceiving of the development of ideals themselves as a tiered developmental process through which, as in the process of individuals' formation, self-realization takes place. However, traits are ascribed to this "spirit" as well as to "reason" that are hard to imagine beyond individuals and their relationships with one another, except in a religious sense.[38] In Hegel, then, "spirit" and "reason" have unmistakable attributes of the divine, which renders understandable the transition to the idea that these entities play an active role in the world.

Like the "living God" of Christianity, it is possible to conceive of an "absolute spirit." This intellectual move is, however, of the profoundest "ambiguity"[39] as far as the Christian faith is concerned. It is unclear whether this entails abandoning Christianity in the traditional sense or justifying it in a new way through the philosophy of history. This ambiguity is also clearly evident when Hegel limits religions, including Christianity, to the sphere of feeling and (mere) imagination, compared to which only conceptual thought—in the shape of philosophy—can help what is merely felt and intuited in religion to assume its full form.

This picture, sketched in bare outline, already shows how difficult it is to resist the pull of the Hegelian conceptual apparatus if one wishes to explain his thinking. It is no accident, then, that the language used in many attempts to build on Hegel sounds like that of the master himself. As I see it, however, we are faced with a fundamental hermeneutical problem if a thinker's ideas are conveyed solely in his own terminology—in Hegel's case, moreover, one invented by the thinker himself. It is precisely the key forks in Hegel's conceptual path that this approach fails to bring out. If a thinker's concepts cannot be formulated or are extremely difficult to formulate in a language other than his own, this should not be taken as an indication of their unsurpassable profundity, but as the sign of a problem requiring resolution.

The basic outline of Hegel's philosophy of history thus consists of a conception of "spirit" that differs from (unspiritual) nature and, in constant struggle with its previous forms of realization, strives to go beyond them until it has found its own appropriate form of realization, that is, until it has realized itself. This is the foundation underlying the edifice of Hegel's philosophy of history, which, while working through a sizeable quantity of contemporary knowledge, traces the major historical stages in the emergence of the state as a form of the positive realization of freedom, first in the "Orient," then in the emergence of ideas on the freedom of the citizen (and only of the citizen) in the Greek world and subsequently in the unrestricted freedom that takes wing in the Roman world, the "place of birth" of the Christian religion.[40] In the history of Christianity, for Hegel the German Lutheran, it is then "the German nations"[41] that contribute decisively to the historical development of this freedom, and it is the Reformation in particular that restores the Christian understanding of freedom in all its purity vis-à-vis the aberrations of the Middle Ages, while exercising a formative effect on the (early modern) state. Enlightenment and revolution, Hegel explains, then give rise to the political phenomenon of the freedom-guaranteeing state, which finds its historically highest and ultimate form in Prussia in the wake of the reforms implemented in response to its defeat at the hands of the Napoleonic army. In his *Lectures on the Philosophy of History*, Hegel's systematic philosophy thus takes the form of a grand narrative that has rightly been called the "great epic of European modernity."[42]

Since Hegel's time, polemical critiques have repudiated this great epic and even held it up to ridicule in the most varied range of ways. Not all the objections raised are equally important to my argument here. The present book concentrates on what I consider to be four key issues, giving rise to its four-part structure: (1) the criticism that Hegel suffers from an intellectualistic understanding of religious faith; (2) the questioning of Hegel's ideas about the connection between religion and political freedom, here chiefly in light of what occurred in the eras after Hegel, especially the twentieth century; (3) new impulses that can shape our understanding of freedom in a way that leads beyond Hegel; and finally (4), overcoming Hegel's Eurocentric and Christianity-centric understanding of world history. Taken together, these four aspects are intended to demonstrate the validity of my claim of a Hegelian dead end in the theory of religion.

(1) The assertion of an intellectualistic understanding of faith in Hegel's work may seem unjustified at first sight. In his early work—and especially compared to Kant's moralistically attenuated conception of faith—Hegel did take into account the dimensions of feeling, intuition, and imagination. In the *Phenomenology of Spirit*, however, as already recognizable in the book's basic architecture, he leaves us in no doubt that there must be an "absolute knowledge" that is higher than the spirit even of revealed religion. For Hegel, not only must faith not remain at this preconceptual level. For him it is crucial that such preconceptual subjective religiosity is—in and of itself—open to content of any kind. This is the systematic point at which, regardless of the personal dimensions of their relationship, Hegel and Schleiermacher differed radically. If Schleiermacher defined religion by means of a feeling, namely that of "absolute dependency," then for Hegel this was wholly inadequate. In a famous jibe, Hegel remarked that a dog must be the best Christian because it lives with a constant feeling of dependency on its master, while the receipt of a bone triggers "feelings of redemption."[43]

What sounds like a masterful rebuff, however, simply fails to do justice to Schleiermacher's sophisticated understanding of faith. The latter therefore consciously refrained from responding publicly to Hegel's statement. There is a difference, one that must surely have mattered to Hegel, between a person capable of freedom recognizing themselves, in all their self-confident freedom, as absolutely dependent, and a dog perpetually limited by its natural dependence. The key question is whether, in religious feeling or, as it was to be expressed by later thinkers, in religious experience, certain cognitive content is always present in such a way that it can and must be articulated, in which case there can be no question of feeling or experience being random vis-à-vis their forms of articulation. Also crucial, however, is how we envisage the limits to conceptual articulation. The understanding of such limits strips this articulation of any notion of self-evident superiority to other symbol systems, underlining that it is always in some measure also one-sided and impoverishing.[44] Here we touch on critical issues relating to the interpretation of Hegel and, above all, to the anthropological foundations of the theory of religion. This is why the present book repeatedly airs the prospect of a different understanding of human corporeality than that inherent in the conception of "spirit."

(2) The claim that Hegel's ideas make a poor fit with the experiences of the twentieth century may also seem trivial or unfair at first sight. Yet ultimately it is quite reasonable to critically review a comprehensive reconstruction of world history in light of later developments. The Prussian constitutional state may have been unsurpassed in Hegel's time in normative terms (though who would now seriously espouse this idea, however critical a view they might take of France, Britain, or Austria at the time?). But the later course of history, and in particular the totalitarianisms of the twentieth century, must surely prompt us to rethink any confidence in the securely established nature of political freedom. Prussian-German history and Christianity's entanglements with it are in fact a striking example of why this is necessary. This rethinking raises fundamental doubts about the future-focused, prognostic value of a teleological reconstruction of history. It turns history from a great supra-personal process back into a contingent one, in which the future depends in significant part on action in the present, on situationally apt and morally imperative actions under conditions that are never entirely controllable.

While Hegel's philosophy is an expression of the radical temporalization and historicization that began in the eighteenth century, this approach immediately rigidifies again if history as a whole is thought of as a single necessary process and the phases of the past are envisaged as stages in an identifiable development. This turns contingency into a surface phenomenon by which the philosopher must not allow themself to be distracted as they contemplate historical necessity. On this premise, they do not talk about history as a whole in bold and risky statements that may be refuted empirically and practically through confrontation with events. Instead, they adopt the tone of a (second-rate) theology of revelation, the pretense of having certain knowledge of past, present, and future and of the ultimate purpose of world history. Here, too, Hegel's ambiguity with regard to secularization, as highlighted by Karl Löwith, is palpable. What appears from one perspective as the dissolution of belief in divine reason and the embrace of a purely mundane world history turns out to be, from a different vantage point, a sacralization of reason, which is articulated with all the fervor of the true believer certain of their salvation.[45]

(3) The question has repeatedly been raised, not least among Hegelians themselves, of the extent to which Hegel's conception of freedom does justice to the intersubjective perspective inherent in his philosophy. In a general sense, this question need not interest us here. But it touches on Hegel's conception of political freedom in that it reveals a highly ambivalent relationship to the idea of the public sphere. In his early work *The Structural Transformation of the Public Sphere*, Jürgen Habermas already highlighted the illiberal statism that prevails in Hegel's work in this regard; in line with this, the moment Axel Honneth turns to the democratic public sphere in his theory of justice, he expressly distances himself from the model of Hegel's philosophy of law, from which he otherwise takes his lead.[46] This suggests that we might need to understand freedom differently than Hegel did at least when it comes to religion in the public sphere—in other words, public religion. On this premise, there is no getting away from the fact that the search for an appropriate understanding of public religion will also have an impact on one's understanding of faith as a whole.

This brings out the problematic nature of simple ideas about Christianity as such or even about Protestantism as such and their respective effects in history. Different believers and different religious groups will relate their faith to politics or politics to their faith in different ways. Controversies and influences will arise beyond the boundaries of religious communities. Specifically with reference to Hegel, one of the things this means is that his anti-Catholicism requires revision. However we may now assess Catholicism in Hegel's day, we are left with the impression of an undifferentiated and static judgment that points to underlying problems. I believe the origins of these problems lie in an exaggerated notion of the autonomy of reason and in a failure to consider the idea of "indebted freedom." What then emerges is that only an even more pragmatic and hermeneutical conception of reason than that found in Hegel and an even more consistent relativization of the ideal of self-determination, through reflection on its constitution, are compatible with the ideals of political freedom. Part III of this book does not, therefore, present a break with Hegel, but seeks to further develop themes that are already present in his work, but were only developed consistently after him.

(4) No one today would seriously dispute that Hegel's philosophy of history is Eurocentric to its core. The introduction to one of the pioneering works of modern global historiography laments the belief, imparted by schools, that

the West has a genealogy "according to which ancient Greece begat Rome, Rome begat Christian Europe, Christian Europe begat the Renaissance, the Renaissance the Enlightenment and the Enlightenment political democracy and the industrial revolution."[47] Such a scheme of historical development, we are informed, is misleading for two reasons. It transforms history into a "race in time in which each runner of the race passes on the torch of liberty to the next relay," which leads to a "tale about the furtherance of virtue" that enables the winners of history to view themselves as vehicles for the achievement of moral objectives. At the same time, interest in history is reduced to a concern with the "precursor(s) of the final apotheosis"[48] instead of sensitizing us to the true conflicts and developmental possibilities of history.

If the Renaissance were replaced by the Reformation and the reference to democracy and the industrial revolution removed, these statements could have been aimed at Hegel. This is because, in taking up and carrying forward the historiography of his time, Hegel composed an epic that spawned a particular stylistic tradition. Though modified in the detail, its basic structure endured in the work of later thinkers. Tellingly, Hegel deals with pre- or anti-state societies in his introductory observations on "geographical foundations" because, it would appear, he is unwilling to dignify them with their own history. For Hegel, history begins with the state and writing, and history in this sense (allegedly) starts with China. But what he has to say about China is marked by a profound denigration of its traditions, both state and religious. Hegel's view is centered on ahistorical patriarchal despotism, undergirded by a religion, Confucianism, that he thinks embodies the opposite of the idea of freedom.[49] India too is depicted as completely ossified in its caste system and thus as captive of fundamental social inequality.

While it would be wrong to condemn Hegel for the views and knowledge gaps characteristic of his time, in this case he was not simply a victim of prevailing prejudices but contributed significantly to the "disenchantment of Asia." Hegel played a major role in confining "the world-historical importance of Asiatic civilizations to their distant past,"[50] and he endorsed the European subjugation of Asia. Without blinking an eyelid, he predicted that China, too, would "some day or other, be obliged to submit to this fate."[51] So although it would be unfair to make excessive empirical demands of grand philosophical schemas, we should not pretend that a philosophy remains untouched by the deficient assessments of reality that entered into it or are based on it.

My concern here is with more than just correcting specific statements. I seek to question Hegel's philosophy of history in a crucial respect. What I have in mind is the same point that exercised Ernst Troeltsch when, in relation to the history of Christianity, he drew on Ranke rather than Hegel.[52] Ranke's often-sneered-at statement that every era is immediate to God is described by Troeltsch as profound because it teaches us not to view eras simply as stages in a development that realizes an ideal, but as independent attempts to realize ideals that are, however, never fully realized and to whose unrealized aspirations we must always react anew in our own particular circumstances. This means we not only have to break with Hegel's Eurocentrism, but also with the idea that Christianity is the absolute religion. Distancing ourselves from Hegel's philosophy of history points to the need to adopt a humbler relationship to Christianity and a more curious and open-minded relationship to other religions; it also highlights the need to adopt a critical distance to secularist Hegelians' tendency to transfer Hegel's salvific certainty to their own secular worldviews.

Schleiermacher and Ranke are in fact two of the thinkers who had to admit defeat in the face of Hegel's overpowering influence, but who gained the upper hand in the subsequent history of the humanities. Of course, this description does not apply to philosophy, in which, to this day, the great theologian and the great historian tend not to be taken very seriously.[53] The present book, however, does not focus on these scholars, whose lifetimes overlapped with that of Hegel, as alternatives to him, but rather on later thinkers who referred to Hegel from a historical distance when they formulated their alternatives, or who simply ignored him. They were mostly influenced by a changed intellectual atmosphere, in which Hegel's impact had been supplanted or eclipsed by Nietzsche's provocations. And many of them contributed to overcoming the Eurocentric view of the history of religion, a process initiated in rudimentary form in the work of Schopenhauer, among others, but that only really bore fruit in the twentieth century.

My reference to Nietzsche's provocations here is deliberately ambiguous. On the one hand, what I have in mind is the overly polemical tone of Nietzsche's critique of Christianity, which is often quite understandable as a reaction to certain suffered forms of this religion, but whose untenable generalization and excessively harsh formulation can sometimes be repellent. On the other hand, I am thinking of the profound intellectual challenges emanating from Nietzsche, which became a productive force propelling a new understanding of history and morality as well as Christianity. While

I have concentrated entirely on Hegel in this introduction, in the book's conclusion I seek to make good on the promise, inherent in its subtitle, that it will, by grappling with the latter, provide an account of the preconditions for theory of religion after Hegel *and* Nietzsche.

As already mentioned, in the four main parts of this book I present individual portraits of thinkers on religion whom I consider significant to the project of exploring religion and political freedom in history beyond the Hegelian grand narrative. The book closes with a look at an issue inherent in this alternative, namely the prospects for a global-historical genealogy of moral universalism. Here Nietzsche's methodological impetus enters into the concept of a genealogy without requiring us to embrace his substantive views of history. It is only in this form—as I assert at the end of the book—that we can retain what is worth saving in Hegel's philosophy of history through a specific conceptual shift.

PART I
A NEW UNDERSTANDING OF RELIGION IN THE EARLY TWENTIETH CENTURY

PART I

I, 1
Introductory Remarks

As early as the second half of the nineteenth century, a new understanding of religion that went beyond Schleiermacher, Hegel, and Feuerbach was slowly gestating; it then broke through in full force in the early twentieth century. In 1963, the great American historian of religion Wilfred Cantwell Smith stated that "in the decades before and after 1900" the definition of religion had become a major topic,[1] and although, even today, many would probably dispute the definitive nature of that theoretical turning point, there can be no doubt about the epoch-making character of the new understanding that arose during this period. The key terms characteristic of this turn are "religious experience," the "interpretation" or "articulation" of such experience, and "sacredness" in the sense of a power or force that is pre-reflectively ascribed to objects, people, and ideational content through religious experiences. It is this turning point that I am concerned with here because it entailed the breakthrough to a nonintellectualistic understanding of religious belief.

Thinkers concerned with religion now moved beyond the idea that it can only be justified in its conceptual, ultimately philosophical form—a notion that, as shown earlier, had found its most radical expression in Hegel. Of course, this turning point was not without precursors. As always happens when innovations are made in the history of science and scholarship, earlier thinkers were rediscovered and reevaluated.[2] The most important forerunner, a figure who therefore attracted a great deal of new attention, was Friedrich Schleiermacher, whose understanding of faith Hegel had once so ignominiously dismissed.[3] But this certainly does not mean that all of the main protagonists associated with this turning point derived their inspiration chiefly from Schleiermacher or that they all had an uncritical relationship with him. Assuming simple influence or the restaging of old battles takes us no further here. Instead, what we can discern is something truly new—a perspective beyond the intellectual possibilities of an earlier era.

For every fundamental turning point in the history of science and scholarship, we can identify external causes and internal reasons. I will touch only briefly on the possible external causes. As far as the "sacredness" discourse is concerned, two challenges of the era seem to have been decisive. First, the confrontation with non-Abrahamic religions became more intense, chiefly due to the intensified colonization of Africa during this period;[4] second, the rise of a secularist labor movement, which developed its own symbols and ritual forms without being religious, impelled a reversal of the relationship between "sacred" and "religious." The sacred was no longer thought of solely as part of traditional religions; conversely, religions could now be interpreted as attempts to stabilize and transmit experiences of sacredness.[5]

It is processes of religious individualization that are likely to have been responsible for the turn to "experience," in particular individuals' experience within their solitary relationship with the divine. Dissatisfaction with religious communities, which demand obedience to doctrines that individuals find intellectually unacceptable, or that enforce a moral conformity that is experienced as an obstacle to individuals enjoying a meaningful life, may engender a resolve to find one's salvation in secularist convictions. But it may also strengthen efforts to explore individual "spirituality"—as it came to be expressed in contrast to institutional religion—as well as reinforcing the tendency to defend one's own experience against institution and doctrine and engage with older traditions of mysticism that more convincingly make room for the associated experiences.[6]

Two nineteenth-century shifts within scholarship stand out. The first of them only truly comes into focus when we extend our attention beyond the history of philosophy to take account of the full range of the humanities. In these disciplines, the burgeoning corpus of empirical knowledge underlined the need for systematization and reinforced the awareness that the available philosophical constructions must without exception be inadequate; the enthralling but undisciplined and megalomaniacal new ideas put forward by Friedrich Nietzsche, especially his criticism of Christianity, played an important role here too. In a development characteristic of the era, theologian and historian of Christianity Ernst Troeltsch distanced himself equally from two major adversaries of the classical period, Hegel and Schleiermacher, using the term "purely dialectical" to castigate both of them for failing to move beyond philosophy-of-history constructions. In one of his early literature reviews on the state of the philosophy of religion and theology, he refers to the book version of the Gifford Lectures by Dutch scholar of religion Cornelius Tiele:

> One only has to compare its content with Schleiermacher's philosophy of religion, which develops in purely dialectical fashion and strives only to

secure Christianity's special status as the exclusive religion of redemption, or with Hegel's no less dialectical philosophy of religion, which strives only to equate the absolute idea with Christianity, in order to recognize how much historical-empirical research has now relocated these problems.[7]

I return later to certain particularly clear instances of problems "shifting." Before doing so, however, it should be mentioned that in addition to the challenge posed by the unforeseen or only superficially acknowledged diversity of religious phenomena and the novel rejections of Christianity, a fundamental methodological challenge arose. I am thinking of the radical questioning of the philosophy of consciousness by American pragmatism and German historical hermeneutics during this era. Ideas about knowledge and reason change fundamentally when the individual subject and their perception of reality no longer form the starting point for philosophical reflection, not even for the knowing subject's reflection on themself, but rather the collective, symbolically mediated action of large numbers of people in a world that they encounter through their corporeality and that they experience as the unproblematic background of every arising problem.[8] This severely deflates philosophy's aspiration to act as a guide for all the scholarly disciplines and for everyday life; the same must go for its relationship with theology and above all with human experience—everyday, ordinary experience, but also extraordinary experience, as assimilated chiefly by religions.

The number of those who contributed to this shift toward a modified understanding of religion, one centered on experience and action rather than consciousness and thought, is considerable, and I do not, of course, seek to provide a comprehensive overview of them here. In this part of the book, I portray three of these thinkers, but first I briefly discuss two others, who remain in the background in my account but who were of tremendous importance to the three main figures portrayed. I include consideration of their explicit arguments with Hegel or their implicit relationship with him.

One figure who played a crucial role in paving the way for this shift in the German-speaking world is Wilhelm Dilthey, one of the greatest scholars living at the time of the Wilhelmine Empire. Though he rarely referred directly to the issue of an appropriate understanding of religion,[9] his work made a key contribution to this turning point. The first outstanding feature of his oeuvre is his biography of Schleiermacher, which was planned as a massive work but ultimately remained a mere fragment. For two intertwined reasons, this biographical project was to become a lifelong preoccupation for Dilthey. As he saw it, Schleiermacher was, first, the pioneer of a way of thinking capable of rendering fluid a religion that Dilthey believed had become institutionally and doctrinally congealed—by illuminating it from a fresh perspective in light of people's "inner experience" as its source. But since, for Dilthey, one of the greatest exponents of the comprehensive historicization of all human phenomena, this experience was necessarily a historically situated one, the biographical reconstruction of a thinker who helped facilitate the breakthrough of "experience" also became a crucial challenge when it came to the self-application of the associated method. Second, while working on Schleiermacher, Dilthey inevitably found himself confronted by Hegel time and again—as Schleiermacher's adversary and as a philosophical challenge for Dilthey himself.

For Dilthey, "The problem of Hegel was one of the factors that obstructed completion of the biography at the time and that initially prompted him to seek systematic clarification."[10] He applied his experience-centered and genetic approach to Hegel too, producing a study of his early development that interpreted his early texts, then available only in handwritten form, in a pioneering way. Dilthey found two aspects of these early writings particularly exciting. First, they gave him access to the experiential basis of Hegel's oeuvre, especially with regard to religion and Christianity—an experiential basis not yet rendered unrecognizable by Hegel the systematist's conceptual apparatus and a dialectics that had developed its own dynamic. Second, according to Dilthey, the surviving fragments of early Hegel make an "invaluable contribution to a phenomenology of metaphysics."[11]

This statement only makes sense if we bear in mind that Dilthey's oeuvre includes not only the great studies in intellectual history of Schleiermacher, Hegel, and others, but also sophisticated outlines detailing the specific character of the humanities and the methodology appropriate to them. These methodological studies, however, are in turn linked with his extensive treatments of the history of metaphysics as the foundation of the humanities and as the reason for their hegemony and decline.[12] For Dilthey, Hegel was both a representative thinker as far as the breakthrough of the historical consciousness was concerned, as well as one of the last figures to embrace metaphysics before its "euthanasia."[13] Understanding Hegel, then, meant comprehending a late type of metaphysics, but rather than doing so in Hegel's wake, Dilthey developed a historicizing approach that included him.[14]

One traditional criticism of the turn to experience paints it as a mere background irrelevant to questions of validity. On this view, it may well be that biographical studies help us access the meaning of great philosophical and scholarly edifices; yet such retreat into biography tells us nothing about their validity. Hence, Hegel's objection to Schleiermacher's notion of "feeling," namely that this gives rise to no specific idea, seems also to apply to every new attempt to build on Schleiermacher. Of course, this objection has always been based on a one-sided reading of Schleiermacher's concept of feeling. This becomes completely clear in Dilthey's development of the concept of experience. His objective is never to transition from cognitionless affect to affectless cognition. Instead, he is constantly in search of a conception with a different take on the transition from experience to concept, namely as a transition from a pre-reflective-holistic mode to a reflective-differentiated mode.

This transition takes place by way of expression, that is, the attempt to give an experience a form that renders it understandable to other people. In his early efforts, Dilthey still thought of this process of finding an appropriate expression or "articulation"[15] as an occurrence within the individual. Subsequently, however, it became increasingly clear to him that this is a process that relies on supra-individual media, and not only in the sense that expression has to take on a generally accessible form, but also because the available means of expression already have an effect on the articulation process. Expressing oneself does not mean describing oneself neutrally. It means making something out of the material given in one's own experience, something in which one recognizes oneself while also being accessible to others. Hence, in addition to the subject and the expressive event, another key element is the role of available forms of expression, for which Dilthey uses the term "objectivation."

With this turn to objectivations, one of Hegel's concepts became important to Dilthey in a new way, namely "objective spirit." The manner in which he appropriated this Hegelian concept is highly instructive if we wish to grasp the interplay of proximity and distance in Dilthey's relationship with Hegel. Dilthey praises Hegel's term as "an insightful and happy coinage,"[16] but rejects the metaphysical construction according to which the world spirit realizes its freedom through its development. Dilthey cannot accept progressively self-realizing reason as his leitmotif; the point of departure must be what is given, in all its ambiguity and contingency:

> The contemporary analysis of human existence fills us all with a sense of fragility, with the power of dark instincts, with the suffering caused by

mysteries and illusions, and with the finitude shown by all that is living, even where the highest creations of communal life arise from it.[17]

Thus, for Dilthey, no ideal construction can lead us to an understanding of this objective spirit, only the exploration of real history. But this renders obsolete the distinction made by Hegel between the "objective" and the "absolute" spirit. For without Hegel's philosophy-of-history construction, art, religion, and philosophy also emerge as objectivations of human action, along with those phenomena Hegel had considered aspects of the objective spirit: family, civil society, and the state.

Dilthey's abandonment of the Hegelian conception of the absolute spirit is associated with a significant methodological gain as well as a grave normative loss when it comes to theory of religion. The benefit is that Dilthey is sensitized to the way in which Hegel's youthful writings on the emergence of Christianity emphasize the early Christian community and its sense of being a community. For Dilthey, one could now come to grips methodologically with something that had been puzzling from the vantage point of individual psychology, namely how the Christ myth came into being—by transferring the transcendental-idealist theory of the creative nature of the subject to the Christian community: "It is the very fact that Hegel and Schleiermacher conceived of the community as the myth-forming subject that renders resolvable the great historical problem of the emergence of the Christian world of faith."[18] Here we can discern an idea fundamental to the sociology of religion (as distinct from an individualist psychology of religion), an idea with a rich effective history.[19] It is the pursuit of this perspective in (Protestant) church historiography that subsequently led this field away from Hegel's constructions and toward historical sociology.[20]

The price Dilthey had to pay for empiricizing Hegel's conception of the objective spirit was the now irresolvable issue of validity: his notion of the "community" as myth-forming subject was of course not meant simply as a critique of religion. Yet how exactly did this notion relate to faith? Dilthey himself saw the tragic predicament into which his work had led him as a dilemma in this sense. In his famous address on the occasion of his seventieth birthday, he gave classic expression to this tragedy. If it is the definitive conclusion of the "historical worldview" that everything is relative, including religions, ideals, and philosophical systems, then what might be the source of universally valid knowledge? Where can we find "the means of overcoming the anarchy of beliefs that threatens to erupt"?[21] He himself could make out no route to a solution. As I see it, Ernst Troeltsch—building on Dilthey but also going far beyond him—was the first to identify such a route.[22]

American philosopher and psychologist William James contributed far more directly than Dilthey to the methodological revolution at issue here in the study of religion. His stylistically brilliant 1902 book *The Varieties of Religious Experience* is considered the founding document of the psychology of religion, but it is much more than this.[23] In a very general sense, it paves the way for the notion that in the first instance religions are neither doctrinal systems nor social institutions. Of course, this does not imply that scholars should not concern themselves with religious doctrines and organizations. It means that we ought to shift the starting point of research toward the study of human experience. The idea here is to recognize religious teachings as (always inadequate) attempts to articulate intensive, extraordinary experiences, and to grasp that churches and religious communities of all kinds are organizational attempts to place such experiences and their symbolizations and interpretations on a permanent footing while making them accessible to others. James's book, like perhaps no other of its era, exuded a spirit of sweeping curiosity about the infinite variety of religious phenomena, whether attractive or repellent. It took aim at all attempts to airily dismiss these phenomena as the mere expression of power relations and oppression or of psychopathology. His attempt to describe religious phenomena in meticulous detail is sometimes referred to as "phenomenology," although James himself was not a member of this branch of philosophy but was in fact a leading exponent of another school of thought, namely pragmatism.

With unprecedented sensitivity, James studied experiences of being "seized" that wrench people from their everyday lives, while also examining the enduring changes in people's relationship with the world anchored in such experiences. In his accounts it emerges that the affective and the cognitive cannot be neatly separated. The pre-reflective conviction, for example, that one is "by loving forces wonderfully sheltered" (Dietrich Bonhoeffer) is neither mere thought nor mere feeling. Experiences often convey insights that are difficult to transfer into the medium of conceptual language but whose inherent authority nonetheless propels our argumentational efforts. In line with this, for James the alternative to religious belief is not the secular worldview—because this too attains its plausibility and appeal on the basis of experiences whose subjectively convincing articulation it facilitates. Instead, the alternative to a way of life guided by ideals—whether of a religious or secular nature—is a weakening of motivation, a dwindling willingness to be, melancholy, depression, and a loss of existential meaning. Prayer too, as an active turning to a life-sustaining personal counterpart, eludes the displeasing alternative between rational discourse and mere emotional expression. The impulse emanating from James's ingenious book was immediately taken up far beyond the United States and has yet to be exhausted. Wilhelm Dilthey, like all three thinkers discussed in more detail in this part of the present book and many others besides, was one of those who took up this impulse.[24]

In sharp contrast to Dilthey, James had no need to first work his way gradually out of Hegel's systematic philosophy or to break free from the orbit of classical German philosophy, although he was surrounded by thinkers who saw themselves as the heirs to idealism. For the most part, however, he regarded them as his intellectual opponents. He saw himself as located far more in the tradition of Anglo-Saxon empiricism and thus of David Hume, though his ambition was to revolutionize the understanding of experience underpinning Humean-style empiricism. As he saw it, the empiricists had been entrapped in dead ends by an impoverished conception of human experience. This is why he called his own thinking "radical empiricism"[25]—it was supposed to be rooted more radically in the phenomenology of human experience than the Humeans had ever been. Kant's transcendental philosophy did not appear to him to be the inevitable step in the right direction beyond Hume, because the transcendental ego was too incorporeal for him, a mere "I think" that must, after all, be preceded by an "I breathe."[26] What he believed was required, especially for the analysis of religious phenomena, was this kind of profoundly body-focused understanding of creative and *receptive* subjectivity.[27]

Hence, Hegel's thinking was not a deep internal challenge for James, but essentially an external one. He wrote about Hegel at a time (1882) when the latter's influence was strong in the English-speaking world but fading at German universities. The tenor of his remarks was that of a warning to his US-American compatriots. Hegel's system, he contended, resembled a mousetrap, "in which if you once pass the door you may be lost forever. Safety lies in not entering."[28] In a casual tone, James fleshes out this warning by stating that it is better to reduce one's expectations of philosophy somewhat and to abandon the notion that all knowledge can be synthesized in such a way as to definitively nullify the contingencies of the world and the contingencies of knowledge of the world.[29] For James, as evident in an unsettling appendix to his article, Hegel's philosophy could ultimately be rendered understandable only from the outside as an expression of an attitude to life, a "very powerful emotion" centered on the "togetherness of things in a common world," which in Hegel's case takes the form of the idea of a "self-developing process."[30] This characterization is similar to that found in Dilthey, who referred to the young Hegel's "mystical pantheism."[31]

A "theist" resistance to such pantheism, however, is the prevailing theme in James's later blueprint for a "pluralist" metaphysics, his most extensive and serious discussion of Hegel.[32] For James, his "pluralistic view" arose from his "radical empiricism." Its main opponent in philosophy, James states, is the "philosophy of the absolute," which he fought against in the neo-idealism of his time and, above all, in the work of Hegel. He agrees with the associated philosophers in their anti-materialism.

> But whereas absolutism thinks the said substance becomes fully divine only in the form of totality, and is not its real self in any form but the *all*-form, the pluralistic view which I prefer, to adopt is willing to believe that there may ultimately never be an all-form at all, that the substance of reality may never get totally collected.[33]

At this point, James first repeats his praise for Hegel's intuitions, this "strange and powerful genius,"[34] but also underlines his inability to understand what Hegel calls "logic" and uses as an argumentative approach. The question of how justified James's specific objections to Hegel are must be left to one side here, and the same applies to the relationship between the other classical thinkers of American pragmatism and Hegel.[35] But what is highly significant to issues in the theory of religion is how James links abstract philosophical questions to a specific view of religion.

His main concern is

> to distinguish the notion of the absolute carefully from that of another object with which it is liable to become heedlessly entangled. That other object is the "God" of common people in their religion, and the creator-God of orthodox Christian theology. Only thoroughgoing monists or pantheists believe in the absolute. The God of our popular Christianity is but one member of a pluralistic system.[36]

James invokes not only lived faith and official theology (of the kind not influenced by Hegel or Hegelianism) but also bases himself on the (Old Testament) prophets:

I can hardly conceive of anything more different from the absolute than the God, say, of David or of Isaiah. *That* God is an essentially finite being *in* the cosmos, not with the cosmos in him, and indeed he has a very local habitation there, and very one-sided local and personal attachments. If it should prove probable that the absolute does not exist, it will not follow in the slightest degree that a God like that of David, Isaiah or Jesus does not exist, or may not be the most important existence in the universe for us to acknowledge.[37]

James's critique of Hegel is driven by his rejection of the "absolute" as a rival, indeed an enemy, of the traditional Judeo-Christian conception of God. While, for James, the philosophy of the absolute poses the speculative problem of evil and of evils in the world without being able to solve it, in the pluralist metaphysics of pragmatism problems arise only from a practical, not speculative point of view. What James has in mind is a metaphysics that ascribes to human activity a history-shaping force:

> Not why evil should exist at all, but we can lessen the actual amount of it, is the sole question we need there consider. "God," in the religious life of ordinary men, is the name not of the whole of things, heaven forbid, but only of the ideal tendency in things, believed in as a superhuman person who calls us to co-operate in his purposes, and who furthers ours if they are worthy.[38]

These observations lay bare the inner connection between James's pluralist metaphysics, which we might describe as post-metaphysical,[39] and his pragmatist orientation toward human action, as well as his pioneering work in the psychology of religion. To protect the phenomena of religion from intellectualist distortions, we need to glean them inductively from factual experience rather than deductively from conceptual constructions. However much one may try to express these phenomena in concepts, they are never fully captured by them.[40] Without really having a conception of "articulation" to match that of Dilthey, here James marks the very point at which Dilthey's notion becomes relevant. The empirical exploration of the diversity of religious phenomena (in James) and the sense of the historical dynamics of experience, expression, and understanding (in Dilthey)—in other words, the psychology of religion and the historically oriented humanities—need each other if the goal is to develop a nonintellectualist understanding of religion.

In what follows, I provide more detailed accounts of three thinkers whose work is rooted in the situation described above. First in the series is Ernst Troeltsch. Though he referred to Dilthey as his "teacher," the evidence shows that he did not attend any of his lectures and there appears to have been no other form of close or direct contact between them.[41] In particular, after being appointed to a position at Berlin University in 1915, Troeltsch explicitly described his studies as a "continuation of Dilthey's work," "in line with his own wishes, as he expressed them to me."[42] Furthermore, Troeltsch responded with sustained enthusiasm to the publication of James's work in the psychology of religion. However, in the following chapter I do not seek to reconstruct how the motifs central to the work of Dilthey and James, and many others, were combined in Troeltsch's wide-ranging oeuvre. Instead, in the first instance I am solely concerned with a single early work by Troeltsch. What is exciting about this text is that, without any influence from the United States, it picked up the threads of late German idealism, which in themselves pointed to the "independence of religious phenomena."

"Independence" is not, as it might seem, meant in a causal sense, that is, the determination of social processes by something that is of a completely different origin. What is meant, in a somewhat anti-Hegelian manner, is the independence of religious phenomena vis-à-vis their rational-discursive penetration, that is, with respect to their sublation in the concept. In this text and in many other places in his oeuvre, Troeltsch adds a sociological argument to the philosophical and psychological arguments against an intellectualist understanding of religion. For him, the intellectualization of religion is a phenomenon typical of the educated classes whenever they seek to mark their boundaries with those lower down the social hierarchy. In 1912, in his thousand-page historical sociology of Christianity, he was to write that "it is the lower classes which do the really creative work, forming communities on a genuine religious basis"; in the early history of Christianity, he contends, this marked a clear contrast with the new religious forms of Platonism and Stoicism.[43] Nietzsche's vicious, condescending description of Christianity as "Platonism for the People" is thus radically inverted.[44]

Troeltsch's outstanding importance to the questions pursued in this book is also evident in the fact that I not only discuss him in Part I due to his early treatise "Die Selbständigkeit der Religion," but also in Part III, in which I analyze his long-term dialogue with Ernst Cassirer and the understanding of freedom it reveals. I also investigate his work in the concluding part in light of his criticism of Nietzsche and his opening up of an empirical perspective on an alternative to Nietzsche's assertions about the genesis of Christianity.[45] I thus refrain here from providing a comprehensive overview of Troeltsch's work, limiting myself for the time being to discussion of one topic, namely the attitude toward Hegel's philosophy of history inherent in his theory of religion.

There is no text by Troeltsch specifically on Hegel, but it is obvious that his respectful attempt to get to grips with the latter is a recurring motif in his oeuvre, always involving confrontation with Kant, Herder, and Schleiermacher on the one hand and a comprehensive knowledge of the state of the empirical sciences of religion on the other. Using literary terminology, reference has been made to Troeltsch's "skeptical modification of a paradigmatic fiction,"[46] namely Hegel's philosophy of history. Troeltsch's skepticism seems to have been present from the beginning but grew ever stronger in the course of his oeuvre; it originally arose from an insistence, reminiscent of James, on the significance of lived faith or, put differently, an existential need for meaning that cannot be satisfied by history. Crucial to this modification, however, are two motifs that we might call contingency[47] and ideal formation, that is, the transcending of this-worldly realizability.

Like many other thinkers who came after the Young Hegelians and Kierkegaard, Troeltsch deplores the teleological character of Hegel's philosophy of history and the associated de-individualization of facts. With regard to the history of religion in particular, he writes trenchantly:

> The history of religion, with its terrible atrocities and its stupid and selfish folly . . . cannot possibly be described as a whole and everywhere as a necessary divine self-movement. The boundless egotism and monstrous unreason at large within it cannot be praised in every case as a necessary step. Its progress is by no means the calm and gradual advance of logical thinking, which from all sides strives continuously toward a pure speculative grasp of the idea of God, but entails the wholly incommensurable flaring up of great religious impulses that dominate the masses for centuries.[48]

Hegel, we are told elsewhere, derived the development of religion "in an overly doctrinal and rigid fashion from the logical necessity of the movement of thought, which has detracted from the purely original factuality of its various developments and its mysterious power."[49] Religions arise in history in unpredictable ways. We might refer to the "fact of ideal formation" as the central phenomenon of history.[50] Specific ideals characterize specific historical phases; history is reconstructed in their light and new things appear in the past. But there is no predetermined development of ideals themselves, no teleology running through all of history, no conclusive perspective on world history. One can certainly try, Troeltsch concedes, to determine the laws of historical development and study historical formations as individual entities relating them to measures of value.

One cannot, however, recombine these two into a unified organic development according to which both the necessity of the sequence and the value gradations of the stages might be abstracted from one uniform law of the whole. This notion, popular even today due to the influence of Hegel, is not practicable in this form.[51]

If historically emergent ideals such as those of Christianity are related to reality, then the distance between ideal and reality, the difficulty or impossibility of realizing the ideal, becomes unmistakable. But Troeltsch's second strong motive for distancing himself from Hegel is that Troeltsch—as Ranke once did—denies the possibility of the complete this-worldly realization of the ideal.[52] What might be misunderstood as an empty quietist promise of a hereafter is in fact a way of critiquing every triumphalist self-image cultivated by a religious community or political order. Neither Christianity nor any other religion or secular worldview within a particular era ever attains a form we could describe as the definitive and complete realization of an ideal; the same goes for all future embodiments. Every form of every religion is a historically particular one. The same applies to political orders in their relationship to ideals shaped by religion.

Through this radical rejection of the instrumentalization of a religion to legitimize a political order with reference to the supposedly successful realization of a religious ideal, Troeltsch also makes us aware of the diversity of religions. In his reply to a criticism of his ideas on the "independence of religious phenomena" he refers to the "power and vibrancy of piety, which in its strength of feeling in no way differs from the Christian variant and claims to have the same direct access to God." But the parallels in terms of content, "the pull toward universalism," Troeltsch contends, are also unmistakable in different religions:

> Only those who roam the history of religion solely as apologetic hunters, merely lying in wait for the quarry that demonstrates the inferiority of

non-Christian religions, but not those who traverse this sublime world of wonders as silent and reverent wanderers, can carry their supranaturalism home unscathed from such forays.[53]

Troeltsch's distance from Hegel's philosophy of history, in which the history of religion and the history of political freedom were interwoven, not only marks a fundamental empirical opening to the diversity of Christianity and of religions, but also a more skeptical understanding of the historically secured nature of political freedom. In the powerful denouement of his text on the importance of Protestantism to the emergence of the modern world, the "first great philosopher of history Germany has seen since Hegel"[54] expresses doubt that the preconditions for "freedom" are likely to be favorable for much longer. For Troeltsch, a "new bondage" loomed in the economy, while the armed forces and bureaucracy were becoming increasingly powerful, scholarship was becoming ever more specialized, philosophy was jaded, and art was merely propagating hypersensitivity. Here there are unmistakable echoes of Max Weber's heroic pessimism and of his research, which was guided by the question of how freedom might be secured in view of historical tendencies toward sweeping bureaucratization and rationalization. Unlike Weber, however, Troeltsch hopes for the recovery of the force of faith in God "whence freedom and personality come to us." This he sees as the best hope of safeguarding freedom, "otherwise the cause of freedom and personality may well be lost in the very moment when we are boasting most loudly of our allegiance to it, and of our progress in this direction."[55]

With his book *The Idea of the Holy*, Protestant theologian Rudolf Otto achieved great and sustained success with a broad reading public in Germany, much as William James did with his work on the psychology of religion in the English-speaking world. First published in 1917, new editions of Otto's book have appeared ever since.[56] As controversial as the turn to experience in the study of religion has repeatedly been, especially in theology, it is indisputable that the focus on experiences gives the broader public easier access to the study of religious phenomena. It is not difficult to demonstrate how smoothly Otto's work fits into the line of tradition that I am tracing here. This is evident, first, in light of his importance to the reception of Schleiermacher. The most significant text when it comes to the turn to experience was Schleiermacher's *On Religion: Speeches to Its Cultured Despisers*, published in 1799. In the course of the nineteenth century this text was published again and again, initially after Schleiermacher himself had reworked it in an attempt to moderate his arguments. But it was not necessarily his most influential work during this period. This only changed when Rudolf Otto rereleased the book in its original form on the centenary of its publication,[57] adding detailed interpretations of his own that already contained, in embryonic form, many of the ideas explored in his later work. Although Otto, as his oeuvre developed, explicitly acknowledged his debt to a now virtually forgotten philosopher of the classical era of German philosophy (Jakob Friedrich Fries), there can be no doubt about Schleiermacher's constitutive influence on his thinking.

Otto dedicated his edited Schleiermacher volume to none other than Wilhelm Dilthey, whose biographical research on Schleiermacher made a key contribution to the shift toward experience I have been describing. Just as clear as Otto's closeness to Schleiermacher is his proximity to William James, though Otto himself makes virtually no reference to him. Ernst Troeltsch, however, recognized in his 1918 review that Otto's book was fully congruent with his early work "Die Selbständigkeit der Religion" and that it chimed almost perfectly with James in terms of the psychology of religion, although not in an epistemological sense.[58] The following chapter on Otto is less concerned with his dependence on these precursors and more focused on systematic issues. Particularly important is how his theory of the sacred looks in light of the dimensions of experience and articulation and how he might contribute to an understanding of sacredness under conditions of secularization.

No discussion of Hegel's philosophy as such is to be found in Otto's writings; he appears to have considered it extraneous to his work, and it apparently failed to inspire him to engage with it. Nevertheless, it would be wrong to regard Otto's oeuvre as valuable only because it functions as a corrective to an intellectualist understanding of faith, though this of course it is thanks to his conception of the sacred. But the importance of his writings extends far beyond this. Otto's idea of rationalization in the numinous entails a rejection of the idea that we should try to write the history of religion on the assumption that the "numinous," that is, the nonrational dimension of religion, has been gradually overcome. Rationalization, according to Otto, depends on "the numinous [which] is at once the basis upon which and the setting within which the ethical and rational meaning is consummated."[59] This idea, however, renders obsolete the notion of Christianity overcoming other religions in a linear historical process, as Hegel had envisaged. It is thus no coincidence that Otto, who became a leading expert on the religious history of India over the course of his life, was also to become a pioneer of the Axial Age thesis.[60]

There is no trace, then, of Hegel's pronounced Eurocentrism in Otto's work. One of the few passages in which Otto distances himself directly from Hegel's philosophy of history concerns the latter's understanding of a saying of Jesus in the Gospel of John: "God is spirit" (John 4:24). "This was the text," contends Otto, "on account of which Hegel held Christianity to be the highest because the most truly spiritual (*geistig*) religion. But Hegel meant by 'spirit' the 'absolute reason.'"[61] But this, Otto states, is a misinterpretation of this passage. The Greek word in the original Gospel text is *pneuma*, and this, Otto explains, in no way means reason, but rather something that contrasts with the world in its entirety, including all understanding and all reason. It is not reason but the "numinous" that is meant here. So "this saying, apparently wholly 'rational' in import, is itself the strongest and clearest indication of the non-rational element in the Biblical idea of God."[62] In other words, if Christianity relies entirely on the rational element in the Christian idea of God in its worship, propagation, and doctrine, without securing their substrate, it is lost.[63]

All the contributors to the experiential shift in theory of religion discussed so far were Protestant theologians (Schleiermacher, Troeltsch, and Otto) or thinkers deeply influenced by Protestantism (Dilthey and James).[64] At first glance, it might seem as if this turn was limited to Protestantism, with its emphasis on the individual's relationship with God. The distance between such a theology and faith in the form of a grand neo-Scholastic doctrine for which the church claims supernatural authority, such that believers must simply fall obediently into line, could not be greater. But neither the authoritarian-hierarchical understanding of the church nor the supranaturalist rationalism of neo-Scholasticism went uncontested in the Catholic world. Of course, various thinkers made their voices heard in the so-called modernism dispute prior to the First World War, making points similar to those of Protestant advocates of an experiential turn. But to the extent that they were subject to the authority of Rome, they were silenced by draconian measures such as the infamous oath against modernism instituted in 1910 by Pope Pius X. I will consider these thinkers no further here. But it was necessary to mention this state of affairs briefly because it forms the background to Max Scheler's extremely ambitious attempt to renew the Catholic philosophy of religion.

Scheler—according to his own assessment, but also that of many contemporaries—seemed to have found an ingenious way out of the unfortunate opposition between the psychology of religion and the conceptual edifice of Scholasticism. This way out arises from Scheler's manner of building on phenomenology, while extending it to the attempt to use its tools to make statements not just about subjective experiences, but about "things themselves." This aspiration, moreover, is directed not only at knowledge of the world but also at feelings and value judgments. Scheler was able to build productively on Schleiermacher, James, and Otto through this phenomenological approach. Although he tends to combine this with polemical attempts to distance himself from these thinkers' philosophical and theological backgrounds, his proximity to them, at least methodologically, is unmistakable. Scheler, then, represents the exciting case of a Catholic attempt to overcome the intellectualist understanding of faith. When I investigate his work in this book, therefore, I will be particularly concerned with whether his sensitive analysis of the experience of subjective feelings of self-evidence, the underpinning of all faith and all secular value commitments, can in fact demonstrate the self-evidence of specific value systems.[65]

It was not Hegel but Kant who represented the great philosophical challenge for Scheler. He fully agreed with Hegel's criticism of Kant's ethics, centered on the moral "ought," but in his "material ethics of value," which took aim at "formalism," he was in search of a completely different approach than Hegel's.[66] He had no time for a teleological philosophy of history and no interest in examining human beings primarily in terms of their capacity for reason. He described Hegel's philosophy of history as "the last, highest, most highly developed theory of history within the framework of an anthropology of 'homo sapiens.'"[67]

Scheler called his ethics "personalism" because he, like Kant, was concerned with securing human dignity, above all other values, but also because, contra Kant, his ethics was one in which the human being is not identified primarily as a rational person.[68] For Scheler, what had remained ambiguous in Kant—personhood beyond the capacity for reason—becomes clear, in a problematic way, in the work of his German successors, especially Hegel. Here "the person becomes in the end an indifferent thoroughfare for an impersonal rational activity."[69] Similar wording crops up time and again in Scheler's writings. He thus established a connection between what he saw as the weakening of the concept of the person within the framework of a metaphysics of reason and the depersonalization of the idea of God.[70] Hence, for Scheler, the defense of human personhood in a sense that goes beyond the rational and the defense of a personalist theism against a philosophy of history anchored in a metaphysics of reason are one and the same thing. Of course, we do not have to agree with this identification.

In his philosophy of religion, which is discussed in more detail in this book, Scheler went so far as to describe the view "that an unfolding of ideas is what lies at the heart of religion's history, which according to what they consider the nature of religion is first and foremost the gradual unfolding in the human mind of the divine self-consciousness,"[71] as a core feature of pantheism. For all theisms, on the other hand, it is fundamental that there cannot be one "law of evolution" that explains the emergence and decline of religions. As in the work of James and Troeltsch, for Scheler the fact of ideal formation remains irreducible.

Akin to Rudolf Otto and much more clearly than Troeltsch and Dilthey, Scheler too bridled at the one-sided "Europeanism" of Hegel's historical thought.[72] In his later work this became an increasingly important motif in part because he changed from a combative theist to a sympathizer with Asian spiritual traditions. This obliged him to fundamentally alter his thinking—a process that remained fragmentary due to his early, unexpected death. What we have to go on are speculations that brought him closer to Hegel (though he did not share his ideas about reason), speculations on world history as the self-realization of a divine spirit, understood as the history of the becoming God, and on evolution as progressive spiritualization.[73]

When Max Scheler died in 1928, Martin Heidegger honored him at the beginning of a course of lectures with the words: "Max Scheler was . . . the strongest philosophical force in present-day Germany, no, in present-day Europe—in fact in contemporary philosophy as such."[74] He also dedicated his 1929 book on Kant "in memoriam Max Scheler."[75] Subsequently, however, he did little to keep Scheler from being forgotten. In general, it is in fact fair to say that the thinkers dealt with here have had a broad effective history in the empirical sciences of religion and in theology, whereas in philosophy, outside of Germany, Dilthey and James, Troeltsch, Otto, and Scheler have long been eclipsed by Heidegger and his student Hans-Georg Gadamer—to such an extent that they have ceased to exercise much of an influence beyond narrow circles.

I am unable to examine the reasons for this development here. But the reader has probably grasped that I intend this book to contribute to the revision of this development, a revision that is desirable far beyond issues in theory of religion as narrowly understood. In theory of religion's understanding of action and experience, intersubjectivity, corporeality, and creativity, we can discern a nonrationalist understanding of human beings and, in this sense, an anthropological conception of their freedom that is illuminating for many other fields as well. At this point, however, the crucial thing is that theory of religion after Hegel and Nietzsche, as developed among the thinkers dealt with here, does not draw a sharp line between philosophy and other forms of scholarship or between knowledge and faith. Instead, it establishes a nuanced relationship between them. Empirical research, philosophical reflection, and vibrant religious faith, rather than failing to achieve their respective goals, thus even have the potential to strengthen one other.

I, 2
The Independence of Religion: Ernst Troeltsch

In a world increasingly beset by virulent religio-political controversies, casting an eye over past debates might be one way of injecting some objectivity into this discourse. Various thinkers have taken us down certain unproductive paths several times over, while some of the more astute past interpreters of religion warned of the dangers of a reductive view of religious phenomena—and underlined the independence of religion—with greater nuance and insight than many present-day authors. It seems to me that few past thinkers have as much to offer us in these respects as Protestant theologian, historian of Christianity, sociologist of religion, and cultural philosopher Ernst Troeltsch. I intend to bring this out through a meditation on just one of his texts ("Die Selbständigkeit der Religion" or "The Independence of Religion").

Troeltsch did not include this essay, originally published in 1895–1896 in the *Zeitschrift für Theologie und Kirche*, in the four-volume selection of his collected writings (*Gesammelte Schriften*), nor was it reprinted anywhere else until the publication of the corresponding volume of the *Kritische Gesamtausgabe* in 2009.[1] As a result, over the last few decades and within the international debate, this text has received even less attention than the other writings of this major thinker. No English translation has so far appeared. And his essay does not make things easy for the reader, particularly a present-day one. If we apply the standards that increasingly hold sway today and that go a long way to determining the career prospects of up-and-coming scholars through the process of publication "in refereed journals," we soon realize that Troeltsch flagrantly violated every one of them. What present-day journal would accept a 165-page essay entirely devoid of subheadings and of any sort of easily graspable structure, a text whose long and complex sentences interleave the examination of factual issues with critical commentary on numerous thinkers of past and present? At best the editors would surely respond with "revise and resubmit." Troeltsch himself later described his early texts as "studies born of struggle and toil," "a patchwork that betrays its cobbled-togetherness."[2] Nonetheless, I believe this text to be a virtually inexhaustible source of still inspirational and stimulating ideas on the topic of religion and thus an apt medium for presenting my own perspective—an indirect mode of expression that precisely mirrors Troeltsch's own style. The key questions are: What is the main thesis of the "Independence of Religion" essay directed against? What risks does it entail? And how can we deal with these risks? Before providing a more detailed analysis, I will briefly describe the two antagonistic fronts one finds oneself sandwiched between the moment one asserts the "independence of religion."

The thesis of the independence of religion is a means of resisting every form of *reductionism* in the study of religion, in other words, every approach that, while recognizing that religious phenomena exist, ultimately views them as the mere expression of something else. In his great work on the psychology of religion, *The Varieties of Religious Experience*, William James wrote vividly of all forms of reductionism as "nothing but" explanations.[3] These are at work whenever religious phenomena are understood as the mere consequences of, for example, social or sexual repression or an overwrought imagination. We will see in a moment what a broad spectrum of possible reductionisms Troeltsch had in mind. It is also important that we reflect historically on how such reductionisms came to hold sway. To quote Charles Taylor, they presuppose the ascent of a "secular option."[4] Only when religion seems dispensable can we expect to find reductive explanations. In other words, the idea that comprehensive secularization is possible is the tacit precondition for "nothing but" explanations of religion. Their explanandum is religion rather than secularization. But if, against these explanations, one defends the independence of religion—in a sense that must, of course, be pinned down more precisely—then one runs the inverse risk of *essentializing* religion. We may forget that the concept of religion is itself the product of specific historical constellations and, moreover, is an abstraction from the concrete diversity of lived religious beliefs, from individual and collective practices of prayer and worship, for example. But even if we keep in mind this status of the concept of religion, it may be that specific religions such as Christianity, or even the cultures shaped by them, appear as fixed entities that, entirely self-contained, either persist over time or develop solely on the basis of their original motifs. These too are analytically detrimental essentializations. I see Troeltsch fighting a battle on two fronts against both reductionism and essentialism in the study of religion, and I see this dual battle as just as relevant now as it ever was.

But this doubly negative definition does not yet provide us with a methodological program, which of course requires positive formulation in its own right. Attempting to flesh out such a program inevitably means expressing our views on religious beliefs' truth claims and certain religions' claims to absolute validity, such as Christianity or Islam. This in turn inevitably throws up the question of how religions might meaningfully communicate with one another and what kind of relationship there might be between religions and the claims of a staunchly secular (or even secularist) reason. I believe Troeltsch addresses this entire agenda of issues in his wide-ranging early essay. While neither exhaustive nor conclusive, his answers are worth examining and reworking for the present day.

The background to his entire train of thought was his keen awareness of the intellectual challenges confronting Christianity in any given era. Troeltsch took up this challenge with great self-assurance. His deep faith that Christianity had nothing to fear from intellectual challenges spared him the need to indulge in shabby apologias. In fact he was convinced that the Christian faith could even be renewed and invigorated by such challenges, as it had so often been in the past. From his early to his late work we find attempts to catalogue these intellectual challenges and to identify which element of Christianity was in particular need of rearticulation in light of them. If we examine Troeltsch's efforts here we soon find that he did not see the real challenge as coming from the progress of natural science, Darwinism, or a dogmatic or skeptical materialism that invokes the natural sciences. I think this assessment is just as correct today. You have to be grossly ignorant of Christian doctrine and theology to suppose—like Richard Dawkins, the well-known critic of religion—that present-day Christians see the myth of the Creation as a paleo-ontologic theory. It is of course important to refute naturalistic reductions of key elements of the concept of the person—in response to the denial of "free will," for example—by exponents of a new neurophysiological determinism. But well-developed counterarguments have been put forward since the nineteenth century, and here we can identify an alliance between defenders of the Christian view of humanity and secular thinkers who also advocate a sophisticated understanding of human behavior, reason, and the person.

Troeltsch perceived a far greater challenge emanating from the humanities of the nineteenth century—in the shape of the sweeping historicization of all validity claims. In this context, the shock waves produced by historical Bible criticism were still being felt. But far beyond this, at work here was the tremendous increase in knowledge of the history of Christianity and the history of other religions—and the increasingly radical questioning of whether anything enduring at all can emerge from the flow of history. Does the contingent genesis of validity claims inevitably render any notion of timeless validity illusory? For the rest of his career, up to and including the composition of his unfinished magnum opus *Der Historismus und seine Probleme* ("Historicism and Its Problems"), Troeltsch was to work on his answer to these questions.[5] What this answer means for the study of religion is that we must take seriously the claim made by religions of revelation that they speak of a God who reveals himself in historical events, but without succumbing to a "revelatory positivism." That is, it is impermissible to remove this revelation entirely from history, viewing it as the mere incursion of something nonhistorical into the realm of history.[6]

Notably, however, both here and in other writings Troeltsch identifies three more key challenges for Christianity. These are, first, the triumphant advance of what he called an "empiricist-utilitarian ethics of welfare" (365/362), that is, the tension between the Christian ethos of love and the idea of the human being as utility maximizer and pursuer of self-interest—an idea that has been all but institutionalized in the discipline of economics and has also spread to the social sciences and sections of philosophy; second, a tendency—once again in Troeltsch's words—toward "advancing immanentization" (366/363), that is, the decline of the idea of transcendence, and here we should note that Troeltsch discerned this tendency before it had become fully manifest in the militant, so-called political religions of the twentieth century; and third, those tendencies toward expressive individualization that allow us to envisage spirituality, if at all, merely in an individualistically constricted form, reducing the church to a "cultic association" and thus losing sight of the extent to which religious institutions are the prerequisite for individual faith.

There is no room here to explore this broad palette of challenges and their present-day relevance.[7] But I had to mention them because they form the background to Troeltsch's alertness to attempts to reduce the religious sphere even when they are far from obvious. It is of course to be expected that Troeltsch rejects all "illusionist" explanations of religion, such as analyses of religion as a kind of overextension of the "desire for causality." For Troeltsch, the supposedly constitutive character of this overextension is impossible to prove because attributions of causality are always already bound up with traditional ideas about higher powers, and the "satisfaction of the need to think" (387/384) is in no way decisive to the genesis of religion. Troeltsch was more forgiving of the theory that religious ideas represent the projection of human capacities onto a "humanlike power" (388/385) because here at least the emphasis is on the "enjoyable and tangible content of human life" rather than the "need to think" (388/385). This, of course, is a conception of the kind initiated by Ludwig Feuerbach and disseminated by Sigmund Freud in the twentieth century, one that present-day thinkers continue to use with astonishing thoughtlessness. Troeltsch disputed that religion emerged from a single type of feeling, including Schleiermacher's "absolute dependence" (*schlechthinnige Abhängigkeit*), and instead tried—with the aid of the concept of "awe" (*Ehrfurcht*)—to get to grips with the inherently complex constellation of feelings associated with the "sacred," as William James, Émile Durkheim, and Rudolf Otto were later to do with momentous consequences for the study of religion in the twentieth century.

But far more fascinating than his predictable rejection of "illusionistic" explanations is Troeltsch's critique of explanations that reduce religion to metaphysics, morality, or aesthetics. For him it is wrong to view religion as nothing but metaphysics because religion is chiefly concerned with how we live on a practical level rather than the systematic, speculative interpretation of the world. Troeltsch opposed attempts to reduce religion to morality chiefly with reference to Kant's philosophy of religion.[8] As much as he admired Kant's moral philosophy, he believed it a mistake to try to ground religion in moral philosophy. According to Troeltsch, this is merely to add another postulate to that of moral freedom, which he already considered flawed; Kant thus attains "a mere analogue to religion" (459/82) rather than lived religion itself. Kant's religion is no more than "human reconstructing and positing, a theoretical supplement to an only directly experienceable moral world order rather than the living and experiencing of the community of God" (459/82). The many passages critical of Kant here and elsewhere in Troeltsch's work clearly show that, at least during this phase of his intellectual development, he was not only no neo-Kantian but in key respects not even a Kantian, and in fact saw his work as a way of overcoming Kant. At the same time, he was aware that Kant's book on religion rapidly stimulated developments that went far beyond it. But neither Schleiermacher, whom he saw as lacking any sense of history, nor Hegel, whom he praised for his grasp of the stuff of history (based on what was known at the time) could provide much guidance here. In the case of Hegel, Troeltsch sensed the danger of an intellectualist misapprehension of religion and the even greater danger of "comprehending the religious process as a purely human movement of thought and abandoning any attempt to ground religion in its divine factor" (370f./369), making it easy for Hegel's materialist or naturalistic successors to dismiss "the living self-revelation of the divine personality" (371/369) as an illusion while advocating a purely immanent and at the same time intellectualist conception of religion. For Troeltsch, the aestheticizing "Bildungsreligion" or religion of the educated in the nineteenth-century German-speaking world is the last place to look for genuine communion with God.

Troeltsch rejected all these explanatory paths. For him, it was wrong to assimilate the religious sphere into the realms of logic, morality, or aesthetics: apart from anything else, the history of religion has shown that it was not closely linked with these realms during the early stages of its development. The distinction between these fields was important to him with respect to the present because only in this way can we grasp the difference between religion and every culture, the sense in which the religious message exceeds the features particular to a given culture. Though every attempt to articulate faith is tied to cultural realities and the general state of intellectual development, for Troeltsch religion is not just one cultural field among others. Here his tone becomes notably sharper: "it is pure superficiality to see nothing but the cultural ideal in the religious ideal. . . . Demonstrably, there is always a certain tension between every profound and vibrant faith on the one hand and culture on the other, not because, losing faith in its own strength, this faith neglects to realize its goals itself and leaves them in the hands of the gods, but because it seeks something other and higher in the first place" (406/404). It also seems to me that this emphasis on the culture-transcending character at least of all transcendence-focused religion clearly shows that it is a mistake to include Troeltsch among the exponents of so-called Cultural Protestantism, at least if this is assumed to be largely forgetful of transcendence. It is this culture-transcendent character that his resistance to the reduction of religion intends to salvage.

This resistance itself requires a positive definition of what constitutes this irreducibly religious sphere and therefore how we should proceed methodologically when studying religion. For years I have advocated the idea that we have William James to thank for a revolutionary shift in the history of the study of religion.[9] His fundamental methodological innovation was to make religious experiences the starting point for the study of religion. With confident one-sidedness, in his book of 1902 he proposed that we comprehend theological doctrines and church institutions as secondary phenomena that must be viewed methodologically from the perspective of the primary phenomenon, namely the religious experience. From this vantage point, religious faith is not primarily a cognitive believing-to-be-true that comes about as a result of persuasive arguments and can be argumentatively unsettled. Instead, it is an attitude toward reality undergirded by a secure sense of the presence of a greater power. James compared faith with the vital basic attitude typical of lovers, whose entire relationship to the world, even when their attention is fixed on other objects, is underpinned by a sense of the continuous presence of the loved other. Faith is thus grounded in experiences of what I call self-transcendence that leave us with a sense of certainty—despite the difficulties involved in articulating this experience. There thus arises a willingness to be that may be lost in states of melancholy or depression. What particularly interested James about conversion and prayer is their nonvolitional character: they involve an active search for communication with the very power from which the individual's life force flows, yet this communication cannot be forced but only graciously address and reveal itself to us.

Troeltsch was one of the first to pay tribute to James's book as the "masterpiece" that it is, engaging deeply with it in a number of texts.[10] But it would be wrong to view his work merely as a continuation of James's. The essay "The Independence of Religion" clearly reveals the extent to which Troeltsch, long before the appearance of James's book, was already headed in the same direction. And this is not all. The numerous theologians, philosophers, and historians, most of them now forgotten, whom Troeltsch referred to in his essay and accompanying book reviews represent a kind of polyphonic choir preparing the ground for the paradigm shift in the study of religion. Troeltsch himself, of course, contra neo-Kantianism and attempts to renew idealist systematic philosophy, had called for a return to Kant *and* Schleiermacher because their writings at least provided the starting point for a "psychological analysis." For him too, religion rests upon experience (419/414), and, very much in analogy to what James was to call his radical empiricism, Troeltsch advocated an undogmatic, rich concept of experience that is itself, as it were, open to experience. He mentioned Dilthey as his role model, with some reservations, and certain others such as his teacher Gustav Claß, along with Hermann Lotze and Wilhelm Wundt, all thinkers who played a key role in the early work of George Herbert Mead, for example,[11] and Georg

Wobbermin, who was soon to translate James's book into German.[12] Here, in exemplary and processual form, we see the convergence, within the study of religion, of pragmatist and historical-hermeneutic developments in the second half of the nineteenth century.[13]

It seems to me that it is only if we acknowledge this convergence that we begin to grasp the value of the lengthy passages on concepts such as will, ideal, sense impression (*Empfindung*), and representation (*Vorstellung*) in the writings of nineteenth-century philosophers and psychologists. In this connection, Troeltsch seems to be making tentative efforts to free himself from the (neo-)idealist semantics of spirit (*Geist*) and, like the pragmatists, to conceive of a concept of action that is not geared toward means-ends relations or compliance with norms but that instead foregrounds the creative character of human action. What Isaiah Berlin and Charles Taylor have so insistently highlighted over the last few decades—the German tradition of an "expressivist" model of action—is central to Troeltsch's thinking. This conception of action is closely entwined with the historicist sensitivity to the endless diversity of cultural phenomena. Troeltsch needed such a model of action because it is only with its help, against all reductionisms, that he could introduce his definition of religion as a "practical self-relation to a living deity" (398/396). Here the emphasis is on the practical dimension, which can only ever be grasped incompletely in any process of reflection, and the "aliveness" of the deity, which he described as its turn to the human being, its intervention in history and our lives. For Troeltsch, religion is based on the "experience of a power that compels, sustains and generates us."[14] So any understanding of religion that disregards this existential-practical dimension or that fails to take seriously—at least on the phenomenal level—believers' experience that they get answers, and that their devotion makes them the vessel of a higher will, must be seen as flawed from the outset.

This definition of religion will look like an apologia to some. But this was not Troeltsch's intention, any more than James's. It seems reasonable to assume that both were looking for a methodological level that is neither apologetic nor hostile to religion, that is, one that neither introduces specific religious presuppositions helter-skelter into the study of religion nor demands that the study of religion be based on secularist presuppositions if it is to avoid being dismissed as crypto-theology. The task must be to avoid both these things, and both Troeltsch and James supposed that they had satisfied this desideratum through a psychological analysis of those human experiences that believers interpret in religious terms. They were also aware that it is part and parcel of these experiences that their content is experienced as "inexpressible as such" (423/417). Religious experience attains its specific form through "media" of expression, and this explains "how absolutely everything that might serve as a means of triggering and expressing religious experience may become an enduring symbol and vehicle of one's conception of God" (423/417)—every conceivable natural phenomenon, every imaginable event in human life, every correct or erroneous conception of the powers, forces and laws in the cosmos, every experience of beauty and of moral laws.

While Troeltsch still lagged behind contemporary pragmatism when it came to the definition of action and experience, his work is undoubtedly superior to that of James in at least one respect. Troeltsch's oeuvre is the culmination of generations of work on the history of religion, and this enabled him to ground his contribution to the study of religion in a dual sense, in terms of both the psychology and the history of religion. We should understand his great speech of 1904 in St. Louis, during his trip through the United States with Max Weber, as the weaving together of these two threads.[15] His comprehensive education in the history of religion inoculated him against essentializations of religion as such or of specific religions. He expressly rejected (425/419) all attempts to determine the "essence" of religion and countered them by stating, "We respect the infinite variety of life, which yields to no definition." His accounts were intended as the beginning rather than the end of the study of religion. He opposed Hegel's "omniscience" (*Allwissenheit*) with the "renunciative devotion to reality" (470/93).

There is no contradiction between the experience-focused definition of religion on which the thesis of the independence of religion is based and the rejection of essentialist definitions because, conceived like this, the study of religion seeks to design its concepts in such a way that we can grasp the endless variety of religious phenomena in their specific contexts. That is, every specific religion or, to quote Troeltsch, every "productive conception of God" that underpins a religious community, "entails, not on the basis of reflection but as a matter of fact, a sense of the world, a mentality, that constitutes a unified, practical whole, a specific, fundamental relationship to God, world and human being" (439/429). This is at work in religious traditions not as enduring cause or fixed telos but as a "germinative principle"[16] that cannot be definitively transformed into a doctrine either by scholars or the faithful themselves. As unavoidable as the doctrinal formulation and institutional shaping of a given basic religious inspiration are, dogmatic torpor and organizational forms that have become "lifeless" (436/427) may represent a danger to faith. One of Troeltsch's key theological motives was to demonstrate the "entanglement of Christian and non-Christian elements,"[17] rather than seeking to separate Christianity off from the history of religion. Significantly, in his great work on *The Social Teaching of the Christian Churches*,[18] Troeltsch elucidated these methodological principles in more detail, but above all he applied them impressively to the history of Christianity, the "endlessly changing and fracturing intellectual world of Christianity,"[19] which "can only be understood in light of the entirety of its realizations and whose creative plenitude may impact on future realities in unforeseeable ways."[20] Elsewhere I have called for comparative studies of the "political ethics of the world religions" informed by this insight.[21]

As a field of scholarly endeavor, the study of religion must be free of tacit presuppositions of both an apologetic and secularist character; it should neither simply presuppose the truth claims of a particular religion nor declare every truth claim of every religion to be illusory. If this is so, then the study of religion must bring out the specific character of religious truth claims—which differ both from cognitive and normative validity claims and do not coincide with the mere claim to subjective truthfulness either—and analyze how a reasonable debate on such religious truth claims might be possible. Troeltsch approached a closer definition of the specific truth claim characteristic of religious convictions via the concept of "a sense of ideal values" (392/390). He tried to distinguish between two types of generality of judgment: cognitive judgments that may be detached "from all subjective varieties of feeling" (393/391) and "ideas" or "ideals" that can "never be detached from their attendant feelings of value and excitations of will" and whose self-evident character rests "not merely on their presence in the mind as such, but especially on their power to elevate and guide the mind, a power one must surrender oneself to if one wishes to prevent the seeds of these ideas from drying up" (393/392). These ideals are indissolubly linked with individuality but this does *not* mean they have no "tendency toward generality" but merely that this tendency is a quite different one than in the case of purely discursive-argumentative rationality.[22] Troeltsch is circumspect enough to recognize that even within this realm of values religion is something special, that is, something more than "the mere imaginative sensualization of the ideal law of reason" (396/394), that—as set out earlier—religion is in fact a practical relationship to a deity that we experience as a force that bestows salvation or calamity. In Troeltsch's work, it should be noted, the analytical distinction between factual and value judgments does not imply that they can in reality be neatly separated from one another.[23]

So religions may be "true," though here "true" does not have the same meaning as in scientific propositions or cognitive assertions in general. But how do we find out which religion is true? How can we engage with religions' truth claims without fundamentally missing the specific character of religious truth claims? Troeltsch makes it clear—in his polemic response to Herbert Spencer, for example—what he considers to be the wrong approach, one, as it happens, that he also sees in the work of Hegelians. This is the notion of a "syncretism of all religions that condenses what they have in common," the "amalgamation and merging of all individual religions in which their common core then emerges as the universally valid and teleologically conclusive element" (450/74). For Troeltsch as a historicist, it is the "unfortunate and confusing, absolutist cult of general concepts" that leads us astray in this way. All that ever comes of such attempts is a "cautiously conceived metaphysical idea," never a "viable religion." We can be fairly sure that Troeltsch would have had similarly strong reservations about the search for the lowest common ethical denominator in the world religions or the idea of the philosophical translatability of the "germinative principle" inherent in religious traditions or inspirations. As he sees it, there is only one way forward: to penetrate the "specific historical manifestations of religion" (372/370) themselves and to participate in the dynamics of interreligious debate oneself. But in this early work he does not really deliver—as Karl Jaspers was later to do[24]—the foundations of a theory of reasonable communication about statements on transcendence, but instead pursues an "idealist evolutionism." That is, through an investigation in the history of religion, he attempts to identify immanent laws of religious development that do not prove, but lend plausibility to, Christianity's claim to be the highest and ultimate form of the universal religious phenomenon. Through reflections on the development of the idea of God, world, and soul, he aims to show that "the inner dialectic of the religious idea [points] in the direction of the completely individual and thus universalist religion of salvation" (515/200).

While I by no means view ideas about religion's evolution toward universalism and individualization as misconceived,[25] I believe these (theological) concluding passages of Troeltsch's great essay to be his most outdated. Despite a number of attempts to engage with Buddhism and Islam, Troeltsch's horizon remains what I would call "Mediterranocentric," to the point that he asserts that world culture was essentially "created" in the associated region

(532/216). And we find numerous statements here that infer, in light of a devout faith in God, that there is an inherent, positive, teleological tendency in history. Troeltsch no longer expressed such ideas after the First World War and the shocking experience of historical contingency associated with it. It is striking that he appears to oscillate between an illusion-free view of religious history "with its terrible atrocities and its stupid and selfish folly" (471/95), a history, he believed, that could not be written as a history of progress but showed only "the utterly incommensurable flaring up of great religious impulses that dominate the masses for centuries" (471/96) and an idealist, teleological philosophy of history. Here, just as in his specific notion of the character of religious experience, there is a shift of emphasis in Troeltsch's subsequent development. But in order to avoid succumbing to the myth of an unavoidably relativist historicism and of the necessity for an existentialist break with this approach, it is important to be aware of this internal tension in Troeltsch's work even at this early stage.

If we fail to do so, Troeltsch's comprehensive research program vanishes behind the old and oft-revived division between the theological and secular-scientific study of religion. I see his program, which I have tried to bring up to date here without adhering to the structure of Troeltsch's early essay, as a brilliant attempt to make a distinction between theology and the study of religion while also closely linking them. This program meets with the disapproval of certain schools of theology and of every philosopher and humanities scholar who identifies scholarship with the embrace of a secularist worldview. But for those keen to overcome this unproductive, mutual ignorance, Troeltsch is surely a prime candidate for consideration as a great thinker in the theory of religion.

I, 3
Secular Sacredness: Rudolf Otto

Rudolf Otto's book *The Idea of the Holy* appeared in 1917—while the First World War was still ongoing and shortly before the epoch-making political and cultural sea change in Germany brought about by this war. It was immediately and enduringly perceived as a book of "liberation" and "breakthrough." These were the phrases used by Paul Tillich to articulate the sense—widely shared beyond his subjective view—that here, in the field of philosophy of religion,

> under all the rational rigidities and encumbrances borne not only by the ecclesiastical but also the philosophical-idealist consciousness of the last few decades, the primordial fire of the vital stirred, and those petrified layers began to shake and tear asunder.[1]

The book's impact extended "into the sphere of personal piety," whether it was read at the front—Tillich himself read it in Champagne—or at home and after demobilization. Rudolf Otto (1869–1937) had envisaged reaching such a readership, far beyond the academic world, and wrote his book in suggestive prose, which differed significantly from the compilation of exotic facts (as in Wilhelm Wundt's *Völkerpsychologie* or folk psychology) and the development of abstract philosophical ideas (as in Wilhelm Windelband's study of the sacred). Otto's work has been called "the best-selling book of theology or religious studies of the modern era."[2] While I do not know the sales figures, the statement does not seem implausible to me, and I can think of only one competitor that might possibly have attracted even more readers: William James's *The Varieties of Religious Experience* of 1902. In the English-speaking world, the truly revolutionary breakthrough in the study of religion is attributed to James's book rather than to Rudolf Otto. While "sacredness" does not occupy the same core conceptual position in James's work as in Otto's, a cursory glance at both texts reveals methodological similarities with regard to the analysis of religious experience.

Was Otto's book a breakthrough only from a limited national perspective? In what sense can we call it a breakthrough at all and perhaps even today? If we distance ourselves from Otto's self-stylization and the perspective of his contemporaries, is there anything left in Otto's work of ongoing relevance?

In this chapter, I set myself to the task of exploring the topicality of Rudolf Otto, but not in the simple sense of extracting individual elements of his ideas from his oeuvre as a whole and scrutinizing their utility for the analysis of present-day phenomena. What I have in mind is a more demanding, dual endeavor of probing his topicality through a historical contextualization of his work while seeking, through reflection on today's changed theoretical situation, to determine what Otto might still be able to add to it. In the first instance, then, I try not to treat Rudolf Otto as a solitary figure in the religious studies landscape, but rather to embed him in the broad discourse on "sacredness" that developed internationally from the middle of the nineteenth century onward; I am particularly interested in establishing how this discourse managed to get off the ground during that era.

I then relate Otto's understanding of the sacred to the current theoretical situation, in which other authors—Émile Durkheim, Max Weber, and William James—play a greater role, at least in the social sciences, than Otto does when it comes to the dynamics of processes of sacralization (and desacralization) in the history of religion, especially under conditions of radical secularization. My own theoretical efforts come into play here as well. Methodologically, these two steps are held together by the idea that historical contextualization is not the opposite of updating, but rather its prerequisite. This was the argument made by Ernst Troeltsch when he sought to lay the ground for the enlivening of the Christian faith by probing the history of religion, recommending this approach, far beyond religious questions, as a way out of the dangers of relativism characteristic of historicism.

Rationalization in the Numinous

Otto's contemporaries already noticed that in his bestseller on the sacred he scarcely mentioned more recent literature, referring almost exclusively to sources and thinkers from the classical period of German philosophy, especially Kant, Schleiermacher, and the otherwise largely forgotten Jakob Friedrich Fries,[3] who was undergoing a brief period of rediscovery and about whom Otto had published a book in 1909. Was he unfamiliar with the contemporary literature, or did he want to cover the tracks that would allow the reader to reconstruct the route he had taken to his ideas? Let's consider William James as our first example. He appears only three times in Otto's book (25, 51f., 68),[4] always in a marginal way and twice with rather negative comments. In particular, James's pragmatism or "radical empiricism" is given short shrift, as was customary in Germany at the time when dealing with US thinkers.[5] Otto dismisses James's approach as a primitive aberration that obstructs all access "to a recognition of faculties of knowledge and potentialities of thought in the spirit itself" (25). Even at the time, an expert on James such as Troeltsch was struck by how inappropriate this was. In his review of 1918, he stated that Otto's work stood in close proximity to that of James to the extent that the American thinker remained purely a psychologist, and like James, Otto adheres "essentially to the subjective religion underlying the objective formations of myth, dogma, worship, etc., and above all . . . presupposes the material collected by James, to which he adds from the Bible, the Koran, mystics, Luther and Indian religion only a few, but well-chosen, supporting passages."[6]

Troeltsch also highlights Otto's closeness to Dilthey, but above all to his own observations, largely in line with Dilthey's thinking, in his wide-ranging essay "Die Selbständigkeit der Religion"; he calls Otto's book, possibly with a slight reproach, "a complete parallel" to this text, which was more than twenty years older.[7] Even more curious than Otto's taciturnity when it comes to James and Troeltsch is that while he briefly mentions two other key contributors to the international discourse on sacredness within religious studies and theology (Robert Ranulph Marett and Nathan Söderblom; 29, fn. 1), he does not identify them as forerunners or true pioneers (though he goes so far as to describe Marett's work as groundbreaking) but as a "very welcome" subsequent "confirmation" of his own assertions in his dispute with Wilhelm Wundt of 1910. Several things are puzzling about this. Most of Marett's studies of "mana," taboo, and pre-animistic religion had been published and widely received before the appearance of his essay collection in 1909.[8]

Meanwhile, Otto mentions his review of Söderblom's book *Das Werden des Götterglaubens* of 1915 (mysteriously dated to 1925 in my edition), yet analysis of Otto's correspondence[9] has revealed that the two theologians came into contact immediately after publication of Otto's Schleiermacher edition of 1899, that Otto visited Söderblom in Paris in 1900, and that they remained in touch, while Söderblom's own influential writings on the sacred, especially his contribution to the *Encyclopedia of Religion and Ethics* of 1913, refer quite openly to the work of Émile Durkheim and his students Marcel Mauss and Henri Hubert.[10] Marett had mentioned their work on magic of 1904[11] as a systematically superior parallel to his own research, so it would be surprising if Otto had not followed up on this. It also appears that Otto was aware of Durkheim's 1912 work *Les formes élémentaires de la vie religieuse*, without, however, mentioning it.[12] Prior to the work of Marett, Söderblom, Durkheim, Hubert, and Mauss, earlier studies had been published on Greco-Roman (Fustel de Coulanges) and Semitic (Robertson Smith) religion, which, from a history-of-religion perspective, pointed in a similar direction to William James from a psychology-of-religion standpoint: religions are not to be understood primarily as doctrinal systems or institutions, but as systems of collective and individual ritual practices and the experiences these facilitate.

I have no wish to delve further here into the intricate pathways of influence characteristic of the discourse on sacredness around 1900.[13] I am certainly not out to clarify questions of "copyright" or claims of precedence in the history of scholarship. But grasping that Otto's work was a significant tributary to a broad river but not its source relativizes the importance of autobiographical statements about motives, such as Otto's claim that his intellectual development was crucially inspired by the far from rationalistic "peasant's son" Luther or by an ecstatic experience in a Moroccan synagogue. In general, it relativizes the significance of each individual contributor to this broad discourse, which could develop only once the ground had been laid for it through an array of historical changes—to which a variety of motives can then be linked. It is this array that I wish to scrutinize.

Two historical changes seem to me crucial here. One concerns the rise of the secular option in broad circles of the bourgeoisie and working class during this period—for example, in Germany and France. I prefer to refer to people embracing the secular option—borrowing from Charles Taylor's terminology[14]—rather than to "secularization," to make it clear that this was not a quasi-inevitable process that affected everyone equally, but rather a series of events that affected individuals in very different ways in line with their sociocultural milieu and political orientation, an occurrence molded by their subjective interpretations of the situation. This rise of the secular option made numerous observers aware that the widespread departure from traditional religious communities could not be equated with a move away from all "religiosity." The secular option represents something new entering the world, something that certainly takes up space but does not conquer it without resistance. In any case, this renders faith itself an option; it loses the taken-for-grantedness it may have had, becoming faith in the presence of the possibility of unbelief.[15]

This insight was sometimes put to empirical use, as when William James, for example, paid attention to religious revival movements and the emergence of new religions. It was also utilized to normative and programmatic ends, through efforts to promote a post-Christian "religion de l'humanité" in the work of Émile Durkheim, which featured the idea of human rights as the sacralization of the person and of the nation as a means of realizing these rights. Empirically, in the work of Marcel Mauss, but especially later in that of Eric Voegelin, Raymond Aron, and others, attempts followed to conceptualize the secular national and social movements of the nineteenth century, but above all the totalitarianisms of the twentieth century, as political or secular religions, as replacements or substitutes for religion, as pseudo- or crypto-religions—and thus with a great deal of conceptual fluctuation.

What all these intellectual approaches have in common is that they did not simply respond to the mass embrace of the secular option or at least (in the United States) to the progressive individualization of religion with an apologia asserting that religion is anthropologically indispensable. But nor did they proclaim, on the basis of a shallow secularism, the elimination—without substitution—of outdated "superstition" and the overcoming of uncivilized "fanaticism," two key terms in the arsenal of the Enlightenment critique of religion. Instead, they undertook to determine the specific qualities of human experience that underlie all religion and that do not simply vanish with the rise of the secular option. The term that became widely established to convey this experiential quality was that of the sacred. Religions thus inevitably appeared as systems that organize the experience of the sacred—"l'administration du sacré"—but the sacred itself appeared as "l'idée mère de la religion" (Henri Hubert),[16] such that the previous conception, which arises from the internal perspective of a religion (and from a critique of religion that merely denigrates this inner perspective), is turned upside down analytically. The "sacred" is thus detached from the institutional and doctrinal contexts suggested by the term "religion."

As different as the politics of religion in Germany were from that of Durkheim's France or William James's United States, what Rudolf Otto and these thinkers had in common was their attempt to respond to the proliferating criticism of religion not simply with apologias but by redefining the level at which the discourse on religion could be conducted methodically in the first place. It is especially true of James and Otto that they were looking for a level at which one might pursue a science of religion whose statements are plausible both for believers of different faiths and for secularists. This required an equal distance, on the one hand, from a theology that simply selected otherwise undeducible "revelatory positivist" propositions as a starting point for its statements, and on the other hand, from reductionist religious studies that can in principle recognize religious phenomena only as expressions of other phenomena—what William James called "nothing-but" explanations.[17] Crucially, the secular option is the tacit prerequisite for such reductionisms; in them, religion as such rather than just a certain faith becomes the *explanandum*. Without irreligiousness, this conceptual framework and such a quasi-external view of all religion would be quite impossible. Meanwhile, against apologetics and reductionism, the turn to "experience" makes it possible to define a field of phenomena about which we can make statements that have a certain independence from religious or antireligious grand interpretations.

The second development that set the tone of the discourse on sacredness around 1900 was the growing realization that terms derived from the Abrahamic religions (Judaism, Christianity, and Islam) are poorly suited to grasping the nontheistic or less theistic religions of South and East Asia as well as the religions of Africa and the South Pacific, for which terms such as "naturism," "animism," "pre-animism" and "totemism" emerged. At the end of the nineteenth century, colonialism and imperialism intensified a cultural confrontation that had set in earlier but whose intellectual impact long remained highly limited.[18] The knowledge possessed by leading eighteenth-century thinkers on religion—from David Hume to Friedrich Schleiermacher—was still meager in this regard, and even Ernst Troeltsch a hundred years later, unlike Max Weber, was largely unfamiliar with non-Christian religions.

This applied neither to Rudolf Otto, a veritable expert on Hinduism, nor to the other leading contributors to the discourse on sacredness. Durkheim and Mauss were concerned with the universal history of religion and focused, for example, on the indigenous peoples of Australia and North America. Marett developed his ideas about pre-animist religion, which were central to the discourse on sacredness, through the study of Melanesians and sought to identify the imaginative material out of which notions of gods can initially form, the "common plasm" or "theoplasm."[19] Concepts such as "god" and "gods," and even more so "the supernatural," were soon understood to entail far too many implicit presuppositions. In search of truly fundamental structures, scholars came across "taboo" and "mana," which are impersonal forces; in a variety of ways, these thinkers established relationships between such phenomena and the concepts derived from them.

But the intellectual processing of the rise of the secular option and the intensified confrontation with nontheistic religious experience were by no means completely separate. As early as the eighteenth century, the Enlightenment vogue for China was partly rooted in the interpretation of Confucianism as a purely secular corpus of wisdom,[20] and for decades in the nineteenth century the Australian Aborigines were considered a virtually nonreligious culture.[21] The possibility of irreligiosity in the past or at earlier stages of humanity's development appeared to strengthen the prospect of developing a purely secular culture in the future as well.

Focusing on religious experience, and in particular the experience of sacredness, changed the parameters of the broad range of debates on religion in highly innovative ways. For Otto, even more than for James, this meant pursuing a new opportunity to revitalize the Christian faith. As Otto saw it, the psychology-of-religion and history-of-religion perspectives did not render Christianity's truth claims irrelevant in relativistic fashion. While he, like Max Weber, referred to "a process . . . by which the numinous is throughout rationalized and moralized" (90), for him—in contrast to Weber—this did not amount to progressive "disenchantment," because, as he put it, "this moralizing and rationalizing process does not mean that the numinous itself has been overcome, but merely that its preponderance has been overcome. The numinous is at once the basis upon which and the setting within which the ethical and rational meaning is consummated" (90).

This idea dovetails perfectly with one of the leitmotifs in what is perhaps the most important contribution to historically oriented sociology of religion of our time, namely the formula "nothing is ever lost" in Robert Bellah's studies.[22] On this view, for example, theoretical rationality does not replace the mimetic-ritual or mythical-narrative dimensions, but is added to them as the question of which history we can legitimately narrate and also as the critical reconfiguration of all existing histories. This is why, in elaborating the numinous in Christianity, Otto does not simply have the past in mind. For him, "This atonement mystery is a 'moment' which no Christian teaching that purports to represent the religious experience of the Christian and

Biblical tradition can afford to surrender" (71). "It will be the task for contemporary Christian teaching to follow in his traces and again to deepen the rational meaning of the Christian conception of God by permeating it with its non-rational elements" (125). But since Otto does not simply place the irrational in opposition to rationalization, but thinks in terms of rationalization *in* the numinous, he emphasizes that

> The God of the New Testament is not less holy than the God of the Old Testament, but more holy. The interval between the creature and Him is not diminished but made absolute; the unworthiness of the profane in contrast to Him is not extenuated but enhanced. That God nonetheless admits access to Himself and intimacy with Himself is not a mere matter of course; it is a grace beyond our power to apprehend, a prodigious paradox. To take this paradox out of Christianity is to make it shallow and superficial beyond recognition. (71f.)

It seems to me that some scholars have failed to grasp the potency of this ultimately Christian-religious impulse in Otto's work when, like Carsten Colpe, they interpret his book on the sacred as a mere attempt to provide consolation following the collapse of Cultural Protestantism and nation-centric hopes.[23] While this may be true of some recipients, it fails to capture the author's intention. Hans Gerhard Kippenberg also goes too far in reducing Otto's ideas to a mere longing for the sacred in an era of disenchantment—a longing, that is, which was bound to be disappointed.[24] More fitting, it seems to me, was the response to Otto of the young Leo Strauss, who recognized that theology's stance had to change profoundly as a result of the progressive proliferation of the secular option. In a world of faith, it had to give the rational its due, but now

> in a spiritual world dominated by reason, [it must] make "the irrational in the idea of the divine" alive to the age through the medium of theoretical consciousness. Earlier theology speculated in a religiously closed vault— the new theology lives in the open air and must itself do what it can to assist in the construction of the vault. In the past, the first fact was God. Today it is: world, man, religious experience.[25]

In this methodological respect, Otto and the entire discourse on sacredness of his era are undoubtedly still highly relevant, especially since the two developments I have mentioned during this period—the spread of the secular option and increased confrontation with nontheistic religiosity—have if anything gained in importance. As I see it, the analysis of sacralization processes of all kinds in past and present is a core topic not only in the sociology of religion but far beyond it. Nevertheless—something that always astonishes me at a subjective level—my assertion here is typically assumed to entail a confessional slant. Is reference to sacredness Catholic in some way? If we include the discourse on sacredness in all its breadth, this assumption seems outlandish. The key contributors to this discourse, as mentioned, were French Jews such as Durkheim and Mauss as well as Otto the Lutheran German theologian and Nathan Söderblom, later Lutheran archbishop in Uppsala, Sweden. Confronted with this assumption, Rudolf Otto would likely have pointed out that "the feeling of the numinous" is indeed "a living factor of singular power" in Catholicism,

> in Catholic forms of worship and sacramental symbolism, in the less authentic forms assumed by legend and miracle, in the paradoxes and mysteries of Catholic dogma, in the Platonic and neo-Platonic strands woven into the fabric of its religious conceptions, in the solemnity of churches and ceremonies, and especially in the intimate rapport of Catholic piety with mysticism. (110)

Yet Otto also knew that the official doctrines of Catholicism were subject to a very "strong rationalizing influence," "to which, however, actual living religious practice and feeling never conformed or corresponded" (110). He perceived the tension between the rational and the irrational, the prospect of rationalization *in* the numinous and the risks of the rationalization *of* the numinous in all Christian confessions and in every religion, to the extent that it had become subject to rationalization in the first place. However, this does not answer the question of whether this is anything more than wishful thinking on the part of those keen to see the emergence of a vital modern religion or whether, after the Enlightenment, the Christian faith must distance itself from all religion and sacredness. Before I can delve into Otto's topicality in this regard, having embedded his conception of the sacred in the intellectual context of the time, I must now examine more closely the specific features of this conception within the aforementioned broad discourse and seek to determine whether his thinking can fit meaningfully within today's theoretical landscape.

Subjectivity and Objectivity of the Sacred

As the starting point for the more specific emplacement of Rudolf Otto within the broad discourse on sacredness that unfolded in the decades around 1900, I choose the question of how Otto envisages the relationship between the subjectivity and objectivity of the sacred. To put it more simply, can everything in the world be sacralized, or can people not avoid perceiving certain experiences as an encounter with something intrinsically sacred? Can the latter happen only if this something is sacred in and of itself, independent of all human experience? The contributors to the sacredness discourse differ greatly on this question. We find the entire spectrum of views here, ranging from a completely objectivist standpoint to a way of thinking according to which the sacred is nothing other than the collective ascription of this quality. I see the objectivist pole as occupied by the most important Catholic contributor to the sacredness discourse of the era, namely Max Scheler. In his philosophy-of-religion magnum opus, *On the Eternal in Man*, he praises Rudolf Otto for the phenomenological analyses in his "profound and beautiful" book, but upbraids it for allegedly concluding by lapsing "a conception of the holy, leaning on Kant and Fries, as a subjective rational category 'coined' for certain sense-data (and so not pre-existent as an attribute of the object)."[26] At the other pole stands Émile Durkheim, for whom there is no intrinsic relationship between sacredness and materiality:

> A rock, a tree, a spring, a stone, a piece of wood, a house, in other words anything at all, can be sacred. A rite can have this sacred character as well; in fact, no rite exists that does not have it to some degree. There are words, speeches, and formulas that can be spoken only by consecrated persons; there are gestures and movements that cannot be executed by everyone.[27]

In the work of both Scheler and Durkheim, their specific personal attitude toward the religious sphere is clearly responsible for their conceptual strategy when it comes to the sacred. As superb as Scheler's own phenomenological analyses of moral feelings and religious experiences are, he overestimates their scope. Just as, for him, laying bare the subjective certainty about values became proof of the objective experience-independent preexistence of values, the fact of religion indicates the existence of God. For him, then, both Otto and James fail to grasp that there are "the ontic features of absolute holiness which are firmly established in Christ's person and there discovered," which means for him they are not formed or constructed.[28] The mirror image of this self-assurance is the work of Durkheim, who claimed to have revealed the secret of all religion sociologically by putting all sacredness—as Nathan Söderblom already critically noted[29]—down to nothing other than the "objectivation und idealization of the social." In both cases, therefore, the analysis of religious experience is used to apologetic or secularist ends; this clashes with William James's idea that the analysis of such experience could constitute the common framework of a science of religion relatively independent of religious presuppositions.

While in Scheler the fundamental philosophical aspiration of his phenomenology of essences (*Wesensphänomenologie*) is open to question, that is, we have to ask whether analyses of believers' subjective sense of self-evidence can provide objective evidence of characterizations of the divine, Durkheim's narrow view of the emergence of sacredness in the collective ecstasy of rituals is amenable to empirical verification. Subsequent research on the Australian Aborigines has clearly shown that the idea of an arbitrary attribution of sacredness based solely on the dynamics of rituals is misconceived. In fact, the experience of the world among the Aborigines consists at its core of perceiving the world as pervaded with symbols that point to a meaning inherent in it.[30] Nor is individual religious practice among the North American "Indians" derived solely from collective ritual. Visions sought in solitude, that is, experiences of self-evidence, in fact play a crucial role.[31] During Durkheim's lifetime, Marett contended that the former was wrong to assert that the ritual-based idea of impersonal sacred forces emerged before that of personal sacred beings[32]—another conceptual constraint, of course, arising from Durkheim's secularist proclivities. Nor can Durkheim's idea of the experience of fusion in ritual, important as it is, explain why this experience extends far beyond sociality to become an "oceanic" feeling of unity with the cosmos.

I will forgo delving further into all of this because the key question here is where to locate Otto within our overarching intellectual frame. I see him lying, like James, somewhere between the two poles, and comparison with James is an instructive means of pinning this down. This approach makes it clear that Otto is closer to the objectivist pole than James is, as already evident in their differing answers to the question of whether there is such a thing as specifically religious feelings. James regards the term "religious sentiment" as "a collective name for the many sentiments which religious objects may arouse in alternation." He believes there exists a whole range of feelings related to religious objects, but no specifically religious feeling: "There is religious fear, religious love, religious awe, religious joy, and so forth. But religious love is only man's natural emotion of love directed to a religious object."[33] The same, in his view, goes for fear and awe. Religious feelings, he contends, are of course empirically distinguishable from other specific emotions, but "there is no ground for assuming a simple abstract 'religious emotion' to exist as a distinct elementary mental affection by itself, present in every religious experience without exception."[34]

Otto, conversely, tries to identify the origin of religious history in numinous awe, a point of origin that supposedly remains intact regardless of how highly developed one's understanding of the numinous becomes, as is apparent in the power and allure of "shudder": "there is something non-natural or supernatural about the symptom of 'creeping flesh'" (30). For him, numinous awe is a feeling sui generis and not, for example, an intensified form of "natural fear," but instead qualitatively different from all analogous feelings (23). While Otto is interested in the full spectrum of numinous emotions, which can of course range from quiet solemnity to wild ecstasy, he believes that here he has found the core of the experience of sacredness, whereas James explores the diversity of religious experience in all its breadth, including feelings, because for him the core of this experience does not lie in a specific feeling at all, but elsewhere, a point I will return to later.

Hence, what looks at first glance like an extreme difference between these two scholars appears less so on closer inspection. James does in fact limit the range of possible religious feelings when he declares solemnity and a specific enthusiasm that goes beyond mere morality characteristic. Grins and giggles, he tells us, are never religious, and the same goes for the total rejection of the cosmos. And in the chapter on mysticism in his great book he states explicitly that certain aspects of nature seem to have a special power to arouse mystical moods.[35] Conversely, in an argument with Söderblom,[36] Otto asserts that the feeling of sacredness "is indeed born of a thoroughly distinct, emotional form of valuation," but "may attach itself to the most varied of things, whether they be objects of inanimate or animate nature, both physical and mental, and to states, capacities, and events as well as to objects." Yet the closer proximity between the two thinkers than first impressions suggest does not mean they had truly clarified the problem at hand. Proximity may also point to shared shortcomings.

I do in fact believe this to be the case. In other words, I contend that the relationship between subjectivity and objectivity in the experience of the "sacred" (Otto) or the "divine" (James) fluctuates in the work of both and ultimately goes unexplained because they worked on the assumption of a dualistic relationship between the experiencing-knowing subject and the experienced-known object rather than a triadic structure of the interpretation of something by someone for someone. We might call this a hermeneutic or even semiotic deficiency in the work of both. In James, for example, myths and dogmas appear as spontaneous products of religious experience, while interpretations in general appear as mere emanations of experience. His friend and Harvard colleague Josiah Royce already upbraided him for this in his late writings, a failing he tried to overcome with a theory of his own.[37] Royce had recognized that the fundamental understanding of the symbol-mediated nature of the human relationship with the world also radically alters our ideas of "self" and "community." It was, he believed, vital to abandon the idea that we have access to ourselves in a way not mediated by symbols, a pure sense of ourselves; "communities" must be recognized as the result of processes of communication. If our relationship with ourselves, including our most intimate experiences, and with others, including those closest to us, is symbolically mediated, then interpretation—of symbols—becomes an essential element of people's everyday life. On this premise, every interpretation always immediately becomes a new symbol in the world and potentially subject to new acts of interpretation.

But such ideas on the articulation of experience remain marginal in James's work. Likewise, in Otto's oeuvre there is always the danger that—as philosopher Matthias Jung writes—"the inner relationship between act and content [is transformed] into a deterministic external relationship, in which the substance constitutes its modes of apprehension."[38] It is true that religious experiences entail an element of passivity, that they are receptive in character. In other words, nobody can interpret their own religious experience as a self-constituted phenomenon while simultaneously viewing it as an encounter with the divine. Yet this does not mean that religious conviction simply grows out of experience. Symbolically structured expectations and patterns of perception always already enter into experiences, and the experiencer must always distance themself from the immediate experience in order to identify it as a particular experience and articulate it to others. Experience is geared toward articulation, calls for it, even compels it.

In my opinion, a work is only of contemporary theoretical relevance if it manages to avoid both a quasi-structuralist arbitrary conception of the sacred à la Durkheim and a purely objectivist notion of the numinous. No hazy middle way can help us here, only a conception that allows us to conceptualize the mediation of experience, articulation, and cultural repertoire.[39] Of course, in his specific studies, Otto constantly comes up against this problem, which his conceptual framework is poorly equipped to resolve. This is most intriguingly manifest in the chapter "Means of Expression of the Numinous" (75–86), but it also occurs wherever he refers to "ideograms," which is his term for a tentative attempt at articulation conscious of its inadequacy. The "nihil" of the Western mystics and the "emptiness" of their Buddhist counterparts are, for him, "numinous ideograms of the 'Wholly Other.'" Only through the "notation of interpretive ideograms" does it become possible to at least "hint at" the "fascinans" of the numinous.

But when, at one level of abstraction higher, he cites Kant's concept of schematization (60ff.) in an attempt to comprehend the "relation of the rational to the non-rational element in the idea of the holy" (60), he makes a categorical error, as contemporary critics already noted ("as inappropriate as possible" was Troeltsch's assessment).[40] This lapse is due to his inadequate understanding of articulation. We might say that here the lack of a nuanced conception of symbolic articulation was detrimental to the phenomenology of religious experience. But it is not enough to correct Otto's reference to Kant because the latter offered no solution to the problem of articulation. Herder and Schleiermacher had already made the same argument.[41]

We can go further still. The hermeneutic or semiotic shortcoming in the work of James and Otto not only renders inadequate their conception of the articulation of feelings or experiences, but also partially blocks any attempt to grasp the core of religious experience. What we find in James is that he is in fact quite unwilling to locate this core at the level of perception but seeks instead to place it within a psychology of the self; for him, this core thus lies in experiences of "self-transcendence," as I have called it,[42] though James himself did not use this expression. While a term such as "self-surrender" was central to his psychology of religious experience, he did not take the decisive step toward a theory of the symbolically mediated constitution of the self, as Charles Horton Cooley and George Herbert Mead later did.

Meanwhile, when Otto distances himself from Schleiermacher we can discern an insight into psychological realities that is testimony to a deeper understanding. He disputes that we can derive religion from the "feeling of absolute dependency" with the compelling argument that on this premise the religious feeling would be "directly and primarily a sort of *self*-consciousness, a feeling concerning oneself in a special determined relation, viz. one's dependence" (24); it would, as Otto underlines, take an act of logical inference to identify the cause of this dependence. This turns our attention toward the idea of experiences that precede the constitution of the self and that represent a primary directedness toward something outside oneself, but Otto's focus here is not really the constitution of the self or experiences of self-transcendence but—once again—only the feeling of numinous awe as such, whose "shadow" is the sense of creatureliness (*Kreaturgefühl*).

Yet the hermeneutic deficits in the work of James and Otto do not mean we can dispense with them. After the "linguistic turn" in philosophy and the "cultural turn" in the social sciences, we often find a tendency to drop the idea of an experience that is not culturally mediated, and this tendency often takes such a radical form that experiences now seem completely determined by cultural patterns of interpretation; in other words we encounter a failure to leave any room for the individual articulation of experience. But—to quote Matthias Jung's concise formulation—"mediation does not do away with immediacy, but makes it articulable."[43] Rather than losing their value after the transition to a conception of articulation, self-formation, and self-transcendence, James's impressively vivid descriptions and Otto's often very brief but deeply penetrating analyses provide a counterweight to mere culturalism.

Otto's sensitivity to the affinities between material determinacy and experience can stimulate a more precise description of the situational conditions under which experiences of self-transcendence may occur. One example will have to suffice at this point. Otto dedicates some pleasing sentences in his book to the experience of the desert (84), whose vast emptiness he calls "the sublime in the horizontal" and whose role in Chinese architecture, with its staging of the quiet expanse, he highlights. The contrast to famous desert aviator Antoine de Saint-Exupéry is worthy of note here. When the latter writes about the desert, his focus is not simply on the sense of the numinous but also on the intensified experience of the self:

> As the desert offers no tangible riches, as there is nothing to see or hear in the desert, one is compelled to acknowledge, since the inner life, far from falling asleep, is fortified, that man is first animated by invisible solicitations. Man is ruled by Spirit. In the desert I am worth what my divinities are worth.[44]

Here the experience of the desert is not, as in Otto's work, a mere feeling of the sublime, but entails a situation of heightened experience of the energy field in which we lead our lives and that constitutes us. This insight, however, presupposes an idea of the self that is constituted through social relationships but that always opens itself to its own transcendence as well.

Rudolf Otto's Topicality

I have highlighted the internal diversity of the discourse on sacredness in the scholarship on religion around 1900, a discourse in which we must locate Otto's work. Further, I have emphasized how much James and Otto—unlike Durkheim and Scheler—strove to attain a methodological level that is neither a source of apologias for religion nor the secularist. But I have also pointed out that Otto and James saw no contradiction between such a conception of religious studies and efforts to help revitalize religion. To conclude, I would like to return briefly to the religious nub of Otto's work.

Both James and Otto and before them Schleiermacher—and in fact virtually every exponent of the turn to experience in the study of religion—were repeatedly excoriated for supposedly running the risk of fostering an aestheticist and sentimentalist reductionism with respect to religion.[45] This is undoubtedly unfair with regard to these two thinkers' motives. Even more than James, Otto makes it clear that he intends his work to lay the ground for the reinvigoration of key components of a biblically based Christian faith. It is thus no accident that his book on the sacred ends with the proclamation of higher stages of sacredness, namely of the prophet and of the Son of God. Yet the prophets are also particularly renowned for their capacity for critique of false sacralization, for their desacralizing impetus. If we seek to determine Otto's present-day religious relevance, we are touching on the problem of whether the prophetic statement represents an overcoming of the mere numinous or its transformation. For Otto, the answer is clear: rationalization is not that *of* the numinous, but, as mentioned earlier, *in* the numinous. Christianity is thus part of the history of religion and not a complete break with it or a matter of paving the way for such a break. But here conceptions of religion diverge, within Christianity as elsewhere.

For some, Rudolf Otto's work and the entire discourse on sacredness in the scholarship on religion are indispensable and of the utmost topicality because they represent the only way to understand those phenomena of sacralization that still exist despite the mass embrace of the secular option, and at the same time provide the only means for Christianity to secure its foundation. Others, however, fear that this perspective does away with Christianity's truly radical aspirations and that the faith will be placed on the same level as all other religious and quasi-religious phenomena in past and present. My own view in this regard is clear. Especially under conditions of secularization, we need research into sacredness because this is the only way for us to consider the multitude of experiences of self-transcendence both within and outside of religions—for example, in art, nature, and eroticism. This is an indispensable prerequisite for the dialogue between believers and exponents of secular worldviews.[46] But we also require an understanding of the reflexive refraction of sacredness, prototypically, for example, in the case of the prophets, in order to do justice to the complex history of the relationship between religion and politics and if the dialogue between believers of different religious traditions is to be productive.[47] With respect to both tasks, Rudolf Otto's work is, mutatis mutandis, a classic text of enduring relevance.[48]

I, 4
Self-Evidence or Sense of Self-Evidence?: Max Scheler

Max Scheler (1874–1928) is one of the few great European thinkers of the early twentieth century who were not exponents—or perhaps we should say victims—of the so-called secularization thesis. In our era, scholars have increasingly questioned this thesis; in other words they have problematized the assumption that modernization processes, through a kind of inner necessity, lead to secularization in the sense of a decline in religion. It thus behooves us today to pay greater attention to those thinkers who did not sign up to this widespread conception, which is woven into the basic assumptions of the cultural and social sciences. These few included American pragmatist philosopher William James, also the founder of the empirical psychology of religion, and German Protestant theologian Ernst Troeltsch, who can also be described as the father of a historical sociology of Christianity; unfortunately, his work was outshone almost entirely by the dazzling international reception of Max Weber. Another such figure was Swiss cultural historian Jacob Burckhardt. Without assuming any necessary historical trend, he distinguished the three "powers" of state, religion, and culture, developing his *Reflections on History* in strictly combinatory fashion out of the resulting "six conditionalities"; hence, religion comes into play as conditioned by state and culture, but also as a condition for them.

Max Scheler is one of these scholars not bound by the secularization thesis whom we need to take a fresh look at today. Not all thinkers of the era were "religiously unmusical." Oddly enough, almost no one ever seems to reflect on the literal meaning of this expression, which first became known through Max Weber's melancholy self-description in a letter and, later, when Jürgen Habermas used it to describe himself in his sensational Frankfurt Peace Prize speech. Many contemporaries introduce themselves with no timidity as "religiously unmusical" before going on to talk and write about religion at great length. How would we perceive someone who described themself as completely unmusical in the literal sense, before proceeding to present us with a study on the history of symphony or opera or an interpretation of Beethoven's late string quartets? In any case, Max Scheler himself rejected this expression with the quasi-theological argument that it contradicts "the content of every arguable idea of God, inasmuch as a God who grants to one group of men special 'talents' for knowing him which he refuses to other groups could be anything but a God."[1] On this premise, nobody is entirely religiously unreceptive.

Yet such sentiments already show that the ideas of Max Scheler are particularly difficult to appropriate in light of the overcoming of the secularization thesis. There are two reasons for this. The first has to do with the pronounced religious aspiration, so palpable in the above quote, which is inherent in Scheler's philosophy of religion. William James remained extremely cautious in this regard, Jacob Burckhardt pursued no affirmative religious goals at all, and Ernst Troeltsch propagated a free Christianity in which there must be room for multiple interpretations even of the core of the faith. Scheler's religious aspiration, meanwhile, was prodigious. It is no exaggeration to say that he saw himself in a role not unlike that of St. Augustine: as a fundamental renewer of the message of faith during an era of tremendous historical upheaval. He saw it as his mission to use the tools of phenomenology to renew the Christian message of love after the First World War, which was perceived as a profound shock to European Christianity, if not as having bankrupted it entirely.

What "the positivist," Scheler wrote, considered a "universal human tendency"—that is, the idea of necessarily advancing secularization—was, in his view, "but an episodic and—in the frame of world-history—momentary diversion of the merely European mind from its religious destiny" (355). Scheler's point of view and self-image were quite widely shared in Catholic circles. Many hoped he might be the "pioneer of newly awakening religiosity"[2] who could free Catholic thought from the neo-Thomist rigidities of the nineteenth century while shielding it from the softenings of modernism. The power of Scheler's ideas as a force for renewal was still to be felt decades later (for example, in the work of leading Catholic theologian Heinrich Fries in 1949).[3] No present-day examination of Scheler's thinking on religion can simply disregard this aspiration.

But there is another difficulty. Not long after Scheler had presented his philosophy-of-religion magnum opus, *On The Eternal in Man*, in the early 1920s, he himself underwent a religious upheaval. I have no wish to speculate here about its biographical underpinnings or precise character. What is certain is that while Scheler did not suddenly become a secularist, we can no longer describe him as a Catholic Christian or indeed any kind of Christian, even if we were willing to use the term in a very broad sense. It was after his religious upheaval that Scheler wrote most of his studies in the sociology of knowledge, sociology of religion, and philosophical anthropology, which were received in disciplines beyond philosophy and theology and for a time earned him such renown as a sociologist that he was mentioned in the same breath as Max Weber (by Karl Mannheim, for example).[4] Since his emphases in these writings were quite different than during his intensely Catholic phase, and since what matters today is to come up with a theory of religion that is acceptable regardless of its author's religious or secularist assumptions, we need to keep the different phases of Scheler's thinking from blurring into one another when we interpret him.[5]

My remarks so far are probably enough to characterize my particular approach. To put it in cursory terms, my intention is to probe the significance of Scheler's pronouncedly Catholic philosophy of religion to the empirically oriented study of religion. At a deeper level, this means determining how Scheler fits into the methodological upheaval that convulsed the scholarly engagement with religion in his day, while not omitting to examine his religious aspirations. This explains the title of this chapter. I ask whether Scheler managed to go beyond the descriptive ascertainment of the fact that religious faith is based on feelings of self-evidence and succeeded in demonstrating the self-evidence of certain religious beliefs, of a particular faith in fact. Or did Scheler simply invert the claim of self-evidence put forward by critics of religion when they asserted that they had unveiled the true character of faith, thus overplaying his hand? I explore this question in both the philosophical and sociological fields and by contrasting Scheler's ideas with pragmatist philosophy and theory of religion.

The Phenomenology of Religious Acts

Regardless of Scheler's religious aspiration, his philosophy of religion consists to a large extent of a phenomenology of religious acts. Quantitatively, other issues, such as the relationship between philosophy and religion or the significance of the Christian idea of love in the modern world take up more space in *On the Eternal in Man*. But at the point (270) where he terminates his phenomenology of individual religious acts, Scheler declares his intention to produce another book ("Religionsphänomenologische Analysen" or "Analyses in the Phenomenology of Religion"), in which he wished to continue these studies. Just as many today find that, when it comes to moral philosophy, Scheler's wonderful essays on moral feelings such as shame and humility may have withstood the ravages of time better than his systematic book on the material ethics of value,[6] in the field of religion also an important part of Scheler's argument is to be found in these phenomenological analyses themselves and not just, or less, in the far-reaching ontological consequences he gleans from them. When Scheler himself admits that it is necessary and possible to "characterize the religious act in so far as it is immanent" (247), I feel authorized by the man himself to begin by putting his religious aspirations to one side.

The first chapter of Scheler's philosophy-of-religion magnum opus is one of his masterful essays on a moral feeling, one with a special significance to religion: repentance. In a sensitive interpretation of a feeling with which almost everyone is familiar, and while astutely distancing himself from false theorizations of this feeling, Scheler shows that repentance is neither a matter of "spiritual deadweight" (39), that is, a simple case of a rejected past living on in the present, nor of "a mere symptom of mental disharmony," as if repentance merely indicated an individual's inability to come to terms with the past. Nor is it "an absurd attempt on the part of the human soul to cast out what is past and immutable"; it only appears this way to someone who thinks that nothing about the past can be changed. This is of course true of the reality of the past, but not of the meaning and value of past events. Meaning and value change time and again in light of the present. But this means that the past not only remains subject to the future, that historical facts remain unfinished, but also that they remain dependent on individuals' ability and will to relate to them anew. If, for example, we not only regret a past deed as if it were something purely external to us, but are appalled "that we then were such a person as could do that deed" (46), then truthfulness toward ourselves can lead us to expel the past deed, as Scheler states, along with its root, that is, its motive, "out of the living center of the Self" (42), and thus liberated, to act in new ways as a changed person. A sense of self-evidence is connected with this intense experience, namely the sense of being able, in principle, to carry out morally better acts, to truly live up to one's ideals. For Scheler, this experience also lends plausibility—as I will discuss in more detail later—to the notion that in the conscience that admonishes us a "divine Judge" (35/38) does in fact speak to us, pointing to an invisible order, and that this is not just a contribution from the "interiorization of yesterday's policeman" (38). Thus, for him, the sense of self-evidence entails a more far-reaching form of religious self-evidence.

Scheler devotes himself to no other religious feeling or act at this point in such detail, but he does repeatedly list what he considers the still outstanding analytical tasks and goes into somewhat more depth in certain passages. He calls "belief, worship, veneration, avowal of insufficiency or redemption" (132) religious acts. He also states that many acts, which often have earthly addressees, are carried by our spirit beyond all of them, contending that in acts such as "praise, thanks, fear, hope, love, endeavor, striving for perfection, indictment, judgment, forgiveness, wonder, veneration, petition, worship" we are aiming at something beyond all finite things (253). Religious hope pertains to a something "we have never experienced and of which we know that we could never have experienced it" (252), just as religious gratitude is thanks for something "in relation to which what we have acquired is only a sign, indication or symbol, and not the proper object of the thanks" (252).

From Rudolf Otto's book *The Idea of the Holy*,[7] Scheler (171) cites the Pauline phrase "What no eye has seen, what no ear has heard" (1 Cor 2:9) to convey the certainty felt with regard to something that has never been experienced and in this sense is not based on any experience. When he draws a clear boundary between religion and metaphysics, Scheler again argues in light of the specific self-evidential character of faith for the believer. Religious belief, like interpersonal trust, cannot be lived hypothetically; if a belief or trust is hypothetical, it is, strictly speaking, nonexistent. Faith and trust are based on the "free option of the person, the innermost person, for the religious truth and benefit held out to faith" (151). They are characterized by a "rocksteady certitude" that is fundamentally different from cognitive feats in which the willingness to hypothesize and falsify is an achievement. Faith-based knowledge is subjectively self-evident.

With this claim, Scheler effectively aligns himself with the empirical psychology of religion founded by William James. In his analysis of mystical experiences, James had already analyzed the specific feeling of certainty that is associated with them and is largely immune to reason. For the subject concerned, such experiences are not emotional states of some kind devoid of epistemic content (James's "noetic quality"),[8] but rather sudden illuminations, insights, and revelations that are difficult or impossible to put into words but that exude an intense authority. To dispel any impression that he was sacrificing rational argument for the irrational authority of such experiences of self-evidence, James immediately added, "Mystical truth exists for the individual who has the transport, but for no one else."[9] In other words, one cannot argue with this truth any more than one can with sensory certainty as such, but this does not mean that it cannot be grasped and investigated empirically as a property of certain human experiences. Such an empirical approach to analyzing religious phenomena beyond the mere examination of religious doctrines or institutions is precisely what the revolution in the scholarly engagement with religion in this era was all about, a revolution whose initial spark some believe they can already discern in the work of Schleiermacher.[10]

However, it is not only Scheler's phenomenology-of-religion analyses in the narrower sense that matter here; his understanding of phenomenology as a method itself unmistakably has an at least vaguely religious character.[11] This method is not only intended to bring out the intrinsic structures of religious experience and religious action against all reductionisms and failures to recognize the "independence of religion," but is meant to provide a phenomenology of the essence of religion that furnishes us with two things (161) in addition to a theory of the religious act, namely the "essential nature of the divine" and the "study of the forms of revelation in which the divine intimates and manifests itself to man." Phenomenology, then, is certainly more than a mere method, so Scheler cannot assent to Husserl's program of "philosophy as a rigorous science." Accordingly, he excoriates Husserl (81) for using the term "science" in two ways: both for inductive empirical science and for "self-evident knowledge of essences" that must be gleaned phenomenologically.

For Scheler, phenomenology is a way of switching off the will in relation to the objects of knowledge and surrendering oneself entirely to "to the absolute reality" (98) of these objects. This brings it into proximity with mystical techniques, to which he had already shown an open-minded attitude in other writings: from techniques of tolerance and suffering to those of contemplation (30, fn. 1). Scheler, bursting with plans, wanted to address these topics systematically at a later point. His objective was not to violate things, indeed being itself, through a practical approach, but to let them speak. This impulse extends into his definition of philosophy's mission. However much he may differ from Plato in the detail, we can still hear echoes of the entire (Axial Age) pathos associated with the emergence of philosophy. Who in a present-day philosophy department would define the discipline as a "love-determined movement of the inmost personal Self of a finite being toward participation in the essential reality of all possibles" (74) and thus describe a philosopher as a person "who takes up this attitude to the world . . ., in so far as he does take it up"? Philosophy in this emphatic and nonprofessional sense is based on a personal willingness to "detach, at least in a functional sense, the act-center from the psycho-physical nexus" (92, fn. 1), to transcend oneself. Brash Berliner Alfred Döblin puts the same idea like this: "I intend for every turnip to come into its own."[12]

His ambitious understanding of philosophy and his elated sense of having found a new and reliable approach in the shape of phenomenology gave Scheler the self-confidence to dissociate himself sharply from all other thinkers who might be thought to have similar things in mind. His objections to Schleiermacher (284ff.), whose critique by Rudolf Otto he embraces, must certainly be taken seriously; they seem a little unfair only in the sense that Scheler fails to acknowledge Schleiermacher's merits in his day. With his repeated portrayals of Kant as a subjectivist, Scheler seems to me to be making a concession to the Catholic apologetics of the era, in which this misleading view was widespread; Scheler knew better in his book on formalism.[13]

In our context, Scheler's efforts to dissociate himself from William James's pragmatism are of particular interest. As far as the latter's psychology of religion is concerned, Scheler first declares it a mere empirical science, from which we can infer nothing about the validity claims inherent in religious convictions. He declares the psychology of religion *in toto* (129) a "subordinate" branch of the study of religion. In sharp contrast to the Pragmatists themselves, Scheler ranks the empirical sciences lower than philosophy—a classic position among members of the educational aristocracy and indicative of academic struggles for distinction. Although James's influence is unmistakable right down to Scheler's wording, the latter distances himself from James and from pragmatism as a whole in wild polemics. James, we are told, has absolutely no principles of a theory-of-religion nature that might have allowed him to bring order, in an evaluative sense, to his abundant material; instead, he seeks to replace such a principle by "an utterly worm-eaten pragmatism forming a quasi-biological if not downright utilitarian touchstone: the happy issue of convictions in practical life" (292). Disregard for an ontology of the essence of the divine, ignorance of religious collectiveness, "an unhealthy penchant for the pathological and coarsely 'sensational'": these are the other entries in James's catalogue of sins. Among the attempts to "cast doubt on the self-sufficiency of religious self-evidence and truth" (309), Scheler states, the "saddest, most wrong-headed attempt of all was made by William James and his pragmatical disciples." Scheler's own project simply has "nothing in common" with this endeavor (291).

It cannot be denied that there are significant differences between James and Scheler;[14] the question of the exact status of "self-evidence" revolves around these differences. It is also indisputable that James's understanding of religion was overly focused on individuals "in their solitude" and that Scheler thought more sociologically in this regard. I will be going into this in a moment. But his emphasis on his differences from James is not only polemically overheated but also wrong in the substance. The misunderstanding of the pragmatist conception of truth as biologistic or utilitarian had in fact become the main obstacle to the reception of pragmatism in Europe at the time.[15] This was an ill-willed misunderstanding in that James's book-long attempt to clear things up in *The Meaning of Truth*, the follow-up volume to his pragmatism lectures, was simply ignored continuously. James's own comment on his "failure in making converts" to his conception of truth was that every "common choleric sinner would curse God and die, after such a reception."[16]

But it is not only Scheler's general characterization of pragmatist philosophy that is fundamentally wrong; so is his interpretation of the status of James's psychology of religion. We now know that James wanted to follow up his first lecture series, which became famous as *The Varieties of Religious Experience*, with a second, whose working title was "The Tasks of Religious Philosophy." The first part of the *Varieties* is written with these tasks in mind, to which James alludes time and again. James's papers even include an outline of the planned sequel.[17] He intended to relate this analysis to his metaphysical ideas, which he later published in *A Pluralist Universe*. It would thus be quite wrong to claim that James wished to provide only a descriptive psychology of religion from which we can infer nothing about the validity claims inherent in religious convictions, or that he had no philosophy of religion at all. Scheler was wrong here or did not want to admit publicly how close he truly was to James. When it comes to the crucial issue ("self-evidence or sense of self-evidence"?), we will see that there is in fact a difference between the two, but it is not the one identified by Scheler.

Sociological Consequences

Scheler's philosophy of religion—and not just his later explicitly sociological work—is shot through with sociological insights and food for thought. These are nowhere presented coherently but are scattered throughout the book. In the present context, a brief systematic overview plus critical commentary can shed much useful light.

Nobody can accuse Scheler of concentrating—as is often the case with philosophers—exclusively on religious beliefs. This is already evident in his key concept of the "religious act," and even more so in his remarks explaining that it is in the nature of these acts "not to confine itself within the human interior but to manifest itself to the outside world in two ways through the medium of the body: purposive conduct and expressive action" (264). For this reason, Scheler contends, every religion entails specific forms of ethos and particular practices of worship. He is also aware that referring to the manifestation of a religious belief in action is misconceived in that religious convictions do not simply precede their expression in worship but are molded and transmitted in and through worship. On this view, the performance of the moral and worship-related acts prescribed by a religion is often what leads to religious conviction in the first place. Unlike James, for Scheler the religious act is always a social act as well: *unus Christianus, nullus Christianus*.

Scheler fleshes out this insight by asserting the existence of necessary connections between the seminal idea inspiring a religious community and the sociological structural forms this community uses or engenders. Akin to Ernst Troeltsch,[18] Scheler has a sense of the novelty and improbability of the "church" as a social entity produced by Christianity. If love is the core idea of Christianity, Christians must seek to create a community of love; if the love of God applies equally to every person, this community of love can only be understood in such a way that "no man or group of men can act as substitute for any other man or group" (267).

Scheler's next step is particularly original. He outlines a typology of *homines religiosi*: "The wizard, the magician, the seer, the sage, the prophet, the lawgiver and judge, the king and hero, the priest, the savior, the redeemer, the mediator, the messiah" (162) and finally puts forward the idea of the Son of God as essential to the notion of the person. Further types arise if we take into account the only derivative *homines religiosi* such as the apostle, the saints through the imitation of Christ, the church father, the doctor of the church, the reformer or the witness, and if we consider overlap with other types of charismatics such as the hero or genius. Scheler uses this typology, which is fertile in itself, as a hinge to establish affinities between certain religions and some of these types of *homo religiosus*. It thus seems evident to him that under pantheistic conditions the teacher of salvation is the core embodiment of the religious message, while under theistic conditions it is the saint who enjoys this status. This immediately brings the aspect of social inequality into play. The god of theistic faith is a god of the people, not the "cerebral god of the 'intellectuals'" (134); it is not the scholars who recognize him best, and religious insight of the theistic kind is, therefore, not found "on a throne or academic chair, [but rather] in an ass's stall—or something of like degree" (338).

Ultimately, Scheler considers the historical succession of forms of revelation of the divine to be a key focus of his phenomenology of the essence of religion: he seeks to develop a theory of religious evolution, as we would put it today. For this theory, too, Scheler derives the crucial assumptions from the inspirational core of a religion, not from an external vantage point. In the chapter on repentance, titled "Repentance and Rebirth," he already contrasts every notion of linear progress, so dear to the nineteenth century, with a historical rhythm of collective insight into guilt and moral regeneration. His historical examples are late ancient Christianity, which distanced itself from the heroic values of antiquity, but also from its hedonistic proclivities, and the profound new beginning marked by the monastic reform movements of the eleventh century, when a fundamental renewal of the church and its liberation from subordination to worldly power was articulated in terms of penance for the sinful paths taken. The waves of revivalist movements in North America—which were vital to the establishment of the United States as a republic, the abolition of slavery, and the achievement of full civil rights for blacks—would fit into this schema; in a sense, here Scheler developed the model of social movements that follow a logic of moral mobilization.[19]

In his work, this model is relativized only in that he views the success of such mobilization as dependent on God's help. Just as he expresses skepticism about linear conceptions of progress, he also criticizes the notion, still widespread today, that religion represents "merely the vital, as yet undifferentiated unity of the spirit informing culture and civilization" (319) and is thus bound to dwindle as a result of advancing differentiation or become limited to specialized religious functions. He counters by asserting that "religion itself, with its goods and values, undergoes differentiation just as art, government, and science do for their part" (320). This is an extremely interesting idea (though unfortunately Scheler does little to pursue it further), which could form a counterweight to the notion of the functional differentiation of religion, one that extends from Max Weber to Niklas Luhmann.[20]

In contrast to ideas of advancing secularization, Scheler is aware that the Christian ethos's loss of hegemony in Europe is not simply a "subtraction story" (Charles Taylor); that is, this loss is not a matter of the internal weakening of a Christianity that was replaced by nothing else. Scheler discerns that other "spiritual forces" (365)—other sacralizations, as I would put it—emerged to take the place of Christianity, in a mutually reinforcing way in some cases. He counts among these phenomena modern political nationalism; the elevation of the idea of state sovereignty; socialism and a one-sided individualism; a secularist humanitarianism, "The bourgeois-capitalist economic ethos of unrestricted production and accumulation of capital" (366); the transposition of all sociality to special-purpose associations, and the idea of the boundless autonomy of culture. Scheler wrote in depth about these matters, particularly the dynamics of nationalism, in other contexts.

At this point it also becomes clear that his rejection of the secularization thesis—to which I alluded in the introduction to this chapter—differs from that found in the work of James, Troeltsch, and Burckhardt in that he fully accepts that the capitalist age has a rationalizing and secularizing effect (276). For him, this alleged state of affairs does not support the secularization thesis only because, like many of his contemporaries, he considers the overcoming of this age to be possible, indeed imminent. He agrees with Ferdinand Tönnies's idea that all social life is being transposed from community to society, to special-purpose and class-based associations, and he infers from this that the social conditions for the emergence of new religions are no longer in place.

This, of course, means that all one can do is "to preserve, vivify and reform, [those forms of religious community that arose in creative eras, in other words the church] and at best to bind them more tightly and deeply together, by striving for the union of Churches" (355). In political terms, for Scheler this means, quite consistently, that salvation can only come from a Christian socialism. And he announced plans for a book on how this might be realized (439, fn. 1). In more concrete terms, this means the detachment of the church from its remaining solidarity with "outworn political forms of bourgeois dominance" (441), a new engagement with social democracy, an orientation not only toward the state but toward the wide variety of forms of community ("civil society" in today's language), decentralization within the European nation-states, and a new legal order in Europe. It is typical of Scheler, the visionary, that he adds to these political innovations a religious vision, namely a new opening toward Asian, especially East Asian, culture.

"The excessively active, bustling European needs—I would say—a rest-cure in the profundities, the sense of eternity, in the repose and dignity of the Asiatic spirit" (429).

I will make no comment on this perception of Asia or on the problems entailed in Scheler's view of capitalism, which makes a poor fit with the religious vitality of the United States. Scheler presents many of the sociological assertions mentioned here as if he had proven their validity through phenomenological reflection. What he gets right is that there may be a deep internal logical connection between a religion's inspirational core on the one hand and, on the other, the institutional structures that it generates, the role models and leaders that are appropriate to it, the worship practices and ethical forms through which it is expressed, and the potential for social change inherent in it, a connection Scheler tries to reconstruct. But it is also undeniable that Scheler's assertions entail empirically questionable value judgments that he fails to establish through rigorous argument and that are perhaps little more than idiosyncratic.

Philosophy of Religion and the Study of Religion (*Religionswissenschaft*)

In order to answer the question "self-evidence or sense of self-evidence?" to which I now return, it is crucial to mark precisely the point at which Scheler's empirical description of believers' sense of self-evidence passes over to the demonstration of the self-evidence of beliefs (or supposedly does so).[21] This problem already arises in Scheler's philosophy of religion when he defines religion in general. He not only sought to present a phenomenology of religious experience and religious action, but to set out the basic determinants of the divine revealed to the believer in such experience. Scheler does not claim to prove the self-evidence of the Christian faith. In fact, he explicitly rejects such an endeavor and in the foreword to the second edition of his book he responds sharply to this misunderstanding, which was very widespread in the first responses to it. He emphasizes that he had even put forward "proof of the unprovability of God as a person" (334), since the belief in a personal God implies that God—like all persons—cannot simply be accessed through one's own acts of cognition, but only "by a free act of self-revelation" (334). Yet in Scheler's definition of religion, the notion of the personhood of God appears as a constitutive characteristic (146, 246). This definition differs profoundly from the attempts by contemporaries such as William James, Émile Durkheim, Rudolf Otto, Nathan Söderblom, and others to make the "sacred" the core definitional hallmark.

Scheler's work is close to these attempts insofar as he considers it necessary for the religious consciousness to link the idea of the divine with the "value-modality known as holiness, with all its attendant wealth of value-qualities" (168). But while, in their definition of religion, the other thinkers mentioned allow for the idea of an apersonal sacred force or a multitude of personal gods, what Scheler already has in mind in his definition is a personalist monotheism. Contemporary attempts by missionary priest Father Wilhelm Schmidt to provide ethnological proof of a primordial monotheism seem to have played a role here (352, fn. 1). Scheler's ontology of essences includes as hallmarks of the divine other ideas going beyond the notion of God's personhood, such as that of universal love and omnipotence as well as a "world-transcending character" (250) of the divine, which he distinguishes radically from all that is finite and this-worldly—attributes that today's scholars believe apply only to religions that arose in the Axial Age or on its foundation.[22]

At one point, Scheler makes use of the distinction between myth and religion in order to defend a narrower concept of religion against the objection (320f.) that much of what is allegedly proven to be self-evident does not apply to the early phases of religious history or to the religion of tribal societies. Yet in many other passages he refers to the religion of "primitives" or to religion during every phase of human history. It would of course be fatal to the ontology of the essence of the divine that he propagates if it could be shown to entail a latent Christian "programming." Incidentally, Scheler completely ignored Islam, which ought to have been a prominent theme given his concept of religion.

For Scheler, proof of the independence of religion coincides with proof of the existence of God and a kingdom of God. As he sees it, we are faced with the following alternative. Either we assert that religious phenomena can be explained by nonreligious factors, or we assert that they are irreducible. In the first case the beliefs found in religions are fictitious; in the second case, real. To quote a key passage in his work,

> If the genesis and intentional aspect of religion can be explained in terms of extra- and pre-religious facts, if its object is to be regarded as a fiction or a synthesis derived from phantasmagorical distortions of mundane experience, then the truth of religion is a lost cause. If it is not susceptible of

such explanations, then we are obliged to assume a domain of reality corresponding to religious acts with exactly the same right as that with which we posit the external and internal worlds, and the consciousness in fellowmen, as spheres of existence. (264)

As a result of this perspective, Scheler—as described above—opens up a chasm between the scholarship on religion and his philosophy of religion. For good reasons, he rejects an explanatory, Humean psychology of religion as a secularist project. But he also allows meager room even for a descriptive, Diltheyan psychology of religion, namely to the extent that this psychology functions as a religious community's internal self-interpretation. For Scheler, these two variants of the psychology of religion are joined by a "concrete phenomenology of religious objects and acts" (159), on which the historiography of religion depends. But he views his own project as fundamentally different from all these disciplines concerned with religion; what he seeks to achieve is the "essential philosophy of religion." This is

not metaphysics, neither is it natural theology, nor epistemology, nor explanatory and descriptive psychology, nor the concrete phenomenology of religion, but it is the ultimate philosophical foundation of all and every other philosophical and scientific study of religion. (160)

We might say that Scheler views his phenomenology of essences as fundamental philosophy par excellence.

At the level of religious phenomena, we find backing for Scheler's view in the fact that religious experience is in fact impossible in the absence of an epistemic claim. No one can interpret their own religious experience as a merely psychological phenomenon while at the same time viewing it as an encounter with the divine. Interpretations are always already inherent in religious experience, which is why not just any old interpretation seems plausible to the experiencer. As Scheler rightly perceived, feelings have an intentional content, and an experience-based value commitment is not experienced as a choice or decision, but as the convincing articulation of the self-evidence of a good or bad thing.

Viewed from an observer's point of view, however, this self-evidence remains subjective self-evidence devoid of any claim to intersubjective authority. Subjective self-evidence may certainly become intersubjective; this is what happens when the charismatic founder of a religion attracts disciples or when witnesses of faith make their voices heard. Yet this intersubjective articulation always remains a shared subjective form of self-evidence; it never becomes philosophically attained religious self-evidence as such that can be defined once and for all. That religious phenomena cannot be reduced to nonreligious ones does not mean that there is a philosophical route to their interpretation that lies outside concrete debates on faith—that is, interreligious dialogue, the dialogue between believers and exponents of secular worldviews, and outside—or foundationally underlying—the scholarly disciplines concerned with religion.

In a letter that is unfortunately no longer extant, one that Scheler mentions in the preface to the second edition of his philosophy of religion (22), Ernst Troeltsch seems already to have pointed out the problem that Scheler leaned much too heavily on the "epistemological principle of self-evidence" and that other men, the writer says, "who live in other circumstances or have other types of character also know other kinds of self-evidence." For Troeltsch, then, Scheler overstretches such subjective self-evidence to the point of implying universal validity. Scheler defends himself against these objections by first trying to sharply distinguish his conception of self-evidence from subjective certainties and feelings of self-evidence. His concern, he states, is with the "objective entities or values" that reveal themselves in knowledge, as it were, only through their thusness in the same way they do through their presence when they resist our actions.

Second, Scheler contends, the individual-personal dimension should not be equated with the merely subjective. In the understanding that characterizes the individual, insights may be revealed that are absolutely true for this individual and their way of life without necessarily applying to others. He thus radically limits the range of universally valid knowledge in an attempt to ensure that metaphysics and religion retain their necessary relation to the personal. Then suddenly (25) Scheler refers to the history of religion as a generator of complementary "Seitenansichten" of the inexhaustible abundance of the godhead. The knowledge of God gained in different ages, nations, peoples, and persons must be brought together "in solidary cooperation and intercompletion." Yet this does not clarify the status of the potentially universal self-evident character that Scheler nonetheless claims for his religious philosophy. Elsewhere, it sounds as if Scheler thinks it necessary to provide "a methodological complement" to phenomenology with the aid of metaphysical considerations.[23]

The impression that Scheler is ultimately unable to sustain the foundationalist philosophical aspiration of his religious philosophy, namely that it can demonstrate the self-evidence of definitions of the divine, is reinforced if we look at the shifts in his sociological claims about religion following his religious reorientation.[24] What had only just counted as self-evidence he now interprets sociologically almost as we would expect from a secularist sociology. While, for example, the church was derived from the essence of the religious act in Scheler's philosophy of religion, it now appears merely "as the form of its organization in the political age" and as a "large institution of salvation," an authoritarian, dogmatic entity that does more to impede than foster the dynamism of religion.[25] Religion now appears as a reflection-limiting enemy of free thought. Worst of all, as he now sees it, is the "deification" of a religion's founder. What he once understood as the apogee of a personalist understanding of God—Jesus as the Son of God—now appears as demonic reification by the official church.

There seems to be no way to get from the claim of religious self-evidence to the deification thesis except by performing a complete U-turn—unless we consider fundamental philosophical claim and sociological reductionism to be two sides of the same coin. If we do so, we can recognize that the pragmatist theory of religion presented by William James rejected both simultaneously. Here philosophy is no longer assigned a foundational role, but nor are the empirical disciplines limited to the purely empirical. From this point of view, every religious experience entails a claim to religious truth. But no one is equipped to take possession of this truth outside of human dialogue. In contrast to Scheler, the erratic genius of German thinking on religion in the early twentieth century, in James's work the modest and democratic pragmatist attitude remained his compass even when it came to salvation and redemption. Rather than proclaiming certain salvific knowledge, James foregrounded the receptive, curious, and tolerant search for it.[26]

PART II
SECULARIZATION AND THE MODERN HISTORY OF FREEDOM

PART II

II, 1
Introductory Remarks

The history of religion and the history of political power are closely linked. This applies whenever religion provides the justification for specific forms of political rule or for the claim to power of individual rulers, but also whenever religion represents a source of inspiration for resistance to rulers or systems of rule and helps change such systems. Of course, as Marx wrongly generalized, religion can be the "opium of the people," but it can also, as Werner Stark countered, produce "adrenaline." Because this close connection exists, the history of secularization, if it means more than just a decline in religious interest and is driven by criticism of a specific religion or all religion, cannot be understood without considering political history. Political motives are among the key elements that influence whether people find a religious community attractive or repulsive. This is not to say that religions merely conceal or stand in for the truly decisive "material" interests of an economic or political nature. It is mostly the case, however, that "spiritual" motives— that is, religious impulses in the exclusive sense—can be pursued in a variety of ways and that a rough, holistic impression of a religious tradition or institution may be crucial to a person's decision to follow a particular path.

I will look at these interconnections in more detail in Part IV of this book. My focus for now is on the fact that the close connection between political and religious motives is found not only at the concrete level of developments in the history of religion but also at the more abstract level of the competition between grand narratives describing the connection between religion and the history of political freedom. In Part I of this book, I presented approaches to overcoming an intellectualist conception of religious faith, based on an aspect of the extremely influential Hegelian philosophy of history. My next step is to consider Hegel's teleological conception of history, according to which Christianity inevitably leads to modern political freedom and is realized within it. Problems arise here at every level: with regard to one's understanding of the position of Christianity among religions, the connections between religious and political history, and the fundamental potential for a teleological construction of history.

It might be helpful to begin by relativizing the narrative of continuity between Christianity and political freedom by exposing it to comparison with other narratives. Protestant theologian Martin Laube has proposed a useful typology to facilitate an overview of possible narratives in this field.[1] The first type, embodied prototypically in the work of Hegel, he refers to as that of continuity. What this means is exclusively continuity between Protestant Christianity and "modern" political freedom. Hegel expressly denied that Catholic Christianity possessed this aptitude for freedom; with it "no rational constitution is possible" since it provides no guarantee that it will not oppose "a rational political constitution."[2] There should, Hegel avers, be nothing in the convictions of the citizenry that claims to be higher and holier than the convictions of the state. In principle, he concedes, although religion may "be looked upon as higher and more sacred" than the state, "it must contain nothing really alien or opposed to the Constitution."[3] As brusque as Hegel's rejection of a religious reference point beyond loyalty to the state is, he offers high praise for the Reformation. Luther, he asserts, gave freedom, in the sense of the individual relationship to God, its rightful place vis-à-vis the church's claims of authority, and in the proclamation of these principles

> is unfurled the new, the latest standard round which the peoples rally—the banner of the *Free Spirit*, independent, though finding its life in the Truth, and enjoying independence only in it. This is the banner under which we serve, and which we bear. Time, since that epoch, has had no other work to do than the formal imbuing of the world with this principle, in bringing the reconciliation implicit [in Christianity] into objective and explicit realization.[4]

From this point of view, the French Revolution can be seen as a step toward the realization of the Reformation, and the same goes for every step taken in the same direction without the chaos and terror of the Revolution, in particular the reforms implemented by the Prussian state after the defeat against Napoleon and liberation from his dominion.

In Hegel's construction, the Reformation is of course preceded by a specific affinity of Christianity with freedom, which distinguishes it from other religions. This assumption might be countered by the fact that experiences of political oppression are stored mythologically in all religions, as are experiences of resistance. A representative example is the exodus motif in the Jewish tradition, the departure from "Egypt, the house of slavery." But the presence of such a theme does not in itself make freedom a central value in a religious tradition. In Christianity, by contrast, a Jewish–early Christian religious interpretation was in fact already articulated by Paul in terms of an ancient Greek conception of freedom. In particular, Paul's letter to the Galatians has been cited time and again whenever the goal was to declare Christianity the religion of freedom.[5] There is much to suggest that this emphasis does in fact represent a specific feature of Christianity. But it would be a mistake in this context to project onto the term "freedom" all the aspirations entailed in the modern political notion of freedom. To put it in a nutshell, Paul was no fighter for democracy or even for the elimination of slavery.[6]

But Hegel's presupposition was not, of course, that modern freedom had already taken on succinct form in the thinking of Paul (or Jesus), but that it did so in the writings of Luther. It was on this assumption of continuity between the Reformation and political freedom that "liberal" Protestantism after Hegel based itself in the broadest variety of ways—up to and including a number of officious declarations made in the context of the five hundredth anniversary of the Reformation in 2017. Hegel is not necessarily mentioned by name in such cases. The continuity narrative has become important in its own right as a pattern of cultural self-interpretation, quite independently of a particular thinker.

How far from being self-evident this narrative is, however, is apparent if we look at the second type, which emerged among Left Hegelians shortly after Hegel's death and took on its most potent historical form in the work of Marx and Marxism. We might call this the hypothesis of radical discontinuity or incompatibility between Christianity and political freedom. For Marx and a huge number of left-wing cultural critics in his slipstream, but also for Nietzsche and his followers, what Hegel extolled about Luther—namely the inner freedom of the believer—is just another step deepening control over people. After all, when control is external, individuals typically enjoy broad leeway to evade it or to deflect pressure through lip service and outward conformity. But if control impinges on one's inner life, there is no more scope for evasion, not even for those with no particular ambition to comply with religious norms. Luther, as Marx asserted in the introduction to his early *Critique of Hegel's Philosophy of Right*, "transformed the priests into laymen by changing the laymen into priests. He liberated man from external religiosity by making religiosity that which is innermost to man. He freed the body of chains by putting the heart in chains."[7]

In the case of Marx, these strident, polarizing statements do not, of course, express a tragic sense of inescapability, as in the case of the later "critical theory," but rather the ardor of a revolutionary who aspires to emancipate human beings from political oppression and concurrently from all religion—and considers this possible. For, Marx goes on,

> But if Protestantism was not the real solution it at least posed the problem correctly. Thereafter it was no longer a question of the laymen's struggle with the priest outside of him, but of the struggle with his own inner priest, his priestly nature. And if the Protestant transformation of the German laity into priests emancipated the lay popes—the princes together with their clergy, the privileged and the philistines—so the philosophical transformation of the priestly German into men will emancipate the people.[8]

Of course, a blunt anti-Hegelian claim of the discontinuity and incompatibility between Christianity and political freedom must by no means assume a revolutionary Marxian form. It may also be expounded by Christians who regard modern political freedom as a major threat to Christianity and thus seek to oppose its spread. From a Catholic vantage point, if one accepts the alleged nexus of Reformation and political freedom, this way of thinking may result in a view of the Reformation as the point where Christians set off down the wrong path, one they can only leave by taking inspiration from the Middle Ages—in other words, the time before the Reformation. Among Protestants, this perspective tends to take the form of reinterpreting Luther and his understanding of freedom, that is, highlighting the ways in which, rather than setting the individual free, Luther bound them in the strictest of senses—to God's word and to worldly authority. Such binding force can then be seen as a source of hope for a disintegrating political and social order. A Christianity of this kind, whether Catholic or Protestant, will also exercise a magnetic pull on those—who may otherwise be rather distant from Christianity—in search of authority and a new sense of binding commitment.

The two types mentioned so far have in common the assumption that the relationship between Christianity and political freedom has a clear sense of historical direction. In spite of his revolutionary orientation, Marx was ultimately no less teleological in his understanding of history than Hegel, and one might classify his critique of Hegel as trumping rather than simply contradicting him. But if we do not assume such a sense of direction, at least as a clear-cut phenomenon, then neither of the two poles will disappear from history. Instead, there will be a permanent tension between the two. This will entail Christianity changing its self-understanding under the influence of political freedom just as the institutions and theories of political freedom will change by taking ever-new inspiration from Christianity. A scenario of this kind at least opens up the intellectual possibility of including such factual changes in our view of things. This third type is, therefore, referred to as that of mediation.

Historically, there can surely be no doubt that in successful democratic societies, for example, there are strong impulses to bring Christian and other religious communities closer to the modern democratic ideal in their internal structures and to reformulate theological teachings in such a way that they do not contradict this ideal. By the same token, even non-Christians have found inspiration time and again in the Christian emphasis on the "creaturely finitude" of human beings; in the Christian sensitivity to indisposability and to the dangers that may lie in unbounded freedom which risk turning it into its opposite; and in liberation from feeling forced to be free.[9]

Even without a teleological view of history, the exponents of such a concept of mediation cannot avoid assessing empirically the actual historical processes of mediation in a generally more optimistic or pessimistic way. In its optimistic variant this type thus approaches Hegelianism. Although this entails conceding the existence of secularization processes, which are at first glance bound to appear as a weakening of Christianity, these are interpreted as possible instances of its realization. This even finds expression in the term "secularization" itself, which in this connection may mean both the "weakening of religion" and the "realization of religion." The anti-Hegelian notion of an "opposition" between the Christian and modern understandings of freedom is thus nullified in quasi-Hegelian fashion.[10]

The more pessimistic variant of the mediation type is more alive to the risks involved in this tense relationship for both sides. This may take the form of increased calls for political and moral engagement, because on this premise trust in history as such is unsustainable.[11] But it might also prompt attempts by critics of Christianity to further extirpate the influence of Christian ideas, for example in bioethics and family law, or lead to complaints from those skeptical of democracy that the entry of democratic principles into the church dilutes doctrine in line with the prevailing zeitgeist.

The fourth and final type does not stop at the prospect of a relationship of tension that will continue to exist for all of historical time but proclaims an eschatological perspective. Christianity is thus imbued with visions of a political utopia, a left-wing utopia whose concrete features are for the most part strongly influenced by a Marxism that is also interpreted in a utopian and messianic way. This fourth type is referred to as that of outdoing.[12] It is somewhat similar to Marx's discontinuity thesis, but without his criticism of religion. When revolutionary hopes reached their apogee in the 1970s, strong forces streamed in this direction. At present such visions have faded, with the impulses of Latin American liberation theology, for example, being stripped of their utopian exuberance without completely drying up.

The typology outlined here seems useful not just in providing an overview of theological or theory-of-religion positions. We might also relate it to standpoints within political theory and the history of liberalism.[13] This need not be pursued further here. A different aspect is key to the thrust of this part of this book. Fundamentally, all the types mentioned so far make modern political freedom, once established, appear firmly anchored. It may be regarded as more or less desirable, and assessments of Christianity or religion may differ widely, but its collapse or reversal seems to be absent as future possibilities. Yet this finding does not correspond to reality; it merely arises from a typology that fails to pay sufficient attention to possible threats to freedom.

In the United States in particular, with its complex balance between liberalism and Christianity, there is a broad stream of self-critical and anxious questioning of the optimistic mediation type. One of the most impressive voices of this kind was that of H. Richard Niebuhr. In the late 1930s, he wrote that no theology of mediation of this nature had ever really succeeded in reconciling these diverging tendencies:

> As time went on liberalism began to outweigh Evangelicalism more and more. At the same time the former tended to become increasingly secular, to speak more accurately, to lose the sense of the broken relation between God and man, between the present and the coming kingdom. In the course of succeeding generations the heritage of faith with which liberalism had started was used up. The liberal children of liberal fathers needed to operate with ever diminishing capital.[14]

Here we have a clear expression of the idea that political liberalism subsists historically on a religious capital that it seems unable to renew on its own. But if this is so, how can it be secured for the future? Niebuhr was not the only figure in his country to ask this question, and there is a veritable tradition of such questioning in the other Western countries as well. In France, Alexis de Tocqueville is one of the key thinkers in this regard, as is Émile Durkheim.[15] In Germany, the now classic topos for this questioning dates back only to the period immediately after the Second World War. This is the so-called Böckenförde dilemma: "The liberal, secular state is sustained by conditions it cannot itself guarantee." Ernst-Wolfgang Böckenförde, the great professor of constitutional law, originally added the following explanation to this oft-quoted sentence:

> That is the great gamble it has made for the sake of liberty. On the one hand, as a liberal state it can only survive if the freedom it grants to its citizens is regulated from within, out of the moral substance of the individual and the homogeneity of society. On the other hand, it cannot seek to guarantee these inner regulatory forces by its own efforts— that is to say, with the instruments of legal coercion and authoritative command— without abandoning its liberalness, and relapsing, on a secularized level, into the very totalitarian claim it had led away from during the confessional civil wars.[16]

Read in its original context, it quickly becomes clear how Böckenförde's statement differs from the tradition of questioning that he is in certain respects perpetuating. It is palpable throughout this passage that he is posing this question after the experience of the collapse of a liberal-democratic state as a result of the Nazi seizure of power in 1933, and it is unmistakably addressed not so much to a general public for whom the role of the churches is to be made palatable, but rather to Christians themselves, who ought not to strive for a "Christian" state, whatever that might be. Rather, they should "no longer see" the liberal-democratic, secularized state "in its secularity, as something alien, hostile to their faith, but as a chance for liberty, the preservation and realization of which is also their task."[17] Böckenförde himself would surely not have classified his question, to which there can be no definitive answer, as such an epoch-making achievement as others have, prompting them to elect him the "Einstein of constitutional law."[18] He himself made reference to Hegel, who, Böckenförde felt, had contemplated the relationship between state and religion at a level never subsequently reached.[19]

Precisely because there is a rich tradition of questioning in this field, an exhaustive treatment here is not an option. The chapters of this part therefore only deal with a small number of contributions that impress due to their originality and depth. I pay particular attention to the extent to which a given thinker tries to base their ideas about secularization and the modern history of freedom on a nuanced understanding of religion.

The first chapter considers an American thinker who rose to become the most influential public intellectual in the United States in the first half of the twentieth century: John Dewey. He had begun his intellectual development as a Christian neo-Hegelian before the close of the nineteenth century, then broke away from the Christian faith while also transforming his Hegelianism into a variant of American pragmatism through a progressive process of naturalization. Like no other philosopher before him, democracy stood at the center of his thinking as a political ideal, but also as a moral guideline in other areas of life. While his view of history was optimistic-progressive before the First World War, this changed as a result of the war. For him, it was above all the Great Depression and the profound convulsions it triggered even in the democratic states that lent such urgency to the key question: can democracy develop the binding forces it requires on its own, without recourse to the traditions of Christianity? The foreseeable destabilization of democracy raised the question of what the conditions for its stabilization might be, and this question refocused Dewey's attention on religion—above all in the form of a "faith" shared by the citizenry. In line with this, the title of his 1934 theory-of-religion book was *A Common Faith*.[20]

This book itself goes a long way to advancing the theory of religion. Dewey builds directly on William James's psychology of religion but drives it from its individualist starting point in an intersubjectivist direction. This is true on several levels. He is interested in shared, extraordinary experiences, in an understanding of the self as constituted intersubjectively and in the presence of an ideal of successful intersubjectivity in everyday communication. His expositions—discussed in more detail in this chapter—seem to prefigure Charles Taylor's ideas on the necessary connection between "value" and "self" and Jürgen Habermas's philosophy, with its focus on communicative rationality.[21] For Dewey, this conception of intersubjectivity and democracy opens up the prospect of viewing tendencies toward secularization not as symptoms of moral decay but as entailing liberation from dogmatism and the elimination of artificial barriers within a polity. He works on the assumption that the dismantling of religious institutions and the emancipation of the "religious" from religious institutions can stabilize democracy. The chapter on Dewey discusses how plausible this solution is, especially against the background of his own theory of religion.

The following chapter is a bit different from the others in that it deals with an author who has achieved renown primarily through his narrative work: Alfred Döblin. Yet he also published a wealth of journalistic and philosophical-speculative works. Most important in the present context are the two "religious dialogues" that Döblin wrote in 1942–1943 and 1950–1952. They are so extremely important because, in the literary form of a dialogue between a (believing) older man and an (unbelieving) younger one, they articulate in argumentative form Döblin's journey from the secular Judaism of his early years to the Catholic Christianity of his later life. This is a path not to a restorative Christianity, but to what I call a "post-totalitarian" Christianity shaped by the experiences of totalitarianism and the history of violence of the twentieth century. Döblin does not advocate feigning continuity where there is none but seeks a new beginning in Germany, Europe, and in Christianity itself.

Döblin's series of publications on religion began with a trenchant critique of religion, composed during the First World War and published for the first time in 1919. He appears to have been planning a pamphlet titled "Los von Gott" ("Away from God"), of which we have only the introduction, "Jenseits von Gott" ("Beyond God").[22] Döblin was strongly influenced by Nietzsche but sought to go beyond his analysis: "One should not say that God is dead for unbelievers." God, for him, is no longer alive, but also not really dead; instead, God is 'something that neither lives nor dies" and is thus a "ghost."[23] Döblin also wanted to eliminate the underlying factors that enable the concept of gods to take on new life again and again.

Despite his polemics against every recent attempt to "somehow accommodate God," which seemed as embarrassing to him "as eagerly using a rusty machine of antiquated design rather than throwing it on the scrap heap,"[24] the beguiling allure of religious practice shines through very clearly in his texts, an appeal Döblin acknowledged. "I feel the sweetness that lies in devotion, in prayer, the invigoration that follows such submission, the equilibrium it elicits, the lure of surrender and abasement."[25] But for Döblin, both the living conditions of the modern city and the development of philosophy and other branches of scholarship seemed to rule out an intellectually honest and viable faith for all time.

There is no space here to trace the twists and turns of Döblin's religious biography.[26] Critics of religion have often interpreted his conversion as a regrettable expression of the overwhelming problems with which he struggled in exile and in light of lack of success and blows of fate. Döblin refuted this in his inimitable cadence: "I am not ill, was not ill and will not be ill."[27] The dialogue he composed on religion furnished him with an ingenious means of rendering intellectually comprehensible the difficulties involved in talking about faith and his own path to faith. This has captured many readers' imagination, confronting them not so much with ready-made answers as with a process of moving forward. Döblin himself saw it as his task to come up with a new language for Christianity; the old one, he was convinced, was falling on deaf ears. He considered this task more urgent than any other if there were to be any chance of "immunizing [the culture] against economic, racist and nationalist fanaticism."[28]

The following chapter operates on a different level than that of the in-depth understanding of religion and faith, seeking to come to grips with the theory of history put forward by German historian Reinhart Koselleck. His writings come into play here because, like perhaps no other body of work, they articulate a radically contingency-aware understanding of history—an understanding that has erased any trace of teleological (or even evolutionist) philosophy of history. In a sense, Koselleck removes a foundation stone from the Hegelian conception, not with respect to the understanding of religion or freedom, but in terms of the understanding of history. In the relevant chapter I discuss in more detail the biographical elements and intellectual influences crucial to Koselleck's approach here. But the true point of my interpretation emerges when we consider the connection between Koselleck's emphasis on contingency and his ideas on secularization.

What we find is that, in a surprising way, Koselleck and thus the project of conceptual history ascribe greater inevitability to modern European secularization than the empirical evidence supports. Of course, no one should take the deep-seated causes of European secularization lightly or declare them simply reversible. But Koselleck in particular, who so astutely exposed claims of historical inevitability, so dear to Enlightenment thought, as weapons in the battle of political opinion,[29] failed to reflect enough on the fact that this might also apply to the assumption of a historically necessary and ineluctable weakening of religion. This observation of inconsistency in Koselleck's work is in part an attempt to point up the fruitfulness of his history of concepts to the historiography of religion and historical sociology; I will be explaining this in more detail from a number of perspectives. But in opposition to both him and Karl Löwith, I also seek to show that the question of the connection between *Heilsgeschehen* ("salvation events") and "world history" has not simply become obsolete but can be posed productively in a new way.

These three chapters are followed by a fourth, devoted to the (probably indisputably) most important present-day thinker when it comes to the relationship between secularization and the modern history of freedom. I am referring to Canadian philosopher Charles Taylor, who makes no attempt to conceal the connection between his thinking and his Catholic faith. In this field he is the leading opponent of German philosopher and sociologist Jürgen Habermas. Profoundly influenced by Protestantism, however much the latter may criticize militant secularism, his conception of reason and faith includes elements that make it hard for believers to recognize themselves. This applies even to his vast late oeuvre. Suffice it to say at this point that his thinking has remained remarkably untouched by almost all the thinkers and scholars dealt with in this book.[30]

I consider Taylor's work in the chapter dedicated to him solely in relation to his monumental 2007 study *A Secular Age*. It should be remembered, however, that for many decades Taylor was by no means regarded primarily as a religious thinker, but rather as a political theorist and philosophical anthropologist, and above all as a leading interpreter of Hegel's philosophy. The conceptual clarity Taylor had gained through his training in analytical philosophy helped him make Hegel newly accessible in the English-speaking world; when it comes to his own contributions, Taylor also took inspiration from Hegel's work (while not stripping it of its religious dimension). The understanding of freedom was crucial here. It is no coincidence that Axel Honneth chose the title *Negative Freiheit?* ("Negative Freedom?") for a German edition of key essays by Taylor in the 1980s: Taylor was one of the leading critics of the idea that a liberal-democratic political order is solely compatible with an understanding of freedom that ascribes to the individual a form of self-determination limited only by the freedom of their fellow human beings.[31] In Hegel, Taylor saw the most brilliant of attempts to link two far-reaching but competing conceptions of freedom, that is, "to realize a synthesis that the Romantic generation was groping towards: to combine the rational, self-legislating freedom of the Kantian subject with the expressive unity within man and within nature for which the age longed."[32]

Even at this early point in his development, however, Taylor was not an orthodox Hegelian. With explicit reference to Dilthey's distancing from Hegel's philosophy of absolute spirit, Taylor initiated a project that, in both form and content, took him even further from the mere reiteration of Hegel's intellectual edifice.[33] As far as I know, he himself has never given a detailed account of this step-by-step modification; nor has anyone else.[34] This will not be the task of the relevant chapter in this book either. Without examining its genesis, it seeks to get to grips with Taylor's mature history or theory of secularization. However we might assess its individual elements, it is certain that—like the other ideas dealt with in this part of the book on the relationship between secularization and the modern history of freedom—this history or theory is not a teleological one, either in the sense of the triumph of Christianity or of final liberation from it.

II, 2

The Sacralization of Democracy: John Dewey

John Dewey's 1934 book in the theory of religion, *A Common Faith*,[1] cannot be compared with the great works of his late philosophy (on nature and art, logic and ethics), for it succeeds all of them in terms of its sheer brevity, the richness of its argument, and the amount of attention that it received. The leading Protestant theologian among Dewey's contemporaries in the United States, Reinhold Niebuhr, called *A Common Faith* quite understandably a mere footnote to his impressive oeuvre.[2] Nevertheless, the three lectures that Dewey (1859–1952) published in this volume are extremely significant, and in order to do them justice, it is in my view necessary to distinguish between two levels. On the one hand, it represents the attempt to intervene in debates on religion taking place in the United States during the 1930s between liberal Christians, fundamentalist currents, those who sought to place fresh emphasis on the concepts of evil and sin, and secular humanist enterprises.[3] In this context, Dewey expresses his personal views on the contemporary state of religion, on its effects and its future. On the other hand, Dewey's book on the theory of religion extends his theory of action and experience to encompass a further area of inquiry in which one can see at least an application, perhaps even a further development or culmination, of his own thought, and thus of the approach inaugurated by William James.[4] It is on this level that we can expect to find Dewey's more systematically important contribution. For this reason, we shall first turn our attention to Dewey's theory of religious experience, before then discussing his peculiar attempt at a sacralization of democracy.

Like William James, Dewey separates at the very beginning of his discussion—in the lecture titled "Religion versus the Religious"—the "religious" from institutionalized forms of religion, which he defines as "a special body of beliefs and practices having some kind of institutional organization, loose or tight" (9). Thus, his approach to the phenomenon of the religious is intended to run parallel to the argument he had employed in his book on aesthetics, where it had proved fruitful not to start out from ossified art hanging in museums, or its professionalized or commercialized forms, but to investigate "art as experience."[5] Dewey immediately defends himself against a possible misunderstanding. Under no circumstances does he intend to trace cultural forms back to their origin in human experience merely in order to reproduce conceptually, by distinguishing types of experience, the rigid boundaries between the culturally differentiated value spheres. Hence Dewey did not believe in a specifically "aesthetic" or "religious" form of experience, but in aesthetic or religious dimensions of human experience. This distinction seems to Dewey to be of fundamental importance as far as religion is concerned, even greater than its significance in the domain of art. He views every assumption of a separate kind of experience that is uniquely religious as disguised theology. Any theory starting from the premise of such "experience" would perpetuate the dualism of the natural and supernatural that Dewey had resisted throughout his entire career. Theories of religious experience had become almost fashionable during the decades separating James's pioneering achievement and Dewey's book—that is, between 1902 and 1934.[6] Dewey sees two reasons for this development. First, the old ontological, cosmological, and teleological proofs of the existence of God had been discredited not only by Kant's epochal critique, but also by the realization that such rationalism was unlikely to inspire religious motivation. Second, in a scientifically oriented age the prospect of justifying religion in an analogous way to science is an enticing one—that is, as based on a separate type of experience clearly distinguishable from the scientific type. Just as the scientists "rely upon certain kinds of experience to prove the existence of certain kinds of objects, so the religionists rely upon a certain kind of experience to prove the existence of the object of religion, especially the supreme object, God" (11).

But this proof from experience, Dewey argues, does not really produce the desired result. Like Durkheim seeking to differentiate his own position from that of James,[7] Dewey objects that experience does not itself determine its correct interpretation. On no account does he wish to doubt that experiences of the kind documented in accounts of religious experience actually occur. However, a person who has such experiences obtains his or her interpretations of them from the culture in which he or she has grown up. Dewey does not put forward his own interpretation with quite the same unshakeable belief in its truth as does Durkheim; but neither does he admit all the interpretations made by those involved, as James did in the spirit of investigative curiosity. Rather, in a manner that is clearly directed against institutionalized and traditional religions, he wants to put the religious interpretation of such experiences in the narrower sense firmly in its place. Thus, at first sight, the real origins of these experiences remain obscure. As a pragmatist, Dewey approaches the question of origins by illuminating the effects: we first ascertain a phenomenon on the basis of its effects. With respect to religious experience, this means that the existence of such experiences cannot prove their "supernatural" origin, but only the fact of "an orientation, that brings with it a sense of security and peace" (13).

Shattering Intersubjectivity

If Dewey rejects the notion of a separate type of religious experience and the proof of the existence of God based upon it, in what, then, does the religious quality of experiences consist for him? What is the essence of the reorientations in life brought about by such experiences? Dewey's first step in answering these questions is to introduce a conceptual distinction. He distinguishes three kinds of such orientation in life and offers three different concepts for them: "adaptation," "accommodation," and "adjustment," all of which are commonly employed as synonyms. Yet to do so is to ignore the fundamental differences Dewey wishes to address, and insufficient attention to this distinction has frequently hindered the understanding of pragmatism.[8] All these terms imply a coming to terms with unalterable circumstances; we always act under given conditions and must always take account of these. Dewey refers to a predominantly passive reorientation of particular modes of conduct to such conditions as "accommodation"; if this unavoidable form of reorientation is generalized and determines our whole behavior, we call it fatalistic resignation or submission to circumstances.

A second form, clearly distinguishable from the first, could best be described as the world adapting to us, its "recasting in a form beneficial to life" (Arnold Gehlen). Dewey terms this second type of reorientation "adaptation"; what stands out here is the active element in the organism's relation to its environment. The third form, which goes beyond either of these two, is what Dewey calls "adjustment"; it is the goal of his conceptual distinctions to clarify the specificities of this third type. The main difference between this third type and the two others lies in its holistic character. Here our whole person is at issue, and not only individual desires or needs in their relation to environmental conditions. Because of their holistic character, Dewey maintains, such modifications to our person are enduring and robust enough to survive despite changes in our environment. It is no simple thing to compare "adjustment" with the other two types of reorientation in terms of activity and passivity. Although fundamental reorientations of our person can be called voluntary, they are not so in the same way that our volitions are. Not only does something change in and through our will, our will itself changes in them. "It is a change *of* will conceived as the organic plenitude of our being, rather than any special change *in* will" (17). There is quite clearly a passive element in the voluntariness here. This should not be confused with a stoical resolution to remain calm in the face of the vicissitudes of fate: this attitude is "more outgoing, more ready and glad" (16) than mere stoicism. It is still rather unclear what kind of experiences Dewey wants to capture through these terminological distinctions and tentative descriptions. We are inevitably reminded of William James's vivid descriptions of the liberating effects of religious experiences. Dewey does indeed have in mind the claim made by religions that it is through them that such holistic and permanent transformations take place in a person's attitudes. However, in keeping with his objective of distinguishing between experience and interpretation, he is at the very least unwilling to take this claim for granted. His method is therefore to reverse the relationship between cause and effect. He thus does not attribute fundamental reorientations in values to a person opening himself or herself up to supernatural influences in religious experiences; instead, he simply designates as religious every such fundamental change in orientation. "It is not *a* religion that brings it about, but when it occurs, from whatever cause and by whatever means, there is a religious outlook and function" (17).

At first sight this move can seem like a mere pseudo-solution to the problem, circumventing it by redefining the terms. We can quite happily concede to Dewey that it is by no means only religions in the usual sense of the word that can bring about fundamental reorientations in a person's outlook; the same goes for the fact that religion only permeates into superficial regions of many believers' characters, so that the influence of religion on personal development can also be easily overestimated. If this were all that Dewey wished to assert, then we would have no qualms in agreeing with him; perhaps we might only want to object that one doesn't necessarily make things any clearer by terming all such reorientations "religious," particularly those that are not connected with institutionalized forms of religiosity.

Dewey could then even have done without the distinction between "religious experiences" and the "religious dimension of experiences," since for him the concept of the religious would have abandoned all relation to institutionalized forms of religion, let alone to a supernatural realm. But such an interpretation would entirely underestimate the profundity of Dewey's thought. We can avoid this underestimation only by reading Dewey's account against the background of his understanding of action and experience. His roundabout way of dealing with the concept of the religious is not merely pedantry or a consequence of his difficult relationship with organized religion. It stems, rather, from his attempt actually to identify in the potentially religious dimension of all experience a phenomenon that differs from the fragmentation of everyday experience, and yet that also represents more than the situation-bound overcoming of this fragmentation through aesthetic experience.[9]

Dewey's crucial step consists in connecting religious experience with the *imaginary* orientation to a *whole self*. Before Dewey, both William James and Georg Simmel had already thought along these lines. James had interpreted conversion as a transformation of the self from a state of division and turmoil to a newly unified one; Simmel had recognized the self's awareness of its finitude as the vital coordinating point in the genesis of ideal validities, and had elaborated the value-relatedness of self-formation.[10] But neither succeeded in translating these insights from intuitions into clear concepts. Dewey at least contributes to the clarification of their approaches.

He makes it clear that the idea of a whole self is thoroughly imaginary. The holistic self no more preexists somewhere—say in a person's inner being, in static perfection waiting to be realized in practical life—than do values exist in a transcendental ideal realm.[11] There is no possibility of ever perceiving the self as a whole through the senses—visually, for example. Neither is a holistic relation to ourselves possible in any practical activity, or in an act of reflection. Even our interaction with other people in everyday life always touches on only one aspect of our person.

Yet we still speak of a whole self or of self-realization, which only makes sense if the present real self can be ascribed something not yet realized, something that nevertheless must somehow have already existed before, and is not first produced in, its realization. Dewey does not attack the notion of the given self in order to destroy the idea of wholeness and self-realization,[12] but in order to underscore the "imaginary" character of this idea. "The *whole* self is an ideal, an imaginative projection" (19). This emphasis on the imaginary should not be understood as reducing this ideal to the status of mere illusion; Dewey resists such a misunderstanding by pointing out that it is only through our imagination that we can perceive any kind of possibility (43).[13] The dualism of the real and the possible simply does not exist for Dewey; rather, the real contains possibilities, and the imagination is an organ through which human beings can apprehend the possible. Dewey praises his contemporary and adversary George Santayana for having introduced into the understanding of religion the dimension of the imaginary in this sense. Dewey describes as a "penetrating insight" (18)[14] Santayana's interest in the difference between an "intervening" and a merely "supervening" role of the imagination, instead of seeking an essential difference between the aesthetic and the religious. The question is whether the imagination merely adds something to our life, or whether it permeates and transforms life; this, however, can happen through art *and* religion, just as art *and* religion could remain merely superficial accessories adorning one's conduct of life. Without a "creative movement of the imagination," all perception remains limited and all discipline mere repression. With it, however, the ideals arise that pervade our perception of the world and our morality. By insisting on their relation to the imaginary, Dewey can recognize ideals without attributing to them a separate, prior existence. In an earlier work he had already asserted, "The ideal is not a goal to be attained. It is a significance to be felt, appreciated."[15] But now he extends this definition through the idea that values or ideals are *the product of creative processes in which contingent possibilities are idealized.* An ideal arises, Dewey writes,

> when the imagination idealizes existence by laying hold of the possibilities offered to thought and action. . . . The idealizing imagination seizes upon the most precious things found in the climacteric moments of experience and projects them. We need no external criterion and guarantees for their goodness. They are had, they exist as good, and out of them we frame our ideal ends. (48)

Dewey has far more in mind here than merely a clever modification of goals in response to the conditions for their realization; he sees the genesis of values as the creative work of our imagination.

At the same time, however, this insight brings him closer to understanding the ideas of the whole self and of self-realization. Amid all the contradictions between our desires, or between duty and inclination, and amid all the anguish we feel over missed opportunities and unrealized potential, creative idealization allows us to imagine a wholeness that never existed, never will exist, and yet still seems to us to be more real than all partial realizations of our self. It seems real to us because we have experienced it as real with the greatest intensity. This can happen in religious experiences, or for Dewey in any experiences that involve this kind of religious dimension because they "completely interpenetrat[e] all the elements of our being" (18) and give our self meaning and coherence. When, in intense emotional experiences, we have this feeling of breaking through to our own wholeness, this "sense of values" sustains us through "periods of darkness and despair to such an extent that they lose their usual depressive character" (14f.). Lack of success in our practical endeavors, blows of fortune, or failures in meeting the moral demands we make on ourselves—none of these can destroy this core of our self. Ideals make permanent that which briefly flares up in these fleeting experiences: ideals integrate. To believe in them is to unify our self

> through allegiance to inclusive ideal ends, which imagination presents to us and to which the human will responds as worthy of controlling our desires and choices. (33)[16]

However, the unification of the self should not, Dewey argues, be understood as cutting the self off from the world. It is only possible for a person to experience themselves as a unity amid all their actions and the events that befall them, and even vis-à-vis their unrealized possibilities, if the world is introduced into the process of self-unification.

> The self is always directed toward something beyond itself and so its own unification depends upon the idea of the integration of the shifting scenes of the world into that imaginative totality we call the Universe. (19)

He defines the "Universe" as the totality of conditions with which the self feels itself to be connected. The wholeness of this Universe has the same imaginary character (in Dewey's sense) as the wholeness of the self. Dewey is well aware that all religions are characterized by the feeling of "absolute dependence"[17] on something greater existing beyond our self, supporting and sustaining our endeavors. For this reason, he designates as areligious only those views that attribute human achievements exclusively to humanity itself and ignore the cooperation of its environment.

> Our successes are dependent upon the co-operation of nature. The sense of the dignity of human nature is as religious as is the sense of awe and reverence when it rests upon a sense of human nature as a co-operative part of a larger whole. (25)

Dewey describes this profound quasi-religious sentiment toward the environment as "natural piety," a term whose origins lie in English Romanticism. He does not wish this term to be misconstrued as Romantic nature worship as such or as a fatalistic belief in natural determinism, for a sense of what is specifically human in nature can certainly be combined with this kind of piety toward nature as a whole.[18]

The recognition of the imaginary wholeness of self and universe also leads Dewey to emphasize the active-passive character of such an experience of wholeness, which he had already delineated when introducing the concept of "adjustment." Like all feats of the imagination and all creative actions, a firm will does not help to bring about this experience. "An 'adjustment' possesses the will rather than is its express product" (19). For this reason, we cannot directly strive for and deliberately attain experiences of wholeness. Rather, they require an openness to forces that flow from sources beyond conscious deliberation and purpose (ibid.). For Dewey, this explains the affinity of such experiences with "supernatural" interpretations. The traditional way of articulating this state of affairs is that religious experiences and the faith that grows out of them are themselves expressions of divine grace. Wholly independent of all theological contexts, Dewey—like James—advocates a concept of faith premised not on a cognitive holding-to-be-true of facts, but rather on a conviction of the presence of ideals that attract us and guide our conduct. This conviction is the product of being seized, not of a conscious decision, and although cognition and reflection are involved, they do not constitute its essence. "Conviction in the moral sense signifies being conquered, vanquished, in our active nature by an ideal end; it signifies acknowledgment of its rightful claim over our desire and purposes" (20).

Thus, Dewey's answer to the question of the genesis of values rather resembles that given by the other thinkers. Like James and Durkheim, but also like Simmel and Scheler, he anchors the genesis of value commitments in experiences of self-transcendence and self-formation. Far more clearly than these other authors, he establishes the connection between the theory of values and the theory of self-formation, yet his description of the phenomenal form of the experiences in which value commitments have their origin is less clear. Dewey does not give any lucid metaphors that might guide us and might be comparable to James's descriptions of prayer and conversion, Durkheim's account of collective states of ecstasy, Simmel's reflections on death and immortality, or Scheler's phenomenology of moral feelings. Scattered over many of his writings from all phases of his work, and drawn from various contexts, we find examples of experiences with a religious dimension. To these belong experiences of fusion with nature, aesthetic experiences, and mystical intuitions, just as much as do shattering moments of compassion and love, or feelings of togetherness that accompany happy, communal life. But experiences—with the exception of aesthetic experiences—are rarely analyzed in detail; rather, they are merely enlisted for conceptual arguments or as pathos-rich tools for concluding an argument.

It is in his great work of natural philosophy, *Experience and Nature*, that the experiential content of Dewey's philosophy of value-constitutive experience probably finds its most concrete expression, above all in the chapter on communication.[19] Here Dewey imbues the anthropological theory of the specifics of human communication, as it had been developed by his friend George Herbert Mead, with a quasi-religious meaning:

> Of all affairs, communication is the most wonderful. That things should be able to pass from the plane of external pushing and pulling to that of revealing themselves to man, and thereby to themselves; and that the fruit of communication should be participation, sharing, is a wonder by the side of which transubstantiation pales.[20]

He regards communication not only as a functional arrangement for coordinating the action of different people, but as an event that can open up individual human beings to others; in doing so, it itself makes possible the experience in which value commitment arises. When communication leads to "shared experience," Dewey sees it as a way of overcoming self-centeredness. In his early work, he had still appealed to the Christian concept of love to support this idea.[21] Yet even if he no longer establishes the connection in this way in his later work, it is still evident that Dewey advocates an emphatic conception of altruism. He understands it not as renouncing one's own interests to increase others' utility, nor as selfdevelopment through one's commitment to others. Instead, Dewey understands it as the radical readiness to let oneself be shaken by the Other in order thereby to realize oneself with and through other people: as shattering intersubjectivity.

I want to emphasize two aspects of Dewey's argument at this point. First, it becomes clear that, by focusing on communication, intersubjectivity, and shared experience, he finds a way out from the inadequate dualism of individual and collective experience as found in the work of James and Durkheim. Although James's work contained the seeds of an intersubjective interpretation of solitary religious experience,[22] these had remained scattered and of little consequence for the construction of his theory. Dewey, in contrast, is so heavily influenced by George Herbert Mead's anthropological theory of communication that he links the structure of extraordinary experiences to the intersubjectivist understanding of human action in general. Dewey construes the opening of the self, which James and Durkheim also described as crucial to extraordinary experiences, as the decentering of the actor toward another—even where this other is nature or God. We should immediately add the rider, however, that although Dewey constantly appeals to the genesis of the self in ordinary and extraordinary intersubjective experiences, he never really delves into the latter.[23] Although he initiates the linkage of an intersubjectivist theory of the self with questions about the genesis of value commitments, he does not take this idea very far.

The second aspect to stress is that Dewey not only maintains that extraordinary experience has an intersubjective character; he also holds that it is possible to find in everyday communication itself an ideal worthy of reverence. Participation in a conversation can itself yield the experience of wholeness. The attitudes of participants requisite for a successful dialogue resemble the opening of the self that he described in the analysis of religious experiences. In turn, the genesis of these experiences in dialogue becomes more likely through that very opening of the self. The opening of the self is both the precondition for and consequence of the experience of shattering intersubjectivity. For Dewey, conversation or dialogue is the place where we are confronted with the values of others, and, when we truly open ourselves up, where we consider our own values anew. At the same time, however, provided that it grants us this experience, dialogue produces a value commitment to engaging in intercommunication itself.

With his description of communication as being simultaneously means and goal, instrumental and final, Dewey repeatedly expresses the possibility of experiencing a "religious" dimension in dialogue itself.[24]

Communication is an exchange which procures something wanted; it involves a claim, appeal, order, direction or request, which realizes want at less cost than personal labor exacts, since it procures the co-operative assistance of others. Communication is also an immediate enhancement of life, enjoyed for its own sake.... Language is always a form of action and in its instrumental use is always a means of concerted action for an end, while at the same time it finds in itself all the goods of its possible consequences. For there is no mode of action as fulfilling and as rewarding as is concerted consensus of action. It brings with it the sense of sharing and merging in a whole.... Shared experience is the greatest of human goods.... Because of its characteristic agency and finality, communication and its congenial objects are objects ultimately worthy of awe, admiration, and loyal appreciation. They are worthy as means, because they are the only means that make life rich and varied in meanings. They are worthy as ends, because in such ends man is lifted from his immediate isolation and shares in a communion of meanings. Here, as in so many other things, the great evil lies in separating instrumental and final functions.... When the instrumental and final functions of communication live together in experience, there exists an intelligence which is the method and reward of the common life, and a society worthy to command affection, admiration, and loyalty.[25]

Dewey's emphasis here is on the experience of communication, on communication as experience. He identifies the transition from interpersonal relationship to the value of community and democracy not in the justification of democratic principles in an idealized discourse, but in the genesis of a value commitment to the practice of communicating, which is itself rooted in the experience of communication.[26] For Dewey, the unlimited nature of everyday communication and its institutionalization in the form of the procedures and institutions of democratic society become the highest ideal. Replying to critics of his philosophy in 1939, in an essay that simultaneously served as a retrospective on his intellectual development, Dewey could claim that he had endeavored all his life to make explicit the religious values implicit in the spirit of science, and likewise "the religious values implicit in our common life, especially in the moral significance of democracy as a way of living together."[27] Democracy becomes Dewey's secular religion. Should we give our allegiance to him as the prophet of this religion?

Democracy and Religion

With this question we return to that contemporary line of thought in *A Common Faith* that we bracketed off at the beginning of our discussion of this work. To facilitate our understanding of his argument, it is useful briefly to recall at what stage of his life Dewey wrote this theory-of-religion book. In his neo-Hegelian, still Christian, early phase, he had indeed, as he set out in his retrospective, already ascribed a quasi-sacred character to pragmatic intelligence and democratic willformation. At first glance, the sermon he delivered to Christian students in Michigan in 1892[28] reads like an attempt at a Christian justification of democracy. As it proceeds, however, it becomes increasingly clear that Dewey is interested in far more than just this; in keeping with the character of American spirituality, by positing a radical relation of the divine to the everyday life of humanity, he opens up the perspective of surpassing Christianity in a sacralized democracy. The spirit of revelation is then "sublated" in scientific inquiry, as the incarnation of God is "sublated" in the democratic community. Dewey asks himself whether religious institutions, with their origins in a predemocratic and prescientific age, can welcome their replacement by democracy and science, or whether, in defending their independence, they are condemned to ossify because they can only look backward to the past. For Dewey himself, it was already clear by this time that the future could belong only to the sacralization of science and democracy. After the end of his neoHegelian phase, he only rarely comments on religion and its place in democracy,[29] but when he does so, his early optimism about the process of secularization is couched in even more radical terms.[30] Specifically, he does not interpret progressive secularization as a symptom of moral and cultural decay; instead, he understands it as a change in the way religious motifs are expressed, as their liberation from dogmatic doctrine and narrow forms of institutionalization.

According to him, the disappearance of individual churches as institutions need not represent a loss; such a development might instead express the universalization of Christian impulses and thus historical progress. This combination of declining interest in religion and democratic optimism did not, to be sure, withstand the turmoil of the twentieth century. After the First World War, and particularly after the beginning of the Great Depression, Dewey became increasingly convinced that his philosophical conception of democracy would not stand up to the events of the age if it did not also find the means of seizing the hearts and minds of the people and inspiring them to make the necessary radical reforms.[31] Therefore, Dewey's attempts to attribute a sacred character to democracy itself already began in the 1920s, and found their culmination in *A Common Faith,* his book on religion.

In Dewey's view, the most important thing is to avoid the infelicitous association of the religious with a belief in supernatural forces. Since modern science has gradually reduced the cognitive claims of religion to represent a knowledge of such forces and has devalued such a knowledge altogether, for Dewey this linkage leads to a poor alternative: either to remain a believer, but then pay the price of defending conceptions of the world that have lost their credibility—or, as a scientifically minded atheist, to become unable to find any meaning at all in religious ideals. Those who refuse to accept this poor alternative, as Dewey is well aware, will be denounced by both sides—with the religionists seeing an opponent of their doctrines and the militant atheists a half-hearted adherent of a religion that is beyond rescue. Dewey, however, thinks he has found a way out from this alternative, which is to uncouple the notion of ideals and values from the cognitive belief in supernatural forces. If it is possible (and this is exactly what the theoretical nub of his argument was driving at) to preserve a rational core at the center of the religious by interpreting experience and action in a new way, and yet simultaneously to cast off all the mythological and dogmatic baggage that has weighed down traditional religions, then the path is clear for the sacralization of the everyday social relationships of human beings and their action in nature. What Dewey finds repellent about mere atheism is that, in rejecting the supernatural, it also tends to devalue the natural. In the belief in a "supernatural" realm, however, he sees the prototypical case of a rupture between the ideal and the real, which he had sought his whole life long to repair. Dewey would have us believe that the catalogue of the misdeeds perpetrated by religions is long. By hypostatizing all that is ideal into the notion of a prior existing being, "God," they distract us away from everyday action, lull us into a false sense of security, and seduce us into idleness; they impoverish our everyday life because they discourage our recognition of its potential; they divert our attention from other people because they fix our gaze on individual salvation; and they delude us into believing in unattainable objectives, thus overtaxing and suffocating our natural powers. All this can be laid squarely at the door of a belief in a "supernatural" being. Moreover, further problems arise because this belief assumes the form of institutionalized churches, each one of which claims a monopoly on our religious experience. In doing so, they hinder such experience rather than facilitating it, competing with one another and thereby erecting artificial boundaries within a community. In order to protect their untenable claims, they obstruct unprejudiced scientific research and the free communication of democratic citizens.

On no account does Dewey express his opposition to all these consequences of religion by proposing a program for its abolition by coercive let alone violent means; his goal is not to destroy religion, but rather to recast it. He defines this recasting as the emancipation of the religious dimension from the institutional forms of religion. For the first time in the history of humanity, "the religious aspect of experience will be free to develop freely on its own account," (2) and people who feel "repelled from what exists as a religion by its intellectual and moral implications" will become aware "of attitudes in themselves that if they came to fruition would be genuinely religious" (9). In this new form of religiosity, the word "God" would no longer designate a particular being beyond the human world, but instead the "*active* relation between ideal and actual" (51). If this were to become the new meaning of the term, then even Dewey, the atheist, would be ready to accept again the notion of a "God."[32] There would then arise, he maintains, a "common faith of mankind" (87), a faith that has always resided *in nuce* in human beings but has been awaiting explication.

But can anyone believe in such a God? Is it really true that organized religion has always inhibited intellectual and moral progress? Can we today, more than eight decades later, still share Dewey's optimism that the deinstitutionalization of religion will release and emancipate authentic religious impulses? The answer to all three questions must surely be "no." The idea that a philosopher's decision to use or to admit the concept of "God" to denote an intellectual abstraction could prompt anyone to do anything, and would trigger the transformation of their person, seems highly presumptuous. But if we strip away Dewey's attempt to recast the concept of "God," the sociological hole in his argument looms large. Admittedly, he asked which ideals today "can direct action and generate the heat of emotion and the light of intelligence" (51f.) in order to buttress democratic institutions in particular. Yet his answer to this question of where the deep affective roots of democracy could lie in individuals and societies remains weak and abstract. Likewise, it is all too easy to read Dewey's objections to the cultural and social impact of institutionalized religion as a fallacious generalization of his experiences of the pietist Protestantism of his childhood and youth. After all, religion has often been not an obstacle, but rather the impetus for intellectual and moral progress. Dewey had never studied the history and sociology of religion in the kind of depth necessary to advance such far-reaching theses. One need only think of Max Weber's intensive studies of the active or passive features, this-worldly or otherworldly orientations, of the major world religions for it to be clear that, if the consequences of institutionalized religiosity are to be assessed, we require more evidence than that which Dewey adduces.[33] Hence not only does he offer no interpretations of concrete religiosity; nowhere does the particular style of his account betray the passionate curiosity for the variety of religious phenomena that was so characteristic of James's work. Dewey brings the debate to a close before it has even begun.[34] In stark contrast to his constant efforts to avoid all stark dualisms in philosophy, he sets institutionalized religion against the free-floating religious in the experience of democracy without seeking to mediate between them. However much he may have been right in individual cases with his critique of the churches' claim to exclusivity, or with his assertion that religious institutions may hinder religious experience, he overshoots the mark with his plea for radical de-institutionalization of the religious sphere. Today it could be said that this de-institutionalization does not, in all probability, lead to the consequences Dewey expected, namely the sacralization of democracy, but rather to a subjectivization of religion—to what the group around Robert Bellah has described as "Sheila-ism."[35] This term refers to a purely personal form of religion, where the only person who currently holds such a belief proclaims her idiosyncratic mixture of views drawn from various traditions to be a new variant of religion. This kind of religiosity, however, largely cuts itself off from the rationalizing effects of the intersubjective assimilation of religious experience, from the richness of traditions spanning millennia and the wisdom of specialists in religious experience. Whoever wishes to be religious without following a particular religion ends up in the same paradox as one who would like to speak without using a particular language.[36]

Dewey's sacralization of democracy[37] thus ends in a paradox. The same thinker who related the questions of the genesis of values or ideals to the value-forming experience of communication eschews any attempt at clarifying particular binding forces. He skips over the particularism of each individual experience and lands, with his "common faith of mankind," in an empty universalism of the democratic ideal, the motivating force of which remains unfathomable.[38] This leads to what Charles Taylor has harshly and accurately called "post-Enlightenment banalities."[39] When it comes to the theory of religion, then, our task now is to continue and go beyond what Dewey started—the combination of the theory of valuegenesis with a theory of self-formation—yet without at the same time ending up in his paradoxes or embracing his vision of the de-institutionalization of religion as a means of securing democracy.[40]

II, 3
Post-totalitarian Christianity: Alfred Döblin's Religious Dialogues

Who could possibly be against a dialogue between believers and nonbelievers?[1] It seems only too obvious that such an exchange is always helpful. In reality, however, dialogue of this kind often proves difficult, even unrealizable. After the rise of the "secular option" in eighteenth-century Europe,[2] any attempt at such a conversation was encumbered by two suppositions. Many critics of the church, Christianity, or all religion viewed their opponents as living in the past and as undeserving of a future that they would certainly be denied. From this perspective, believers inevitably seemed backward, while defenders of the faith appeared as historical relics, even as "reactionary." Conversely, champions of faith tended to view their adversaries as morally dangerous. Since they expected the weakening of religion to engender moral decay, they were bound to perceive critics of religion as naive contemporaries inadvertently fostering such decline, if not as Mephistophelian forces seeking to ensure the triumph of their own sinister agenda.

Both these assumptions have largely lost their credibility today because the anticipated victory of secularism in the wake of modernization has largely failed to materialize outside of Europe, while the often highly secularized societies of Europe have not experienced the predicted moral decline. It is true that these two ideas have not completely disappeared from public life, but they are more rarely put forward today with that great self-confidence typical of the religio-political debates of the nineteenth and twentieth centuries. Despite this changed situation, the after-effects of the old mutual stereotyping can still be felt, and there is meager interest in open dialogue between believers and nonbelievers.[3] An awkward silence often sets in if religious themes arise in discussions or conversations. This may have to do with the fact that there are so few cases of successful dialogue of this kind, while both sides worry that talking about such matters will set in motion a dynamic that can only end in division.

There is thus an increased need for role models—for examples of successful dialogue. Against this background, it might be beneficial to focus new attention on literary works that present us with such dialogue—as fiction, of course. There have been attempts of this kind since Voltaire and Lessing in the eighteenth century. In the twentieth century, Alfred Döblin (1878–1957) produced an outstanding work in this genre. To be more precise, he composed two interrelated texts: *Der unsterbliche Mensch* ("The Immortal Human Being") and *Der Kampf mit dem Engel* ("The Struggle with the Angel").[4]

Both of Döblin's late-oeuvre "religious dialogues" take place between an "older" and "younger" man. The interlocutors are not named, no doubt in part because Döblin has both of them articulating views that he himself expounded at different stages of his life. Both works were written after Döblin's conversion to (Catholic) Christianity, the first during his Californian exile in 1942–1943, the second after his return to Germany and before his second, voluntary exile in France between 1950 and 1952. Döblin did not have to try to put himself in the shoes of another person with a quite different attitude toward matters of faith than he, a task that may sound easier than it actually is. But empathizing with one's former self is undoubtedly a great challenge in itself, especially given that converts are not known for their sympathetic accounts of their pre-"enlightenment" years. This, of course, applies no more and no less to those who have found their way to religious faith than to those who have broken away from it.

Döblin's dialogues, then, take place between an "older man" who has found his way to faith and a "younger" counterpart who, in the first instance, rejects this path out of hand. It should immediately be pointed out that these dialogues are not structured in such a way that the older believer starts out with proselytizing intentions. On the contrary, initially the older man is clearly reluctant to enter into the dialogue at all, and later to continue it. Toward the end of the first dialogue (258), in a retrospective monologue, he makes the sad statement that he has no wish to have such conversations again. The older man does not, therefore, feel called to be an apostle. What makes him hesitate, and why does he feel so uncomfortable from time to time and in retrospect? There are in fact two reasons for this, which vary in importance at different stages and are addressed in a verbal skirmish (11) prior to the real debate.

One reason is that the older man feels misunderstood from the outset in light of the premises underlying his younger counterpart's initiative. The trigger for the entire event is in fact the younger man's deep disappointment with his older interlocutor. The former believes that, as a result of his evident religiosity, the latter has betrayed the common cause of progressive politics and the fight against fascism and Nazism. What is more, he accuses his once-respected friend of having voluntarily renounced freedom and rationality as a believer. He has excluded himself from the circle of free persons and is now abandoning himself to "dark feelings" in a way that is unworthy of him, feelings that "everyone carries within himself but represses because they are atavistic vestiges of earlier times" (12). It is precisely as a free spirit that the younger person feels committed to the value of tolerance. He does not believe that his accusations against his opposite number contradict this: he feels obliged to set limits to tolerance in cases of the voluntary renunciation of freedom.

The older believer thus finds himself directly confronted with a whole bundle of assumptions in which he cannot recognize himself. Sometimes ironically, sometimes reproachfully, he rejects these assumptions and categorically refuses to enter into the conversation in the first place if he is effectively supposed to speak from the dock. If one's faith raises suspicions that one has deserted (20) a good cause or is in need of a psychiatrist's help, this eliminates the most elementary prerequisite for a successful dialogue, namely the fundamental recognition of the other and their soundness of mind. "If we don't conduct our religious dialogue without ulterior motives, by which I mean honestly, face to face, person to person, then we might as well forget the whole thing" (23).

The nonbeliever, then, must at least be prepared to question the idea that believers are less interested in rational insights and truth than he is, that they are more passive with regard to social changes, more eccentric, more easily fall victim to illusions and ideologies, and are generally weaker in character. Similarly, the believer must be willing to understand where this picture of faith comes from and the extent to which it is based in reality. Hence, the origin of human rights already comes up in the dialogue partners' preliminary skirmish. As the younger man sees it, these stem from the French Revolution. Previously, he argues, there were "only gods' rights, God's rights over man, as championed by the clergy, for which the rulers rewarded them. It is true that the existence of human rights is mentioned in the Bible, but little was ever made of this" (17). Suddenly, however, without reference to the Bible and solely on the basis of the revolutionaries' armed might, people were declared free, something that has "oppressors around the world gnawing at their fingernails to this day" (ibid.).

But it is not just these politically charged ideas about the character of faith that impede dialogue about it. Conversation may become impossible not only if those involved are so caught up in grappling with mutual prejudices that they never get to the meat of the subject, but also because faith is not simply a matter of propositions that can be dealt with argumentatively. Faith is bound up with the person's innermost, even intimate core. No one wishes to be forced to expose this or is willing to expose it if the other has no other intention than "sniffing at" it, let alone "tearing it down" (31). Even if the believer has the courage to speak about faith, they will sometimes hesitate to do so because what is believed generates a sense of "awe" (42). Who is certain that they have penetrated their own faith completely? Is it not immodest and lacking in humility to be so sure of one's own faith that it need only be proclaimed? Toward the end of the first book, a letter from the older man to the younger one quotes an old monk's wise remark: "The less a person thinks about converting the world and the more he seeks to convert himself, the more likely it is that the world will be converted through him" (274).

I have already mentioned that Döblin repeatedly inserts into the dialogue monological interludes, namely the interlocutors' individual reflections and correspondence between them, both of which seek to calmly bridge the gulf that has opened up in their relationship. There is certainly no steady rapprochement between the two overall. Döblin was much too experienced as a person and too masterly an author to reduce the tension of the dialogue to simple didactics. This is why speculative flights of fancy and pontificating passages are repeatedly interrupted by sobering references to contemporary realities. This is also why both interlocutors are ascribed self-doubt and both relapse to earlier views despite the consensus they have already achieved, a development sometimes welcomed euphorically as liberation through the "unholy spirit" (245). It is far from certain that the older man consistently represents Döblin's views, denying the reader a comfortable vantage point. Again and again, meanwhile, the idea that argument is the right form of dialogue in this field is fundamentally called into question. From a certain point onwards, the older man suggests praying together and he is aware that their conversation about faith is not enough to convey the experiences constitutive of faith. He increasingly places his hopes in shared reading of the Bible: "To learn about his [Christ's] life across the millennia and to hear the cadence of his words is something greater than arguments, something fuller, truer, more real and thus more plausible and convincing" (201).

At the end of the first book, we thus find a discussion of the forty days between the resurrection and ascension of Christ, and the fifty days between Easter and Pentecost. The second book, which is somewhat less intense than the first, even bears the subtitle "A Walk through the Bible," because it is largely a meditation on the Old Testament and to a lesser extent the New Testament—through a mode of appropriation that I will return to later.

It is part and parcel of Döblin's pathos to trace the differences between people back to their self-encapsulation and to long for an escape from the prison of the ego through prayer, but also through a life shared with other human beings. This general relativization of differences is reinforced in these religious dialogues by the fact that the two participants, despite all that divides them, can also be understood as embodying the same person at different stages of development. Clues are clearly laid when the older man mentions that he allowed his younger counterpart to engage him in dialogue "because he reminded me of myself" (213), indeed, that he himself had previously "walked the same paths" (255) as the younger man. These hints can be read biographically but are surely intended to convey something beyond the contingencies of the author's biography, pointing to a fundamental understanding of dialogue, one in which we recognize something of ourselves in the other.

The biographical interpretation is, however, quite natural and plausible. Alfred Döblin came from an already strongly secularized Jewish milieu, from which he further distanced himself when he left the Jewish community of Berlin in 1912. Only when jolted by the anti-Semitic pogrom in Berlin of 1923 did he resolve to learn more about his ancestors' faith and way of life. His report on his trip to Poland, which he undertook for this reason, is a testament both to his distance from the lived Judaism of East-Central Europe and to his budding fascination with it.[5] This fascination went beyond the Jewish to the Christian realm, which he encountered in Poland with its intense Catholic piety and great religious works of art. Despite Döblin's distance from religion during this period, it would thus be quite wrong to call him "religiously unmusical." His literary works and a multitude of autobiographical texts show that, more than almost any other intellectual of the twentieth century, he engaged with the religions of the world in a tremendously productive way.

This engagement includes his early novel about a Daoist-inspired peasant rebellion in China (*The Three Leaps of Wang Lun*), a preoccupation with Buddha, and his editing of a volume on Confucius in the

United States.[6] He also studied the myths of the indigenous peoples of the Amazon, the Indian and Babylonian gods, the medieval mysticism of Johannes Tauler, and the Jesuit state in Paraguay. His views on individual religions or on religion as a whole, however, changed time and again; a religious search no doubt underlay his boundless interest. At a young age, in a famous letter to Else Lasker-Schüler of November 10, 1904, following a visit to the Freiburg Minster, he wrote, "It occurs to me that I might once again become very religious."[7] Around 1920, he professed his faith in a highly polemical critique of religion, in which God figures as a "phantom" from which one must finally free oneself. At the same time, the typical forms of enlightened liberalism repelled him. His intensive reading of Søren Kierkegaard's writings in the course of the 1930s, but also his experiences during his flight from Nazi troops in France, were decisive to his conversion to Catholic Christianity, which was the trigger for the composition of the religious dialogues.

For the reasons identified above, this conversion can in no way be interpreted as a case of complete discontinuity in Döblin's life. What is contested, and obviously depends on interpreters' attitudes, is whether Döblin's conversion was a mere phase in his religiously muddled and erratic personal development, as the author of the most extensive Döblin biography to date argues,[8] or whether it is "the end point of a long road, the becoming visible of a long-existing tendency," as asserted by the author of one of the most thorough studies available on religiosity in Döblin's character and oeuvre.[9] Both perspectives probably overstate things, but this is not the place to settle that question. Döblin's later novels and stories (such as *November 1918: A German Revolution, Tales of a Long Night, Der Oberst und der Dichter oder Das menschliche Herz* ["The Colonel and the Poet or The Human Heart"] and *Die Pilgerin Aetheria* ["Aetheria the Pilgrim"]),[10] like the two religious dialogues, invite us to be challenged by Döblin the Christian. However we may assess his biography, this challenge must not be reduced to it.

The Immortal Human Being

In any case, for both believers and nonbelievers, the dialectical richness of the first religious dialogue in particular, and the refreshingly disrespectful tone with which old and new philosophy, scholarship, and politics are discussed, does in fact pose a true challenge. Döblin, a doctor and scientist, who ascribes a scientific past or present to both interlocutors, begins his unfolding train of thought with the "scientistic" worldview that classifies religion as "pre-scientific thinking" (24) and distinguishes three zones of knowledge: one already illuminated by science; a second in which this illumination will eventually take place; and a third, into which science cannot penetrate and about which no meaningful statements can thus be made. In opposition to this tripartite worldview, the older man reflects on the knowing subject in their bodily existence; he wishes to show that no one can maintain this neat division of zones in their self-relationship and self-understanding, that even in cases of profound skepticism about the "supernatural" and "miraculous," a sense of overwhelming wonder arises when people delve deep into their own existence. This train of thought is followed by reflections on the "feeling of gratitude" engendered by one's existence (37) and on the helplessness and hollowness that typify it (41). On this basis, Döblin develops ideas on the connection between one's individual person and a more comprehensive process of life:

> And when I see how I must absorb water and salts from the earth, how my lungs exchange gases with the air, how substances from animals, plants and minerals mix with my body and move back and forth through it so that it can survive and endure for the short period of time that makes up its existence, I recognize that I am a person, but not a boundary. We do exist as individuals, but within a large, powerful body. (36)

Even an ordinary strip of grass by the side of the road or a few ants in the sand (71) can be experienced as a pointer to the immeasurable multiplicity of living beings and their ultimate unity.

Döblin's train of thought develops along a second path of reflection, by looking not at the living beings around us but at our own inner life. This trained psychiatrist does not conceive of this inner life as a well-ordered realm subject to complete control by the ego, but as a

> mollusk, a gelatinous mass that I am unable to grasp, and if I do grasp it, I squash it. There, though I do not know from where or out of how many sources and channels, imaginings, images and ideas flow and seep. Threads of emotion accompany them, perceptions sink in. And from time to time eddies form, impulses of will pierce through, and the light of a lighthouse—the consciousness—flickers in fits and starts as if over a dark, restless sea. (37)

The sense of untamable richness that surpasses the self is at its strongest in the experience of one's own creative activity, in the production of beauty (80) and ideality. For Döblin, it is in this experience of one's own creativity, but also in the ability to resist one's drives and instincts (138), that one's sense of being a person is ultimately rooted.

Up to this point, the older man's train of thought cannot be described as religious in a narrow sense. In many cases it is more in line with the kind of philosophical reflections put forward by phenomenologists and pragmatists, philosophers of life (*Lebensphilosophen*), and exponents of philosophical anthropology. It would require in-depth research into Döblin's reading to reconstruct direct connections and influences and to gauge what stood in continuity with his philosophical inclinations before his conversion and what was rooted in his subsequent concern with medieval Christian philosophy. His tone is often the same as during his period of speculation in natural philosophy. But this continuity now ends at the point where he relates a positively assessed human personhood to a personal conception of God.

For a long time, the dialogue made no mention of "creation" but of the "ultimate ground" in order to avoid any covert reference to the beliefs of Judaism or Christianity. But the point comes where this issue can no longer be avoided. If the previous steps, which the older man certainly presents as a strict sequence, have been completed, should this "ultimate ground" of all existences remain a "mere abstraction" or simply be viewed as "the continuous order and regularity of the world" (157)? Or should this ultimate ground itself be ascribed features with which we are familiar from the experience of our own personhood? The older man feels justified in taking a further step here: "Now this is an immense phrase, and you will not enjoy hearing it: 'The ultimate ground is the person.' You will recoil from this because you will discern the truest form of 'anthropomorphism'" (157). This is where the leap into faith takes place within the dialogue, though this is not meant to be a leap into an intellectually unjustifiable supposition.

Immediately before introducing the concept of the person and justifying the idea of interpreting the "ultimate ground" itself as a person, the dialogue moves in an unexpected direction. The older man, building on the paradise myth in the biblical account of creation and the appearance of "angelic beings" in the book of Genesis, develops the idea of an original, ideal form of the human being. A way of life is poetically imagined in which people had not yet lost their "openness to the ultimate ground, their unbroken connection with it" (138), such that reason and free will were available to them within the framework of a harmonious creation and not merely, as was the case later, as "a paltry, narrow, lightless reason together with the freedom to choose, without knowing what" (147). Döblin quite obviously conceived of this vision of the ideal form of the human realm—a form that, as he believed, reverberates in all later ages and within every human being—as the centerpiece of the first religious dialogue; there is no other plausible explanation of the title "The Immortal Human Being." Would a religious dialogue titled "The Mortal Human Being" have been conceivable, in which the believing interlocutor articulates the Christian hope of resurrection?

Let us leave the status of this vision of original ideality to one side for a moment. I will mention, however, that this vision should not be misunderstood as equating with the kind of creationism expounded by Protestant fundamentalists or radical Catholic antimodernists. Döblin uses it to criticize Darwinist explanations and an evolutionary anthropology only insofar as he accuses them of diverting our attention from the improbability of the emergence of human personhood. But this is an argument related to the turn toward grasping the miraculousness of one's own existence or that of other living beings. As the dialogue proceeds, the Jews' hopes of a messiah are derived from the vision of the ideal form of the human realm, and this Jewish conception is presented as giving rise to the figure of the Son of God, which both fulfills this hope and—with regard to earthly expectations of salvation—refutes it.

Once again, however, the dialogue immediately challenges us to scrutinize what has changed in a worldly sense through the coming of the Savior. The older man recalls a religious dispute that took place in medieval Spain in 1263, when the rabbi Moses ben Nachman put it to his opponent, a Dominican, that "nothing in the state of the world points to the conclusion that a Messiah has appeared" (240). This leads to the question of whether there is any demonstrably positive legacy of Christianity. While reflections on the nature of faith and the origins of the Church appear at the end of the first religious dialogue, it is above all the second book that fleshes these out.

The Struggle with the Angel

This book ("The Struggle with the Angel"), written about ten years later, continues the dialogue after the same interval of time. It is again the younger man who takes the initiative. The older man had left letters unanswered; only now, weakened by age, is he once again prepared to receive his younger counterpart as a guest and conduct longer conversations, as opposed to discussions, with him. The younger man's motive is not, as one might expect, a relapse into doubt and uncertainty after finding a path to Christianity at the end of the first book. Instead, he is driven by the suffering entailed in the extreme challenge posed by Christianity. The Christian faith woke him up, we learn, but now he can find no peace, as his conscience constantly compels him to engage in radical self-examination and fills him with anxiety. If the world has not changed decisively through Christ and if most Christians are proud of themselves and their righteousness like the Pharisee in the synagogue, full of self-assurance because they see themselves as quite different from sinners (287), what was the point of Christ's coming (286)? Is the only consequence the despair of those who take his unrealizable morality seriously? Does this make Christianity an illness? Does a Christian have to be sick (285)?

Here the younger man's utterances gain an edge reminiscent of Kierkegaard, a radicalism that, far from rejecting political changes, seeks to surpass them:

> People shouldn't come to me with minor acts of charity, social reform or bloody civil wars and class struggle. These revolutions are not enough for me, none of them tackle true reality.... Only the teaching of Christ can do that. Who is going to take on the task of draining the swamp of this docile society sunk in lethargy and hatred? (288)

The younger man's radicalism repeatedly prompts him to consider breaking off his "Bible study" (339), dethroning the Ten Commandments in Nietzschean style (344), and returning to paganism with its "shameless gods" (350). The main thrust of the second book is, however, the description of a shared meditative reading of the Bible. Now the drama is no longer generated by the dynamics between the dialogue partners, but by the reading material. Because the older man takes the lead unchallenged, there are more and more passages in which his younger counterpart appears as a mere stooge for his interpretations. At the end, the two begin to use the informal word for "you" with each other; they jointly celebrate, in eucharistic fashion, the opportunity for people to come together in the Lord's Supper, and they sing a song of praise to the triune God.

One of the second book's leitmotifs is Jacob's struggle with the angel (Genesis 32:25–32), which serves to capture humans' grappling with faith in a single image. In the first book, the meaning of religious belief is already distinguished from the uncertain knowledge typical of the everyday use of language, "that paltry category" (240). While struggle metaphors play a role in the second book, it would be wrong to assume that what Döblin saw in faith was chiefly the suppression of reason's insights. In fact, the older man advises against a fixation on the will:

> Cease to want anything for a while. Get on with your life and do what is necessary in the moment. Do not fall for the idea that God insists that we think of him in concepts, or even that we are conscious of him in our feelings.... There is no need to pester the one who is always there. He offers himself. (247)

This voice of wisdom thus advises surrendering rather than pressuring oneself. The struggle only becomes a part of what is happening insofar as surrender faces resistance, namely from fear or from the self-imposed shackling of one's own feelings and experiences. The understanding of faith presented in this text also underpins its conception of the community of believers. It is no accident that the prayer Jesus Christ himself taught the disciples refers to "our Father" rather than "my Father," because "The troubles of others, whom you must help, call upon you and free you from your ego" (595). Döblin contrasts the church above all with any notion that a particular state, nation, or people is in any way situated above others. In the social form of the church, Döblin discerns a concrete universalism, but he does not idealize the church, mentioning the Crusades and Christian anti-Judaism (562) as self-contradictory transformations of this concrete universalism back into a particularist ideology: "You can count yourself lucky not to stand in the shoes of those Jews, ... and we thus prove ourselves pure and innocent by cursing them and through actions such as conquering the Holy Sepulchre" (562).

Akin to Döblin's perspective on the church, stand-alone questions of justice are posed again and again in light of the Bible reading: Why did God not accept Cain's sacrifice? Why did God not love the Egyptians as well, instead condemning them to a gruesome fate in the Red Sea? Could the flood really have been his will? Does a close look at human history not put paid to any notion of divine planning and providence? Is this history not in fact "the adventure of a horde ... that throws itself into one bout of raving madness after another, falls over and picks itself up again, but only to stagger on, over the skeletons and piles of skulls left behind by the past" (388)?

No one should expect Döblin's religious dialogues to provide a definitive, let alone authoritative, answer to all such questions. The strength of these texts lies in their capacity to stimulate readers' own thinking in multiple ways and to unsettle certainties, both religious and secular. If we try to characterize Döblin's approach in the two religious dialogues, two things stand out: a quasi-systematic philosophical approach, especially in the first book; a distance from historical biblical criticism, especially in the second book; and, bound up with this, the neomythological elaboration of the idea of the "immortal human being" in both.

The philosophical approach we can glean from the first book is that of step-by-step reflection on the conditions of possibility for experiences constitutive of faith. Despite all Döblin's engagement, in his late work, with the thought of Thomas Aquinas, the similarities seem to me rather superficial, with Döblin's own thinking essentially shaped by the philosophy of life (*Lebensphilosophie*). What must the character of the cosmos be, how must man's nature be constituted, for there to be believers? Even the sharpest critic of religion cannot deny the empirical fact that some people fit this description. Certainly, some things are conceptually vaguer in Döblin's work than in that of professional philosophers or theologians. Yet he can describe experiences with the greatest intensity, leaving terms such as "self-transcendence" that seek to capture them looking arid in comparison:

> Sometimes beauty appears in dynamic form, and it may be a source of dread and confusion. The individual effectively loses his bearings, that world in which he had been reposing comfortably and operating within. There is the beauty granted the opposite sex, which refuses to let us rest and holds us in its power. It urges beings to approach beauty and abandon themselves to it, to merge with it. (80)

A similar picture prevails when it comes to his descriptions of the enjoyment of day-to-day living and of the kind of ideal formation that outstrips all experienced good.

Because Döblin thus defends a conception of nature that tries to do justice to what is specifically human, he sees himself as an opponent of all "naturalism." He mockingly rejects the pseudo-solution to the problems of anthropology provided by the idea that the brain is responsible for human symbols and action (27f.). Döblin's dissociation from this naturalism is, however, so stark that he not only misses the intellectual possibilities of a nonreductionist naturalism,[11] but must forgo the opportunity to truly anchor the concepts so central to his view of the human being, such as "freedom," "will," and "reason," in the corporeality of the human being, rather than simply treating them as substantive essences in their own right.

When it comes to the reading of the Bible, which dominates most of the second book, the question arises as to Döblin's position in the field of tension between the meditative and historicizing treatment of biblical texts. Evidence of inconsistencies, for example between the Gospels, the later redaction and attribution of the prophetic books, the fictional nature of historical events in the Bible's chronicle-like parts, unsettling correlations with other religious traditions—all of this was bound to shatter any literal understanding of the Bible as "the word of God." To this day, therefore, there is vehement resistance to any such historicization—for example, within so-called Protestant fundamentalism. Yet leading theologians around 1900, such as Ernst Troeltsch, already recognized this historicization not as a threat to the faith but as an opportunity to reappropriate it under the conditions of a modern consciousness molded by naturalism *and* historicism.

Döblin's religious dialogues contain several instances of marked dissociation from the historicizing approach (see, for example, 293f.). The older man wishes to prevent future generations from looking down on the Bible because they believe their scientific, historical, and philosophical knowledge vouches for their superiority (296). Meditative reading is all about introducing people, in the first instance, to this book's superiority over their own wisdom. This superiority, however, lies in the intensity and greatness of the human experience of God, which is reflected in the Bible. The interlocutors themselves repeatedly historicize the text when it otherwise makes no sense to them—for example, when considering the Egyptian magicians (427ff.). Time and again, the older man emphasizes that his approach to the Bible has nothing to do with denouncing reason, science, and technology (361, 588), but instead serves to lay bare another way in which human beings deal with the world—just as a particular approach to a forest can open hearts and minds (291f.) if it is treated as more than just timber.

The broad depiction of the paradise myth in the first religious dialogue does not claim, as I have mentioned, to assert a scientific fact. "One will dig in vain for the 'Garden of Eden' ... on the earth of today" (359). But it would be wrong to see in Döblin's embellishment of a biblical myth a general turn toward myth. On the contrary, Döblin criticized "mythomania" among contemporary writers as a "widespread affliction."[12] He viewed it as an avoidance of Christianity: "One walks on crutches because one has forbidden oneself to use one's legs." For him, Christianity does not represent one myth among many others, any of which one might make use of, but rather the truth, to which other myths merely approximate. Döblin often mockingly contrasts the ancient Greek god myths with Christianity—for example, comparing the adulterer Zeus in the Amphitryon saga to the Annunciation.

Döblin researchers have speculated in a variety of ways on whom Döblin drew, or may have drawn, as he developed this line of thought. From Origen through Pascal and Franz von Baader to Teilhard de Chardin, a number of authors have conjectured and made assertions about Döblin's reading and sources. We would surely have to add one of the most powerful volumes of Catholic apologetics of the twentieth century (at least in the English-speaking world), namely Gilbert Keith Chesterton's 1925 book *The Everlasting Man*, an alternative to H. G. Wells's secularist philosophy of history, which had reached a broad readership, and to the understanding of religion cultivated by the academic discipline of comparative religion.

Strikingly, the German translation of this book by the convert Chesterton, published in 1930, bears the same title chosen by Döblin for his first religious dialogue, *Der unsterbliche Mensch* ("The Immortal Human Being").[13] But far beyond this commonality, it is characterized by uncanny parallels in terms of content. Chesterton vehemently rejects the idea that the specific features of the human world differ only by degree from those of animals and emerged gradually. Even the "man in the cave," he states, was conspicuous, for his drawings and had "art" and "religion."[14] In the history of humankind, we are told, an original monotheism was followed by a division between the divine and the heavenly. All in all, Chesterton contends, the implications of the view that the human being is an animal are far more untenable "than if he were treated as an angel."[15] But this is not the place to delve into these parallels.

As I see it, more important than the question of whether Döblin was familiar with this book and was guided by it is the fact that Chesterton's text was part of a broader movement that endeavored to counter the demythologization of Christianity by invigorating its truth claims. This invigoration also applied to the status of the mythical—indeed, the goal was to engender new forms of mythical expression. This dimension of Chesterton's history of influence is often overlooked with respect to the reception of his writings by C. S. Lewis, whose Narnia adventures are among the great Christian children's books, and above all in relation to the worldwide success of J. R. R. Tolkien's books. If the connection between his religious dialogue and Chesterton can be proven, Döblin's exploration of the immortal human being stands in proximity to such efforts to forge new myths.

A New Language for Christianity?

In his autobiographical work *Destiny's Journey*, Alfred Döblin clearly expressed his motives in writing the first religious dialogue. Top of the list was the specific way in which he personally appropriated Christianity following his conversion:

> So that I might possess it completely, I had to look at it and translate it into my own language.... The test would be how I put it into sentences, into my language, and to the degree that these ideas penetrated my sentences, they would penetrate me more strongly and steadfastly.[16]

While writing, however, a second task had presented itself to him:

> The path I took was not to be mine alone. It was surely also the path many others took. I was not a writer merely to enlighten myself, I also had a responsibility to speak out.... It was clear to me that I had taken a positive but very dangerous position. I could foresee the arguments against me, against my ideas and my stance.[17]

Finding a new language for Christianity after the old had begun to fall on deaf ears—this is Döblin's "good" but "dangerous" undertaking. There are highly divergent views on whether he succeeded. Protestant theologian Dorothee Sölle, for example, in her broad and stimulating attempt to come to grips with Döblin, surprisingly stated that in *Der unsterbliche Mensch*, in contrast to his literary work, he had become bogged down in "religious clichés" and taken "flight into traditionalist language."[18]

These statements make no sense to me. Sölle mentions the reaction of a Berlin journalist to a speech by Döblin in 1948 in Charlottenburg Palace: one had so often heard the same thing or something very similar, and it became "no better" just because it was put forward by "a famous writer and infrequent visitor." Although her source for this is Döblin's *Destiny's Journey*, she makes no mention of Döblin's reply, which is reproduced in the book: "You've never heard it. And if you heard it with your ears you didn't comprehend it, and you'll never comprehend it because you don't want to."[19] Even the most authentic attempt at a new language depends on listeners' receptiveness, and this may be refused. The assessment of a reviewer in the *Süddeutsche Zeitung* newspaper shortly after the publication of *Der unsterbliche Mensch* was in sharp contrast to Sölle's. In a brilliant review, Wilhelm Hausenstein described what is surely felt by many readers even today: "In Döblin's book, Christian arguments are expressed in an entirely original and thus new way. . . . Through his immense personal strength in his defining literary artistry in the dogmatic field, the book brings things up to date across the board—taking on a peculiarly radical missionary force."[20]

The search for a new language always takes place in a specific historical context; the more radically this has changed, the more urgent this search becomes. Alfred Döblin, who witnessed and suffered the history of violence in the twentieth century to an extreme degree, leaves us in no doubt about the historical situation he is concerned with: that of Christianity following the Nazi seizure of power. Right at the start of the dialogues, when the younger man accuses his older opposite number of abandoning himself to atavistic feelings, the latter retorts that he is championing his faith publicly precisely "in order to attack the enemy with discernment, clarity and acuity" (13): "I would surely be guilty of an unforgivable crime were I . . . not to go on hurling myself against the corrupters, incendiaries and obscurantists by all means available to me" (12).

While the irreligious younger man still praises "the new Russia, under the leadership of the Marxist Lenin" (18) "as the first example of the application of reason," his older counterpart sees in the renewal of faith an important means of strengthening resistance to all dictatorships. The younger man extends his view beyond the European history of violence to "the unparalleled sufferings of the black peoples, whom the white conquerors," seeking to enslave them, "fell upon in earlier centuries." He makes statements of great bitterness, for example about the present, which we have been "damned" (89) to live in, and about the earth, which is fortunately no bigger, because otherwise people would have even greater opportunity to do evil to one another (62). The concentration camps (93) and the "unprecedented atrocities" committed against "millions of innocent people" (389) are mentioned, culminating in the younger man's declaration that the tyranny in Germany is a reflection of the "bankruptcy of Christianity" (178). In sharp contrast, for the older man, who does not deny the indifference of the bourgeoisie under Nazi rule or their role as "hypocritical beneficiaries and accomplices" (274), the Nazis' racial fanaticism drew its arguments "from the naturalism to which we used to adhere" (ibid.). The new language Döblin seeks for Christianity is meant for a faith that has experienced the totalitarianism of the twentieth century, both its oppressive effects and seductions. This is a post-totalitarian Christianity.

The second religious dialogue ends with an allusion to a new threat of war. It was written in the early 1950s when, to Döblin's horror, rearmament was being discussed in West Germany. Döblin's Christian faith could not be assigned to a political current that claimed Christianity for itself. For him, the history of secularization is in part a history of Christian guilt. If the churches side with the rich and powerful, we read (275), they should not be surprised when the people and the intellectuals lose their faith. This prompts the younger man to conclude, "Unfortunately, Christianity's past stands in the way of its future" (276). His older counterpart replies that religion "is not refuted by any past, for it is always present and future" (ibid.). It alone is "capable of immunizing [people] against economic, racist, and nationalist fanaticism" (275). This sentence has lost none of its relevance. Of course, Döblin does not simply mean religion as such. In fact, his religious dialogues develop a sophisticated understanding of what religion can mean in a universalist sense. If it means what he thinks it does, then it represents a crucial break with every instance of a state's or people's self-sacralization, but also—let's not forget—with the self-sacralization of economic systems, to which there are supposedly no alternatives and to which we have no choice but to adapt.[21]

II, 4
The Contingency of Secularization: Reinhart Koselleck's Theory of History

The empirical social sciences soon come up against their limits when examining the topic of contemporary trends in secularization, and even more so when discussing the links between "secularization" and "modernization." It is true that the knowledge methodically compiled by these sciences, on such things as membership figures for religious communities, the distribution of religious attitudes, or the frequency of religious practices, is wholly indispensable. So initiatives aimed at replacing the patchwork quilt of individual surveys with a comparative international report on religion are very welcome indeed.[1] And it is equally essential to link this knowledge of religion with indicators for other social developments, such as "modernization," if we wish not only to record how things stand at a particular point in time, but also what changes are occurring and what is causing them.

But such research comes up against its limits because it is confronted with two questions that it is ill equipped to tackle. First, those who reflect seriously upon their own experiences quickly realize that it is very difficult for scholars of religion to make empirical statements that are not molded by specific underlying religious (or antireligious) presuppositions. Often, researchers acquire their ideas on practices and organizational forms from one tradition, mostly Christianity, which then have a distorting effect when applied to other religious traditions. At times, assumptions relating to such things as "transcendence," which apply only to certain religions, slip unnoticed into the very definition of what religion is. Beyond one-sided ideas about religions, the question also arises as to how we might control methodologically for secularist assumptions about religion and the development of religion that may as well slip unnoticed into our work.

Now it may seem that we can remedy this problem quite simply through clear definitions of the terms used. It may be true that the term "secularization" is used in a confusing variety of ways and that unfortunately things are just as bad with the term "modernization." But none of this is inevitable, and the author of a given text could at least set out clearly how she is using a given term. Nietzsche already made the profound observation that only concepts that have no history can be pinned down clearly through definitions.[2] Any serious definitional work that hopes to get a hearing must consider the conceptual field as a whole and pay attention to a term's history. Otherwise, we will inevitably experience the wide range of possible meanings of one and the same concept as mere confusion and fail to bring order to the conceptual field. Thus a lack of experience with conceptual history is the second limit that empirical research comes up against both here and elsewhere.

From this perspective, conceptual history emerges as anything but an irrelevant field pursued by esoteric historians of ideas, a field of no significance to the practice of the empirical social sciences. Quite the reverse: terms such as "secularization" and "modernization" are neither value-neutral nor can they be pinned down through acts of definition. They are replete with historical assumptions or even those drawn from the philosophy of history. It is especially important to recognize these assumptions if constant innovations are occurring within a given conceptual field. One need think only of the debate kicked off by Peter Berger on the "desecularization of the world" or the debate on "post-secularization," which developed in response to a talk by Jürgen Habermas,[3] to see that the field of secularization is particularly prone to such innovation.

The focus of the present chapter, however, is not on the findings of research in the conceptual history of "secularization" that we are so fortunate to have at our disposal. Hermann Lübbe, Hermann Zabel, and Giacomo Marramao have long since completed the crucial work in this field.[4] Instead, what I want to do is give the reflective screw a few more turns. With all due respect to the project of conceptual history, I want to investigate whether specific religious or secularist premises have slipped unnoticed into this project itself. Even research in conceptual history is not free of presuppositions. I shall be exploring this issue with reference to the life's work of a historian who, in intellectual and organizational terms, had no equals as a practitioner of conceptual history—at least in the German-speaking world. My focus is on Reinhart Koselleck's explicit and implicit view of secularization and its consequences for the project of conceptual history as a whole.

As already mentioned, the really comprehensive studies in the conceptual history of secularization were not carried out by Reinhart Koselleck (1923–2006) himself. So when he set out his views, he was initially dependent entirely on the results of others' work. One of the findings of this work is that the great extension in the meaning of the word "secularization," from a legal term for the change in the status of clergy or the expropriation of church property, to a key term of general cultural analysis, took place from 1800 on. Koselleck could easily take this as confirmation of his general ideas on the significance of this historical era (Saddle Period or *Sattelzeit*). The conceptual historians themselves did not take on the task of linking the secularization of 1803 more closely with its intellectual prehistory, and neither did Koselleck.[5]

Koselleck's only study explicitly devoted to the topic of secularization is quite different in nature.[6] But as we shall see, it is of tremendous relevance to the issue of the religious presuppositions underpinning the project of conceptual history.

Secularization and Acceleration

Koselleck's point of departure in this study is the observation that there are disturbing similarities between early Christian ideas about a speeding up of time in the face of an imminent apocalypse and notions of technological progress in the sense of an increasing acceleration of social life. This observation tallies with motifs that crop up frequently in Koselleck's writings. First, though, we must attempt to clarify the observation itself. This is not difficult in the case of the statement regarding technology. It has become a commonplace to trace the acceleration of our lives back to modern means of communication and transport, and the experience of this acceleration is a common one.[7] The idea of a preapocalyptic acceleration of time, meanwhile, is rather hard to relate to for many people today. Koselleck found evidence of this idea not only in early Christianity, but extending into the era of the Reformation and in Luther's own interpretation of the dramatic chains of events, which he himself had set in motion, as a sign of the imminent end of days. Today, it seems to me, the easiest way to begin to get across this idea is to imagine the psychological consequences of an increased awareness of our own finiteness, as in old age or when we are confronted with a medical diagnosis that drastically limits our life expectancy: time seems to pass ever more quickly; constantly accelerating, it races toward the end. There remains an unmistakable difference between these two experiences of acceleration. In the case of apocalyptic anticipation, the idea is that time itself is shortening; God himself is compressing time. In the experience of modern technology, an unchanging physical time is assumed. Here, the feeling of acceleration consists solely in the fact that human actions "use up" less time.

What Koselleck was primarily interested in was whether, despite this unmistakable difference, we may state that the modern perspective represents a secularization of Christian apocalyptic thought. There is no need to recapitulate his expositions in detail here. His key conclusion in this regard is that the modern idea is not simply a secularization of the old Christian idea. For Koselleck, the modern perspective rests on the experience of modern technology itself. This result of his reflections is in accordance with his general—and in my view justified—methodological approach of not regarding traditions as something that, as it were, perpetuate themselves, but as something that must be actively continued and appropriated afresh under ever new conditions. While this prevents a merely intellectual history perspective, for Koselleck a connection does emerge, in mediated form, between Christian conceptual presuppositions and the history of their secularization. The modern experience of acceleration, after all, played a role in the development of a historical-optimistic worldview, according to which technology brings a progress that fulfills hopes of redemption. For Koselleck, secular hopes of redemption could "crystallize around" the fact of technological progress.[8] But in this sense, a technology-centered understanding of progress could be described as the secularization of Christian hope. He added that this very fact reduced Christian ideas of redemption to a mere secondary phenomenon.

Now this is a highly stimulating line of thought. But it seems to me to suffer from a tendency toward overgeneralization. If the key dimension is the modern experience of technology itself, then all interpretations of this experience are important. But these interpretations were and are by no means always optimistic in nature. Furthermore, time and again even the optimistic interpretations have to process disappointed hopes of redemption, hopes geared toward technological progress. While this processing may transfer these hopes to future progress, it may also lead to a rupture with historical optimism. In light of this, we would have to study in depth the interplay between the experience of technology and religious experience and investigate the related systems of interpretation before making generalizations.

Another problematic overgeneralization of his findings, so it seems to me, creeps into Koselleck's work when he identifies, as a general historical tendency, the subordination of Christian hopes of redemption to the optimistic ideology of technological progress. This subordination can surely have occurred only in those places that have seen a general process of secularization in the sense of a weakening of religious attitudes. But this process is by no means universal. In the United States—to take only the best-known example of a religiously vital modern society—we can certainly not refer to a unilinear transformation from religious to secular worldviews. So what we require is investigation of the embedding of interpretations of modern technology in contemporary religious worldviews. Overhasty claims of secularization merely distract from this. Koselleck, who saw acceleration as *the* key characteristic of modernity, went so far as to describe it as a "post-Christian" category—while making no attempt to justify the claim of a historical rupture with Christianity that this entails.

So interpretation of the only text in which Koselleck explicitly developed a thesis on secularization leads us to an ambivalent result. He was careful to avoid presenting his arguments on secularization solely in terms of intellectual history, but seemed inclined to false generalizations, positing a comprehensive process of secularization on the basis of meager evidence.

Before we examine the implicit assumptions about secularization in other writings by Koselleck, it is probably a good idea to briefly consider his way of thinking in light of two of his academic teachers or mentors, who are among the key figures in the twentieth-century debates on secularization: Carl Schmitt and Karl Löwith. Beginning with his doctoral thesis, Koselleck always gratefully acknowledged Schmitt's influence on his work. There is also no doubt that Schmitt's views on the development of a sphere of political action in the absolutist state, a sphere that was neutralized with respect to the bloody religious conflicts of the post-Reformation era, was of constitutive importance to Koselleck's doctoral thesis *Kritik und Krise* (*Critique and Crisis*).[9] Carl Schmitt's thesis that all modern political concepts are secularized theological concepts was described by Hans Blumenberg[10] as "the strongest version of the secularization theorem." Koselleck referred repeatedly to this notion.[11] Yet both of Schmitt's ideas are highly problematic. The modern state was by no means neutral toward the confessions,[12] and, against Schmitt's assertions, the origins of theological concepts themselves—such as divine sovereignty—often lay in the political language of the Roman Empire.[13] This is not the place to go into these questions, as we are concerned with Koselleck rather than Schmitt. Throughout his life, Koselleck thought it highly unfair when his interest in Schmitt was interpreted as political proximity—as, for example, in an early review by Jürgen Habermas.[14] As his sympathetic analysis of leading English Christian historian Herbert Butterfield shows,[15]

Koselleck also drew on other sources to articulate his own basic moral and political sense. With respect to Butterfield, he underlined that because for him every war is a sin, on the basis of Christian motives he vehemently rejects the idea

> that one party alone can monopolize the law. Everyone shares in sin, even the just. Should the roles of guilt and innocence be allocated in an overconfident way, then what we are dealing with is extreme irresponsibility, a particularly intractable sin of the holier-than-thou variety, the sin of unadulterated self-righteousness. The consequence is a moral simplification of the complex historical reality. The enemy becomes a criminal, the self-righteous becomes at once party and judge. A clear case of utopian arrogance in other words.[16]

Koselleck ascribed tremendous significance to Butterfield's theological reflections here when applied to politics. Since war cannot be permanently overcome even through a great punitive war, the crucial issue is its containment. Koselleck did not share Butterfield's view of the strategic significance of the Christian message of love in the politics of the time. Nonetheless, I see clear evidence here of Koselleck's motives, deeply rooted in his biography, motives that also drew him toward similar arguments by Carl Schmitt. Schmitt's intentions were no doubt originally quite different.[17] But as recounted persuasively by Reinhard Mehring, biographer of Carl Schmitt,[18] Koselleck received Schmitt's "existentialism" and "decisionism"— against the background of his experience as a soldier in World War II—as a moral questioning of the possibility of justifying violence as such. So the de-normativizing notion of violence as the basis of law generates the moral idea that violence cannot be justified even as the basis of law. What Mehring sees at work here is the war generation's skepticism toward every justifying interpretation of violence and toward all great constructions in the politics of history.

But I believe Karl Löwith is far more important than Schmitt to understanding Koselleck's view of the topic of secularization. Löwith was not only one of the examiners of Koselleck's doctoral thesis. Above all, Löwith's book *Meaning in History: The Theological Implications of the Philosophy of History* had a profound influence on Koselleck.[19] The book's key aim is to interpret modern philosophy of history and notions of progress as the secularization of the Christian view of history. It first appeared in English in 1949. In an interview in 2002,[20] Koselleck described how, as a student, he translated significant portions of this book to his own ends; he felt that the three months he spent on this endeavor amounted to perhaps the most instructive bout of intellectual work of his entire life. Löwith's influence on the third chapter of *Critique and Crisis* in particular is unmistakable. Löwith's own anthropological orientation—against Heidegger and Gadamer—has also been correctly identified as one of the reasons why Koselleck attempted to give his theory of history an anthropological foundation.[21] Koselleck wrote the foreword to Löwith's autobiography[22] and first published one of his most important and influential essays ("Historia Magistra Vitae") in the festschrift for Löwith.[23] In the famous dispute between Karl Löwith and Hans Blumenberg he unambiguously backed Löwith.[24] Blumenberg in turn saw clearly how close Koselleck was to his adversary and rejected Koselleck's view of the experience of acceleration and the eschatological origins of political utopianism.[25]

So for all kinds of reasons, it seems likely that Löwith's theory of secularization played a constitutive role for Koselleck.[26] The link to Löwith is soon apparent in *Critique and Crisis*. The beginning of the chapter "The Philosophy of Progress and Its Prognosis of Revolution" develops the book's key idea, namely that the gulf between the bourgeoisie's sense of moral superiority and their de facto political powerlessness in the absolutist state was bridged by the construction of a philosophy of history that made the desired power seem the inevitable result of future history.

> The moral citizen, whether expressly stated or not, was always safe in a philosophy of history which by name alone was an eighteenth-century product. It was largely the successor to theology. Christian eschatology in its modified form of secular progress, Gnostic-Manichaean elements submerged in the dualism of morality and politics, ancient theories of circularity, and finally the application of the new laws of natural history to history itself—all contributed to the development of the eighteenth-century historico-philosophical consciousness.[27]

The Freemasons, to whose attitude toward religion Koselleck devoted much attention, made particular efforts to replace "religion [with] morality" and "theology [with] the philosophy of history."[28]

It is only by grasping this idea of the development of a secular philosophy of history that trumped theology—as the crucial hinge between the situation of the bourgeoisie in the absolutist state and the development of a political utopia—that we can understand the deeper meaning of another of Koselleck's particularly influential ideas. I am referring to his assertion that during the same period and shaped by the same conditions, the "collective singular" of history now arose out of the earlier idea of a multiplicity of histories, all of them overarched by the one *Heilsgeschichte* (history of salvation). There is a real need for this idea of the one history beyond the many individual histories if this one history itself is to be ascribed something like its own logic, indeed a kind of inherent subjectivity. Rather than merely the product of countless human actions and experiences, history can then be conceived as a subject which itself acts, has a will, provides certain actors with a mission, and so on. The intention of Löwith's book had been to invalidate this idea. Jürgen Habermas interpreted this as a "stoic retreat from historical consciousness,"[29] which would have been paradoxical if this retreat could be performed only through a comprehensive study in intellectual history. In this respect we must agree with Hermann Lübbe. Far from seeing a liberation from history at work in Löwith's oeuvre, he sees a resistance to "the unreasonable ideological demand that we ought to recognize 'history as argument' in a way that merely assumes meaning."[30]

This seems to me to apply to Reinhart Koselleck as well. In an appreciation of the postwar thought of Karl Jaspers, he brought out how much Jaspers remained a Kantian in the republican principles of his political thought—but without sharing his or any other version of liberal philosophy of history. For Koselleck, Jaspers no longer saw "the prospect of a linear forward projection of increasing freedom. He strictly rejects all the forms of reinsurance once capable of finding hope in history itself."[31] So it is a misunderstanding to conceive of the fight against the philosophy of history as a rupture with historical thought or, even worse, the value of freedom. On the contrary, its aim is to achieve a view of history anchored in a radical awareness of contingency, one that has erased all traces of teleological or evolutionist faith in the progress of political freedom or in its future stability and security. It is precisely this that makes Koselleck's work so incredibly topical and important to the elaboration of an alternative to Hegel.

Secularization and Temporalization

But do these points also apply to Koselleck's understanding of secularization? There is good reason for doubt on this front. Experts have expressed major doubts about Koselleck's account of the development of early modern historiography and the supposed transition from the theology of history to the philosophy of history. Stefanie Stockhorst points out that for the period of interest to Koselleck, we must at least work on the assumption of the "coexistence of traditional and innovative concepts."[32] Basing himself on research by Adalbert Klempt, Matthias Pohlig, and Arno Seifert, Stephan Schleissing states that if we fail to factor in the Protestant "self-secularization" of history since Melanchthon, we end up with a false picture of the Enlightenment-inspired rupture with Christian notions of history.[33] Jan Marco Sawilla observes incisively that Koselleck underestimates the longevity of biblical chronology, which persisted well into the nineteenth century. Sawilla also shows the implausibility of interpreting universal historian August Ludwig Schlözer as confirming the assumption that in the late Enlightenment "as transcendence was dispensed with, for the first time mankind was addressed as the prospective subject of its own history in this world."[34] On the contrary, "for Schlözer, the primary use of universal history, as the 'servant of religion,' [was rooted] in a concept of history and God anchored in a rational theology."[35] Sawilla even establishes a link with the influence of Löwith when he writes that "the search for secular derivatives of the old *Heilsgeschichte* (history of salvation) begun by Löwith, [led] to the paradoxical result that the existence of explicitly religious interpretations was long overlooked."[36]

This finding does not apply only to Koselleck's own studies but is characteristic of the project of conceptual history as a whole. The *Geschichtliche Grundbegriffe* ("Basic Historical Concepts"), as Olaf Blaschke has already pointed out,[37] were conceived with an awareness of an inexorably advancing process of secularization. While the series does include one important article on the term "Christianity" (by Trutz Rendtorff) and of course the entry on "Säkularisation/Säkularisierung" (by Hermann Zabel), there is no entry on "religion"! The simplistic assumption of an advancing process of secularization runs through all Koselleck's writings. We shall have to make do with a few examples in support of that claim. In his theory of temporalization, Koselleck clearly wants to describe how the quasi-spatial distinction between a transcendent and mundane sphere—in other words, transcendence in contrast to all that is worldly (a distinction that arose in the Axial Age) was converted into a temporal distinction between past and future. So *Verzeitlichung* or temporalization even seems to him a better term than *Verweltlichung*—an equivalent of the term "secularization" found in nineteenth-century Germany, in the work of Marx, for example. But what of all the thinkers who wrote on temporalization but were not supporters of secularization? It is not just among non-Christian thinkers that we find a tendency to espouse radical temporalization in the eighteenth and nineteenth centuries. Was Hegel not a significant exponent of temporalizing thought—and would we not then have to determine the complex relationship between his ideas on religion and the temporalization in his philosophy of history, rather than simplistically declaring that the latter superseded the former? It would be even more vital to make this distinction if we include the history of philosophy in America, especially American neo-Hegelianism and the philosophy of time produced by pragmatism.[38] Koselleck also made it clear that he believed there is common ground between his critique of historical utopias and the critique of theological eschatologies. In one of his programmatic statements, he went so far as to underline that it was the aim of his studies on temporal structures to demonstrate the *unreality* of both ways of understanding history: "This would involve finding the temporal structures which could define as unreal the empirical content of both theological eschatology and historico-philosophical utopias."[39] What I want to highlight is that he made no attempt to first argue the case for the "unreality" of theological eschatology. All his efforts were directed toward critiquing the utopias produced by philosophy of history; this other critique was simply assumed as something long since completed. In this sense we may state that his entire research program was underpinned at the very least by the assumption of secularization.

Koselleck's late studies on remembrance of the war dead, as nowhere else in his work, vividly explored the loss of ideas and conceptions of the beyond.[40] Yet even here he views this loss as simple fact—without even beginning to seek an understanding of transcendence of contemporary relevance, now that it is no longer presented through spatial metaphors. All of Koselleck's studies on the eighteenth century are pervaded by statements on advancing secularization. Yet Koselleck was familiar with the entire spectrum of attitudes toward religion in the age of Enlightenment—from the German Enlightenment, which remained essentially religious in nature,[41] to predictions of the disappearance of Christianity, as found for example in one of the political testaments of Frederick II of Prussia. Particularly interesting in this connection is his 1982 study "Aufklärung und die Grenzen ihrer Toleranz" ("Enlightenment and the Limits of Its Tolerance"). Here Koselleck rejected any self-satisfied view of the Enlightenment, as if it had invented tolerance—a view that has left a deep impression in modern Protestantism. Building on the work of another of his academic teachers, Johannes Kühn,[42] he pointed out that Christian thinkers had fostered the shift to the primacy of autonomy of conscience, so central to the postulate of tolerance, at a far earlier point in time. "In terms of the history of influences, many Christian minorities of a mystical, spiritualist, or rational persuasion, from Luther onward, have fostered a freedom of conscience of this kind." He was well aware of the great gulf that opens up when the nexus between autonomy of conscience and faith in revelation dissolves. Then, of course, there is a need for a new counterweight to the individual's reference to his conscience, which otherwise seems mere arbitrary subjectivism. "Natural law, natural feelings and the natural heart, rational insight, common sense and generally reasonable theories of morality are *apparently* at our disposal as we seek to find a religiously neutral, confessionally indifferent platform, on the basis of which the sum of all individual conscience might find a new commonality."[43] But the real point of his remarks is to demonstrate what a hard time the Enlightenment had "practicing the tolerance it had demanded for itself."[44] This begins with John Locke's exclusion of Catholics and atheists from tolerance and extends from the intolerant state religion that began to emerge in the work of Rousseau to attempts to make the demand for freedom of religion a vehicle "for propagating a new social order while disregarding the Christian religion."[45] This actually meant "tacitly setting new limits of intolerance." So the basic thesis of Koselleck's highly multifaceted diagnosis is that "any kind of tolerance leads us back to aporetic situations that cannot be resolved in any obvious way.... Even the paradigm shift... of the 18th century, from the disputes over religious revelation to the postulates of a new social order, entailed resulting costs which we are still paying to this day."[46]

Seen against the background of this sensitive analysis of the aporias of secular conceptions of tolerance, it seems absurd to impute antireligious intentions to the secularist implications of Koselleck's thought that I aim to demonstrate here. Yet these assumptions are present—they are the tacit premises of his thought. They take palpable form in terms such as "post-Christian" and "post-theological age."[47] Taking Koselleck as our guide, this inherent presumption of inevitability cannot be read as the mere value-free reporting of an empirical tendency. After all, since *Critique and Crisis*, Koselleck's analysis of Enlightenment thought had clearly taught us that historical assertions of inevitability must themselves be understood as weapons in the battle of opinion. According to Koselleck, in the Enlightenment the political battle against the absolutist state was superseded by a historico-philosophical interpretation of its outmoded status. Demonstrating the inevitability of its disappearance thus becomes a weapon, whose character as such is not acknowledged. But precisely the same applies to the Enlightenment prognoses of the disappearance of Christianity or of religion as a whole, and this continues to apply into the present. Repudiation of faith is replaced by the thesis that it is outmoded, backward, behind the times. It is peculiar that Koselleck himself seems never to have drawn this conclusion from his analysis of the Enlightenment with respect to religion. But this fact does not show that he himself was trying to deploy the thesis of secularization as a weapon. It merely shows that in this field an assumption of historical inevitability, not constructed by him, seemed to him self-evident. As a result, the great champion of historical contingency failed to see the contingency of religious history and the contingency of secularization.

Now that we have examined the religion-related premises of Koselleck's conceptual history, let us return to our point of departure, namely the relationship between "secularization" and "modernization." There are three obvious conclusions of relevance to the social scientific study of these questions:

First, Koselleck's "deconstruction" of the idea of one "history" is an important step in deconstructing falsely homogenizing concepts of "modernity" and "modernization," and therefore an antidote to the "fetishism of modernities." This is the term deployed by Canadian political scientist Bernard Yack—building on Herbert Schnädelbach's critical interpretation of the *Dialectic of Enlightenment* by Horkheimer and Adorno—to describe totalizing concepts of the modern age and modernity as "social myths" that turn a multiplicity of different social processes and phenomena into a single object. Without the concept of one history, there can be no myth of a singular process of modernization. But the entire thesis that modernization inevitably leads to secularization presupposes this *singular* process of modernization. I suggest that we take one step back from this conceptual simplification.[48] If there is no single process of modernization, then neither the history of secularization as it has come to pass in large parts of Europe nor the American experience of enduring religious vitality reveals *the* secret of the *one* modernity.[49] This would leave us merely with specific sets of circumstances, with national (or regional) processes of religious change.

In this case, we cannot even be sure that secularization in different eras should really be regarded as one and the same process: in the France of the late eighteenth century or in Germany during the industrialization of the late nineteenth century or among the educated middle classes of Western Europe after 1968.

But of course the deconstruction of a falsely unifying concept is not the last word in the empirically oriented social sciences. The reconstruction of the diverse paths of secularization and their explanation on the basis of institutional realities and historical experiences certainly leads to identification of certain patterns that apply in many cases. David Martin made an early attempt to distinguish between an Anglo-Saxon and a Latin-European pattern, for example, meeting the demand for a "general theory of secularization"[50] with far greater success than modernization theory. If we also acknowledge that there may be interactions between these patterns—that Latin America, for example, has now come under the influence of the US-American pattern of religious pluralism or that in the age of globalization immigrants have a religious influence on their country of origin—it is evident that the deconstruction of false uniformity gives rise to a need for a new totalization. To date, I believe this case has been made most convincingly by Paul Ricœur in *Time and Narrative*.[51] He draws on the work of Koselleck in order to escape the Hegelian temptation of total mediation. The alternative for him is

> an open-ended, incomplete, imperfect mediation, namely the network of interweaving perspectives of the expectation of the future, the reception of the past, and the experience of the present, with no *Aufhebung* into a totality where reason in history and its reality would coincide.[52]

But unlike Koselleck, rather than an anthropological theory of temporal structures, on this basis he outlines a post-Hegelian program of empirically backed partial mediations of a singular history, a history that nonetheless includes difference and mutual influences. This mediation, of course, always occurs in specific situations and is undertaken by specific subjects.

Second, the deconstruction of falsely homogenizing concepts of history, modernization, and secularization points beyond precise historical analysis of specific processes and sets of circumstances to the foundations of historical action and historical experience. As already mentioned, Koselleck has an action-oriented understanding of tradition. Traditions must be actively perpetuated; the repetition of an action is always a new action. In this sense—as Swedish historian Bo Stråth writes in a review of Koselleck's book *Zeitschichten* ("Temporal Strata")—even enduring repetitive structures are unique in every situation. "The long-term structures, which make change possible, change themselves with the changes they have initiated."[53] So Koselleck's conceptual proposals go beyond a simple contrast between social structures and human action. The impression that Koselleck's conceptual history had less affinity with the social sciences than the writing of social history (which he also practiced of course),[54] could only arise if the writing of social history saw itself as "structuralist" rather than anchored in action theory or if it reduced its understanding of action to rational action and the pursuit of self-interest.

Third, if we try to overcome the unthinking perpetuation of certain assumptions about secularization in Koselleck's work, this also opens up new ways of understanding the history of salvation, which only ever appears in the work of Löwith and Koselleck as a thing of the past that can have no serious legacy in the present. As in Enlightenment polemics, their work too conceives of the idea of a history of salvation solely in the sense of a nonempirical pseudo-knowledge that is maintained by authoritarian institutions against all rational evidence. "Salvation" and "redemption" are contrasted with worldly happiness. Yet there have long been theological attempts to overcome the notion, which is in fact obsolete, "that the history of salvation is a special history within the general history of humanity, in line with the notion of salvation as a special religious topic and as something that stands in contrast to worldly life."[55] Wolfhart Pannenberg and Trutz Rendtorff are the key Protestant thinkers here, and Karl Rahner the leading Catholic one.[56] The theological questions themselves cannot, of course, be discussed here. But the reference to "salvation" and "redemption" opens up the prospect of thinking history not in terms of rationalization, however understood, but in the light of those mundane experiences viewed as a foreshadowing or sign of redemption. If such experiences—as in the so-called salvation religions—are also interpreted as the gift of a transcendent deity, then the focus of attention shifts to their genesis—as in the work of Max Weber and research on the Axial Age—and their fate since then, in the present and in the future. "The special status of Israel and of Christianity does not somehow appear 'vertically from above,' but as the historical particularization of religious life, a process of particularization whose peculiarity lies in the fact that it enabled the historicity of the topic of salvation itself to become explicit for the first time."[57] Then, though, the question of the connection between *Heilsgeschehen* (salvation events) and "world history" also appears in a different light than in the work of Löwith and Koselleck—not, that is, simply in the sense of the supplanting of one by the other, but as a new integration of the two. In nontheological terms, this means that studies of processes of religious history or secularization must reflect upon their specific religious or secularist premises; such studies must also identify those experiences from which people gain the ideas of what is good that come to guide their action—but also those experiences that lead to the insight that human action is not enough, in and of itself, to realize the Good. Koselleck's reflections in historical theory open up the way for such studies—though he himself might not have joined us for the journey.[58]

II, 5

The Secular Option, Its Rise and Consequences: Charles Taylor

The term "secularization" is notoriously ambiguous. In my previous work on the subject, I have distinguished seven different meanings of this word and expressed the belief that some of the controversies over secularization are due to misunderstandings, to confusions that arise from the ambiguity of the term.[1] Two of the seven meanings are legal in nature (the transition of a religious priest into the secular priesthood and the expropriation of church property); two articulate genealogical connections between modern culture and the Judeo-Christian tradition and differ essentially in whether they take a mainly affirmative or critical view of this religious tradition; and three are common in the social sciences, but these too are far apart in meaning (decline of religion, retreat of religion into the private sphere, and the liberation of parts of society from religious control). In his great work *A Secular Age*, eminent Canadian philosopher and Catholic Charles Taylor (b. 1931) adds another meaning to these seven.[2] His specific interest is the changed conditions for everyone, including believers, brought about by the emergence of the possibility of unbelief, what he calls "the secular option."

There are in fact good reasons for adding this eighth meaning. From the outset, it undermines mere religious triumphalism, which interprets the current crisis afflicting the theory of secularization in a purely apologetic way, as if a mere intellectual aberration had finally reached its predictable end. This is consonant with my belief that while secularization theory is currently gripped by crisis, the old assumptions of religious apologetics have also lost their credibility, according to which people—for anthropological reasons, for example—cannot be nonreligious over the long term or that social cohesion, in the sense of a shared orientation toward unconditionally valid values, is bound to erode in the absence of religion.

In reality, Taylor is not the first to emphasize this eighth meaning of secularization. In sociology, he was preceded by Austrian American sociologist of religion Peter Berger, who in several works, perhaps most clearly in the book *A Far Glory: The Quest for Faith in an Age of Credulity*, put forward a strong hypothesis on the social-psychological consequences of cultural pluralism, and in *The Heretical Imperative: Contemporary Possibilities of Religious Affirmation* asserted that the modern Westerner is subject to an imperative of choice.[3] Berger often described this situation in economic terms because, as he believed, they capture its character so precisely, and Taylor's notion of the secular option, which, Berger tells us, has existed as a possibility for large sections of the population since the eighteenth century, is no doubt influenced by this usage. But Taylor emphasizes (833, n. 19) that his train of thought differs from Berger's in a crucial way and is, therefore, not subject to my critique of Berger.[4]

Berger, of course, had assumed that constant encounters between believers of different kinds—as inevitable under conditions of pluralism, but especially believers' encounters with people without religious beliefs—have relativistic consequences. As he sees it, religious faith can only be passed on under conditions of cultural homogeneity and the authoritarian exclusion of alternatives; under other conditions, he contends, an ever-larger breach opens up in one's worldview, the self-evident nature of religious truths dwindles, and the intensity of one's commitment to them diminishes. Relativism then articulates the belief that all beliefs are equally good or at least equally unfounded. But since relativism is hard to bear psychologically, it also provides fertile ground for "taking the initiative" in a defensive way—for example, through the voluntaristic shoring up of certainty through various forms of fundamentalism. This line of thought may sound psychologically plausible at first, but on closer inspection it turns out to be neither theoretically nor empirically sound. In fact, empirically it appears to be the case that the confrontation with other worldviews and value systems increases people's interest in religious knowledge without reducing the intensity of their commitment to faith. The theoretical reason for this lies in the fact that religious commitments do not come about through rational argumentation—either of a discursive nature or centered on the calculation of benefits.

Religious commitments, then, tend to remain essentially unaffected both by discursive objections as such and unfavorable cost-benefit calculations. The appeal of a religion can only arise from alternative interpretations of the experiences that originally led to a religious commitment. In the passage mentioned above, Taylor explicitly distances himself from Berger's assumption of the intensity-reducing effect of cultural pluralism or the presence of the secular option. Instead, he refers to "fragilization," which conveys the idea that the easier availability of alternatives prompts more people to "convert" to religion or to secularism over the course of their lives or to join a different religious community than the one their parents belonged to. I do consider this an important field of empirical analysis. Even more important, however, is Taylor's impulse to reconstruct the intellectual and experiential conditions that religiously committed people and others *share* with each another today.

Taylor's primary interest is in the rise of this secular option. How did this option come to be available in the first place? We have to keep reminding ourselves—especially in eastern Germany, world champion of secularization—that for most of human history this option did not exist, and if it did, then at most for small cultural elites, as in the thinking of Epicurus and Lucretius, and not for the broad mass of the population. To portray this rise of the secular option Taylor must tell a story, and it is useful to reflect briefly on its status. For Taylor, the narrative dimension is not an accessory to his argument, which could do just as well without it; this is no "optional extra," as he puts it,[5] but a necessary component of any attempt to understand our values. This is bound up with his view that we can define an identity only with reference to qualitative distinctions, especially strong evaluations. Taylor famously elucidates the relationship between the person and their values through spatial metaphors.[6] He refers to a moral space and its topography and draws on the spatial metaphors of everyday language, in which we distinguish higher and lower values, deeper and more superficial persons, and inward and outward orientations. If we envisage our values as occupying a place within a moral space, then it is inevitable that we will wonder where we stand at a given point in time in relation to the place of our values.

Hence, we cannot avoid asking where our life is going, the extent to which it can be interpreted as striving, and whether our striving is successful at a certain point in time. The quasi-spatial structure of our relationship to values thus gives rise to a temporal dimension in our self-understanding. We ascertain the current "place" of our striving by telling our life as a story. With reference to *Sources of the Self*, Martin Seel once spoke of Taylor's anti-genealogy,[7] and I myself came up with the term "affirmative genealogy" to convey, in the field of human rights for example, the crucial interweaving of narration and argumentation, as well as the character of such genealogical arguments, which by no means necessarily destroy values and may well support them.[8] When Taylor contrasts a time of highly intensive religious debate in Europe without a secular option (around 1500) with a secular age (around 2000)—in other words, an age in which this option exists—then he is explicitly out to do more than just compare two points in time. His goal is to establish the connection between them, and this makes a narrative structure inevitable:

> Our sense of where we are is crucially defined in part by a story of how we got there. In that sense, there is an inescapable (though often negative) God-reference in the very nature of our secular age. (29)

What Taylor means is that this narrative is often written as one of progress, insight, and enlightenment. It can of course also be written as one of error, loss, and sin or—with Weberian melancholy—as one of inevitable but existentially difficult to endure "disenchantment."

Taylor's own narrative has two hallmarks. First, it takes aim, with no lack of acerbity, at all those narratives he calls "subtraction stories"—accounts asserting that something additional, such as the belief in supernatural or transcendent forces and beings, ceases to exist or is eliminated at some point in the course of historical development. In contrast, he seeks to write a narrative of the emergence of something, as a result of which the conditions for understanding transcendence or immanence, the natural and supernatural, have changed in such a way that some consider one half of these pairings to be dispensable, while others feel a pressure to reformulate their religious faith. Second, Taylor cannot avoid putting his own cards on the table in his narrative. For a long time, as George Marsden put it, "only the most acute readers might surmise that the author is Catholic, if they did not know that already."[9] This only changed in the second half of the 1990s, chiefly through the publication of *A Catholic Modernity*. His great work in theory of religion, however, constantly makes it clear that the narrative it presents is in part a defense of the possibility of the monotheistic, especially Christian, and in particular the Catholic faith under today's intellectual conditions. This had never before been such an explicit feature of Taylor's work as it is in this book.

It would be well beyond the scope of this chapter to attempt to retell Taylor's extremely rich narrative in detail. For example, Taylor describes the emergence of the modern concept of nature, the switch from "cosmos" to "universe." This sounds like intellectual history, and of course it is in part, although again it is astonishing, as in *Sources of the Self*, how Taylor ignores important precursors—in this case, for example, Wilhelm Dilthey's investigations into the emergence of the "natural system of the human sciences."[10] But Taylor wishes to offer far more than a history of ideas; we might say that his goal is to produce a history of experience, prompting him to delve deep into research in cultural and social history.

Here he gets his guiding concept from Max Weber: "disenchantment." Taylor describes an initial state of affairs in which people located themselves within a cosmos of spiritual beings, the social realm was integrated through shared sacredness, and secular time was related to a sacred dimension (through "eternity" and "salvation history"). The partial loss of carnivalesque forms of structural dissolution is also particularly important to him, and he has profound things to say about the extent to which the modes of experience typical of "anti-structures"[11] have now shifted into the private sphere. The process of social disciplining is presented in just as much detail as the spread of secularism to large sections of the population in the "age of mobilization," that is, in the nineteenth and twentieth centuries. Instead of an extensive retelling, I will concentrate on a few points where I find Taylor's conceptual constructions and his historical narrative problematic. I foreground one questionable point from his analysis of the rise of the "secular option" and one from his account of its effects.

Sacredness and Transcendence

My difficulties begin right at the start of the book (14f.) when Taylor briefly defines his use of the term "religion." Here he takes the distinction "transcendent/immanent" to be fundamental. But this is by no means self-evident. The entire debate—which has been going on since the publication of the original German version of Karl Jaspers's book *The Origin and Goal of History* in 1949—on the historical emergence of the idea of transcendence in the so-called Axial Age (in the middle of the last millennium BC), draws our attention to the fact that the religious history of humankind was long devoid of conceptions of "transcendence" in the strict sense.[12] This is of more than religio-historical interest, because the religious tendencies of the present include "detranscendentalization," a return to pre–Axial Age forms.

Without this distinction, it is difficult to capture present-day modes of belief at the fringes of established religions—as the Bertelsmann Stiftung's *Religion Monitor* clearly shows.[13] A distinction between two forms of the localization of sacredness, one immanent and one transcendent, would have made more sense to me. Religion would then (as in the work of Durkheim) be defined via the concept of the sacred rather than that of transcendence.

To characterize the premodern world, Taylor uses the term "enchanted world." This is of course derived from the common English translation of Max Weber's concept of *Entzauberung* as "disenchantment"; Max Weber himself had no such counter-concept. The problem with this is that Taylor embraces the dichotomous notion of an "enchanted" and "disenchanted" world, which is consistent within Weber's framework but runs counter to his own intentions. What I mean by this will become clearer when fleshed out through a brief historical rundown.

In his book, Taylor illustrates the "enchanted," "magical" world almost exclusively with reference to the practices of medieval Christianity, especially in its popular form. I find this unfortunate because medieval Christianity is after all a post–Axial Age religion—in other words, a transcendence-focused, antimagical religion that, by expanding into circumstances that it would not have produced on its own, was compelled to enter into a whole array of compromises with spontaneous popular religiosity. Medieval Christianity thus existed in a state of extreme tension between Axial Age program and pre–Axial Age practice.[14]

With tremendous skill, Taylor characterizes the ways in which this tension finds expression—for example, through compromises, such as the idea of hierarchical complementarity between clergy and laity. A key part of his narrative also describes how the Axial "thorn" in this form of religious life made its presence felt time and again, and not only in the course of the Reformation but since the eleventh century at the latest, in ever-new attempts at monastic and church reform. The change in the image of Christ during this era, from ruler of the world to suffering person, the centering of the veneration of relics on Christ and Mary, the rejection of object-related ideas of a coercion of God in favor of the ethical aspirations in the teachings of Francis of Assisi and through the establishment of religious orders that foregrounded them—all these are early manifestations of efforts at "reform" prior to the "Reformation."

Taylor also attaches particular importance to the increasing individualization of the consciousness of death, and of notions of judgment upon the individual immediately after their death and not only on the Day of Judgment, and he shows how the social embedding of this individualization, namely prayer for remission of punishment for the sins of relatives in purgatory, was meant before its corruption, "and in the end set fire to the whole structure of the mediaeval church" (69). In principle, I fully agree with Taylor on this point. But I think it would have been better to illustrate the features of tribal religion and archaic religion in general or with reference to pre-Christian Europe.

Even more importantly, I think it was a mistake to subtly reinterpret the inner tension of medieval Christianity as a "vector" of the Reformation, which was supposedly brewing for centuries, and as a vector of the constitution of the modern sense of immanence, a process that takes us beyond the Reformation. That is exactly what Taylor does, as a result of which the extraordinarily productive idea of a constant, unresolved Axial Age tension in medieval Christianity moves imperceptibly into the vicinity of the idea of a special (Western) European path determined purely by culture. Here Taylor postulates a development of Latin Christianity continuing since the time of Pope Gregory VII in the eleventh century, without really having an explanation as to why this vector should be so powerful. "What keeps this vector going is a question which is hard to answer, but I think its general direction is undeniable" (786, n. 92). It is true that reforms, even if their advocates often envisaged them as a return to a primordial form of Christianity, could become "an engine of genuine novelty and unprecedented change" (ibid.), but I believe the contingency of these processes and their determination by factors other than cultural ones to be far greater than Taylor appears to assume. It is surely a retrospective illusion to infer an enduring movement from repeated endeavors, some of which built on one another or invoked forerunners in an attempt to shore up their own legitimacy.

Religious Experience Today

This is also important because the answers to these questions will determine how we assess the present-day prospects for religious experience in the Axial sense. In contrast to Charles Larmore, who criticizes Taylor by citing Weber's thesis of disenchantment, with only slight modification, as an empirical fact,[15] I would advise Taylor to move even further away from Weber's construction. Although many aspects of Weber's work can be seen as a precursor of Jaspers's idea of the Axial Age, Weber did not make a clear and consistent distinction between the pre-Axial "magical" dimension and the post-Axial "sacramental" realm, instead tending to join them together with a hyphen ("magical-sacramental") as if they were practically the same.[16]

When Weber explicitly called the sacrament of the Eucharist "essentially magic," this is inadequate in terms of the sociology of religion and should be understood as part of a Calvinist-inspired confessional polemic. For Weber, Catholicism was, so to speak, pre-Axial, and his implicit denigration distorts his image of Lutheranism as well. This perspective caused him to miss the innovative potential of, for example, the liturgical movement of his time, while also preventing him from grasping the potential of sacramental experience in past and present. Taylor, of course, has the opposite goal in mind, but as I see it he ought to have done more to elaborate conceptually the constant tension between the Axial Age "thorn" and the loss of transcendence in religious contexts, the analogous tension between universalism and particularism in secular contexts—and the varied range of ways in which these tensions can be resolved.[17]

This brings us to the consequences of the presence of the secular option. Here, too, Taylor has groundbreaking things to say. Some of this is already familiar from his earlier works, such as the significance of an originally religiously motivated affirmation of ordinary life and reflections, reminiscent of Durkheim, on the roots of the autonomization and sacralization of the individual. When I stated at the end of the chapter on Taylor in my book *Do We Need Religion?*[18] that Taylor's publications had whet my appetite for more detailed elaboration from his pen of the opportunities and risks of expressive individualism in the field of religion, then all I can say now is that my appetite has been more than appeased by *A Secular Age*. One problem, however, continues to be thrown up by Taylor's distinction between paleo-, neo- and post-Durkheimian linkages of religion and state.

What Taylor means, first, is societies in which religion is not truly distinguished from the rest of life ("paleo"); second, those in which it is a distinct realm but at the same time symbolizes a larger whole (such as the nation-state) ("neo"); and finally, those dominated by a form of radical individualism without any social embedding ("post"). If Taylor's goal here is to draw attention to the problems engendered by radical individualization, this is no doubt useful. But once again, the term "paleo-Durkheimian" does not seem to me to capture the nature of medieval Christianity, given that the tension between church and empire, between pope and emperor, was always inherent in it. This is further evidence of the shortcomings of Taylor's conception. As far as the present is concerned, however, the question is whether the post-Durkheimian condition truly exists. Who really joins a denomination voluntaristically? Who fails to live their expressive individualism in appropriate social forms? Taylor clearly dissociates himself from conservative jeremiads about the growth of "free-floating spirituality" by highlighting the "spiritual costs" (513) of its other forms: religious hypocrisy, the fusion of faith and power, and more besides. But like many interpreters of the contemporary world, he too seems to me to exaggerate the quantitative significance of the "post-Durkheimian" phenomenon and to overstate its representative character when it comes to the religio-cultural analysis of today's world.

But while these passages in Taylor's book may be sociologically superficial, there is a profound theological argument at play here. His text is pervaded by reflections on what the "church" actually is in today's language. The meaning of this term is not easy to articulate under the conditions of a prevailing individualist perspective. It seems to have become a matter of course that social entities must be based on the voluntary association of their members, and therefore, even in the case of religion, they represent at most a kind of club, a "cultic association," as Ernst Troeltsch put it.[19] The idea of the church as an entity that is superordinate to individuals and that makes it possible for them to become believers and to become themselves in the first place is thus deeply out of keeping with the times. Taylor calls the church a network of *agape*,

> a skein of relations which link particular, unique, enfleshed people to each other, rather than a grouping of people together on the grounds of their sharing some important property (as in modern nations, we are all Canadians, Americans, French people or, universally, we are all rights-bearers, etc.). (739)

Here we can clearly perceive his closeness to theological critics of an antimodern, authoritarian-centralist Catholic understanding of the church, such as French theologians Henri de Lubac and Yves Congar, and their tendency to draw on (mainly Greek) church fathers (847f., n. 39). This is of sociological and social philosophical interest because Taylor himself thus opens up at least the possibility that the institution of the church may be characterized by tremendous modernity:

> The church is in this sense a quintessentially network society, even though of an utterly unparalleled kind, in that the relations are not mediated by any of the historical forms of relatedness: kinship, fealty to a chief, or whatever. It transcends all these, but not into a categorical society based on similarity of members, like citizenship, but rather into a network of ever different relations of agape. (282)

He immediately adds, realistically, that the church often "lamentably and spectacularly fails to live up to this model, but this is the kind of society that it is meant to be" (282). This idea also stimulates us to reflect on the social forms appropriate to non-Christian traditions of moral universalism.

A brief discussion of open questions and controversial issues cannot do justice to the richness of Charles Taylor's monumental book. In particular, a more detailed discussion would have to demonstrate the relevance of the points I have criticized to other periods examined by Taylor. His tendency to construct a cultural determinism to explain the reformist tendencies of medieval Christianity, an approach I have criticized here, is also present in his analysis of modernity, when he (299ff.) refers to a "nova effect": "It's as though the original duality, the positing of a viable humanist alternative, set in train a dynamic, something like a nova effect, spawning an ever-widening variety of moral/spiritual options" (299). While the emergence of options can certainly be construed in this way, the attempt to explain the perception of these options by individual and collective actors requires an analysis that looks more closely at specific political constellations, reconstructs links between interests and religious (or antireligious) orientations, and takes into account the often mythical form in which such constellations enter the collective memory and influence attitudes to specific religions or religion in general. The Enlightenment of the eighteenth century, the liberalism and socialism of the nineteenth century, and the cultural upheavals of the 1960s and 1970s did not simply have secularizing effects as such. Taylor would surely agree with this. But his book is crying out for sociological and social historical supplementation.

Waves of Secularization

My last remark indicates the direction in which I believe research needs to go if we wish to tease out the causes of secularization processes. By overcoming the secularization thesis, we free up space for such investigation. Studies in intellectual history à la Taylor elucidate the emergence of an option, but, as I have already underlined, they cannot explain the varying inclination to embrace this option. While Taylor did endeavor (in Part IV of his book) to take account of sociological and historical writings on the subject, many threads are still to be stitched together in this regard.

Methodologically, my thesis is that secularization can be explained neither in terms of intellectual history nor in light of different levels of economic development, but only if we focus on the level of institutional arrangements encompassing state, economy, and religious communities. Crucial here is the position of religious communities and churches on the national question, the social question, democracy, civil rights and liberties, and on religious pluralism itself, and the way in which this position is reflected in the institutional configurations of state and church. All economic conditions, all scholarly and cultural developments are experienced and interpreted within these fields of tension and thus impede or foster secularization.

We owe this insight to British sociologist David Martin, who presented it in his 1978 book *A General Theory of Secularization*, in what I believe to have been a pioneering way, though his observations made little impact at the time.[20] Of course, it could be said that this insight was already inherent in the work of Max Weber, but this rather misses the point: Weber's own view of Christianity, of disenchantment and rationalization, led him to make assertions that seem quite untenable, especially with regard to the method I am foregrounding here. These are highly complex questions that I will refrain from delving into further at this point. Instead, I will briefly illustrate how the historical events leading to secularization appear from this perspective.[21]

My contention is that secularization is not a uniform, linear, continuous process that has continued (for example) from the eighteenth century to the present day. Instead, we can identify three historical spurts or waves through which this process has largely played itself out. The first and third of these surges in particular are crammed into a relatively short span of years. The first wave, I assert, chiefly washed over France, in addition to a number of other places, between 1791 and 1803; the third wave can be discerned between 1969 and 1973 in Western Europe (but, by contrast, in the late 1950s in Eastern Europe). The second wave, which extended over a somewhat longer period of time, I place between 1848 and 1880 in Germany.[22]

These strong claims immediately require qualification. It is not obvious that these three waves all form part of one and the same process of secularization. It could be that the three phases are so different from one another that this umbrella term implies a false commonality. Further, the identification of three waves should not be taken to mean that between them the process of secularization was merely interrupted; were we to make that assumption, there would be no doubt about the direction of travel, however much the velocity might vary during the different phases. In fact, the periods between the waves may feature massive countermovements as well as modernizations, revitalizations, and retraditionalizations of faith. Ultimately, of course, any such statement is dangerous if not specified on a regional or class basis. I can neglect this here because I am merely seeking to illustrate a methodological approach.

Let's take a closer look at the first of these waves. The conventional view that the eighteenth-century Enlightenment was anti-Christian and was a major source of ideological inspiration for the French Revolution in this regard can be countered by the observation that in the first instance religion was not a major theme in the Revolution.[23] The revolutionaries who stormed the Bastille are said to have sung a Te Deum in thanks, and in the first few years of the Revolution thanksgiving services were held on the anniversary of this event on July 14. At first it was only the general impulse to abolish feudal privileges that was directed against the church; in other words, the issue was its role as landowner.

It was not this that was crucial to the fate of religion in France, but the fact that the Revolution soon began to focus less on the separation of church and state and more on establishing a kind of national church, that is, on the nationalization of the church. This drove priests, monks, and nuns, as well as many believers, into a deep clash of loyalties, while the pope (Pius VI) responded by condemning every aspect of the Revolution, including the declaration of human rights. A conflict escalated that took violent forms: acts of violence by revolutionaries against priests who refused to take the oath of loyalty and violence by believers against priests loyal to the regime. When fears of a counterrevolutionary military intervention by Austria reached hysterical proportions in 1792, hundreds of priests were murdered and hundreds more the next year; the *terreur* reached its climax, and forcible de-Christianization was systematically pursued.

While these efforts soon came to an end and Napoleon sought to establish a new modus vivendi in the relationship between church and state, it is fair to say that France has never recovered from this extreme polarization. All those countries culturally oriented toward France, especially Spain and Portugal, as well as parts of Italy, were drawn into this polarization, which shaped the entire nineteenth and parts of the twentieth century and is still making a clear impact today—in Spain, for example. My goal here is to bring out the highly contingent character of this polarization and thus of the secularization process.

The history of Protestantism in Prussia from 1848 onward demands analogous interpretation. There are direct parallels in the revolutionaries' history of disappointment and alienation vis-à-vis the Protestant state church, in which the sovereign was the supreme bishop. In this case, we must also factor in the history of rapid urbanization and industrialization, but again, not as a simple cause of secularization, but in the sense of a challenge to the church arising from new social developments—one it failed to recognize, let alone meet. This inability to respond to contemporary realities was initially evident, as in England during the industrial revolution, at the logistical level: a lack of church buildings in the cities, sartorial expectations among bourgeois-dominated milieus that were unrealizable for the lower classes, and so on. This is why Berlin was considered the most unreligious city in the world as early as 1881.

The subsequent church-building offensive was, however, much less successful than in England, where church attendance reached an all-time high around 1900. In Prussia-Germany, after the founding of the Reich, Protestant "pastoral nationalism" intensified the alienation of working-class men, who in turn sacralized a secular utopia and scientific-technological progress. The secularization of proletarian women, however, was yet to materialize; this is probably the main reason why organized movements to leave the church, initiated again and again, remained fairly unsuccessful. Here, too—I would argue—things might have turned out very differently, a point that seems backed up by comparison with the Catholic Church's far greater ability to maintain ties with workers in the Rhineland and the Ruhr region, for example.

We can also extricate the most recent rapid surge in secularization in the late 1960s from the apparent determinism of an epoch-making process. The early stages of the German student movement were in part strongly Christian in character; this is exemplified in the figure of Rudi Dutschke, the best-known charismatic leader, as well as in the infrastructure of the movement in the form, for example, of Protestant student congregations. I cannot offer a methodologically sound explanation for Christianity's later precipitous decline within this history of cultural and political transformation. But here too, international comparison shows that the "expressive revolution" of the 1960s did not necessarily have a secularizing effect. In the United States during this phase, tendencies toward the sacralization of eroticism, for example in the hippie movement, and toward the reception of Asian forms of spirituality played at least as important a role as tendencies toward secularization perceived as "European," a phenomenon still apparent today.

This sketch of an explanation for processes of secularization, in which a great deal is undoubtedly missing and certain other things are only hinted at, must suffice for now. The secular option, which first saw the light of day in the course of this history, will not go away. An end to optionality is inconceivable. Taylor is surely right to foreground within his thinking the question of how faith changes and must change once the secular option has entered believers' consciousness and the Christian faith itself has thus become one of several options. This situation throws up unprecedented challenges because faith must be articulated in new ways, yet these challenges can be experienced as motivating rather than intimidating. Those who distance themselves from Christianity or all religion must of course also recognize the optionality of their own secular orientations.

This is the unsettling effect of the death of the conventional secularization thesis. Over the last two decades, those who contributed, for example, to the debates in Berlin on the relationship between religious and ethical education or to discussions in Brandenburg on the new school subject of lifestyle, ethics, and religious studies, surprisingly often put forward arguments featuring untenable ideas about the church as historically obsolete. In other words, they refused to accept the notion of optionality and presented their views as historically guaranteed. Present-day discussions of the secular option and of faith as an option are reopening a field of debate long sealed off by modernist or antimodernist ideas of history. With his historically and philosophically rich account of the rise of the secular option, Charles Taylor has changed the terms of the debate on these questions in an epoch-making way.[24]

PART III
THE SEARCH FOR A DIFFERENT KIND OF FREEDOM

PART III

III, 1
Introductory Remarks

However much we may agree that freedom is a key value or the highest value in a certain cultural tradition or ought to have this status everywhere, in all cultures, this by no means tells us precisely what freedom is. Clarity seems to prevail only if freedom merely means individuals' unrestricted power of disposal over themselves, their actions and property, even their bodies and lives. On this premise, the freedom of the individual seems to be limited only when the self-determination of other individuals—claiming or deserving of freedom—is affected. As a result, philosophical and political debates are shifting from attempts to precisely define the concept of freedom as such toward clarifying the relationship between freedom and equality. If it seems obvious that everyone has the same right to freedom, then the focus must be on the institutional and other preconditions for guaranteeing freedom for all, at least in a particular polity and perhaps even beyond it. Today, many find this equal right to freedom of all people self-evident, though it must be remembered that even the Western tradition is pervaded by ideas about differing entitlements to liberties enjoyed by different social classes, "races," and genders.

If the search for "a different kind of freedom," to which the title of this third part of the book alludes, meant nothing more than an effort to find an alternative to the "negative" freedom of individuals in the sense I have just set out, then Hegel's philosophy would be one of the mainstays of such efforts rather than being a body of ideas that we need to revise and move beyond. In the thinking of Charles Taylor, Robert Pippin, and Axel Honneth, to which I referred earlier,[1] Hegel is the most important source of inspiration for a nuanced understanding of freedom that goes beyond the merely negative version without ignoring the good sense inherent in demands for self-determination. Nor does this sophisticated conception declare these demands historically superfluous, glossing over specific power relations as the fulfillment, at long last, of dreams of freedom. The search for "a different kind of freedom" must, therefore, mean more than the Hegelian critique of the negative conception of freedom. Those conducting this search must have in mind elements of the understanding of freedom not found in Hegel's work, elements that are indispensable to an adequate understanding of religion and faith.

In the following four studies I aim to elaborate two such elements in particular. The first and longest chapter in this part investigates whether the demands central to the Western tradition of political freedom are in fact based on a conception of autonomous and secular reason, as claimed by certain leading thinkers from Hegel to Habermas. If this were true, then any understanding of reason that disputes its autonomy, and thus any search for a different, less reason-centered understanding of freedom, would be suspected of undermining or endangering political freedom. This would apply even to such tendencies within the Western cultural tradition—for example, in American pragmatism—but a fortiori in cultures (such as that of Germany) in which liberal-democratic political traditions are perceived as less firmly anchored than in the heartlands of the West. Even Hegel's search for a historical understanding of reason and freedom, which to some seems the epitome of a metaphysics of reason, would then be suspected by others of entailing a freedom-threatening tendency of this sort.

Conversely, the "deflation" of reason—for example, in the thinking of the neo-pragmatist Richard Rorty—may be perceived as a prerequisite for stable political freedom—or once again as a threat to it, because he hedges in the universalist claims inherent in demands for freedom in a culturally relativist way. A large, multifaceted web of questions opens up here that I am unable to address exhaustively at this point.[2] The focus in our context must be on the problems of the theory of religion and the understanding of faith. The crucial question here, then, is whether a postulate of human freedom in the Kantian sense can serve as the starting point for the theory of religion and the understanding of faith in such a way that the certainty of God must also be based on this postulate, or whether, conversely, we may need religious faith in order to gain a sense of ourselves as beings endowed with freedom of action. The following three shorter chapters all revolve around this alternative, namely the idea of "indebted freedom." All the thinkers portrayed consider an understanding of freedom inadequate if it fails to incorporate this motif of indebtedness.

Debates on freedom, reason, and religion are frequently charged with energies stemming from a particular definition of national and cultural identity. They often revolve around questions about dependence on the "West" or distance from it, especially in cases where membership of the West is not a matter of course. In France, the United Kingdom, and the United States this affiliation may be beyond doubt; yet even in these countries, the question is often to what extent one's tradition is still viable or is endangered under new conditions and of what exactly it consists. Especially with regard to its relationship with religion, the notion of a unified West is grossly misleading, as immediately apparent in the utterly different role of religion in the political culture of France and the United States.

In German intellectual history, for two centuries an important role was played by the question of independence from the West, of a "German idea of freedom," which is meant in a self-confident and delimiting way, or a "special German path" (*Sonderweg*), which has generally been a target of critique. Although Germany's "long road west"[3] may have resolved this issue historically, the motifs that were articulated here at a more abstract level have by no means disappeared in the present. Today they crop up in varying configurations in Eastern Europe and Russia, in the Islamic world and China. A look back in this respect is, therefore, of more than antiquarian or national interest. The way in which I am tracing these motifs in twentieth-century German thought may seem unusual at first glance but is imperative in light of the intellectual presuppositions informing the present book. What I wish to highlight are the different ways in which "Western" and "German," "rationalist" and "expressivist" motifs are linked in the work of Ernst Troeltsch and Ernst Cassirer, the former one of the leading representatives of the historicist tradition and the latter a prominent and extraordinarily productive Kantian.

Foregrounding this comparison between two thinkers may appear unusual because another comparison, between Cassirer and Martin Heidegger, has attracted enormous attention in recent years. The dispute between the two in Davos in 1929 has been stylized as a fateful moment in the history of continental philosophy and is enveloped in a variety of myths.[4] In the present book, meanwhile, I regard Troeltsch as a key figure in the development of the theory of religion "after Hegel and Nietzsche";[5] hence, the additional insights garnered about his ideas through comparison with Cassirer are as worthy of our attention as the Davos clash.[6] In this case, however, we are not dealing with a confrontation at a specific point in time, which can be dramatically imbued with the status of generational conflict and historical turning point. This was a decades-long relationship between two scholars, based on friendship, in which they respectfully acknowledged each other's writings on an ongoing basis, constantly modifying their own views in the process.

I find this mutual engagement, with its many twists and turns, particularly exciting for two reasons. First, these were two fascinating attempts not simply to take one of two sides—"rationalist" or "expressivist"—but to factor the relative legitimacy of the other side into one's own philosophy. Specifically, this means that as he increasingly took account of the aesthetic dimension and of classical German literature, the thinking of the Kantian, republican, and cosmopolitan Cassirer developed into an extensive philosophy of symbolic forms and an anthropology centered on the use of symbols. Meanwhile, after the First World War at the latest, Troeltsch set about the project of breaking with the "anti-Western" mixture of Romanticism and militarism in Germany and finding his own new and potentially superior way of supporting the ideal of human rights by drawing on the tradition of German thought on individuality and history.[7]

The second reason lies in the comparison of the two thinkers' positions—not on Hegel's, but—on Kant's philosophy of morality and religion. Despite his willingness to develop classical Kantian transcendental philosophy further through a theory of signs and to reflect historically on his own philosophical position, Cassirer remained a strictly orthodox Kantian when it came to normative issues. The postulate of people's moral freedom remained his core intellectual lodestone. On this premise, religion comes to the fore primarily or exclusively as a factor that strengthens the motivation for moral action. For Troeltsch, who tried to express himself in the idiom of German neo-Kantianism only during certain phases of his oeuvre but drew his real intellectual motifs from other sources, this perspective is completely unacceptable. Even the definition of the moral takes a different form in his work in that he regards the historical development of ideals—the fact of ideal formation, not that of conscience—as crucial.[8]

This strips the history of morality of any trace of teleology. For Troeltsch, a religion that is extrapolated conceptually from morality is far distant from truly "living and experiencing communion with God." Scholarship on religion, he believes, rather than reducing it to acts of thinking, ought to focus on the fact that people are seized by it. On this premise, experiences are also constitutive of commitment to the value of freedom. This idea can be used to criticize every form of—as Troeltsch puts it—"messianic rationalism."[9] But here Troeltsch merely wishes to question the way in which its exponents understand this philosophy of freedom, not to dismiss its demands. Instead, he develops a more historically reflective way of historicizing moral universalism and a better grounding of subjectivity in the reality of our corporeal character and physical environment. Moral freedom necessarily highlights the preconditions for its own constitution. This is in fact the bridge to the second component of a "different kind of freedom," namely the idea or the experience of its indebtedness.

As I will show, this idea is already inherent in the work of Troeltsch. But it was first elaborated systematically by a thinker who occasionally referred to himself as a student of Troeltsch: Paul Tillich. I have nevertheless placed the following portrait of Tillich—which is fairly extensive in order to shed light on his productive contribution within the field of tension between theology and sociology—under the title "indebted freedom," because I believe his reflections on "theonomy" are of crucial strategic importance to a theory of religion "under the spell of freedom."[10] In order to make this point clear, I will first explain what is at stake here in everyday—that is, nonphilosophical and nontheological—language.

The starting point must be the question of whether, and if so to what extent, we do in fact perceive ourselves in our everyday lives as beings capable of making our own decisions and taking consequential actions. The sense that we do seems not to be equally pronounced in all people, nor does it seem equally strong in every phase or at every moment of life. We may be so constrained by the force of circumstance or others' power that while we do not doubt our ability to act in principle, we do doubt that it can be realized under prevailing conditions. Yet we may also doubt that we have this fundamental ability, at least with respect to aspects of our conduct of life, if we perceive ourselves as entirely driven by natural impulses or addictions, as an object of our own compulsivity or if we feel empty inside, that is, devoid of any motivating impulses at all. All such experiences show us that neither our fundamental ability to act nor our concrete scope for action are self-evident givens. They depend on certain enabling conditions, which we can try to apprehend through reflection.

If, on the other hand, we perceive ourselves as free in a pleasurable, perhaps even euphoric, way, in the context of play, creative achievements, or successful interaction, this too may prompt reflection on the conditions of possibility for this feeling. Precisely because in the case of play, creativity, or the success of a relationship we depend in part on obliging "fortunate" coincidences, while our own inspirations delight and surprise us, we are pushed beyond the mere attribution of our actions to ourselves. Even the most secular intellect will presumably trace back their own ability to act freely to their parents' love and the way they were brought up or to favorable conditions at school, in a sports club, political youth organization, or perhaps even in a church community, and possibly to the peaceful character and political culture of their home country. Such reflections, however, do not easily come to an end, since we can query, in terms of their own enabling conditions, how our parents brought us up and how our teachers educated us, and the same goes for role models and group structures. We can take such deliberations as far as the question of the capacity for freedom of the human species and its general preconditions.

This, however, means that the insight into the indebtedness of our capacity for freedom takes us beyond our immediate environment and the present era, and that it makes sense to identify preconditions for this capacity that even transcend human beings. Hence, an innocuous feeling of gratitude for freedom may give rise to the questions of anthropology, in turn prompting even more far-reaching questions of a metaphysical and religious kind. Because in fact, in reflecting on the indebtedness of freedom, the majority of people are probably not chiefly interested in its ancestry or in its history, let alone the "ladder" of nature and the "great chain of beings" as envisaged by premodern natural philosophy. What moves them more strongly are existential matters. What does it mean for my conduct of life that I have not made myself a free being? What does the unavoidable insight into my vulnerability and the finiteness of my existence mean for the way I live my life? Does the fear of suffering and death paralyze me in such a way that it restricts my ability to act and make decisions? Or does faith free me from this fear, thus enhancing my ability to lead my life? Am I sufficiently aware of my dependence on others, and do I consistently incorporate others' dependence on me into my self-understanding as a free person capable of acting?

In Christianity, though by no means exclusively, the idea of indebted freedom has played a central role and has a long tradition since Paul. The best-known passage in this regard can be found in his letter to the Galatians: "It is for freedom that Christ has set us free" (5:1). Or translated differently: "Christ has freed us, and he wants us to stay free. So stand firm and do not submit again to the yoke of slavery."[11] But from what and how did Christ, according to Paul, set us free? If we look at the immediate context of this passage, it clearly seems to be about liberation from Jewish "law," from the need for Christians to be circumcised and all other ensuing obligations. But this interpretation would be too narrow, especially since the recipients of the letter (the Galatians) were not Judeo-Christians at all. The letter soon goes on to designate God as the liberator and to identify the freedom involved as freedom from selfishness and freedom to love: "Do not use your freedom to indulge the flesh; rather, serve one another humbly in love" (Galatians 5:13). But Paul (Galatians 5:14) immediately goes on to mention the commandment of love explicitly as the epitome of the "law," placing the Gentile Christians in clear continuity with the Torah.[12]

Thus, Paul Tillich—who liked to call himself *Paulus*, as Paul the Apostle is known to German speakers—is certainly not the first to put forward this tradition-steeped idea. But it seems to me that Tillich's merit lies in the way he introduced it, in a new and impactful manner, into the debates within classical German philosophy on the "autonomy" of the morally capable and rational person. The Kantian tradition, as mentioned, throws up the problem that religion seems to occupy a secondary status vis-à-vis autonomy in a moral sense, and attains even this status only if it serves as a source of motivation for moral action. If it fails to do so, then religion is bound to appear as a threat to human autonomy, as submission to commandments and laws imposed by an outside authority or to the will of a feared superhuman being. In the Left Hegelian tradition, religion thus became the epitome of heteronomy, and overcoming it was viewed as a crucial prerequisite for advances in political autonomy.[13] This is at complete variance with Latin American–style liberation theology, in which religion and especially Christianity are ascribed a key role in acquiring political freedom, and not in an abstract sense, but with direct reference to mobilizing the faithful to engage in political struggle from within their church communities.

It would of course be absurd to deny—and Tillich did not deny—that faith may in fact be heteronomy, that individuals may fail to realize or avoid their autonomy through obedience to the church, for example. But it would be just as absurd to view all resistance to religious belief as safeguarding autonomy. Tillich recognized that the conceptual pair autonomy/heteronomy is simply not enough to clarify these issues. According to him, we need a third concept that emerges from the "deepening of autonomy in itself to the point where it points beyond itself."[14] This is exactly what opens up to us when we reflect on the conditions constitutive of our freedom. Tillich referred here to "theonomy," because he saw a path to God in this reflection on the conditions of our freedom, a path that does not contradict the ideal of autonomy.

"Theonomy" is absolutely not intended to denote blind submission to a sacred law or divine will, but rather a becoming aware of the indebted character of freedom. In such a turn to God as the source of one's capacity for freedom, the aspiration to freedom remains undiminished. It is, however, changed from within, in that the free individual is no longer fixated on their own autonomy and the free collective is shielded from the hubris associated with the wholesale planning and organizing of every sphere of human life. This also engenders an inner freedom when dealing with external pressures and with social and political orders. It gives rise to a respect for the indisposability of the other and of nature, even of one's own life.[15] Hence, however much we might prize the value of self-determination, it is not the only or self-evidently highest guide when it comes to moral reflection.

In a masterly essay, French philosopher and Protestant Paul Ricœur took up this idea of the relationship between theonomy and autonomy and developed it further.[16] Tracing this relationship from the New Testament back to the revelation of the Mosaic Law, especially in the concentrated form of the "Ten Commandments,"[17] his starting point here is the "entangling of the bestowal of the law with the story of liberation"[18] from enslavement in Egypt and the development of an idea of loving obedience. A "theonomy" understood in this way, Ricœur tells us—and this is the crucial point in the present context—is not opposed to autonomy but dialectically interwoven with it.

In Ricœur's language, what we are dealing with here is the interplay between "love" and "justice." According to him, the ethic of love does not break with the demands of justice, but modifies them in a range of ways while also being modified by them.[19] The chapter "Sieve of Norms and Holy Scripture, Theonomy, and Freedom" in the present book, which is dedicated to Ricœur, first shows how he develops out of these elements a conception in which the Kantian-Habermasian motif of moral universalism is affirmed and preserved, but is mediated by the emergence of our value commitments out of contingent experiences and the narrative constitution of our selves. Second, I seek to illuminate how Ricœur thinks of the relationship between religious experience and religious language, between "manifestation" and "proclamation," between extraordinary individual experience and communication.

In the case of the next thinker portrayed here, German Protestant theologian Wolfgang Huber, my initial focus is on this motif of intersubjectivity and communication. He does not build on the influential theory of communicative action developed by Jürgen Habermas or the concept of recognition formulated by Axel Honneth, but on the idea of "communicative freedom" as found in the work of a leading Christian Hegelian of our time, Michael Theunissen.[20] It certainly cannot be said of Theunissen, in contrast to many other contemporary Hegelians, that faith and Christianity were a blind spot in his reconstruction of Hegel's philosophy;[21] at the same time, like Habermas and (later) Honneth, he was aware of the relative narrowness of Hegel's conception of intersubjectivity and, through his broad reception of the Jewish and Christian philosophy of dialogue, made a key contribution to overcoming this conception.

Theunissen drew on Kierkegaard, so his work already includes the motif of becoming oneself, not only out of the structures of intersubjectivity, but also through insight into one's relation to God—a motif that, for our purposes, I address as that of indebtedness and place in a context that is not exclusively Christian or religious. In my portrait of Huber's "theology of liberation," I aim to elaborate, first, how he develops the motif of indebtedness within the framework of this conception. Second, I ask critically to what extent Huber has succeeded in consistently linking the various strands of thinking on freedom that appear in his work.[22]

In my remarks so far on the "search for a different kind of freedom," I have referred to the problems entailed in the assumption of an autonomous reason and to the need to reflect on the indebtedness of freedom. To conclude, I aim to relate these two lines of thought to one another as I seek to establish the potential for such reflection in the first place. If we assume the autonomy of reason, it may appear that the subject is able to freely decide to reflect on the conditions of possibility for its own capacity for freedom. This was conceivable under the conditions of classical German philosophy; Fichte's thinking in particular has often been interpreted in this way.

If, on the other hand, we think of individuals' reflections not as initiable at will, but rather as compelled or at least suggested by real action situations, the question arises as to when a subject feels the need to experience itself as capable of acting and when it experiences itself as such. On this premise, we are dealing not with an act of decisionist self-positing by an ego, but with a readiness to open oneself to forces not produced by one's ego.[23] These forces may be, but are not necessarily, thought of as coming from God or a god. In the present day, it makes more sense to many people to view them as forces of the unconscious.

It was thus only consistent that William James not only examined the concrete preconditions for a sense of self that entails a belief in one's capacity for action in many of his writings, but also systematically left open the question of the sources from which individuals acquire such capacities not generated by themselves. He wanted to be neither an apologist for faith nor a critic of religion, but rather to remain, in terms of his "scientific" work, at the level of the phenomenology of religious consciousness. When he went, quasi-metaphysically, beyond the level of "science," he fell back on metaphors. His favorite metaphor for the experience of being imbued by forces that are not generated by the subject itself but enable it to be itself is that of the "mother-sea."[24] What James no doubt had in mind here was the great sea that sustains all its bays and flows into them as the tides change. In James's speculations, this idea has to some extent not theistic but pantheistic or "panpsychic" features. Even the Apostle Paul's train of thought did not simply grow out of faith in Christ or Jewish monotheism but was shaped in significant part by the Greek Stoics.[25] While the experience of the indebtedness of our freedom certainly requires us to interpret its source, it allows for more than one such interpretation.

Yet this experience may be absent or not taken seriously. In this case, the capacity for self-determined action appears given in nature and the world seems chiefly a place of restrictions for the individual. One's relationship with other people is transformed from one saturated with gratitude to one of reproach and enraged efforts to push through one's own wishes and demands. The idea of freedom of action, which is crucial to political freedom, turns into a threat to the preconditions for free coexistence because the individual no longer feels any responsibility to safeguard the underpinnings of a free and democratic order. In this sense, the ideas of Troeltsch, Tillich, Ricœur, and Huber—the focus of this part of the book—are much more than just a pleasing embellishment of sober political conceptions of freedom. They point to a necessary break with exaggerated notions of the autonomy of reason and the moral person, a move vital to securing political freedom over the long term.[26]

III, 2

A German Idea of Freedom?: Cassirer and Troeltsch between Germany and the West

After 1945, reeling under the impact of catastrophic military defeat and the exposure of the horrific crimes perpetrated by the Nazi regime, Western Germany turned decisively toward the political and cultural traditions of Western Europe and North America. For German intellectuals and scholars of the postwar period, this turn to the "West" complicated their relationship to those traditions that had long been perceived as specifically German within and outside Germany. An unbroken continuation of these traditions was out of the question for most. Only a few, however, opted to turn abruptly away from all German, let alone all "Continental," ways of thinking. Many looked for untainted figures in the German tradition itself and believed they had found them, for example, in Immanuel Kant or Max Weber or the Frankfurt School. More productive than such borrowings, which were often plagued by an excessive need to identify with the thinker in question, was to place oneself in the unavoidable field of tension between German ideas and those emanating from outside the country, to combine the greatest openness to, say, American, British, and French works with a new appropriation of German intellectual history as well. Ironically, international observers tend to pay greater attention to such efforts than in the case of the mere repetition of motifs that are well known in their countries of origin. As far as the perpetuation of the motifs characteristic of "Critical Theory" is concerned, Jürgen Habermas in particular has thrown the windows wide open and done much to ensure the reception of ways of thinking that had played virtually no role in earlier stages of this tradition or had been devalued from a critique of ideology perspective. Axel Honneth has followed him in this in the next generation. With great intellectual independence, he has built on Critical Theory and integrated new elements into it, demonstrating the vitality of this tradition of thought even today. Karl-Otto Apel meanwhile, has done more than anyone else to make the philosophy of American pragmatism known in Germany and to relate it systematically to German traditions of thought. In no way should we regard these complicated efforts at mediation as over and done with. Many tasks remain, and present efforts also shed new light on the period before 1945.

Two Cases of Mediation between Germany and the West

The attempts at mediation between Germany and the West, it must be admitted, have a much longer history. Two German thinkers, whose thinking cannot be understood without this tension and whose achievement cannot be judged without scrutinizing the success of their mediation efforts, have returned to prominence in recent years in an almost triumphant manner after decades in which they seemed almost forgotten: Ernst Cassirer and Ernst Troeltsch. Today, Ernst Cassirer (1874–1945) has become an unmissable subject for all those interested in twentieth-century German philosophy in general and in the symbol-theoretical or semiotic transformation of transcendental philosophy in particular, thanks to his important works in intellectual history, but even more so to his philosophy of symbolic forms and his philosophical anthropology. Ernst Troeltsch, meanwhile, had for decades been received almost exclusively by theologians. In the social sciences, the fame of his longtime friend and colleague Max Weber almost completely overshadowed his work, and in philosophy he was perceived more as a late representative of historicism than as its creative overcomer in the sense that he solved the problem of relativism. Ernst Troeltsch died, not yet sixty years old, before completing his major work.

At the age of fifty-eight, Ernst Cassirer was forced to leave his country in order to escape from the Nazis and their racial persecution. The fact that he was of Jewish origin had already impeded his academic career in the much-praised scholarly world of Wilhelmine Germany: it was not until after the revolution of 1918–1919 that he managed to attain a professorship at the newly founded University of Hamburg. His election as its rector for the academic year 1929–1930 was only the fourth election of a Jewish rector in the history of German academia. After his emigration, which interrupted a delayed but then brilliant academic career, Cassirer found a new home as a scholar and as a human being first in Sweden, at the University of Gothenburg, and then in the United States.

To contextualize their works historically is consonant with the interest in the history of ideas that Cassirer and Troeltsch shared; to relate their thinking to important contemporary problems is in line with their own attempts to intervene in public debates.

Cassirer's work has often been contrasted with that of a thinker whose ideas he had grappled with intensely, as reflected in the famous Davos debate between Cassirer and Martin Heidegger in 1929.[1] That year, the alleged "neo-Kantian" Cassirer and the young sensation of German philosophy at the time, Martin Heidegger—who had risen to prominence at least since the publication of *Being and Time* two years before—clashed in front of an international audience of two hundred people over seemingly esoteric questions relating to the interpretation of Kant: the relationship, that is, between epistemology and metaphysics in this thinker's work. The witnesses of this clash already seem to have experienced the event as a sort of epochal rupture. Among them were such subsequently famous figures as Emmanuel Levinas, Joachim Ritter, Eugen Fink, the Jesuit Erich Przywara, Otto Friedrich Bollnow, and (as rumor had it) Leo Strauss and Herbert Marcuse—plus, as we now know, even Rudolf Carnap.[2] Shortly after the discussion and in the same venue where it had taken place, some of them replayed in satirical fashion the struggle between the philosophical titans. Bollnow played Heidegger, while Levinas imitated Cassirer. In this role, Levinas uttered the same sentence over and over: "I am a pacifist," whereas Bollnow's Heidegger made nonsense statements drafted by Levinas such as, "To interpret something means to turn it upside down." What must have seemed like rarefied student hijinks in 1929 looks hideously frivolous in hindsight, and Levinas is said never to have forgiven himself for the role he played in this cruel performance. But the young philosophers' flippancy also reveals that they did not invest the collision between Cassirer and Heidegger with all the meanings that we today tend to project onto it. For us, this dispute may look like a clash between rationalism and irrationalism, humanism and (antiliberal and anti-Semitic) antihumanism. It is therefore very difficult to unearth the substantive questions that were at stake here and that necessarily arise in any encounter between transcendental philosophy and historicist hermeneutics—to dig them out from beneath all the political and ideological layers above them.

This is one of the reasons why I have chosen a different path. Here I will confront Cassirer with one of the greatest representatives of the German hermeneutic-historicist tradition: Ernst Troeltsch. Cassirer and Troeltsch studied each other's writings and reacted to them over decades. The focus of my discussion of their intellectual relationship will be the topic of human rights and their foundation—a topic that is of the highest moral and political relevance. The comparison of Cassirer and Troeltsch allows me to connect philosophical and moral-political questions, but without all the connotations of Heidegger's particular case. And it allows me to reconstruct not just one moment of collision in the life of two thinkers, but an interconnection of two learning processes, a mutual mirroring of intellectual developments. The differences and commonalities of the two thinkers can thus become visible; although their points of departure clearly were very different, we should not exclude the possibility that their development led to a sort of convergence. What is the exact relationship between transcendental philosophy and hermeneutics in the works of these thinkers, and what is the political relevance of this relationship, in particular with regard to the understanding of political freedom and its relation to the history of religion? This is the question I have in mind when I analyze the position of Troeltsch and Cassirer between Germany and the West and the "German idea of freedom"—and when I tell the story of a tense intellectual friendship.[3]

I will not, however, proceed in a strictly chronological manner, because the best way for me to clarify my main question is to start with Troeltsch's late writings. Let me begin my reflections by presenting you with a specific scene. It is October 24, 1922, in downtown Berlin. In Schinkel's Bauakademie building, the German School of Politics ("Deutsche Hochschule für Politik") held its second annual celebration that evening. The president of the Reich, Friedrich Ebert, and outstanding figures in Berlin's academic-intellectual life—such as historians Friedrich Meinecke, Erich Marcks, and Hans Delbrück—had accepted the invitation from this newly created institution, which had set itself the goal of promoting adult education in the spirit of democracy and therefore had a somewhat difficult task in the early years of the Weimar Republic. The keynote address was given by one of the greatest scholars of the old *Kaiserreich*, the Protestant theologian, historian, and philosopher Ernst Troeltsch; his topic was "The Ideas of Natural Law and Humanity in World Politics."[4] Contemporaries were fascinated by Troeltsch's argument in his lecture. After reading the text, Thomas Mann responded with a detailed essay that appeared in the *Frankfurter Zeitung*; Friedrich Meinecke dedicated his book *Die Idee der Staatsräson* ("The Idea of Reason of State") to Troeltsch, devoting the final chapter of the book to Troeltsch's lecture; and Leo Strauss, the emigrant political philosopher, took it as the starting point for his 1949 lectures at the University of Chicago, in which he warned America against the relativistic influence emanating from defeated Germany, and out of which he developed his influential book *Natural Right and History*.[5] Even today, Troeltsch's vision continues to fascinate, and perhaps it can only now be fully understood—by us, several generations later.

What was so special about this lecture? Its unique contribution lies in a remarkably productive confrontation between the Western human rights tradition and a sophisticated conception of individuality, creativity, and self-realization that was developed primarily in Germany. Troeltsch's tone was entirely sober and level-headed. During the first years of the war, Troeltsch had been one of the most avid composers of the nationalistic tracts produced by top German academics, a keen contributor to the heated public debates of the time. He had mostly emphasized the differences between Germany and the West. Though highly knowledgeable and generally above crude stereotypes, he was mainly interested in evoking an impassable cultural and political boundary. But the war's events and outcome, including the collapse of the monarchy, did not drive him further in the direction of nationalistic radicalism, as they did others, such as Oswald Spengler. Troeltsch neither simply conformed to the new circumstances for external or strategic reasons, by adopting the guise of a "republican of reason" (*Vernunftrepublikaner*), nor did he throw himself into the arms of the West that he had previously disparaged in a complete about-face. He attempted, by means of genuine and deep-reaching self-criticism, to undo the disastrous alliance that had formed in Germany between an ambitious understanding of individuality and the glorification of *raison d'état* and power politics. To reach this goal, he first showed clearly that the ideas of natural law and humanity were not, as was often assumed at the time in Germany, "merely modern or merely West European concepts," but rather "ideas of great antiquity . . . and of general European scope; ideas which are the basis of our European philosophy of history and ethics; ideas which have been closely connected, for thousands of years, with theology and humanism."[6] He further argued that Catholicism had always remained much closer to this "common tradition of Europe,"[7] the Romantic image of Catholicism notwithstanding. What was really new and modern, according to Troeltsch, were the—typically German—conceptions of the Romantics and Historicists that essentially emerged out of a revolt against natural law, which, in its modern form, was perceived as a fusion of utilitarianism and morality. The Romantics and Historicists, for their part, focused "on the particular, the positive: on what is eternally productive of new variety, constructive, spiritually organic, on plastic and super-personal creative forces."[8]

Indeed, since Herder and Humboldt, a significant strand of German thought had conceived of the human person neither as a utility-maximizing individual nor as a subject largely following the dictates of a rational morality, but rather as a being that expresses itself, and in this sense realizes itself, in its utterances and acts.[9] On this view, individuals are not just so many identical atoms, whose relationships to each other are subject to universal laws; rather they are highly unique personalities who undergo complex developmental processes as they seek out a path to self-realization through their own actions. This epochal transformation in thought also resulted in a new and different understanding of "community," which is sharply distinguished from contractual relationships; of humanity, which is conceived as the struggle of the national spirit; and of history, which is not interpreted as linear progress. Troeltsch was quite clear that for him—and he believed for all of us—this transformation cannot simply be undone, any more than this demanding new understanding of all individuality, including our own, can be renounced. Hence, such renunciation is the last thing he has in mind. Instead, he was convinced of the need to probe assiduously whether the political manifestations of the expressive German conception of individuality are in any way justifiable and whether their opposition to Western universalism makes any sense. In retrospect, Troeltsch tended to see the consequences of the grandiose innovations of the classical period of German thought as a history of decline:

> But the conception of a wealth of unique National Minds turns into a feeling of contempt for the idea of Universal Humanity: the old pantheistic deification of the State becomes a blind worship of success and power; the Romantic Revolution sinks into a complacent contentment with things as they are. From the idea of the particular law and right of a given time, men proceed to a merely positive acceptance of the State: morality of the spiritual order, transcending bourgeois convention, passes into moral skepticism, and the urgent movement of the German mind toward a political form and embodiment ends merely in the same cult of imperialism which is rampant everywhere.[10]

Troeltsch explicitly distanced himself from Germany's fatal antipathy toward human rights and the League of Nations.

> The theory of the Rights of Man—rights which are not the gift of the State, but the ideal postulates of the State, and indeed of Society itself, in all its

forms—is a theory which contains so much of the truth, and satisfies so many of the requirements of a true European attitude, that we cannot afford to neglect it; on the contrary, *we must incorporate it into our own ideas.*[11]

The key point is to be found in the last clause. Troeltsch is not only out to conquer the anti-Western blend of Romantic excess and the militaristic mania for order in Germany; he also wants to draw on the tradition of German thought concerning individuality and history to place the ideal of human rights on a new, proper, and potentially superior foundation.

And here lies the challenge, still unmet, that emanates from his text even today. It might at first appear as if Troeltsch's text simply documents, as so many others have done, Germany's long and arduous path toward the West. Initially, of course, this path led still deeper into anti-Western resentment, so that during the Third Reich, one historian (Wilhelm Ihde) would go so far as to argue that the idea of human rights was derived from a "decadent and pathological type of human."[12] After the step-by-step process of Westernization that occurred in Germany following the catastrophes of the Second World War and the Holocaust, first in the Federal Republic of Germany and then in Germany as a whole, Troeltsch's passionate concerns might seem outdated. But this would be a crude simplification of reality. For the West was never as homogeneous as its critics or the advocates of complete Westernization believed; the differences among the Western countries and their political camps and cultural traditions can only appear negligible when viewed from a great distance. What is more, the cultural tensions that exist within the West clearly resemble the ones that were employed to construct a fundamental difference between Germany and the West. For example, the French Declaration of the Rights of Man and of the Citizen of 1789 *simultaneously* proclaims the inviolability of individual freedoms and the sovereignty of a common will, without really resolving the tension between the two principles. If one follows French sociologist Alain Touraine's "critique de la modernité,"[13] the tension in the declaration can be seen as rooted in a tension between two fundamental principles of modernization: a process of progressive rationalization on the one hand, and a process of progressive subjectification on the other. While this tension was indeed contained from time to time, it broke out into the open again and again, and certainly during the cultural upheavals of the 1960s experienced by all Western societies. This shows that Troeltsch's search for an alternative to utilitarian and rationalistic justifications of human rights has, in fact, become *increasingly* relevant, even in the West, in part because of the massive and historically unparalleled diffusion of the value of creative self-realization. Troeltsch's question posed in 1922 can thus be rephrased today as follows: How can a belief in human rights and the universal dignity of the human person be linked to an ethos of self-realization? And how, under these new conditions, might people be affectively bound to universalist moral values?

If we take these questions explored by Troeltsch, which he had posed partly in light of the self-critical revision of his own thinking after the First World War, and look back from this vantage point at Ernst Cassirer's development, the first thing that is striking is the enormous difference between the two thinkers' points of departure. In the intense and historically informed debates on modern culture that took place before the war and that are linked with the names of Jacob Burckhardt, Max Weber, Werner Sombart, and Troeltsch, Cassirer had not played a major role. In his writings on Descartes, Leibniz, and Kant, despite all his sensitivity to the history of ideas and history of science, the antihistoricist effort to find certainties beyond history clearly prevailed. These certainties were a Kantian understanding of the moral freedom of the human being, and—with respect to politics—the concepts of republicanism and cosmopolitanism associated with it. Cassirer thus belonged to that rare species in the German professoriate of the time that sympathized with the Enlightenment and the French Revolution, with a value-rational liberalism and the resistance to nationalism.[14] But Cassirer did not propagate these ideals in a militant way; they were implicit in his philosophical writings, which therefore remained rather marginal in public debates in comparison with the dominant tendencies of historicism and nationalism and their alliance. But Cassirer's position already began to change prior to the First World War. He recognized more and more clearly that Kant's epistemology had essentially been informed by the natural sciences and thus could not simply be transferred to the humanities—an insight that brought Cassirer closer to the problematique that had become so decisive to hermeneutics—for example, to Wilhelm Dilthey's oeuvre—namely the construction of the historical world in the humanities. In much the same way as Hannah Arendt decades later with regard to political philosophy, Cassirer first tried to posit such a logic of the humanities while remaining within the framework of Kant's philosophy—which seemed possible if one focused on Kant's *Critique of Judgment*. While Cassirer had barely mentioned Kant's so-called third critique in his interpretation of Kant as set out in the second volume of his history of the problem of knowledge in 1907, almost one-quarter of his 1918 book on Kant was devoted to it.[15] A much richer diversity of human activities came to the fore through this widening of perspective, while the creative character of human action received much more attention than it ever could within the dualism of moral freedom and a pure reason that posits the laws of nature.

But in another connection Cassirer took a considerable step further toward the German historicist-hermeneutical tradition—and it is obvious that he did so under the influence of the First World War. I have in mind his great book *Freiheit und Form*, published in 1916,[16] which first made Cassirer a public figure. This book is a product of the war not only in the trivial sense that Cassirer wrote it when he worked in the German Ministry of Propaganda, analyzing French reportage on the war. The book is also rightly seen by many commentators as an expression of Cassirer's understanding of his patriotic duty to defend the authentic intellectual heritage of Germany against anti-German propaganda, but also against the nationalistic self-misunderstandings in German war-related writings. This authentic heritage was, for Cassirer, a strong cosmopolitan orientation—in line with the principle that it is un-German to be nothing but German (Friedrich Meinecke):

> Even in these days German culture will not allow itself to be diverted from its original course—neither by the distortions and insults of its adversaries nor by a narrow-minded intellectual chauvinism.[17]

Cassirer's book begins with short introductory chapters on the Renaissance concept of personhood in Dante, Montaigne, and Erasmus and on the "religious individualism" of the Reformation, but it is essentially an intellectual history of Germany in a prolonged eighteenth century—from Leibniz to Hegel, with masterful chapters on Leibniz, on eighteenth-century aesthetics, Kant's understanding of freedom, Goethe, Schiller, and the political philosophy of German idealism. Cassirer attempts to identify a fundamental tension in this history—the tension, as the title of the book puts it, between "freedom" and "form." As Cassirer sees it, the pole of freedom is rooted in Luther and Renaissance humanism, while it finds its clearest articulation in Kant's understanding of moral freedom. The other pole, namely "form," thus relates to the question of how, under this condition of individual freedom, order (the sphere of the general) might be possible. Cassirer stresses that he is not seeking to convey this tension through a conceptual scheme imposed on German intellectual history, but to inductively reveal a basic tension that is characteristic of German thought, though not restricted to it—which means that all cultures are familiar with it and that German intellectual history is grappling with a tension of universal relevance. The writings of Kant and Goethe thus appear as unsurpassed attempts to identify a solution; it is, supposedly, merely the tension between these two different attempts that remains for us to resolve. Cassirer's book is clearly a contribution to German identity-exploration and identity-formation; in its homogenizing of national cultural traditions it shares an important feature with wartime publications in general. But it is also a significant philosophical work that goes beyond the framework of neo-Kantianism insofar as Goethe receives the same degree of attention here as Kant, if not more.

How is Cassirer's effort mirrored in Troeltsch's thinking? Among the many book reviews Troeltsch wrote we can find several on Cassirer, starting in 1904.[18] Troeltsch praised Cassirer's first book, the monograph on Leibniz, as an "extraordinarily competent and instructive work," indeed as the true foundation for an adequate understanding of Leibniz. But he also pointed out that Leibniz is interpreted by Cassirer as a precursor of Kant's thought, which—as in the writings of his teacher Hermann Cohen—is presented as "the definitive and only canonical system of philosophy." Troeltsch emphasized that Leibniz had developed his main ideas "in a theological-metaphysical form," whereas Cassirer seemed to assume that he "could break off from them the metaphysical substance without injury to the basic character of Leibnizian thought."[19] Troeltsch, who had himself published a remarkable study on "Leibniz and the beginnings of Pietism" in 1902,[20] defends his own "interpretation of Leibniz from the perspective of the history of theology" as "historically as justified" as Cassirer's interpretation, "rooted in logic and epistemology." But the conclusions of the two interpretations point in opposite directions. Whereas in Cassirer's presentation Leibniz's metaphysics is merely a remnant of a tradition, for Troeltsch it is Leibniz's true concern. Whereas Cassirer, like Kant and the neo-Kantians, is interested in overcoming all substantialist metaphysics, in Troeltsch's interpretation of Leibniz the substantiality of God and of the monad in its devotion to God remains the source of orientation— and for Troeltsch, the theologian, this is inevitable against the background of religious belief. Accordingly, he calls Cassirer's interpretation the "forcible Kantianization of Leibniz,"[21] and he generalizes his reservations into a critique of a Kantian rationalism in general, which, he contends, impedes an adequate view of the "irrational dimension of the substance that is independent of consciousness yet relates to it, that is, above all, the irrational dimension of the concept of God, of an alien consciousness, and [hinders a convincing conception of] the irrational dimension of individuality in its many forms and of the emergence of the new in its many forms."[22] In a condensed formula, here we have four important hints about possible limitations of Kantian thought: the question of God, and the problems of intersubjectivity, plurality, and creativity. In this controversy over the relationship between epistemology and metaphysics in Leibniz we can discern an early sign of the coming controversy between Cassirer and Heidegger about this relationship in Kant.

Cassirer's book *Freiheit und Form* is addressed in several texts by Troeltsch. Two of them are of particular importance here. He published a review of the book in 1917, but he also commented on it at length in his great 1916 speech on education policy: "Humanism and Nationalism in Our Educational System."[23] There is a dangerous temptation to reduce these texts to their political message. When Troeltsch introduces his discussion of Cassirer with the remark that "almost all modern literary and intellectual histories of the German people" use "Classicism and the Renaissance as their self-evident yardstick" and that this approach demonstrates its absurdity in exemplary fashion in Cassirer's work "because its inability to truly grasp German life and to vividly determine the German future, is laid bare here,"[24] then it would be all too easy to read this as a sort of exclusion of the Western-oriented Cassirer from true "Germanness"—as if Cassirer's attempt to determine the specific features of the German history of ideas had prompted Troeltsch to reject his thinking out of hand. But this view is too simplistic, not least because Troeltsch again has a lot of positive things to say about Cassirer's erudition and elegant style. So let's focus on the substantive issues.

Troeltsch first takes issue with the temporal limitations of Cassirer's account. It says nothing about any of the history *before* the Reformation (other than the few remarks that appear in Cassirer's portrait of Luther) or the period *after* Goethe. This isolation of a "good" phase of German history with both ends cut off makes Troeltsch suspicious. He refers to the "deification" of a specific historic moment, a "theology of humanism," and this for him is one of the substitutes produced by the modern mind, which will never attain the heft of the monotheistic religions. It is indeed strange that Cassirer completely ignores the time after Goethe and Hegel and extending up to his own day in *Freiheit und Form*: not a word on Romanticism; the history of political thought in the nineteenth century; the attempts by Marx, Kierkegaard, and Nietzsche to break radically with prevailing beliefs; hermeneutics or

"Lebensphilosophie." But nor does Cassirer's notion that Luther's alleged "autonomous religion of conscience" functioned as a source of support for the Renaissance and was a major hallmark of incipient modernity find Troeltsch's approval. We are confronted by an ironic situation in which the Protestant theologian and historian of Christianity disputes the "modernizing" view of Luther proposed by a Jewish intellectual. Since his first major publication (on Melanchthon), Troeltsch had emphasized the "still fundamentally medieval character of the thinking of the Reformation."[25] Accordingly, he makes a sharp distinction between old and new Protestantism. What he means is the thinking of the Reformation period itself, in which the medieval-Catholic vision of the full-scale Christian penetration of culture remained, and the synthesis of Enlightenment and Protestantism in the eighteenth century, in which the secularization of the state and the ideal of the autonomous development of personhood first took hold. The two centuries in between he thus interprets as a long threshold phase, indeed as the "late blooming of the Middle Ages." Troeltsch expresses this idea in a particularly pointed way when he remarks that Luther himself strongly opposed the abolition of serfdom and points out that the new wave of serfdom among the peasantry of the East Elbian provinces from the sixteenth century onward faced no resistance from Lutheranism, which in fact promoted it.[26] For Troeltsch this contradicts the retrospective illusion of Luther as a harbinger of the Enlightenment.

Religion and Autonomy

But these differences in Troeltsch's and Cassirer's assessments of intellectual history are merely the expression of deeper, systematic differences that had yet to be overcome. There are three of them. First, Troeltsch considers it symptomatic that both in his book on Leibniz and then in his history of German thought, Cassirer underestimates and misinterprets the "importance of the religious element in German intellectual history." "As things stand now in Cassirer's work, the religious dimension essentially appears only as metaphysical background or as a kind of postulate emanating from philosophical-artistic autonomy."[27] One may see this difference as a mere reflection of the difference between theology and philosophy, but when we consider the adequacy of Cassirer's view of Luther or his account of the "religious element" in Leibniz and classical German philosophy we are in fact dealing with serious empirical questions. The second difference concerns the concept of autonomy itself. The relative marginality of religion in Cassirer follows quite logically from the emphasis he places on the concept of autonomy, "particularly if this concept is essentially derived from science and art," as Troeltsch states. But—he continues—"then Luther can hardly be incorporated into such a development." For Luther, he underlines, the unconditional validity of Scripture and not the autonomy of the individual was what really mattered. Here we can see the philosophical significance of what might have looked like Troeltsch's merely historically motivated resistance to Cassirer's view of Luther, resistance that is of course related to the entire question of the "significance of Protestantism to the rise of the modern world." I cannot go into this here. Troeltsch's views seem to fluctuate, or he seems to emphasize different aspects depending on the context.[28] Besides the question of the correct interpretation of the Reformation era, another issue is decisive here: the relationship between "theonomy" and "autonomy." While in the critique of religion, faith is often interpreted as heteronomy, as incomplete or evaded autonomy, modern religious thinkers tend to ask how to facilitate autonomy and interpret faith as a reflexive insight into the divine constitution of autonomy and thus as a means of guarding against human hubris and a fixation on autonomy.[29]

But most important is the third sense in which Troeltsch and Cassirer differ, which is fundamental. This has to do with their views of the alternative to the ideal of autonomy that Cassirer declares his key paradigm and that is supposedly rooted in the Renaissance and Reformation. Just how much their notion of this alternative differed is strikingly evident in their views of the Middle Ages. In a view informed by the Renaissance, Cassirer inevitably perceives the Middle Ages as an era of "self-imposed immaturity." For Troeltsch, meanwhile, the Middle Ages are not a time of indissoluble ties, but of "infinitely individualized freedom," by which he was probably attempting to highlight their lower degree of social disciplining. As Troeltsch sees it, modern freedom, including expressive freedom, is present here in seminal form, which is not the same as moral freedom in the Kantian sense. Due to this difference, Cassirer's title *Freedom and Form* led Troeltsch to expect things the author never intended: "One would think," writes Troeltsch, "that his fundamental question must be how the impetuously irrational imaginative drive of Gothic man that we have inherited from the Middle Ages can find form and shape amid the needs and fortunes of recent history, this tragic history of the German struggle for redemption from formlessness ever since its Gothic form was shattered and an alien principle of form imposed on it."[30]

But, Troeltsch underlines, Cassirer says nothing at all about this. Troeltsch's vocabulary must surely sound odd today; it is certainly imbued with an ethnic essentialism when he ascribes to the Germans a near-untamable vigor, one that cannot, in any case, be accommodated within Latin-Roman forms. But the problematic aspects of this notion of the "Gothic" character of the Germans should not blind us to the fact that Troeltsch introduces a motif here that has played a crucial role in German thought since Herder and at the very latest since the Romantics. Following Isaiah Berlin and Charles Taylor, we might call it "expressivism," an expressivist anthropological model of human action, and consequently, of "freedom" and "form." Troeltsch himself refers to Hamann and Herder, Goethe and Jean Paul, but also to German "ideals of social life," religiosity and art. If my translation of Troeltsch's language into the contemporary philosophical idiom is justified, then there is indeed a problem with Cassirer's understanding of "form." It cannot be accused of being one-sidedly Kantian in the sense of the conception of autonomy inherent in Kant's pure and practical reason. Such an accusation would fall flat given Cassirer's subtle grasp of "the discovery of the aesthetic world of form" in Hamann, Herder, and Winckelmann and the way he takes his lead from Goethe and Schiller, the interpretation of whom takes up most of *Freiheit und Form*. But both the "general form of reason" and the particular "aesthetic form" that reshapes the former are, according to Troeltsch, treated by Cassirer only as "general matters of formative reason." Troeltsch recognizes that Cassirer takes account of their specific fate in Germany, but underlines that he fails to consider how these forms are filled with "the substance of German life," restricting his analysis to "humanity in all its generality."[31] Translated into today's language, Troeltsch's critique can perhaps be rephrased as follows: Cassirer's integration of the expressive dimension leads him beyond the formalism of Kantian moral philosophy, but he fails to take it as far as Troeltsch believes necessary. This is because Cassirer sees the formation of the expressive dimension as relating to a structure that is conceptualized as universal in the same sense as cognitive and normative validity claims. Troeltsch, however, indicates that for him the addition of the expressive dimension does not simply add another universal problem with its own particular structure but that here the relationship between form and content is fundamentally different. We can understand what he means if we consider the fact that "values" are connected with "identities" in different ways than cognitive and normative validity claims. This means that when it comes to values, genesis and validity are less amenable to separation. We have a confrontation between two ways of thinking here. While Cassirer can only view the history of a nation as the contingent genesis of universal validity, Troeltsch uses the inseparability of genesis and validity when it comes to values to argue against the potential universality of their validity. At least at this point in their intellectual development, then, both fail to achieve the level of reflection at which it becomes clear that even universalist values can only have specific and particular forms of expression.

But as my summary of Troeltsch's 1922 lecture showed, this story does not end here. The thinking of both philosophers developed with tremendous vigor after the war, and they published the texts we now consider their magna opera. In the 1920s, Cassirer brought out in rapid succession the three volumes of his great *Philosophy of Symbolic Forms*, which not only made a major contribution to the philosophy of language, philosophy of religion, and epistemology, but also took a big step toward "detranscendentalization" and thus hermeneutics. Jürgen Habermas aptly characterized the inner logic of this move in his 1995 speech on Cassirer. We must bear in mind

> that the semiotic turn not only does away with the reference point of an objective world, but also the transcendental subject beyond the world. As soon as the transcendental operations are transferred to different systems of symbols, then the transcendental subject loses its place beyond the empirical world. It loses its pure intelligibility and autonomy. It is drawn, along with its symbolic embodiments, into the process of history and fragmented into a pluralism of languages and cultures.[32]

Of course, Cassirer was by no means in favor of the relativism that the semiotic turn threatened to usher in. But it was entirely unclear in his book how he might avert this risk, whether, for example, the various symbolic forms ought to constitute a narrative of progress and on what the requisite normative judgments should be founded. Ernst Troeltsch, meanwhile, published his magnum opus *Historicism and Its Problems* in 1922. Here he tried to overcome the problems of relativism inherent in the German historicist-hermeneutic tradition, which he recognized more clearly than any other proponent of that approach. He intended to show that historicism itself could provide a new route to universalist values. As Troeltsch envisaged it, this book was to be the first of two volumes. It is first and foremost a preparatory, methodical reflection on the essence of the problems at hand. His sudden death prevented him from writing the second volume, which was to present his solution. As sources indicating how his thinking might have developed and the kind of answer he had in mind, we have only the essays that were published posthumously under the title *Christian Thought: Its History and Application*[33]—apart from the final chapters of the first volume, his speech on natural law, and his many substantial studies on European intellectual history, which also appeared posthumously as the fourth volume of his *Collected Writings*.[34] As it happens, in 1921, in a review of the third volume of Cassirer's *Das Erkenntnisproblem in der Philosophie und Wissenschaft der Neueren Zeit* ("The Problem of Knowledge in the Philosophy and Science of the Modern Era"), which had been published shortly before, Troeltsch described the first volume of his series on historicism as a conscious "though much more modest counterpart" to Cassirer's book.[35] Politically, in the few years granted to him after the end of the war, Troeltsch increasingly grew into the role of leading German political intellectual, one who both held political offices and did all he could to help bring about an intellectual reorientation, a complete rethinking of "the entire historical, political, and ethical world characteristic of the imperialist, unboundedly capitalist and nationalist period [that has held sway] until now."[36] Again, I cannot trace every aspect of the relationship between Troeltsch's and Cassirer's intellectual development during this period. I restrict myself to an exemplary study of their views of the crucial topic of human rights, their history, and their underlying rationale, while also probing the role of religion in their ideas.

With regard to Troeltsch, there is no need to belabor the relevance of this comparison. I began this chapter by highlighting his plea for a novel incorporation of human rights into the "expressivist" tradition. But Cassirer, too, foregrounds time and again the problem of human rights in key passages of his writings. This is true even of *Freiheit und Form*, but especially of his *Philosophy of the Enlightenment* and his last book, *The Myth of the State*. The most explicit presentation of his thinking on this subject—which changes only slightly over the years—is to be found in his speech "The Idea of a Republican Constitution" of 1928.[37] Here, Cassirer begins by observing that Kant's main writings were published not long before the French Declaration of the Rights of Man and of the Citizen (August 26, 1789). Cassirer asks whether this chronological proximity is mere coincidence or has a deeper significance. This, of course, should not be misunderstood as a question about Kant's biography or about Kant's (nonexistent) influence on the French revolutionaries. The question Cassirer had in mind was "whether and if so to what extent the fundamental intellectual tendency characteristic of Kant's theoretical philosophy and his ethics converges with those tendencies that gave rise to the revolutionary movement in France."[38] But this question

> cannot be answered as long as we simply juxtapose the "revolution of thinking" that Kant achieved in philosophy and the great political transformation. We must go back to the sources [of both] to find the true point of confluence.[39]

To this end, Cassirer describes the French Revolution as mostly driven by ideology—a view that has long been shared by many, but that is deeply in dispute today. Nevertheless, Cassirer recognizes that Rousseau cannot have been the originator of the ideology underlying the Revolution, at least not this aspect of it. Since Rousseau's theory of the social contract contained the assumption that individuals completely renounce their original rights as soon as they enter into the contract, it cannot have been the source of the idea of *inalienable* individual rights. Cassirer relies here on the research of Georg Jellinek, the great legal historian and a close friend of Troeltsch. The above insight into Rousseau prompts Jellinek and Troeltsch to deny any French primacy in the history of human rights. They instead contend that this concept originated with the leaders and declarations of the newly independent North American states (Virginia, Pennsylvania, and so on). They view the demand for religious freedom as the first historical form of a sacred, that is, inviolable and inalienable subjective right.[40] Cassirer, meanwhile, offers a new and surprising historical explanation of his own making. For him, as the leading authority on this thinker, none other than Leibniz was "the first among the great European thinkers to emphatically and resolutely assert the principle of inalienable basic rights of the individual, both in the foundation of his ethics and in his political and legal philosophy."[41] Leibniz, Cassirer states, could draw inspiration from Stoicism and Hugo Grotius, but it was in Leibniz's work that these motifs found "a firm and determinate form":

> He does not create the *substance* of this idea, for this was already present as the heritage of ancient, particularly Stoic philosophy and ethics. But the new form that this idea now took on, the systematic formulation and *foundation* that it received, made it effective in a new way that radiated throughout the intellectual universe.[42]

Cassirer goes so far as to construct a line of influence running from Leibniz to the systematization of his insights by German Enlightenment philosopher Christian Wolff, then to the reception of Wolff's writings by English legal theorist William Blackstone, the American declarations, and finally—through the role of the latter as a model for France—to the declaration of 1789. I will not discuss here whether this hypothesis of influence constructed by Cassirer is historically correct. Suffice it to say that it has never played a major role in the historiography of human rights. But the political message of his construction is absolutely clear, and Cassirer minces no words:

> What I wanted to bring home to you is that the idea of a republican constitution as such is by no means foreign to German intellectual history as a whole, let alone an external intrusion into it. This idea in fact grew in German soil and was nourished by its own inherent forces, namely those of idealist philosophy.[43]

But this political message also has a philosophical side. By putting so much emphasis on Leibniz's alleged authorship and Kant's unshakeable "reason-based" belief in the idea of a republican constitution, he protects this idea from defilement by the concrete history of the revolution and from Jellinek's and Troeltsch's claim that religious motives—rather than a "faith of reason"—stood at the beginning of the history of human rights. This also comes across in Cassirer's other texts from the same period. His 1931 essay "Germany and Western Europe in the Mirror of Intellectual History"[44] appears, in its typology of cultures, similar to Troeltsch's numerous older studies on this subject. But as if in response to Troeltsch's earlier criticisms, Cassirer now describes the religious understanding of inwardness as characteristic of Germany. Luther—in contrast to Erasmus—is now characterized as the implacable advocate of the thesis of the "unfree will" and divine omnipotence. This requires that Kant be defined in contrast to Luther. Kant's "autonomy of practical reason"—according to Cassirer—

> no longer recognizes any absolute metaphysical power that might cause it to founder, in light of which it might shatter or come to grief. For now even the divine being has lost this sort of omnipotence. Even the latter is subject to the "Copernican turn." Instead of assuming the being of God as dogmatic certainty and posing the question of human freedom on that basis, Kant takes the inverse route. He starts with freedom; he sees in it the only

possible means of access, and gateway, to the realm of intelligible being. Although God is seen as the centerpiece of this intelligible being, he too is subject to the condition posited in the pure idea of freedom. Hence, the moral idea of freedom no longer breaks down due to the basic religious claim of the will's total dependence on God. Instead, conversely, religious certainty, the certainty of God, is now founded on the certainty of freedom and moral self-legislation.[45]

Once again, then, Cassirer declares Kant the culmination of German intellectual history, and not just the German variety. In 1931 (!) Cassirer even manages to describe European intellectual history—following Goethe—as a grand fugue in which powerful dynamic tensions always ultimately find resolution in harmony. But the strongest expression of Cassirer's tendency to evoke harmony, especially under conditions that most seem to contradict it, is his book on the Enlightenment.[46] When this book came out in English in the 1950s, it was characterized as overly harmonizing by none other than Isaiah Berlin, a man under no suspicion of antiliberal or anti-Western views. All great thinkers of the eighteenth century are presented in Cassirer's book "as a band of happy fellow workers" among whom there are no major conflicts. Meanwhile, Cassirer ignores completely all the undercurrents of, and countercurrents to, the Enlightenment, which led to its rapid demise. A mechanism appears to be at work here that has been brought out by Stephen Toulmin with regard to the rationalism of Descartes and the Vienna Circle: in all these cases, the valorization of rationality emerges not out of a culture in which it is clearly at work, but out of historical phases in which some thinkers, despairing at the irresolvable conflicts around them, find a source of support and consolation in a hypostasized reason.[47] In Cassirer's case, this led to an idealizing return to an era—the Enlightenment—in which his ideals were (allegedly) beyond dispute.

No other contemporary scholar is quoted in Cassirer's book as often as Troeltsch. With regard to the relationship between Protestantism and the Enlightenment and between Christian and modern natural law, Cassirer now relies completely on Troeltsch and accepts his conclusions. This does not apply to the Enlightenment itself, which appears much more tension-ridden and unstable in Troeltsch's work. It seems that Cassirer went a decisive step further only in the very last phase of his life. His last book (*The Myth of the State*) dealt with the conscious manipulative use of myths in modern totalitarianism. In one of his last texts, what Cassirer invokes in opposition to this totalitarianism is not the Enlightenment, but monotheism as established by the Jews.[48]

Cassirer might have moved once again toward Troeltsch in this regard. We do not know how the latter would have reacted to the temporary victory of totalitarianism, and there is no point speculating about it. Rather than continuing to write the history of the dialogue between Cassirer and Troeltsch on the basis of guesswork, I would now like to summarize what we today can learn from this partly real, partly fictitious dialogue in political as well as philosophical terms. I have juxtaposed two German thinkers, both of them admirable in their sweeping erudition and in the potency of their concepts. We have traced their dialogue, which repeatedly conveys the impression of a convergence that never ultimately occurred. What is the remaining difference between them, and what does it mean for us today?

I believe that Cassirer, whose work started out rooted in Kant, went further than any other German thinker toward the semiotic transformation of transcendental philosophy. In order to avoid the relativist risks of this transformation, however, he clung to a strictly Kantian position with respect to normative questions. Kant's postulate of moral freedom remained for him the benchmark for all normative questions. That is why he could write the history of ideas up to and including Kant as a history of progress. For him, after Kant the insight into the moral freedom of human beings could be blurred, forgotten, or attacked—but this was merely the historical fate of truth, leaving its core unaffected. Even religion, for him, could only be justified on the basis of this postulate of freedom. Its role was limited to strengthening the motivation to act morally.

Messianic Rationalism?

Troeltsch was skeptical about all these ideas centered on what he would have called "messianic rationalism."[49] For him, the Enlightenment era was not the high point of intellectual history, where philosophical thinking comes into its own, but merely a period of transition between the unquestioned validity of Christianity and the incipient historical and cultural relativization of all certainties, a period of the "denial or at least limitation of the historical dimension through rational construction," a "final dam holding back the emerging historical consciousness yet reluctantly adapting to it in manifold ways."[50] On this view, the progressive historicization and psychologization of every sphere of life is a continuation of the Enlightenment but one that is now washing over even this final dam. Kant's rationalism is in Troeltsch's perspective a "secularized echo of religious absolutism."[51] What it can produce, Troeltsch believed, is always restricted to what can be deduced from the formal character of the "ought." This, he underscored, should not be underestimated, insofar as it does in fact entail universal traits of what Troeltsch calls a "morality of conscience." But "a substantive system of reason-based values as the yardstick and guiding thread of historical life"[52] has proved impossible to establish on this foundation. For Troeltsch, from a historically informed perspective, every notion of "natural rights" ultimately melts away:

> The so-called natural standards are in no way more firmly fixed than the standards we call supernatural; and all attempts to fix the one from the side of the other are illusory, from whichever side we may care to start our labor.[53]

For Troeltsch, then, any attempt to found religion in moral philosophy is doomed to failure. Such an endeavor would mean placing a further postulate on top of what is no more than the postulate of moral freedom. In this way, as Troeltsch saw it, Kant could achieve a "mere analogon of religion" rather than lived religion; Kant's religion is "never more than human reasoning and postulate-making, a theoretical complement to the moral order of a world that is the only one that can be experienced without mediation; it is not the lived experience of communion with God."[54] In contrast to Cassirer, lived religion is front and center in Troeltsch's theory of religion.

Troeltsch, then, had to proceed in a different way than Cassirer. His treatment of the history of ideas had to be much more sociological. In line with this, his analysis of the "German idea of freedom" had to investigate economic, political, social, and military conditions in an attempt to explain the specificities of German intellectual history, while carefully identifying what constituted German backwardness that had to be overcome and what might be a potential form of superiority that might even be attractive to others.[55] At a crucial point, Troeltsch had to go beyond the limitations of Kantian transcendental philosophy, even in the form it had taken on through Cassirer's semiotic transformation.

This decisive point arises from Troeltsch's understanding of religion. As I mentioned, for him religion is not deducible from the postulate of moral freedom. According to Troeltsch and many other great philosophers of religion from Schleiermacher to William James, the experience of vibrant communion with the divine is characterized by a sense of being "seized," of being overwhelmed, a feeling of self-surrender. Troeltsch expressed doubts early on about whether such self-surrender can even be grasped within a framework oriented toward subjects ordering whatever happens to be in their consciousness at a given moment. "Here, the fundamental presupposition of religion, that a finite being can experience its seizure by an infinite power in the mode of self-surrender or shuddering awe, is utterly meaningless and redundant."[56]

Although he respected Kant's achievement of having stressed the subjective component in the structuring of reality and thus strictly limited the potential for assertions about transsubjective reality, Troeltsch also emphasized that "human consciousness is only a small particle of an immeasurable reality that produces and nourishes it."[57] And for Troeltsch this reality is that of human action in the world, action from which there must be no dogmatic exclusion of action vis-à-vis the divine and the experience of an encounter with the divine. We might call this the pragmatic transformation of transcendental philosophy. It supersedes a dualistic anthropology, modifies the "empirical-phenomenal notion of causality" in Kant, and is thus "geared toward the penetration [of consciousness] by powers of a different kind that act upon it." It is this step that, according to Troeltsch,

> pulls the rug from under the attempt of the Marburg Kantian School [from which Cassirer emerged] to grasp critical thinking and thus philosophy as the scholarly production of a law-governed unity that is universally valid and, therefore, the first truly real instantiation of such a unity, an idea bound up with the reduction of religion to the notion of reason characteristic of the law-governed unity of the world that is generated by the progress of thought.[58]

Here, then, we find a marked difference rather than convergence between the two thinkers. This is because Cassirer's admirable semiotic transformation of transcendental philosophy was insufficiently pragmatic. Both transformations are necessary, but they are not identical. When Cassirer calls the symbolic forms "autonomous creations of mind," as Matthias Jung has convincingly argued,[59] the transcendental philosopher in Cassirer once again gains the upper hand over the hermeneuticist. Rather than positing "the mind," we have to accept that there is an irreducible plurality of individuals who create meaning through singular acts, which are inevitably situated, in contingent ways. And this meaning is always connected with action. We cannot do justice to religion in all its plurality if we interpret it—like myth—as an ultimately unitary symbolic form.[60]

This difference between Cassirer and Troeltsch should not be reduced to that between faith and absence of faith. Such a theological (or antitheological) reductionism would be as misguided as the merely political interpretation of other differences between Cassirer and Troeltsch. When Troeltsch refers to the "religious *apriori*," it may sound as if he is arbitrarily putting forward the anthropological postulate that religious faith is an inevitable part of the human condition. In fact the opposite is true: Troeltsch developed this concept because he wanted to avoid the mere postulate of freedom. He wanted to replace this postulate in the philosophy of Kant and the Kantians in its systematic function with the experiences of (self-)transcendence and "the irrationality of creative action,"[61] the experience of one's own ability to be free. If this operation he has in mind is successful, the difference between this project and rationalism can be redefined. Then we would no longer consider religion to be a mere addition to the rational foundation of morality through nonrational sources of motivation. We would recognize that rationalism is itself a faith.

> That in which one finds values, goods, welfare, or progress can never be rationally justified and enforced. Even the mere affirmation of an "ought," which by no means exhausts the world of values, is nothing that is rationally enforceable, but rather a recognition and a faith.[62]

On this premise, the validity of universalist norms also depends on specific values; the history of human rights depends on the history of social movements, the commitment to values, and the experiences of violence and liberation; the justification of values depends on narration; and the semiotic transformation of transcendental philosophy depends on breaking with its concept of the subject by bringing in experiences of self-transcendence, whether they are articulated in religious or nonreligious ways.[63]

III, 3
Indebted Freedom: Paul Tillich

In 2008, the Max Weber Centre for Advanced Cultural and Social Studies in Erfurt, of which I was director at the time, awarded an honorary doctorate to Robert N. Bellah of the University of California, Berkeley, perhaps the greatest historically oriented sociologist of religion to emerge in the second half of the twentieth century. In preparing my laudatory speech, I tried to come up with a pithy phrase that would bring out the special features of Bellah's theoretical and methodological approach to the universal history of religion, even to those barely familiar with his oeuvre. The formula I settled on was that his work represents "the synthesis of Talcott Parsons and Paul Tillich."[1]

In the 1950s, Parsons the sociologist was regarded worldwide as the leading theoretical mind in his subject, while during the same period the Protestant theologian Tillich (1886–1965), originally from Germany—after some initial difficulties in American exile—rose to become one of the most influential representatives of his discipline and one of the leading public intellectuals in the United States.[2] That the core conceptual impulses of these two prominent thinkers could be fused was by no means obvious.

Following the celebrations marking the award of his honorary doctorate, Robert Bellah told me he approved of the formula I had chosen and stated, to my relief, that he could easily recognize himself in it. Both Parsons and Tillich, he explained, had influenced him as his academic teachers at Harvard in the late 1950s. However, it turned out that I was not the first to come up with this form of words; that distinction, Bellah revealed, belonged to Barrington Moore, a Marxian sociologist and social historian who also taught at Harvard. For him, however, Parsons was the epitome of bourgeois sociology, an academic variant of the conformist consensus in the United States after the Second World War, while Tillich, as a theologian, could not be taken seriously as interlocutor in any case. "The synthesis of Parsons and Tillich": what Moore meant as a scathing put-down, I had uttered as an expression of the highest recognition.

Under the Spell of Freedom. Hans Joas, Oxford University Press. © Oxford University Press 2024.
DOI: 10.1093/oso/9780197642153.003.0013

I will come back to the exact meaning of this accolade later. In the first instance, it helps me elucidate the specific perspective on Tillich's work that informs my argument at this point. What does Tillich's theology look like if it is not only embedded in the history of theology (and perhaps even philosophy) but is also related to the history of the social sciences? The history of theology and that of sociology are hardly ever linked, although developments in the two subjects feature many interdependencies. This is mainly due to sociologists' sweeping and sometimes aggressive ignorance of theology; in some disciplinary histories, the overcoming of religion, religious thought, or theological influences is celebrated straightforwardly as progress. Against this background, four topics seem to me to be central to a present-day perspective on Tillich: (1) his understanding of time and history; (2) his theory of signs or symbols; (3) his reflections on the relationship between religious traditions, primarily Protestant and Catholic Christianity; and (4) his conception of the conditions constitutive of human freedom.

Before I begin my run through these subject areas, an additional complication needs to be mentioned. We cannot be concerned solely with the effect of Tillich's theology on the social sciences, as Tillich himself had already taken up crucial impulses from sociology and, above all, was influenced by a theological teacher who, during his lifetime and in early retrospectives on the genesis of German sociology, was himself cited as a leading sociologist: Ernst Troeltsch. Troeltsch himself saw at least his gigantic volume *The Social Teachings of the Christian Churches and Groups* (to give the literal translation of the German title of the book) as a radical sociologization of church historiography of a kind that had not previously been attempted.[3] While this book managed to make some impact on sociology here and there, Troeltsch's other writings, most of which are not even available in English translation, have been completely overshadowed by the great Max Weber or have remained completely unknown. Paul Tillich can thus also be seen as an intermediary between German historical sociology of religion from the beginning of the twentieth century and its US-American counterpart from the early twenty-first century, in other words as a bridge between Troeltsch and Bellah. In addition to the question of what sociology and theory of religion learned from Tillich in these four subject areas, the task is thus to uncover to what extent Tillich succeeded in going beyond Troeltsch or merely introduced his insights and advances into US discourse.

Kairos

Let's start with Tillich's understanding of time and history. He coined one of the most important catchwords in twentieth-century theological debates by declaring *kairos* a key term, one he first mentioned in 1922:

> *Kairos* means "fulfilled time," the concrete historical moment and in the prophetic sense "fullness of time," the breaking into time of the eternal. *Kairos* is therefore not the moment filled in whatever way, the ever-changing slice of the course of time, but is in fact time itself, insofar as that which is absolutely meaningful is fulfilled within it, insofar as it is destiny. To regard a time as *kairos* is to see it as entailing an inescapable decision, an unavoidable responsibility; it is to behold it in the spirit of prophecy.[4]

Tillich traced the term *kairos* back to ancient Greek philosophy, the Gospel of Mark (Mark 1:15), and the Apostle Paul (2 Corinthians 6:2); but even before Tillich's appropriation, thanks to the circle around Stefan George it had become a virtual buzzword in German intellectual and artistic circles. The emphasis on the fateful moment, which, as discontinuous, differs from the continuity of passing time, a moment in which one's own decision essentially determines what the future brings, in which meaningfulness is not the product of reflection but comes about through prereflective certainty—these elements of the *kairos* concept captured with great intuitive certitude and suggestive force the attitude to life typical of contemporaries who had experienced the First World War and the postwar period as a break with all that was traditional, as an era that imposed existential risks and a pressure to make decisions and show resolve.

Hence, parallels with Tillich's ideas about *kairos* in the work of other thinkers, particularly those on the intellectual right during the Weimar Republic (Ernst Jünger, Carl Schmitt, and Martin Heidegger), have often been pointed out.[5] And the essence of the important idea of the "demonic" in Tillich's work is also found, for example, in the writings of Rudolf Otto and in the George circle. This notion serves to prevent any moralistic narrowing of the dynamism of the "creative depth of every moment,"[6] that is, it allows for the diversity of human impulses and highlights the possibility that a decision may be made against God or against the good.

The ideas of the theologian Tillich differ from the various forms of decisionist or voluntarist thinking about the "present" as the key to understanding time and history common on the political right in that he foregrounds the passive or receptive aspect. His reference to the "prophetic" dimension serves to relate the moment of decision to something that is granted to the recipient at that moment, something they decide to do only insofar as they open or surrender themself to it and are prepared to act according to the instruction received. In Tillich's conception of *kairos*, then, the true subject of the event is not the resolute human being, but God, who reveals himself to human beings through his grace. Opening oneself to the "breakthrough" of the event of revelation—this is what Tillich has in mind in his pathos-laden conception of *kairos*.

Time and again, history-of-theology studies on Tillich in the Weimar era have placed his work, with good reason, in the context of the "antihistorical" or "antihistoricist" revolution[7] in the German Protestant theology of the time. In this context, Tillich's relationship with Troeltsch is crucially important. Several excellent studies are available on the subject,[8] and they clearly show what we can already gather from Troeltsch's and Tillich's primary texts: it would be grossly misleading to paint a picture of polarization in which the historicism embodied by Troeltsch was supplanted by an understanding of time and history focused on existence and the present in Tillich's work. Tillich himself was well aware of this. In his 1924 review of Troeltsch's book *Der Historismus und seine Probleme*, he refers to the historical consciousness of young people as a "consciousness of standing in history, of being responsible for history to come and thus of having to look back on past history while interpreting it and endowing it with meaning."[9]

Although Tillich too refers to a "crisis of historicism" in this context, in no way does he suggest that this new historical consciousness among the young is opposed to that of Troeltsch; on the contrary, he explicitly attributes to Troeltsch the view that the crisis of the present has provided "new impetus [to tackle] the key problems in philosophy of history."[10] Yet he says nothing about the fact that Troeltsch himself mentioned him and the *kairos* idea in the reviewed text, in a brief footnote probably inserted immediately before going to press—namely when Troeltsch states that in this earthly life, at every moment, "the task arises anew to form the coming history out of the past."[11] Troeltsch refers to Tillich in such a way that his notion of *kairos* appears explicitly as a realization of the very idea he is advocating.

The difference between him and Tillich, then, at least from Troeltsch's perspective, did not lie in Tillich's emphasis on the present as the situation in which pasts are reconstructed and futures anticipated, but in the substantive definition of the historical moment. Tillich wanted (in Troeltsch's words) "to justify a religiously imbued socialism as a demand of *kairos* and not as one of dialectics or natural law."[12] As I understand it, Troeltsch shares with Tillich a distance from dialectical materialism as well as from an ahistorical–natural law justification of socialism; here, then, Troeltsch differs from Tillich only in his simultaneous distance from all forms of socialism. Eduard Spranger's posthumous characterization of Troeltsch's historical thinking as "existential historicism" fits this interpretation.[13] Troeltsch had of course already grappled with Kierkegaard and his notion of the "leap." Without completely rejecting it, he suggested that this idea overstates the indisputable element of decision and risk that always comes into play when actors have the will "to form their own ideals in a responsible way"[14] and thus consciously commit to values whose claim to validity is experienced as subjectively self-evident.

Here, then, it is certainly not historicism and existential ideas that are presented as polar opposites, but rather a historicism (which is given an existential turn in Troeltsch's work even after the teleological-idealist remnants have been cleared away) and a notion of *kairos* that emphasizes—more forcefully but also more one-sidedly—the existential relevance of all historical reconstructions. Tillich himself presented this, however, not as merely a new emphasis, but as a way out that Troeltsch had sought in vain.

This way out was called "overcoming historicism." It seems obvious that there is a need to question this recurring form of words, which was unfortunately even chosen as the title of Troeltsch's "lectures for England and Scotland" by the editors of the associated volume after his death;[15] its exact meaning must at least be clarified. Troeltsch certainly never wanted to overcome historicism in the sense of a radical insight into the historicity of all human phenomena; it seemed to him an indispensable perspective that it was crucial to uphold. For him, the only version of historicism to be overcome was what we might describe as a relativism with regard to all ideals and norms or a relativism that implies an impotence of judgment. His late magnum opus was dedicated to overcoming this phenomenon, and my contention is that it succeeded.[16]

Tillich, conversely, consistently presented Troeltsch as a thinker who, however great and deserving of admiration, was entangled in irresolvable aporias and was thus a tragic failure.[17] Due to his great influence in the United States, he did much to consolidate this idea.[18] As Tillich saw it, Troeltsch had stopped just when the decisive step had to be taken, namely beyond human phenomena into the sphere of divine action. Troeltsch, he believed, was incapable of understanding the divine not only as the "ground and purpose of cultural life" but as a "breakthrough through cultural life."[19]

One might understand Tillich's objection to Troeltsch here as reflecting a contrast between a stronger and weaker faith, between a theology that reduces revelation to a phenomenon of cultural history and one that takes the divine character of revelation seriously as an incursion into cultural history. Outside of theology, however, this difference would be of little interest. Anyone who does not believe in a revelation or at least feels obliged to disregard revelations methodologically in their scholarly work will take a skeptical view of Troeltsch's willingness to allow for divine revelations as phenomena of cultural history, while perceiving Tillich's objections to Troeltsch as nothing less than a regression from historicism into theological dogmatism.

At this point it might be helpful to look beyond theology and beyond Germany. Tillich's notion of *kairos* and the broader reception of the philosophy of existence were by no means the only forms of "presentism" in the understanding of time and history during this era. Such a way of thinking had also developed on the other side of the Atlantic, beginning as early as the nineteenth century, but becoming more radical, especially after the shattering experience of the First World War. The first element crucial to this new perspective was Darwin's theory of evolution, which impelled a break with all teleological philosophy of history. In contrast to the popular reception of Darwin, the leading thinkers here did not derive an evolutionism from the theory of evolution. On the contrary, they rejected the idea that the laws of organic evolution lead to a predictable, higher form of development in a definable direction.

The associated ideas took their most mature form in a book by George Herbert Mead, which appeared in 1932, a year after his death, under the title *The Philosophy of the Present*.[20] The title is a play on words as it initially sounds like a mere overview of the situation of philosophy around 1930, but then it becomes clear that the book in fact puts forward a dual critique of teleology and evolutionism. Here teleological historical thinking is classified as the "philosophy of the future" because it can only conceive of the present as a stage in a process that moves through it and whose utopian or apocalyptic endpoint is fixed. Evolutionism as faith in progress, meanwhile, Mead tells us, is the "philosophy of the past," since here the present necessarily appears as the mere effect of past causes.

Mead contrasts both variants with a radical presentism, which he goes on to develop further in connection with the rival philosophical interpretations of Einstein's theory of relativity. I am unable to delve further into this here. I just want to add that Robert Bellah, although he does not base himself directly on these studies by Mead, calls his project of a universal history of religion "religion in human evolution" rather than using the title of his earlier, famous essay "Religious Evolution."[21] This modified title was intended to avoid any appearance that he was putting forward an evolutionist understanding of the history of religion of the kind commonly found in the nineteenth century; his goal was instead to embed the history of religion in the cultural and natural history of humankind without teleological (or evolutionist) assumptions.

This brief aside will have made it clear that we can only understand Tillich's *kairos* idea in connection with the broader turn to "presentism" in the philosophy of history.[22] This turn began decades before the First World War—as Tillich concedes time and again.[23] It is already evident in Nietzsche's polemic in the second of his *Untimely Meditations* ("On the Uses and Disadvantages of History for Life") and in the philosophy of time developed by Henri Bergson and William James. While this shift was intensified and radicalized by the experience of war, it was not wholly inspired by it, though this wartime experience was to some extent stylized later as a means of reinforcing the plausibility of an intellectual change that was already underway.[24] This also explains the relative continuity between the late Troeltsch and the early Tillich. But what, in this respect, did Tillich's embrace of the *kairos* idea achieve?

Certainly less than Tillich would have liked. On the negative side, one could argue that Tillich's prophetic gesture risks becoming an empty one. Here, of course, everything depends on the plausibility of his vision being fleshed out through the postulate of "religious socialism." For me, "religious socialism" is more clearly recognizable in a negative than positive sense. It is clear what from this perspective must be overcome, namely mammonism and militarism, but we are furnished with no sophisticated program of political and economic change, nor with an empirically substantial analysis of proletarian living conditions or forms of consciousness. If the proletariat is primarily ascribed a "power to shape the future,"[25] this is surely correct in that ideas about the future play a major role in the organized labor movement. It is also an existential fact that people are future-oriented and, if their sense of a future is threatened—for example, by fear of death—they can barely cope with their present. But this does not mean that people, including proletarians and the terminally ill, live in the future. They live in their particular present. Although Tillich himself accused dialectical theologians of making empty prophetic gestures and thus of "disempowering"[26] critique, I am tempted to suggest that he himself indulged in a kind of meta-prophecy, proclaiming the prophetic as such rather than specific commandments or guiding principles.

As has frequently been observed, for Tillich the prospect of "religious socialism" plays the same role as did the European cultural synthesis for Troeltsch.[27] And it is remarkable that Tillich's criticism of Troeltsch here does not pillory his limitation to Europe, but in fact perpetuates it. During this period, both had in common a broad ignorance of the non-European world and, above all, of the effects of the "subjugation of the world" by Europe, on the Continent itself and outside it.[28] There can be very little justification for this limitation, either in Troeltsch's program of "universal history" or in Tillich's "socialist" perspective. From an empirical point of view, with regard to his understanding of history, Tillich seems to have taken a step backward compared to what had already been achieved above all by Max Weber, but even by Troeltsch. If one wanted to give these limitations a positive spin, one might say that a conception of "religious socialism" based primarily on a "total experience of negativity"[29] is apt to reinforce awareness of the role of such experiences in history.

It is indeed the case that revolutionary changes are often not initiated and propelled chiefly by clearly thought-out ideals. At the very least, the unification of different groups of actors is easier to achieve on a negative than a positive basis. But even more important, it seems to me, is an idea put forward by Tillich that appears in the *kairos* studies but is properly elaborated elsewhere, namely where he delves deeply into the dynamics of religious belief.[30] This idea bridges the gap between the theory of time and the conception of faith in Tillich's work. As he puts it, "If any present has meaning it has eternity."[31] Here, the meaning-saturated moment is not thought of, in line with a "positivism of revelation," as a simple incursion of the divine into the earthly. To the contrary, viewed in this light every experience of a meaning-saturated present creates a belief in something that, through this experience, emerges as unconditionally good (or bad) and—because of its unconditionality—timeless. This is a step toward a conception of the experience of unconditional meaning that, phenomenologically or psychologically, goes far beyond what we find in Troeltsch's analyses of processes of ideal formation and prefigures Tillich's later books, inspired by depth psychology.[32]

Sign and Symbol

In Tillich's symbol theory, to which I now turn, we are in fact presented with an important step beyond Troeltsch, which is of key importance to the history of Tillich's impact on sociology and theory of religion. While the roots of Troeltsch's work lay in the grand German hermeneutic tradition of the nineteenth century, like many of its representatives he remained transfixed by methodological questions when interpreting canonical texts and largely ignored the phenomena of everyday human understanding. It should be emphasized, however, that at the end of his great work on historicism, in the section on "history and epistemology," he advanced to the insight that the "knowledge of other minds," which is fundamental to historical understanding, cannot be gained through pure intuition, but necessarily remains bound to "ordinary or inferred sensory mediations."[33] Translated into today's philosophical language, this means that human intersubjectivity is necessarily symbolically mediated and that the methods of historical scholarship are based on the assumptions of a semiotic anthropology.

But Troeltsch got no further than this fundamental point in this respect. A key insight of semiotics with regard to the field of religion had, however, become clear to him early on, namely that here we are dealing with signs or symbols that are necessarily inadequate to their object: in principle, what is designated by the sign cannot be fully conveyed by it. Troeltsch had encountered this notion in the work of French Protestant theologian Auguste Sabatier under the heading of "critical symbolism." For Troeltsch, this conception necessarily leads to denial of the idea of "a fixed revealed doctrinal truth" and as such itself represents "an inner transformation of religion . . . , which, on this premise, must perceive itself differently than before."[34]

This was the starting point for an emphatic contribution by Tillich. He seems to have been crucially inspired to present the ideas in his 1928 essay "The Religious Symbol"[35] by the publications of Ernst Cassirer,[36] who was working on his three-volume *Philosophy of Symbolic Forms* during this period. Ideas of importance to Tillich's theory can in fact be found in those of his studies referring directly to Cassirer.[37] In "Mythos und Mythologie," Tillich presents his own approach as overcoming the opposition between a metaphysical theory of myth, as he discerns it particularly in the late Schelling, and the kind of epistemological theory he finds in Cassirer. As he saw it, his overcoming of this opposition extracts the realism from the metaphysical theory and embraces the intellectual constructionism of the epistemological theory. Tillich calls this a "symbolic-realist" theory:

> On this view, the myth is the symbol, built up from elements of reality, of the unconditional or the realm beyond being that is intended in the religious act. The myth has reality, for it is directed toward the unconditionally real. This is the truth of the metaphysical conception. But this myth does not have the reality of the likeness: for it lives in symbols which, of course, are not arbitrary, but, depending on how one conceives of the unconditional, are subject to a certain—and, moreover, a general—regularity. This is the truth of the epistemological conception.[38]

In the theory of the religious symbol, Tillich emphasizes the properties of all symbols, above all in contrast to what he calls signs—a terminological approach to which I have not so far adhered in this account. It is crucial to this distinction that Tillich ascribes arbitrary interchangeability to signs, in line with Ferdinand de Saussure's famous phrase "Le signe est arbitraire."[39] The symbol, on the other hand, has "innate power," "a power inherent within it"; religious images, for example, "were originally charged with a magical power that sets them apart from mere conventionality. Such symbols are by no means necessarily religious; they may also be political or aesthetic. Tillich cites as an example of a political symbol the concept of "surplus value" in Marx's critique of political economy, which has become a "symbol of economic exploitation"[40] in the consciousness of the proletariat. Religious symbols differ from other symbols in that they *visualize* "that which is unconditionally beyond the conceptual sphere, they point to the ultimate reality implied in the religious act, to what concerns us ultimately."[41]

In this phase of his development, Tillich evidently shared with Cassirer a relatively narrow concept of religion. In Cassirer's work, of course, religions are only those forms that transcend the mythical, an effect of the growing understanding of the symbolicity of symbols (the difference between God and the image of God or statues of a deity), as a result of which notions of sacredness have developed into those of transcendence.[42] Cassirer never elaborated the theory of religion beyond myth, but since his time the distinction between pre- and post–Axial Age religion, first made by Karl Jaspers, has become the centerpiece of research in the universal history of religion. Hence, the difference Tillich has in mind between symbols of all kinds—pre-Axial and secular—and religious symbols in the sense of the symbolization of transcendence assumes tremendous strategic importance.[43] Numerous questions arise here about both the history of scholarship and factual matters. How does Tillich's symbol theory differ from that of Cassirer on the one hand and that of American pragmatism on the other? What are the implications of Tillich's symbol theory for the historical sociology of religion pursued by Bellah and Parsons and thus for empirical questions about the universal history of religion? Keeping my answers brief, I will now try to respond to these questions.

When it comes to Cassirer, we find illumination in Tillich's own writings. Cassirer's "critical idealism" holds that religion—in the narrow sense I have just set out—moves into opposition to myth at a certain point in human development, combats it, and finally overcomes it, a view that failed to explain what distinguishes the transcendence-oriented religions from philosophy. Against this idea, Tillich postulates that myth has by no means died off due to the emergence of ideas of transcendence, but has merely changed form:

> The struggle of the Jewish prophets against pagan mythology was a struggle of the ethical henotheism of the old religion of the desert against the ecstatic polytheism of agrarian religion, a struggle of Jahwism against Baalism.[44]

However, the position of the mythical within religion changes when myth is ruptured by ideas of transcendence and, I would add, by theoretical reflection (in philosophy and scholarship). But the ruptured myth remains a myth. "Nothing is ever lost" is a constantly recurring motif in Robert Bellah's work, one that seeks to highlight the persistence of both ritual and myth in the history of religion as well as in secular worldviews and value systems.

It seems to me that Tillich blazed a crucial trail here. But if we contrast this with the semiotics of pragmatism, a school of thought that went unacknowledged by both Tillich and Troeltsch,[45] we will immediately notice that he had to pay a price for his sharp distinction between the conventional sign and the "self-authorized" symbol, namely the complete discontinuity between everyday communication and the world of religion. As Hermann Deuser has tried to show, building on the theory of signs put forward by American pragmatist Charles Sanders Peirce,[46] it is at least possible and potentially more fruitful when it comes to Tillich's own intentions to assume continuity between the everyday use of signs and religious symbolism, between propositional speech in scholarly texts and the articulation of the qualitative experience of the world in poetry and painting, for example. This is not to deny the distinction proposed by Tillich. But it should not prompt us to conclude that cultural spheres can be completely separated from religion.

Finally, Tillich's symbol theory was of decisive importance to Bellah's sociology of religion. Bellah even adopted Tillich's term, "symbolic realist," to characterize his own sociology when he moved from Harvard and away from his teacher Parsons to Berkeley in 1967. Here I must finally clarify the phrase "synthesis of Parsons and Tillich" mentioned at the beginning of this chapter. The concept of value was central to Parsons's sociology, and he occasionally referred to himself as a "cultural determinist." But when it comes to the empirical apprehension of the values that guide real people, to differentiating between levels of awareness of these values and to interpreting the complex and intrinsically inconsistent cultures of various major civilizations or nations, Parsons's conceptual apparatus was far too rigid and schematic. Building explicitly on Tillich, Bellah developed the basic outline of an analysis of the mythical structures of contemporary societies, in his case using the example of the United States. Here myths were not treated as self-contained, consistent entities, but as complex and tension-filled structures[47]—as in the 1975 book *The Broken Covenant*, whose original subheading was to have been "Studies in the Mythic Dimensions of American Culture."[48] Tillich's ideas on the specific features of *religious* symbols were crucial to Bellah's historical sociology of religion.

> Every religion must use symbolism, even when, like Zen Buddhism, it is only to break the symbolism. It is the principal task of the study of religious symbolism to determine the axes along which such symbols are organized, and thus to arrive at a typology of religious symbols.[49]

Parsons, inspired by his pupil Bellah, even integrated this core Tillichian motif into his late work,[50] which explores how the experience of unconditional meaning that in principle transcends temporality can itself be articulated. In other words, he investigates the forms of symbolization through which people can pass on this experience and this meaning over time, from one generation to the next.

The Interplay of Religious Traditions

This symbol theory developed by Tillich is vital to an adequate understanding of the relationship between different religious traditions and the position of individuals in relation to these religious traditions. Troeltsch's remarks on the effects of "critical symbolism" on the understanding of dogma and revelation had already given an indication of the transformative impact of such a symbol theory. Indeed, Troeltsch's perspective was consonant with his readiness, quite unusual among Protestant thinkers at the time, to approach Catholic Christianity, in all its internal diversity and contradictoriness, in an informed and unprejudiced manner. He followed the fate of Catholic modernism with a good deal of sympathy.

Paul Tillich's work, however, puts forward a much stronger vision of the reciprocal correction of different variants of Christianity than we find in Troeltsch's writings. But one of the key ideas in Troeltsch's *Social Teachings*, which Tillich had studied thoroughly,[51] may have been a source of inspiration here—namely, the idea that the major forms of the social organization of Christianity, "church" and "sect," should not be viewed straightforwardly as opposed to one another, but as emerging from one another repeatedly over the course of history.

Tillich's symbol theory is quite obviously influenced by his criticism of contemporary Protestantism; it enables him to counter the "antisymbolism" in that branch of Christianity. His studies on Protestantism and the "permanent significance of the Catholic Church for Protestantism"[52] are pervaded by the motif of the mutual correction of the prophetic and sacramental, the shielding of Catholics from remagification and Protestants from self-secularization.[53]

In terms of the theory of religion, what matters here is whether the dissolution of the simple opposition between the confessions leads to greater awareness of their internal contradictions. The idea of mutual correction could, after all, be associated with the stereotyping of the two institutional traditions. Yet neither is the Protestant tradition consistently skeptical of rituals and antisacramental, nor is the Catholic tradition purely sacramental and unprophetic, let alone magical. We could cite various examples of this, such as founders of religious orders, including Francis of Assisi and Ignatius of Loyola, as well as the shift initiated by the Second Vatican Council, which Tillich lived to see and to which he rightly responded that the future would show whether the Catholic Church is in fact capable of upholding the principle of constant self-reform.[54]

In terms of methodology, when it comes to the interplay between confessional or religious traditions, Tillich introduces the idea that the theoretically distinguishable types are in reality not static, but change as they grapple with the other types, for example, by adapting to one another or distinguishing themselves from one another. He calls this a "dynamic typology" with respect to the history of religion,[55] and it is true that this idea may embody a very important consequence of the grounding of the theory of religion in a theory of signs or symbols, because it means making a systematic distinction between the inspirational core of a tradition and the specific ways in which this core is articulated. Tillich attributes to his idea of a "dynamic typology" "a decisive advantage over a one-directed dialectics like that of the Hegelian school in that it does not push into the past what is dialectically left behind."[56] It is particularly noteworthy that he fleshes out the advantage of his perspective over that of Hegel with reference to the latter's view of Buddhism:

> For example, in the problem of the relation between Christianity and Buddhism, Hegelian dialectics considers Buddhism as an early stage of the religious development which is now totally abandoned by history. It still exists, but the World-Spirit is no longer creatively in it. In contrast, a dynamic typology considers Buddhism as a living religion, in which special polar elements are predominant, and which therefore stands in polar tension to other religions in which other elements are predominant. In terms of this method, for example, it would be impossible to call Christianity the absolute religion, as Hegel did, for Christianity is characterized in each historical period by the predominance of different elements out of the whole of elements and polarities which constitute the religious realm.[57]

It is easy to imagine Tillich rejecting the idea that Catholic Christianity is historically obsolete in the same way. As mentioned, one of his central concerns was with the potential for the two major Christian confessions to learn from one another. Only one point seems to me to be problematic in Tillich's conceptualization of such learning processes. Tillich refers to the "sacramental" not only with reference to Catholic Christianity, but to the entire history of religion as well. Yet it would make sense to distinguish clearly here between the "sacred" and the "sacramental." The sacramental dimension in Catholicism is not, after all, a relic of the pre-Axial or pre-Christian "sacred," but the transformation of the sacred within the context of transcendence.

When Tillich writes of the "antisacramental" protest of the prophets or the Stoics,[58] he misses the opportunity to distinguish between the rejection of pre-Axial sacredness through transcendence-oriented prophecy and the transformation of sacredness into a transcendence-focused religion. This distinction would have been better aligned with his observations on the transformation of myth. Because he fails to make this distinction, once again the Catholic realm tends to be devalorized as primitive—in a way akin to Max Weber's constant references to the "magical-sacramental." Yet the mutual correction that goes on between the Protestant and Catholic realms is based on a common foundation in the understanding of transcendence and incarnation. This is not a matter of correcting the prophetic through the sacred as such.

In numerous studies, Robert Bellah built directly on Tillich's criticism of individual "Protestantisms" and of tendencies toward antisymbolism and antisacramentalism, the best-known example being his essay "Flaws in the Protestant Code."[59] In Bellah's student days, Tillich was already vital to his turn away from the Marxism of his youth and reconversion to Christianity;[60] these impulses now became important to his path from Reformed Christianity to the Episcopal Church, the American variant of Anglicanism. It is therefore almost "symbolic" in itself that the text of his Paul Tillich Lecture is probably the last one Bellah completed in his lifetime, just under three months before his death.[61] But Tillich was crucial to Bellah's scholarly work in another respect that I have not so far mentioned—a dimension of which most Western theologians are perhaps no more than marginally aware. I am referring to his understanding of religious developments in East Asia. Bellah is the author of a social science classic on Japan (*Tokugawa Religion*) and many other relevant studies in this field.[62] Yet he stated repeatedly that the decisive impulse for his understanding of Japan came from Tillich.[63]

This does not mean that Tillich himself was a great expert on East Asia. He did develop a certain interest in Zen Buddhism and in Christian-Buddhist dialogue late in life. But many of his remarks—for example, on the secular character of Confucianism and the way this supposedly facilitated the victory of communism in China—seem simplistic and in need of revision given the revitalization of religious traditions in today's China and the rapid Christianization of South Korea.[64] What Bellah found eye-opening was Tillich's overcoming of an understanding of faith focused primarily on religious institutions. Just as Tillich believed modern Western individuals must develop a relationship to structures of unconditional meaning on their own, as Bellah saw it, religious traditions in East Asia have never been fixed casings between which individuals had to choose and to which they had to unambiguously affiliate themselves. From a religious point of view, East Asia appears less exotic when features of the confessional age in Europe and America lose their taken-for-grantedness. Under Tillich's decisive influence, Bellah's oeuvre not only embraced the perspective of mutual correction between

Protestantism and Catholicism, but, to a far greater extent than in Tillich's own work, considered the possibility of mutual correction among all Axial religious traditions, especially Christianity and those currents so influential in East Asia of Confucianism, Daoism, and Buddhism.[65]

Theonomy

In working through the topics of "time," "symbol," and "religious tradition," I have brought together what I believe to be the most important elements in Tillich's work that entered into his synthesis of theological and philosophical traditions. The key idea underpinning this synthesis is an understanding of religious faith as the "state of being ultimately concerned."[66] But given the modern dominance of the value of freedom—that is, the fact that we live "under the spell of freedom"—the emphasis on the passive dimension of being seized and the unconditionality of what seizes us inevitably require us to ask what the position of faith might be within the field of tension between autonomy and heteronomy. Tillich's response lies in another of his key concepts, namely that of theonomy. His relationship to the understanding of freedom as self-determination depends on the precise meaning of this suggestive yet ambiguous term.

Here Tillich's key move differs from the one discussed in the previous chapter with reference to Troeltsch. Troeltsch, as I demonstrated, had endeavored to explicate a "German" idea of freedom, which entailed overcoming utilitarian and Kantian conceptions of freedom on the basis of ideas about expression and self-realization. His attempt in his late work to reformulate the idea of human rights in this framework, which we today would call "expressivist," holds great appeal.[67] What is little known is that Troeltsch had already taken up the idea of theonomy in other parts of his work, thus paving the way for Tillich's thinking in this regard. We know from Troeltsch's Heidelberg lectures of 1911–1912, published posthumously as *Glaubenslehre*, that he interpreted the autonomy of moral reason in the Kantian sense itself as the presence of God in the human being: "Christian autonomy is at the same time theonomy."[68]

He articulated this conception in varying ways, referring to the "autotheonomy" of the human being.[69] His question was whether the interpretation of autonomy as God's presence gives rise to anything substantial in ethical terms or whether this is still no more than a formal definition of human freedom of choice. His answer consisted of finding "guidelines" in an understanding of autonomy that does not disregard its constitutive preconditions, "guidelines that are based on the rigor of self-surrender to God, on detachment from the entanglement of the world, and very much on brotherly love.... The Christian moral law is always something to be formed anew, but it is also always something that has a certain goal in mind."[70] In another lecture from the same period, Troeltsch states with great clarity that autonomy and theonomy are only in opposition if religious demands are traced back to an "externally revealed, statutory law," but not if theonomy merely means the "emphasis on the religious presuppositions contained in the idea of autonomy itself."[71]

These observations can certainly be seen as laying the ground for relevant writings by Tillich during the Weimar Republic. In the context of his endeavors to advance a "religious socialism," Tillich looked for an alternative to both "capitalist autonomy" and "ecclesiastical heteronomy" and to their interplay. He called this alternative "theonomy," by which he meant the "free devotion of finite forms to the eternal."[72] In the great postwar and postrevolution crisis, he turned this into a rallying cry for a new, offensive role for Christian theology in the fight not against the autonomy of culture but against its "profanation, exhaustion, and disintegration."[73] The decisive step toward this alternative is the notion of reflecting on the preconditions for autonomous action. In a 1931 encyclopedia article on "theonomy," Tillich referred to the "deepening of autonomy in itself to the point where it points beyond itself."[74] For Tillich, what mattered was the insight into the finitude of our freedom and into the preconditions of our capacity for self-determination. In a comprehensive study, *Religion als Freiheitsbewußtsein* ("Religion as Consciousness of Freedom"), Christian Danz has related Tillich's ideas to the reflections of classical German philosophy, defending Tillich convincingly against Hegelianizations or Hegelian criticisms of his work.[75] The only thing Danz fails to sufficiently clarify is the relationship between Tillich's step and other postidealist intellectual programs of a similar hue.[76]

The concept of theonomy always risks being misunderstood as denoting a special form of heteronomy. "At least," wrote Tillich's successor in Chicago, Paul Ricœur, "at first blush, the idea of a legislation of divine origin must appear as a form of heteronomy, diametrically opposed to the presumed autonomy of moral conscience."[77] This misunderstanding can only be overcome if the limitations of autonomy, which come into focus when we understand the constituted character of our autonomy, are not misinterpreted as implying heteronomy. While Tillich had distanced himself from the "religious socialism" of his early days, in his voluminous work *Systematic Theology*, which he wrote in the United States, he held fast to the concept of theonomy while outlining it more clearly. Here he specifies that what he advocates is a culture in which an orientation toward the divine does not stand in opposition to the "autonomous forms of the creative process" but opens them from within to the "experience of holiness, of something ultimate in being and meaning."[78]

If, for example, we understand life as a gift, then as one consequence of this idea we will deal with and have to deal with our lives differently than if we regard them as our property, to do with as we wish. In the late Parsons's sociology of religion and medicine, several studies revolved around this idea of life as a gift and the potential to reformulate it in an era when the notion of human beings as the "children of God" had lost its meaning for many.[79] In his empirical studies on American culture, including the bestseller *Habits of the Heart*, Robert Bellah (together with his coauthors) presented the overcoming of utilitarian and expressivist individualism—that is, a culture that gives primacy to utility maximization and self-realization—as vital to the survival of democracy in the United States.[80] In his last text, the aforementioned Tillich Lecture, he explained what he believed theonomy can meaningfully denote today: respect for the dignity of all people in a form that prevents lapses into the privatization and instrumentalization of the idea of human rights to particularist ends.[81]

This he found expressed in the idea, coined by Émile Durkheim and elaborated in my book on the history of human rights, of the "sacredness of the person." In my book, wrote Bellah, I had moved into proximity to Tillich without knowing it. Bellah was right. But in this connection it is worth mentioning that I subsequently found in Tillich, namely in *The Religious Situation*, the statement that recognition of the "sacredness of personality," the "faith in human rights and human worth," have been the principal forces for liberation in the history of bourgeois society.[82] This belief in the "sacredness of the person," in the "sacredness of personality," exists in religious and secular forms, just as the violation of human rights and human dignity can be motivated by both secular and religious beliefs. What is certain is that we will misunderstand the present era if we look at it solely from the perspective of secularization processes and fail to consider such new or intensified instances of sacralization. If "theonomy" in its religious form means grasping the indebtedness of our freedom, it sets a normative standard for the evaluation of sacralizations.

I have used this chapter to discuss the work of Paul Tillich in light of its importance to the theory of religion and in particular to a social scientifically based universal history of religion. To this end I have consistently compared it, across four subject areas, with the thinking of Tillich's outstanding predecessor Ernst Troeltsch and his most important successor, Robert Bellah. I have not, therefore, mentioned other sociological influences on Tillich or other effects of his work in sociology.[83] Tillich's theological work is interwoven with the history of sociology in manifold ways. It is therefore astonishing how sweeping Tillich's understanding of capitalism was, especially in his religious-socialist phase, while his notion of the proletariat as a "mechanized mass" with its "instinctive movements" lacked a sound empirical basis.[84] Just as sociology has much still to learn from Tillich's understanding of religion, theology—including those of its variants that build on Tillich—needs to ground its statements in a better knowledge of social reality. Only then will the claim made by an American sociologist of religion in 1963 be fully realized: if Billy Graham, the well-known preacher, can be called the Elvis Presley of religious life, then in his field Paul Tillich is the Arturo Toscanini.[85]

III, 4
Sieve of Norms and Holy Scripture, Theonomy, and Freedom: Paul Ricœur

In his much-discussed book *Return to Reason*, Stephen Toulmin, the famous British-born American philosopher, tells of a colleague in the Jesuit order. For many years he had denied that there could be any real conflicts between values or between moral obligations for Christians. God, he firmly believed, had surely arranged the world in such a way that conflicts of this kind simply do not arise to confuse believers. From such a perspective, other value systems—in this case, non-Christian ones—can only be perceived as a failure to grasp true values or, at best, as approximations of that which is recognized, in unsurpassable form, in one's own Christian faith. With British understatement, however, Toulmin immediately adds, "He has now revised his opinion."[1]

With this self-correction, his Jesuit colleague had probably come to embrace the insights at large within the broad current of present-day value pluralism. We may assume that he not only relaxed the holism of his earlier worldview but learned to regard his earlier belief in unambiguity and moral objectivity as problematic in itself. Many contemporaries find value pluralism appealing because they—or perhaps I should say "we"—are guided by an ethos of tolerance and tend to question themselves, their nation, religion, and culture, which is what makes them skeptical of any kind of culture-independent universalism, even if it appears in the guise of contract or discourse theory. At the same time, however, many of us feel repelled by mere particularisms and are aware of their political risks. Hence, we cannot avoid asking whether liberal values, the values privileged by democratic constitutional states, the rule of law, but above all human rights and universal human dignity, are really nothing but one cultural option among countless others. If one trusts these intuitions, value pluralism and universalism by no means appear to be logically exclusive alternatives. Clarifying their exact relationship and examining their linkability, however, requires some effort and a large number of steps. A stark opposition is certainly not the last word here.

In my book *The Genesis of Values*, I investigated which types of action and experiential contexts might be the source of the subjective feeling that something is a value.[2] The short version of my answer is that values arise through experiences of self-formation and self-transcendence. The book delves deeply into the phenomenology of such experiences of self-transcendence while also reflecting on the theoretical means of understanding and conceptualizing such experiences. My phenomenology of experiences of self-transcendence ranges from individual prayer to collective ecstasy in archaic rituals or in nationalistic enthusiasm for war; it includes moral feelings and the opening of the self through dialogue and through the experience of nature. I will, of course, not be repeating these ideas here.

But I aim to build two bridges from them to the work of Paul Ricœur (1913–2005), the most profound and systematic thinker on religion in the French phenomenological and hermeneutical tradition. The first question I want to pursue here is whether such an emphasis on the genesis of our value commitments in contingent experiences forces us to deny the possibility of a universalist morality. On this premise we would be unable to pursue the task of linking value pluralism and universalism. People are quick to assume that this is what one means if one emphasizes the dynamics of value-constitutive experiences. The thinkers of American pragmatism have of course suffered this fate time and again.

When Paul Ricœur develops the concept of "narrative identity" set out in *Time and Narrative* into an ethics as he works his way toward his later book *Oneself as Another*, he too becomes entangled in this problem. If the self ultimately constitutes itself in the form of the narrative, then its relationship to moral norms must also be embedded in this narrative structure. But Paul Ricœur does not allow himself to be seduced by this insight, as did Alasdair MacIntyre in his influential book *After Virtue*, into opposing a universalist conception of morality.[3] In the first part of this chapter, I will specify how Ricœur proceeds here and what his attempt at synthesis looks like, reformulating it in my own language. In doing so, I largely adhere to the arguments presented in *The Genesis of Values*.

The other question I grapple with, however, goes well beyond them. It has to do with the connection between religious or generally value-constitutive experience and the interpretation of this experience. Here I will trace Ricœur's thinking, as manifested in certain texts concerned with this question, while also making some critical comments. Of course, my approach to these two questions is extremely selective in relation to the philosophy of

Paul Ricœur with its impressive range[4] and especially in relation to the tasks of a philosophical ethics as a whole. But any ethics that is not limited to the rational grounding or justification of norms and encompasses values in addition to norms—that deals with the good as well as the just, while also making a serious attempt to illuminate the experiential basis of our commitment to norms and values—will succeed only if it clarifies these two issues.

The Sieve of Norms

"Le crible de la norme"—the "sieve of norms"—is the name of an ingenious concept put forward by Paul Ricœur that articulates the basic thrust of his linkage of universalist moral philosophy and a contingency-conscious conception of the good and identity. The term appears first at the beginning of the seventh treatise of *Oneself as Another* and is then elaborated more broadly in the eighth. The first occurrence is in the context of programmatic remarks on the potential for a synthesis of Aristotelianism and Kantianism in ethics, "an Aristotelian heritage, where ethics is characterized by its *teleological* perspective, and a Kantian heritage, where morality is defined by the obligation to respect the norm, hence by a *deontological* point of view." While Ricœur, sounding like Aristotle, tells us that ethics enjoys priority over morality, he also emphasizes "the necessity for the ethical aim to pass through the sieve of the norm,"[5] which sounds like Kant. When I read this sentence for the first time, I felt a sense of epiphany. It made it clear to me why the pragmatist thinkers could expound a theory of the universal structures of human action, especially interpersonal action, while also emphasizing the contingency of the emergence of value commitments, elaborating this last point in their studies in the theory of religion. This was possible because they conceived of the theory of action in terms of a universalist anthropology, while thinking of ethics from the perspective of the actor.[6]

From a standpoint such as this, there is in fact no higher authority than discourse when it comes to the justification of norms. German discourse ethicists Karl-Otto Apel and Jürgen Habermas built on this insight put forward by Charles Sanders Peirce, the founder of pragmatism—though in a one-sided manner. From the perspective of the actor who constructs their actions under contingent conditions, what is paramount is not this justification but specifying the good or the right in action situations. Even if we as actors want to give clear primacy to a particular good or to the right as we understand it, we do not have definite knowledge of what this requires us to do. We can seek honestly to increase the good or to act exclusively to advance the right, but this gives us no certainty that we will succeed through the actions we decide to take and in light of all the consequences and side-effects we thus induce.

Every conception of the good or the right will potentially require revision if we factor in the consequences of action. Nor do new attempts to specify the good or the right furnish us with a way out. An unambiguous conclusion is inconceivable, since the situations in which we act are always new and our longing for certainty will never be satisfied. *In abstracto*—that is, in discourse detached from action situations—we can establish certainty that in light of specific assumptions about our priorities we should focus on certain objectives. But in the concrete reality of action situations, though we may often achieve a subjective feeling of certainty, this amounts to no more than plausibility at an intersubjective level. Retrospectively, with the benefit of hindsight, we can find out more about the appropriateness of our actions, but even this does not constitute a definitive, certainty-providing judgment, because the future will bring forth further consequences of our actions and points of view that jeopardize our assessment once again.

Now some may admit that our actions have the character described here but nevertheless deny that this clarifies the relationship between the good and the right. To what extent is this emphasis on the "creativity of action" meant to indicate the nature of this relationship? At first it may appear that this emphasis is at best banal and at worst dangerous. It is dangerous if it underlines only the situatedness of our decisions, opening the door to unprincipled and arbitrary conduct. It is banal if it merely highlights what no one, even the most ardent exponent of an ethics of conviction (*Gesinnungsethik*), has ever denied, namely that good intentions do not always lead to correct deeds. But as I see it, the way in which we ought to put forward arguments about the creativity of our actions in ethical contexts does not grant unlimited scope for arbitrary conduct but merely declares certain revisions and specifications acceptable. And it is far from banal to incorporate into the concept of good intentions itself the moral duty to attend to the empirical preconditions for realizing these intentions. As a consequence of such an understanding of action and an ethics structured on the basis of the actor's perspective, the restrictive aspect of the right must inevitably appear in the action situation itself, but only as one standpoint existing alongside the guidance provided by the good.

This dual assertion needs further explanation. The right must feature in this conception because it represents the anthropological-universal coordinates required by social action; these are unavoidable because action is always embedded in social contexts. This social embedding of all action is inevitable because the ability to act itself is socially constituted, and our cooperation is not only aimed at individually attributable, but also at irreducibly social goods. Across the panoply of our orientations, this aspect of the right is always present: the situational revision of our objectives does not degenerate into arbitrariness because it has to pass a test. This is Ricœur's "sieve of norms."

For Ricœur, the right can only appear as one point of view among several in the actor's situation, because this potentially universal "sieve of norms" would have nothing to assess in the first place if the actor were not oriented toward various ideas of the good, which they cannot be sure are acceptable from the standpoint of the right. Though a moralist who demands too much of themselves and is utterly determined always to prioritize the universalizing approach in their conduct of life may aspire to neutralize their inclinations, they will only be able to examine their ideas about possible actions through this approach. One of the key elements underpinning the emphasis (including my own) on the creativity of action is precisely the insight that actions cannot be derived from the universalizing standpoint itself; we can only check whether a possible action is acceptable from this point of view. So even if one could somehow rid oneself of one's inclinations, this would not eliminate the candidates for the test represented by the universalizing rule. These candidates are our ideas of our duty on the one hand, and our strivings on the other; they too entail a potentially universal validity claim.

If in the reception of Kant it is sometimes unclear whether the universalization test entailed in the categorical imperative is aimed at our inclinations or at the maxims underpinning our actions, then this—as Ricœur argues, referring to Otfried Höffe's interpretation of Kant[7]—is due to a deficient understanding of the interplay between our prereflective strivings and our conscious intentions. If, on the other hand, one proceeds on the basis of a theory of action that anchors intentionality in situated reflection on our prereflective strivings, then it becomes clear that these inclinations can only ever become subject to the universalization test in the form of the universality claims inherent in maxims and that the right can only ever be a testing authority, unless it becomes a good itself, that is, the value of justice.

In the action situation, then, there is no primacy of the good or the right. There is no relationship of superordination or subordination here, but rather complementarity. In the situation of action, the irreducible orientations toward the good already inherent in our strivings come up against the testing authority of the right. What we can achieve in these situations is only ever a reflective equilibrium between our orientations. To be sure, the extent to which we subject our orientations to this test may vary. Hence, the perspective of the right and the universalization test entail an everlasting, inexhaustible potential that also impacts on changes in our ideas of what is good. But the universality of the right neither means that in action situations we must self-evidently give it priority over all other considerations, nor that we should not do so.

The debate on whether we should give primacy to the good or the right must be clearly distinguished from the debate on the universalizability of the right. From the perspective adopted here, there is no need to conduct a debate on the universalizability of the right—not because this possibility is rejected, but because it is declared indisputable given the premises of the anthropological theory of action. The emphasis here on the situatedness and creativity of action in no way denotes skepticism about the idea of the universality of the right. But it does not follow from this idea that within the action situation we must obviously prioritize examination of our orientations in light of the universalization principle above all other considerations.

Ultimately, we would have to relate these observations, developed with a view to the individual actor, to acting collectives and institutions, indeed to entire societies. After all, they too exist within a field of tension between their contingent—indeed particular—value systems and the potential of a morality that pushes us toward universality. "Particular" does not, of course, mean "particularist"; cultural specificity is not tantamount to an inability to take universalist viewpoints into account. On the contrary, from the perspective of the universality of the right, the question is which particular cultural traditions we might build on, and how other cultural traditions can be creatively perpetuated and transformed from this universalist point of view.[8]

Religious Experience and Religious Language

Rather than pursuing this path further here, as stated earlier I will now turn to the theory-of-religion question of what the relationship between religious experience and religious language looks like in the work of Paul Ricœur. For every ethics that foregrounds the constitution of value commitments in the manner described earlier, it is crucial to ask how people make the prelinguistic force of value-constitutive experiences communicable and integrate it into the interpretive schemas of everyday life, or to what extent these experiences already embody linguistically and culturally preformed, even predetermined expectations.

Paul Ricœur addresses this question at various points in his oeuvre, including in the context of the Gifford Lectures, out of which his great book *Oneself as Another* emerged. But he did not include his concluding remarks in this book. One reason for this, as he himself openly admitted, was to defend his "philosophical writings against the accusation of cryptotheology."[9] The text I am citing here was published elsewhere under the title "Expérience et langage dans le discours religieux" ("Experience and Language in Religious Discourse").[10] In this essay, Ricœur first addresses the obstacles to a phenomenology of religion. He does not see these as arising chiefly from the fact that the concept of intentionality as found in phenomenology entails a degree of subjective control over phenomena, which would inevitably clash with the character of religion as an insight into the dependence of all subjectivity on something higher. As Ricœur sees it, phenomenology has certainly developed the ability to reconstruct experiences in which the subject opens up to this wholly other ("une altérité intégrale"), and immediately after putting forward this argument, in his sketch of a "phenomenology of praying" he himself shows how such a self-opening toward the divine can be understood in an active sense.

In fact, Ricœur considers the main difficulty for a phenomenology of religion to be the linguistic mediation even of experiences that seem to epitomize the direct seizure of our entire person. Here, too, he concedes that phenomenology long ago left behind the stage in which it construed language only as an unproductive additional layer above the truly essential layer of experienced meaning, but precisely this insight, he writes, "condemns phenomenology to run the gauntlet of a hermeneutic and more precisely of a textual or scriptural hermeneutic."[11] He also demonstrates the culturally mediated nature of even the most powerful religious experiences by highlighting the impact on the interpretation of such experiences of ideas concerning the immanence or transcendence of the divine and its personal or anonymous character, notions of the individualist or "communitarian" orientation of faith, and assumptions of activism or passivism.

For Ricœur, the consequence of this, among other things, is that there can be no true phenomenology of religion as such, but only a hermeneutic tracing of the broad lines of an individual, specific religion, in light of which, on a comparative basis and in the spirit of a "hospitalité interreligieuse"—that is, "interreligious hospitality"—insights can then be applied in a scrutinizing manner to other specific religions. With respect to the Christian tradition, Ricœur himself develops the hermeneutic circle that pertains to this religion and perhaps, despite all their differences, to all religions based on a "Holy Scripture," in other words also to Judaism and Islam. This hermeneutic circle in these cases encompasses the poles of divine word and Holy Scripture, of Scripture and community of interpretation, of interpretive tradition and every new situational concretization (or "miniaturization," as Ricœur puts it).

With tremendous sensitivity, his subsequent remarks show how religious self-discovery is possible through the reading of the Holy Scriptures, how the book can become a mirror for the reader. This path is doubtless possible, and it is evident that Paul Ricœur himself is speaking on the basis of the most intensive personal experience, which he has transmitted so powerfully to others in his biblical hermeneutics.[12]

But one step in his argument irritates me, a non sequitur that seems surprising coming from such a careful author as Ricœur and perhaps points to something deeper. I have no objection to the argument that a phenomenology of religion is only possible as a hermeneutic endeavor, but I do not understand why such a hermeneutics should first and foremost be a hermeneutics of sacred texts and not a hermeneutics of texts about religious experience. Even the step toward a hermeneutics of texts may be premature, as this soon tends to blot out the interpretation of oral and nonlinguistic articulations of religious experiences. But more important in systematic terms and more pressing under present-day religious conditions is to distinguish clearly between a religious experience that is, as it were, first constituted through the medium of scriptural interpretation, and a religious experience that seeks appropriate articulation, however much experience and articulation may already be influenced by the content of the Scripture-based tradition.

More than eighty years before Ricœur, another scholar delivered the famous Gifford Lectures and chose the very approach I am pressing for here. William James's book *The Varieties of Religious Experience* uses autobiographical texts as its empirical basis—texts by religious virtuosos such as saints and founders of religions but also by people like you and me, in which they talk about conversion and loss of faith, experiences of prayer and mysticism.[13] James's book, whose roots do not lie in phenomenology as a school of philosophy, has been lauded as a better phenomenology of religion than those works describing themselves as such.[14] The study of autobiographical narratives of religious experiences also fits perfectly with Ricœur's emphasis on the formation of selves through narrative. The more individuals go their own way in creating religious meaning, the closer we have to get to the associated experiences.

Conversely, the type of experience foregrounded by Ricœur presupposes that study of Holy Scriptures is central to the religious life of individuals and communities, though this has surely become a rarity today. Moreover, even for those well acquainted with these Scriptures, his emphasis sounds a little like the Protestant privileging of scriptural interpretation over all other sources of religious experience.[15]

There is, however, a text by Ricœur that goes beyond this perspective: *Manifestation et Proclamation*, published in 1974.[16] This text virtually set out to mediate between a hermeneutics of proclamation and a phenomenology of the manifestation of the sacred. Ricœur's reference authors with respect to the phenomenology of the sacred are Rudolf Otto[17] and above all religious scholar Mircea Eliade, originally from Romania—but, once again, not William James. Here, too, this decision is highly consequential, since the goal from the outset is to produce a phenomenology of the sacred but not a phenomenology of religious experience or the experience of the sacred. Unlike James (and Émile Durkheim), for whom there is no inherent relationship between the quality of objects and their sacredness, Otto and Eliade insist on a description of the numinous as a quality inherent in objects themselves. This is a strength because it brings into play a wealth of specific questions central to research on religion, but also a weakness because the power of sacredness, which potentially pervades all objects in the world, tends to take a back seat.

Clearly influenced by Eliade, his longtime Chicago colleague, in the text mentioned above Ricœur elaborates how little in many religions the experience of the sacred itself is linguistically constituted and language-centered. Of course, Ricœur tells us, there is a relationship between manifestations of the sacred on the one hand and myth on the other—and thus a linguistic representation of the sacred. But what we have here, he goes on, is merely a sort of minimalist hermeneutics; rather than a text underpinning sacredness, sacredness is the foundation of the linguistic form. In the work of Ricœur, unlike that of Eliade, a hermeneutics of proclamation is opposed to rather than incorporated into this phenomenology of the sacred, which is intended to apply primarily to so-called primitive and nonscriptural religions (and not to the religious experience of modern people). This occurs mainly through an interpretation of the Old Testament prophets as radically antimagical, "desacralizing" actors who help give the Word the upper hand over the numinous.

Ricœur's image of the religion of ancient Judaism is therefore very similar to that of Max Weber. It is, however, subject to the same objections as Weber's analysis, the latter having been accused of projecting Protestantism back into ancient Judaism.[18] But Ricœur opposes the tendency to take this line of thought too far, as in Rudolf Bultmann's project of demythologizing the Bible and Dietrich Bonhoeffer's vision of a "religionless" Christianity. Ricœur—the great thinker of mediation—seeks to elucidate the mediation between manifestation and proclamation—for example, through the dialectic of sacrament and sermon in the religious service. From this point of view, the Word is not only the overcoming of the merely numinous, but its transformation. In the sacraments in particular, Ricœur contends, the (primitive) sacred ritual is transformed into a symbolization of the history of salvation. Without such a manifestation of sacredness, however, as Ricœur states at the end of his text, the Word itself becomes abstract and intellectualistic.

Hence, oddly enough, this older text turns out to be less language-centered than the later one. Its perspective is consonant with that put forward by Paul Tillich with regard to the mutual learning processes between the Christian confessions or between religions.[19] Here Ricœur opens up a Scripture-centered understanding of religious experience at least to sacramental experiences. Robert Bellah, a student of Tillich and leading US-American sociologist of religion, would also see in this step a slight convergence between Protestant Word-centeredness and Catholicism, which he regarded as an apt quid pro quo for a certain Protestantization of present-day Catholicism as a result of the growing affirmation of religious individualization even in this community-oriented tradition.[20] I would like to go further still, incorporating an even broader array of religious experience in order to then probe how Christianity might function as a language for articulating these experiences—through an unprejudiced confrontation with the full range of these phenomena.[21]

Even less than in the other chapters of this book can I claim that these two brief discussions of parts of Ricœur's oeuvre amount to an exhaustive treatment of the thinking of one of the twentieth century's great theorists of religion. Ricœur's work does at least appear time and again in other parts of this book as a key point of reference. I would like to remind the reader of the two most important instances of this. First, nobody has done more to reintroduce into philosophy the theological discourse on "theonomy," which I discussed in this part of the book mainly with reference to the writings of Paul Tillich, but also those of Ernst Troeltsch.[22] This goal of the complex relativization of the ideal of autonomy—or better, of demonstrating the dialectical interweaving of the aspiration to autonomy with insight into its indebtedness—was already unmistakable among these theologians, but here Ricœur built a bridge between theology and philosophy far more clearly than any of his predecessors.

Second, in the chapter on Reinhart Koselleck I pointed out how Ricœur took up the impulses of his theory of history in order to avoid the "Hegelian temptation" of constructing a teleological philosophy of history in whatever form. Here a specific conception of the human being and their freedom seems to inform Ricœur's understanding of both autonomy and history, a perspective he already developed in his early days when grappling with, but also distancing himself from, existential philosophy. It was not Heidegger, Jaspers or even Sartre that were central to his ideas here, but rather the Christian thinking of Gabriel Marcel, in whose work, in Ricœur's words, "the freedom of response goes beyond the freedom of choice."[23] On this basis, we might already discern in his work a responsive or communicative understanding of freedom.

III, 5
Communicative Freedom and Theology of Liberation: Wolfgang Huber

Wolfgang Huber (b. 1942) is without a doubt German Protestantism's most prominent public intellectual of our time. He did not achieve this influential position with all its diverse demands by demonstratively distancing himself from the institution of the church. Instead, in an admirable way, over many years he has combined the exercise of church offices, up to that of the bishop and council president of the Evangelical Church in Germany, with astute statements on an array of topics central to public political and moral debates. In addition, over decades of academic activity, particularly in the field of ethics, he has succeeded in developing his own theological approach, which underlies his public interventions and endows his ecclesio-political action with aspirations going well beyond a merely pragmatic approach. If the Protestant Church in Germany presents itself today as the "church of freedom," Wolfgang Huber's understanding of the church as the "realm and advocate of freedom," developed in numerous publications, has certainly played some role in this. "Freedom" is the central concept in his theology and also figures in the title of one of his books, which brings together essays and speeches from more than three decades.[1] The following discussion focuses on this book, although that volume cannot be regarded as the sum of his diverse writings. I thus consider Huber's other publications in a number of asides without discussing them in depth.

"Freedom" may, of course, be an empty phrase that sounds good and is easy to applaud but commits no one to anything in particular. Hence, what we need to probe is how Huber constructs his key concept in the detail, how his definitions relate to competing ones, and whether the concept of freedom can truly bear the burden placed on it here. Since I am not a theologian, I will not proceed through comparison with rival theological approaches. Instead, I will investigate the meaning of Huber's ideas on freedom in a context by no means alien to him, namely that of social philosophical and social scientific debates. At the same time, I will take a critical look at the author's claim that his concept of freedom expresses the core of the Christian message and the Reformed faith.

Wolfgang Huber is a vigorous advocate of the idea that even in the twenty-first century the Christian faith represents a "plausible way of life" (11) amid the "multiplicity of present-day options." He disagrees with those for whom only the secular option remains in the present and who therefore regard the Christian faith merely as a relic of bygone times that should finally be overcome or perhaps, somewhat more benevolently, as a cultural source of modern achievements that must nevertheless be detached from their wellspring. In Wolfgang Huber's oeuvre, this future orientation does not consist in the simple continuation of traditions. Every line of his writings is undergirded by an awareness of the terrible crimes of German history in particular, of which Christians are not innocent, and by a keen awareness of the dangers of the present.

For me, this makes him an exemplary representative of what I call post-totalitarian Christianity.[2] This term is an attempt to highlight the status of Christians who are well aware just how much, within this history, the overcoming of Christianity formed part of the pathos of modernity typical of totalitarianism. Precisely because Christianity has a future and secularization trends cannot simply be projected into the future, he believes, the question of the relationship between religion and freedom is one of the key issues of our time, at least if the great importance of the value of "freedom" in our time is recognized and we cease to assume the fusion of the "liberal-democratic" with the anti-Christian, the "free-thinking." Like few others, Wolfgang Huber, exemplarily in his sociologically well-informed book *Kirche in der Zeitenwende*[3] ("The Church at the Turn of Eras"), has helped ensure that the church (of whatever tradition) not only views itself within the frame of a "simplistic church/state duality" (161), but as an actor in civil society, albeit a very special one. This is akin to the thinking of Spanish American sociologist of religion José Casanova,[4] and I will not pursue it further at this point.

Huber and Theunissen on Communicative Freedom

Since the late 1970s, Wolfgang Huber has defined the concept of freedom so central to his thinking more precisely as "communicative freedom." Here he draws on the thinking of philosopher Michael Theunissen, who coined the term in the context of his interpretations of Hegel.[5] Drawing on Theunissen was a good choice, for at least three reasons. First, in his important 1964 postdoctoral thesis submitted at the Free University of Berlin,[6] which was published under the title *Der Andere* ("The Other"), Theunissen set out the basic features of a philosophy of intersubjectivity, whose key idea is that we can only find and develop our selves through the encounter with the other and by dedicating ourselves to them. This book takes up motifs mainly from the Jewish-inspired dialogics of Martin Buber but develops out of this an incredibly astute critique of the inadequacies in the conception of intersubjectivity espoused by Husserl, Heidegger, and Sartre. In Theunissen's work, Buber's motifs are also developed into a Christian interpretation of the "between"—the space that subjects share with one another, but which cannot be ascribed to any of them in the manner of property—as the kingdom of God in our midst.

In the work of all the important thinkers on intersubjectivity in Western intellectual history, including Ludwig Feuerbach, George Herbert Mead, and Jürgen Habermas, one can undoubtedly discern a religious inspiration informing their sensitivity to the structures of intersubjectivity. Their intention, however, particularly clearly in the case of Mead and Habermas, was to overcome religion in the spirit of its rational legacy. The same did not go for Theunissen, and this is the second reason why his thinking helped shape Huber's theology. Drawing on Kierkegaard, Theunissen thinks the possibility of self-becoming not only within the structures of human intersubjectivity, but much more radically as dependent on the insight that the self recognizes itself as originally posited by a wholly other, namely God.[7] Viewed through this lens, the freedom that may be experienced in human communication is always already underpinned by a liberation that may be devotedly embraced or defiantly spurned. Third, Theunissen's thinking is not limited to the sphere of the individual and their communication with their fellow human beings and with God but addresses the problems of a social theory by grappling with Marx and with Hegel's theory of institutions.

In all three of the above-mentioned respects, traces or preexisting affinities can be found in Huber's theology. If we consider how modestly Theunissen himself refers to his concept of "communicative freedom," freely admitting that there is a need to clarify more precisely how freedom and communication relate to one another,[8] it is of course even more appealing to view Huber's theology as a further development, rather than merely as an application, of this philosophy of communicative freedom. In the first-mentioned respect it is quite clear that for Huber freedom reigns where "the other is no longer a barrier to my self-realization, nor is [he or she] merely an opportunity for or the object of my moral probation" (63); instead, "each person experiences the other as an enrichment of the self and as a responsibility central to one's own life" (ibid.).

Freedom and love of one's neighbor thus move into close proximity; an understanding of freedom pervaded by the ethic of love informs Huber's thinking here. Service to one's neighbor is expressly understood "not as the abnegation but as the realization of the self." (119) With reference to Luther, Huber states that freedom cannot be a "personal possession" but rather "presses for ramifications in relation to others" (26). Fundamentally, Huber thinks in terms of a relational anthropology, whose key historical reference figures, alongside Buber and Theunissen, are surely H. Richard Niebuhr and George Herbert Mead.[9]

The second point concerns one's relation to God as a prerequisite for becoming oneself. The first striking aspect here is how often this relation is tacitly truncated in present-day philosophy and social theory—for example, in Habermas's distinction between human beings' three relations to the world (the material, social, and subjective worlds) in his magnum opus *The Theory of Communicative Action*[10] or in other interpretations of Hegel not penned by Theunissen. It is truncated not only in the self-understanding of thinkers who consider a relation to God to be an illusion, but often even with regard to their own subject matter, that is, the possible relation to God of the people they are writing about. Wolfgang Huber, conversely, develops this idea in a pleasing and emphatic way.

When he states that the remembrance of a liberation is constitutive of the Christian understanding of freedom, "by virtue of which people perceive themselves as limited and can renounce fantasies of omnipotence" (25); that Christian freedom crucially entails "liberation from the compulsion to justify oneself" (26); and that this liberation gives rise to "existential strength" (42), freedom from "the ballast of self-affirmation," a deep sense of gratitude (105), and the certainty of being able to start anew (120)—then in all these passages Huber's written style palpably reflects and articulates his core personal convictions.

And third, Huber's attempt, which dominates Part II of his book *Von der Freiheit* ("On Freedom"), to arrive at an ethics of institutions, to focus on law while not overlooking its grounding in less fixed, everyday practices, can be considered a realization of Theunissen's social theoretical aspirations, but in a form that is less fixated on Marx and Critical Theory than in Theunissen's work. Crucial here is the idea of a necessary increase in human beings' power over their own power, as formulated in Catholic theology by Romano Guardini soon after the end of the "Third Reich."[11] But power over one's own power means increased responsibility. Responsibility is in fact a leitmotif of Huber's understanding of freedom more generally.[12]

The term "communicative freedom" is clearly not identical with the various common understandings of freedom, and Huber construes it in a way that underlines how it differs from other notions of freedom. I would like to distinguish two kinds of such demarcation. First, Huber puts forward a definition of freedom in general as communicative as opposed to merely negative freedom or falsely understood positive freedom. Second, he seeks to illuminate the constitution of communicative freedom, its "indebtedness" beyond immanence.[13]

Huber's "communicative freedom" is most clearly different from a merely negative understanding of freedom, one that attained its classic form in the early modern period in the work of Thomas Hobbes. According to him, a free person is one who "in those things, which by his strength and wit he is able to do, is not hindered to do what he has a will to."[14] Quite contrary to Hobbes's own intentions, thanks to this conception's tremendous effective history it has largely become a cultural matter of course in the West to demand freedom to pursue the most idiosyncratic goals and even to regard the critique of such goals as a restriction on one's freedom. Huber is aware that it would be unfair to reduce the negative concept of freedom entirely to such arbitrary freedom. What may seem completely lacking in substance as negative freedom must often be understood as a certain kind of negation: "As a rule, demands for freedom acquire their substantive specificity from the experience of forces preventing one's development, of coercion and imposed inequality" (102).

In line with what has been said so far, it is above all the pursuit of whatever an individual may perceive as utility at a given moment that Huber attacks as an overly narrow conception of freedom. But he distances himself not only from this kind of utilitarian individualism but also from the expressivist variant, in other words the idea that freedom simply exists in the realm of self-realization, in the individual's unrestricted opportunity to discover, articulate, and realize their own intrinsic telos on a singular basis. This, of course, as Robert Bellah and his colleagues convincingly demonstrated in their 1985 US-American cultural analysis *Habits of the Heart*, merely results in a different type of egocentricity, not so much the "managerial" as the "therapeutic" kind, which is not to say that we cannot often find both types nowadays combined in one person.[15] Huber's understanding of freedom, pervaded by the ethos of love, allows him to recognize such a self-centered understanding of self-realization, in which others merely become a means because there is no real decentering of the self, as deficient.

Least pronounced is Huber's distinction between the idea of "communicative freedom" and a Kantian concept of freedom that privileges the moral autonomy of the individual and a social order based on it. In light of the Christian ethos of love, two questions arise here that are, in my opinion, clearly distinguishable and have been discussed in a wide range of ways in the history of ideas. First, the insight that love cannot be commanded leads to the question of whether love of neighbor can be meaningfully thought of as a moral obligation.[16] Second, we must ask how exactly we are to conceive of the transition from a normatively substantial idea of self-determination to insight into the indebtedness of human freedom and what the moral consequences of this transition might be.[17]

The first question is concerned with the precise relationship between rationally comprehensible moral duty and the enthusiastic devotion to others intrinsic to the ethos of love. In his reflections on love and justice, Paul Ricœur, for example, pointed out that in the writings of St. Luke the Evangelist, the commandment to love one's enemy and the Golden Rule appear close together (6:27 and 6:31).[18] His point here is to show that a subtle dialectic between the ethos of love and the pathos of justice is embedded in Christianity, which cannot be resolved within either of these two frameworks, either in the sense of an "acosmistic ethics of brotherliness" (Max Weber) or of a universalist moral philosophy. When related to Wolfgang Huber's "communicative freedom," however, this means that there is a fundamental need to clarify the relationship between the effusive understanding of freedom inherent in the notion of self-realization through devotion and the legally and morally disciplined understanding of equal freedom for all through just institutions, something the book *Von der Freiheit* fails to do. Elsewhere, however, Huber has set out in detail the foundations of a Christian "ethics of right," partly by building directly on Ricœur.[19]

The second complex, freedom and "indebtedness," is likewise only hinted at in Huber's slim volume. If it is to be understandable, the fundamental Christian idea that we must see our freedom as a gift giving rise—as with every gift—to obligations of reciprocity must be clearly articulated today through dialogue with representatives of secular worldviews as well as dialogue among believers. When Christians grapple with secular beliefs, it is important not to present this idea of freedom as a gift as if this notion would obviously be inaccessible without prior Christian belief. I found this to be the exemplary feature of Michael Sandel's book on bioethics, *The Case against Perfection*.[20] And this is also how I understand Wolfgang Huber's writings in this field, namely as attempts, very much aimed partly at secular minds, to bring out the sensitivity to indisposability inherent in these ideas and the risks that ensue from the loss of these conceptions.[21] In dialogues among believers, this must mean countering the dilutions quite common among German Protestant intellectuals as a result of "self-secularization" (Wolfgang Huber); when it comes to euthanasia or suicide, for example, in many cases the idea of life as a gift has become incomprehensible to these thinkers, who (like their secular counterparts) disqualify as irrational any notion of a value higher than that of free self-determination.[22]

Value Monism and Value Pluralism

But even more important than these two issues, it seems to me, is the need to clarify in a broader sense the relationship between the concept of communicative freedom and the competing concepts of freedom that are claimed by Huber to be deficient. Even if there is more to our understanding of freedom than Hobbesian negative freedom, we still intuit that there is something worth defending about it. As plausible as it is to illustrate true freedom with reference to our devotion in relationships of love, this still leaves many other social relationships to consider—let's say with the person behind the kiosk counter who sells you your monthly travel pass. Here, although we must never view the other person merely as a means to an end, it would be inappropriate to orientate ourselves toward the ethos of love. And the same applies to the other variants of the concept of freedom, such as that of expressive individualism.

From this it follows that a higher-level concept can and should be held up against the deficient concepts. But at least when transitioning to institutional ethics, it is crucial to discuss in which social sphere we perceive compelling reasons to institutionalize which variant of the value of "freedom." This will not always entail the institutionalization of communicative freedom.

Wolfgang Huber's ethics highlights a complex architectonics characteristic of the institutions of legal, moral, and social freedom, as we might put it in light of Axel Honneth's distinction.[23] However, this cannot be Honneth's architecture itself, as it, like John Dewey's conception of the public sphere and democratic culture, which greatly influenced Honneth, ignores to a stunning degree the institution so central to Wolfgang Huber's work: the church.

In debates on Islam, Europeans often note with astonishment that it knows no church, which makes it difficult to regulate its relations with the state. Wolfgang Huber too refers to this fact on numerous occasions. Yet Islam is not the exception among religions here, but the rule. After all, there is no such thing as a Jewish, Buddhist, Confucian, or Hindu church. I sometimes think we all need to rediscover the ability to be amazed that Christianity managed to produce a totally unprecedented social entity called the church. Perhaps this astonishment has passed some of us by because this church has, again and again, leaned too much on other entities such as the state or has adapted itself to them; but it has also repeatedly detached itself from them and shown the potential to point beyond ties to family, nation, state, and a specific civilization.

Within Wolfgang Huber's work, I see the clearest approach to a nuanced institutional ethics, one that neither conceals functionally necessary distinctions through an overly emphatic concept of freedom nor ignores the church, in his reflections on a "public church within plural public spheres" (158ff.), which he has developed more broadly in numerous other writings. There he distinguishes between four "reference areas" of the public sphere:

> The exercise and oversight of state authority, the satisfaction of needs and pursuit of interests as mediated by the market, the configuring of conditions common to all citizens and finally the production of publicity through cultural communication. (166f.)

It must be possible to develop out of this distinction a theory of different spheres of freedom, that is, spheres of different kinds of freedom.

The need not simply to submerge the competing concepts of freedom in a superior concept of communicative freedom, but to recognize their legitimacy in social life, may certainly raise doubts as to whether we are right, in our debates on values, to present the value of freedom as the highest source of orientation. Here Wolfgang Huber seems to show a tendency toward value monism when it comes to freedom. "Liberty, equality, fraternity" was the famous slogan of the French Revolution—three values, not just freedom, were proclaimed. "This was only conceivable," writes Huber,

> because freedom was understood as disposal over oneself, which now required a community-oriented counterbalance in the shape of fraternity. To supplement the Christian concept of freedom with that of brotherhood, conversely, must appear meaningless. (150)

Again, though, we might ask whether we can really imagine a social life in which we are expected to live up to this ambitious normative expectation across the board, not only as the highest point of reference of all spheres, but also within spheres such as economy or politics, that is, in which we must focus not on our disposal over ourselves but on the indisposability of the other. This would mean that all values except freedom play an ancillary role; security, for example, is declared the "political prerequisite for freedom" (146). This tendency is found even more prominently, as I explained in the introduction to this book, in the aforementioned volume by Axel Honneth. He too does not understand a value such as that of equality, which one might view as in tension with that of freedom, as a value in its own right, arguing that "it can only be understood as an elucidation of the value of individual freedom, as the notion that all members of modern societies are equally entitled to freedom."[24]

But here both Huber and Honneth resolve real value conflicts or tensions between values merely at the verbal level. If we can want equality only in the shape of equal freedom, this does not mean that in concrete instances we do not have to choose between doing without a certain amount of freedom or equality. Much the same goes for tensions between freedom and security. What is the status of values that were once so important, such as obedience, willingness to make sacrifices, and humility? I can understand the idea of grounding these values too in freedom, but the voluntary forgoing of freedom that they entail must nevertheless remain recognizable. What is needed is sensitivity to genuine dilemmas, including cases of conflict between competing understandings of freedom with their relative legitimacy, along with an awareness of those instances when freedom comes into conflict with other values. Meanwhile, a relationship of tension exists between the proposition that the meaning of freedom is always contested, and the rather different proposition that today there is only one great value—namely, freedom.

In opposition to a "value monism" of freedom, I would thus like to propose a "value pluralism," not in the sense of the mere acceptance of a plurality of socially existing values, but as suggested by one of the most important philosophers who have written about the concept of freedom, namely Isaiah Berlin. For him, value pluralism means that "ultimate human values are objective but irreducibly diverse, that they are conflicting and often umcombinable, and that sometimes when they come into conflict with one another they are incommensurable."[25] For Berlin, such a pluralism of values means that there can be no perfect society in which all genuine ideals are simultaneously realized, and not because such a goal is utopian but because it is intrinsically incoherent.

Berlin was consistent enough to infer from this that even a liberalism that sees itself as guaranteeing political salvation is dangerous. In Berlin's philosophy—in contrast to that of John Rawls—the value of justice is, therefore, not the incontestably highest value that must be upheld when establishing a polity, but a value that is in constant conflict with other values such as freedom, equality, community, and peace. Such a pluralism of values has an elective affinity with a tragic conception of history—tragic at least in the sense that even our most reasonable decisions will doom to destruction something in the world that is of value and has features worth preserving, and no form of political progress is conceivable that would definitely rule this out.[26]

What is more, value pluralism requires paying a great deal of attention to actors' decision-making situation. If a value's top position in a hierarchy of values has not been secured once and for all through abstraction from concrete action situations, then real, risky predicaments will always arise in contexts of action in which we have to weigh things up, unique constellations in which we have to prioritize different values at different times. Then we will regularly find ourselves in situations of the kind Max Weber was thinking of when he referred to an "ethics of responsibility."

As mentioned earlier, "responsibility" and an "ethics of responsibility" are also crucial categories for Wolfgang Huber. In his book on freedom, he identifies

> a number of substantive criteria for responsible action . . . : providing for a shared natural, social and cultural space for people to live in together; fairness to the weaker . . . ; self-limitation out of consideration for the rights of future generations and the dignity of nature; respect for others' freedom of conscience. (93f.)[27]

That makes perfect sense to me. But my point is that we have to strike a—sometimes tragic—balance and that while an anthropology of freedom teaches us that we will face such moments of weighing things up, the value of freedom furnishes us with no clear criteria determining how we should go about this in a given case.

My skepticism, which I have at least hinted at here, regarding the central position of the freedom motif also fuels a certain reservation about designating Christianity in general and Protestantism in particular as the religion of freedom. First, as I have mentioned, we have to ask whether Christianity, which also aims to be a religion of love and justice and obedience to God, can be all of this and at the same time a religion of freedom. The last thing I wish to do is question the central role played by the message of freedom at least since Paul's letter to the Galatians. But in my view the tensions between freedom, love, justice, and devoutness do not melt away as unambiguously as the emphasis on freedom suggests.

Second, of course, this points to the need for an honest empirical-historical assessment of the broad topic of Christianity's freedom-promoting or freedom-hindering role. Wolfgang Huber is well informed about the dark sides of this history and even begins his book by remarking that the term *Obrigkeit* ("authority" or "authorities") became a familiar feature of the German language thanks to Martin Luther (13). Even Max Weber—a point missed by many of those who now refer to his notion of the "Protestant ethic" in the manner of an apologia—saw Lutheranism primarily (and certainly one-sidedly) as the source of a quietist German subservience, prompting him to describe this strand of Christianity in a letter to Adolf von Harnack as "the worst of all horrors,"[28] regardless of his profound rejection of Catholicism (which he also found fascinating in some ways).

Yet Wolfgang Huber's work also features many passages that are rather quick to assert affinities between Protestantism and democracy (35), the Enlightenment (192), and other good things—in a way that fails to fully integrate the kind of qualifications we have just considered. The risk here is that a selective reconstruction of the past will serve to emphasize the superiority of one's own traditions. Is it permissible for Christians to do this with regard to their Christianity? Even if we leave this moral question aside, are we doing justice to history? The great early modern historian Wolfgang Reinhard brought out in a brilliant way how the right to resist and thus an element of modern freedom was indeed "invented" and first propagated by Lutherans in the middle of the sixteenth century

> until they no longer needed it thanks to the legal protection provided by the Peace of Augsburg. In the meantime, it had "migrated" to the Calvinists. Due to the tribulations of the Huguenot Wars, especially after the St. Bartholomew's Day massacre, they presented themselves as "monarchomachs," although John Calvin's political doctrine was hardly less authoritarian than that of Luther and he would have dearly loved to impose his gospel with the help of crowned heads in the style of a state church. However, when Henry of Navarre, who was originally Calvinist, became the most promising contender for the French Crown, the Catholics suddenly became opponents of the monarchy, even embracing the theory and practice of tyrannicide, while the Calvinists, under the protection of the Edict of Nantes—much like the German Lutherans in the past—turned into absolutists, until the tide turned again in the seventeenth century with the revocation of the Edict of Tolerance. Under such circumstances, can one still claim that a particular group is on its way to modernity, or does this apply to all or to none?[29]

Much the same applies when it comes to the history of human rights. Like Wolfgang Huber, I take the view that the struggle for freedom of religion and conscience was an important first stage in achieving the entrenchment of such rights, but if we look at key figures in this history, such as Roger Williams in North America, we find that in this case their Protestant motives made them outsiders within Protestantism and they barely managed to resist the pressures imposed by the—Calvinist—majority.[30]

In order to advocate something in the present, one does not have to claim that one's own religious or value-based tradition has always advocated it or did much to bring it about. And my impression is that Wolfgang Huber has no wish to contribute to the idealization of Protestantism. When he writes that "we must now develop the legacy of the Reformation as a 'theology of liberation'" (17), his goal is not to promote a past-oriented cultural Protestant complacency, but rather to renew our awareness of the prophetic core of the legacy of the Reformation, making it a stimulus for action in the present:

Those who understand Christianity only as a culture will see their task primarily as preserving a "tradition" and administering an "inheritance." Those who call to mind the source of these cultural influences will seek to understand the vital force that seizes their own life and whose cultural outgrowths are thus capable of renewing themselves. (43f.)[31]

The distinction between "religion" and "culture" implied here is crucial not only to the problems of ethics, but especially to a historical sociology of religion of the kind I address in Part IV of this book.

PART IV
THE PROJECT OF A HISTORICAL SOCIOLOGY OF RELIGION

PART IV

IV, 1
Introductory Remarks

Almost a century after Hegel's Berlin lectures on the philosophy of history, which amalgamated contemporary knowledge on the history of religion and political freedom, the great studies in the sociology of religion emerged in Germany and France; these were to be of fundamental importance to the emergence of the discipline of sociology. The same year, 1912, saw publication of Émile Durkheim's epoch-making study *The Elementary Forms of the Religious Life* and Ernst Troeltsch's pioneering work in the historical sociology of Christianity, titled *The Social Teachings of the Christian Churches and Groups*. Around the same time, Max Weber began a vast project in which he sought to go beyond his controversial thesis on the connection between the Protestant ethic and the spirit of capitalism, investigating the economic ethics of all world religions. This simultaneously nudged him away from the issue of the emergence of modern capitalism, as exacting as this is, to the even greater problem of how the phenomenon of "Occidental rationalism," pervading all areas of culture and society, could come about. He published his first studies on this set of themes from 1916 onward in a journal, the *Archiv für Sozialwissenschaft und Sozialpolitik* ("Archive of Social Science and Social Policy"), and then collected them in three volumes, to which further texts were added and that appeared in 1920, the year of his death.

The premises underlying the study of religion had, of course, changed considerably in the nearly one hundred years since Hegel. In his review of Hermann Süskind's book on Schleiermacher, Ernst Troeltsch summed up Hegel's and Schleiermacher's outdated conceptual presuppositions as follows: "The East is still to be discovered, Schopenhauer and Nietzsche do not yet exist, and Strauss is yet to write the life of Jesus."[1] Here Troeltsch was highlighting the fact that at that time Western scholarship was yet to truly grapple with the non-monotheistic religions of Asia, while a "pantheistic-pessimistic religiosity" was yet to appear as a competitor to Christianity in European culture itself. In particular, however, Troeltsch underlined, those who had begun to historicize Christianity, even after questioning the miracles described in the Bible, had yet to critically examine the life and words of Jesus himself in the same way.

None of the three great founders of a historical and comparative sociology of religion, however, could avoid or wished to avoid these new challenges. This is not the place to portray this in detail. But it is crucial to note that the way back to the assumption shared by Hegel, Schleiermacher, and their contemporaries was cut off for all three—namely the contention that "Christianity is undoubtedly the highest ethicization and spiritualization of the common ground" of all religions.[2] In Durkheim's work, Christianity as such appeared as a thing of the past, one replete with historical merits, but no more than a tool and weapon of reactionary politics in the present. His evolutionist assumptions drove him to refrain from developing his theory of religion on the basis of a study of Christianity or any other "world religion." Instead, he went back to the "most elementary" form of religion, of which there were still living examples in his day, and he believed he had found this among the Australian Aborigines and certain North American Indian tribes. He thought he could describe their religious practices and ideas as "totemism." By studying totemism, he was convinced, one could gain insights that would be of significance to a post-Christian age. Reflecting the context of the time, he was primarily concerned with the social cohesion of a nation and with general respect for human rights as captured by the notion of the sacredness of the individual or person.

Ernst Troeltsch, on the other hand, limited himself entirely to Christianity in his great book of 1912. The question of how an empirically defensible historicization of this religion could coexist with the claim to truth or even absoluteness resulting from faith pervades his entire work, starting with his first book (after his dissertation), titled *Die Absolutheit des Christentums und die Religionsgeschichte* ("The Absoluteness of Christianity and the History of Religions").[3] It was only in his late work, twenty years later, that he was to find what he considered a satisfactory answer to these questions, now generalized in the question of how historically contingent ideals can claim universal validity in the first place.[4] Christianity was for him by no means a thing of the past. On the contrary, he believed in the possibility of a future age in which people would look back at the atheism of Feuerbach and Marx, Schopenhauer and Nietzsche as a historical phenomenon.[5] His work was crucially informed by the attempt, as a Christian, to meet the intellectual challenges of the time and to achieve a new gathering of religious forces through far-reaching reform of the church.

Finally, Max Weber went further beyond the horizons of Christianity and Europe than any other German scholar of his time, far more than Wilhelm Dilthey and Troeltsch, for example. Despite the ultimately fragmentary and often empirically untenable character of his assertions, this is an achievement that must be permanently upheld. From this point of view, his distance from Hegel and Schleiermacher is huge. However, another hundred years later, we cannot ignore two shortcomings that Weber's work shares with Hegel's philosophy of history. Although Weber was very far removed from any historical teleology centered on the self-realization of spirit and while he viewed history as the contingent result of the interweaving of human actions, he looked out from the Europe of his time at its history and that of all other civilizations and pondered why what had emerged in Europe (or the "West") had not arisen outside of it. But this is by no means an inevitable perspective. The question of why modern capitalism or other (alleged) expressions of "Occidental rationalism" did not appear elsewhere is problematic for two reasons.

First, it inherently privileges long-term cultural prerequisites over contemporary constellations. In this way, the researcher's gaze is directed toward cultural turning points far in the past, rather than toward the political, economic, military, and, of course, cultural realities of a specific present.[6] In our time, when, for example, the capitalist economy has powerfully established itself in East Asia, even in the People's Republic of China, still nominally under communist rule, the assumption of an insufficient affinity between "Asian" culture and "Occidental rationalism" is rapidly losing plausibility. Of course, one might point out that the emergence of a phenomenon requires different conditions than its spread. But explanations of its origins that foreground long-term cultural developments lose their persuasiveness if the cultural resistance to the new proves weak.

Second, a "deficit-oriented" perspective on non-Western societies and cultures is also problematic because it scarcely allows one to discover anything in them that might enrich "Western" culture. The example of vegetarianism may serve to illustrate this. In the West today there is growing skepticism about meat consumption and the conditions of meat production. This might inspire us to look with curiosity and admiration at the traditions of India, where, for longer than in Christian cultures, the sacredness of all life has prompted certain conclusions about human nutrition. This example is not meant to suggest that we simply reverse the "deficit perspective"—that we exclusively emphasize our own guilt and missteps. But it does show that when comparing cultures, we must eschew any standardizing reduction to one point of view that prevails over everything else.

Weber's perspective was certainly not characterized by a seamlessly positive assessment of Western developments—quite the opposite. He combined the notion of an undeniable superiority of Occidental rationalism with a melancholy ambivalence toward the culture of his time. On the one hand, he welcomed the political freedom that had developed in Europe and North America; on the other hand, in view of world-historical tendencies toward comprehensive rationalization, which he believed he had identified, he could not believe in its future viability. This resulted in a deeply value-conscious "heroic agnosticism"[7] and historical pessimism. Durkheim's conscious atheism and politically militant laicism amounted to a call for the—absolutely achievable—firm institutionalization of human rights, at least in France. Troeltsch, meanwhile, in view of the dangers he perceived of a "new bondage" in the capitalist economy and given the pressures he discerned emanating from the armed forces and bureaucracy, saw the only opposing force as the preservation of a "religious metaphysic of freedom and of a faith based on personal conviction," above all within Protestant Christianity in his case.[8] But Weber's project was bound to end aporetically here, namely as an ethos of freedom without a religious or optimistic-areligious foundation, an affirmation of free political institutions without the possibility of identifying the social forces that might defend them. Some find this unsatisfactory, while others consider it admirably free of illusion.

These brief remarks are intended to demonstrate that the original project of a historical sociology of religion was not simply a matter of establishing a special, perhaps somewhat esoteric, field of research, but was centered on questions of tremendous and far-reaching importance. But what was the subsequent fate of this "discourse"? Nobody would deny that after the generation of Durkheim, Weber, and Troeltsch this scholarly project petered out rather than flourishing. Volkhard Krech and Hartmann Tyrell, two of the leading experts in this field, have taken some of the drama out of this observation by underlining that the sociology of religion was from the outset a wholly European—in fact, exclusively French and German—affair, while Max Weber's work was a "grandiose one-man project" that no one could have carried on after its tragically premature end.[9]

Yet both remarks must be taken with a grain of salt. As far as the United States is concerned, the above picture pertains if we look only at the prevailing tendencies in the discipline of sociology itself without considering the reception of sociology in historically oriented theology or the theological writings of sociologists.[10] In France too, to paint a realistic picture we would have to include full consideration of Durkheim's impact not just on sociology—for example, in the work of Marcel Mauss and the entire Durkheim School—but also in other subjects such as Sinology and ancient history.[11] Max Weber's most important direct student in this field, Paul Honigsheim, has been completely forgotten today, although he made a signal contribution to sociological research on Jansenism, scholasticism, and mysticism, among other topics.[12] Later independent perpetuators of Weber's and Troeltsch's ideas, such as Benjamin Nelson, are also part of this picture.[13] An even remotely satisfactory history of scholarship in this regard has yet to appear. I cannot remedy this major shortcoming here. The lack of such an account is just another symptom of the fact that a project that had got off to a flying start had surprisingly little influence in the period that followed.

As a consequence, in a peculiar way, while the writings of Weber and Durkheim, especially their contributions to the sociology of religion, were to become an enduring focus within sociology,[14] the relativization of Weber's and Durkheim's views within specialist fields on the basis of today's superior level of knowledge has made virtually no impact on the overall discipline. Hence, teaching and theory building within sociology carry a great deal of conceptual baggage that has long since proven untenable. It seems to me that the only way to remedy this is to once again fuse the project of sociology wholeheartedly with developments in historical scholarship and ensure that the sociology of religion in particular retains its capacity for dialogue with theology.

But I do not wish my message at this point to be dominated by laments over disciplinary missteps. On the contrary, this part of the book is focused on identifying outstanding figures who continued and advanced the project of a historical sociology of religion with great independence and in full awareness of the importance of the questions constitutive of this project. As we will see, one of the things at play here is a substantial topic identifiable in the work of these scholars, a topic that revolved, as I would put it, around the history of moral universalism. The main aim of this part of the book is to give this theme a sharper profile and flesh it out empirically; it would be quite wrong to understand it as centered on marginal figures in the history of sociology. Before concisely characterizing the scholars whose often little-noticed oeuvres are my focus here, we need to reflect briefly on the phenomenon alluded to above: the great beginning and rapid weakening of the attempt to produce a sociological analysis of the world history of religion or, to put it the other way round, a sociology whose categories and whose understanding of the present might prove tenable when confronted with this world history of religion.[15]

I have referred elsewhere to the seemingly paradoxical fact that, in the shape of Weber and Durkheim, two scholars who espoused a universal approach to history and for whom the history of religion was a core part of universal history became classical figures in a discipline to which neither of these characteristics apply.[16] Sociology became ever more unhistorical, dwindling to the study of contemporary society, which simultaneously lent impetus to the genre of *Zeitdiagnose*, the analysis of the contemporary world, and thus to speculations about the present and future that have often been difficult to verify empirically. The sociology of religion was increasingly pushed to the margins of the subject and declared irrelevant by many; this was true even where new trends toward historicization set in, but religion was, for example, subsumed under the term "ideology," thanks to economistic and power-centered approaches.[17]

What needs to be explained about this development is why a discipline that moved so far away from its founders, rather than simply discarding them, increasingly placed them on a pedestal and venerated them. The solution to this riddle seems clear to me: the writings of Weber and Durkheim themselves encouraged this development. This is because they themselves made assumptions about religion's progressive loss of importance and about the specificity of the new era of "modernity"—to which much of what applied in earlier ages would supposedly no longer apply. But if "modernity without religion" constitutes the real subject of sociology, the importance of everything premodern and of all religion decreases prodigiously. On this premise, when it comes to religion the only remaining question is the nature of its role in creating the conditions for the emergence of this modernity without religion. This explains the key role played by Max Weber's essay on the Protestant ethic and by Émile Durkheim's theory of change in the character of law and in forms of social cohesion generally. The subsequent far-reaching ignorance of Troeltsch's masterpiece can be explained in the same way.

Over the last few decades, however, the assumption of "modernity without religion" has lost credibility because, above all outside Europe, rapid modernization spurts have taken place unaccompanied by secularization. Historical research, furthermore, has increasingly shown the history of European secularization to be multifaceted rather than marked by inevitable trends. These shifts have led to a change of perspective. To the extent that a discipline is based on the idea of modernity without religion, such a new perspective is bound to have a profoundly unsettling effect on it. Under these changed premises, what is interesting about Durkheim's work is not so much the assumption of secularization and of the surmountability of Judaism and Christianity as his approach to explaining modern phenomena of sacralization—whether of the nation, "race," and party, or of the person, quite independent of their deeds and achievements.

On the same premise, what is most impressive about Max Weber's work—I would argue—is his sensitivity to the competition between different forms of self-transcendence, between aesthetic, erotic, and religious experience, for example, or the competition between moral universalism and particularist "brotherhood," rather than the idea of the progressive differentiation of value spheres.[18] The work of Ernst Troeltsch was at first self-evidently counted among the classic founding texts of German sociology, but then largely faded into obscurity in this discipline since it came from a theologian of all things—one who, moreover, made no secret of his desire to illuminate the preconditions for a modern Christianity. From the new vantage point outlined earlier, his writings can suddenly attract attention again and have the potential to become a methodological model.[19]

This is the background against which the following five chapters must be read. My first portrait is of one of the leading US-American theologians of the twentieth century, H. Richard Niebuhr. As we will see, his thinking is guided by two motifs, both of which are hugely relevant in the context of the present book. First, more than anyone before him, Niebuhr took the specifics of US religious history seriously in a systematic way. Certainly, he was preceded by Max Weber with his brilliant essay on the Protestant sects.[20] But Niebuhr developed in greater breadth and depth the idea that the United States, in contrast to the European model of state-supported territorial religious monopolies, is characterized by an inherently pluralist religious system, for which he introduced the term "denominationalism." In line with this, he was concerned with the development of this system and the reasons for its differentiation into the various denominations.

His view of the concrete form taken by this denominational pluralism was mainly negative: he could discern in the denominations no more than a reflection of the dividing lines to be found in social reality. This mirroring, however, seemed to him incompatible with the idea, which he strongly advocated, that Christianity should never be identified with a particular class, nation, or any other kind of social entity. In this respect, Niebuhr took very seriously a motif that assumed radical form in Europe in protest against "Cultural Protestantism," namely that God transcends all specific religions and cultures. But it was not only in the new "dialectical" theology that Niebuhr saw this motif at work. It can in fact also be found in the work of Ernst Troeltsch, who is wrongly regarded as the epitome of Cultural Protestantism. This chapter describes how Niebuhr takes up motifs from Troeltsch and Weber, fleshing them out through a sociologically highly significant typology of the relationships between moral-universalist religion on the one hand and culture on the other.

But his thinking is guided by a second motif as well. Niebuhr was one of the great mediators between German and US-American intellectual traditions, specifically German historicism and US-American pragmatism. Two traditions that I presented in the first part of this book as crucial to the development of a nonintellectualist understanding of religion came closer to one another in his work than in that of any other thinker. This is particularly evident in Niebuhr's study of revelation, which I seek to decipher as an impressive attempt to convey universalist validity claims through contemplation of the historical particularity of those who make them. This theologian, who drew much of his inspiration from Troeltsch, finds the resources for this project in the philosophy of sociality and time developed by George Herbert Mead.

In his late writings, Niebuhr developed out of this a (never more than fragmentary) ethics, based on a pragmatist understanding of action. Concrete action in specific situations is never merely the application of preexisting norms or values. The concept of the responsibility-bearing self became crucial for Niebuhr, a self that, however much it may strive to pursue a universalist approach, can never shed, and must not ignore morally, its particularity. Naturally, in a theological ethics some things will remain normative that a sociologist might have elaborated in a different way. No surprise, then, that others have taken up Niebuhr's potential sociological impulses and developed them beyond anything appearing in his own writings.

In sociology, however, recognition for Niebuhr's achievements came after a considerable delay. Tellingly, his book was not reviewed in the leading sociological journal when it was published, but the same publication thought it necessary to self-critically mention and celebrate the new edition a quarter century later.[21] Over the course of time, both theology and sociology generated significant studies that creatively embraced Niebuhr's ideas and updated his findings.[22] In the first instance, however, the most important task for these disciplines was to discern and fill an obvious gap in Niebuhr's arguments. His books on denominationalism and on visions of the kingdom of God in American history were devoted almost entirely to Protestantism. Catholic Christianity appeared almost exclusively in its medieval form as a historical foil and not as a contemporary US-American reality. Judaism was absent, as were all forms of secularist humanism.[23]

The key step toward remedying this was taken by Russian-born Jewish theologian and sociologist Will Herberg, who had broken away from the atheistic communist convictions of his early days under the influence of the Niebuhr brothers. His brilliant book *Protestant, Catholic, Jew* from 1955 represented much more than a mere reflection of the fact that the basic Protestant consensus that had long prevailed in the United States had changed into a generally Christian and then even "Judeo-Christian" one by the time of the Cold War at the latest.[24] Herberg raised the debate on the social organization of Christianity to a new level, beyond attempts to characterize the denominations.

Central to Herberg's account was the term "religious community." By this, he meant that in the 1950s neither denominations nor ethnic groups provided the most important classificatory principle in US-American society, but rather the three major religious milieus of Protestants, Catholics, and Jews, between which there was virtually no switching of affiliation or even dialogue. Each of these milieus was ethnically plural, but ethnicity was relativized by religious affiliation, which could be shown empirically, for example in marriage behavior and its milieu-dependency. In place of the notion of the United States as (ethnic) melting pot, Herberg asserted that in reality the country consisted of three coexisting melting pots. But, he contended, individuals were at a disadvantage if they did not belong to one of the three. Non-Christian Asians, Orthodox Christians, and secularists, Herberg claimed, had a hard time feeling like real Americans under these circumstances.

Herberg viewed this development with the utmost skepticism. President Eisenhower's declaration that "our form of government" was based on a deeply felt religious faith, but that it did not matter which one,[25] must, according to Herberg, appear to European believers like a deplorable heresy. For this statement revealed that what was meant here was not the specific moral demands of a particular belief in God, but merely trust in the socially integrative effects of religion as such; in a sense, Herberg contended, this was not a matter of belief in God, but of belief in religion. This meant that the growing membership of religious communities was not a reliable indicator of growing piety, but merely signaled an increased need to belong to a national community.

Such a shift in core loyalties from a universalist to a particularist orientation was exactly what Niebuhr had "prophetically" called into question. Herberg followed his example, explaining in detail how the Americanism of all three milieus affected the associated religious traditions. His analysis of American Judaism in terms of its own division into "denominations" and institutional structures was particularly original. The final chapter of his book then presented a biting critique of the transformation of all religious traditions in the United States into cultural religions, marked by a complacent nationalism, and critical remarks on the loss of a strong understanding of moral universalism and transcendence. The same sociological factors that moved people to join the religious "communities," that is, milieus crosscutting the various denominations, thus emerged as the driving forces of a process of internal secularization. The result, Herberg stated, was secularism in religious guise.[26]

In retrospect, this book comes across as an astute, historically well-founded analysis of the religious situation in the United States in the 1950s, but also as a child of its time: it is blind to the specific situation of blacks and "Hispanic" Catholics and fails to recognize the major religious upheavals of the era. The book is devoid of the merest hint of awareness of the civil rights movement and the new spiritual currents later entangled with the cultural convulsions of the 1960s. Yet the civil rights movement in particular cannot be accused of cheapening the aspiration to transcendence and moral universalism. Nevertheless, Herberg's work is another milestone in the history of a historically oriented and "universalism-sensitive" sociology of religion.

But in addition to Niebuhr's Protestant and Herberg's Jewish perspective, another study in historical sociology appeared that concurrently represented a plea for the fulsome preservation of moral universalism as a key aspiration. The 1960s saw the publication of an extremely ambitious work by a Catholic scholar in the form of a five-volume (English-language) historical sociology of Christianity. I am referring to the sociologist Werner Stark, of Bohemian Jewish origin, who converted to Catholicism during his British exile and wrote this great work in the United States. From a history-of-scholarship perspective, this text is a peculiarity in that when it was published both the author and others had high hopes that it would attain classic status. Not only did it fail to achieve this, but it was marginalized and forgotten to such an extent that this phenomenon itself seems to require explanation.

But this is not the focus of the relevant chapter in the present book, which is concerned with more specifically sociological issues. Since Stark distanced himself from the Protestant one-sidedness of Max Weber's sociology, I will first discuss the validity of his criticism of certain Weber-based ideas that gained canonical status. I then turn to the alternatives Stark proposes, especially his ideas on the potential institutionalization of charisma in the church and the renewed focus he advocates on the role of monasticism and religious orders in the history of Christianity. Finally, the true structuring principle of his work turns out to be a distinction that cannot be expressed through the conventional typology of church versus sect—namely that between the universal church and a church established at the national level. Stark sees an unabridged Christian universalism as present institutionally only in Catholic and Calvinist-Reformed Christianity, but not in Lutheran and Orthodox Christianity. My broad discussion of Stark's work is not intended as a sweeping affirmation of his theories but does seek to open up debate on this sophisticated work, which has been unjustly forgotten.

My next study, on British sociologist of religion David Martin, also begins with Max Weber. In contrast to Werner Stark's perspective, the key question here is not the extent to which Weber's Protestant background distorted his scholarly work. Instead, the starting point is the possible discrepancy between Weber's de facto research in historical sociology and his famous notion of a world-historical process of rationalization and disenchantment. I call David Martin "more Weberian than Weber" because he adheres to Weber's research methods but is skeptical of his grand statements about historical tendencies. I characterize Martin's work as a political sociology of religion because he declares the attitude of churches and other religious communities toward key political issues—but above all the fundamental, enduring patterns that typify the relationship between political power and religion—the crucial dimension that helps us explain processes of secularization, as well as religious change and religious revitalization. No one has challenged the thesis that modernization necessarily leads to secularization as early and consistently as David Martin, and no one has elaborated an alternative general theory of the development of religion in recent history in the same breadth and depth.

However, in its original form this theory was limited to Europe and North America, apart from a few glances at Latin America. One of the most stunning religio-political phenomena of the second half of the twentieth century—the rapid growth of the so-called Pentecostal movement in Latin America and Africa, but also in East Asia—prompted Martin to significantly expand his research horizon and to focus specifically on the dynamics of this global expansion of a particular form of Christianity. His studies on this topic have proven highly controversial, but nonetheless essential to the broadening of scholarly horizons beyond Europe and North America. Another aspect of Martin's research has also proved productive, namely his investigation of the relationship between religion and violence in history. Martin's main focus here is not on the causes of violence but on the preconditions for a religiously motivated rejection of violence. This leads him to important observations on the relationship between universalist ideals and particularist forms of political and religious institutionalization.

David Martin's contribution is that of an outsider who, with admirable independence, broke away from many widely held views and, over the decades, developed an alternative to them, which only received broad recognition in the wake of the general questioning of the secularization thesis. But the importance of his work to social theory as a whole is yet to be fully recognized. The situation is quite different when it comes to the self-confident and persistent attempts by Israeli sociologist Shmuel Eisenstadt and his US-American colleague Robert Bellah to attain the intellectual level already reached by the classical sociological figures of Weber and Durkheim, and to revive the project of a comparative historical sociology of religion.

Both build in significant ways on the work of Talcott Parsons, whose variant of modernization theory greatly influenced Western sociology in the 1950s and 1960s. The discipline probably never came so close to cleaving to a clear-cut paradigm, either before or after. This state of affairs came to an end due to the critiques of this hegemonic theory put forward from a broad range of perspectives in the late 1960s and 1970s. But not everyone abandoned the goal of producing such a theory. Eisenstadt in particular set about a step-by-step revision of Parsonian sociology that took account of criticisms without sacrificing its core.[27] This revision primarily sought to honor the fact that modernization does not necessarily equate with Westernization. The major civilizations of the world may, according to this perspective, modernize economically, technologically, and scientifically. But they do not do so by breaking completely with their deepest religious and cultural traditions. To convey this perspective, Eisenstadt coined the term "multiple modernities," which proved to be a magnet for many intellectual projects of a similar hue.[28]

But which of the world's civilizations have such a core from which innovative adaptations can emerge under radically changed conditions? To answer this question, from the 1970s onward Eisenstadt drew on an idea first conveyed by German philosopher Karl Jaspers, who coined the term "Axial Age" during the Second World War, though conditions in Germany meant that it appeared in his published work immediately after that conflict.[29] This idea itself is far older: it had been expressed in different variants since the late eighteenth century and was also hinted at by Max Weber. It revolves around the assertion that in ancient Greece, Israel, China, and India (and perhaps Iran), there were independent breakthroughs to moral universalism and notions of transcendence, a shift that ultimately laid the ground for all world religions and philosophy. Even if one was unable to prove the simultaneity of these breakthroughs, the important question would remain of when, where, how, and why these (multiple) breakthroughs can be identified in history. This prompted Eisenstadt himself and some of his students to produce analyses of individual non-European modernization paths (particularly in Japan) as well as comparative studies—for example, on the institutionalization of religious virtuosity in Buddhism and Christianity.[30] It would be fair to say, however, that he continued to be guided by a desire to revise modernization theory, rather than focusing on the history of moral universalism or the assessment of every case of modernization in light of Axial Age ideals.

The other great scholar who developed Parsons's legacy, Robert Bellah, proceeded in a different way, which is why I devote another chapter of this book to him. Through his training in Japanese (and Chinese) studies, from the outset his interests extended beyond the "West." But his first, now-classic study in this field was still guided by a question unmistakably molded by Max Weber's halfhearted overcoming of Eurocentrism.[31] In the 1950s, he asked how the only non-Western country capable of competing with the West at the time, namely Japan, had managed to progress without the "Protestant ethic" supposedly so decisive in the West—in other words, what its "functional equivalent" in Japan had been. His studies on the United States, for which he became particularly famous, emerged in the backwash of this intellectual decentering, which had greatly sharpened his awareness of features specific to the United States.

In his early years as a scholar, Bellah had already briefly outlined a theory of the universal development of religion, which he named "religious evolution." Though this was not his intention, this sounded like the return of unilinear evolutionist ideas of the kind so common in the nineteenth century, which had enjoyed a brief renaissance after the Second World War. But when Bellah set about elaborating his theory on a broad basis in his later years, no one could now impute to him such simple beliefs about evolution (or even progress), which he had never held anyway. While he based his ideas about religion on a psychological theory revolving around levels of cognition and the use of signs, he did not mean that this was a necessary development or that we should embrace a stage model in which earlier levels become insignificant when higher levels are reached. Nor did he press entire religions into a stage model. In line with this, he no longer referred to "religious evolution" at all, but only to "religion in human evolution." Even more consistently than Eisenstadt, he foregrounded the links and tensions between religion and political power.

The death of Robert Bellah, however, terminated this epoch-making project soon after the completion of the first volume. As for the sequel, all we have to go on is a fragment and an original table of contents that had clearly become obsolete in the course of the project. But the extant materials compare the constitutive conditions of religious development in China, India, and the "West" in an unprecedented way. Bellah thus moved decisively beyond both Hegel's philosophy of history and Max Weber's historical sociology.

The final portrait in this part of the book is of Spanish American sociologist José Casanova, another outstanding figure pursuing the project of a comparative historical sociology of religion. He is world-famous for his 1994 book, *Public Religions in the Modern World*, which marks a true paradigm shift in the sociology of religion, putting paid to the notion of the advancing privatization of religion, a close relative of the secularization thesis.[32] In his later studies, he first extended the investigation of the public role of religion to other societies. Second, he examined the development of transnational religious relationships under the conditions of globalization. Taking up Niebuhr's idea, he refers to our present as a time in which territorial religious monopolies in general, and not just in the United States, have become impossible and a "global denominationalism" is emerging.

For the first time in world history, Casanova tells us, all world religions are in principle devoid of fixed territorial ties and are reproducible outside the areas in which they developed historically. What was already evident in the Pentecostal movement is increasingly becoming a general phenomenon. At present, Casanova is going beyond consideration of the globalization of Christianity and other world religions: his interests now extend to the entire history of the interrelationship between globalization and the history of religion. He has made this topic workable by concentrating on the history of the Jesuits as pioneers of globalization. In Casanova's work, too, we can make out the tendency to revive an approach that, as mentioned earlier, played a constitutive role in the founding phase of sociology.

But as I have emphasized, I am only indirectly concerned here with the history of a scholarly discipline. What matters more is that we can discern in this history and in the output of the scholars whose work I probe a shift of focus away from Christianity-centric and Eurocentric ideas toward a global historical perspective on moral universalism in all its multifarious forms. I will be returning to this by addressing the future prospects for research in this area in the conclusion of the present book.

IV, 2

Religion Is More Than Culture: H. Richard Niebuhr

American pragmatism and the German tradition of hermeneutics and historicism were long perceived as fundamentally different traditions of thought. The mere fact that it is customary in both cases to label these schools of philosophy with a national tag certainly indicates that both are strongly influenced by the cultures in which they originally developed. Furthermore, the US-American "civilization" of the nineteenth century was certainly very different from the German "culture" of the time. Yet this first impression is also misleading in many respects.[1] Under its influence we easily overlook the deeper similarities behind the superficial differences. The impression of difference seems to me to have three main causes. First, the disciplinary backgrounds of the two schools were different. While classical pragmatism developed out of the natural sciences (geodesy and astronomy in the case of Peirce, biology and physiological psychology in that of James and Mead), hermeneutics and historicism emerged from the humanities, above all the historical-critical study of the Bible and an engagement with the history of religion, law, and literature.

In both cases, then, the starting point lay in the most respected and influential disciplines, but which of them enjoyed this elevated status in the two countries differed greatly. Second, we cannot overlook the cultural difference between a strongly future-oriented progressive historical optimism in the United States and the German focus on the past and history in the context of struggles over national identity and unity. Third, their relationship with Christianity was very different. In neither case was it primarily critical, let alone destructive, but in the United States it was oriented chiefly toward contemporary religious experiential possibilities, spirituality, and practical results, and in Germany more toward history and religious doctrine.

But these conspicuous differences are undergirded by a commonality, which can be characterized most simply as a shared opposition to Cartesianism. Just as Charles S. Peirce, the founder of pragmatism, wanted to replace the Cartesian principle of methodical doubt with real-world, situational doubt and thus with an understanding of human action as a creative way of dealing with problems, so the hermeneuticians shed light on the understanding of texts as a process that never begins without presuppositions and is necessarily creative. They showed that we always already approach the text that we are trying to understand on the basis of a plethora of assumptions that we have brought along with us, and that our interpretation of the text gives us a better understanding of it, but also of ourselves and the world. What both schools have in common, then, is the insight into the situatedness of all knowledge. In both cases, this insight also changes ideas about the relationship between philosophy and other disciplines. Philosophy can no longer be thought of as a path to timeless knowledge that furnishes other scholarly fields with their foundation. From now on, reference is made to a non- or anti-"foundationalist" role for philosophy. For both pragmatists and hermeneuticians, problems are always specific, contexts holistic, and solutions creative.

Beyond the assertion of such a fundamental similarity, it can be argued that the two schools changed in the course of their development in such a way that they grew increasingly similar. Especially after the First World War, the rapprochement was so great as to constitute genuine convergence. This thesis applies above all to the work of two of the greatest representatives of the schools of thought in question, who made fundamental revisions in their own traditions and thus, without knowing about one another, reached a point that was almost crying out for dialogue or even synthesis.

I am referring to pragmatist George Herbert Mead and his philosophy of temporality developed in the 1920s, and to historicist Ernst Troeltsch and the realization in his late work that an appropriate understanding of history depends on an anthropology that declares human beings' use of signs fundamental. Fusion of the "semiotic anthropology" generated by pragmatism and the "affirmative genealogy" arising from historicism and hermeneutics would have made the synthesis of the two traditions possible.[2] For contingent reasons, however, there was no dialogue between, let alone synthesis of, these traditions in the 1920s. After that, from the 1930s onward, both schools lost the intellectual hegemony they had enjoyed in their respective homelands. This did nothing to enhance the prospects of a new attempt at synthesis.

But there was one major exception, a thinker who, from the early 1920s onward, pursued a theoretical program that could be described as the synthesis of Troeltsch and Mead—that is, the combination of the most mature forms of pragmatism and historicism at a time when both were increasingly considered outdated. However, since this thinker was a theologian and theology is often marginalized or left out in accounts of modern intellectual developments, his achievements, apart from a small number of writings, have remained almost unknown outside of theology. Within theology, meanwhile, it seems to me that there has been a general failure to recognize the full scope of his ambition. The scholar in question is H. Richard Niebuhr (1894–1962). He was the younger brother of Reinhold Niebuhr, probably uncontestably the most prominent Protestant theologian in the United States in the twentieth century. At this point, the following biographical remarks about him are merely intended to lend provisional plausibility to the thesis that this is an oeuvre dedicated to achieving a synthesis of Troeltsch and Mead, of historicism and pragmatism.

Niebuhr wrote his doctoral thesis on Ernst Troeltsch's philosophy of religion. This extensive work, submitted to Yale University in 1924, has unfortunately never been published,[3] though it represents—if I am correct—the earliest and most comprehensive study in the United States on Troeltsch or any representative of the German historicist-hermeneutic tradition. Troeltsch remained a key, lifelong point of reference in Niebuhr's work, even when the former suffered a dramatic loss of prestige in Protestant theology due to the "anti-historicist revolution."[4] The first mentions of George Herbert Mead, meanwhile, are not to be found in Niebuhr's publications until the year 1945, but his name crops up regularly after that. In contrast to the statements often made by other authors, these are not mere sweeping references to the concept of "self," but also deal intensively with the theme of temporality and the temporal dimension in the constitution of the self. However, the influence of pragmatism on Niebuhr was not limited to Mead, as he also thoroughly studied many of William James's writings and especially the late work of Josiah Royce, which pointed in a similar direction to Mead.[5]

But there are other biographical facts that reinforce the intuition of a synthesis of Troeltsch and Mead in the work of Niebuhr. In 1921 and 1922, Niebuhr studied sociology, first at Washington University in St. Louis and then at the University of Chicago,[6] where Mead taught. Though we have no evidence that Niebuhr attended Mead's courses, one of his lecturers in St. Louis was a direct student of Mead's named Walter Bodenhafer, who had submitted a dissertation to Mead on the concept of the group in US-American sociology.[7] Hence, at least one indirect early encounter with Mead's ideas seems to have taken place before Niebuhr composed his doctoral thesis on

Troeltsch. While it is customary in the history of theology to locate Niebuhr in the field of tension between Ernst Troeltsch and Karl Barth—as Niebuhr himself occasionally did[8]—it seems to me that underlining his connections with Troeltsch and Mead does more justice to the deeply sociological and philosophical character of his oeuvre.[9] Further, this is the only way to understand why some of his writings became classics of the sociology of religion and how his influential ethics and its conception of responsibility are anchored in a "relational anthropology."[10]

The convergence of pragmatism and hermeneutics over time would be a big topic and must be left aside here. William James's psychology of religion in particular was of course received intensely by leading German thinkers such as Wilhelm Dilthey and Ernst Troeltsch, while Mead studied under Dilthey and his encounter with him was probably a significant factor inspiring his efforts to anchor a *Verstehen*-based psychology in biology.[11] Troeltsch's comprehensive study on the history of Christianity, the thousand-page work *The Social Teachings of the Christian Churches and Groups*, was in turn received by Royce as early as 1913, and when it appeared in English translation in the late 1920s its foreword was by none other than Niebuhr. It is fair to say that the topic of religion was of central importance in this mediation of pragmatism and historicism or hermeneutics; it is thus no coincidence that it was a theologian who picked up the associated threads when they were dropped in philosophy and sociology.

From the point of view of a possible synthesis of pragmatism and historicism I will highlight three areas of Niebuhr's oeuvre. First, I will show how Niebuhr, in his first books and in his 1951 volume *Christ and Culture*, attempted to build on Troeltsch's historical sociology of Christianity but also to go beyond it. I then discuss Niebuhr's most important contribution to systematic theology, namely his 1941 book *The Meaning of Revelation*. Since some nontheological minds are likely to be disinclined to engage seriously with a theology of revelation, I must immediately add that this book could also be described as an attempt to mediate intellectually between the universality of validity claims and the historical particularity of all those who make such claims. This is a potent theme even for nontheologians. What we can see here is that the spirit of pragmatism already plays an essential role in Niebuhr's solution to a problem in Troeltsch's work.

Third and finally, I turn to the book *The Responsible Self*, published posthumously in 1963, which Niebuhr surely did not intend to be his final word in its existing form but which nevertheless represents the most mature version of his synthesis of Mead and Troeltsch. In this section I will also discuss whether and if so to what extent Niebuhr's attempt at synthesis was successful. The organization of the chapter reflects my systematic intent. It proceeds from Troeltsch and the history of Christianity to a reworking of Troeltsch's historical thinking (in the spirit of a new understanding of self and temporality) and then to a moral-philosophical work whose full meaning we can grasp only if we take account of its foundations in Niebuhr's earlier writings.

Beyond Troeltsch: Niebuhr's Contribution to the Historical Sociology of Christianity

In Ernst Troeltsch's sociologically inspired history of Christianity, the distinction between three types of social organization of Christians emerged as the core conceptual lodestone, namely church, sect, and "mysticism"— or the loose spiritual community. In his 1951 book, Niebuhr praised Troeltsch for having taught him "to respect the multiformity and individuality of men and movement(s) in Christian history, to be loath to force this rich variety into prefashioned, conceptual molds, and yet to seek *logos* in *mythos*, reason in history, essence in existence."[12] Deeply impressed by Troeltsch's typology and its explanatory power when applied to the history of Christianity, the young Niebuhr, confronted with the social reality of Christian life in the United States, could not shake the feeling that an additional social form had arisen in his home country, one that does not fit into Troeltsch's conceptual framework. Niebuhr was interested in the type referred to in the United States as the "denomination" and wished to explain the phenomenon of "denominationalism"—in other words, the fact that in the United States all social forms of Christianity, even if they originally understood themselves as churches or sects, had to adapt to the "denomination" type.

This phenomenon is one of the most important characteristics of the US-American religious landscape. While the religious situation in almost every part of Europe was long characterized by the monopoly of a single Christian confession (Catholic, Protestant, or Orthodox) supported by the state,[13] US-American Protestantism has always consisted of a multitude of different religious communities. To this day, even the smallest of towns usually host several churches of different kinds; a recent ethnographic study of a poor, mostly black neighborhood in Boston found at least twenty-nine Christian congregations in an area of approximately 1.5 square kilometers,[14] most of them based in commercial storefronts. Niebuhr himself wrote of about "two hundred varieties of Christianity which flourish in the United States."[15] He emphasized that this diversity cannot simply be deduced from European religious history, since many of these communities arose in the United States and many others owed the development of their separateness and individuality to the impact of social forces in their new environment.[16]

But what is the reason for this diversity? It seems immediately obvious that the absence of a state-supported church monopoly, as guaranteed in the United States since the adoption of the Constitution at the end of the eighteenth century, is the main factor underpinning the system of denominational pluralism. But in itself this does not explain the specific way in which the denominations differentiated. The answer certainly does not lie in the different theological views of these groups and organizations, according to Niebuhr:

> The effort to distinguish churches primarily by reference to their doctrine . . . appeared to him to be a procedure so artificial and fruitless that he found himself compelled to turn from theology to history, sociology, and ethics for a more satisfactory account of denominational differences.[17]

It is true, Niebuhr states, that the "attitude of Christians toward such institutions as private property, democracy, and slavery" as well as their opinions regarding the correct organization of the church are purportedly always derived from biblical texts, but only "the purest novice in history" will accept these justifications at face value. Rather than the *theological* sources of denominationalism, Niebuhr thus probed the *social* sources. His 1929 book, *The Social Sources of Denominationalism*, became one of the classic works in the sociology of religion. Far beyond the intimations in Max Weber's work and more than any of his US-American predecessors, in this text Niebuhr opened up the United States as a specific object of investigation. He examined in depth the role of the ethnicity of the various immigrant populations, of social stratification, and what he calls the "color line"—that is, racial segregation and racism—within the country's religious landscape. For Niebuhr, the differentiation of denominations is a consequence or a mirroring of the structures of inequality in US-American society, and he assails this fact in the tone of a prophet:

> The division of the churches closely follows the division of men into the castes of national, racial, and economic groups. It draws the color line in the church of God; it fosters the misunderstandings, the self-exaltations, the hatreds of jingoistic nationalism by continuing in the body of Christ the spurious differences of provincial loyalties; it seats the rich and poor apart at the table of the Lord, where the fortunate may enjoy the bounty they have provided while the others feed upon the crusts their poverty affords.[18]

Niebuhr's criticism of the system of US-American denominationalism is driven by a strong desire for Christian unity and a radical understanding of the moral universalism found in the gospel. There is a subtle difference here between him and Troeltsch. For Troeltsch, the ideals of the gospel inevitably encounter insurmountable resistance to their realization in the political, economic, and military realities of the "world." Forms of social organization are therefore never simple translations of these ideals or emanations of them, but neither are they pure reproductions of a given social structure. Rather, they are the result of attempts by people to preserve their ideals under adverse circumstances, to pass them on to new generations, and to organize ritual forms that allow an experience of the ideal, at least in a transitory way.

However, according to Troeltsch, this will never be possible in a single organizational form that is binding for everyone, since churches, for example, will always be forced to make all sorts of compromises with their social environment; this in turn leads to individuals or entire social groups interpreting these compromises as a betrayal of the ideals and organizing themselves into stricter "sects." These will be felt by some to be so narrow and restrictive that they will join churches again or shift the organization of the sect in a churchlike direction.

Where Niebuhr laments the lack of unity among Christians, Troeltsch tends to praise the pluralism of the organizational forms of Christianity. Where Niebuhr criticizes the reproduction of the social structure in Christianity, Troeltsch analyzes the influence of the various forms of organization on the "social teachings" of the Christian churches and groups. As useful as Niebuhr's expansion of Troeltsch's typology is, his negative assessment of denominationalism is one-sided. He did not see the positive aspects of the coexistence of a large number of Christian denominations, which fundamentally respect each other and do not deny each other's legitimacy. Later research in history and sociology did not follow him in this evaluation.[19] At the very end of his study, however, Niebuhr seems to have had doubts about the desirability of an organizational unification of the churches in the United States. There he expresses the fear that a US-American national church could lead to an even greater subordination of the ethics of Christianity to a "nationalist ethic" and thus to even greater tensions between Christians of different nations.[20]

Soon after the completion of his first book, Niebuhr himself seems to have recognized some of its weaknesses. However, he now took the relative simplicity of his own understanding of sociology—tracing religious organizations back to socio-structural conditions—to be a weakness of sociology as a whole. It seemed to him that the discipline was only capable of helping explain why the "religious stream" runs along certain "channels"; it could not explain the stream itself. Sociology, he concluded, can only approach the churches as institutions, but not Christianity as a historical movement from which these churches emerged. Its object, Niebuhr contended, is always religion in its dependence on culture, but it "left unexplained the faith which is independent, which is aggressive rather than passive, and which molds culture instead of being molded by it."[21]

Again, a comparative look at Troeltsch shows how narrow Niebuhr's understanding of sociology is here. For Troeltsch it was precisely the fact of ideal formation that was central; the processes of ideal formation should not, however, be thought of as a mysterious incursion into a culture, but rather as a culture's self-transcendence under certain cultural conditions. Therefore, in line with Niebuhr's views, religions are in fact more than culture; they arise from certain cultures to which they do not, however, have to be restricted. For Niebuhr, the analysis of these processes required the transformation of historicism in sociology.[22]

But despite these unsatisfactory methodological comments, it is fair to say that Niebuhr's 1937 book *The Kingdom of God in America*, which began with his self-critical remarks, is characterized by a great sensitivity to the problem of the institutionalization of universalist ideals in a particular culture and the transformations of this institutionalization over the course of history. More specifically, this book sought to trace the ideal of the "kingdom of God," which was so central to Jesus's preaching, in US-American history. For Niebuhr, this ideal took on three major forms within this history: first, in early Puritanism, that of an exclusive emphasis on the sovereignty of God; then, in the time of the Christian Enlightenment, revivalist movements and revolution that of a fraternal, novel kind of body politic centered on Christ; and finally, from the late nineteenth century onward, that of a kingdom of

God to be realized on earth in the "social gospel" movement. The crucial aspect here is that for Niebuhr the kingdom of God in the United States is neither an ideal nor an organization; it is a

> movement which, like the city of God described by Augustine in ancient times, appears in only partial and mixed manner in the ideas and institutions in which men seek to fix it.[23]

As I see it, here Niebuhr is articulating the insight that we should not regard ideals as something that ever exist in a clearly defined form, but rather as holistic and essentially prereflective orientations that are, therefore, articulated very differently under different conditions. A culture in which universalist ideals are found is thus never simply identical with itself. It is always subject to the yardstick of the ideals it itself espouses and must always define the appropriate relationship between itself and these ideals. Universalist religions transcend any given culture and also seize people of other cultural backgrounds. It is therefore a key task of sociological-historical research to study the emergence of culture-transcendent ideals and movements, while probing the attitudes to specific, discrete cultures of those who are seized by such universalist ideals.

Niebuhr set himself to this task in another book, which was intended to overcome the one-sidedness of both earlier works. His *Christ and Culture* of 1951, in Niebuhr's own words, was in a certain sense merely meant to "supplement and in part to correct" Troeltsch's work on the history of Christianity,[24] with the correction involving a stronger emphasis on a relation to God that transcends all history. The decisive step here was to examine the fate of universalist ideals at a higher level of abstraction. Niebuhr was no longer just concerned with the social organization of Christians in churches, sects, or denominations, but much more fundamentally with the possible relationships between the universalist, culture-transcending ideals of Christianity and any given culture. Niebuhr distinguished five possible types, which he described in theological language as "Christ against culture," "Christ of culture," "Christ above culture," "Christ and culture in paradox," and "Christ the transformer of culture."

Translated into secular language, we could sum up the five types as those of a radical rejection of the world, a fundamental affirmation of the world, an organic social ethic, a moralization that pulls the rug from under itself, and a reformist-conversionist understanding of faith. This translation should make it clear that the importance of Niebuhr's ideas is not limited to Christianity or theology or the situation of Christian believers. Whether those seized by a universalist ideal ought to realize it by withdrawing from the world as part of a small circle of those similarly seized or through activities in the world, whether or not they already perceive tendencies toward the realization of these ideals in this world, whether or not they assent to a graduated sequence of ideal realization, whether or not they can perceive the danger of moral self-righteousness in their own ideal-related demands—all these questions arise equally with respect to all universalist ideals, both religious and secular.

Niebuhr's rich, complex reflections on the five types cannot be traced in detail here. Instead, I will merely identify the three aspects that make the ideas in Niebuhr's book profoundly and systematically important to the theory of religion. First, the assertion that one and the same religion can lead to five different attitudes toward the world is superior to all attempts to derive a single "path to salvation" from the core of a religion, a path that then determines the relationship of this religion to the "world." Max Weber's research program on the world religions largely succumbed to the latter temptation.[25] But it can easily be shown that, for example, the attitude of Confucians to capitalism, Buddhists to violence, or Muslims to politics is extremely variable and that it would be wrong to declare one such attitude the only consistent form of expression of the religious tradition in question. In this way, Niebuhr reinforces the pluralist understanding of Christianity initiated by Troeltsch and paves the way for a correspondingly pluralist understanding of the other "world religions."

Second, Niebuhr uses the insight into the fundamentally culture-transcendent character of religions featuring moral universalism to examine the forms of particularist regression to which these religions may be subject. Each of them may degenerate into the self-sacralization of its own particularity. In his book *Radical Monotheism and Western Culture*, published in 1943, Niebuhr wrote that the main rival of monotheism in our day is not polytheism, but "that social faith which makes a finite society, whether cultural or religious, the object of trust as well as of loyalty, and which tends to subvert even officially monotheistic institutions, such as the churches."[26] Nationalism is obviously the characteristic modern example of such an orientation, but subnational entities such as tribes or regions may also be "the value-center and the object of loyalty,"[27] as may supranational ones, such as an empire or an entire civilization. Niebuhr interprets Marxism as a non-nationalist self-sacralization of a particular collective. He is also critical of secular universalisms, in which only humanity (and not creation as a whole) is declared the highest benchmark. He condemns cruelty to animals as sinful along with the commercial profanation of creation and its beauty.[28] There can be no definitive safeguard against relapse into the self-sacralization of the collective in one of these forms. The tension between moral universalism and cultural particularity will always remain.

Third, it should be emphasized that Niebuhr's understanding of the role of his typology vis-à-vis the moral orientation of the individual is much more complex than is usually appreciated. Time and again, it has been assumed that Niebuhr's true objective was to defend the fifth type, that is, the idea of a gradual transformation of culture in the direction of a partial institutionalization of universalist ideals. This assumption prompted some to accuse him of partiality in his characterization of the four other types and inspired a decidedly negative view of the entire book. "Few books have been a greater hindrance to an accurate assessment of our situation than 'Christ and Culture,'" wrote Stanley Hauerwas, one of the most prominent US-American evangelical theologians of our time.[29] What is forgotten is that Niebuhr's typology draws explicitly on Weber's method of constructing ideal types.

Above all, though, there is a failure to recognize the ethical conclusion he himself drew in light of the plurality of Christians' possible attitudes toward the world. For him, every individual bears the "burden of freedom"[30] and must make their own personal existential decisions. In line with this, the book ends on an existentialist note; the title of the last chapter, "Concluding Unscientific Postscript," even borrows directly from a text by Søren Kierkegaard. An existential decision, according to Niebuhr, cannot be "reached by speculative inquiry, but must be made in freedom by a responsible subject acting in the present moment on the basis of what is true for him."[31] But Niebuhr also makes it very clear where he differs from Kierkegaard. For Niebuhr, like Mead and Troeltsch, the questions of existence are not purely individual. In their most passionate form, they are not posed in solitude, but in the context of our relationship with others. These are the existential questions that confront people who only have a self because of and through their relationship with others.[32]

For Niebuhr, our responsibility is deeply social and tied to a specific present. This presentness, again in contrast to Kierkegaard, is not understood as one that lies in an unhistorical present devoid of any connection to past and future. As right as it is to emphasize freedom of choice, Niebuhr tells us, we must still recognize that "we exercise this freedom in the midst of values and powers we have not chosen but to which we are bound."[33] Niebuhr by no means privileges any one of the five types. He does not claim that any of them represent the only justifiable type of Christianity, but rather ascribes to individuals the freedom, but also the responsibility, to make their own existential decisions regarding the relationship between faith and the world. For this very reason, his thinking also drives him to examine more closely the existential requirements for the reconstruction of history and the processual character of the social constitution of the self.

Universalist Validity Claim and Historical Particularity: Niebuhr's Conception of Revelation

As mentioned, Niebuhr's book on revelation is about the tensions between the universal character of validity claims and the inevitable historical particularity of those who make them. According to Ernst Troeltsch, even the strictest universalist does not have the ability to foresee the perspectives of later generations. Everyone must therefore expect those born later to uncover their blind spots, unconscious biases, and repressed dark sides. This unsettling state of affairs prompted Niebuhr to address one of the key issues in the discourse on religion, especially in the eighteenth century, namely the question of the relationship between "reason" and "revelation." These had long been thought of as complementary in Christianity; human reason in particular was considered a gift from God. But in the wake of the Reformation and especially during the Enlightenment era there was a tendency to view them as opposites. "Reason" became the watchword of progressive forces; in line with this, invoking revelation was often perceived as merely defensive.[34] In fact, such talk of revelation increasingly came to appear dangerously irrational, a defense of arbitrary assertions through reference to supernatural sources of knowledge and authorities, a demand for obedience, and a refusal to expose validity claims to the process of rational argumentation.

To this day, a corresponding image of the discipline of theology holds sway among an astonishing number of philosophers and scholars, while in secular circles there is still a tendency to caricature those who profess a belief in revelation. The tenacity of these ideas is astonishing because the parameters of the debate had already changed fundamentally by the end of the eighteenth century—through Kant's critical philosophy of reason and through the shift toward a subject- and experience-centered understanding of faith in the work of Schleiermacher and others. A seemingly outdated idea thus took on new plausibility. It was now possible to investigate when insights to which individuals and collectives ascribe the highest importance to their own existence are thought of as something received or given rather than something self-made or independently achieved.

However, this subjective turn in the understanding of revelation aggravated the problem of the validity claim. Instead of one revelation, whose validity is a matter of dogma, did it now make sense to refer to an endless array of subjective revelations, none of which is truer than the others?

That is the context in which H. Richard Niebuhr produced the 1941 book with which I am concerned here. He was deeply influenced by the experience-centered tradition of the understanding of faith, but also took seriously Karl Barth's concerns that this risked diluting God into a mere phenomenon of the human imagination, with the meaning of revelation as the self-revelation of God potentially being lost. As he writes in the foreword, in this book he tried to achieve a synthesis of Troeltsch and Barth, that is, he was concerned with an appropriate and undiluted understanding of revelation informed by an experience-based and nonintellectualist understanding of faith.

His decisive move here is to take as his starting point the undeniable historicity of all revelation, such as the historical locatability of the prophets and the Messiah. This requires us, however, to make a distinction in the concept of history. The focus cannot be on what Niebuhr called "external" history, which is often experienced as Shakespeare's Macbeth put it: "[Life] is a tale / told by an idiot, full of sound and fury, / signifying nothing."[35] What we perceive in external history is "particularity, finiteness, opinions that pass, caprice, arbitrariness, accident, brutality, wrong on the throne and right on the scaffold."[36] By contrast, what Niebuhr had in mind is the "internal history" that comes into play when we are participants rather than observers, when we reconstruct our own life with a view to the events that have been meaningful to us, when we tell "the story of our life," to quote the title of the second chapter of Niebuhr's book.[37]

If we were to experience our entire life as devoid of meaningful events, that is, if we perceived it as meaningless, we would be unable to go on living; we would lose the "willingness to be" of which William James spoke. This means that we inevitably talk about our own life in light of the meaning it has for us. We thus reconstruct our life story against the background of the events and changes in which the meaning of life shone through to us. Hence, what we mean by revelation is that something has happened to us in our history which conditions all our thinking and that through this happening we are enabled to apprehend what we are, what we are suffering and doing and what our potentialities are. What is otherwise arbitrary and dumb fact becomes related, intelligible and eloquent fact through the revelatory event.[38]

The same idea appears elsewhere in almost aphoristic form: "Revelation means this intelligible event which makes all other events intelligible."[39]

Obviously, if revelation is understood in this way, it is not a "substitute for reason."[40] It does not belong in a history of external events recorded by an uninvolved observer, but rather in a person's own history, a "history of selves."[41] Niebuhr's idea of an "internal" history is based on the concept of self developed by no one as potently as George Herbert Mead. In his book on revelation, however, Niebuhr does not mention Mead, but relies on Martin Buber's philosophy of dialogue, perhaps because this deeply religious Jewish thinker appealed to him more in this context than the secular naturalist Mead. Nevertheless, and given the similarities between Mead and Buber, it can be argued that Niebuhr goes beyond Troeltsch here because he has a better understanding of the "self."[42]

But what does this turn mean when it comes to the universality of validity claims? Obviously, their meaning cannot be the same in statements about "internal" history as in those about "external" history. We cannot be dealing with purely cognitive validity claims as in natural science (or metaphysics). The universality of the existential understanding of narration can only be achieved through a universalization of the self, through expansion of the self in the direction of a universal community. To convey this idea, Niebuhr again provides us with a shorthand formula, one that is likely to be difficult for secular minds to accept, though it could be translated into secular terms:

> To be a self is to have a god; to have a god is to have history; that is, events connected in a meaningful pattern; to have one god is to have one history. God and the history of selves in community belong together in inseparable union.[43]

Of course, this does not mean that atheists do not have a self. It means that the formation of a self is interwoven with the formation of ultimate values, that ultimate values require a narrative about their genesis—what I have called an "affirmative genealogy"—and that the overarching orientation of different people toward one and the same source of value fuses them into a community. In this way, even people who do not belong to a particular ethnic or political collective can be joined together to make a community. Hence, in Christianity and other forms of moral universalism, solidarity goes beyond membership of a community.

Entering into such a process of universalization of the self is no easy matter. It is a painful process because it requires one to appropriate the wrongs that have been perpetrated by those who belong to one's group, to feel responsible for them. Within the universalist framework this becomes a responsibility for the entire history of humankind: "Through Christ we become immigrants into the empire of God which extends over all the world and learn to remember the history of that empire, that is of men in all times and places, as our history."[44]

It is not just his appropriation of the Meadian conception of the self but this entire attempt to make the subjectivity and historical relativity of all validity claims the starting point for gradual and always incomplete universalization that brings Niebuhr close to pragmatism here. Like the pragmatists, he draws no skeptical or relativistic conclusions from the turn to subjectivity. Thus, for him, speaking about God does not mean making statements about a metaphysical entity, but rather talking about "my God." Revelation is therefore not simply something that took place at a certain past point in history, as if we were discussing the publication date of a divine message.[45] Revelation must be an event in the ongoing process of divine self-revelation; this is why Christians refer to the "living God." Here, too, an illustration drawn from the interpersonal realm is useful: there is no substitute in objective knowledge for the self-revelation of the other in the context of love.

Niebuhr's book ends with ethical conclusions that I will discuss in the next section but I want to preempt the discussion of one of these ideas. So far, I have referred only to the internal relationship between "self" and "value," to the interweaving of self-formation and value formation. But we always become objects of evaluation by others as well. While some of our reference persons appreciate us, others do not. What is universalization supposed to mean in this regard? Should the requirement be that we must value all our fellow human beings in the same way, whether they value us or not? This would be a highly artificial norm or, as Niebuhr writes, "a wild imagination of the heart."[46] But this contrasts with the fact that the central certainty of Christianity is the belief in the infinite or sacred value of all human beings.[47] Yet we humans, unlike the divine, infinite self, cannot treat all souls as equally valuable. Nor can we simply regard this divine perspective as irrelevant to our human actions. How, then, can necessarily particular beings meet the demands of moral universalism without overburdening themselves morally and, through ignorance of their particularity itself, violating moral demands? Niebuhr grapples with this question in the book *The Responsible Self*, which is the most mature version of his synthesis of historicism and pragmatism.

Self and Responsibility

So far in this account, Niebuhr's historicism has been easier to recognize than his pragmatism. Connections with Mead's theory of the self and time have been unmistakable, as has the general impetus toward a universalization of the self. But it would be a gross exaggeration to claim a central position for pragmatism in his oeuvre up to the point we have considered so far. After 1945 this seems to have changed, with his references to US-American intellectual traditions becoming ever clearer. The first evidence is an essay on the theme of "conscience," in which he elucidates this key concept in Christian moral thinking with the help of Mead's intersubjectivist conception of the genesis of the self.[48]

In the foreword to a book about Mead and Buber, Niebuhr calls the insight of both into the "interpersonal nature of our human existence" one of the most fruitful of recent ideas.[49] He tries to identify other intellectual endeavors evincing the same direction of travel and names Ernst Cassirer's *The Philosophy of Symbolic Forms*, Charles Horton Cooley's sociological pragmatism and Harry Stack Sullivan's synthesis of Mead and Freud.[50] Josiah Royce had long been important to him.[51] The interpersonal dimension and the semiotic dimension became ever more significant in Niebuhr's work. This is also reflected in Niebuhr's characterization of his theology and ethics as "relational." In his clearest and most powerful acknowledgment of the roots of his theory of value, he stated, "Philosophically, [it is] more indebted to G. H. Mead than to Aristotle, theologically it is closer, I believe, to Jonathan Edwards ... than to Thomas Aquinas."[52]

His avowal of a relational anthropology is underpinned by an understanding of human action informed by pragmatism. The central ethical concept in Niebuhr's work, meanwhile, is "responsibility." But this concept he defines in terms of action theory, stating that it is based on "the idea of an agent's action as response to an action upon him in accordance with the interpretation of the latter action and with his expectation of response to his response; and all of this is in a continuing community of agents."[53]

This definition contains at least four densely packed components that deserve to be emphasized individually:

(1) For Niebuhr, both models of human action dominant in the Western philosophical tradition are inadequate. He sets out in detail why he wishes to adhere neither to the Aristotelian teleological model, in which the good has priority, nor to the Kantian deontological model, in which the right enjoys primacy. For him, both suffer the same shortcoming, detaching the individual actor and the individual action from the specific interpersonal situations in which they are embedded. Yet action is always situated and is neither guided entirely by internalized values nor by norms. The human being, for Niebuhr, is "an answerer," engaged in dialogues, responding to actions that affect her or him.

(2) Responses are mediated by interpretations. This is the fundamental difference between the behaviorism that long dominated psychology and Mead's interactionism. There can be no doubt which side Niebuhr is on in this regard. In his understanding of interpretation, he tries to avoid any one-sidedness. Interpretations, for him, are neither automated reactions to a stimulus nor "simply an affair of our conscious, and rational, mind, but also of the deep memories that are buried within us, of feelings and intuitions that are only partly under our immediate control."[54]

(3) Neither the good nor the right is suitable as supreme benchmark in this understanding of action. An ethics of responsibility sees this benchmark in the "fitting action," the situation-appropriate action, as we might put it, an action that "fits into a total interaction as response and as anticipation of further response." Only a situation-appropriate action is "conducive to the good and alone is right."[55] It goes without saying that situational appropriateness is not intended to replace the orientation toward the good and the right; without it, however, neither the good nor the right is achievable.

(4) Not only is our perception of the world and ourselves structured by past experiences, but these experiences also generate expectations and anticipations of the future, to which we already respond in the present. Since our actions are carried out not by part of us but by our whole person, each individual must deal with the fact that they are faced with a multiplicity of situations, both simultaneously and over time. There is no self without a certain continuity "with a relatively consistent scheme of interpretations of what

it is reacting to."[56] And this also applies to continuity within a community of actors to which the person belongs.

Niebuhr first develops such a pragmatist understanding of action,[57] which is only hinted at here, in the first chapter of *The Responsible Self*, before further elaborating it in the following chapters. The second chapter, "Responsibility in Society," is the most Meadian. Niebuhr follows Mead in understanding sociality not only as entailing an external aggregation of individuals but also as constituting the preconditions for the development of individuality. The potent metaphor Niebuhr uses here is that of the "womb," that is, society as the maternal body:

> To say the self is social is not to say that it finds itself in need of fellow men in order to achieve its purposes, but that it is born in the womb of society as a sentient, thinking, needful being with certain definitions of its needs and with the possibility of experience of a common world. It is born in society as mind and as moral being, but above all it is born in society as self.[58]

For the ethicist Niebuhr, this fundamental relationality is not simply a matter of the gradual development of the self, but of all the action situations in which the self is involved. His focus, as with his emphasis on the situational appropriateness of action, is on a concrete ethics, in this case a morality oriented toward the concrete other. The reason he is so critical of Kant's understanding of conscience is that he believes it abstracts from the specific otherness of one's interaction partner. This emphasis on the moral importance of the other's uniqueness has been seen as anticipating the ideas of Emmanuel Levinas.[59] One can already discern the same tendency at work in the ethics of John Dewey, when it confronts the phenomenon of "shattering intersubjectivity,"[60] though it would certainly be going too far to claim that Dewey and Mead developed this idea in depth. Niebuhr thus went beyond the classic pragmatists in this respect.

Niebuhr believed he had also gone beyond Mead in two other ways. He emphasized the triadic rather than simply dyadic structure of the interaction between two people, insofar as they tend not to simply concentrate on one another, but also on some "object" they have in common. Here Niebuhr clearly distanced himself from Martin Buber's philosophy of dialogue, but erroneously seemed to equate Mead with Buber, although Mead, like Royce, emphasizes this shared "object" no less than Niebuhr. Consonant with this object-orientation of interaction, Niebuhr also underlined that our relationship to nature is necessarily socially mediated and, by the same token, that our relationship to others is mediated through our relationship to nature. It is jarring that here, too, Niebuhr seemed to have been unaware of the central role these ideas played in Mead's studies on the constitution of the "physical thing" and in his "philosophy of the act" in general.[61]

Like Mead, Niebuhr was interested in the dynamics of moral universalization. However, as mentioned earlier, he was opposed to any conception of this that entails an abstraction from concrete others or implies a switch to a monological and situation-inappropriate orientation toward universalist norms or ideals. His focus was thus on a moral universalism that must be lived under concrete, particular conditions. This means that he foregrounded the need to strike a balance between the demands of a universalist morality and those tangible and particular demands made of us that cannot be subsumed under the universalist dimension.[62] But while Mead, albeit in a rather simple way, tried to clarify empirically the role of the advancing global division of labor in the history of moral universalism, Niebuhr remained entirely at the normative level. When he wrote about the preconditions for the development of moral universalism, he clearly saw this as somehow inherent in a radically understood monotheism. Yet he paid no serious attention to the religious or cultural dynamics that may have been at work here, let alone to the economic, political, and military influences in the history of moral universalism.[63]

The remaining three chapters of the book serve to apply Mead's conception of the self and temporality to the problems of the philosophy of history and theology. The name Troeltsch is conspicuous by its absence despite his central role in Niebuhr's intellectual development. The reason is obvious: when he wrote this book, Niebuhr was mainly interested in existentialist philosophy. These chapters were written in the context of an implicit or explicit dialogue with Heidegger, Jaspers, and Gabriel Marcel—with Kierkegaard as a key figure in the background for all of them. As already mentioned, the book *Christ and Culture* had ended with Niebuhr characterizing his own thought as "social existentialism." But now the emphasis is not only on sociality versus individuality but on historicity and, as we have seen, an apt understanding of the temporality of the self.

For Niebuhr, the extreme existentialist philosophers exaggerate the idea of freedom, presenting the human being as a creature that, at every moment, creates anew, chooses, and is capable of defining itself. This, as Niebuhr sees it, is to take abstraction from the factual embedding of human beings in historical continuities as far as it could possibly go.[64] Niebuhr regarded his concept of co-presence ("compresence") as an alternative to this. We share our present with others. If we abstract entirely from these others, Niebuhr contended, we also lose ourselves and the sense of time. But if our routines are ruptured and this causes us to experience the present moment as sharply differentiated from the before and after, then we share it with something that happens to us—"in threatening or promising form."[65] Through the encounter with others, the self experiences itself as "absolutely dependent in its existence, completely contingent, inexplicably present in its here-ness and now-ness."[66]

This may sound like Heidegger but is in fact deeply opposed to him. Niebuhr denied that we have to think of our lives as a matter of having been "thrown" into existence or that we "maintain" ourselves by our "own power." He considered it more apt to state "that I am being lived than that I live."[67] The entire fourth chapter of *The Responsible Self* is in fact dedicated to exploring responsibility in the context of "absolute dependence," in other words that which Schleiermacher declared the basis of all faith and, for Niebuhr, characterizes an adequate understanding of human existence. Like the existentialist philosophers, Niebuhr emphasized our ability to make choices. But for him there was more to say than just that this ability is exercised under conditions we ourselves have not chosen. He also emphasized more than the existentialist philosophers that we can interpret the fact that we have not chosen our existence ourselves within the framework of a "reasoning faith," that is, in such a way that we regard our existence as a whole, our capacity for rationality and sociality, as a gift we have received. This shifts our understanding of freedom in a fundamental way toward the idea of responsible freedom.[68]

H. Richard Niebuhr left behind many important fragments. Even the book *The Responsible Self* is not the systematic ethics its author had in mind but a collection of manuscripts Niebuhr used for a series of lectures at the University of Glasgow in 1960 and later on other occasions. Many questions thus remain open. Furthermore, if we read his work as an incomplete attempt at a synthesis of historicism and pragmatism, a whole range of questions arise about the sustainability of his interpretation of these two traditions, such as the work of Mead and Troeltsch, and about the factual validity of his assertions—for example, on the distinction between internal and external history or teleological and deontological ethics. I was unable to address all these issues in this chapter. But in two respects, this attempt at synthesis seems particularly relevant today.

First, it plays an important role for a historical sociology of religion, especially that of Christianity, that is crying out for revitalization, a scholarly endeavor to which the theologian Niebuhr perhaps contributed more than any of the sociologists working during the same period. Second, it directs our attention to a critical juncture in the history of ideas in the twentieth century and thus to a path not taken by the dominant intellectual forces. The synthesis of historicism, hermeneutics, pragmatism, and existentialist philosophy, as I have sought to bring out, entailed an opportunity that was missed in the thinking of Heidegger and his followers, which emerged from a similar tension between traditions. We might describe Niebuhr's synthesis, in all its differentness, along with Troeltsch's existential historicism, Tillich's theology, and Ricœur's philosophy, as collectively laying the ground for a fundamental alternative to Heidegger's thinking when it comes to the understanding of human freedom and the Christian faith.[69]

IV, 3
Christianity and the Dangers of Self-Sacralization: Werner Stark

Today, Max Weber and Émile Durkheim are regarded the world over as the great classical figures in the sociology of religion. Clearly in their shadow, we would also have to mention Weber's longtime colleague and friend Ernst Troeltsch, and Durkheim's nephew and collaborator Marcel Mauss. Let's take these formative figures in sociology as a whole, and in the sociology of religion in particular, and place them within the field of European religious history. On the German side we are dealing with two scholars who were deeply influenced by Protestant Christianity, one of whom (Troeltsch) was in fact originally a theologian, while the other (Weber), despite his distance from Christianity, owes much of his renown to his attempt to demonstrate links between the "Protestant ethic" and the "spirit of capitalism." On the French side, in contrast, it was two Jewish thinkers who played the lead role. These two intellectuals were strongly secularized, even militantly laicist to some extent, but both came from families that had produced rabbis over many generations.

In general, and especially in the case of great scholars, there can be no question of simply tracing back their scholarly oeuvres to their religious (or antireligious) biographical background. Still, it is striking that Catholic scholars seem largely absent from the early years of the sociology of religion. This no doubt reflects the Catholic Church's difficulties, in the late nineteenth and early twentieth centuries, with the modern scholarly disciplines as a whole, and especially with those that specifically scrutinized dogmatically proclaimed teachings or the institution of the church, an institution that, according to its self-image, was founded not by humans but by God. Nevertheless, we cannot rule out the possibility that the writings constitutive of the sociology of religion contain biases—that is, confessional or secularist prejudices—that might have been avoided if Catholic Christians had been more involved in the associated scholarly debate.

Under the Spell of Freedom. Hans Joas, Oxford University Press. © Oxford University Press 2024.
DOI: 10.1093/oso/9780197642153.003.0018

A Forgotten Catholic Classic?

A great deal could be said about the relationship between the Catholic Church and sociology—both with respect to the institution's position in relation to the discipline and in terms of attempts to analyze the church as an institution with the tools of sociology.[1] My goal here, however, is not to provide an exhaustive treatment of this subject, but merely to examine the possible accomplishments of a significant but largely ignored attempt to write a Catholic-inspired historical sociology of Christianity. I am referring to the five-volume work by Austrian émigré Werner Stark (1909–1985), composed between 1963 and 1971 and published in English between 1966 and 1972.[2] This highly ambitious text, which initially attracted a great deal of attention and was reviewed by leading figures in the field, was soon so completely forgotten that today, even in historical reviews and encyclopedic overviews, there is practically no mention of it. One is tempted to speak of a kind of *damnatio memoriae*, an erasure from the disciplinary memory, and as we will see, this dovetails with the witheringly negative appraisals in some contemporary reviews.

Just as the history of an author's reception and their gradual canonization represents an exciting challenge in the sociology of knowledge or scholarship, this also applies to their total excommunication from the canon. In the case of Stark, a number of studies[3] have sought, among other things, to assess the extent to which his Catholic faith played a role in the suppression of his work. This I will only touch upon here rather than tackle in depth. Nothing should distract from the task of evaluating the systematic importance of Werner Stark's writings.

Scholarly studies can of course be forgotten for good reason. But I am going to argue that this does not apply in Werner Stark's case. I claim that, after the oeuvre of H. Richard Niebuhr,[4] Stark's multivolume work represents the most important attempt in the twentieth-century sociology of religion to write the history of Christianity through the lens of moral universalism and the problems of its institutionalization. It is, therefore, quite unacceptable that Stark's achievements are not even recognized. As will be shown, I have no wish to sweepingly vindicate all his ideas, but I do call for scholars to engage critically with his work rather than condemning it wholesale or casting a veil of silence over it.

A glance at Stark's personal history shows how poorly he fits the stereotype of Catholic obscurantist. Born in 1909 and raised in a well-to-do,

German-speaking, secularized Jewish family in Bohemia, he studied law and social sciences at the University of Hamburg from 1928 to 1934 and wrote a dissertation in economic history on so-called feudal capitalism in his home country of Bohemia. Politically, like his father, he was inclined toward the socialists; in particular, his father had links with the famous Austromarxist Karl Renner, Austria's first state chancellor after the collapse of the Habsburg Empire. Since Stark's Jewish origins ruled out any prospect of a career in Nazi Germany, he moved to Prague, where he worked as business editor of a daily newspaper and as a bank clerk.

After the invasion of German troops in 1939, Stark fled to England; there, in unpropitious circumstances, he succeeded in building an academic career. His knowledge of economic history and the history of the discipline of economics was crucial in this regard. With the help of probably the most famous economist of the day, John Maynard Keynes, he was appointed to a teaching post at Cambridge University and was entrusted with editing the economic writings of Jeremy Bentham.[5] After serving in the British armed forces during the Second World War, he held posts at the universities of Edinburgh and Manchester; in 1962, he moved to the United States. Jesuit-run Fordham University in New York offered him a professorship in 1963 on the recommendation of Robert Merton, which he held until his retirement in 1975.[6] After completing his major work in the sociology of religion during this period, Stark's scholarly interests shifted toward the sociology of knowledge and a theory of fundamental social forms (*The Social Bond*); on both these subjects, as well as the sociology of religion, he produced exacting multivolume works. He spent his retirement in Salzburg, where he died in 1985.

This Jewish scholar, then, was certainly not destined at birth to embrace Catholicism or develop an interest in the history of Christianity. In the foreword to the first volume of his great sociology of religion, he traces his interest back to his studies, specifically to the lectures delivered by leading modern historian Justus Hashagen at the University of Hamburg on the Reformation and Counter-Reformation, as well as to courses on canon law at the University of Prague in the 1930s.[7] In this work he makes no mention of the fact of his conversion to Catholic Christianity in 1941, during his English exile. More detailed biographical research would be required to fully illuminate this turning point in Stark's life. At an intellectual level, his reading of John Henry Newman's writings seems to have been decisive to his conversion,[8] but of course a conversion is caused by shifts in layers of personhood lying deeper than a simple reading experience.

I will not speculate about this deeper dimension here. But an indication of the driving force—and simultaneous prefiguring—of Stark's project in the sociology of religion can be found in an essay of the late 1950s that he dedicated to Cardinal Newman, himself a convert from the Anglican to the Catholic Church. Newman, according to Stark, felt repelled by the social selectivity of the established church and by the "division of the faithful into hostile sects according to their social standing." Neither an established church that takes the side of the privileged nor a sect that organizes a certain type of underprivileged group could embody the universalist aspirations of Christianity, but only the "all-comprehensive fold of Rome"—in other words, the Catholic Church—if it truly lives up to the catholicity its name implies.[9] I therefore tend to interpret his conversion as such as occurring for a variety of reasons. But I interpret his conversion to *Catholic* Christianity as a step away from all religious and secular particularisms, especially from nationalism, from Zionism as Jewish nationalism, and from liberalism and socialism to the extent that they are unaware of their own particularism.

The similarity to H. Richard Niebuhr's trenchant polemic assailing the fragmentation of US-American Christianity into particularist socially and ethnically based groupings is unmissable.[10] Stark's embrace of Catholicism, then, appears to have been inspired by a search for a true universalism. Yet his scholarly reception imputed to him a fiercely particularist, reactionary ideology, a return to the Middle Ages or the Counter-Reformation, to Golden Age Spain under Philip II and the spirit of the Jesuit order, which emerged during that era. Even if these assumptions were justified—whether or not they are remains to be discussed—it is still astonishing that Stark's critics were so blind to the fate of this Jewish émigré. Even if Stark's work were to show a streak of the overzealousness so often attributed to converts, respect for his biography and life's work might have prompted a less polemical approach.

Routinization of Charisma? Stark's Critique of Max Weber

Stark's writing of his sociology of religion was continuously accompanied by critical engagement with Max Weber and, to a lesser extent, Ernst Troeltsch. It seems plain to me that he wished to go beyond Weber by freeing the latter's work from distortions stemming from Protestant prejudices toward Catholicism and a limited understanding of the dynamics of religious experiences. Stark's ambition was not to substitute a "Catholic sociology" for a strictly empirical one, as was occasionally imputed to him.[11] In fact, he expressly distanced himself from such a project, whose absurdity he underlined by comparing it to a "communist mathematics" or "Jewish physics."[12] In his interpretations of Weber, he was not concerned with the latter's person or his complex biographical relationship with Catholicism, but exclusively with the theoretical and empirical dimensions of his sociology of religion.

Stark took umbrage primarily at two aspects in Weber's rendering of Catholic teaching and practice.[13] He vigorously disputed that the cult of saints should be understood as a relic of polytheism or as a relapse into it. Stark conceded that Weber was aware of the difference between the two at the level of official doctrine and was commenting exclusively on the practice of ordinary believers. Yet, he contended, Weber's account of the latter was also incorrect when he presented the saints as if they appeared in believers' consciousness as "independent deities who have undergone a semi-involution,"[14] rather than friends of God and sinners' advocates. Stark also vehemently rejected Weber's application of the term "magic" to sacramental practice and forms of worship in the Catholic Church.

In both respects, there are now additional good reasons to agree with Werner Stark in his opposition to Weber. The classical studies by historian of Christianity Peter Brown on the origin of the cult of saints have—probably definitely—empirically refuted the thesis of polytheism, which dates back to the work of David Hume and Edward Gibbon.[15] Likewise, research on the emergence of ideas of transcendence in the "Axial Age" has paved the way for a radical distinction between "magic" and "sacrament."[16] For Stark, however, behind Weber's shortcomings in the detail lay a more fundamental weakness. With his theory of the routinization of charisma, Stark believed, Weber had put forward an important idea. But he had not seen that it failed to do justice to the specific institution of the church and its practice. This point is so important to everything that follows here that we need to take a closer look at it.[17]

For Stark, the background to Weber's lack of understanding of the role of the saint in the Catholic tradition and of sacramental practice and its alleged proximity to magic lies not only in Weber's confessional prejudices and aversions, but also in a fundamental design flaw in his theory of charisma and its routinization. For Weber, "charisma" appears primarily as a revolutionary force, a break with traditions, but tragically, if it succeeds at all, it can never escape the fate of rigidifying back into tradition.

Now nobody would deny that charisma-based new dawns, triggered by prophets or political leaders, cannot themselves be perpetuated in all their zeal and ecstatic enthusiasm. But the question is whether elements that mitigate the cooling of the enthusiastic spirit can be built into the structure of those institutions that are based on a charismatic awakening, thus keeping this spirit alive. As is well known, part of the background to Weber's theory was the history of canon law composed by staunchly Lutheran legal historian Rudolph Sohm.[18] In acerbic polemics aimed chiefly at the Catholic Church, Sohm portrayed the mere existence of canon law as contradicting the essence of Christianity. Early Christianity, he declared, was based exclusively on personal participation in the charisma of Christ's teachings, without fixed membership rules, leadership structures, financial organization, administration, or, of course, juridification. Through this lens, the development of the Christian church since early Catholicism appears as a break with early Christianity, indeed as a reversal of its basic impulse: the office is no longer based on charisma, but vice versa.

For Weber, too, charisma of office (*Amtscharisma*) was a transformation of the original personal charisma and was more a matter of reversal than preservation. While for Sohm the Reformation represented a regaining of the impulses of early Christianity, Weber turned a single element of Sohm's analysis, namely a distance from the realm of tradition (by no means intended in a revolutionary sense), into a type identifiable throughout history, namely a revolutionary antitraditionalism and its predictable tragic downfall.

Werner Stark was fully aware of the connection between Weber's theory of charisma and the Protestant polemics penned by Sohm.[19] Based on later research, he took issue with Sohm and Weber by pointing out that Jesus was certainly not fundamentally hostile to law. Not only do the Gospels themselves contain guidelines setting out how Christian communities were to deal with conflicts and misdeeds (Matthew 18:15–17), including sanctions extending to the exclusion of a member, but the first (Jewish) Christians could also draw on and invoke the legal thought of their own tradition as a matter of course.[20]

For Stark, just as biased as Weber's portrayal of a purely charismatic primordial Christian community that did entirely without law is his analysis of what happened as the Christian communities expanded and became ever more firmly established and independent institutions. Stark conveys the one-sidedness he assails with a pleasing metaphor: when it comes to the transmission of the founder's charisma, Weber had thought only of Peter and his office—in other words, the papacy—and not of John, the true "personal companion of the Lord".[21]

In Peter and John we thus recognize, admittedly only in rudimentary form, the two types that are to sustain the Church to come: the administrator and the mystic. Certainly, the administrator should also be a mystic and the mystic should not be so unworldly as to be unable to administer if necessary. The personalities need not and should not be separated, but the functions should. It was Max Weber's most critical error to see only the presence and the coming of the administrator, but not the being and the recurrence of the mystic who, through his love of God, his Johannine nature, allows ever new life, ever new warmth to flow into the persisting structure.[22]

The history of the church features an impressive line-up of such innovators, such as Benedict of Nursia, Francis of Assisi, Ignatius of Loyola, Carlo Borromeo, and many others; we might almost refer to a tradition of renewal, paradoxical as this sounds. In various works, which cannot be discussed in detail here, Stark endeavored to demonstrate from various angles the implausibility of a conception that sees nothing but routinization. This he did, for example, by analyzing the tension between quasi-legal casuistry in the confessional and the dynamism of open, substantive communication between the confessor and individual believers; the tension between intellectuality and mysticism in the work of the greatest theologians, such as Augustine and Thomas Aquinas; and similar tensions in religiously inspired art. All these arguments boil down to the idea that Weber's intellectual presuppositions only allowed for a path from individual charisma to the religious collective's charisma of office, while ignoring the path from the religious collective's traditions to the ever-new emergence of charisma out of it. If one remedies Weber's bias here, it also becomes clear that we cannot extrapolate from the empirically indisputable cases of routinization of charisma to a schema of a necessarily recurring pattern of development, let alone a world-historical tendency for charismatic awakenings to peter out.[23]

In Stark's critical engagement with Weber, especially his understanding of the (Catholic) church, and in Stark's alternative conception of charisma, we can already discern where he was going with his major corrections to Weber's sociology of religion. Stark wished to correct, in two key respects, the dichotomous distinction, which goes back to Weber, between types of the social organization of Christianity (church versus sect) as well as the triadic typology dating back to Ernst Troeltsch (church, sect, and spiritual communities). First, he declared Weber's and Troeltsch's concept of church to be inadequate, because it could not express the essential difference between a territorially limited church (called the *Landeskirche* in German with reference to the Protestant Church) and a universal church. Second, he upbraided Weber and Troeltsch for failing to pay sufficient attention to the role of "orders" in church history and thus for their lack of understanding of the differences and similarities between "sects" and "orders." In my opinion, both are criticisms of the greatest systematic relevance.

Stark's attempts to revise the classical typology of the social forms of Christianity were the latest in a long line of similar intellectual projects beginning with H. Richard Niebuhr's analysis of US-American "denominations";[24] thanks to Joachim Wach's efforts, these led to the introduction of more new types such as that of the "established sect" and the "cult."[25] However, this development produced an ever larger number of alleged types, "a proliferation of type labels increasing almost directly with the number of scholars actively interested in the problem."[26] Each contributor thus tried to attract interest in their work by introducing new types and subtypes. This inevitably triggered a countervailing reaction, such that the typological debate, which had long been extremely lively, came to an end. For decades, it has played virtually no role in the sociology of religion and has been supplanted by ethnographic studies of individual religious groups or quantitative research in which types are generated on the basis of groups of variables. Both trends, the gratuitous increase in types and their methodological reduction to correlations between variables, evinced a lack of understanding of the logic of type formation at work in the writings of Weber and Troeltsch.

Their relevant studies were not simply attempts to bring conceptual order to a large quantity of data. They represented an action-oriented perspective, an attempt to illuminate how people who are seized by radical ideals such as those of Christianity, faced with the difficult task of realizing these ideals, can create forms of community and institutions that allow them to maintain hope, to preserve and pass on ideals rather than cynically renouncing them, and to realize them within these institutions and in the world around them (more strongly in the former and more weakly in the latter).[27] Werner Stark's critique of the typologies of Weber and Troeltsch retained this action-oriented character. His emphasis on religious orders served to demonstrate the church's inner power of renewal. There is absolutely no need to view this emphasis as the addition of a type; it can instead be seen as a correction to a picture of the church that—as in Weber's work—emphasizes its character as a hierocratic institution. Nor does the distinction between a universal church and a church established at the individual state level serve to produce a typology of greater explanatory power. Rather, it brings out the moral universalism in Christianity and raises awareness of its endangerment through (as Stark saw it) inappropriate forms of institutionalization. Evidently, when his work was published, it was no longer possible for an approach reminiscent of that deployed by the classical figures of sociology to gain a sympathetic hearing from "explanatory" sociologists of religion.[28]

Stark could no doubt have done a better job, in an interpretive sense, of backing up his claim to have outdone, in two respects, the typologies of Weber and Troeltsch. As far as the distinction between the universal church and "established church" is concerned, his most important source is the great medievalist Ernst Kantorowicz, not a representative of Catholic theology.[29] But Stark does not explore in detail whether we cannot in fact find a feeling for the difference between territorial and universal church in the writings of the classical German sociologists of religion, at least in their accounts of the Middle Ages.[30]

With regard to monasticism and religious orders and their comparison with sects, meanwhile, Stark takes up a suggestion made in one of the earliest works of British sociologist David Martin.[31] There are enough passages in Weber that Stark is right to critique—for example, when, in his sociology of domination (following Adolf von Harnack), he describes monks as the specially disciplined "troops of the monocratic head of the church," simply subordinating them to the church's (alleged) character as a form of hierocratic rule. But, as is not uncommon with Weber, he also shows an awareness of opposing tendencies and refers to the "tensions" between monasticism and the charisma of office, and even to monasticism's *negation* of the exclusive importance of the charisma of office.[32] This is quite close to Stark's proposed correction. So while Stark's argument needs to be more solidly substantiated, there is no reason to declare his impulses misguided or attributable solely to apologetic motives.

The Sacralization of Political Domination

This brings us to Stark's core decision when it comes to the structure of his multivolume work. The guiding thread of his macrosociological volumes is gleaned from his revised typology of the social forms of Christianity. The first volume is devoted to all forms of "established religion," more specifically to all basic forms of the sacralization of political domination. In a dialectical countermovement, the second volume deals with the sociology of sects, which are interpreted as rebellions against the fusion of political power and religion under the conditions of "established religion." The third volume, far more extensive than the two previous ones, then presents the two major variants of Christianity that, for Stark, have retained the faith's universalist aspirations in fundamentally undiminished form and thus defended the ideal of the universal church: Catholicism and Calvinism. He discusses both in terms of their conservative and revolutionary aspects, tracing back the distinction between them to the difference between "community" and "society," between a more communitarian and a more individualist-aggregative social form. While all three volumes are thus geared toward a seemingly static typology, they provide a movement, namely from a thesis and antithesis toward a synthesis.

This movement is not that of world history as such, as if Stark were claiming that history is heading ineluctably toward the triumph of the universal church. Instead, he constructs a movement arising from attempts to realize the ideal of moral universalism—which is drowned out again and again by particularisms, but, having once appeared in the world, has never entirely lost its appeal. In this respect, we can also read Stark's work as a story with a moral, as a warning of the dangers of particularization and as an attempt to build on exemplary ways of regaining the universalist spirit. For Stark, the strongest role models lie in the history of the Catholic Church; there can be no doubt about that. Even those who do or do not entirely share this view should not evade the challenge of Stark's arguments by ignoring them. The task must be to correct the picture he has drawn through a realistic picture of the Catholic Church and by referring to other sources of moral universalism, both religious and secular. In what follows, by examining Stark's substantive analyses more closely, I aim to do this with greater precision with respect to the history of Christianity, which is the only religion he examined.

The first volume, which, as mentioned, is dedicated to "established religion," is fairly expansive despite its general limitation to the history of Christianity. This broader horizon is not chosen arbitrarily: Stark is concerned with the sacralization of politically constituted human social forms in general, and this phenomenon did not first enter world history with Christianity. For Stark, Christianity in fact represents a break with the self-sacralization of particularist social forms; in this first volume, however, he is primarily concerned with relapses into particularism, with the loss of universalism within states influenced by Christianity. As a foil for the tensions in Christianity, he discusses the pre-Christian, archaic self-sacralization of political domination in Egyptian civilization and to a lesser extent its Mesopotamian counterpart, while also examining the history of the Japanese Empire. The political subtext can hardly be missed. Stark aims to sensitize his readers to the various forms of Christian sacralization of rulers and peoples over the course of history by pointing up its overlap with twentieth-century Japanese imperialism and with modern totalitarian forms of the sacralization of leaders as found in the cults of Hitler and Stalin.

Stark does not mention forms of collective sacralization before the emergence of archaic statehood. He is, however, aware that the sacralization of the ruler (or "chief") already began under the conditions of "tribal societies."[33] These rudiments, however, became exponentially more important with the emergence of archaic empires and in response to them. The sacralization of the ruler is thus a universal phenomenon, that is, it can be found in many different eras and all over the world—"from China to Peru."[34] The sacralization of the ruler always faced competition from the self-sacralization of the people, but for over three thousand years—according to Stark (I, 15)—the latter was always in the shadow of the former, until modern revolutions, which entailed a partial or complete break with the sacralization of the ruler. Drawing on the comparative study of religion, Stark distinguishes three main types of sacralization of rulers.[35] First, the king may be presented as a god or at least the descendant of gods or as becoming a god upon his death. Second, the king may be regarded not as divine himself, but as sent, chosen, exalted, or anointed by gods—that is, as a person who is in special proximity to the divine. And third, in continuity with the connection between the offices of chief and high priest in pre-state societies, the king may be primarily or exclusively viewed as the supreme or even the only priest.

But this typology and the discussions connected with it, including those on ancient Judaism and the Germanic peoples before Christianization, serve only as a background to analysis of the fusions of Christianity and the sacralization of rulers. Stark sees the three main forms of such fusion in the history of the Byzantine Empire, which he explores in particular depth; in the history of tsarist Russia, where he is particularly interested in the nexus of modernization and increasing sacralization of the ruler; and in English history, with its tradition of stylizing the ruler as a miracle worker and healer, as classically examined by Marc Bloch,[36] and in light of the emergence of an Anglican Church independent of Rome. Stark also pays ongoing attention to France, as it of course has traditions similar to those of England in many respects and, in the shape of "Gallicanism," developed a partial analogy to Anglicanism. Strikingly, Lutheranism, another way in which Christianity was inserted into the framework of discrete political territories, mostly remains outside Stark's field of perception.

I am unable to discuss the empirical details and validity of Stark's analyses in detail here. It is remarkable with what intensity he noted and incorporated into his conceptions key works of historical research that emerged after the generation of the classical sociological figures. The core focus of Stark's analyses of these texts is the reparticularization of Christian moral universalism as the state hedges in Christianity in various ways. He often refers to "caesaropapism" as a threat to Christianity, while inventing the term "populopapism" (I, 164) for the sacralization of the people, which was long the weaker phenomenon but then gained the upper hand. He shows that often it is not the "people" alone that is the subject of sacralization, but that the soil, the constitution, or the law may also attain sacred status. In a nuanced account and, with regard to the Middle Ages, based on the pioneering studies of Ernst Kantorowicz,[37] he elaborates on the links between the sacralization of rulers and the sacralization of the people; he then goes on to elucidate the modern, revolutionary nationalist and often secularist forms of exclusive sacralization of the people, for example in nineteenth-century Italy.

In addition to these two main types of particularist political sacralization, Stark is interested in the emergence of the idea of a sacred mission. Conspicuously, he does not take the usual approach of identifying its emergence in the Axial Age religions,[38] but in the archaic states themselves. This is important because, contrary to a widely held view, he rejects the idea that the moral universalism of the Axial Age is the origin of the concept of mission. Instead, a messianism that Stark describes as ethnocentric already seems to be inherent in the expansionist tendencies of archaic empires. To develop his idea here he draws mainly on important studies of Egypt,[39] where the expansion of its empire was already justified in religious terms—albeit in the sense of the superiority of its gods and the need to dominate others, not in the sense of a mission to propagate a universal truth.

But again, Stark brings out the susceptibility of Christianity, which is actually opposed to ethnocentrism, to legitimizing an expansive empire: "The pax Augusta and the pax Christi had a tendency to coalesce" (I, 107). Stark's analysis of British colonialism and imperialism is particularly detailed and trenchant, especially when it comes to the cloaking of interest-driven politics and claims to civilizational superiority in Christian garb. In many passages, we can clearly see his repugnance at the moral tone so typical of the struggle between imperialisms. Ideally, Stark would have presented a more detailed argument comparing British with French, Spanish, or Japanese imperialism to avoid the impression of a one-sided critique of the British variety. But the entire anti-imperialist thrust of Stark's account makes a rather poor fit with the notion of a conservative apologist for Catholicism.

Some have countered Stark's sharp distinction between the universal Catholic Church and the various forms of caesaropapism by highlighting the phenomenon of the Papal States, which, after all—more perhaps than any other form of political rule that was justified with reference to Christianity—represented a fusion of political and sacred power.[40] While Stark does not address this polity, in connection with (Mazzini's) secular Italian nationalism he does mention the fall of the Papal States in 1871 (I, 200); he calls this event, which many Catholics and the Church experienced as a painful loss, "a blessing in disguise." Only in this way could the pope cease to be perceived, in Italy and elsewhere, as a regional potentate, and instead be viewed as a "spiritual leader on a world-wide scale." Nor does Stark interpret the French Revolution, with its antichurch excesses, from a backward-looking perspective, but as providing impetus for the church's self-renewal and its re-embedding in the broader population, from which it had become detached long before the Revolution.

One point of great theoretical relevance must be added. With explicit reference to Durkheim and his claim to have uncovered the true secret of religion in the self-sacralization of society,[41] Stark writes that while it is wrong to explain the idea of God in this way, this perspective does enable us to shed light on the idea of the god-king as "society writ large" (I, 137). A non-atheist Durkheim might have put forward the same kind of argument, although it is certainly not the last word on the complex genesis of notions of God and their interaction with structures of domination. For Stark, the appeal of "monarchical religion" remains in force as long as the fundamentals of society are organized on a collective basis. But here he overlooks the fact that the very emergence of kingship and the archaic state represented a break with the community form. This is the price he pays for having begun the history of collective self-sacralization with sacred kingship and failing to pay more attention to nonstate societies.

Social Conflicts and Sectarianism

As I see it, despite all such possible criticisms and Stark's controversial empirical assessments, which I leave aside here, it is undeniable that the first volume of *The Sociology of Religion* makes an important contribution to the historical sociology of sacredness and power. As I have indicated, the second volume relates to the first in the manner of antithesis to thesis. For Stark, it is beyond doubt that "established religion"—that is, the fusion of religion with state power and social privileges—is bound to repeatedly trigger a reaction from the disadvantaged and dissatisfied, which—given that all actors express themselves in religious terms prior to the rise of the secular option—will itself take religious forms. This, he believes, is exactly what sects are.

Sects, as Stark states after H. Richard Niebuhr (II, 2), are religious "conflict societies" that we can only understand in light of their opposition to the dominant "church." Although every sect can also be described at the level of theological doctrines, Stark contends, theological differences with the church are usually not responsible for their secession but are based instead on experiences of disadvantage and disregard. These experiences may result from the classic forms of social inequality, but also from ethnic, geographic, gender-related, and generational forms of discrimination. Finally, Stark claims, in contrast to Niebuhr, that sectlike secessions may be rooted in individual psychology, such as inferiority complexes that trigger demands for compensation. By adding this last-mentioned source of the dynamics of such breakaways, Stark safeguards his argument against criticism in a problematic manner. Even if a social explanation seems unconvincing in a particular case, he can still defend his general claim.

In his selection of cases, Stark focuses mainly on the same territories he considered in the first volume. He justifies this by stating that it is where the religious "establishment" is strongest that sectarian protest and resistance are most pronounced. For him, it thus makes sense to declare the "caesaropapist" countries of England and Russia as particularly fertile soil from which sects were bound to sprout, while classically Catholic areas—he mentions Austria, Bavaria, and Spain (II, 59)—provided no inducement for religious secession due to their strict orientation toward a universal church.

Right from the outset, two doubts must be raised about Stark's guiding theoretical construction. On any account, there is a need to clarify how we might explain the case of the United States on this premise, a country in which the establishment of a "state church" was rendered impossible with the adoption of the Constitution at the end of the eighteenth century, but at the same time one that is host to a particularly large number of religious communities. How do these so-called denominations relate to sects? And why is this phenomenon found in the United States in particular? Stark gives a detailed answer to these questions, to which I will return. The second doubt has to do with the homogeneously Catholic countries without a nationalized church. In Stark's construction, it looks as if social protest there was not articulated in the form of sectarian movements.

This, however, fails to acknowledge that in addition to the formation of sects, which did in fact occur, another nonreligious form of secession from the Catholic Church took place from the eighteenth century onward. The question is whether, under the conditions of a Catholic religious monopoly, the equivalent of sect formation is the division of society into a religious part and often militantly secularist part. There is much to support this assumption in Spain, in the France of the nineteenth and twentieth centuries, and in Austria. David Martin refers to political sectarianism[42] and calls for "an integrated taxonomy of both religious and political attitudes, beliefs and structures, and also a discussion of the way they relate to each other in different cultures."[43] We might say that the more we adduce the political and economic causes of sect formation, the more we have to take them into account in general, including when examining churches, if we are to avoid an analytical imbalance.

In the entire first part of the second volume, which is devoted to the emergence of sects, Stark attempts a complicated balancing act between a political sociology explanation of sect formation and a theoretical approach that by no means seeks to reduce religious convictions to the mere reflection of interests. He expressly distances himself from such an idea (II, 69) and counters the Marxist notion of religion as the opium of the people by stating that it is often better characterized as a stimulant, as "adrenaline" (II, 57). But there are passages that sound reductionist in this sense—for example, where Stark views the success of a social movement as the cause of a weakening of religion (II, 59). Here Stark's empirical example is also implausible: he asserts that the success of the black civil rights movement in the United States is increasingly emptying the churches, a claim for which there is no evidence.

He repeatedly gets bogged down in unproductive quarrels when, contrary to ample evidence, he asserts that Methodism in particular was originally sectarian in character, or, similarly, claims that "anti-masculinist" resentment played a major role in the emergence of Christian Science (II, 31). David

Martin's question as to why Stark, as a Catholic sociologist, should be more Marxist than the Marxists when analyzing sects[44] is therefore not unjustified. We would only have to modify it by noting that Stark's heavy emphasis on the psychology of resentment adds a Nietzschean note—one mediated by Max Scheler—to his Marxist impulses.

Once again, I must leave aside the details of Stark's analyses in this first part of the second volume. The theory of the inversion of the sacralization of rulers in sects (II, 83ff.), developed chiefly with reference to Russian sectarianism—in which the tsar is defined as the antichrist and leaving the church is declared a sacred duty—seems to me an important addition to the first volume. This brings the specific theological ideas held by these sects more clearly back into play. If sacralization is an ambiguous term because it can refer to the divine as well as to the diabolical and demonic, then we must view even this inversion as a form of sacralization.

In line with the strongly typologizing approach of the entire work, the second part of the volume is dedicated to a typology of sects. The first key aspect here is the distinction between messianic and nonmessianic sects. If, as I have asserted, not all messianism is driven by moral universalism, but all moral universalism must be missionary—at least in the sense of a mission to propagate moral universalism as such, not necessarily its specific form— then the degree of universalism should be evident in whether the salvific goal is viewed as attainable for all. As Stark sees it, from this point of view many sects turn out to be far from universalist, because the expectation of salvation is restricted to a small number of people, that is, an elite, while the damnation of those who have refused to be converted may even be noted with satisfaction. The concept of predestination espoused by Augustine and Calvin occupies a problematic intermediate position here, according to which salvation is not granted to all, but the judgment upon individuals' eternal fate does not depend on the moral qualities of their action.

Stark does not discuss this conception in particular but devotes considerable attention to its rejection—for example, in early Quakerism and among the Methodists, who, he contends, came close to turning the doctrine of a distant God into pantheistic and pre-romantic ideas. Early Methodists, he underlines, were suspected of being, and caricatured as, crypto-Catholics, and we can discern interrelationships with the intensification of piety associated with St. Francis de Sales within the framework of the "Counter-Reformation" (II, 154f.). In this context, Stark also proposes two interesting corrections to Max Weber's famous thesis, according to which the inscrutability of one's future salvation is causally related to the pursuit of economic success. Stark argues that since there are sects without a belief in predestination, but with a clear orientation toward activity and disciplined effort, the connection cannot be so straightforward. The crucial element, he avers, may have lain not just in the "inscrutability of God's will," but also in the "inscrutability of one's own experience," in the impossibility of finding out to what extent one's own conversion experience has truly brought one closer to God. And activism, Stark goes on, was not necessarily centered on the striving for economic success but may also have manifested itself in an active approach to public life in general (II, 171ff., 274ff.). For Stark, then, the relationship between sects and capitalism is far less clear than it seems in Weber's work.

Stark also offers a correction worth considering to a key thesis expounded by Troeltsch and H. R. Niebuhr. Both emphasized the strongly emotional character of the lower classes' religiosity. Stark (II, 137) interprets an emphasis on rationality not only as the usual attempt by the upper classes to obtain distinction, but in certain cases also as a form of sectlike distancing from emotionality, if this has become an important characteristic of a religious community. This is his explanation for a certain breakaway from the Methodists. With this thesis, whether it applies in a specific case or not, Stark directs our attention to the "contracultural" character of many sects, as he puts it using a term fashionable in the 1960s (II, 128). Everything that seems characteristic of the dominant culture may become the object of passionate rejection, including beauty, good manners, and manner of speaking, not to mention, of course, courts, taxes, education, and the armed forces.

In elaborating his typology, Stark works with the three polarities of "retrogressive versus progressive," "rigoristic versus antinomian," and "violent versus nonviolent." Sects may long for or strive for the return to an (imagined) former state of things as well as for progress toward a dreamed-of future. They may, with regard to sexuality, for example, aspire to the strictest abstinence (extending to self-castration), just as orgiastic-Dionysian practices may become prevalent. Violence against the enemies of the envisaged kingdom of God may be perceived as justified, just as radical nonviolence may be demanded, even in the form of a refusal to defend oneself against violent attackers. Sometimes one and the same movement may switch from one extreme to the other, as when—Stark tells us—the violent Hussites were transformed into the nonviolent Bohemian and Moravian Brethren. Whether such a change actually took place is often historiographically controversial, because a certain genealogy is of course then perceived as embarrassing. Rigorist and nonviolent sects, Stark states, are easier to integrate into the existing order than antinomic and violent ones.

Stark's accounts are rich in empirical illustrations of the types he develops. His entire argument here can also be read as a further development of the ideas in Max Weber's famous "Intermediate Reflection," namely as a typology of the tensions between the universalist fraternal ethic and different cultural values or alternative possibilities for sacralization, but, unlike Weber, without assuming a developmental dynamic. Stark says nothing to suggest a necessary tendency toward progressive functional differentiation.[45]

Sects often have a short life, as the reasons for secession may cease to apply or at least lose much of their force. Secessions from sects themselves resulting, for example, from different degrees of radicalism in renouncing the "world" or re-embracing it may reduce the potency of these groups (II, 298). Sects may also shrink due to a shortage of young members if the motives for establishing them are not imparted to the next generation. And they may fall victim to their own success, as their adherents' economic achievements alter their disposition. A passage in the writings of John Wesley, the founder of Methodism (II, 267f.)—one that had also caught the attention of Max Weber and H. Richard Niebuhr—plays a major role in Stark's argument here.[46] Wesley states that religion inevitably generates diligence and thrift, but thus also wealth, which in turn intensifies worldliness and thus weakens religion. While Weber saw this as backing for his hypothesis, it must be remembered that Wesley was neither seeking to confirm his own salvific predestination nor making a point about capital accumulation. Instead, he was urging Christians to donate more as a means of fostering their own salvation.

But what becomes of sects if they do not disappear? To refer to "established sects," as has been proposed,[47] Stark considers an unhelpful contradiction in terms. Instead, he concurs with Howard Becker, who decreed in 1932 that "denominations are simply sects in an advanced stage of development and adjustment to each other and the world."[48] This formula seems to answer two questions at once, namely "What becomes of sects?" and "How do denominations arise?" With reference to multiple examples, Stark illustrates the routinization of sectarian life, the gradual acquiescence in previously rejected regulations such as payment of priests, the preparation and ritualization of church services, and the use of organ music and rehearsed singing. In line with this, the group's self-designation also shifts from an emphasis on nonconformism and dissent to the "Free Church" (II, 287), and, Stark contends, sociological terminology must take account of such changes. As he sees it, the diversity of religious communities without a strong missionary zeal then facilitates a system of mutual tolerance.

Since denominations are typical of the United States, this is the point at which Stark must take up the question I posed when we first turned to the topic of sectarianism: namely how a country without an "established religion" could also have been a breeding ground for sectarianism. His answer is based essentially on a study in the historical sociology of religion—also influenced by Niebuhr—by Will Herberg.[49] In short, Stark's explanation has three components: the specific conditions on the frontier, where no established upper class existed; the consequences of mass immigration, which turned even churches accustomed to a monopoly into sects in the United States; and the emergence of an ideology of Americanism in which democracy and the US-American people were sacralized. As exemplary as the mutual tolerance of the religious communities is, Stark states that the "American ideology" poses a threat of its own to the moral universalism of Christianity. Volume II ends with a warning of this threat—the self-sacralization of the United States.[50]

The Universal Church

The third volume of *The Sociology of Religion*, conceived as a synthesis of the first two, now focuses on the two currents of Christianity in which, for Stark, universalism has been most strongly preserved: Catholicism and Calvinism. The author repeatedly emphasizes that Calvin's Geneva was intended to replace Rome as the center of a universal church, refers to "the great Genevan" (III, 244), and even describes it as his book's main thesis that "in Calvinism we encounter a third form of religious tradition, different from both established and sectarian religiousness" (III, 113). While England repeatedly serves as an example of "established religion," Calvinist Scotland appears in a far better light. Stark is well aware of the influence of the (Calvinist) Presbyterians in the history of England (III, 119), but overall, he fails to paint a truly nuanced picture of English constitutional history.[51]

Nevertheless, the idea that Stark is merely writing an apologia for Catholicism is undermined by this strong appreciation for Calvin and primordial Calvinism as well as his account of ancient Judaism in the introductory part of the third volume (III, 28–45). The latter is empirically untenable today. The role of the prophets is so hypostatized that it seems as though there was already a kind of separation of church and state in Judaism; no one would now defend this notion.[52] But a sympathetic interpretation will see this, as well as his appreciation for Calvin and Catholicism, as an attempt to invoke moral universalism.

As mentioned, Stark has been accused of idealizing the Middle Ages, Spain's Golden Age under Philip II, and the Catholic Church as a whole. A fairer assessment might be that medieval Christianity serves him as a point of orientation because it was a pre-national era (III, 13). It is his anti-nationalism that aroused in him the longing for a time in which a different relationship between "neighborhood community" and "world unity" existed than in the era of the "all-importance of nationhood." However, what prevented him from idealizing the medieval church was his equally pronounced sense of the risk to which it was undoubtedly subject, namely of an "all-too-close alliance" with the feudal system (III, 14).

He sees this fusion as a (legitimate) source of the Reformation. Despite all its meritocratic traits, the church, Stark asserts, repeatedly capitulated to the status system of feudal society (III, 246). Without idealization, Stark thus searches for the first attempts to relativize state power in the church reforms of the Middle Ages. With Alois Dempf, he refers to an effective prefiguring of the English Magna Carta in the struggle between Pope Gregory VII and Henry IV, Holy Roman Emperor.[53] It is certainly anachronistic and misleading when Stark speaks of the church's "democratic" tendencies, when these were essentially theocratic and egalitarian. But again, one might appreciate his attempt to tell a different story of freedom than that typically narrated by Protestants and in the Anglo-Saxon world.

How risky this attempt was is evident above all in the reactions to Stark's appraisal of Spain. He himself knew that Philip II had long been and still was widely regarded as "the symbol of tyranny or even the symbol of all that is evil" (III, 160). Once again, he wished to give any hint of idealization a wide berth, and he even criticized the famous book by German poet and novelist Reinhold Schneider as far from immune to this danger (III, 160).[54] His key focus was on a crucial criterion, namely the extent to which the justification of a king's rule places him above or under the law and to what extent the ruler internally accepts this justification.

Particularly fruitful in Stark's interpretation of Spain is his appreciation for the intellectual approaches of so-called late Spanish Scholasticism, the dramas of Pedro Calderón de la Barca, and his in-depth study of the history of Spanish colonialism. From the point of view of racism and race relations, the Spanish Empire seems to him no worse overall than the United States (III, 232). All in all, one could interpret the entire first part of the third volume as an attempt to analyze the threat to universalism arising from the incorporation of the universalist churches into particularist orders. A church, that is, may be de facto rather than de jure identified with a particular state (III, 249).

The second part seeks to illuminate how the church can liberate itself from the tentacles of the world if these impede its universalist mission. In the context of a study in the sociology of religion, this means looking again for forms of movement and organization in which such endeavors can take on institutionalized form. This prompts Stark to turn to the great church reformers and in particular to monasticism and the religious orders. For him, these are the intrachurch equivalent of the rebellious and revolutionary sects. In a wide-ranging account, he depicts the emergence of monasticism (in Egypt) before the conversion of Emperor Constantine, Benedict of Nursia's efforts to organize monastic life, and in particular, the medieval monastic reforms and the emergence of the Franciscan order. The monastic reforms emanating from Cluny are especially consonant with his idea of the church's independence from local power structures and specific ties to social classes (III, 269).

The guiding thread here is the question of "the periodic rebirth of universalism in the church body."[55] For Stark, it is indisputable that an element of anticlericalism always played a role in the emergence of the religious orders (III, 409) and that the church did not itself found the orders. Hence, it was often a far from foregone conclusion—in the case of Francis of Assisi, for example—whether a religious awakening would lead to a sect or an order. This was determined through its interplay with the church authorities.

Stark also provides an in-depth examination of the post-Reformation orders, such as the Redemptorists, but above all the Jesuits. He presents Ignatius von Loyola as the initiator of the synthesis of mysticism and organization that the Reformers failed to achieve (III, 372), an achievement that, Stark tells us, profoundly transformed the church as a whole via the Council of Trent.

While Stark's account of the Catholic Church is sustained by his optimistic faith in its capacity for self-renewal—though oddly enough he makes no reference to the Second Vatican Council, which immediately preceded the writing of his book—his portrayal of the other great form of Christian universalism, Calvinism, is essentially a tragic narrative of decay. This decline, according to Stark, was a danger from the very beginning in that the associated "drive for universality" began at a time "when the compass of development was set in the direction—fostered, if not indeed released, by the Reformation itself—of nationalism, of world-disintegration, of splintered religiosity" (III, 426). The division of Calvinism into Presbyterians and Congregationalists, based on class divisions, Stark asserts, weakened its universalist potential (III, 429). Calvinism's adaptation to the bourgeois-capitalist order or even—in South Africa and the United States—to a slavery-based economy (III, 243), Stark goes on, then stripped it entirely of this potential in certain countries.

The question, of course, is whether these assessments, at the time Stark wrote them and looking back from a historical distance, were plausible arguments or an expression of personal beliefs that have no place in a scholarly work. It would have been better if Stark had clarified the status of moral universalism as a benchmark for all Christians, which any and all of them may fail to live up to. His overall assessment could then have been empirically nuanced without implying the superiority of Catholicism. But if he did wish to emphasize this confessional perspective, he could have been more critical of the specific dangers of the Catholic tradition. Catholicism's greater, though by no means omnipresent, distance from nationalism and the sacralization of the nation may, after all, go hand in hand with a greater willingness to sacralize a ruler than is typically found in Calvinism. Up to the present, in the words of Karl Rahner, the Catholic Church has been a global church more *in potentia* than *in actu*,[56] and the specific risk of Catholicism has always been the self-sacralization of the church.[57] Stark says nothing at all about this.

His work, then, certainly has multiple shortcomings. But these call for constructive resolution, not for the author's exclusion from the scholarly community. Nor is Stark's prose devoid of purely rhetorical elements. Yet he also succeeds in articulating certain ideas with brilliance and in conveying deep insights. Of Stark's contemporaries, David Martin seems to me to have judged his work most fairly. In 1973, he wrote—in the *Jewish Journal of Sociology*—that an understanding of Catholicism from the inside was no more calamitous for scholarship than the taken-for-granted cultural assumptions of the Protestant-based, Anglo-Saxon world as they crop up routinely in its self-analyses. But he also predicted that Stark's work would probably be fated to stand like an isolated monument, one seldom visited and then only to scrawl disparaging comments on it.[58] I believe it is high time to take a different approach to this Jewish émigré and great Catholic scholar.[59]

IV, 4
More Weberian Than Weber?: David Martin

In 2011, I was asked to write a blurb for the new book by British sociologist of religion David Martin (1929–2019), which appeared under the title *The Future of Christianity*.[1] I tried to come up with a pithy way of conveying the main achievement of his wide-ranging oeuvre and settled on describing him as a pioneer of the "political sociology of religion." Fortunately, the author, who had never presented himself in this way, accepted my characterization. It probably goes without saying that this form of words did not mean that David Martin tended to view religions as the mere distorted expression of people's real "material" needs, their political claims and grievances. A cursory glance at the complex imbrication of empirical historico-sociological knowledge and theological reasoning in this scholar's work is all it takes to dispel this idea.

What I was trying to articulate was that here we have an approach to research in the sociology of religion that eschews any notion of processes of secularization and religious revitalization as the sum of individual acts of conversion, religious experience, or decision-making with regard to religion. Instead, this approach takes proper account of the determinants of individuals' attitudes toward churches and religious communities. Individuals, that is, perceive religious communities of all kinds holistically. As a rule, they are not concerned, at least not primarily, with approving or rejecting theological doctrines or doctrinal systems, but rather with a "locus of self-definition,"[2] to quote the term used in recent research on conversion—in other words, an orientation toward a particular definition of their identity and a willingness to accept a certain moral authority.

This view of individuals' self-assignment to religious communities is consonant with David Martin's thesis that the attitudes of churches and religious communities to key political issues, but especially the fundamental, enduring patterns of relationship between political power and religion, are the crucial dimension when it comes to the sociological explanation of religious developments and secularization. These core political issues include the national question, the social question, the democratic question, and the issues of individual rights and religious pluralism; when it comes to relations between power and religion, it is the institutional arrangements governing the relationship between state and "church" that stand out. This list of political questions or issues is neither exhaustive nor has it been stable across history. In our era, for example, in some countries at least, the question of gender equality can be perceived as absolutely crucial—or at least as far more important than it ever was before.

Of course, the urgency of the "national" question depends on whether a country has, for example, been divided up by external powers or is oppressed as a whole, or on whether national unity seems undisputed and secure. All these questions involve the subjective perception of urgency.[3] This focus on political questions in the broadest sense is not meant to imply that economic processes or intellectual and cultural developments are irrelevant to the history of religion. But it does suggest that the effects of all these changes, as well as the dynamics resulting from experiences of religious certainty or the impulses of religious doubt, must necessarily pass through fields of political tension. Only in this way do they take on secularizing or desecularizing force, and it is this political dimension that determines the appeal of religious communities as they compete with one other.

David Martin is the pioneer of a political sociology of religion understood in this sense. He himself states that the sociology of religion and political sociology are "joined at the hip"[4]—grown together like Siamese twins from the outset. For him, then, the history of nationalism and the history of religion, for example, must be examined within a shared framework. This means that the myths and rituals of secular states can be properly understood only if we view them partly as transformations of religious myths and rituals or as the result of opposition to them.

This call for an integrated perspective on the dynamics of sacralization and the dynamics of power does not mean that nationalism or secularism should be declared objects of the sociology of religion as substitutes for religion, quasi-religions, or "political religions."[5] That would presuppose the unhistorical idea that all people have religious needs and that every case of the suppression of religion can therefore only lead to the displacement of these needs. This contrasts with the notion that people can indeed live without religion, but not without sacralization.[6] However, everything that is perceived as "sacred" has consequences in the sphere of power, and no political power can be stabilized without belief in its legitimacy. This legitimacy always entails a reference to the sacred, whether in the form of the charisma of a leader figure, the sacred aura of a tradition, or formal procedures whose results are respected only if these procedures themselves are considered legitimate.

At this point, some readers will feel moved to comment that what I have said so far is nothing new. Max Weber, they will underline, had already consistently linked the sociology of religion and domination, and he developed the associated typology of forms of legitimate domination to which I have just alluded.[7] There are in fact good reasons to call David Martin a Weberian. In addition to the reasons mentioned above, importantly, the whole style of his historical-comparative research is reminiscent of the great role model of Max Weber. Yet Martin was not a member of a school inspired by Weber, nor was he greatly concerned with the debate on this classical figure's writings. I would describe him as "more Weberian than Weber."

Again, this label can easily be misunderstood. If we call someone "more Catholic than the pope" it tends not to be a compliment. Likewise, the apocryphal quote from Marx, "Moi, je ne suis pas Marxiste" ("I am not a Marxist myself"), is chiefly intended to upbraid individual Marxists or all of them for a narrow-mindedness or dogmatism of which the master himself was allegedly not guilty. I have the opposite idea in mind with my characterization of David Martin. Martin is not among those scholars who use Weber's canonical status and tremendous reputation to give their own approach or "paradigm" an unassailable status. He works like Weber, but this has also compelled him to highlight the differences between his findings and Weber's.

It seems to me that the decisive factor in understanding this is the tension between Weber's research as such and his famous characterizations of long-term tendencies of social change. Weber's claims of a world-historical process of rationalization, disenchantment, and bureaucratization became more influential than his research itself. That need not have been a problem if his major claims could be viewed as empirical discoveries arising from methodical research. This is how the literature on Weber often presents things. As an alternative to this conventional view, however, it is possible to argue that at a certain point in the development of his oeuvre, as his studies grew increasingly fragmented, Weber imposed on them ambiguous and excessive claims about tendencies, that is, he resorted to what David Martin called "dangerous nouns of process."[8]

My goal is not to delve into these differences in perspective on Weber's work.[9] All that matters here is that, against this background, we can view

David Martin's political sociology of religion both as a culmination of Weber's historico-comparative research program and as a way out of possible dead ends arising from his analysis of modernity and its genesis. If this description is correct, then it is anything but trivial to call Martin's work "more Weberian than Weber." Because then its significance is not limited to the field of the sociology of religion.

This is the guiding thread of the following account. I do not seek to provide a complete overview of Martin's work. Instead, I am going to focus on three areas: first, his attempt to produce a general theory of secularization, to quote the title of his 1978 book; second, his investigation of the global expansion of Pentecostalism and of Christianity; and third, Martin's even broader historical framing of his theory of religion, as evident in his studies on the so-called Axial Age and the problem of violence in and through religions.

A General Theory of Secularization?

Despite his modest beginnings and the meandering course of his early education, David Martin, born in London in 1929, soon made a name for himself in the academic world.[10] He was still a student when he wrote the now classic essay "The Denomination" in 1962. Engaging critically with the work of H. Richard Niebuhr, he demonstrated both that the Christian organizational type known as the "denomination" did not first emerge in the United States, but in Great Britain, and that it is quite wrong to claim that denominations necessarily originate in (rebellious) sects.[11] In another early essay (from 1965), Martin caused a stir by calling for nothing less than the elimination of the term "secularization" from the vocabulary of sociology.[12] Against this background, it inevitably seemed odd when, more than a decade later, the same author set about writing a general theory of secularization. Even decades later, this book was described as "one of the most gloriously mistitled works in our field."[13]

Martin was unhappy about this mockery and also felt misunderstood. In calling for the elimination of the concept of secularization, his goal was neither to ban the word nor forbid analysis of the associated realities. Instead, his focus was on the term's false definitude and its political charge; he also wanted to help make a better fit between research and its object by putting forward an alternative conceptual apparatus to illuminate the different levels of meaning involved. As far as the claim of a "general theory" is concerned, everything obviously depends on what such a theory might mean within the social sciences. This is by no means clear. If, building on the positivism of the nineteenth century and the logical positivism of the twentieth century, we take it to mean propositions about lawlike relationships between causal variables and their effects, then we can formulate such propositions as hypotheses independently of the empirical research itself. These propositions, which are in themselves unhistorical, then have to be applied—from the outside, so to speak—to the researcher's historical-empirical material, which leads to their falsification or (always necessarily provisional) verification. On this view, it is irrelevant to the understanding of an object of investigation whether or not it represents human action and history.

There is, however, an entirely different understanding of "general theory." This emerged chiefly in the German traditions of historicism and hermeneutics. On this view, there are no unhistorical laws of human activity. The dream of a "social physics" will never be realized. Scholars operating on this premise always study individual cases, but in such a way that, through careful comparison with other cases, they gradually formulate generalizing statements that then establish a guide for the explanation of developments in a subsequent case. If this new case cannot be described in the expected way, this in no way means that our previous generalization is completely falsified. But we are compelled to modify our explanatory model in such a way that it now encompasses the new case as well. In this way, step by step, our theory becomes more historically rich, but not ahistorical or suprahistorical. This is the logic of historical-comparative research in the nonpositivist tradition. Again, there is no need here for a discussion of whether Max Weber correctly portrayed this logic and his own approach in his methodological writings.[14]

I had to set out these observations in a fair degree of detail at this point because David Martin seems to fluctuate between the two meanings of this term in his "general theory," which makes it harder to understand. At bottom, Martin tends toward the historical-hermeneutic approach, but he tries to articulate his findings in a quasi-positivist theoretical framework. His book thus begins with the statement that previous research has demonstrated certain tendencies toward secularization in industrialized societies and that these are viewed as "fairly well established"[15] and can be presented as quasi-laws. Religious institutions, Martin tells us, are weakened to the extent that a region is dominated by heavy industry, especially if its population is homogeneously proletarian. Religious practice, he goes on, declines in proportion to the urban share of the population.

Yet these supposedly well-established empirical findings are neither undisputed nor self-evidently plausible. They are based on certain assumptions about "industrial society" and about functional differentiation that defy the spirit of a "political sociology of religion," which, for example, does not simply view the working and living conditions of the industrial proletariat as responsible for its secularization, if such can be established. The experiences of workers and their social movements with the churches play a crucial role. In no way does Martin wish to simply repeat the conventional claims about lawlike regularities but he accepts them as correct, "other things being equal." Yet he immediately adds, "But things are not equal—ever."[16] And it is central to his argument, he underlines, that this applies above all in view of the "particular cultural . . . complex within which they [such regularities] operate." For him, then, a general theory must relate universal processes to a typology of cultural contexts and then specify the type of "refraction" that these processes undergo within such contexts.

This formulation sounds like a mere compromise between the two versions of general theory discussed earlier. Those adhering to the stricter conception because they are unwilling to abandon the goal of uncovering social laws were suitably dissatisfied. Conversely, more historically and hermeneutically oriented sociologists found Martin's case analyses and comparisons highly illuminating but wondered why he tried to squeeze them into a framework that failed to question the basic assumptions of the theories of industrial society and functional differentiation.

The real advantage of Martin's approach lies in the elaboration and application of a typology of fundamental patterns of the relationship between political power and religion. While at first sight the term "political sociology of religion" might seem to imply a subdiscipline concerned solely with the attitude of religious communities to specific events and political issues, it now becomes clear that while Martin is interested in this topic—something I will return to later—his main focus is on enduring patterns and configurations.

Of course, these enduring patterns are themselves rooted in constitutive events. With respect to the recent history of European and North American Christianity, Martin highlights the success or failure of the Reformation; the outcome of the English Civil War between 1642 and 1660; and the impact of the American, French, and Russian Revolutions, but also the absence or failure of revolutions in Lutheran territories.[17] For the Briton Martin, the starting point for his typology is his own country, whose religious situation he characterized (in the 1970s) as "institutional erosion, erosion of religious ethos, maintenance of amorphous religious beliefs."[18] The underlying institutional constellation, he asserts, is that of the partial dissolution of the established church's monopoly through the presence of independent religious organizations and a merely slight political charging of the distinction between religious and secular. Martin continually contrasts the British case with two other models, namely the US-American and French.

The US-American case is typified by the early separation of the state and religious communities—as fundamentally guaranteed by the Constitution when the state was founded in the late eighteenth century—and thus by the absence of any form of established church. In the history of religion in the United States, despite all the equally unmistakable tendencies toward the secularization of its guiding ethos, we can observe the notably high presence of religious attitudes and even a sustained expansion of religious institutions over long periods of time. While there are certain continuities and similarities between the British and US-American cases (denominationalism), the French case is completely different. In France, but in other "Latin European" countries as well, there is a bifurcation of culture and society ("les deux Frances"). In one section of the population, religious beliefs and the associated institutional and ethical forms are strong. But they contrast with the equally intense secularist convictions and institutions of the other part of the population.

In these circumstances, religion easily becomes the subject of political conflicts. These conflicts may escalate and intensify social polarization; but mitigating elements may also come into play, which Martin observes chiefly in Italy, though not in Spain. The Latin American model is influenced by the Latin European one but differs from it due to the specific conditions of the region's (much later) Christianization. The presence of a Catholic left on a greater scale than in Europe, Martin contends, helped reduce the secularist militancy of the rest of the left. Martin added a "Russian" variant to the main models, which he understood—with reference to conditions under Soviet rule—as a simple reversal of the fusion of state and religious power in the form of a Marxist orthodoxy as state ideology. Here religious belief and religious institutions were profoundly repressed by the state. Faith and ethos continued to exist within religious institutions if they managed to survive.

Having made a fundamental distinction between these models, Martin's approach to them in his individual analyses is far from schematic. By taking account of the specialist research on particular nations and regions as well as on specific historical periods, he brought other aspects into view that are not adequately addressed either in conventional secularization theory or in theories that focus solely on the different variants of the state–church relationship.

Admittedly, these aspects were not presented in a coherent manner anywhere in the book; we have to glean them from Martin's analyses of individual cases. I want to highlight five of them here. First, Martin continuously paid attention to the international or geopolitical embedding of national developments. Hence, his explanatory efforts repeatedly address the topic of wars and their consequences for religious developments. Just as a religious community may be perceived as shielding national identity against threats or, conversely, as an agent of oppression, it may also be viewed as complicit in a lost war that it supported or as insufficiently loyal. In France, after the defeat at the hands of Prussia-Germany in 1870 and in Spain after its defeat by the United States in 1898, the church was affected by the overall decline in loyalty to institutions, while in Austria after 1945 the clear separation of the political camps was somewhat attenuated as a result of its defeat.[19]

Second, of course, it is always possible that churches and religious communities will undergo learning processes that diminish their support for institutional arrangements that they have so far endorsed or defended. This is especially likely to be the case if a church is organized supranationally. Then a learning process at the global level may also influence the church in those countries that would not have undergone the change involved on their own. Martin devotes an entire chapter of his book to what he calls "reactive organicism,"[20] that is, a religiously based departure from liberalism and the secularization of the state. Others refer to "antimodern" forms of religio-political rule. Here Martin's book focuses mainly on Spain and Portugal, where this model came to an end when he was writing his book, and on organizations such as Opus Dei—but he also treats the Catholic opposition to this organicist reaction in a highly nuanced way.

The third feature of Martin's theory I wish to highlight here encompasses aspects commonly referred to as "ecological," though here the meaning of this term differs from its common use. The focus here is not on the human–nature relationship, but on social environments; in this specific case, the question at issue is, for example, not only whether there is a religious minority in a country, but also whether it is territorially concentrated or is scattered across the country, and how large it is in relation to the majority society.

Fourth, David Martin tries—albeit, as he himself laments, at a relatively late point in his work[21]—to incorporate into his analyses the ideas about center and periphery put forward by Edward Shils, with whom he had worked on higher education policy. In the work of Shils, these ideas were not simply focused on the "geographical" or "ecological" dimension of social realities but shone a light on their respective proximity to or distance from the sacred core of an established system of legitimation. Martin's question in this context is what contribution a religious community makes to the legitimation of the state order and how great the distance is between this community's official contribution and the life of the people, so to speak. In the United Kingdom, for example, the public role of the Anglican Church may be substantial, but its distance from the general population may also be great.

Fifth and finally, it should be mentioned that Martin elaborated an idea that only became fashionable in sociology and the history of technology a few years later as a result of other impulses.[22] Martin states that societies develop a framework within which future developments necessarily take place. "There is a contour of dykes and canals set up at a crucial turning point in history and the flow of events then runs according to that contour."[23] The term that has become fashionable to convey this today is "path dependency," which is often explained with reference to the far from functional arrangement of letters on a typewriter, which is also standard on today's computer keyboards. A more or less random initial constellation may be sustained over the long term through self-reinforcing mechanisms.

As I have mentioned, these components of Martin's theory are abstracted from his rich analyses. These probe not only individual societies or religions, but also systematic issues, such as the consequences of migration for migrants' religiosity. Here Martin specifies that the outcome depends on many factors—for example, whether we are dealing with seasonal labor migration, whether entire families are involved and whether the conditions in the host country make it possible for migrants of the same origin to settle in the same place; another crucial issue is whether the religion of the host country differs greatly from that of the country of origin, whether there is a history of conflict between these religions, how large the number of migrants is, whether other markers of identity such as language are involved, whether patterns of endogamy are ruptured by social mobility, and whether specific characteristics of an external nature prove to be a particular hindrance to integration.[24]

Again, Martin's synthesizing impulse and nuanced analysis are impressive. Yet this does not really amount to a "general theory of secularization." The findings overshoot the theoretical framework with which Martin began, and he does not forge the new elements into a new framework. The fact that he considers only Christianity in Europe and North America must further limit his claim of a general theory. Since he proposes no coherent counternarrative to that of secularization, moreover, the book made little or no impact among a broader public. This has been put forward as the reason for David Martin's relative lack of global renown outside specialist circles.[25]

But these critical remarks do nothing to change my view that he made an epochal contribution to the sociology of religion. There was certainly nothing superior to his work at the time. To a considerable extent, Martin's later writings can be viewed as empirical and theoretical attempts to remedy the shortcomings of his first attempt at a "general theory." This applies explicitly to *On Secularization*, which appeared in 2005 with the subtitle *Towards a Revised General Theory*,[26] but also to many of his other publications. I will now outline three of these subsequent developments.

The first concerns the "Russian" pattern of secularist monopoly. This disappeared with the collapse of the communist systems of rule in Europe, which no one had foreseen. Here the challenge for Martin was to explain religious developments after communism with the tools of his theory. Clarifying the great differences between countries was especially challenging. While religious revitalization occurred in certain nations (such as Romania, Bulgaria, Serbia, and Albania), in others (East Germany, the Czech Republic, and Estonia) the level of religious practice remained extremely low, or an extremely high level during communist times (Poland) declined slightly after the collapse. Martin's studies begin with the precommunist institutional order to explain, against this background, the success or failure of the state's forcible secularization and the subsequent dynamics of religious revitalization, as well as the highly variable role played by religion in the different countries in the upheavals that led to the end of communism.[27]

A second challenge arose not from a world-historical upheaval, but from an obviously flawed prediction he had derived from his theory. Unhappily, this related to Martin's own country of the United Kingdom. As he himself had to concede in retrospect, his expectations about the stability of religious beliefs and practices turned out to be wrong. In his book *A Sociology of English Religion*, Martin attributed to the churches of England an astonishing resilience, ascribing to individuals an evident attachment to religious practices such as attending church.[28] In this book he did not consider the cultural developments of the 1960s or the effects of the Second Vatican Council. Thirty years later, he attributed these lacunae to the fact that he had completed the research for the book in the mid-1960s; when he finished the manuscript, he had not registered the epoch-making changes happening at the time.[29] The question that inevitably arises, then, is whether these changes were as unpredictable as the collapse of communism twenty years later, or whether they reveal flaws in Martin's theory.

How one answers this question, something I cannot do conclusively here, obviously depends on how one describes and explains the development of religion in the United Kingdom since the 1960s. One dimension of this development could certainly not have been foreseen in terms of its extent. I am referring to the importance of immigration to the country, which primarily affected urban areas. While the rural areas were traditionally more religious than the cities, this has now been reversed by migration: in the former, secularization advanced, while in London, which still epitomized the notion of the "secular city" in the early 1960s, the number of new Christian places of worship being opened is now greater than the number of old ones closing.[30] The "feminization" of unbelief (or the end of the feminization of faith)—that is, the diminishing number of religiously committed women—has repeatedly been identified as one of the main causes of the undeniable, rapid secularization, a shift that also eliminated one of the greatest countervailing forces to the secularization of men.

Above all, though, controversy reigns over how we should conceptualize the religious effects of the cultural changes of the 1960s. All over Europe, the evidence seems to point to secularization through an increase in expressive individualism. But the self-evident way in which such an effect is assumed is shaken if we take a comparative look at the United States. There, the most important social movement of the era, the civil rights movement, was strongly influenced by religion, but even the more expressively individualist movements (such as the hippies) were generally not antireligious but tended to embrace the practices of Asian spiritual traditions.[31] At the time, David Martin was sharply opposed to the cultural upheavals affecting the universities and churches. One might speculate about the extent to which his polemical rejection of these changes prevented him from properly appreciating the fragility of traditional religious institutions.

The Pentecostal Movement and Its Global Expansion

But David Martin's third and most important step beyond the "general theory" of 1978 saw him shift his research focus to an entirely new and rapidly growing sector of Christianity, namely the Pentecostal movement. It would be an overstatement to declare him a pioneer in this field, since a considerable number of specialized studies had already appeared by the time he became interested in the subject. But he can rightly be described as a pioneer in the synthesis of this research and as a builder of bridges between these studies and the general sociology of religion.[32] His work in this area proved so consequential in part because it powerfully remedied the sociology of religion's near-exclusive preoccupation with Christianity in Europe and North America. For a long time, non-European Christianity had only been considered through the lens of "missiology." The widespread expectation that missionary activity, and Christianity along with it, would become less important in the relevant countries after the end of colonial rule reinforced the marginalization of this research field.

Martin made a major contribution to bringing to the attention of the West the tremendous global expansion of the Pentecostal churches and other evangelical and charismatic forms of Christianity; we are talking about several hundred million believers. For him, it is not only typical of the deep-seated and often largely unconscious assumptions held by exponents of the secularization thesis that they failed to foresee this growth of religious communities. He goes so far as to refer to "forbidden revolutions" (the same term he uses to describe the religiously inspired resistance movements in European communist societies),[33] upheavals that not only came as a surprise, but in the minds of many should not have happened at all—an unloved, unwanted strengthening of religion.

This is not the place to delve into the history and developmental dynamics of this religious "movement" itself. The name, of course, alludes to the outpouring of the Holy Spirit fifty days after the resurrection of Christ—the experience of early Christians that their faith overrode ethnic and linguistic boundaries and united them spiritually, as impressively depicted by the Acts of the Apostles in the New Testament (Acts 2) and celebrated by Christians in the form of Pentecost. Time and again in the history of Christianity, believers' hopes centered on a return of this experience. Ecstatic occurrences during church services, surprising healings of physical and mental illness, and a breakthrough to a new attitude toward life in association with others could all be interpreted in this way. After a first wave in the United States and parts of northern Europe in the early twentieth century and later attempts to revive the movement when it waned, the global upswing with which David Martin was concerned began in the 1970s, first in Latin America, then in Africa and East Asia and gradually in South Asia as well.

This upswing itself and the research on it are matters of extreme political controversy. This reflects the fact that many political statements by representatives of this movement are on the right edge of the political spectrum and there is undoubtedly a wide range of support for it from similar religious communities in the United States. Some left-wing critics—especially those with secularist leanings, but also left-wing Catholics—see the Pentecostal movement as a kind of Trojan horse for "US imperialism." Martin was accused at least of naivety, if not of supporting authoritarian regimes in Latin America.[34] For some, these suspicions were fueled by the fact that it was well-known sociologist of religion Peter L. Berger who initially facilitated the financing of Martin's studies in this field and then wrote the foreword to his first book on the topic. In this foreword, Berger placed the Pentecostal movement in the context of the idea that Protestantism's "this-worldly asceticism" (Max Weber) was key to the social advancement of individuals, the development of a bourgeoisie, and the collective growth in prosperity.[35] This can in turn be read as an apologia for capitalism and as reducing macroeconomic issues to those of individual morality.

David Martin often felt deeply misunderstood by these interpretations and imputations of political motives. His affinity for the Pentecostal movement was initially religious. He recognized in it the motifs and practices of the English Methodism of his childhood home. While he had moved away from this (toward Anglicanism) in his own life, he still felt a connection with it and held it in high regard. What enduringly fascinated him was a Christianity based less on clerical hierarchy than voluntary self-organization, one less dependent on the state or its own statelike structures and more on an entrepreneurial missionary spirit, one that was less churchlike and more "denominational." He was intrigued by the strong and independent role of women in these religious movements and the latter's tremendous affinity for modern media and creative commitment to "evangelization."

For him, these religious forms represented an ideal adaptation of Christianity to the living conditions of poor migrant families in the megacities of the global South, as well as those of Europe and North America. As he saw it, they brought to the world of Latin America, which had been characterized by a monopoly Catholicism featuring strongly hierarchical institutional structures, a shift toward Anglo-American denominationalism. In no way does he deny the possible downsides of this development—here too we find "machismo" in remnant form, corruption, financial exploitation of believers, and political instrumentalization. But for him it was quite wrong to underestimate, because of these downsides, how much many people had gained in terms of individual agency and freedom.

A very different criticism than that emanating from a politically motivated left is directed at Martin's implicit image of Latin American Catholicism. Many commentators pointed out that the Pentecostal movement should not primarily be compared with traditional Catholicism but with the "basic ecclesial communities," inspired by liberation theology, that developed in Latin America during the same period and represented a significant force in the struggle against military dictatorships. In his critical engagement with David Martin, José Casanova thus refers to "parallel reformations." As he sees it, by altering its view of itself with regard to the state and religious freedom, the Catholic Church opened up the space in which the Pentecostal movement could then proliferate and a general denominationalization could occur.[36] Others go so far as to discern in the rise of a Protestantism remote from the state a decisive factor in avoiding the "Latin European" path of a division of society into a religious and a secularist milieu.[37] In this view, Catholic and Pentecostal-evangelical movements are essentially in the same boat, with both contributing to the religious vitality of these societies.

Martin clearly considered any imputation of subtle remnants of anti-Catholic prejudice in his thinking highly offensive, and in his replies he highlighted his own recognition of the role of liberation theology.[38] Above all, though, he was more interested in the level of religious practice than that of institutions or doctrines. At the practical level, Martin noted, one of the great strengths of Catholic Christianity has always been its tendency to integrate popular practices and hopes of salvation into its own forms of religious life, thus "Christianizing" them, rather than seeking to extirpate them from the top down in rationalistic fashion. This was particularly important when it came to Latin American Catholicism and the indigenous population. Typically, traditional Protestantism has always struggled to forge a productive relationship with indigenous traditions—and official Catholicism, too, if it tries to become more "rational," may alienate the faithful from their church. For Martin, this also opened up a "gap in the market" for the

Pentecostal movement, which "sets itself against the demons of popular religion even while drawing on its forms."[39] While, for instance, the cult of saints is rejected at the level of doctrine, many practices—such as the sacralization of the Bible—are consonant with its structure.

Obviously, at this point my goal can only be to consider the significance to his theory of this part of David Martin's oeuvre, which was central to the last three decades of his work, rather than to attempt to resolve empirically the questions raised above. The Protestantization or religious pluralization of parts of Latin America posed a challenge to his theory that it proved amply capable of meeting. In addition, the mere existence of a religious movement that is not a relic within processes of modernization but highly modern in many respects (such as its affinity for technology and its religious individualization) was a triumphant confirmation of his resistance to the secularization thesis. Of course, we must also ask whether his theory does justice to other regions of the world than Latin America. When it comes to African countries south of the Sahara, this theory must be expanded to include the case of poorly developed or failed statehood.[40] Martin's remarks on other regions of the world are sketchy and require others to elaborate and test them out.[41] We also have to ask whether the growth these movements have seen in the last few decades will continue or whether they are transitional phenomena. What we do observe are reactions on the part of the religious competition, in the shape of a strengthening of charismatic practices in the Catholic Church, for example. But what has happened again and again in the history of European Protestantism may also occur: decline due to Protestants' own economic success.[42]

Religion and Violence

The relationship between religion and violence is another of David Martin's long-standing foci. It would of course be surprising if a political sociology of religion did not explore violence. Crucially in this regard, in his autobiographical texts Martin not only talks about his religious and scholarly paths, but also about a fundamental shift in his understanding of politics. He identifies this change as the second major conversion of his life,[43] namely from the Christian pacifism of his youth not to secular pacifism but to a Christian realism, especially with respect to international politics and issues of war and peace.

The intellectual trigger for this conversion is clearly identifiable: his encounter with the writings of famous US-American Protestant theologian Reinhold Niebuhr, above all his book *Moral Man and Immoral Society*.[44] In the English-speaking world, Niebuhr and this book are of enormous importance to many intellectuals to this day. This is because it opens up the possibility of a Christian justification for the use of violence in the political sphere, particularly when it comes to war between states. Niebuhr's work never had a comparable effect in Germany or France. This may have something to do with the fact that the Catholic tradition of thinking on just war and Protestantism's proximity to the state prevented Christian pacifism from becoming as strong in Europe as it was in the United States.

The abstract justification of the possible legitimacy of the use of violence cannot, of course, be the last word on the matter. Apart from anything else, the sharp distinction between "moral man" and "immoral society" can hardly be considered a convincing basis for Christian realism in the political realm. It was none other than Reinhold Niebuhr's younger brother Richard who immediately expressed this doubt and self-evidently located evil at the level of the individual as well. This shows, however, that the distinction between individual and political ethics must not be equated with the problem of the moral ambivalence of action.[45] The younger of the two brothers firmly rejected the (allegedly Christian) activist approach to foreign policy espoused by his older sibling, without being a strict pacifist.[46]

But even more importantly, a general justification for violence and a Christian realism should not straightforwardly be taken as justification for specific forms of violence in specific situations. In several extensive works, David Martin grappled with the relationship of Christianity to violence and with the question of whether religions contribute to peace or to violent conflicts.[47] As important as these works are with their criticism of blanket suspicion of all religion, they remain relatively vague with respect to the exact normative criteria involved or empirical assessments. One may well be a "Christian realist" in principle, but still consider the destruction of the Japanese cities of Hiroshima and Nagasaki by nuclear weapons or the bombing of German cities like Dresden, far beyond any strategic military utility, to be unjustified. Here every sentence leads to normatively charged empirical questions such as how strategically important Dresden was or why no medical aid had been prepared for the survivors in the Japanese cities. We might even suggest that, in an odd way, Martin's turn to Christian realism, due to its conviction-based distancing from pure pacifism, diverted his interest from more concrete engagement with Christian approaches to conflict avoidance and conflict de-escalation or the building of the structures crucial to a stable peace.[48]

In one respect, however, David Martin suggested a valuable and innovative approach to this topic. More than any other contributor to the discourse on the "Axial Age," he paid attention to the emergence of the ideal of nonviolence and its preconditions.[49] While others have carried out research (or speculated) on the emergence of ideas of transcendence, moral universalism, or systematic reflexivity in this context, Martin scrutinized the break with the ever-lurking potential for violence in human relations. In doing so, he turned the question around: away from the conventional perspective, which focuses on the causes of violence, to one that foregrounds the causes of its rejection in principle.[50] The ideals that emerged in the Axial Age clash with social realities, and it is fruitful to probe the relationship to violence found in Axial Age cultures. We can find such an investigation in embryonic form in Martin's late work, where he referred to varying "angles of transcendence."[51]

While the studies of Israeli sociologist Shmuel Eisenstadt on the subject of the Axial Age and "multiple modernities," as well as Charles Taylor's great work on the development of religion in Europe from 1500 to 2000, have received broad international attention, the same cannot be said of David Martin's publications, at least not to the same extent. There are many similarities between these authors, but also considerable differences. Martin was certainly much more positive about the Pentecostal movement than Eisenstadt, whose work is dominated by concerns over a new religious "fundamentalism."[52] More than Taylor and in this respect similar to Eisenstadt, Martin thinks in terms of a permanent tension between Axial Age ideals, the cultural forms of their articulation, and political orders.

In contrast to Taylor's thesis of a "vector" of development in Latin Christianity,[53] Martin asserted that we should write the history of Christianity as one of waves of attempted Christianization. Christianity became established, for example, due to "its adoption by monarchs seeking to accede to what was for them the civilised centre in Rome or Byzantium, its promotion by friars preaching in hall churches to the urban masses, and attempts to universalize monastic aspirations in Puritanism, Pietism and Evangelicalism."[54] As this brief reference to the differences between Martin's work and other more influential analyses is intended to show, the theory-of-religion potential of his writings is considerable when it comes to assessing diverse forms of "modernity," but by no means has it been fully exploited in the key debates.[55]

IV, 5

Religious Evolution and Symbolic Realism: Robert Bellah

Robert N. Bellah, who died in 2013, was one of the leading sociologists of religion in the world and one of the most important analysts of the contemporary United States. He wrote a book that, like no other, laid the foundation for a truly global-historical theory of religion. To understand this, I begin by taking a look at his biography, before going on to highlight the key features of his late work.

Born in the town of Altus, Oklahoma in 1927, Bellah was raised in a Presbyterian family of Scottish descent; his father was the editor of the local newspaper. After the latter's untimely death, Bellah grew up in Los Angeles and, moving well beyond the confines of southern Protestantism, came into contact with the progressive social gospel and a multitude of other religious cultures and subcultures. After attending Harvard University and completing eighteen months of military service, he earned a BA in social anthropology in 1950. His thesis on the kinship structures of the Apache won an award and was published as a book in 1952.[1] At Harvard University, Bellah came under the decisive influence of Talcott Parsons, unquestionably the leading sociological theorist at the time, and the interdisciplinary group of social scientists and humanities scholars that formed around him.

In retrospect, Bellah's keen early interest in the culture of the Native Americans emerges as one of his attempts to distance himself from postwar US-American culture, which he increasingly perceived as problematic. The roots of two other biographical developments lay in this experiential background and in his perception of a great tension between US-American values and society. As a university student, Bellah briefly joined a communist organization and became a Marxist. In the era of McCarthyism, this hindered the advancement of his career. When Parsons offered him a postdoctoral fellowship at Harvard, the university made his appointment conditional upon the denunciation of other communists. Bellah chose not to comply with this condition and left Harvard for McGill University in Montreal.[2]

While Bellah's Marxist phase was very brief, a third instance of cultural exploration and searching was to permanently shape the course of his life. As a student, Bellah began studying Japanese and Chinese and exploring the history of East Asia. In his doctoral thesis (published in 1957) he pursued the ambitious goal of applying Max Weber's approach in his comparative studies of the economic ethics of the world religions to Japan. The resulting book, *Tokugawa Religion*, is considered one of the most important ever written on Japan and an exemplar of the achievements of modernization theory in the 1950s.[3] It was first and foremost a groundbreaking historical study of certain value patterns in Japan that enabled this Asian country to go a long way toward catching up with the West by the end of the nineteenth century. In Japan and thus outside European-American culture, Bellah was looking for functional equivalents of the Protestant ethic with its dynamic consequences, which were supposedly decisive to the rise of capitalism in Northwestern Europe.

But his study was important for another reason as well. It showed that the industrialization processes that occurred in Japan were completely different in character than, for example, those in the United States. While economic values held primacy in the latter's industrial society, this did not seem to have been the case at all in Japanese modernization. In Japan, the political sphere played a crucial role, and economic values were constantly subordinated to political ones. Specifically, this meant that the industrialization and modernization process was pushed through by political elites, and in a way that must have seemed alien to Western observers, especially Anglo-Saxon ones: Japan's breakthrough to modernity took place on the basis of narrow, particularist ties binding all social elites to the imperial family and through efficiency-oriented militaristic values, which had pervaded Japanese society in the nineteenth century.

Bellah's conclusion here posed a challenge to the assumption, embraced by almost all modernization theorists, that we can make a neat distinction between "traditional" and "modern" values. Particularist value orientations, as this example shows, cannot be straightforwardly attributed to tradition alone. This simultaneously problematized the thesis that modernization moves in a culture-independent, unambiguous direction. Modernization, according to Bellah, does not simply lead to the undisputed dominance of rational or secular values. For him, this also means that religion, for example, does not simply disappear as modernization advances, but may take on new forms and appear in new settings. From the outset, then, Bellah did not espouse a simple secularization thesis in the manner of many modernization theorists. Parsons too maintained a distance from such ideas, but at this early stage the young Bellah already moved beyond his teacher's views when he attempted to write a theory of "religious evolution."

Bellah continued to work on the sociological analysis of Japan throughout his career; his publications and teaching in Japan sparked intense controversy there. In the 2003 book *Imagining Japan*, Bellah looks back on these debates, masterfully combining analysis of the institutional and intellectual specifics of Japanese history.[4]

Biographical developments, however, prevented Bellah from concentrating exclusively on East Asia. The scholarship from McGill University, which enabled him to continue his career despite his distressing experience at Harvard, came from the Institute of Islamic Studies, and there Bellah began studying Arabic and the Qur'an. This further enhanced his linguistic foundations for a globally comprehensive, comparative sociology of religion and culture. When the McCarthy era was over, Bellah was able to continue his academic career in the United States, first at Harvard and then from 1967 until his retirement at Berkeley, where he was active in sociology, Japanese and Korean studies, and theology.

In the 1960s, Bellah produced studies that are among the most frequently cited in sociology. I will examine his important article "Religious Evolution" in a moment. In the first instance, it was the essay "Civil Religion in America" and the response to it that set the course for his subsequent scholarly development.[5] This text includes an attempt to apply to the United States Émile Durkheim's thesis that a stable social order is based on shared ideas of sacredness. Bellah claimed that the country is characterized by a theistic conception of sacredness, but one that cannot be assigned to a specific denomination, and he demonstrated this with reference to speeches by US-American presidents upon taking office. In the heated political debates of the late 1960s, his perspective here was often misunderstood as defending a cult of the nation and its "manifest destiny"; in fact, Bellah's goal was to draw attention (prophetically) to the universalist and critical dimension of US-American civil religion.[6]

Thanks to this essay and the fierce arguments it provoked, Bellah became a "public intellectual" and a highly regarded analyst of the age, his brilliant rhetorical and writing skills helping him blaze this particular trail. His 1975 book *The Broken Covenant*, which was much more than just a jeremiad assailing the corruption of American civil religion during the Vietnam War, received a lot of attention.[7] The book also represents a methodologically innovative attempt to analyze the internal tensions of cultural myths. While Bellah's teacher Talcott Parsons had called himself a cultural determinist but never carried out truly in-depth analyzes of a particular culture, mostly reducing them to abstract concepts such as norm and value, from the outset Bellah proved far more sensitive to the character of symbols and to the dynamics of symbolization processes. Key to this, in addition to his early engagement with cultural anthropology, were the theological writings of the German émigré Paul Tillich, with whom Bellah had come into personal contact when he attended Tillich's lectures at Harvard.

In his theology of culture, Tillich had distinguished between "symbols" and "signs."[8] For him, signs may be arbitrary and conventional; it makes sense to distinguish between them and the reality to which they refer. But symbols are different; they contribute to the meaning and power of that which they symbolize. They arise or fade away—but they cannot be invented. They are experienced as apt articulations of the meaning of extraordinary experiences, although this sense of appropriateness may be accompanied by the insight that what is to be articulated inevitably goes beyond what can be articulated. No notion of God can ever be the last word on God; he transcends his own name. Consonant with this, Tillich's program amounted not to "demythologization" (Rudolf Bultmann) but to "deliteralization," a rejection of attempts to reduce myths to the level of scholarly statements or technological mastery of the world, that is, of the attempt to comprehend "symbolic" articulations of faith as quasi-cognitive propositions and doctrines. Tillich's theology, which he himself tended to call "belief-ful realism," led Bellah to his own standpoint, which he called "symbolic realism."[9] Earlier than famous cultural anthropologist Clifford Geertz and of great influence on the work of his student, cultural sociologist Jeffrey Alexander, Bellah thus set out the fundamentals of an analysis of the myth, which is not treated as unitary but as "a complex and richly textured mythical structure with many inner tensions."[10]

In the 1970s, Bellah undertook several projects whose goal was to examine the religious dimension of the cultural upheavals of the 1960s.[11] He interpreted the new "counterculture" as a consequence of the inability of utilitarian individualism—that is, a culture in which augmenting individual utility had risen to become the guiding value—to endow personal and social existence with meaning. Parsons too had put forward interesting ideas about the cultural upheavals of the 1960s as a revolution of expressive individualism and as potentially marking the birth of a new religion.[12] Here we find a major difference between Europe and the United States. While the cultural upheavals of the time triggered a rapid surge in secularization in Europe and talk of a religious dimension to protest was mostly part of conservative attempts at pathologization, the secularizing effects in the United States were far less pronounced. There it would be more accurate to refer to increased religious individualization and a new wave of reception of Asian spirituality, such as Zen Buddhism.

In 1973, Robert Bellah's scholarly achievements and his sensational contributions to public debates in the United States earned him the offer of one of the most coveted and respected positions in the US-American academic system: that of Permanent Fellow at Princeton's Institute for Advanced Study. This overture triggered the so-called Bellah Affair. For a number of reasons, several natural scientists and historians put up tremendous resistance to his appointment. Resentment toward the discipline of sociology no doubt played a role. More important, however, was aversion to Bellah's evidently religious—in other words, Christian—convictions and his refusal to split his person into two parts, one purely scholarly and the other only privately religious. Of course, this did not entail ideological distortion of empirical or theoretical research but did involve resistance to implicit secularist assumptions widespread in the academy.[13]

So Bellah stayed at Berkeley, where he gathered around him a group of gifted young scholars (such as Richard Madsen, William Sullivan, Ann Swidler and Steven Tipton).[14] With them, he wrote one of the greatest bestsellers in the history of sociology: *Habits of the Heart*.[15]

Community and Democracy

The starting point of the book is Alexis de Tocqueville's famous thesis in his 1835 volume *Democracy in America* that an intensive relationship between private and public life is decisive to the survival of free institutions: democracy can be and remain vibrant only if citizens are willing to go beyond the immediate private context (family and relatives) and to articulate themselves as persons in the public arena, in circles of friends, associations, political parties, and so on. Retreat into the private sphere, Tocqueville contended, merely courts the risk that an omnipotent and all-regulating state will emerge, ultimately spelling doom for a free and democratic society.

Bellah and his colleagues embraced this thesis, using it as a foil for their analysis and critique of the contemporary United States. To this end, they interviewed around two hundred adults from the white US-American middle class, asking them about certain aspects of their private life (their relationship to marriage, love, and therapy) as well as their "public" life (their involvement in clubs and associations or in local politics). In a sense, the findings confirmed the crisis identified by other so-called communitarians and also led to new insights into the highly diverse forms of modern individualism.

While German sociologist Ulrich Beck, for example, scarcely bothered to distinguish between different forms of individualism in his numerous writings on the individualization thesis, Bellah and his colleagues saw this as their first priority. In their interviews, but also in historical reviews of important figures in US-American intellectual history, they were able to identify a total of four types of individualism: a "biblical" tradition going back to the religiously motivated settlement phase, a republican tradition dating back to the revolutionary era and geared toward a Greco-Roman understanding of politics, and finally a tradition in which two undercurrents must be distinguished, as I will explain in a moment: a utilitarian and an expressivist individualism.

Analysis of the interviews alone, it must be said, tended to paint a picture of cultural impoverishment. While Tocqueville could still observe chiefly religious and republican individualism in his investigation in the 1830s—and, in his view, it was precisely these forms of individualism that were the source of the strength and vitality of the US-American polity and democracy—there is little sign of any of this among those interviewed for Bellah's project. The idea to be found, for example, in the thinking of John Winthrop (1588–1649), the "first Puritan" on American soil, that human beings' freedom is a good that obligates them to feel reverence for God and his commandments, has now lost influence. The same goes for the notion of individuality propagated by Thomas Jefferson (1743–1826); as coauthor of the Declaration of Independence, he considered purely formal freedom insufficient and, drawing on ancient political traditions, considered a polity worthy of respect only if its citizens have a say and actively participate in political events.

The kind of moral language used by a Winthrop or Jefferson to express their ideas was simply absent from most of the interviewees' vocabulary. Individualism in its newer forms—according to Bellah and his coauthors—is either utilitarian, that is, oriented almost entirely toward the attainment of short-term utility, generally defined in material terms, or expressivist, that is, geared toward the satisfaction of emotional needs and the cultivation of oneself. According to Bellah, these two types of modern individualism are associated with two social figures that dominate modern US-American culture (as well as other cultures): the manager and the therapist. They, Bellah tells us, epitomize the utilitarian or expressivist individualism that has become dominant, and this impedes attempts to make oneself understood in the public realm, even if one is oriented toward the biblical or republican forms of individualism.

What is striking about these two radical forms of individualism, according to Bellah, is the following: for the most part, people who act in line with these particular kinds of individualism simply lack the ability to conceive of how their interests might be combined with those of other people. They often suffer, Bellah contends, from an absence of relationships and emotional bonds; furthermore, they are not even capable of defining what a "good" life might be. The interviewees articulated (consciously or unconsciously) an unease about their lack of bonds with others, often going so far as to convey their displeasure at the social hegemony of the "managers" and "therapists." But at the same time, they were unable to express this unease and displeasure in a moral language that could have transcended this utilitarian and expressivist individualism. Hence, according to Bellah, it is important "to find a moral language that will transcend their radical individualism."[16] This, he goes on, is all the more urgent because evidently neither the self-realization through career so typical of utilitarian individualists nor the purely private cultivation of personal proclivities as characteristic of expressive individualists brings true contentment, not least because both types lack social contacts of depth and durability.

Bellah's thesis is that these problems can only be resolved if this radical individualism is replaced, or at least supplemented, by cultural orientations that once played a major role in US-American history but even now have not disappeared entirely, and that facilitate identification with communities and living traditions. According to Bellah, only by engaging with the biblical and/or republican traditions can US-Americans breathe new life into their democracy over the long term:

> If we are not entirely a mass of interchangeable fragments within an aggregate, if we are in part qualitatively distinct members of a whole, it is because there are still operating among us, with whatever difficulties, traditions that tell us about the nature of the world, about the nature of society, and about

who we are as people. Primarily biblical and republican, these traditions are, as we have seen, important for many Americans and significant to some degree for almost all. Somehow families, churches, a society of cultural associations, and, even if only in the interstices, schools and universities, do manage to communicate a form of life, a *paideia*, in the sense of growing up in a morally and intellectually intelligible world.[17]

This, Bellah believed, is the only way to prevent the (US-American) polity from dissolving into a conglomerate of atomized individuals or from becoming an assemblage of "lifestyle enclaves," each of which consists only of like-minded people (the gay community, the white middle class, New Age enthusiasts, and so on) and which, precisely because of this, is no longer even capable of communicating with other communities, let alone undertaking collective political action. As Tocqueville saw, what is needed is a reasonable balance between private and public life in order to ensure the vitality and stability of democracy.[18]

Bellah's call for a richly textured society vibrant with tradition should not be understood as a reactionary reversion to bygone ways of life. Quite the opposite: he wished to see social movements that could spearhead the cultural change toward a vibrant democratic culture, movements that build, for example, on the ideals of the civil rights movement of the 1950s and 1960s. This, after all, did not pursue utilitarian interests or seek to satisfy emotional needs, but rather to create a truly democratic political culture on the basis of which all US-Americans, regardless of race, can contend with one another over how best to organize their shared polity.

The critique of the state of US-American society expressed by Bellah and his coauthors in *Habits of the Heart* and the associated analysis of the contemporary world were translated into concrete proposals for the revitalization of the US-American polity in a book titled *The Good Society*, published in 1991. These range from a call for the dismantling of militaristic state structures[19] to the democratization of workplaces.[20] It seems important to highlight such objectives because in Germany the rhetoric of community characteristic of Bellah and the communitarians has often met with resistance and been viewed as ranging from conservative to reactionary—which is to some extent understandable in light of the Nazis' misuse of the concept of community (as in the term *Volksgemeinschaft* or People's Community). There are, of course, conservative communitarians. But the concept of community has a completely different status in US-American intellectual history than in its German counterpart,[21] which is why US-American progressives or left-wingers can easily embrace it, as evident in the concrete political demands put forward by Bellah and his coauthors.

Bellah called his ingenious linkage of sociological research and an orientation toward broad public debate "Social Science as Public Philosophy." But it would be quite wrong to interpret the books *Habits of the Heart* and *The Good Society* as a matter of Bellah shifting away from professional social science toward journalism. In fact, Bellah spent the last decade and a half of his life working on a voluminous work that could be described as a sociologically inspired world history of religion. This entailed the full-scale revision and extensive elaboration of the aforementioned early article, through which the young Bellah had already made his mark on the history of scholarship: "Religious Evolution."[22]

Global History of Religion

The theoretical starting point of this study was once again the work of Talcott Parsons, but not in the sense of a functionalist sociology of religion, in which religion is simply related to the functions it (allegedly) fulfills for the social system.[23] Bellah was just as interested in the connections between religion on the one hand and culture, corporeality, and personality structure on the other. He drew on ideas predating Parsons by going back to the classical sociological figures of Max Weber and Émile Durkheim. But he read even Durkheim as more than just a functionalist, namely as a thinker of religious "experience" for whom collective experiences of self-transcendence ("collective effervescence") played a constitutive role for religion.

Bellah's early essay outlined stages in the religious history of humanity, but not simply as envisaged by Hegel and other nineteenth-century thinkers, as if the history of religion always strives toward its crowning glory in the shape of Christianity as the absolute religion. Even in this outline account, it is clear that Bellah was not only making parallels between the stages of religious history and the stages of political history, that is, the history of collective human self-organization, but was seeking to integrate them. Consonant with this, his early developmental schema featured five stages: primitive religion, archaic religion, historical religion, early modern religion, and modern religion. The terminology certainly sounds outmoded today, and subsequently

Bellah would not have consistently defended his specific characterizations of religion at these different stages.

The term "primitive," for instance, has fallen out of use for good reasons. In his later writings, Bellah replaced it with the word "tribal," though he was well aware that there are objections to this choice of term as well. It refers to pre-state forms of political organization, which can also be called nonstate or even anti-state if one wants to avoid the slightest hint of a schema of necessary development toward the state or to highlight resistance to state formation. Bellah applied the term "archaic" to the large, mostly imperial states of antiquity. He thus saw the transition to the state as a fundamental date in the history of religion, a transition, as I would put it, from the self-sacralization of a collective to the sacralization of a ruler.

The term "historical" is a nettlesome means of indicating the break with the core symbol systems of the archaic orders. The criterion that, as Bellah saw it, allows us to distinguish one from the other is the emergence and availability of ideas of transcendence. In other words, we are dealing with the era of change that Karl Jaspers called the "Axial Age."[24] If a dimension beyond the mundane comes into play that is more than just a continuation of this world and instead epitomizes the true and the good, then reality is subject to a permanent standard of assessment in a quite different way than it was before. This earthly reality can then become the object of fundamental rejection or of efforts to improve it. This, however, turns the spotlight on changes in political and social conditions, and not just on their mutability, but also their malleability and thus their historicity in a radical sense.[25] At the time, Bellah still identified early modern religion with that of the Reformation era, with a turn to inner-worldly but transcendence-related individualist activism. Finally, Bellah interpreted the immediate present—the time when his essay was written—as the era of modern religion. This differs from early modern religion, Bellah explained, only in the sense that the tendency for individualization and religious pluralization, which had existed since the Reformation, increasingly gains the upper hand.

There is no need to discuss this essay in detail, as it is merely an adumbration of Bellah's later magnum opus. Throughout his life, he contemplated transforming this sketch into a truly mature historical-sociological work on the global history of religion. Through teaching and research, he added ever more positive knowledge to his existing conceptual framework. At the same time, stimulated by this research, he constantly reworked his framework in light of theoretical reflections. When Bellah retired in 1997 at the age of seventy, he resolved to finally write the work he had envisaged for decades. A table of contents that I have at hand dating from the summer of 1998 still exhibits a good deal of continuity with his original article. The title was also the same. An introductory chapter on his understanding of religion was to be followed by two chapters on "social evolution," one extending from the Paleolithic to "historic society" and one from the latter to the present. Tribal and archaic religion were both to be treated in one chapter. Two chapters were planned to examine the "historical religions," the first on the emergence of ideas of transcendence in ancient Judaism and in Greece ("classical Mediterranean"), in India and China, and (with a question mark indicating uncertainty about sources) in Zoroaster's Iran.

A second chapter was then to take account of the fact that the origins of the two largest world religions, namely Christianity and Islam, did not lie in the same period in which the breakthrough to transcendence first took place. They are, however, inconceivable without the "Axial Age" developments in ancient Judaism and in Greece. This is why Bellah, like others before him in the literature on the emergence of the state, referred to "secondary formations," with a slight shift in meaning. But he chose "organic social ethics" as the heading for this chapter. This term goes back to Max Weber and Ernst Troeltsch, with the focus in the former's work being on the analysis of Hinduism, while the latter was concerned in this context with medieval Christianity. What is meant by this is not simply the transfer of organic metaphors to the social and political order, but the fusion of the universal accessibility of salvation with a (corporative) social system featuring profound social inequality. Evidently, this chapter was to address these fusions in Christianity, Islam, India, and East Asia. Bellah then planned to write a lengthy chapter on religion and modernity, with subchapters on Reformation, Enlightenment, and science, and the global dissemination of these innovations. The final chapter was to have explored what might come after modernity, a question of much topicality at the time in light of the debates on postmodernity.

In 2011, a first volume was finally published, which modified the original title in a significant way. This important work was no longer called "Religious Evolution," but *Religion in Human Evolution*.[26] Bellah made this change to finally clear up the misconception that he was asserting the existence of a sequence of steps immanent in religion. He did, however, aim to link the history of religion with a theory of social change, and the latter itself requires a foundation in cosmological and biological evolution, which is what Bellah turned to first. The volume as it exists ends with what was originally planned to be the fifth chapter. The tribal and archaic religions were not dealt with in one chapter, as initially planned, but in three, one each on the two major types ("tribal" and "archaic") and one on the transition between them.

Each of these chapters was associated with a systematic line of inquiry. In the case of tribal religions, this concerns the emergence of meaning; when it comes to the transition to the archaic state, the focus is on the interactions between the constitution of meaning and power; in the case of archaic religions, the spotlight turns to the interwoven processes of the development of concepts of god and ruler in sacred kingship. Of the originally planned five Axial Age topics, the Iranian case, which was considered problematic from the start, was left out. A conclusion sums up the ideas presented throughout the book.

Given the age Bellah had reached when it was published, he could not ignore the fact that there was unlikely to be enough time to elaborate the rest of his vision in similar depth. He thus decided not to tackle the entire history of religion from the Axial Age to the present in a similarly learned work, but in a shorter book working with less evidence. He also wanted to reduce the global historical aspirations of his project to a mere contrast between the "West" and China. This sequel exists as a fragment of around one hundred pages.[27] Bellah's sudden death in the summer of 2013 brought his work to an abrupt end.

I cannot provide a detailed account here of the extremely rich published volume, or of how others have built on and grappled with it.[28] I limit myself to three brief descriptions of the specific features of Bellah's conception.

(1) At an early point in my account of Bellah's development I underlined that he went beyond Parsons's schematic cultural sociology with the aid of Tillich's theory of symbols. In line with this, the essay "Religious Evolution" was already structured in such a way as to indicate affinities with certain forms of symbolization at every stage of the history of systems of political domination. This was still rather vague at the time. For his masterpiece, however, Bellah was able to rely on an evolutionary cultural and cognitive psychology that had developed tremendously since the 1960s.

The main source of inspiration here is the work of Merlin Donald,[29] with the incorporation of this research simultaneously enabling Bellah to build a bridge between human history and primate evolution. Donald undergirds his distinction between three stages of cognitive evolution through an account of the "episodic mind" and the "episodic culture" of primates, that is, the fact that their perception and memory are limited to situations of relatively short duration. He then identifies the three stages of culture as "mimesis," "myth," and "theory." "Mimesis" covers forms of expression centered on the body, that is, representation through gestural communication. The term "myth" refers to the role of storytelling, which relies on a more situation-independent medium than "mimetic" representation, namely language. Finally, the term "theory" arises from action situations in which one can question the truth of traditional narratives. Questions of this kind presuppose the capacity to distance oneself from traditional narratives; answering them requires an even more situation-independent medium than spoken language, namely writing. Writing facilitates recourse to earlier facts and representations, enabling a critical confrontation between past and present.

(2) Bellah now applied this theory of the evolution of cognition and sign use to the history of religion.[30] Here, too, the details of the resulting theory of religious rituals, myths and doctrines must be left to one side. But it is crucial to grasp that Bellah was a theorist of evolution rather than an evolutionist; he did not assume that a given level of development devalues the one that precedes it, let alone renders it superfluous. Instead, one of the leitmotifs of his book is that "nothing is ever lost." Of course, this does not mean that, when it comes to the history of religion, everything is remembered, let alone that it retains its vigor and vitality. This is clearly not the case.

What Bellah was seeking to convey is that none of the stages of evolution ever disappears completely. Even when linguistic communication and feats of memory linked to language come into play, mimesis remains; gestural communication and playful representation are still important. Even with the development of critical and reflective capacities, the importance of storytelling for the individual and for the collective creation of meaning does not disappear. Religions exist on all these levels. A more positive or negative attitude to the ritual or mythical dimensions may be built into them, but no religion will be able to detach itself entirely from these levels. Hence, we can never fully fathom religions if we focus exclusively on their "theoretical" doctrines and theological systems. For Bellah, much the same is true even of secular value systems. However theoretically rational they may be, they too have a basis in experiences, their ritual embodiment, and mythical narration.

(3) Bellah also brought the dimension of political domination or power-backed cooperation into line with the present state of knowledge in his magnum opus. Far from idealizing a primal egalitarianism of tribal societies, he probes how their relative equality may have emerged from the strictly hierarchical social orders of the primates and explores which mechanisms

maintain this equality.[31] The focus of his subsequent accounts is thus on how this relative, by no means idyllic, but nevertheless pronounced egalitarianism of tribal societies could transition into the extreme hierarchization of the archaic empires with their monopolizing of power and sacralization of rulers. Subsequently, Axial Age innovations not only usher in the ethical relativization of these systems of domination but also trigger a revival and universalization of egalitarianism, at least in religious terms. People are no longer just subjects of a ruler, but have their own individual relationship to the divine, and their moral obligations apply not only to members of their own people or state, but to all human beings. Yet Bellah was well aware that the religious ideas that emerged in this way, namely those of universal humanity and of the individual relationship to God, gods, or a sacred cosmos, could and did repeatedly become part of the strategies of political legitimation pursued by states and empires.

The development of this global historical theory of religion is one of the great creative achievements of any scholar in our time. For Bellah himself, it obviously—inevitably, as he himself would have said—had a religious dimension. As early as 1973, in an essay on liturgy and experience, the Protestant Bellah put forward a "Catholic" interpretation of the sacraments as intense spiritual experiences.[32] Over the course of his life, he became ever more critical of what he perceived as "flaws in the Protestant code."[33] He increasingly sought to combine the radicalism of prophetic criticism, which Protestantism has so often brought forth, with the classical Catholic tradition of sacramental experience. Like Tillich, a free-floating prophecy without a sacramental-institutional counterbalance seemed to him impossible in the long run. Through his studies of Japanese militarism and against the background of fascism and Nazism, he was also aware of the risk of a loss of transcendence in modernity, with its possible consequences for the viability of moral universalism. His investigations into US-American culture aimed to determine the current prospects of this moral universalism in relation to utilitarian and expressive individualism and in light of its reliance on the particularity of ties to community. Taking all these motifs into consideration, Robert Bellah's oeuvre can fairly be defined as the successful synthesis of Talcott Parsons and Paul Tillich.[34]

IV, 6
Religion and Globalization: José Casanova

It was in 1969 that a highly gifted boy from provincial Spain, more precisely a village in Aragón, having completed his studies at a church-run high school in Zaragoza, set off for Austria to train as a Catholic priest.[1] We have to imagine what Spain was like in the 1950s and even in the 1960s: governed by Francoist fascists, backed and legitimized by the Catholic Church, generally isolated on the international stage, economically backward, and cut off culturally from the rest of Europe. Still, José Casanova (b. 1951) describes the village of his early years, when he had no thoughts of a brilliant future career in the international sociology of religion even as a distant dream, as a preindustrial lifeworld in which he spent a happy childhood. His path led him away from this familiar environment to studies in Innsbruck, a city he experienced as representative of the modern world. There he acquired the broad foundations of philosophical and theological knowledge that we can discern again and again in his work. His most important academic teacher turned out to be Franz Schupp,[2] successor to the great Karl Rahner in the chair of dogmatics at the University of Innsbruck (Austria).

The spirit of the Second Vatican Council could be felt there far more than in Spain, so much so, in fact, that in 1974, when the mood in Rome had shifted again, the church stripped Schupp of his teaching license. The church's *aggiornamento* with regard to democracy and religious freedom, the broad switch from a natural law to a personalist frame of reference, a de-clericalized conception of the church—these are the motifs that Casanova absorbed at the time. They show up again and again in his writings—for example, when he calls the famous pastoral letters issued by the United States Conference of Catholic Bishops on nuclear arms and economic justice "the closest empirical approximation to the institutionalization of discourse ethics at the general level of civil society"[3] because these texts were not simply placed before believers as a fait accompli, but emerged from a complex process of consultation with experts, interest groups, activists, Catholic dissidents, and of course the Vatican. Course content in Innsbruck covered a broad spectrum, including the great classical and modern theologians of Catholicism, their Protestant counterparts, liberation theology, and critical theory.

In Innsbruck, Casanova also met the woman of his life, Ika, born as the daughter of Ukrainian displaced persons in Bavaria, who was to exercise a major influence on his intellectual and political development. In 1973, Casanova gained his master's degree in theology; it was also at this time that he decided not to become a priest or a theologian, but to devote himself to sociology. This is why he occasionally calls himself, self-deprecatingly, a "late-ordained sociologist."

With all due respect to its academic staff, it is fair to say that the University of Innsbruck was not the ideal place to advance within the discipline of sociology. It was Franz Schupp who gave the up-and-coming young scholar the somewhat paradoxical, and for Germans depressing, advice that anyone wishing to build on the great German tradition of sociology—geared toward universal history and undergirded by philosophy—should not go to Germany to study, but to the United States. From this point of view, German sociology at the time was "Americanized" in a negative sense and in such a superficial way that it had largely repressed its own impressive traditions, while the German heritage was more often preserved and furthered on the other side of the Atlantic. This advice referred specifically to the New School for Social Research in New York, whose graduate faculty had absorbed so many outstanding émigrés from Germany and Austria during the "Third Reich" and had perpetuated these traditions after the Second World War, later taking in Eastern European émigrés as well.

This institution became Casanova's academic home for decades. It was there that he completed his MA in sociology in 1977 and his PhD in 1982. His most influential academic teacher at the New School was Benjamin Nelson, though he died in 1977. Almost forgotten today, he had become known chiefly for his major study on the history of usury, that is, the prohibition on charging interest on loans in the book of Deuteronomy. This study falls within the genre of the broadly conceived sociology of economic and moral behavior anchored in the history of religion, a field that has produced such outstanding works since Max Weber (and Ernst Troeltsch) and probably embodies the ideal that Casanova strives to emulate.[4] From Casanova's earliest publications onward, Max Weber has been a key reference point in his work; while he has shown great interest in the competing interpretations of Weber's work, Casanova has articulated his own views without the fanaticism that has often induced German Weberians to indulge in personal animosity and sectarian schisms.[5]

Modernization, Democratization, Religion

The picture of the young José Casanova that emerges from his first publications is of a sociologist with a clear set of questions in mind and an unambiguous methodological orientation. He was interested in why Spain's history was so different from that of the "West"—why Spain, although located in the extreme geographic west of Europe, took so long to become modern in the Western sense. His methodological orientation was that of Weberian comparative historical research, supplemented by an emphatic understanding of democracy and the public sphere, as developed by the young Jürgen Habermas, and distinguished by its critical distance from the so-called modernization theory that dominated the Western social sciences. In an early essay, Casanova brought out how exponents of this theory attempted to draw lessons for development policy from a profoundly Protestant narrative of the rise of northwestern Europe—lessons in which the postwar United States appeared as the ultimate in social development—with the sort of civilizational hubris that had been typical of the Victorian Britain of the nineteenth century.[6]

The subject of his dissertation, consonant with his intellectual foci and methodological orientation, was Opus Dei, more precisely: "The Ethics of Opus Dei and the Modernization of Spain."[7] In studying Opus Dei he had no interest in conspiracy theories or in posing as a criminologist seeking to uncover the history of a "holy mafia." His goal was to examine how "a reactionary, clerical, traditionalist and anti-modern 'fundamentalist' regime could have contributed to the modernization of Spain."[8] Who exactly were the agents of this modernization? What was the source of their ideas? Why were they relatively successful within the regime? To what extent did Spanish modernization nonetheless remain partial?

One can clearly sense in these questions the school of modernization theory with its core concern: what was the functional equivalent of the Protestant ethic, supposedly decisive in northwestern Europe, in the case of other successful processes of economic modernization? Robert Bellah had exemplified this in his analysis of the (at the time) only successful Asian case, namely Tokugawa Japan (1603–1868).[9] However, in contrast to the views typically held by modernization theorists, Casanova—drawing on Habermas's critique of technocracy—took a critical view of administrative elites.[10] With regard to the success of the organization he was investigating, he argued that Opus Dei succeeded in prompting the Franco regime to embrace administrative rationalization and, in some cases, the rule of law, the goal being to integrate the Spanish economy into the world economy without destroying the regime itself.

Religion, of course, plays an important role in this analysis, but it would be grossly foreshortened to label Casanova's research program, at this point in its development, simply as sociology of religion. It was far more broadly conceived, and if I am correct, it stayed that way. Casanova does not see religion as a small, specialist field, which he investigates much as others study the sociology of sport or nutrition. Without an understanding of the centrality of religion, for him—like the classical figures of sociology, Max Weber and Émile Durkheim—there is absolutely no prospect of gaining an understanding of processes of societal change. Here, however, we are faced with the apparently paradoxical fact that although sociology regards as its classical figures two scholars for whom religion was crucial and who dealt with social phenomena across the entire history of humankind, as a discipline it has for a long time increasingly been shrinking to the status of the "study of the contemporary world," while marginalizing the study of religion. This paradox can only be resolved if we recognize that the two classical figures themselves contributed to this unfortunate development: their writings entailed assumptions about religion's progressive loss of importance in a novel historical formation, that is, about a disenchanted or secularized modernity.[11]

At precisely this point, the train of thought begins that led to Casanova's most important work to date. From the second half of the 1980s, inspired by dramatic historical developments—such as the Shiite-inspired Iranian revolution of 1979, the Catholic-influenced Solidarność movement in Poland, the rise of a Protestant fundamentalist Christian right in the United States, and the productive role of the postconciliar Catholic Church in democratization in many countries, especially in Latin America, including the Sandinista revolution in Nicaragua—Casanova turned to the question of the exact nature, consequences, and legitimacy of such politico-religious mobilization. The resulting book, which was published in 1994, is a groundbreaking achievement. It is no exaggeration to call it a classic in the sociology of religion, one that symbolizes a veritable paradigm shift in research in the field. I am referring to *Public Religions in the Modern World*,[12] whose merits I would like to highlight briefly and somewhat schematically with reference to four key points.

(1) First, more effectively than anyone else, Casanova brought clarity to the tangled morass of secularization concepts, thus furnishing many successors with a suitable vocabulary. All too often, those involved in religio-political debates talk past one another because one debater takes secularization to mean the decreasing importance of religion in general, another its withdrawal from the public sphere, and a third the liberation of spheres of society from religious control. These differences could be neglected only if developmental tendencies in these different respects all pointed in the same direction. But this is far from being the case, as is immediately apparent to anyone familiar with the United States, where a fairly strict and historically early separation of state and church or religious communities has not only gone hand in hand with the enduring vitality of religion but has likely played a major role in bringing it about.

Things are unclear even within the first variant of the concept of secularization, namely the idea of the weakening of religion. People may remain in their church or religious community despite having lost their faith, or they may give up membership despite continuing to believe. Regular attendance at church services is, if at all, a good indicator of the intensity of faith only among Catholics, and so on. For Casanova, the widespread assumption of religion's progressive loss of importance due to modernization processes was empirically implausible from the outset. The regional and national differences are enormous and cannot usually be explained with reference to different degrees of modernization. The separation of state and church seemed to him the plausible aspect of the secularization thesis; above all, he rejected the idea of the advancing privatization of religion.

(2) This is where Casanova truly departs from a tremendously widespread assumption. Of course, here too the term ("privatization") suggests more clarity than it can deliver. When reference is made to a retreat into the private sphere, it is far from clear where this lies: outside the state in civil society, outside state and civil society in families, only in the spiritual life of the individual?[13] Another ambiguity, it seems to me, can be discerned when the investigation of public politico-religious mobilization is condensed into the thesis of the advancing de-privatization of religion. It may be unclear whether the privatization thesis should be considered empirically refuted once and for all or whether it should be described as historically outdated due to new trends away from privatization. There is certainly a need for further

clarification here. This need has become even more pressing due to the complicated shifting of the boundary between the private and the public—for example, in connection with the abuse scandals that have so damaged the reputation of the Catholic Church. Due to his interest in feminist criticisms of an overly simple, quasi-spatial separation between public and private spheres, Casanova was sensitized at an early stage to the conceptual and factual problems at issue here.

(3) His main interest in the 1994 book, however, was in the dynamics of politico-religious mobilization at the level of entire societies. Hence, we can read the chapter on Spain in his great book as a continuation of his previous sociological analysis of Opus Dei, but now with less focus on economic modernization and more on democratization. As Max Weber already saw and articulated in his writings on Russia,[14] advances in capitalism and the progress of democracy are not related as straightforwardly as "modernization theorists" would like to believe. I see Casanova's book as (in this sense) a Weberian analysis of democratization processes in Spain, Brazil, and Poland, with special emphasis on the role of believers and religious communities, while also paying plenty of attention to other actors and to the learning processes of all those involved in such developments. The political goals and doctrines of churches and religious communities in particular are by no means as fixed as they tend to present them in retrospect; in the Catholic Church, too, however hierarchical and centralized it may appear, there are complicated influences flowing from the bottom up.

In a similar vein, Casanova then dedicated two chapters in his book, namely those concerned with the United States (specifically, on Catholicism's path to the status of a respected "denomination" and on Protestant fundamentalism) to the role of churches. This time, however, his focus was on the part they play not in democratization processes but in an established democracy. Here, however self-assured their claims to moral truth may be, they must conduct themselves as mere participants in public debates; they cannot rely on the state to help them exercise power imperiously, bypassing both the convictions of religious believers and those who espouse secular worldviews.

(4) This brings the normative aspect of Casanova's work into play. *Public Religions in the Modern World* is exemplary not only because of the originality of the questions posed, its conceptual clarity, and historical-empirical approach but also—at least as I see it—because it does not shirk the responsibility of coming to normative conclusions on the basis of empirical research. The book makes a clear case for the legitimacy of a public role for religion

and thus rejects a fundamentalist secular humanism (whose proponents often describe it as liberal) that seeks to monopolize the public sphere and, in the idiom of economics, to compel the churches to withdraw into their "core business" of pastoral care. Of course, Casanova also rejects pre-democratic claims made by the churches and their voluntary limitation to those who already agree with them.

Casanova's empirical findings, conceptual suggestions, and normative statements are, of course, not entirely uncontroversial. As it happens, the book's reception was sluggish. Despite a number of efforts, for example, for many years no German publisher was prepared to commit to a translation. In retrospect, this seems like an interesting indication of how little interest there was at least in Germany in the study of politico-religious mobilization as recently as the mid-1990s. This changed radically after the attacks of September 11, 2001. Due to its scholarly quality, Casanova's book now gained wide recognition all over the world. By then, of course, he had developed his ideas considerably and in several different directions. Three such directions are particularly worth highlighting.

(1) *Public Religions in the Modern World* was occasionally assailed for its limitation to Catholic and Protestant Christianity. In fact, his family connections with Ukraine have familiarized Casanova with Orthodox Christianity as well, and in several articles and with increasing frequency he has also written about the religious situation in Ukraine and religious pluralism in postcommunist societies in general.[15] The real challenge to his theories, however, was posed by the major non-Christian religions, especially Islam. Most significant in this context are his ingenious comparisons of the history of Catholicism and Islam and their perception in Protestant or secular public spheres.[16] We should not forget that in many countries, Catholicism was long viewed as nationally unreliable, incompatible with democracy, and impeding the integration of immigrants, much as Islam is often claimed to be today. The successful history of Catholicism in the United States, as the classic country of immigration, prompts Casanova to draw optimistic conclusions about the future of Islam, albeit with a great sense of proportion and sensitivity to the long path that lies ahead.

If we make more analytical space for non-Christian religions, including some of those originating in Asia, the challenges mount with regard to issues of historical depth. For example, the question of whether the concept of the secular, whose roots lie within a Christian framework, can be appropriately applied to other "world religions" requires us to go back to the wellsprings of these religions. As a result, under the influence of Shmuel Eisenstadt and Robert Bellah, Karl Jaspers's concept of the Axial Age has become increasingly important to Casanova.[17] One key concern for him is to clearly separate the three contrastive conceptual pairs of sacred–profane, transcendent–immanent, and religious–secular—because only through this discriminating lens can we truly grasp the specifics of religion in so-called tribal societies and archaic states, the great upheaval involved in the emergence of world religions, and the sacralization of secular content in the nineteenth and twentieth centuries.

(2) The aspect of the conventional view of secularization that Casanova initially considered worth preserving increasingly faded in his later works. I am referring to the "differentiation" of state and religion as a necessary component of modern societies. International comparison has made it increasingly clear that neither the French nor the US-American model can simply be seen as a template for others or as an indicator of modernity. Before his untimely death, German legal theorist Winfried Brugger produced a typology that elaborates the variety of arrangements lying between theocracy and secularist dictatorship.[18] Overall, in any case, the notion of functional differentiation has clearly receded as a guiding thread in Casanova's writings.

(3) In light of his empirical studies of the part played by religion in the integration of immigrants, Casanova has underlined the diversity of conditions in different countries and the correspondingly variable role of specific religions.[19] I will mention just three of the many findings of this research. Traditionally, immigrants to the United States tend to become more religious as a result of migration, but this does not apply to all countries of immigration; while religion is often regarded as a medium of integration in the United States, it tends to be seen as an obstacle in Europe. In the past, the impact of religious pluralism in the United States was limited to the religion of immigrants in the country itself, but today, thanks to the ease of travel and communication, this effect often extends to countries of origin as well.

In general, Casanova has increasingly sought to provide a comprehensive panorama of globalization from a religious standpoint. The Catholic Church in particular, which has always considered itself a global player—though it was long Eurocentric and, in its upper echelons, even Italocentric—has completely new opportunities to make a transnational impact: opportunities, of course, that it may fail to take advantage of. All religions today are becoming available for individual or collective appropriation outside their cultures of origin. At the same time, they are coming under pressure to take a fresh look at the particularisms they have brought along with them from the cultures in which they were previously embedded. Religion, culture, and territory are becoming ever less aligned.

At present, Casanova is not just an analyst of globalization from a religious perspective but also, in the transnational Catholic public sphere, one of the most important voices providing informed commentary on one of the most far-reaching historical developments of our time—the globalization of Christianity.[20] But his global presence and orientation do not prompt him, as postmodern authors have often done, to aporetically link skepticism about the Enlightenment with Enlightenment-inspired skepticism about religious traditions. In a brief, brilliant critique of Zygmunt Bauman's outline of a postmodern ethics, he wrote the confessional line: "Without embeddedness in some particular moral tradition, the morality of the autonomous self has no content and must perforce be vacuous."[21]

In all three thematic fields mentioned here, one particular critique of Casanova's book has proven especially challenging for the author, namely that put forward by anthropologist and scholar of Islam Talal Asad.[22] Asad objected that Casanova was making it too easy for himself by declaring that the thesis of religious privatization had been refuted while cleaving to the concept of progressive functional differentiation.[23] He also asserted that an increased public role for religion is bound to have an effect on subjective religiosity and that attempts to measure this role quantitatively would lose their validity if focused exclusively on "private" religious life. What undermines the theory of differentiation, Asad contends, is that a public religion cannot remain indifferent to crucial issues of economic development or education, child-rearing or scholarship. Casanova's solution of trying to make a neat distinction between the democracy-compatible and antidemocratic politicization of religion, he went on, is much too simple.

But these reservations were not just meant as corrections to a few limited aspects of Casanova's arguments. Asad had more in mind than a radicalization of Casanova's partial rejection of secularization theory. He was asserting that the very concept of the secular, but also that of religion, are products of Christian-European history and that applying these concepts to non-Christian cultures and non-European societies is deeply problematic. Michel Foucault's notion of "genealogy" is key to Asad's own thinking and approach. While Casanova did not embrace Asad's perspective here, he has taken up the challenges posed by his critique in several ways; in fact, they came to play a formative role in the further development of his ideas. As this is still a "work in progress," I can provide only a provisional account of it here.

Globalization of Christianity

Casanova's catchword in this new phase of his oeuvre is no longer "modernization" or "secularization" but "globalization." Unfortunately, this term is as ambiguous as the other two. Obviously, the expansion of global relations of production and trade, the deregulation of international financial markets, the availability of rapid means of transport, the technological enabling of global real-time communication, and migration flows across long distances are not simply aspects of one and the same process, although there are a number of causalities between them. Casanova has yet to bring the same kind of clarity to this term as he did for secularization. His research on religion and globalization has developed in two main directions, one more contemporary and one more historical.

The contemporary phenomenon that interests him most was mentioned briefly when I referred to the loosening of the links between religion, culture, and territory in the context of globalization. The decisive term Casanova coined for this is "global denominationalism."[24] Casanova asserts that the system of denominationalism claimed by H. Richard Niebuhr to be specific to the United States—and also identified by David Martin, mutatis mutandis, as a feature of Britain and postcolonial societies, especially the former British and Spanish colonial empires[25]—is a key aspect of the present-day global religious situation. This idea is evidently stimulated by the contemporary Pentecostal movement, "a highly decentralized religion with no historical links to tradition and no territorial roots or identity, and which therefore can make itself at home anywhere in the globe where the Spirit moves."[26]

This observation is not meant to detract from the fact that under the conditions of globalization new opportunities are opening up to the Catholic Church, a religious institution that has always been globally oriented—and one that, in sharp contrast to Pentecostalism, features a profound connection with tradition, a pronounced hierarchical structure and a clearly identifiable center (Rome). What matters to Casanova is not whether centralism or decentralization increases the chances of religious expansion. The point he is making is that, for the first time in world history, the fundamental universalism of world religions can become—and is becoming—a social reality.

In religions which (from the Axial Age onward) developed an idea of a single humanity and its common history, this idea was always hedged in by their de facto ties to a specific civilization. But mass migration and electronic mass media are altering this linkage. Hence, for Casanova, the famous and infamous diagnosis of a "clash of civilizations" is backward-looking and misleading, precisely because it fails to factor in the deterritorialization of cultures. This present-day "proliferation of deterritorialized transnational, global imagined communities" (Casanova, borrowing the Arabic term for the global Muslim community of faith, also refers to the "global umma") applies to the old universalist world religions, but not only to them. The new situation also fosters the emergence and spread of "hybrid globalized religions like the Bahai, Moonies, Hare Krishnas, Afro American religions, Falun Gong and so on."[27]

In these circumstances, it is plainly apparent that the universalism of all previous religious and secular systems of orientation for humankind has always been a universalism of particular institutions and traditions. Now, however, insights into the coexistence of a plurality of universalisms opens up the potential for increased cross-tradition learning processes, for "intercivilizational encounters, cultural imitations and borrowings, diasporic diffusions, hybridity, creolization and transcultural hyphenations."[28] Of course, these are not the only tendencies we might identify; the goal here is not to trivialize conflict—the erecting of boundaries, homogenization, and fundamentalism—but to pay due attention to these growing universalist tendencies as well. As in the denominationalism of US-American history, these tendencies could provide an opportunity for greater mutual recognition.

In something of a summary of his decades of research, Casanova has now outlined the historical prerequisites for the transnational denominationalism of the present.[29] More than other globalization theorists, he focuses not only on changes in the global distribution of religious practices and beliefs but on changes in, or the establishment of, new institutional structures. In this respect, Casanova's work stands squarely in the tradition leading from Max Weber via the British sociologist David Martin to a political sociology of religion around the globe. David Martin's long-standing intellectual restriction to Europe and North America, which he only partially overcame in his late work by examining the global expansion of Christianity, is finally overcome by Casanova through the inclusion of Islamic countries, China, and Japan and their respective religio-political constellations. As yet, however, some aspects have remained rather sketchy, and Casanova has certainly not consistently expanded his perspective to encompass Chinese and Indian history to the same degree as Bellah did; he has so far mostly added historical depth to our understanding of Christianity in Europe and its former colonies.

Three special features of his argument seem to me to be particularly worth emphasizing, and we can give them a clearer profile by contrasting them with other influential analyses. First, with regard to religion, for Casanova the modern age does not begin, as it does for many scholars, with the Reformation or with pre-Reformation tendencies toward the strengthening of individualized piety. Nor, as in the work of Charles Taylor, does it start in the somewhat arbitrarily chosen year of 1500.[30] Instead it begins in 1492, with the first vigorous attempt to religiously homogenize a European state, namely Spain, a process that entailed the expulsion of Jews and Muslims. Casanova's decision here stems from the assumption that we can understand the history of religion only in light of its interaction with the history of the state, rather than purely with respect to its endogenous tendencies.

Second, in no uncertain terms Casanova also contradicts the widespread liberal historical narrative, according to which modern religious freedom and religious tolerance are a direct result of the bloody European confessional conflicts of the sixteenth and seventeenth centuries. He calls this historical narrative "the basic story of the modern separation of religion and politics" and counters it with the thesis that the so-called religious wars of the early modern era are more aptly described as wars of European state formation.[31] It was not, Casanova tells us, secularization that resulted from these struggles, but the "confessionalization of the state" and the "territorialization of religions and peoples."[32]

Third, Casanova makes a sharp distinction between two types of religio-cultural pluralization today, namely pluralism based on different forms of religion and that characterized by the distinction between religion and secularism. Here the late work of sociologist of religion Peter L. Berger is clearly present in the background.[33] Long one of the best-known exponents of the secularization thesis, and especially of the notion of the progressive privatization of religion, in old age he dramatically abandoned these long-held views and embraced the idea of the progressive pluralization of religion. Casanova builds on this but divides the two forms of pluralism—religious and religious-secular—between different regions of the world. On this view, Europe, to put it formulaically, is characterized by secularization without religious pluralization, the rest of the world by religious pluralization without pronounced secularization.[34] Unlike Berger, Casanova does not assume one single process of modernization leading to pluralization but rather multiple processes with different resulting forms of pluralism.

Certainly, this formulaic thesis and the implicit critique of Berger are still quite schematic. After all, voluntary or forced forms of secularization are not entirely absent outside Europe, and there is some religious pluralization in Europe; we can identify cases of religious pluralism in premodern societies, and pluralization is not exclusively a result of modernization.[35] Migratory movements in past and present have always been a complicating factor, and it would be necessary to distinguish, within pluralism, the mere coexistence of alternatives from an appeal exercised by these alternatives.[36] But Casanova's studies have erected a theoretical frame of reference into which we can easily insert such empirical distinctions.

As historically rich as Casanova's work on "global denominationalism" and its emergence and consequences is, it is centered on sociological systematization rather than historical research. It is thus worth noting that in recent years Casanova has devoted a good deal of energy to a narrower historical subject, though one that is particularly well suited to shedding new light on the history of globalization. I am referring to the Jesuits as a key component of this history.[37] Casanova (together with Thomas Banchoff) portrays the Jesuits as the pioneers of a globalization *avant la lettre*. From their founding until the eighteenth century, no group has contributed as much to the creation of a global cultural network and a global awareness. Casanova describes the order as the first conscious global network,[38] because the cultural knowledge gained on site and the dictionaries and grammars it produced could circulate worldwide in Jesuit educational institutions scattered around the globe. Here globalization comes vividly to life as something that does not simply occur as a result of modernization. In a nuanced account, Casanova evaluates the Jesuits' receptiveness to the various cultures in which they maintained outposts.

This is not the place to go into detail about this research, which has so far been published only in fragments. What matters is that it is an attempt to show how the great historical phases of the Jesuit order and those of globalization mirror each other and to gain new perspectives from each that help us understand the other. What were the preconditions for the Jesuits' pioneering role? What triggered the papal prohibition on the order in 1773 and what led to its reinstatement in 1814? What was the order's position in the history of Europe's imperial expansion in the nineteenth century? What exactly was its position vis-à-vis the nation-state in Europe? To what extent did the order lay the ground for the Catholic Church's self-reform through the Second Vatican Council? What alternatives to globalization as it currently exists does the Jesuit order offer at a time when a Jesuit is pope for the first time in history? And finally, is there a route to the "globalization of brotherhood"?

While the Axial Age religions produced the beginnings of an ethos of humanity for the first time in history, and while the processes of globalization have made the idea of one humanity a social fact today from an economic and technological perspective, many questions remain about the global history of moral universalism. With the help of José Casanova's research on the global history of religion in the present era, as well as the studies produced by Robert Bellah and others on the history of religion, including the Axial Age, we can begin to answer them.

Conclusion: Global History of Religion and Moral Universalism

A Look Back

In this book, I have presented and critically discussed sixteen important theorists of religion of the twentieth and early twenty-first centuries. By recalling the development of their ideas and highlighting their research, the aim was to fundamentally question a notion of history that found particularly systematic expression in the work of Hegel, but which repeatedly asserts itself even without his direct influence. This is a view of the history of religion and political freedom according to which Christianity towers above all other religions as the absolute religion, while the Protestant form of this Christianity is a crucial driving force in the modern history of political freedom.

This view of history is espoused not just by Christians in the manner of an apologia but also by secularists who believe they can defend their claim to superiority over all religion more easily if they can understand the departure from Christianity as the overcoming of the highest form of religion. From this vantage point, the shift toward modern political freedom is an achievement to which Christianity itself contributed historically but for which it has now become superfluous or perhaps even problematic. My motive for "deconstructing" this image of history, meanwhile, is neither critical of Christianity nor is it defined by skepticism about the normative demands of modern political freedom. But the misleading effects of the historical perspective I am questioning here on the understanding of both religion and political freedom are, I believe, so grave that it seems worthwhile putting forward complex arguments to counteract them.

The ideas presented in this book point us toward four desiderata for a more appropriate understanding. The first might be described as a call for scholars to take account of the independence of religion or the independence of any instance of genuine ideal formation. This expression, used by Ernst Troeltsch, does not, as it might appear, imply the inherent causality of ideas and ideals against a materialist understanding of society and history. Rather, contra an understanding influenced by Hegel, it is an attempt to oppose the sublation of religious phenomena into the concept, that is, to resist the idea that the rational-discursive penetration of religion is now the prerequisite for accepting it in the first place.

I believe this idea is based on the misapprehension that only rational arguments, rather than essentially biographical and historical experiential conditions, are constitutive of nonreligious values. Religious and secular beliefs are both attempts, by means of articulation, to give the certainties and subjective self-evidence resulting from experience an intersubjectively credible form. In this book, I treat William James, Wilhelm Dilthey, and Ernst Troeltsch as major representatives of this idea of the independence of religion and ideal formation; I also show that the phenomenology of the sacred and of the experience of self-evidence, as found in the work of Rudolf Otto and Max Scheler, respectively, points in a similar direction. In a similar way, John Dewey, Charles Taylor, and Robert Bellah also seek to understand ideal formation, with Bellah's notion that "nothing is ever lost" being a particularly vivid demonstration of the persistence of ritual and myth, of bodily expressivity and narration.

The second desideratum is a radical understanding of historical contingency. In contrast to a philosophy of history in which the history of religion and history in general seem to follow an iron internal logic, here the emphasis is on the contingency of history.[1] Modern European secularization, in the sense of the weakening of religion, was not inevitable and is not simply being repeated, as long assumed, through modernization processes outside Europe. Conversely, however, this does not mean that its future is secure, thanks, for example, to the anthropological indispensability of religion. What applies to religions also applies to political systems. Even established systems of political freedom remain contingent. They may crumble or perish for internal reasons or due to external pressure.

Of the thinkers I have discussed in this book, John Dewey, Alfred Döblin, Reinhart Koselleck, and Paul Ricœur most clearly show an awareness of such historical contingency. In Dewey's case, it was the experience of the First World War that made him call prewar expectations of progress a "fools' paradise";[2] the consequences for social cohesion of the global economic crisis then demonstrated to him the fragility even of US-American democracy, prompting his plea for a secular "common faith." A particularly interesting case is the great novelist Alfred Döblin, who was drawn toward Christianity in response to war and Nazism, though not in the form of a culturally well-established and culturally saturated Christianity, but rather that of a "post-totalitarian" Christianity that is aware of the threats it faces.[3]

More than any other theorist of history, this insight into historical contingency was the point of departure for Reinhart Koselleck. Oddly enough, however, with his attention focused on the history of war and violence in the twentieth century, he remained rather unreceptive to the signs that the history of European secularization was also contingent. Paul Ricœur, whose "hermeneutics of historical consciousness" was significantly influenced by Koselleck, put forward one of the most balanced discussions of Hegel's philosophy of history and called for scholars to resist the "Hegelian temptation" of a teleological interpretation of history—without forgetting that humanity does in fact have a single, common history.[4] A growing awareness of the contingency of both the history of religion and the history of freedom naturally prompts us to inquire into the precise dynamic relationship between them. What the evidence shows is that no specific religious or secular worldview can be regarded as a secure buttress of political freedom, nor does any political order as such determine what its effects will be on religion and values or how these effects might impact on this order itself.

This raises the question of how we might relativize the value of freedom within a value system as a whole in such a way as to achieve an enduring freedom-based political order. This cannot be done through a purely negative understanding of freedom, since the mere defense against others' interference in individuals' freedoms cannot guarantee a commitment to the value of equal freedom for all. Hegel's philosophy already moved beyond such an understanding in significant ways. Yet we need to move beyond Hegel too through a clearer understanding of the public sphere and communication, as Jürgen Habermas, Michael Theunissen, Charles Taylor, and Axel Honneth, despite their proximity to Hegel, have striven to provide.

In the present book, this idea comes up chiefly in my account of Wolfgang Huber's ideas on freedom. Huber too conceives of individual freedom in relational terms, as something dependent on intersubjective relationships that do not solely represent a constraint on freedom but in fact make it possible in the first place. This is why I call the third desideratum the idea of indebted freedom. As important as the value of individual self-determination is, it is of little use to an order of freedom if it entails no awareness of what enables it. The conditions that facilitate freedom extend far beyond those who brought us up and influenced us directly. Nobody has made himself or herself a being capable of self-determination all on his or her own. In this book, it is Paul Tillich's thinking that chiefly embodies the creative attempt to honor this insight, one with deep roots in Christianity. This idea is also inherent in the work of Troeltsch and was further developed by Paul Ricœur and Wolfgang Huber.

The fourth desideratum is that of a turn toward global history. It is vital to regain a sense of simultaneity and analogy where Hegel saw pastness (*Nachzeitigkeit*) and difference.[5] Christianity never was,[6] nor is it today, a purely European phenomenon; no inner logic of religious history is leading to the progressive Protestantization of the world or the marginalization of Catholic Christianity. I have provided a detailed treatment of two scholars who eschew such a simplified perspective, examining H. Richard Niebuhr's study of the specific features of US-American Christianity and Werner Stark's vigorous defense of the historical role of Catholicism. We can clearly discern in their writings a sensitivity—heightened by the historical developments of the twentieth century—to the dangers of the self-sacralization of states and nations under the banner of Christianity; they also provide a prophetic defense of this religion's moral-universalist message.

Meanwhile, David Martin's work laid the ground for moving constructively beyond the secularization thesis in the form of a political sociology of religion; he also augmented our understanding of Christianity's present-day non-European expansion. More than anyone else, Robert Bellah helped advance a history of religion that truly takes account not only of the Western and Judeo-Christian world but also China and India. Through his exemplary historical sociology, he answered Ricœur's philosophically based call for us to think about that human history without teleological presuppositions. His guiding thread here was an inquiry into the diverse roots of moral universalism and the political preconditions for its stabilization. In his great work *Religion in Human Evolution*, he demonstrated this primarily with reference to the so-called Axial Age. More closely focused on recent history and the contemporary world, José Casanova's ongoing research on the globalization of Christianity and on Christian responses to globalization has a similar goal in mind.

This fourfold revision points us toward an alternative to the tradition of Hegel and Marx, one that also differs from another tradition of thought, long perceived in Germany and Europe but increasingly in the United States too as the most important alternative, namely the ideas of Friedrich Nietzsche.

The subtitle of this book refers to a theory of religion not only after Hegel but also after Nietzsche. For some of the thinkers I have discussed, Nietzsche, more than Hegel, posed the decisive challenge. This applies to Döblin, who was deeply influenced by him in his younger years and even wished to outdo his radical critique of religion.[7] It applies to Max Scheler, whose essay on the psychology of resentment is nothing other than an embrace of Nietzschean motifs in opposition to Nietzsche's critique of religion,[8] and it applies to Ernst Troeltsch, who grappled with Nietzsche throughout his life and regarded him as "the great revolutionary of the age in the field of the humanities,"[9] one whose work had fundamentally shaken the idea of progress and had raised in a new and irrefutable way the problem of the relationship between history and value judgments.

So radically did Nietzsche express his critique of Christianity and religion on the one hand and his insight into the contingency of history on the other that there seemed to be nothing left of Hegel's philosophy of history. But do we have to choose between these two perspectives? Or is there a third way that frees itself from Hegelian constraints in the four respects mentioned above without ending up on a Nietzschean path?

I maintain that such a third way is possible if we transform Hegel's historical-philosophical analysis of the role of Christianity in the history of political freedom into the project of a global historical genealogy of moral universalism, taking into account the four desiderata mentioned above. After a brief reminder of the deep and persistent challenge posed by Nietzsche and with the aid of the critique of Nietzsche's assertions in the writings of Max Weber and Ernst Troeltsch, I will shed light on this project while highlighting how it contrasts with Nietzsche's ideas.

Nietzsche's Challenge

I regard Nietzsche—especially in his 1887 *Streitschrift* or polemic *On the Genealogy of Morality*—as the pioneer of a historical and psychological investigation of the genesis of values.[10] I do not mean this in the relatively trivial sense of opening up a new area of research that had somehow been neglected but in the much deeper sense of a break with all previous notions of history and their relationship to the "good." As long as the good was viewed, in the Platonic tradition, as the highest form of being, the question of its origin inevitably appeared meaningless. This question of origins could, in principle, be posed with respect to all individual beings but not to that being toward which all beings move and that human beings must recognize in order to orient their conduct of life toward it.

The question of the genesis of values therefore presupposed a turn to subjectivity, which is of course why scholars referred ever less often to one good and increasingly to different values, varying from era to era, from culture to culture, from individual to individual. This turn to the subjectivity of evaluation was already performed by the so-called philosophy of value (*Wertphilosophie*) before and alongside Nietzsche. But this is only a necessary, not sufficient condition for the rise of questions about the origin of these values. For in the academic neo-Kantian philosophy of value, the key question was how to prevent the subjectivity of evaluation from becoming a bottomless pit of value relativism. This problem was solved by assuming an ideal realm of valid values that belongs to a different mode of being than the subjects themselves, which is why they can embody and discover values but not produce them. On this view, it is impossible to conceptualize this ideal realm as having arisen from people's actions and experience. Nietzsche, however, took a further, far more radical step beyond the insight into the subjectivity of evaluation, highlighting the historical contingency of values themselves, that is, the nonnecessity of their existence and emergence.

Nietzsche was well—almost excessively—aware of the novelty and boldness of his undertaking and he put forward his ideas with the dramatic air of someone who, as he put it, has traversed "a vast and dangerous land"[11] and knows that few possess his courage, with all lesser and unfree minds refusing to contemplate his message. He himself states that from an early age he not only asked himself where evil actions come from, but also, increasingly, how certain actions came to be evaluated as evil: "Under what conditions did man invent the value judgments good and evil? And what value do they themselves have?"[12] Repelled by Schopenhauer's ethic of compassion—that is, what he mockingly calls his "Euro-Buddhism"[13]—Nietzsche finds himself propelled toward the question of the "value of pity and of the morality of pity" and from there to the project of a "critique of moral values."[14]

This critique has no qualms about questioning the values of "love" and "justice," so central to the Jewish and Christian traditions. In fact, Nietzsche wishes to explore whether, perhaps, the good may be more harmful to humans than evil, "so that morality itself [might be] to blame if man, as species, never reached his highest potential power and splendor," while "morality itself [might be] the danger of dangers."[15] Nietzsche was certainly aware of the sinister nature of his questions, and this quality can be felt to this day, despite the weakening of Christian traditions in Europe. What meant more to him and many of his readers, however, was the liberating effect of such pitilessness, the prospect of mental liberation from increasingly intolerable, religiously based moral pressures.

In two respects, then, Nietzsche's questioning was more radical than any previous thinker's. He probed not only into the origin of individual moral values but also into the genesis of moral evaluation itself—and he did not ignore the historical contingency of such processes of emergence, that is, the true emergence of something new in history, predetermined by nothing. It was in precisely this way that he set himself apart completely from Hegelian or Marxist ideas of history, in which the good is temporalized or historicized but only in such a way that it now appears as the goal of history, toward which this history is more or less inevitably leading.

In the questions raised by Nietzsche and in the method he developed to answer them, which he called "genealogy," I do see an epoch-making achievement. Before beginning to examine the exact character of this method, let alone Nietzsche's theory and its empirical legitimacy when applied (in the work of Nietzsche himself) to the emergence of Christianity, I would like to identify the issue that has always prevented me from simply adopting a Nietzschean perspective and prompted me to try to correct Nietzsche's thinking with the help of a great US-American contemporary of his, namely William James.[16]

This issue may be described as an activist or voluntarist misunderstanding of the process of ideal formation in Nietzsche's work. This is easy to discern in Nietzsche's wording. For instance, he asks his readers whether they would like to get a glimpse into the "workshop" in which "*ideals are fabricated* on this earth" and the procedures governing this process. Or shortly after this: "Bad air! Bad air! This workshop where *ideals are fabricated*—it seems to me just to stink of lies."[17] Perhaps the term "fabrication" can be justified in light of the critical intention of uncovering the sinister plans of those who are held responsible for prevailing ideals. But in Nietzsche's positive alternative, and not only in his criticism, this voluntarism also shines through, namely when he initially locates the origin of the predicate "good"—that is, before it was fractured by Jewish and Christian morality—in the self-affirmation of the superior, in other words in the noble, the mighty, the high-placed and the high-minded, who saw and judged themselves and their actions as good, I mean first-rate, in contrast to everything lowly, low-minded, common and plebeian. It was from this *pathos of distance* that they first claimed the right to create values and give these values names.[18]

Both this original *creation* of values through the self-affirmation of the superior beings on the one hand and the value-positing power of minds freed from morality—a power Nietzsche felt must be regained—on the other entail the idea that it is fundamentally possible to posit, choose, and fabricate values.

But that is the question. If values or ideals are characterized by the fact that they seize us, that we have to be seized by them if we are to feel bound by them, then the idea of self-posited values is as paradoxical as the notion of ideals intentionally produced for others. In the work of William James, in contrast to that of Nietzsche, the phenomenon of "self-surrender" comes to the fore, that is, the commitment to other people we feel when we realize that we love them, or the commitment to ideational content we feel because we experience its truth, in an affectively intense way, as uncontroversially valid for us, as subjectively self-evident. From the outset, Nietzsche failed to see this deeply passive dimension of being seized by a value or ideal.

However much one may admire Nietzsche's pioneering achievement in this field, as I see it there is no getting around this problem. The history of morality and religion cannot be reduced, à la Nietzsche, to a history of power and the positing of potent values. Such a rejection of Nietzsche certainly allows us to do greater justice to the human experiences out of which attachments to people and ideals arise. But as we have to concede to Nietzsche, this perspective in itself is inadequate when it comes to systematically grasping the power dimension in which all processes of ideal formation are in fact embedded. There is a need to clarify the relationship between the dynamics of processes of sacralization and ideal formation on the one hand and the dynamics of processes of power formation on the other. Without reducing the sacred or ideals to power, we must probe the sacralization of power and the power-critical potential of ties to sacredness and ideals.[19] This also compels us to consider the genesis of those values that require the well-being of all to be taken into account. This is what I mean by the genealogy of moral universalism, which I believe must replace the Hegelian philosophy of history.

The Critique of Nietzsche by Max Weber and Ernst Troeltsch

In order to clarify where I differ from Nietzsche, at this point I must return to the concrete way in which he explained the genesis of the values of justice and love in the Jewish and Christian religions. The true nub of Nietzsche's recourse to the self-affirmation of the high-placed and high-minded was that it provided an answer to the question of why this state of affairs came to an end. He believed this was because those who were naturally weaker and inferior could not affirm themselves, but rather, in confrontation with their superiors, developed feelings of envy and hatred—and a desire for revenge. They could not act on this, however, precisely because of their inferior position. But the fantasy of possible vengeance rigidified into resentment, into a grudging view of the qualities of their superiors. According to Nietzsche, this resentment would remain without impact in the absence of agents capable of articulating it and turning it into an entire system of values.

Nietzsche first identifies the priests in the advanced ancient civilizations as the true agents of such systematic devaluation of heroic and aristocratic values. In line with this, he devotes a lot of space to the alleged emergence of ascetic ideals out of the priestly way of life, characterized by cultic purity. But according to Nietzsche, even more historically impactful than the priests in the individual civilizations was a specific people, "a priestly people," as he puts it, namely the Jews, who knew how to obtain satisfaction "through an act of the most deliberate revenge" vis-à-vis their enemies and subduers.[20]

What Nietzsche calls the "slaves' revolt in morality" supposedly began with the Jews. For him, this makes Jesus Christ and the gospel of love the very epitome of what is Jewish. Through Christ and the myth of the crucifixion, Nietzsche believes, the strong lose the innocence of their self-enjoyment; they are preoccupied by feelings of guilt and scruples and contaminated by the weak. Thus, in the form of Christianity, the Jews ultimately conquered the Roman Empire; when "the noble method of valuing" briefly flared up again in the Renaissance, it immediately lost its vigor again: "thanks to that basically proletarian (German and English) *ressentiment*-movement which people call the Reformation."[21] For Nietzsche, the French Revolution in particular is a victory for "Judea"—and the democratic and socialist movements of the nineteenth century are the harbingers of an age of cultural mediocrity and massification.

Although we now know how little Nietzsche had to do with German nationalism and racist anti-Semitism, this should not fool us into believing him innocuous. There can be no doubt that Nietzsche set out to provoke and that his ideas were in fact provocative; the question is how best to deal with this. I would suggest that we neither turn a blind eye to this provocativeness nor flirt with it. It seems to me that the only fitting approach is to put his claims to the test of empirical research. This makes sense even if Nietzsche's empirical posturing was mere window dressing. In addition, such a test will help philosophers avoid echoing untenable claims only because a great philosopher once made them.

It is surely beyond dispute that Nietzsche had astute things to say about the psychology of resentment. Resentment arises whenever people are confronted with the superiority of other people in any sense, and one would have to be completely blind to deny the role of resentment among Christians as well. Max Scheler, himself a Christian, was even prepared to contemplate whether the idea of love might be particularly well suited to providing convenient camouflage for claims to power. Since many contemporaries see themselves as adherents of a secular moral universalism, I would like to submit that this, too, is an apt means of expressing resentment—against the less educated and "provincial," for example. So it is not the existence of resentment that is controversial, but whether we find plausible Nietzsche's explanation of the emergence of the ethos of love out of it.

Analyses accusing Nietzsche himself of deep resentment toward Christianity and of therefore misunderstanding the Christian idea of love range from Scheler to the early work of Maurice Merleau-Ponty.[22] The special feature of this idea that he missed lies in the notion of a God that is not only to be loved but is himself loving, and in a human devotion to others that comes from the feeling of being unconditionally loved, that is, from an abundant capacity for love. Such a turn to others, however, is the opposite of a turning that arises from primal self-hatred or a resentment-driven demand for compensation.

These arguments, important as they are, remain at the level of psychology on the one hand and theology on the other. For an understanding of the approach entailed in a genealogy of moral universalism, however, it is essential to go beyond this and to treat sociologically as well the questions that Nietzsche raised. Max Weber and Ernst Troeltsch were the first to attempt this by grappling directly with his work. I will briefly characterize their approach here in order to open up the prospect of a constructive alternative to both Hegel and Nietzsche.

The name Nietzsche crops up very rarely in Weber's writings. We now know that a famous phrase that appears in quotation marks in his essay on the Protestant ethic ("Specialists without spirit, sensualists without heart; this nullity imagines that it has attained a level of civilization never before achieved"),[23] although often interpreted as such, is definitely not a quotation from Nietzsche and is not compiled from his writings (as Wilhelm Hennis thought). In fact, Weber got it from Gustav von Schmoller's *Grundriß der allgemeinen Volkswirtschaftslehre*, where it is attributed to an unidentified French author.[24] However, Weber repeatedly mentioned one of Nietzsche's texts and frequently subjected it to detailed critique: *On the Genealogy of Morality*.

In the longest passage on this text in Weber's work (in the introduction to his comparative studies in the sociology of religion), he calls Nietzsche's "polemic" (*Streitschrift*) a "brilliant essay" and interprets it as a parallel to the criticism of religion put forward by Marxists. However, he advises extreme caution toward both these radical simplifications of the links between religion and class. With respect to the other great world religion—besides the Judeo-Christian tradition—that puts tremendous emphasis on compassion-centered values, namely Buddhism ("one of Nietzsche's main examples"),[25] Weber rejects completely Nietzsche's explanation foregrounding the collective resentment of the "inferior." He points out that in the Hindu doctrine of reincarnation, individual suffering was not attributed to others but was regarded as one's own fault and that Buddhism, which emerged from Hinduism, certainly did not represent any kind of slave revolt in morality: it arose in privileged circles and is far removed from a doctrine born out of *envy*.

Quite generally, Weber contends, the motives underpinning religious change and the ethical "rationalization" of the conduct of life are for the most part completely different from those undergirding resentment. Only within a very narrow subfield of religious ethics concerned with the evaluation of suffering, Weber tells us, are there phenomena with respect to which Nietzsche's theory, "if properly understood, [might claim] a certain justification."[26]

For Weber, there really was an elemental tendency to exclude human beings "permanently suffering, mourning, diseased, or otherwise infortunate" from communities of worship, especially when suffering was attributed to possession by evil spirits or the rage of an aggrieved deity. Like Nietzsche, Weber takes the self-perception of those not affected by suffering as his starting point. But unlike Nietzsche, he does not assume seamless self-expression, but refers to a "theodicy of good fortune," that is, an original need of the fortunate to perceive their good fortune as "legitimate," even if they do not come under pressure to justify themselves from the less fortunate.

The dynamic of the shift toward a positive interpretation of suffering also takes a different form in Weber than in Nietzsche. For Weber, the "ecstatic, visionary, hysterical... states" that may arise from suffering were repeatedly interpreted as positive forces, and this was even more pronounced when redemption cults developed and redeemer myths appeared, such as that of a savior who guarantees salvation to all who embrace him. On this premise, what is special about the Jewish people is that here "the suffering of a people's community, rather than the suffering of an individual, became the object of hope for religious salvation." Weber comes close to Nietzsche's conception when he affirms the appeal of prophetically proclaimed, savior-focused religiosity, especially for the lower social strata, and emphasizes the affinities between a positive assessment of suffering and a resentment-laden devalorization of happiness. But this convergence occurs despite different starting points: for Weber, neither the question of meaning nor that of justice can be traced back to the dynamics of resentment.

Hence, thanks to his nuanced understanding of Indian and Jewish religion, we can learn a great deal from Weber that is of value to an empirically based alternative to Nietzsche's perspective. Weber also rejects Nietzsche's ideas about the emergence of kingship and the state through the subjugation of one tribe by another as "arbitrary."[27] One senses that Weber the scholar is often repulsed by Nietzsche's tone. He refers to "the negative moralistic pathos which often betrays an embarrassing residue of bourgeois philistinism even in some of his [Nietzsche's] greatest passages."[28] He is even more repelled by the false pseudo-aristocratic air of Nietzsche's epigones, who believe that they can gain "dignity" and "form" under the conditions of democratization through snobbish setting one's self off from the "far too many."[29]

But whether Weber explicitly mentions it or not, his understanding of the modern age and modern culture is closely related to Nietzsche's diagnosis of nihilism. Weber, too, experiences his era, as he puts it, as "alien to God and bereft of prophets," and in an attempt to understand the advent of this period he presents us with the evocative idea of a world-historical process of the disenchantment of the world that has lasted for millennia. As compelling as this analysis is for many, it is hardly the only one on offer. Especially with regard to Nietzsche's genealogy of Christian morality, an alternative was quite conceivable. It can be found in the work of Ernst Troeltsch.

Troeltsch opposed the burgeoning atheism of his time like few other thinkers, though he never came close to being a mere apologist for Christianity. He considered the atheism of the modern socialists—that is, the linkage of their utopias and reformist agenda "with a completely naturalistic atheism of an utterly ruthless kind"—to be historically explicable, but also "quite accidental," and he took the same view of the inverse phenomena of the "unfortunate linkage of [the] frightened property[-owning classes] with the church."[30] But he has grave historical and moral-philosophical reservations about the atheism espoused by conservatives and liberals, who believe that by overcoming Christianity they can build a "purer ethics centered on the wellbeing of society in the most general sense."[31] His thinking here is not rooted in the old Christian-apologetic assumption that there can be no atheistic ethics. Yet dropping the idea of a loving God will not, Troeltsch believes, be without consequences for ethics.

It is precisely at this point that Nietzsche becomes important to him. He had "tirelessly ridiculed those who wish to be educated enough not to have a religion, but who are at the same time lazy enough in their thinking to nonetheless retain an altruism-centered morality that now lacks any foundation."[32] In this respect, Nietzsche's "new morality beyond good and evil, which with full awareness also draws completely new consequences from its new foundations,"[33] is, for Troeltsch, considerably superior to the simple idea of "morality minus religion." At the same time, it leads "into a tremendously dark world of purely individual character enhancement."[34]

For Troeltsch, Nietzsche's deep sense that modern intellectual culture is anything but the proud apogee of world history holds out a certain promise for those seeking to revitalize the Christian religion, while the vapid perpetuation of bourgeois morality offers them nothing at all. In 1913, Troeltsch went so far as to predict that Nietzsche's fate would be much like that of Spinoza, "whom his contemporaries called the *philosophus atheissimus*,"[35] but whom the Romantics celebrated as an essential source of inspiration for a new religiosity. In general, it is remarkable just how much Troeltsch regarded contemporary trends toward secularization as contingent and historically temporary. He suspected that the atheism of Feuerbach and Schopenhauer, Marx and Nietzsche would "one day be a thing of the past,"[36] and took a dim view of those constructions in which atheism and secularization are a virtually inevitable result of religious history or, in line with the thinking of Nietzsche and Weber, a consequence of the Christian value of truthfulness, prophetic hostility to magic, puritan asceticism, and disenchantment.

Troeltsch's expectation of future religious revitalization has not come to fruition in Germany. Nevertheless, it would be imprudent simply to discount his reasons for this expectation. After all, the idea of a coming altruistic morality freed from religion has not been confirmed by twentieth-century German history either. Troeltsch's perspective, however, is not the "new eschatology of the superman"[37] but a constructive version of the genealogical method and a new European "cultural synthesis," that is, a productive continuation of Christianity, but also of other European cultural traditions.

As Troeltsch saw it, Nietzsche, especially in the second of his *Untimely Meditations*, "On the Uses and Disadvantages of History for Life," had "shockingly raised"[38] the question of how to establish a yardstick of historical evaluation, a problem Troeltsch was never to cease grappling with and to which he found a solution, one preferable to Weber's stark contrast between existential value decisions and value-free research. Those writings of Nietzsche to which Troeltsch more often refers are concerned (like Weber) with the genealogy of Jewish and Christian morality. Here, much like Weber, Troeltsch is critical of Nietzsche on empirical grounds, but his emphasis is somewhat different, and he puts forward an argument that is crucial in the present context. I limit myself here to two aspects of his line of reasoning.

First, Troeltsch declares it "very remarkable" that Nietzsche, "who in reference to his own system of morals is very conscious that it is the consequence of the proposition *God is dead*, will not allow that the other system of morals [the Gospel] is the consequence of the proposition *God is alive*."[39] Consonant with this, Troeltsch emphasizes the significance of this glowing core of religious inspiration for Jesus, but also seeks to show that this religious inspiration already existed among the Hebrew prophets and injected vitality into the early Christian communities and the ancient church.

Neither in the case of the prophets nor that of Jesus, Troeltsch contends, are the beatitudes of the poor and suffering the origin of this conception of God. Instead, they are the consequence and product of the "unbreakable nature of faith in Yahweh and a counterposing of the inner world and the outer world of power."[40] Poverty and suffering may lead to humility and trust in God and are therefore extolled; needless to say, resentment may then focus on such religious ideas. This, Troeltsch states, has certainly happened repeatedly in the case of the Jews, as it has in that of the Christians. But, he asserts, even Christian humility should not be seen as the cause of ascetic ideals, but as their consequence, and the emergence of these ideals is incomprehensible without the preceding ethos of love; its setting must in any case be "much more complicated than Nietzsche admits."[41]

For Troeltsch, the history of asceticism as well—in medieval monasticism, for example—cannot be understood if it is conceived purely negatively, in the sense of the mortification of natural needs, without acknowledging the positive sense of the "release of religious feelings." Contra Nietzsche, then, Troeltsch emphasizes that the gospel is much more than asceticism and that this "misreading of its chief religious ideas" must inevitably cause Nietzsche and those of like mind to "underestimate the sociological energies which issue from this leading religious idea."[42] Here, much like Weber, Troeltsch is obviously keen to defend the "independence of religion" against a power-centered reductionism. Just as it was for Weber, for Troeltsch Christianity is not an ancient proletarian movement, as Karl Kautsky and other Marxists claimed. As important as it was to both Troeltsch and Weber to consider the social bearers of religion, they also underlined that religion was more than camouflage for supposedly core material (or power-related) interests.

But if this is so, how are we to explain, against Nietzsche and Marx as it were, a Jewish sect's triumphant advance to the status of world religion? For Troeltsch, and this is the second important aspect of his argument, the explanation lies in the history of the ancient empires. The Diadochian Empires, into which the empire of Alexander the Great had disintegrated, but above all the Roman Empire, had led to the "shattering of the old national religions and the old entrenched relations between peoples."[43] Without them, however, a dual tendency was bound to ensue: toward the individual on the one hand and toward a universalism beyond the particularisms of people and state on the other. "The world empire demanded a world religion and, by destroying the goods of the old civilisation, directed attention toward the supramundane and the otherworldly."[44] Ideas of transcendence and moral universalism thus became more appealing—across all social strata. In the upper class, the needs that arose in this way could be satisfied, for example, through Stoic philosophy. But the lower class needed something other than philosophy, namely a new cult and a new religious organization beyond ethnicity and archaic statehood. Christianity could offer this, while also gradually integrating into its teaching philosophical impulses of a similar hue.

The newly emerging Christian ethos, that is, is not just an expression of the resentment of the weak or of utopian hopes of salvation characteristic of a particular class; it breaks away from all existing sociological structures. Troeltsch left us another important piece of evidence in support of this view.

Before his untimely death, he made many extensive additions to his personal copy of the *Social Teachings*, which he wished to include in a future edition. Among these new insertions, at the end of the chapter on the gospel and before the transition to his account of Paul and the "organization of a worldwide Church, independent of Judaism, founded on the worship of Christ and going out into the world to win the world to Him,"[45] we find what is probably the clearest description of this ingenious insight as Troeltsch once again grapples directly with Nietzsche.

The emergence of Christianity, for Troeltsch, entailed a breaking away from the ties of class, "from the *polis*, from the empire" and the "discovery of the human being and humanity."[46] But, Troeltsch contends, if a group has detached itself from all existing social forms, its members will feel a need to create new ones, which is what generated the social form of the "church." Philosophers' associations and schools of philosophy could certainly not meet the needs of the lower classes.

According to Troeltsch, this is the true core of Nietzsche's well-known remark in the preface to *Beyond Good and Evil* that Christianity is "Platonism for the People." Naturally, this new and potentially universalist social form of the "church" will be commandeered by certain classes more than others, and by certain states and civilizations as well, though time and again it has broken away and distanced itself from them. Beyond Troeltsch, then, the question arises as to what the functional equivalents of the role of the "church" might be in the history of other universalist religious traditions, such as Buddhist monasticism;[47] another key issue is the organizational problems suffered by possible secular forms of moral universalism, if these move beyond intellectual circles to become a social movement.

Future Prospects: A Global Historical Genealogy of Moral Universalism

By this point we should have a clearer sense not only of the constructive alternative to Nietzsche's method, but also of the alternative to Nietzsche's "empirical" explanation of the genesis of Jewish and Christian morality. I borrow the term "genealogy" in this philosophical sense from Nietzsche. What I have in mind here is a historiography that takes enough account of the contingency of historical processes when reconstructing the past, in other words one that is not guided by ideas of progress, whether evolutionist or teleological. Seen in this way, history did not have to lead to us and our values; it will produce radically new things in the future that we cannot foresee and that will seem self-evidently good to people of the future, though they may deviate greatly from our present-day values.

But while Nietzsche's intention in applying this method to the history of morality in Judaism and Christianity was a destructive one—he wanted the scales to fall from our eyes to reveal how the ideals that morally restrict us were once "fabricated"—my goal lies in the opposite direction. I refer to an "affirmative genealogy"[48] because grappling with the contingencies of history may confront us, for example, with past suffering and injustice in such a way that we feel deeply moved and called to take action intended to prevent the recurrence of such suffering and such injustice. I thus deploy Nietzsche's method in a modified form and with intentions far removed from his. Such an "affirmative genealogy" also seems to me the most effective way to evade the conceptual constraints—tending to result in teleological arguments—that I identified and criticized in the work of contemporary Hegelians in the introduction to this book.[49]

What I mean by "moral universalism" is a moral-philosophical orientation that does not measure the good by its utility for a particular human community. I am not talking here about a lowest common denominator of the morality of all human beings. What I have in mind is an idea of humanity that transcends all particularist collectives such as family, tribe, people, nation, state, or religious community. This is a normatively charged concept of "humanity" that, beyond those presently living, encompasses the preconditions for the existence of future people as well. This moral-universalist intuition—which existed long before Kant in the world religions and in philosophical projects such as Stoicism, and which can also be articulated in other ways—found one of its clearest forms of expression in Kant's ideas on the universalization of principles of action through the verification process entailed in the categorical imperative. Kant's writings, however, fail to reflect in historically sufficient fashion on the specifics of this moral-philosophical orientation itself. This is done in a certain sense in the work of Hegel, but his analysis suffers from the very shortcomings so central to the present book.

Hence, the "genealogy of moral universalism" means the empirical question of when, where, why, and how exactly this moral universalism, which has not always existed, emerged, and how it developed after its initial breakthrough; what setbacks it suffered; the various ways in which it was fenced in; how and where it was canonized; how a religious and philosophical ethos of this kind gave rise to forms of law within the framework of individual states or even transnational legal systems; and what the effects of these legal forms of moral universalism might be.

Today, such a genealogy of moral universalism must be a global historical one.[50] For a long time, Christianity or Europe or the West were simply ascribed a monopoly on moral universalism without any serious consideration of, for example, Chinese and Indian history. Fortunately, that changed a great deal in the second half of the twentieth century, although there are still many forms of European or Western triumphalism. A German thinker plays a central role here. He had taken up key impulses from Nietzsche and Weber, but under the influence of Nazism and its crimes he also opened up completely new perspectives beyond Eurocentrism. I am referring to Karl Jaspers and the discourse he initiated on the "Axial Age," in which (between 800 and 200 BC) ideas about "transcendence" and "humanity" arose in several major civilizations. A global historical genealogy of moral universalism must (as in the writings of Robert Bellah) begin with this Axial Age. But it must also extend to the present day and look far beyond the framework of the history of the West or of Christianity.[51]

Troeltsch's method of genealogical historical reconstruction seems to me more convincing than that of Weber. While we must integrate Weber's arguments into the empirical correction of Nietzsche's perspective, Troeltsch went further than Weber—who had already related monotheistic prophecy and state building to one another—in making the connection between moral and political universalism, between religion and empire. Weber, however, extended his view beyond Europe and Christianity to a greater extent than Troeltsch. To draw methodologically and theoretically on both Weber and Troeltsch but go far beyond both in empirical terms: this is what the global historical genealogy of moral universalism needs to do. A theory of religion, as developed subsequent to Hegel and Nietzsche, offers an abundance of additional insights for this genealogy to build on. I see this genealogy as the constructive fusion of the ideas elaborated on in this book with reference to selected thinkers on religion of the twentieth and early twenty-first centuries.

A Note on the Text

Several chapters of this book are based on previous publications, all of which were reworked when integrated into the present volume. Below, I identify where these texts were first published.

Part I
Chapter 2: Christopher Adair-Toteff (ed.), *The Anthem Companion to Ernst Troeltsch*, London: Anthem Press 2018, 25–35.

Part II
Chapter 2: Hans Joas, *The Genesis of Values*, Chicago: University of Chicago Press 2000, 109–123, 208–211.
Chapter 4: Hans Joas and Barbro Klein (eds.), *The Benefit of Broad Horizons*, Leiden: Brill 2010, 87–104.

Notes

Epigraph

1. Alexis de Tocqueville, *Democracy in America: An Annotated Text, Backgrounds, Interpretations*, ed. Isaac Kramnick, New York: Norton & Company 2007, 392.

Introduction

1. Axel Honneth, *Freedom's Right: The Social Foundations of Democratic Life*, New York: Columbia University Press 2015. This wording also appears in Martin Laube, "Die Dialektik der Freiheit. Systematisch-theologische Perspektiven," in Martin Laube (ed.), *Freiheit*, Tübingen: UTB 2014, 119–191, here 119.
2. Honneth, *Freedom's Right*, 15.
3. Charles Taylor, *Sources of the Self: The Making of the Modern Identity*, Cambridge: Harvard University Press 1989, 503.
4. Ibid.
5. Christoph Halbig, "Hegel, Honneth und das Primat der Freiheit. Kritische Überlegungen," in Magnus Schlette (ed.), *Ist Selbstverwirklichung institutionalisierbar? Axel Honneths Freiheitstheorie in der Diskussion*, Frankfurt am Main: Campus 2018, 53–72, here 54, fn. 8.
6. Honneth, *Freedom's Right*, 16.
7. Axel Honneth, "Erwiderung," in Schlette (ed.), *Ist Selbstverwirklichung institutionalisierbar?*, 313–337, here 319; on Halbig's critique, see also ibid., 328–334.
8. John Rawls, *A Theory of Justice*, Cambridge: Harvard University Press 1971.
9. Honneth, "Erwiderung," 319.
10. Honneth, *Freedom's Right*, 18.
11. See my arguments, drawing on Ernst Troeltsch, on an "affirmative genealogy" in Hans Joas, *The Sacredness of the Person: A New Genealogy of Human Rights*, Washington, DC: Georgetown University Press 2013, ch. 4, esp. 114–130.
12. Halbig, "Hegel, Honneth und das Primat der Freiheit," 55. On the issue of value pluralism, which I am unable to pursue systematically in the present book, and on the ideas put forward by the leading exponent of this position (Isaiah Berlin), see Part III, ch. 5, in connection with my discussion of Wolfgang Huber and the literature cited there.
13. Ibid., 66.
14. An overview of the various assessments is provided in the introduction to Part I.

15. Wolfgang Knöbl, "'Das Recht der Freiheit' als Überbietung der Modernisierungstheorie," in Schlette (ed.), *Ist Selbstverwirklichung institutionalisierbar?*, 31–52.
16. Honneth, "Erwiderung," esp. 327. It is also revealing that elsewhere, when it comes to the normative issues arising in this connection, Honneth tends to fall back on a modified Kant rather than on Hegel. See Axel Honneth, "Die Unhintergehbarkeit des Fortschritts. Kants Bestimmung des Verhältnisses von Moral und Geschichte," in Axel Honneth, *Pathologien der Vernunft. Geschichte und Gegenwart der Kritischen Theorie*, Frankfurt am Main: Suhrkamp 2007, 9–27.
17. Rolf Schieder, "Der 'culte de l'individu' als Zivilreligion des Westens. Eine praktisch-theologische Relektüre von Durkheim, Foucault und Boltanski," in Schlette (ed.), *Ist Selbstverwirklichung institutionalisierbar?*, 287–312, here esp. 288f.
18. Honneth, "Erwiderung," 317.
19. Ibid., 320.
20. Ibid., 317.
21. His analysis of Honneth is instructive in this respect: Robert Pippin, "Reconstructivism. On Honneth's Hegelianism," in: *Philosophy and Social Criticism* 40, no. 8 (2014), 725–741. Important studies by Pippin on Hegel and his notion of freedom are collected in Robert Pippin, *Idealism as Modernism: Hegelian Variations*, Cambridge: Cambridge University Press 1997. A German selection of Pippin's articles, *Die Verwirklichung der Freiheit. Der Idealismus als Diskurs der Moderne*, Frankfurt am Main: Campus 2005, contains an overview of the development of his work by Axel Honneth and Hans Joas, "Vorwort"; see 7–13 in that volume.
22. According to one of the best present-day interpreters of Hegel's philosophy of religion. See Thomas M. Schmidt, "Anerkennung und absolute Religion. Gesellschaftstheorie und Religionsphilosophie in Hegels Frühschriften," in Matthias Jung, Michael Moxter, and Thomas M. Schmidt (eds.), *Religionsphilosophie. Historische Positionen und systematische Reflexionen*, Würzburg: Echter 2000, 101–112, here 101.
23. This is the phrasing of Ludwig Siep, not Hegel. See Ludwig Siep, *Der Staat als irdischer Gott*, Tübingen: Mohr Siebeck 2015, esp. 6ff., which provides a compilation of those of Hegel's statements that allow us to refer to the sacralization of the state in his work.
24. Most famously in the work of Richard Rothe, for whom—in the words of Ernst Troeltsch—"the removal of the institution of the church had [already] begun with the Reformation" and "one day, with the spiritualization of all men achieved through the Second Coming of Christ, only the religiously inspired organization of moral reason, Hegel's state, will exist and the last trace of the church will have disappeared." See Ernst Troeltsch, *Richard Rothe. Gedächtnisrede (zum 100. Geburtstag)*, Freiburg: Mohr 1899; also in Ernst Troeltsch, *Schriften zur Theologie und Religionsphilosophie (1888–1902)* (= KGA, vol. 1), Berlin: De Gruyter 2009, 732–752, here 739. This text also includes information on Rothe's writings. Troeltsch refers to a "most outlandish train of thought," but nonetheless describes this as the point of departure for "very profound insights," because Rothe's perspective means that the church is not simply derived from the ideas of early Christianity. This raises the question of whether we have to explain the institutions of Christianity chiefly in terms of the difficulties of realizing Christian ideals rather than in light of these ideals themselves. See Hans

Joas, *The Power of the Sacred: An Alternative to the Narrative of Disenchantment*, New York: Oxford University Press 2021, 104.

25. To quote the powerful engagement with Hegel and his effective history in theology by Karl Barth, *Die protestantische Theologie im 19. Jahrhundert. Ihre Vorgeschichte und ihre Geschichte*, Zürich: Evangelischer Verlag 1946, 343–378, here 343f.

26. Charles Taylor, *Hegel*, Cambridge: Cambridge University Press 1975, esp. 480–509; Michael Theunissen, *Hegels Lehre vom absoluten Geist als theologisch-politischer Traktat*, Berlin: De Gruyter 1970. A chapter of the present book is dedicated to Taylor; see Part II, ch. 5. I return to Theunissen briefly in the introduction to Part III and in more detail in Part III, ch. 5 on Wolfgang Huber.

27. Karl Löwith, *From Hegel to Nietzsche: The Revolution in Nineteenth-Century Thought*, New York: Columbia University Press 1991.

28. Reinhart Koselleck's "Foreword" to Karl Löwith, *Mein Leben in Deutschland vor und nach 1933. Ein Bericht*, Frankfurt am Main: Fischer 1989, ix–xv, here xiii.

29. Löwith, *From Hegel to Nietzsche*, 388.

30. Georg Lukács, *The Destruction of Reason* [1955], London: Merlin Press 1980; Herbert Schnädelbach, *German Philosophy 1831–1933*, Cambridge: Cambridge University Press 1983. Lukács's account is tendentious to the point of uselessness; Schnädelbach's fair and judicious. Symptomatically, both identify 1933 as the historical endpoint of their accounts.

31. Jürgen Habermas, *Auch eine Geschichte der Philosophie*, 2 vols., Berlin: Suhrkamp 2019; for a provisional assessment, see my review: Hans Joas, "Faith and Knowledge: Habermas' Alternative History of Philosophy," in: *Theory, Culture and Society* 37, no. 7/8 (2019), 47–52. On William James's attempts to build on Hume, which do not fit into Habermas's schema, see also the introduction to Part I in this volume.

32. The present book thus takes a different approach to Hegel than my book *The Power of the Sacred* does to Max Weber. In it, I aspired to provide the philologically most comprehensive and most precise interpretation of Weber's conception of disenchantment. I do not seek to do so with respect to Hegel here. Nor do I examine Nietzsche in this introduction. But see my earlier account in Hans Joas, *The Genesis of Values*, Chicago: University of Chicago Press 2000, 22–34, and the Conclusion of the present book.

33. For my examination of this narrative, see Hans Joas, *Faith as an Option: Possible Futures for Christianity*, Stanford: Stanford University Press 2014, 50–62 ("Modernization as a Culturally Protestant Metanarrative").

34. I base my remarks on the following edition: G. W. F. Hegel, *Vorlesungen über die Philosophie der Geschichte*, Frankfurt am Main: Suhrkamp 1970 (= *Werke*, vol. 12). For details on the constitution of the text, see 561–568. For an incomplete English translation, see Hegel, *The Philosophy of History*, Kitchener: Batoche 2001.

35. For a very good study of this, see Magnus Schlette, *Die Idee der Selbstverwirklichung. Zur Grammatik des modernen Individualismus*, Frankfurt am Main: Campus 2013.

36. G. W. F. Hegel, *Vorlesungen über die Geschichte der Philosophie III*, Frankfurt am Main: Suhrkamp 1970 (= *Werke*, vol. 20), 339.

37. Richard Kroner, *Die Selbstverwirklichung des Geistes. Prolegomena zur Kulturphilosophie*, Tübingen: Mohr Siebeck 1928 (cf. Schlette, *Die Idee der Selbstverwirklichung*, 12f.).
38. On the difficulties and opportunities associated with the term "spirit" within the present-day landscape of the humanities, see Hans Joas and Jörg Noller (eds.), *Geisteswissenschaft—was bleibt? Zwischen Theorie, Tradition und Transformation*, Freiburg: Karl Alber 2019.
39. See Löwith, *From Hegel to Nietzsche*, 333.
40. Hegel, *The Philosophy of History*, 337. It is also here that Hegel refers to the knowledge of God as the Triune God, which is the "Angel" ("pivot") around which world history revolves. Jaspers builds on this with his theory of the Axial Age, substituting "Achse" ("axis") for "Angel."
41. Ibid., 32.
42. Albrecht Koschorke, *Hegel und wir. Frankfurter Adorno-Vorlesungen 2013*, Berlin: Suhrkamp 2015, 24. Koschorke approaches Hegel's constructions with the tools of narrative theory, with highly instructive results.
43. G. W. F. Hegel, "Vorrede zu Hinrichs Religionsphilosophie" [1822] (a reference to Hinrichs's book *Die Religion im inneren Verhältnisse zur Wissenschaft*), in G. W. F. Hegel, *Berliner Schriften 1818–1831* (= *Werke*, vol. 11), 42–67, here 58. Cf. Walter Jaeschke (ed.), *Hegel-Handbuch. Leben—Werk—Wirkung*, Stuttgart: Metzler 2003, 279–282, with references to statements by Schleiermacher in correspondence. For a systematic comparison, see Jörg Dierken, "Hegel und Schleiermacher. Affinitäten und Abgrenzungen," in Thomas Hanke and Thomas M. Schmidt (eds.), *Der Frankfurter Hegel in seinem Kontext*, Frankfurt am Main: Klostermann 2015, 251–268; Jörg Dierken, "'Hauskrieg' bei Kants Erben. Schleiermacher und Hegel über Religion und Christentum," in Andreas Arndt and Tobias Rosefeldt (eds.), *Schleiermacher/Hegel*, Berlin: Duncker & Humblot 2020, 19–36.
44. A generous interpretation sees Hegel, in his late philosophy-of-religion lectures, on the way to a less concept-centered perspective. See Paul Ricœur, "Le statut de la 'Vorstellung' dans la philosophie hégélienne de la religion" [1985], in Paul Ricœur, *Lectures 3. Aux frontières de la philosophie*, Paris: Seuil 1992, 41–62.
45. For an incisive account, see Koschorke, *Hegel und wir*, 99 and 131.
46. Jürgen Habermas, *The Structural Transformation of the Public Sphere: An Inquiry into a Category of Bourgeois Society*, Cambridge: MIT Press 1991, 117–123; Honneth, *Freedom's Right*, 254.
47. Eric R. Wolf, *Europe and the People without History*, Berkeley: University of California Press, 1982, 5. Peter Frankopan describes the reading of these sentences as the moment (on his fourteenth birthday) that first kindled his passion for global history. See Peter Frankopan, *The Silk Roads: A New History of the World*, London: Bloomsbury 2015, xiii f.
48. Wolf, *Europe and the People without History*, 5.
49. Hegel, *The Philosophy of History*, 132–155. For a first-rate treatment, see Eun Jeung-Lee, *"Anti-Europa." Die Geschichte der Rezeption des Konfuzianismus und der konfuzianischen Gesellschaft seit der frühen Aufklärung*, Münster: LIT 2003, 274–333.

50. Jürgen Osterhammel, *Unfabling the East: The Enlightenment's Encounter with Asia*, Princeton: Princeton University Press 2018, 29. For a study that takes this approach a step further, see Peter van der Veer, *The Modern Spirit of Asia: The Spiritual and the Secular in China and India*, Princeton: Princeton University Press 2014.
51. Hegel, *The Philosophy of History*, 160.
52. See Leopold von Ranke, *Weltgeschichte*, vol. 9.2: *Über die Epochen der neueren Geschichte. Vorträge dem Könige Maximilian II. von Bayern gehalten*, Leipzig: Duncker & Humblot 1888, 5. On this text, see Ernst Troeltsch, *The Social Teaching of the Christian Churches*, London: Allen and Unwin 1931, 206f.; Joas, *The Power of the Sacred*, 107. It is interesting to note that Koschorke (*Hegel und wir*, 125) comes up with a similar critique without referring to Ranke or Troeltsch.
53. In many ways groundbreaking for the treatment of Schleiermacher as a philosopher are the edited volumes and studies by Andreas Arndt, including *Friedrich Schleiermacher als Philosoph*, Berlin: De Gruyter 2013. To my knowledge, however, his work is yet to find recognition in the writings of present-day Left Hegelians, whose "blind spot" I critiqued earlier.

I, 1

1. Wilfred Cantwell Smith, *The Meaning and End of Religion*, New York: Macmillan 1963, 46.
2. The technical term for this process is "predecessor selection." For the classic treatment, see Charles Camic, "Reputation and Predecessor Selection: Parsons and the Institutionalists," in: *American Sociological Review* 57 (1992), 421–445. This term seems to me more fitting than "influence."
3. See the introduction to the present volume.
4. See Part I, ch. 3 with reference to Rudolf Otto.
5. For an in-depth account, see Hans Joas, *The Power of the Sacred: An Alternative to the Narrative of Disenchantment*, New York: Oxford University Press 2021, 58–87.
6. For a highly informative treatment of the US-American case, which is particularly important in this respect, see Ann Taves, *Fits, Trances, and Visions: Experiencing Religion and Explaining Experience from Wesley to James*, Princeton: Princeton University Press 1999.
7. Ernst Troeltsch, "Religionsphilosophie und prinzipielle Theologie," in: *Theologischer Jahresbericht* 17 (1898), 531–603; also in Ernst Troeltsch, *Rezensionen und Kritiken (1894–1900)* (= KGA, vol. 2), Berlin: De Gruyter 2007, 366–484, here 390. For an account in which Troeltsch distances himself with similar clarity from Hegel and Schleiermacher as radically outdated, see Ernst Troeltsch, "Christentum und Religionsgeschichte" [1897], in Ernst Troeltsch, *Gesammelte Schriften*, vol. 2., Tübingen: Mohr Siebeck 1913, 328–363, here 330f.
8. See Hans Joas, "Pragmatism und Historicism," in Hans Joas and Daniel R. Huebner (eds.), *The Timeliness of George Herbert Mead*, Chicago: University of Chicago Press 2016, 62–81. For an excellent though highly abbreviated account, see Jürgen

Habermas, "Die Philosophie als Platzhalter und Interpret," in Jürgen Habermas, *Moralbewußtsein und kommunikatives Handeln*, Frankfurt am Main: Suhrkamp, 1983, 9–28, esp. 16–18.

9. Wilhelm Dilthey, "The Problem of Religion" [1911], in Wilhelm Dilthey, *Ethical and World-View Philosophy* (= Selected Works, vol. 6, ed. Rudolf Makkreel and Frithjof Rodi), Princeton: Princeton University Press 2019, 295–316.

10. This statement by Dilthey is quoted by his student and editor Hermann Nohl in his preface to Wilhelm Dilthey, *Die Jugendgeschichte Hegels* (= Gesammelte Schriften, vol. 4), Stuttgart: Teubner 1974, v–viii, here v.

11. Ibid., 3.

12. Wilhelm Dilthey, *Introduction to the Human Sciences* (= Selected Works, vol. 1), Princeton: Princeton University Press 1989, 171ff.

13. Ibid., 228. In Dilthey's work the term is used in the sense of "beautiful death," which is no longer possible subsequent to the Nazis' misuse of it.

14. For a pioneering study when it comes to interpreting Dilthey in the context of the turn in the theory of religion around 1900, see Matthias Jung, *Erfahrung und Religion. Grundzüge einer hermeneutisch-pragmatischen Religionsphilosophie*, Freiburg: Karl Alber 1999, 17–133. Jung draws attention (ibid., 30–33) to the fact that Honneth, like Dilthey, emphasizes action-theoretical motifs in the early Hegel "that were superseded in the later system by the metaphysical paradigm of the absolute" (ibid., 31). But, Jung underlines, in the wake of Habermas, what Honneth has in mind is Hegel's early Jena writings rather than his "youthful writings in theology." Honneth makes no mention at all of them, which is congruent with the "blind spot" lamented in the present book's introduction. Another text by Jung worth consulting is Matthias Jung, *Dilthey zur Einführung*, Hamburg: Junius 1996. Very much written in the polemical tone typical of the Stalinist repression of religion, meanwhile, is the account by Georg Lukács, *The Young Hegel: Studies in the Relations between Dialectics and Economics* [1948], London: Merlin Press 1975. Here, Dilthey's interpretation of these writings is described as "a legend created and fostered by the reactionary apologists of imperialism" (16). On the present-day state of knowledge regarding the textual basis and dating of the fragments of Hegel systematized by Nohl, see Walter Jaeschke, "Hegels Frankfurter Schriften. Zum jüngst erschienenen Band 2 der Gesammelten Werke Hegels," in Thomas Hanke and Thomas M. Schmidt (eds.), *Der Frankfurter Hegel in seinem Kontext*, Frankfurt am Main: Klostermann 2015, 31–50.

15. On articulation, see Joas, *The Power of the Sacred*, 244–245 and esp. 338, n. 23 on the history of the term's use in the work of Dilthey.

16. Wilhelm Dilthey, *The Formation of the Historical World in the Human Sciences* [1910] (= Selected Works, vol. 3, ed. Rudolf Makkreel and Frithjof Rodi), Princeton: Princeton University Press 2002, 295–316, 170.

17. Ibid., 172.

18. Dilthey, *Die Jugendgeschichte Hegels*, 173. See also Jung, *Erfahrung und Religion*, 28f.

19. On Adolf Deißmann, Wilhelm Bousset, and Ernst Troeltsch, see Joas, *The Power of the Sacred*, 99.

20. For a detailed account, see Manfred Wichelhaus, *Kirchengeschichtsschreibung und Soziologie im neunzehnten Jahrhundert und bei Ernst Troeltsch*, Heidelberg: Winter 1965.
21. Wilhelm Dilthey, "Rede zum 70. Geburtstag" [1903], in Wilhelm Dilthey, *Die geistige Welt. Einleitung in die Philosophie des Lebens* (= *Gesammelte Schriften*, vol. 5), Leipzig: Teubner 1924, 7–9, here 9.
22. See Hans Joas, *The Sacredness of the Person: A New Genealogy of Human Rights*, Washington, DC: Georgetown University Press 2013, 97–139; see 100 on Dilthey's address.
23. William James, *The Varieties of Religious Experience*, New York: Longmans, Green and Co. 1902. As I have discussed this book in depth elsewhere, I provide only a very brief account here. See Hans Joas, *The Genesis of Values*, Chicago: University of Chicago Press 2000, 35–53, and Joas, *The Power of the Sacred*, 31–57.
24. Dilthey, *The Problem of Religion*, 302 and 312.
25. William James, *Essays in Radical Empiricism*, New York: Longmans, Green and Co. 1912.
26. William James, "Does Consciousness Exist?" [1904], in William James, *Essays in Radical Empiricism*, 1–38, here 37.
27. In the introduction (fn. 31) I already pointed out that the reconstruction of the history of philosophy by Jürgen Habermas suffers, among other things, from the fact that he sees in Hume's work only a reductionist naturalism, while failing to discern that it also includes such an understanding of embodied subjectivity.
28. William James, "On Some Hegelisms," in William James, *The Will to Believe*, New York: Longmans, Green and Co. 1905, 263–298, here 275.
29. Ibid., 294.
30. Ibid., 298.
31. Dilthey, *Die Jugendgeschichte Hegels*, 138ff.
32. William James, *A Pluralistic Universe: Hibbert Lectures at Manchester College on the Present Situation in Philosophy* [1909], Cambridge: Harvard University Press 1977, esp. 43–62.
33. Ibid., 20.
34. Ibid., 43.
35. For an excellent discussion of James's critique of Hegel, see Robert Stern and Neil W. Williams, "James and Hegel: Looking for a Home," in Alexander Klein (ed.), *The Oxford Handbook of William James*, Oxford: Oxford University Press 2018 (Oxford Handbooks Online, DOI: 10.1093/oxfordhb/9780199395699.013.20, accessed March 30, 2020). The ground for this interpretation is laid by David Lamberth, *William James and the Metaphysics of Experience*, Cambridge: Cambridge University Press 1999, esp. 171–174. While James and Peirce maintained a critical distance from Hegel, John Dewey was initially a neo-Hegelian before embracing pragmatism. On Dewey's theory of religion, see the relevant chapter in this volume. Mead's intellectual journey also began with an intensive interest in Hegel, but he was soon more convinced by Schleiermacher, presumably under the influence of Dilthey, "whose instincts were in advance of his time," while Hegel's speculative conceptions "could

be clearly defined and deduced in detail, without going beyond the mental horizon of his own period." See George Herbert Mead, "Review: Gustav Class, *Untersuchungen zur Phänomenologie und Ontologie des menschlichen Geistes*" [1897], in: *American Journal of Theology* 1 (1897), 789–792, here 789.
36. James, *A Pluralistic Universe*, 54.
37. Ibid.
38. Ibid., 60.
39. On the seemingly paradoxical concept of a "post-metaphysical metaphysics," see my examination of the important contributions by Protestant theologian Hermann Deuser in Hans Joas, "Antwort auf Hermann Deuser," in Heinrich Wilhelm Schäfer (ed.), *Hans Joas in der Diskussion. Kreativität—Selbsttranszendenz—Gewalt*, Frankfurt am Main: Campus 2012, 49–55, here 54f.
40. It is at this point that we might build a bridge to phenomenology if this is not conceptualized as transcendent. In the present volume, I do not seriously tap the richness of studies in this tradition of importance to theory of religion; this richness is evident only in the chapters on Scheler and Ricœur. For an overview of this tradition, most of whose exponents are to be found in France, see Jean Greisch, *Le buisson ardent et les lumières de la raison*, vol. 2, Paris: Cerf 2002, 241–372. On one of its leading contemporary representatives, see also Michael Gabel and Hans Joas (eds.), *Von der Ursprünglichkeit der Gabe. Jean-Luc Marions Phänomenologie in der Diskussion*, Freiburg: Karl Alber 2007.
41. Ernst Troeltsch, "Zur Frage des religiösen Apriori" [1909], in Ernst Troeltsch, *Gesammelte Schriften*, vol. 2, Tübingen: Mohr Siebeck 1913, 754–768, here 754. For a nuanced treatment of this topic, see Helge Siemers, "'Mein Lehrer Dilthey'? Über den Einfluß Diltheys auf den jungen Troeltsch," in Horst Renz and Friedrich Wilhelm Graf (eds.), *Untersuchungen zur Biographie und Werkgeschichte* (= *Troeltsch-Studien*, vol. 1), Gütersloh: Gütersloher Verlagshaus 1982, 203–234.
42. Ernst Troeltsch, "Rezension: Wilhelm Dilthey, Gesammelte Schriften, Bd. 2" [1916], in Ernst Troeltsch, *Rezensionen und Kritiken (1915–1923)* (= KGA, vol. 13), Berlin: De Gruyter 2010, 91–94, here 94.
43. Ernst Troeltsch, *The Social Teaching of the Christian Churches* [1912], London: Allen and Unwin 1930, 44.
44. Friedrich Nietzsche, "Jenseits von Gut und Böse" [1886], in Friedrich Nietzsche, *Werke*, München: Hanser 1969, vol. III, 9–205, here 12.
45. I recommend the following up-to-date, brief overview: Friedemann Voigt, "Ernst Troeltsch. Leben und Werk," in Ernst Troeltsch, *Gesammelte Schriften*, vol. 1 [1912], reprinted Darmstadt: WBG 2016, v–xxxiv. Of my own studies on Troeltsch, see Hans Joas, "Selbsttranszendenz und Wertbindung. Ernst Troeltsch als Ausgangspunkt einer modernen Religionssoziologie," in Friedrich Wilhelm Graf and Friedemann Voigt (eds.), *Religion(en) deuten. Transformationen der Religionsforschung* (= *Troeltsch-Studien*, new series, vol. 2), Berlin: De Gruyter 2010, 51–64; on the *Social Teachings*, see Joas, *The Power of the Sacred*, 88–110; on the topic of historicism, see Joas, *The Sacredness of the Person*, 97–139.
46. George J. Yamin Jr., *In the Absence of Fantasia: Troeltsch's Relation to Hegel*, Gainesville: University Press of Florida 1993, 9, with reference to Frank Kermode.

47. For more on this aspect of the revision of Hegel, see Part II of the present volume.
48. Ernst Troeltsch, "Die Selbständigkeit der Religion" [1895/96], in: Ernst Troeltsch, *Schriften zur Theologie und Religionsphilosophie (1888-1902)* (= KGA, vol. 1), Berlin: De Gruyter 2009, 359-536, here 471.
49. Troeltsch, "Christentum und Religionsgeschichte," 359.
50. See Joas, *The Power of the Sacred*, 93ff., and Joas, *The Sacredness of the Person*, 102ff.
51. Ernst Troeltsch, *The Absoluteness of Christianity and the History of Religions* [1902/1912], Richmond: John Knox Press 1971, 102.
52. See the introduction to this book, 32-34.
53. Ernst Troeltsch, "Geschichte und Metaphysik" [1898], in Ernst Troeltsch, *Schriften zur Theologie und Religionsphilosophie (1888-1902)* (= KGA, vol. 1), 613-682, here 623f.
54. Adolf von Harnack, "Rede am Sarge Ernst Troeltschs" [1923], in Friedrich Wilhelm Graf (ed.), *Ernst Troeltsch in Nachrufen* (= Troeltsch-Studien, vol. 12), Gütersloh: Gütersloher Verlagshaus 2002, 266-271, here 268f.
55. Ernst Troeltsch, "Die Bedeutung des Protestantismus für die Entstehung der modernen Welt" [1911], in Ernst Troeltsch, *Schriften zur Bedeutung des Protestantismus für die moderne Welt (1906-1913)* (= KGA, vol. 8), 183-316, here 316.
56. Rudolf Otto, *The Idea of the Holy: An Inquiry into the Non-rational Factor in the Idea of the Divine and Its Relation to the Rational* [1917] (transl. by John W. Harvey), Harmondsworth: Penguin Books, 1959. When Otto's book on the sacred appeared, a similar turn had already played itself out in French sociology and ethnology, particularly in the work of Émile Durkheim and Marcel Mauss. See Joas, *The Power of the Sacred*, 58-87.
57. Göttingen 1899. On its reception history, see Kurt Nowak, *Schleiermacher*, Göttingen: Vandenhoeck & Ruprecht 2001, 97-113; Ulrich Barth, "Friedrich Schleiermacher," in Friedrich Wilhelm Graf (ed.), *Klassiker der Theologie*, vol. 2: *Von Richard Simon bis Karl Rahner*, Munich: C.H.Beck 2005, 58-88, here 68f. On Otto in particular, see Claus-Dieter Osthövener, "Ottos Auseinandersetzung mit Schleiermacher," in Jörg Lauster et al. (eds.), *Rudolf Otto. Theologie—Religionsphilosophie—Religionsgeschichte*, Berlin: De Gruyter 2014, 179-190.
58. Ernst Troeltsch, "Zur Religionsphilosophie. Aus Anlaß des Buches von Rudolf Otto 'Das Heilige' (1917)," in Ernst Troeltsch, *Rezensionen und Kritiken (1915-1923)* (= KGA, vol. 13), 412-425, here 414.
59. Otto, *The Idea of the Holy*, 90.
60. See Rudolf Otto, "Parallelen und Konvergenzen in der Religionsgeschichte," in Rudolf Otto, *Das Gefühl des Überweltlichen*, Munich: Beck 1932, 282-305, esp. 285. On Otto and the Axial Age, see Joas, *The Power of the Sacred*, 170, and Jan Assmann, *Achsenzeit. Eine Archäologie der Moderne*, Munich: C. H. Beck 2018, 135-140. On this topic, see also Part IV, esp. the chapter on Robert Bellah.
61. Otto, *The Idea of the Holy*, 109.
62. Ibid.
63. If we strip Otto's thinking (ibid., 107) down to its essentials. In this context it is also important to note that Otto was a leading critic of a reductionist naturalism, and here his guiding perspective was the human capacity for freedom. See Rudolf

Otto, *Naturalistische und religiöse Weltansicht*, Tübingen: Schwabenverlag 1929, esp. 212–278.
64. I do not discuss those authors within religious studies who represent the tradition of "phenomenology of religion" and whose work features multiple affinities with the themes tackled by the authors I deal with here, such as Gerardus van der Leeuw and Mircea Eliade.
65. See ch. 4 in this Part.
66. Max Scheler, *Formalism in Ethics and a Non-formal Ethics of Values: A New Attempt toward the Foundation of an Ethical Personalism*, Evanston: Northwestern University Press 1973; see my discussion in Hans Joas, *The Genesis of Values*, 84–102.
67. Max Scheler, "Mensch und Geschichte" [1926], in Max Scheler, *Philosophische Weltanschauung*, Munich: Lehnen 1954, 62–88, here 70.
68. Scheler, *Formalism in Ethics*, 370ff.
69. Ibid., 372. For a comparative analysis of Scheler and Hegel, see Evrim Kutlu, "Der Begriff der Person bei G. W. F. Hegel und Max Scheler," in: *Hegel-Jahrbuch* 1 (2014), 276–281.
70. Scheler, *Formalism in Ethics*, 503.
71. Max Scheler, *On the Eternal in Man*, Abingdon: Routledge 2017, 340.
72. Ibid., 355.
73. See Werner Stark, "Max Scheler," in Werner Stark, *Social Theory and Christian Thought*, London: Routledge 1958, 135–174, esp. 152–159. On Werner Stark, see Part IV, ch. 3.
74. Martin Heidegger, "Andenken an Max Scheler," in Paul Good (ed.), *Max Scheler im Gegenwartsgeschehen der Philosophie*, Bern: Francke 1975, 9. On the relationship between Heidegger and Scheler, see Michael Theunissen, "Wettersturm und Stille. Über die Weltdeutung Schelers und ihr Verhältnis zum Seinsdenken," ibid., 91–110.
75. Martin Heidegger, *Kant und das Problem der Metaphysik* [1929], Frankfurt am Main: Klostermann 1988.

I, 2

1. Ernst Troeltsch, "Die Selbständigkeit der Religion," first in: *Zeitschrift für Theologie und Kirche* 5 (1895), 361–436, and 6 (1896), 71–110 and 167–218, now in: Troeltsch, *Schriften zur Theologie und Religionsphilosophie (1888–1902)* (= *Kritische Gesamtausgabe*, vol. 1), Berlin: De Gruyter 2009, 364–535. All page numbers in this chapter refer first to the *Kritische Gesamtausgabe*, then (after the slash) to the original publication.
2. Ernst Troeltsch, *Briefe an Friedrich von Hügel 1901–1923*, ed. Karl-Ernst Apfelbacher and Peter Neuner, Paderborn: Bonifatius 1974, 60 (letter of March 10, 1903).
3. William James, *The Varieties of Religious Experience*, New York: Longman, Green, and Co. 1902, 12: "We are surely all familiar in a general way with this method of discrediting states of mind for which we have an antipathy. We all use it to some degree in criticizing persons whose states of mind we regard as overstrained. But when other people criticize our own more exalted soul-flights by calling them 'nothing but'

expressions of our organic disposition, we feel outraged and hurt, for we know that, whatever be our organism's peculiarities, our mental states have their substantive value as revelations of the living truth; and we wish that all this medical materialism could be made to hold its tongue."

4. Charles Taylor, *A Secular Age*, Cambridge: Harvard University Press 2007.
5. Ernst Troeltsch, *Der Historismus und seine Probleme* [1922], 2 vols. (= *Kritische Gesamtausgabe*, vol. 16.1 and 16.2), Berlin: De Gruyter 2008. See my detailed interpretation in Hans Joas, *The Sacredness of the Person: A New Genealogy of Human Rights*, Washington, DC: Georgetown University Press 2013, 97–139.
6. For more on an understanding of revelation permeated by the insights of historicism, see Part IV, ch. 2.
7. But see Hans Joas, *Faith as an Option: Possible Futures for Christianity*, Stanford: Stanford University Press 2014, 126–137.
8. I will have more to say about Troeltsch's views of Kant in Part III, ch. 2.
9. See Hans Joas, *The Genesis of Values*, Chicago: University of Chicago Press 2000, 58–86.
10. Ernst Troeltsch, review of William James, *The Varieties of Religious Experience*, in: *Deutsche Literaturzeitung* 25 (1904), col. 3021–3027, now in: Troeltsch, *Rezensionen und Kritiken (1901–1914)* (= *Kritische Gesamtausgabe*, vol. 4), Berlin: De Gruyter 2004, 364–371; *Psychologie und Erkenntnistheorie in der Religionswissenschaft*, Tübingen: Mohr 1905, now in: Troeltsch, *Schriften zur Religionswissenschaft und Ethik (1903–1912)* (= *Kritische Gesamtausgabe*, vol. 6), Berlin: De Gruyter 2014, 215–256; "Empiricism and Platonism in the Philosophy of Religion," in: *Harvard Theological Review* 5 (1912), 401–422.
11. On these interconnections, see Hans Joas, *G. H. Mead: A Contemporary Re-examination of His Thought*, Cambridge: MIT Press 1985.
12. William James, *Die religiöse Erfahrung in ihrer Mannigfaltigkeit. Materialien und Studien zu einer Psychologie und Pathologie des religiösen Lebens*, trans. by Georg Wobbermin, Leipzig: J. C. Hinrichs'sche Buchhandlung 1907.
13. On this convergence, see Hans Joas, "Pragmatism and Historicism: Mead's Philosophy of Temporality and the Logic of Historiography," in: Hans Joas and Daniel R. Huebner (eds.), *The Timeliness of George Herbert Mead*, Chicago: University of Chicago Press 2016, 62–81.
14. Ernst Troeltsch, "Geschichte und Metaphysik" (1898), in: Troeltsch, *Schriften zur Theologie und Religionsphilosophie (1888–1902)*, 617–682, here 659. This essay is a response to the critique by Julius Kaftan of Troeltsch's study "Die Selbständigkeit des Christentums" ("The Independence of Christianity"). See Kaftan, "Die Selbständigkeit des Christentums," in: *Zeitschrift für Theologie und Kirche* 6 (1896), 373–394.
15. Troeltsch, *Psychologie und Erkenntnistheorie*.
16. Troeltsch gets this concept from British philosopher Edward Caird, whose Gifford Lectures of 1891/1892 were published in the book *The Evolution of Religion*, Glasgow: James MacLehose and Sons 1894. In Troeltsch's text, see 452/76 and fn. 125 by the editor in the *Kritische Gesamtausgabe* version.
17. Troeltsch, "Geschichte und Metaphysik," 622.

18. Ernst Troeltsch, *The Social Teaching of the Christian Churches*, New York: Macmillan 1931. See my in-depth interpretation in Hans Joas, *The Power of the Sacred: An Alternative to the Narrative of Disenchantment*, New York: Oxford University Press 2021, 90–110.
19. Troeltsch, "Geschichte und Metaphysik," 630.
20. Ibid., 671.
21. Hans Joas, "Society, State and Religion. Their Relationship from the Perspective of the World Religions," in: Hans Joas and Klaus Wiegandt (eds.), *Secularization and the World Religions*, Liverpool: Liverpool University Press 2009, 1–22.
22. See my attempts to grasp the specificity of communication about values in Joas, *The Sacredness of the Person*, 174–182, and *The Genesis of Values*, 161–186.
23. Hilary Putnam, *The Collapse of the Fact/Value Dichotomy*, Cambridge: Harvard University Press 2002.
24. Karl Jaspers, *Philosophical Faith and Revelation*, New York: Harper 1967. On the problems involved in Jaspers's solution (and suggestions on further reading), see Joas, *The Power of the Sacred*, 163–168.
25. See Part IV, ch. 5 on Robert Bellah and the book's conclusion.

I, 3

1. Paul Tillich, "Die Kategorie des 'Heiligen' bei Rudolf Otto" [1923], in *Begegnungen. Paul Tillich über sich selbst und andere* (= *Gesammelte Werke*, vol. XII), Stuttgart: Evangelisches Verlagswerk 1971, 184–186, here 184.
2. Georg Pfleiderer, *Theologie als Wirklichkeitswissenschaft. Studien zum Religionsbegriff bei Georg Wobbermin, Rudolf Otto, Heinrich Scholz und Max Scheler*, Tübingen: Mohr Siebeck 1992, 104.
3. Ernst Troeltsch, "Zur Religionsphilosophie. Aus Anlaß des Buches von Rudolf Otto über 'Das Heilige,'" first appearance in: *Kant-Studien* 23 (1917), 65–76; also in Ernst Troeltsch, *Rezensionen und Kritiken (1915–1923)* (= KGA, vol. 13), Berlin: De Gruyter 2010, 412–425, here 413.
4. Rudolf Otto, *The Idea of the Holy: An Inquiry into the Non-rational Factor in the Idea of the Divine and Its Relation to the Rational* [1917] (transl. by John W. Harvey), Harmondsworth: Penguin Books, 1959. (All page numbers in the main text refer to this book.)
5. Hans Joas, "American Pragmatism and German Thought: A History of Misunderstandings," in Hans Joas, *Pragmatism and Social Theory*, Chicago: University of Chicago Press 1993, 94–121.
6. Troeltsch, "Zur Religionsphilosophie," 414.
7. Ernst Troeltsch, "Die Selbständigkeit der Religion" [1894–1895], in Ernst Troeltsch, *Schriften zur Theologie und Religionsphilosophie (1888-1902)* (= KGA, vol. 1), Berlin: De Gruyter 2009, 359–535, here 413. Cf. in this Part, ch. 2 on Troeltsch.
8. Robert Ranulph Marett, *The Threshold of Religion*, London: Methuen 1909.

9. Jan N. Bremmer, "'Religion,' 'Ritual' and the Opposition 'Sacred vs. Profane,'" in *Ansichten griechischer Rituale. Geburtstags-Symposium für Walter Burkert*, ed. Fritz Graf, Stuttgart: Vieweg & Teubner 1968, 9–32, here 26f.
10. Nathan Söderblom, "Das Heilige (Allgemeines und Ursprüngliches)" [1913], in Carsten Colpe (ed.), *Die Diskussion um das "Heilige,"* Darmstadt: WBG 1977, 76–116.
11. Henri Hubert and Marcel Mauss, *A General Theory of Magic* [1904], London: Routledge 1972; cf. Marett, *The Threshold of Religion*, xii.
12. See Camille Tarot, *Le symbolique et le sacré. Théories de la religion*, Paris: La Découverte 2008, 485, which builds on the work of Henri Hatzfeld, *Les Racines de la religion. Tradition, rituel, valeurs*, Paris: Esprit/Seuil 1993, 27f.
13. This discourse has already been reconstructed in interesting ways on a number of occasions. See, for example, Carsten Colpe, *Über das Heilige. Versuch, seiner Verkennung kritisch vorzubeugen*, Meisenheim: Anton Hain 1990; Arie L. Molendijk, "The Notion of the Sacred," in Arie L. Molendijk and Paul Post (eds.), *Holy Ground: Reinventing Ritual Space in Modern Western Culture*, Leuven: Peeters 2010, 55–89. See also Hans Joas, *The Power of the Sacred: An Alternative to the Narrative of Disenchantment*, New York: Oxford University Press 2021, 58–87.
14. Charles Taylor, *A Secular Age*, Cambridge: Harvard University Press 2007.
15. For a detailed treatment, see Hans Joas, *Faith as an Option: Possible Futures for Christianity*, Stanford: Stanford University Press 2014.
16. Henri Hubert, "Introduction à la traduction française," in Pierre Daniel Chantepie de la Saussaye, *Manuel d'histoire des religions*, Paris: Armand Colin 1904, v–xlviii, here xlvii.
17. See ch. 2 in this Part.
18. On the beginning of this history, see Guy G. Stroumsa, *A New Science: The Discovery of Religion in the Age of Reason*, Cambridge: Harvard University Press 2010.
19. On "common plasm," see Marett, *The Threshold of Religion*, xi; on "theoplasm," see Marett, *A Jerseyman at Oxford*, London: Oxford University Press 1941, 161.
20. Eun-Jeung Lee, *"Anti-Europa." Die Geschichte der Rezeption des Konfuzianismus und der konfuzianischen Gesellschaft seit der frühen Aufklärung*, Münster: LIT 2003, esp. 54–140.
21. William Edward Hanley Stanner, "Religion, Totemism and Symbolism," in Ronald Berndt and Catherine Berndt (eds.), *Aboriginal Man in Australia*, Sydney: Angus & Robertson 1965, 207–237.
22. Robert N. Bellah, *Religion in Human Evolution: From the Paleolithic to the Axial Age*, Cambridge: Harvard University Press 2011, 267 and passim. Here Bellah bases himself chiefly on the studies by Canadian cognitive psychologist Merlin Donald. Cf. by the latter esp. *Origins of the Modern Mind: Three Stages in the Evolution of Culture and Cognition*, Cambridge: Harvard University Press 1991. On Bellah, see Part IV, ch. 5.
23. Colpe, *Über das Heilige*, 46.
24. Hans Gerhard Kippenberg, *Die Entdeckung der Religionsgeschichte. Religionswissenschaft und Moderne*, Munich: C. H. Beck 1997, 249ff. and 192f. An alternative perspective, in which Otto is not viewed through Weber's eyes, can be found in the

outstanding monograph by Todd A. Gooch, *The Numinous and Modernity: An Interpretation of Rudolf Otto's Philosophy of Religion*, Berlin: De Gruyter 2000, 204f.
25. Leo Strauss, "Das Heilige" [1923], in Leo Strauss, *Philosophie und Gesetz—Frühe Schriften* (= *Gesammelte Schriften*, vol. 2), Stuttgart: Metzler 1997, 307–310, here 308.
26. Max Scheler, *On the Eternal in Man*, Abingdon: Routledge 2017, 145. On Scheler, see ch. 4 in this Part.
27. Émile Durkheim, *The Elementary Forms of Religious Life* (transl. by Carol Cosman), New York: Oxford University Press 2001, 36f.
28. See Scheler, *On the Eternal in Man*, 287. See also Hans Joas, *Do We Need Religion? On the Experience of Self-Transcendence*, Boulder: Paradigm 2008, 59f.
29. Söderblom, "Das Heilige (Allgemeines und Ursprüngliches)," 80.
30. See, for example, Stanner, "Religion, Totemism and Symbolism," 213, and Bellah, *Religion in Human Evolution*, 117–174.
31. Roy A. Rappaport, *Ritual and Religion in the Making of Humanity*, Cambridge: Cambridge University Press 1999, 380.
32. Marett, *The Threshold of Religion*, in the preface and introduction to the second edition of 1914.
33. William James, *The Varieties of Religious Experience*, New York: Longmans, Green and Co. 1902, 27.
34. Ibid., 28.
35. Ibid., 394.
36. Rudolf Otto, Review: "Nathan Söderblom, Gudstrons uppkomst," in: *Theologische Literaturzeitung* 40 (1915), col. 1–4, here col. 2.
37. On this critique, see Hans Joas, *The Genesis of Values*, Chicago: University of Chicago Press 2000, 67f. On Royce's alternative, see Royce, *The Problem of Christianity* [1913], Washington, DC: Catholic University of America Press 2001, esp. 273ff. For a commentary on this, see Joas, *The Power of the Sacred*, 44–57. Similar ideas are put forward by Hermann Deuser, "'A Feeling of Objective Presence'—Rudolf Ottos 'Das Heilige' und William James' Pragmatismus im Vergleich," in Jörg Lauster et al. (eds.), *Rudolf Otto. Theologie—Religionsphilosophie—Religionsgeschichte*, Berlin: De Gruyter 2014, 319–333.
38. Matthias Jung, "Religiöse Erfahrung. Genese und Kritik eines religionshistorischen Grundbegriffs," in Matthias Jung et al. (eds.), *Religionsphilosophie. Historische Positionen und systematische Reflexionen*, Würzburg: Echter 2000, 135–150, here 145.
39. See Joas, *The Genesis of Values*, 134ff. See also Matthias Jung, *Der bewußte Ausdruck. Anthropologie der Artikulation*, Berlin: De Gruyter 2009.
40. Troeltsch, "Zur Religionsphilosophie," 421.
41. Deuser makes the same point. See Deuser, "A Feeling of Objective Presence."
42. In Joas, *The Genesis of Values* and *Do We Need Religion?*
43. Jung, "Religiöse Erfahrung," 146.
44. Antoine de Saint-Exupéry, *Letter to a Hostage* [1941], London: Pushkin Press 1999, Part II.
45. Paul Tillich, *Systematische Theologie*, vol. 1, Stuttgart: Evangelisches Verlagswerk 1956, 251.

46. Because Charles Taylor makes the concept of transcendence rather than that of sacredness the starting point of his account of secularization, he struggles to adequately grasp phenomena of sacredness in contemporary culture. This, at least, is the argument made by Peter Gordon and me. See Part II, ch. 5, as well as Peter E. Gordon, "The Place of the Sacred in the Absence of God: Charles Taylor's 'A Secular Age,'" in: *Journal of the History of Ideas* 69 (2008), 647–673.
47. On this point, see the contributions in Robert N. Bellah and Hans Joas (eds.), *The Axial Age and Its Consequences*, Cambridge: Harvard University Press 2012; see also Joas, *The Power of the Sacred*.
48. This relevance is also evident in recent multiauthored volumes on Otto: Lauster et al. (eds.), *Rudolf Otto*; Wolfgang Gantke and Vladimir Serikov (eds.), *100 Jahre "Das Heilige." Beiträge zu Rudolf Ottos Grundlagenwerk*, Frankfurt am Main: Peter Lang 2017. For advice on how to improve an earlier version of this chapter, I owe a debt of gratitude to Matthias Jung. Conversations with Hermann Deuser also helped me tighten up my argument.

I, 4

1. Max Scheler, *On the Eternal in Man*, Abingdon: Routledge 2017, 29. (All page numbers in the main text refer to this book.)
2. Nicolai Hartmann, "Max Scheler (Nachruf)," in: *Kant-Studien* 33 (1928), ix–xvi, here xiv.
3. Heinrich Fries, *Die katholische Religionsphilosophie der Gegenwart*, Heidelberg: Kerle 1949.
4. Karl Mannheim, "Zur Problematik der Soziologie in Deutschland" [1929], in Karl Mannheim, *Wissenssoziologie*, Neuwied: Luchterhand 1964, 614–624, here 614.
5. Though the degree to which Scheler abandoned his Catholic views is subject to contestation. In his interpretation of Scheler, Hans Urs von Balthasar sees his "tragic and titanic turn" away from Christianity as already inherent in his understanding of Christianity during his Catholic phase. See Hans Urs von Balthasar, *Apokalypse der deutschen Seele. Studien zu einer Lehre von letzten Haltungen*, vol. 3, Salzburg: Pustet 1939, esp. 146ff. A similar analysis was put forward by Dietrich von Hildebrand, "Max Schelers Stellung zur katholischen Gedankenwelt," in Dietrich von Hildebrand, *Zeitliches im Lichte des Ewigen. Gesammelte Abhandlungen und Vorträge*, Regensburg: Josef Habbel 1932, 341–364. Conversely, in an interesting essay, Guido Cusinato argues that "Scheler's shift away from Christian theism can by no means be described as a complete and definitive break." See Guido Cusinato, "Werdender Gott und Wiedergeburt der Person bei Max Scheler," in Ralf Becker and Ernst Wolfgang Orth (eds.), *Religion und Metaphysik als Dimensionen der Kultur*, Würzburg: Königshausen & Neumann 2011, 123–134, here 123. For an analysis that discerns an expansive movement toward a "universal vision," see also Werner Stark, "Max Scheler," in Werner Stark, *Social Theory and Christian Thought: A Study of Some*

Points of Contact, London: Routledge 1958, 135–174, here 152f. (On Stark, see Part IV, ch. 3.) An instructive overview of Protestant and Catholic criticisms of Scheler is provided by Gerald Hartung, "Autonomiewahnsinn? Der Preis einer Säkularisierung des Menschenbildes in der philosophischen Anthropologie Max Schelers," in Christel Gärtner, Detlef Pollack, and Monika Wohlrab-Sahr (eds.), *Atheismus und religiöse Indifferenz*, Opladen: VS 2003, 75–92.

6. This is the argument I made in Hans Joas, *The Genesis of Values*, Chicago: University of Chicago Press 2000, 84–102.
7. Rudolf Otto, *The Idea of the Holy: An Inquiry into the Non-rational Factor in the Idea of the Divine and Its Relation to the Rational* [1917] (transl. by John W. Harvey), Harmondsworth: Penguin Books, 1959, 48. On Otto, see ch. 3 in this Part.
8. See Joas, *The Genesis of Values*, 49f.
9. William James, *The Varieties of Religious Experience*, New York: Longmans, Green and Co. 1902, 405.
10. On the question of whether this methodological revolution can be traced back to Schleiermacher or James, see Hans Joas, "Schleiermacher and the Turn to Experience in the Study of Religion," in Dietrich Korsch and Amber L. Griffioen (eds.), *Interpreting Religion: The Significance of Friedrich Schleiermacher's "Reden über die Religion" for Religious Studies and Theology*, Tübingen: Mohr Siebeck 2011, 147–162.
11. Again, von Balthasar already had a clear sense of this: Balthasar, *Apokalypse*, 128f.
12. Alfred Döblin, "Theater in Berlin (November 21, 1921)," in Alfred Döblin, *Ein Kerl muß eine Meinung haben. Berichte und Kritiken 1921–1924*, Olten: Walter 1976, 15–17, here 17. On Döblin, see Part II, ch. 3.
13. I forgo detailed exploration of Scheler's critique of Schleiermacher and efforts to distance himself from Kant. But it is worth mentioning his misleading rendering of the basic ideas of Ernst Troeltsch (144), effectively corrected by Scheler's assertion in the foreword to the second 1922 edition of the German original of his book that Troeltsch had undergone a major shift in his thinking (16).
14. For a more detailed investigation, see Christoph Seibert, "Religion aus eigenem Recht. Zur Methodologie der Religionsphilosophie bei Max Scheler und William James," in: *Neue Zeitschrift für systematische Theologie* 56, no. 1 (2014), 64–88.
15. Hans Joas, "American Pragmatism and German Thought: A History of Misunderstandings," in Hans Joas, *Pragmatism and Social Theory*, Chicago: University of Chicago Press 1993, 94–121.
16. William James, *The Meaning of Truth*, New York: Longmans, Green and Co. 1911, 136.
17. See David Lamberth, *William James and the Metaphysics of Experience*, Cambridge: Cambridge University Press 1999, 106ff.
18. Ernst Troeltsch, *The Social Teaching of the Christian Churches*; London: Allen & Unwin 1931.
19. Hans Joas, *The Sacredness of the Person: A New Genealogy of Human Rights*, Washington, DC: Georgetown University Press, 85–94.
20. For a detailed treatment not of Scheler but of the problems of differentiation theory from a theory-of-religion perspective, see Hans Joas, *The Power of the Sacred: An Alternative to the Narrative of Disenchantment*, New York: Oxford University Press

2021, 195–233; for a more general account of this theory, see Hans Joas, *The Creativity of Action*, Chicago: University of Chicago Press 1996, 209–244.

21. For an interesting take on this question, see Todd A. Gooch, "The Epistemic Status of Value-Cognition in Max Scheler's Philosophy of Religion," in: *Journal for Cultural and Religious Theory* 3, no. 1 (2001), <https://jcrt.org/archives/03.1/gooch.shtml>, accessed August 30, 2023. See also Georg Pfleiderer, *Theologie als Wirklichkeitswissenschaft. Studien zum Religionsbegriff bei Georg Wobbermin, Rudolf Otto, Heinrich Scholz und Max Scheler*, Tübingen: Mohr Siebeck 1992, 193–224. But I would particularly like to highlight the largely forgotten, in-depth article on this topic published by Hanna Hafkesbrink shortly before her forced emigration to the United States: Hanna Hafkesbrink, "Das Problem des religiösen Gegenstandes bei Max Scheler," in: *Zeitschrift für systematische Theologie* 8 (1931), 145–180 and 251–292. Particularly laudable is the contrast she draws between the position occupied by Scheler in his ethics and the one he expounds in his philosophy of religion (263ff.). See also Hanna Hafkesbrink, "The Meaning of Objectivism and Realism in Max Scheler's Philosophy of Religion: A Contribution to the Understanding of Max Scheler's Catholic Period," in: *Philosophy and Phenomenological Research* 2 (1942), 292–309.

22. Robert N. Bellah and Hans Joas (eds.), *The Axial Age and Its Consequences*, Cambridge: Harvard University Press, 2012.

23. Max Scheler, "Vorwort," in Otto Gründler, *Elemente zu einer Religionsphilosophie auf phänomenologischer Grundlage*, Munich: Kösel 1922, i–ii, here ii.

24. Max Scheler, *Problems of a Sociology of Knowledge* (transl. by Manfred S. Frings), London: Routledge, 1980, 82ff.

25. See Fries, *Die katholische Religionsphilosophie der Gegenwart*, 131.

26. In this sense, the present chapter is an elaboration of the few sentences on Scheler in my book *Do We Need Religion?* (Boulder: Paradigm 2008, 59f.). Here I allude to these older remarks.

II, 1

1. Martin Laube, "Die Dialektik der Freiheit. Systematisch-theologische Perspektiven," in Martin Laube (ed.), *Freiheit*, Tübingen: Mohr Siebeck 2014, 119–191, here esp. 124–137.
2. G. W. F. Hegel, *The Philosophy of History*, Kitchener: Batoche 2001, 469.
3. Ibid.
4. Ibid., 435.
5. I found the following book highly informative: Orlando Patterson, *Freedom*, vol. 1: *Freedom in the Making of Western Culture*, New York: Basic Books 1991. For further development of this argument, see Orlando Patterson, "Freedom, Slavery, and the Modern Construction of Rights," in Hans Joas and Klaus Wiegandt (eds.), *The Cultural Values of Europe*, Liverpool: Liverpool University Press 2008, 115–151. See also Hans Joas, "Der Wert der Freiheit und die Erfahrung der Unfreiheit," in

Hans-Richard Reuter et al. (eds.), *Freiheit verantworten. Festschrift für Wolfgang Huber zum 60. Geburtstag*, Gütersloh: Gütersloher Verlagshaus 2002, 446–455. For an informative account of the state of research on the New Testament, see Friedrich Wilhelm Horn, "'Zur Freiheit hat uns Christus befreit.' Neutestamentliche Perspektiven," in Laube (ed.), *Freiheit*, 39–58.
6. Patterson, *Freedom*, vol. 1, 316–344.
7. Karl Marx, "A Contribution to the Critique: Introduction" [1843–1844], in Karl Marx, *Critique of Hegel's "Philosophy of Right,"* Cambridge: Cambridge University Press 1970, 129–142, here 138.
8. Ibid.
9. See Martin Laube, "Tendenzen und Motive im Verständnis der Freiheit," in Laube (ed.), *Freiheit*, 255–267, but also Hans Joas, *The Sacredness of the Person: A New Genealogy of Human Rights*, Washington, DC: Georgetown University Press 2013, 140–158, esp. 143. See also Part III of the present book.
10. Here I borrow from Martin Laube's interpretation of the theology of Trutz Rendtorff in "Die Dialektik der Freiheit," 131 and 133.
11. Laube thus counterposes the "Hegelian" Rendtorff to the "Kantian" Wolfgang Huber (ibid., 175). On Huber's "theology of liberation," see Part III, ch. 5.
12. Laube, "Die Dialektik der Freiheit," 134.
13. See the inklings of this in the "bibliographical essay" appearing in the excellent book by David L. Chappell, *A Stone of Hope: Prophetic Religion and the Death of Jim Crow*, Chapel Hill: University of North Carolina Press 2004, 297–301.
14. H. Richard Niebuhr, *The Kingdom of God in America*, New York: Harper & Row 1948, 194. Niebuhr's famous searing description of a "domesticated" Christianity appears shortly before (193): "A God without wrath brought men without sin into a kingdom without judgment through the ministrations of a Christ without a cross." For a detailed treatment of Niebuhr, see Part IV, ch. 2.
15. Cf. the epigraph of this book from Alexis de Tocqueville, *Democracy in America*, New York: Norton 2007, 392.
16. Ernst-Wolfgang Böckenförde, "The Rise of the State as a Process of Secularization" [1967], in Ernst-Wolfgang Böckenförde, *Religion, Law, and Democracy*, ed. M. Künkler and T. Stein, Oxford: Oxford University Press 2020, 152–167, here 167.
17. Ibid., 167.
18. Heribert Prantl, "Dem Einstein des Staatsrechts. Dem Juristen Ernst-Wolfgang Böckenförde zum 80. Geburtstag," *Süddeutsche Zeitung*, September 18, 2010, 5.
19. Böckenförde, "The Rise of the State as a Process of Secularization," 167, fn. 50, with reference to § 552 in Hegel's *Enzyklopädie der philosophischen Wissenschaften* [1830].
20. John Dewey, *A Common Faith*, New Haven: Yale University Press 1934.
21. On Taylor, see ch. 5 in this Part, and also my review essay on his book *Sources of the Self*: Hans Joas, "Ein Pragmatist wider Willen?," in: *Deutsche Zeitschrift für Philosophie* 44 (1996), 661–670.
22. Alfred Döblin, "Jenseits von Gott" [1919], in Alfred Döblin, *Kleine Schriften I*, Olten: Walter 1985, 246–261. See also Hans Joas, "Auseinandersetzung mit dem Christentum," in Sabina Becker (ed.), *Döblin-Handbuch. Leben—Werk—Wirkung*, Stuttgart: Metzler 2016, 356–366, here 356–358.

23. Döblin, "Jenseits von Gott," 246.
24. Ibid., 251f.
25. Ibid., 247.
26. The most profound interpretation of Döblin's late oeuvre from this perspective can be found in Helmuth Kiesel, *Literarische Trauerarbeit. Das Exil- und Spätwerk Alfred Döblins*, Tübingen: Max Niemeyer 1986. See also Hans Joas, "Ein Christ durch Krieg und Revolution. Alfred Döblins Erzählwerk 'November 1918,'" in: *Sinn und Form* 67 (2015), 784–799.
27. Alfred Döblin, "Brief an Wilhelm Hausenstein vom 31.1.1947," in Alfred Döblin, *Briefe*, Olten: Walter 1970, 364.
28. Alfred Döblin, *Der unsterbliche Mensch / Der Kampf mit dem Engel*, Frankfurt am Main: Fischer 2016, 275.
29. Reinhart Koselleck, *Critique and Crisis: Enlightenment and the Pathogenesis of Modern Society* [1959], Cambridge: MIT Press 1988.
30. See also p. 367 above, fn. 31.
31. Charles Taylor, "What's Wrong with Negative Liberty?," in Charles Taylor, *Philosophy and the Human Sciences: Philosophical Papers 2*, Cambridge: Cambridge University Press 1985, 211–229; Charles Taylor, *Negative Freiheit? Zur Kritik des neuzeitlichen Individualismus. Mit einem Nachwort von Axel Honneth*, Frankfurt am Main: Suhrkamp 1988.
32. Charles Taylor, *Hegel*, Cambridge: Cambridge University Press 1975, 539.
33. Ibid., 538.
34. I have given my views on the stages of this process over several decades. In addition to the text mentioned in fn. 21 of the present chapter and the chapter on Taylor in this book, see esp. Hans Joas, *The Genesis of Values*, Chicago: University of Chicago Press 2000, 124–144; Hans Joas, "A Catholic Modernity? Faith and Knowledge in the Work of Charles Taylor," in Hans Joas, *Do We Need Religion? On the Experience of Self-Transcendence*, Boulder: Paradigm 2008, 81–90.

II, 2

1. John Dewey, *A Common Faith*, New Haven: Yale University Press 1934. (All page numbers in the main text refer to this book.)
2. Reinhold Niebuhr, "A Footnote on Religion," in: *The Nation* 139 (September 26, 1934), 358–359.
3. The best reconstruction of this debate in relation to Dewey can be found in Steven Rockefeller, *John Dewey, Religious Faith and Democratic Humanism*, New York: Columbia University Press 1991, esp. 445–490, here 466.
4. The thesis that Dewey's theory of religion is the pinnacle of his thought, even more than his theory of art, was first and most consistently advanced by Robert Roth, S.J., *John Dewey and Self-Realization*, Englewood Cliffs: Prentice Hall 1962, esp. 100ff., and Robert Roth, S.J., *American Religious Philosophy*, New York: Harcourt, Brace 1967,

85ff. Similarly positive evaluations can be found in Victor Kestenbaum, *The Grace and the Severity of the Ideal: John Dewey and the Transcendent*, Chicago: University of Chicago Press 2002; Sami Pihlström, "Dewey and Pragmatic Religious Naturalism," in Molly Cochran (ed.), *The Cambridge Companion to Dewey*, Cambridge: Cambridge University Press 2010, 211–241. The most important systematic attempt to build on Dewey is in my opinion to be found in the books of Matthias Jung: Matthias Jung, *Gewöhnliche Erfahrung*, Tübingen: Mohr Siebeck 2014; Matthias Jung, *Symbolische Verkörperung. Die Lebendigkeit des Sinns*, Tübingen: Mohr Siebeck 2017.

5. John Dewey, *Art as Experience* [1934], New York: Putnam's 1980. On my interpretation, see Hans Joas, *The Creativity of Action*, Chicago: University of Chicago Press 1996, 138–144.

6. Even more important than James's book for this development, especially in theological circles, was Rudolf Otto's *The Idea of the Holy: An Inquiry into the Non-rational Factor in the Idea of the Divine and Its Relation to the Rational* [1917] (transl. by John W. Harvey), Harmondsworth: Penguin Books, 1959.

7. See Hans Joas, *The Genesis of Values*, Chicago: University of Chicago Press 2000, ch. 4, 61ff. It is worth mentioning that, as early as c. 1915, Dewey engaged in a study of Durkheim's theory of religion (in the original French). His literary remains contain a handwritten excerpt from this work (as communicated to me in a letter dated April 20, 1993, from the archive of Southern Illinois University, Carbondale, IL).

8. Because of this, pragmatism was frequently understood as a philosophy of adaptation, and not as a philosophy of situated creativity. Admittedly, we might ask whether in his early writings Dewey himself always clearly adhered to this distinction. Our assessment of the differences between Dewey and Scheler depends on the answer to this question. See Kenneth Stikkers, "Technologies of the World, Technologies of the Self: A Schelerian Critique of Dewey and Hickman," in: *Journal of Speculative Philosophy* 10 (1996), 62–73.

9. The details of the relationship between the aesthetic and religious dimensions of experience are controversial. Robert Roth (*John Dewey and Self-Realization*) has been particularly consistent in his emphasis not only on the continuity but also the differences between the two. In addition to his books and the monograph by Steven Rockefeller cited earlier, I recommend the following works which deal with the question treated below: Richard Bernstein, *John Dewey*, New York: Washington Square Press 1967; William Shea, "John Dewey: Aesthetic and Religious Experiences," in William Shea, *The Naturalists and the Supernatural: Studies in Horizon and an American Philosophy of Religion*, Macon: Mercer University Press 1984, 117–141; John Herman Randall Jr., "The Religion of Shared Experience," in Horace M. Kallen (ed.), *The Philosopher of the Common Man: Essays in Honor of John Dewey to Celebrate His Eightieth Birthday*, New York: Greenwood Press 1940, 106–145; John Blewett, S.J., "Democracy as Religion: Unity in Human Relations," in John Blewett, S.J. (ed.), *John Dewey: His Thought and Influence*, New York: Fordham University Press 1966, 33–58; Horace L. Friess, "Dewey's Philosophy of Religion," in Jo Ann Boydston (ed.), *Guide to the Works of John Dewey*, Carbondale: Southern Illinois University Press 1970, 200–217; Edward Schaub, "Dewey's Interpretation of Religion," in Paul Arthur Schilpp (ed.), *The Philosophy of John Dewey*, New York: Open Court 1939, 393–416;

John K. Roth, "William James, John Dewey and the 'Death-of-God,'" in: *Religious Studies* 7 (1971), 53–61.
10. See Joas, *The Genesis of Values*, ch. 3, 51ff., on James; and ch. 5, 79ff., on Simmel.
11. Thus argues James Gouinlock, *Dewey's Philosophy of Value*, New York: Humanities Press 1972, 145.
12. In Dewey's neo-Hegelian phase, the concept of self-realization was central to his ethical thought. See John Dewey, "Self-Realization as the Moral Ideal" [1893], in John Dewey, *Early Works*, vol. 4, Carbondale: Southern Illinois University Press 1971, 42–53; Robert Roth (*John Dewey and Self-Realization*) plausibly makes the idea of self-realization a leitmotif of his interpretation of Dewey's entire intellectual development.
13. Dewey's language, probably influenced by George Santayana, resembles that of Cornelius Castoriadis in his important work *The Imaginary Institution of Society*, Cambridge: MIT Press 1987.
14. On Santayana's theory of religion, see the pathbreaking study by Henry Levinson, *Santayana, Pragmatism, and the Spiritual Life*, Chapel Hill: University of North Carolina Press 1992.
15. John Dewey, *Human Nature and Conduct: An Introduction to Social Psychology*, New York: Henry Holt 1922, 263 (also in John Dewey, *Middle Works*, vol. 14, Carbondale: Southern Illinois University Press 1988, here 180).
16. When I use the terms "ideals" and "values" interchangeably here, I am following Dewey, who seems to make no terminological distinction between them.
17. As Schleiermacher famously defined religion. See Dewey, *A Common Faith*, esp. 25.
18. Steven Rockefeller stresses that Dewey was able to erase the traces of a purely instrumental orientation to nature in his early works through his long stay in Asia and his study of Chinese philosophy, especially Daoism. His philosophy from this point onward could gain new currency under the influence of new ecological attitudes. See Rockefeller, *John Dewey: Religious Faith and Democratic Humanism*, 499ff.
19. John Dewey, *Experience and Nature* [1925], London: Open Court 1958, 132–161. But also important to his complex perspective is the chapter "Existence, Ideas and Consciousness," 298–353.
20. Ibid., 132.
21. See John Dewey, *Psychology*, in John Dewey, *Early Works*, vol. 2, Carbondale: Southern Illinois University Press 1967, esp. 282–295; on the significance of this motif to our context, see the chapters on Nietzsche and Scheler in Joas, *The Genesis of Values*.
22. See Joas, *The Genesis of Values*, chapter 3; I do not see such points of departure in Durkheim. It thus remains a mystery to me why Jürgen Habermas in his *Theory of Communicative Action* should describe Durkheim, together with Mead, as the inaugurator of the paradigm shift from "purposive activity to communicative action."
23. This was already recognized by Gouinlock, *John Dewey's Philosophy of Value*, 93, n. 64. He also criticized the fact that Dewey made use of George Herbert Mead's findings without properly acknowledging his contribution.
24. See, for example, Dewey, *Experience and Nature*, 144, 159, and passim.
25. Ibid., 144f., 157, and 159f.

26. I am unable to discuss the relation of this aspect of Dewey's thinking to Jürgen Habermas's and Karl-Otto Apel's discourse ethics in more detail at this point but I do so in Joas, *The Genesis of Values*, ch. 10. On the semantics of the concepts of "community" and "democracy" in Dewey and the American tradition of thought in general, as well as the frequent misunderstandings in Germany, see Hans Joas, "Communitarianism: A German Perspective," Indiana University Institute for Advanced Study, Distinguished Lecture Series, vol. 6, Bloomington, IN, 1993.

27. John Dewey, "Experience, Knowledge, and Value: A Rejoinder," in Schilpp (ed.), *The Philosophy of John Dewey*, 517–608, here 597 (also in John Dewey, *Later Works*, vol. 14, 3–90, here 79).

28. John Dewey, "Christianity and Democracy" [1893], in John Dewey, *Early Works*, vol. 4, 3–10.

29. For a biographical portrait and comprehensive interpretation, see Rockefeller, *John Dewey: Religious Faith and Democratic Humanism*, and Robert Westbrook, *John Dewey and American Democracy*, Ithaca: Cornell University Press 1991. Rockefeller must be given credit for including Dewey's lyric poetry in a study of his religious development. These are important documents attesting to Dewey's search during a time in which his publications are silent about the subject of religion. See esp. Rockefeller, *John Dewey: Religious Faith and Democratic Humanism*, 312ff.

30. See, for example, John Dewey, "Religion and Our Schools," in: *Hibbert Journal* 6 (1908), 796–809 (also in John Dewey, *Middle Works*, vol. 4, 165–177).

31. See Rockefeller, *John Dewey: Religious Faith and Democratic Humanism*, 446.

32. Dewey's obviously idiosyncratic attempt to redefine the word "God" initiated extensive misunderstandings and debates in the 1930s. See also esp. Rockefeller, *John Dewey: Religious Faith and Democratic Humanism*, esp. 512ff.

33. Max Weber, *Gesammelte Aufsätze zur Religionssoziologie*, 3 vols. Tübingen: Mohr Siebeck 1920.

34. Willard Arnett, "Critique of Dewey's Anticlerical Religious Philosophy," in: *Journal of Religion* 34 (1954), 256–266. Also, we should not neglect to mention that Dewey's understanding of Catholicism was largely uninformed and stereotypical. For a refutation, see Blewett, "Democracy as Religion: Unity in Human Relations," 52.

35. Robert N. Bellah et al., *Habits of the Heart: Individualism and Commitment in American Life*, Berkeley: University of California Press 1985, 221. For more on this, see Part IV, ch. 5.

36. According to George Santayana, "Reason in Religion," in George Santayana, *Works*, vol. 4, New York: Charles Scribner's Sons 1936, 3–206, here 4: "The attempt to speak without speaking any particular language is not more hopeless than the attempt to have a religion that shall be no religion in particular." Of course, this in no way rules out "multilingualism," both in the literal sense and in the field of religion.

37. For a critique of this tendency in the United States, see Will Herberg, *Protestant—Catholic—Jew: An Essay in American Religious Sociology*, New York: Anchor 1955, 100ff. I go into more detail about Herberg in the introductory remarks to Part IV of the present book.

38. It might be argued that, in his theory of religion, Dewey thereby contravenes postulates that he himself put forward in his ethics and political philosophy.

39. Charles Taylor, "Reply and Re-articulation," in James Tully (ed.), *Philosophy in an Age of Pluralism: The Philosophy of Charles Taylor in Question*, Cambridge: Cambridge University Press 1994, 213–257, here 229. Taylor's answer to Michael Morgan's essay in this volume ("Religion, History and Moral Discourse," 49–66) and Morgan's contribution itself are generally of the greatest interest to the questions I have discussed here with reference to John Dewey.

40. For a similar line of thought, see Kestenbaum, *The Grace and the Severity of the Ideal*. He convincingly demonstrates that traces of what he calls the "transcendent"—I would refer instead to experiences of self-transcendence—can be identified throughout Dewey's work from the early idealist phase onward. See also Victor Kestenbaum, "Ontological Faith in Dewey's Religious Idealism," in Hermann Deuser et al. (eds.), *The Varieties of Transcendence: Pragmatism and the Theory of Religion*, New York: Fordham University Press 2016, 73–90. A judicious and well-informed monograph has been published by Annette Pitschmann, *Religiosität als Qualität des Säkularen. Die Religionstheorie John Deweys*, Tübingen: Mohr Siebeck 2017. However, in my opinion, even in these extremely insightful interpretations of Dewey, the shortcomings of his theory of religion that I have pointed up here remain unmistakable. Particularly important to a critical assessment of Dewey is Jung, *Symbolische Verkörperung*, 144–163. My thanks to Victor Kestenbaum (Boston) for valuable pointers that helped me improve an older version of this chapter on John Dewey.

II, 3

1. I have tried to avoid referring to nonbelievers or unbelievers in this book, knowing that those with secular worldviews and value systems can easily perceive these terms as insulting and in awareness of the fact that they fail to do justice to the many intermediate forms of searching, doubting, and vacillating. I make an exception only in those cases in which a sharply polarized perspective seems to me to reflect a given author's intentions, and thus chiefly in the present chapter.
2. See the monumental account by Charles Taylor, *A Secular Age*, Cambridge: Harvard University Press 2007; on this book, see ch. 5 in this Part.
3. On the obsolescence of these two assumptions and the new potential for dialogue on faith, see Hans Joas, *Faith as an Option: Possible Futures for Christianity*, Stanford: Stanford University Press 2014.
4. Easily accessible in Alfred Döblin, *Der unsterbliche Mensch / Der Kampf mit dem Engel*, Frankfurt am Main: Fischer 2016. (All page references in the present text refer to this edition.)
5. Alfred Döblin, *Journey to Poland* [1925], New York: Paragon House 1991.
6. *Alfred Döblin Presents the Living Thoughts of Confucius*, Toronto: Longmans, Green and Co. 1940. On Döblin's biography, see Wilfried F. Schoeller, *Alfred Döblin*, Munich: Hanser 2011 (though this text is not always reliable, particularly when it comes to religion). For a comprehensive treatment of Döblin's work, see Sabina

Becker (ed.), *Döblin-Handbuch. Leben—Werk—Wirkung*, Stuttgart: Metzler 2016. I forgo bibliographic references to other literary works by Döblin.
7. Alfred Döblin, *Briefe*, Olten: Walter 1970, 25–27, here 26.
8. Schoeller, *Alfred Döblin*, 16–18.
9. Monique Meyembergh-Boussart, *Alfred Döblin. Seine Religiosität in Persönlichkeit und Werk*, Bonn: Bouvier 1970, 7. This book was long the only penetrating study on the topic. It has now been joined by Christoph Bartscherer, *Das Ich und die Natur. Alfred Döblins literarischer Weg im Licht seiner Religionsphilosophie*, Paderborn: Igel 1997; Friedrich Emde, *Alfred Döblin. Sein Weg zum Christentum*, Tübingen: Narr 1999. For an excellent and sweeping treatment of the topic, see also Helmuth Kiesel, *Literarische Trauerarbeit. Das Exil- und Spätwerk Alfred Döblins*, Tübingen: Max Niemeyer 1986. A highly informative account is provided by Anthony W. Riley, "Nachwort des Herausgebers," in Alfred Döblin, *Der unsterbliche Mensch / Der Kampf mit dem Engel*, Olten: Walter 1980, 661–699. For my own observations, see Hans Joas, *Die lange Nacht der Trauer. Erzählen als Weg aus der Gewalt?*, Gießen: Psychosozial-Verlag 2015.
10. See my interpretation in Becker (ed.), *Döblin-Handbuch*, 361–363.
11. For an exemplary account drawing on Wilhelm von Humboldt, Wilhelm Dilthey, George Herbert Mead, and contemporary authors, see Matthias Jung, *Der bewußte Ausdruck. Anthropologie der Artikulation*, Berlin: De Gruyter 2009.
12. Döblin, "Fragen, Antworten und Fragen" [1950], quoted in Kiesel, *Literarische Trauerarbeit*, 311.
13. Gilbert Keith Chesterton, *The Everlasting Man* [1925], in Gilbert Keith Chesterton, *The Collected Works II*, San Francisco: Ignatius Press 1986, 135–407; *Der unsterbliche Mensch*, Bremen: Schünemann 1930.
14. Chesterton, *The Everlasting Man*, 155–171.
15. Ibid., 318.
16. Alfred Döblin, *Destiny's Journey* (ed. Edgar Pässler, transl. by Edna McCown), New York: Paragon House 1992, 255. Reading this text provides an important supplement to study of the religious dialogues.
17. Ibid.
18. Dorothee Sölle, *Realisation. Studien zum Verhältnis von Theologie und Dichtung nach der Aufklärung*, Darmstadt: Luchterhand 1973, 344 and 343.
19. Döblin, *Destiny's Journey*, 313.
20. Originally appeared in *Süddeutsche Zeitung*, February 1, 1947, reprinted in Ingrid Schuster and Ingrid Bode (eds.), *Alfred Döblin im Spiegel der zeitgenössischen Kritik*, Bern: Francke 1973, 390–393, here 391.
21. For a detailed treatment of the dangers of collective self-sacralization, see Hans Joas, *The Power of the Sacred: An Alternative to the Narrative of Disenchantment*, New York: Oxford University Press 2021, 234–273.

II, 4

1. I am referring to Bertelsmann Stiftung (ed.), *What the World Believes: Analysis and Commentary on the Religion Monitor 2008*, Gütersloh: Verlag Bertelsmann Stiftung

2009. See also my critical discussion in Hans Joas, *The Religious Situation in the USA*, in that volume, 317–334, particularly 321f.
2. Friedrich Nietzsche, *On the Genealogy of Morality*, Cambridge: Cambridge University Press 2007, 371.
3. Peter Berger (ed.), *The Desecularization of the World: Resurgent Religion and World Politics*, Grand Rapids: Eerdmans 1999; Jürgen Habermas, *Glauben und Wissen*, Frankfurt am Main: Suhrkamp 2001. See my critiques in Hans Joas, *Do We Need Religion? On the Experience of Self-Transcendence*, Boulder: Paradigm 2008, 21ff. and 105ff.
4. Hermann Lübbe, *Säkularisierung. Geschichte eines ideenpolitischen Begriffs*, Freiburg: Alber 1975; Werner Conze and Hermann Zabel, "Säkularisation, Säkularisierung," in Otto Brunner, Werner Conze, and Reinhart Koselleck (eds.), *Geschichtliche Grundbegriffe. Historisches Lexikon zur politisch-sozialen Sprache in Deutschland*, vol. 5, Stuttgart: Klett-Cotta 1984, 789–829; Giacomo Marramao, "Säkularisierung," in Joachim Ritter and Karlfried Gründer (eds.), *Historisches Wörterbuch der Philosophie*, vol. 8, Basel: Schwabe 1992, col. 1133–1161; Giacomo Marramao, *Die Säkularisierung der westlichen Welt*, Frankfurt am Main: Insel 1996.
5. See Hartmut Lehmann, "Die Entscheidung des Jahres 1803 und das Verhältnis von Säkularisation, Säkularisierung und Säkularismus," in Hartmut Lehmann, *Säkularisierung. Der europäische Sonderweg in Sachen Religion*, Göttingen: Wallstein 2005, 70–85; Ulrich Ruh, *Säkularisierung als Interpretationskategorie*, Freiburg: Herder 1980.
6. Reinhart Koselleck, "Zeitverkürzung und Beschleunigung. Eine Studie zur Säkularisierung," in Reinhart Koselleck, *Zeitschichten. Studien zur Historik*, Frankfurt am Main: Suhrkamp 2000, 177–202.
7. Most systematically analyzed in several publications by Hartmut Rosa, for example in *Social Acceleration: A New Theory of Modernity*, New York: Columbia University Press 2015.
8. Koselleck, "Zeitverkürzung und Beschleunigung," 194.
9. Carl Schmitt published a short, extremely positive review: Carl Schmitt, review of Koselleck, *Kritik und Krise*, in: *Das historisch-politische Buch* 7 (1959), 301f.
10. Hans Blumenberg, *The Legitimacy of the Modern Age*, Cambridge: MIT 1985, 92.
11. For a detailed discussion of the relationship between Koselleck and Carl Schmitt, see Reinhard Mehring, "Begriffsgeschichte mit Carl Schmitt," in Hans Joas and Peter Vogt (eds.), *Begriffene Geschichte. Beiträge zum Werk Reinhart Kosellecks*, Berlin: Suhrkamp 2011. There is considerable controversy over this issue. In addition to the direct influence we must also consider the indirect one, through Schmitt's impact on Otto Brunner and Brunner's impact on the project of conceptual history, for example. Emphasis on this influence is to be found in the work of James Van Horn Melton, "Otto Brunner and the Ideological Origins of *Begriffsgeschichte*," in Hartmut Lehmann and Melvin Richter (eds.), *The Meaning of Historical Terms and Concepts: New Studies on Begriffsgeschichte*, Washington, DC: German Historical Institute 1996, 21–35, and that of Melvin Richter, *The History of Political and Social Concepts: A Critical Introduction*, Oxford: Oxford University Press 1995, 26ff. This influence is disputed by scholars such as Christof Dipper, "Die 'Geschichtlichen Grundbegriffe.' Von der Begriffsgeschichte zur Theorie der historischen Zeiten,"

in: *Historische Zeitschrift* 270 (2000), 281–308, and also in Joas and Vogt (eds.), *Begriffene Geschichte*, 288–316.

12. An excellent set of arguments contra Schmitt in this connection is provided by Horst Dreier, "Kanonistik und Konfessionalisierung—Marksteine auf dem Weg zum Staat," in Georg Siebeck (ed.), *Artibus ingenuis*, Tübingen: Mohr Siebeck 2001, 133–169. For an important recent take on this topic, see José Casanova, "Das Problem der Religion und die Ängste der säkularen europäischen Demokratien," in José Casanova, *Europas Angst vor der Religion*, Berlin: Berlin University Press 2009, 7–30. On Casanova, see part IV, ch. 6.

13. Wilfried Nippel, "Krieg als Erscheinungsform der Feindschaft," in Reinhard Mehring (ed.), *Carl Schmitt. Der Begriff des Politischen: ein kooperativer Kommentar*, Berlin: Akademie 2003, 61–70.

14. Jürgen Habermas, "Zur Kritik an der Geschichtsphilosophie" [1960], in Jürgen Habermas, *Kultur und Kritik*, Frankfurt am Main: Suhrkamp 1973, 355–364. This reprint of the review is abridged and has the offensive parts removed. The original review was published as "Verrufener Fortschritt—Verkanntes Jahrhundert," in: *Merkur* 14 (1960), 466–477.

15. Reinhart Koselleck, review of Herbert Butterfield, *Christianity, Diplomacy and War*, in: *Archiv für Rechts- und Sozialphilosophie* 41 (1955), 591–595.

16. Ibid., 592.

17. See Hans Joas, *War and Modernity*, Cambridge: Polity 2003, esp. 21–23 and 152–157.

18. Mehring, "Begriffsgeschichte mit Carl Schmitt," 164.

19. Karl Löwith, *Meaning in History: The Theological Implications of the Philosophy of History*, Chicago: University of Chicago Press 1949.

20. Manfred Hettling and Bernd Ulrich, "Formen der Bürgerlichkeit. Ein Gespräch mit Reinhart Koselleck," in Manfred Hettling and Bernd Ulrich (eds.), *Bürgertum nach 1945*, Hamburg: Hamburger Edition 2005, 40–60, here 56.

21. As Reinhard Mehring argues ("Begriffsgeschichte mit Carl Schmitt"); see also Reinhard Mehring, "Heidegger und Karl Löwith," in Dieter Thomä (ed.), *Heidegger-Handbuch*, Stuttgart: Metzler 2003, 373–375.

22. Karl Löwith, *Mein Leben in Deutschland vor und nach 1933. Ein Bericht*, Frankfurt am Main: Insel 1989. Foreword by Reinhart Koselleck. (English translation London: Athlone 1994.)

23. Reinhart Koselleck, "Historia Magistra Vitae," in Reinhart Koselleck, *Futures Past*, New York: Columbia University Press 2004, 26–42.

24. Koselleck, "Zeitverkürzung und Beschleunigung," 193, fn. 28.

25. Blumenberg, *The Legitimacy of the Modern Age*, 31f.

26. I feel confirmed in this regard by Gennaro Imbriano, *Der Begriff der Politik. Die Moderne als Krisenzeit im Werk von Reinhart Koselleck*, Frankfurt am Main: Campus 2018. See also Niklas Olsen, *History in the Plural: An Introduction to the Work of Reinhart Koselleck*, New York: Berghahn 2012, 21–23 and 52–57.

27. Reinhart Koselleck, *Critique and Crisis: Enlightenment and the Pathogenesis of Modern Society*, Cambridge: MIT 1988, 130.

28. Ibid.
29. Jürgen Habermas, "Karl Löwith: Stoic Retreat from Historical Consciousness" [1963], in Jürgen Habermas, *Philosophical-Political Profiles*, Cambridge: MIT Press 1983, 79–98.
30. Hermann Lübbe, *Geschichtsbegriff und Geschichtsinteresse. Analytik und Pragmatik der Historie*, Basel: Schwabe 1977, 82.
31. Reinhart Koselleck, "Jaspers, die Geschichte und das Überpolitische," in Jeanne Hersch et al. (eds.), *Karl Jaspers. Philosoph, Arzt, politischer Denker. Symposium zum 100. Geburtstag*, Munich: Piper 1986, 291–302, esp. 298.
32. Stefanie Stockhorst, "Novus ordo temporum. Reinhart Kosellecks These von der Verzeitlichung des Geschichtsbewußtseins durch die Aufklärungshistoriographie in methodenkritischer Perspektive," in Joas and Vogt (eds.), *Begriffene Geschichte*, 359–386.
33. Stephan Schleissing, *Das Maß des Fortschritts. Zum Verhältnis von Ethik und Geschichtsphilosophie in theologischer Perspektive*, Göttingen: Ruprecht 2008, see, for example, 41.
34. Jan Marco Sawilla, "Geschichte und Geschichten zwischen Providenz und Machbarkeit. Überlegungen zu Reinhart Kosellecks Semantik historischer Zeiten," in Joas and Vogt (eds.), *Begriffene Geschichte*, 387–422, here 418.
35. Ibid.
36. Ibid.
37. Olaf Blaschke, "Das 19. Jahrhundert. Ein zweites konfessionelles Zeitalter," in: *Geschichte und Gesellschaft* 26 (2000), 38–75, esp. 46.
38. See, for example, George Herbert Mead, *The Philosophy of the Present*, Open Court: La Salle 1932; see also Hans Joas, "Temporality and Intersubjectivity," in Hans Joas, *G. H. Mead: A Contemporary Re-examination of His Thought*, Cambridge: MIT Press 1985, 167–198.
39. Reinhart Koselleck, "History, Histories and Formal Time Structures," in Koselleck, *Futures Past*, 93–104, here 103.
40. See, for example, Reinhart Koselleck, *Zur politischen Ikonologie des gewaltsamen Todes. Ein deutsch-französischer Vergleich*, Basel: Schwabe 1998.
41. Reinhart Koselleck, "The Status of the Enlightenment in German History," in Hans Joas and Klaus Wiegandt (eds.), *The Cultural Values of Europe*, Liverpool: Liverpool University Press 2008, 253–264. See also the recent work by David Sorkin, *The Religious Enlightenment: Protestants, Jews, and Catholics from London to Vienna*, Princeton: Princeton University Press 2008.
42. Reinhart Koselleck, "Aufklärung und die Grenzen ihrer Toleranz," in Trutz Rendtorff (ed.), *Glaube und Toleranz. Das theologische Erbe der Aufklärung*, Gütersloh: Mohn 1982, 109–124, reprinted in Reinhart Koselleck, *Begriffsgeschichten. Studien zur Semantik und Pragmatik der politischen und sozialen Sprache*, Frankfurt am Main: Suhrkamp 2006, 340–362, esp. 343. Reference to Johannes Kühn, *Toleranz und Offenbarung*, Leipzig: Meiner 1923.
43. Koselleck, "Aufklärung und die Grenzen ihrer Toleranz," 343 (my emphasis).

44. Ibid., 344.
45. Ibid., 352.
46. Ibid., 344f.
47. The expression "our post-theological age" appears in Koselleck's foreword to *Critique and Crisis*, 3; on the term "post-Christian," see Koselleck, "Zeitverkürzung und Beschleunigung," 195.
48. Bernard Yack, *The Fetishism of Modernities*, Notre Dame: University of Notre Dame Press 1997; Herbert Schnädelbach, *Zur Rehabilitierung des Animal Rationale*, Frankfurt am Main: Suhrkamp 1990, 241; Hans Joas, *Faith as an Option: Possible Futures for Christianity*, Stanford: Stanford University Press 2014, 67f.
49. José Casanova, "Beyond European and American Exceptionalisms: Toward a Global Perspective," in Grace Davie et al. (eds.), *Predicting Religion: Christian, Secular and Alternative Futures*, Aldershot: Ashgate 2003, 17–29.
50. David Martin, *A General Theory of Secularization*, Oxford: Blackwell 1978. On Martin, see Part IV, ch. 4.
51. Paul Ricœur, *Time and Narrative*, vol. 3, Chicago: University of Chicago Press 1988 (on Koselleck, see esp. 207–240).
52. Ibid., 207.
53. Bo Stråth, review of R. Koselleck, *Zeitschichten*, in: *European Journal of Social Theory* 4 (2001), 531–535, here 532.
54. See, for example, Reinhart Koselleck, *Preußen zwischen Reform und Revolution. Allgemeines Landrecht, Verwaltung und soziale Bewegung von 1791 bis 1848*, Stuttgart: Klett 1967. For an important attempt to connect conceptual history and historical sociology, see Björn Wittrock, "Cultural Crystallization and Conceptual Change," in Jussi Kurunmäki and Kari Palonen (eds.), *Zeit, Geschichte und Politik. Zum achtzigsten Geburtstag von Reinhart Koselleck*, Jyväskylä: Jyväskylä University Press 2002, 105–134.
55. Wolfhart Pannenberg, "Weltgeschichte und Heilsgeschichte," in Reinhart Koselleck and Wolf-Dieter Stempel (eds.), *Geschichte—Ereignis und Erzählung*, Munich: Fink 1973 (*Poetik und Hermeneutik* V), 307–323, esp. 315.
56. Pannenberg (see fn. 55). See also "Erfordert die Einheit der Geschichte ein Subjekt?," in Koselleck and Stempel (eds.), *Geschichte—Ereignis und Erzählung*, 478–490; Trutz Rendtorff, "Geschichtstheologie," in Joachim Ritter and Karlfried Gründer (eds.), *Historisches Wörterbuch der Philosophie*, vol. 3, Darmstadt: Wissenschaftliche Buchgesellschaft 1974, col. 439–441; Karl Rahner, "Weltgeschichte und Heilsgeschichte," in Karl Rahner, *Schriften zur Theologie V*, Einsiedeln: Benziger 1962, 115–135. This topic also plays a major role in the documents of the Second Vatican Council and in Latin American theology of liberation, but this is not the place to discuss them.
57. Pannenberg, "Weltgeschichte und Heilsgeschichte," 321.
58. My thanks to Lucian Hölscher, Christian Meier, Stephan Schleissing, and Peter Vogt for suggested modifications.

II, 5

1. Hans Joas, *Faith as an Option: Possible Futures for Christianity*, Stanford: Stanford University Press 2014, 10–12; Hans Joas and Klaus Wiegandt (eds.), *Secularization and the World Religions*, Liverpool: Liverpool University Press 2009.
2. Charles Taylor, *A Secular Age*, Cambridge: Harvard University Press 2007. (All page numbers in the main text refer to this book.)
3. Peter L. Berger, *The Heretical Imperative: Contemporary Possibilities of Religious Affirmation*, Garden City: Anchor 1979; Peter L. Berger, *A Far Glory: The Quest for Faith in an Age of Credulity*, New York: The Free Press 1992.
4. Hans Joas, *Do We Need Religion? On the Experience of Self-Transcendence*, Boulder: Paradigm 2008, 21–35.
5. Charles Taylor, *Sources of the Self: The Making of the Modern Identity*, Cambridge: Harvard University Press 1989, 68.
6. Ibid., 3–24.
7. Martin Seel, "Die Wiederkehr der Ethik des guten Lebens," in: *Merkur* 45 (1991), 41–49.
8. Hans Joas, *The Sacredness of the Person: A New Genealogy of Human Rights*, Washington, DC: Georgetown University Press 2013, 97–139.
9. George Marsden, "Matteo Ricci and Prodigal Culture," in James L. Heft (ed.), *A Catholic Modernity? Charles Taylor's Marianist Award Lecture*, New York: Oxford University Press 1999, 83–93, here 87.
10. Wilhelm Dilthey, *Weltanschauung und Analyse des Menschen seit Renaissance und Reformation* (= *Gesammelte Schriften*, vol. 2), Stuttgart: Teubner 1991.
11. Victor Turner, *The Ritual Process: Structure and Anti-structure* [1969], London: Routledge 2017.
12. Karl Jaspers, *The Origin and Goal of History* [1949], London: Routledge 2010. For an overview of Jaspers's sources and the literature building on his ideas, see Hans Joas, *The Power of the Sacred: An Alternative to the Narrative of Disenchantment*, New York: Oxford University Press 2021, 154–194.
13. Bertelsmann Stiftung (ed.), *Religion Monitor 2008*, Gütersloh: Verlag Bertelsmann Stiftung 2007 (for my critique, see 18–21 in that publication); see also Peter E. Gordon, "The Place of the Sacred in the Absence of God: Charles Taylor's 'A Secular Age,'" in: *Journal of the History of Ideas* 69 (2008), 647–673, esp. 669ff.
14. See Ernst Troeltsch's apposite observation: "The Catholicism of educated antiquity, which married a thousand years of cultural heritage with Christianity and sustained that heritage through Christianity, is separated from the Catholicism of the cultureless, authority-needy and fantastical Germanic-Romanic Middle Ages, and both in turn are separated from early Christianity, by a deep gulf." Ernst Troeltsch, "Geschichte und Metaphysik" [1898], in Ernst Troeltsch, *Schriften zur Theologie und Religionsphilosophie (1888–1902)* (= KGA, vol. 1), Berlin: De Gruyter 2009, 613–682, here 672.
15. Charles Larmore, "How Much Can We Stand?," in: *The New Republic*, April 9, 2008, 39–44.

16. For a critique of Weber, see also the writings of Werner Stark and Part IV, ch. 3.
17. For an in-depth account, see Joas, *The Power of the Sacred*.
18. Joas, *Do We Need Religion?*, 81–90, here 89.
19. Ernst Troeltsch, "Religiöser Individualismus und Kirche" [1911], in Ernst Troeltsch, *Gesammelte Schriften*, vol. 2, Tübingen: Mohr Siebeck 1913, 109–133, here 117. See also Joas, *Faith as an Option*, 116–125.
20. David Martin, *A General Theory of Secularization*, New York: Harper & Row 1978. On Martin's oeuvre, see Part IV, ch. 4.
21. Very important in this regard are the books of Hugh McLeod, *Religion and the People of Western Europe 1789–1989*, Oxford: Oxford University Press 1981; Hugh McLeod, *Piety and Poverty: Working-Class Religion in Berlin, London and New York*, New York: Holmes & Meier 1996; Hugh McLeod, *Secularization in Western Europe 1848–1914*, New York: St. Martin's Press 2000; Hugh McLeod, *The Religious Crisis of the 1960s*, Oxford: Oxford University Press 2007.
22. For more detail on what follows, see Joas, *Faith as an Option*, 37–49.
23. Of the extensive research literature, I will mention just the following overview: Timothy Tackett, "The French Revolution and Religion to 1794," in Timothy Tackett and Stewart J. Brown (eds.), *Enlightenment, Reawakening and Revolution 1660–1815* (= *The Cambridge History of Christianity*, vol. 7), Cambridge: Cambridge University Press 2006, 536–555.
24. The work of Charles Taylor, but particularly his contributions to religion and politics, have met with a strong response around the world. Numerous monographs and edited volumes expressing critical views have appeared, several of them featuring a reply by Taylor. Key addendums and self-corrections are to be found in these replies. I will mention just a few of these titles, while making no attempt at this point to do justice to the arguments they present in detail: Michael Kühnlein, *Religion als Quelle des Selbst. Zur Vernunft- und Freiheitskritik von Charles Taylor*, Tübingen: Mohr Siebeck 2008; Michael Kühnlein and Matthias Lutz-Bachmann (eds.), *Unerfüllte Moderne? Neue Perspektiven auf das Werk von Charles Taylor*, Berlin: Suhrkamp 2011; Michael Kühnlein (ed.), *Charles Taylor. Ein säkulares Zeitalter*, Berlin: De Gruyter 2018; Michael Warner, Jonathan VanAntwerpen, and Craig Calhoun (eds.), *Varieties of Secularism in a Secular Age*, Cambridge: Harvard University Press 2010; Carlos D. Colorado and Justin D. Klassen (eds.), *Aspiring to Fullness in a Secular Age: Essays on Religion and Theology in a Secular Age*, Notre Dame: Notre Dame University Press 2014; Ulrike Spohn, *Den säkularen Staat neu denken. Politik und Religion bei Charles Taylor*, Frankfurt am Main: Campus 2016; Mirjam Künkler, John Madeley, and Shylashri Shankar (eds.), *A Secular Age beyond the West: Religion, Law and the State in Asia, the Middle East and North Africa*, Cambridge: Cambridge University Press 2018; Kieran Flanagan and Peter C. Jupp (eds.), "Symposium on Charles Taylor with His Responses," in: *New Blackfriars* 91 (2010), 625–724.

III, 1

1. See the introduction to the present volume and ch. 5 on Charles Taylor in Part II. Research into the conceptual history of the term "freedom" shows that affiliation with a protective community is one of its fundamental elements. See the entry "Freiheit" in Otto Brunner, Werner Conze, and Reinhart Koselleck (eds.), *Geschichtliche Grundbegriffe. Historisches Lexikon zur politisch-sozialen Sprache in Deutschland*, vol. 2, Stuttgart: Klett-Cotta 1975, 425–542.
2. I have engaged critically with the work of Rorty on many occasions in my studies. On the point briefly addressed here, see Hans Joas, *The Sacredness of the Person: A New Genealogy of Human Rights*, Washington, DC: Georgetown University Press 2013, 137, fn. 16.
3. In allusion to the title of Heinrich August Winkler's monumental work of history *Der lange Weg nach Westen. Deutsche Geschichte I und II*, 2 vols., Munich: C. H. Beck 2000.
4. Peter E. Gordon, *Continental Divide: Heidegger, Cassirer, Davos*, Cambridge: Harvard University Press 2010. For my views, see Hans Joas, "Situated Creativity: A Way out of the Impasse of the Heidegger-Cassirer Debate," in: *History of European Ideas* 41 (2015), 565–570. This issue also includes other reviews and a reply by Peter Gordon.
5. See the introductory remarks on Part I of this book and ch. 1 in Part I, which is dedicated to Troeltsch.
6. Comparison between Troeltsch and Heidegger is also instructive and might be profitably fleshed out. A number of studies have appeared on this comparison and on Heidegger's reception of Troeltsch (and Troeltsch's surviving letters to him). This reception can be seen, for example, in Martin Heidegger, "Einleitung in die Phänomenologie der Religion," in Martin Heidegger, *Phänomenologie des religiösen Lebens* (= *Gesamtausgabe*, vol. 60), Frankfurt am Main: Klostermann 1995, 1–156, here 19–30. The best treatment is Sylvain Camilleri, "A Historical Note on Heidegger's Relationship to Ernst Troeltsch," in S. J. McGrath and Andrzej Wierciński (eds.), *A Companion to Heidegger's "Phenomenology of Religious Life,"* Amsterdam: Rodopi 2010, 115–134. See also Jeffrey Andrew Barash, *Martin Heidegger and the Problem of Historical Meaning*, New York: Fordham University Press 2003, esp. chs. 3 and 4; Gregory P. Floyd, "Between 'Liberale Theologie' and 'Religionsphilosophie': A New Perspective on Heidegger's 'Phenomenology of Religious Life,'" in Gerhard Thonhauser (ed.), *Perspektiven mit Heidegger. Zugänge—Pfade—Anknüpfungen*, Freiburg: Karl Alber 2017, 132–146; Marta Zaccagnini, *Christentum der Endlichkeit. Heideggers Vorlesungen zur Einführung in die Phänomenologie der Religion*, Berlin: LIT 2003, 104–151. I must also mention here that in 1930 Heidegger was appointed to the chair formerly held by Troeltsch at Berlin University—against the will of the faculty, all of whom backed Ernst Cassirer. See Reinhard Mehring and Dieter Thomä, "Leben und Werk. Martin Heidegger im Kontext," in Dieter Thomä (ed.), *Heidegger-Handbuch. Leben—Werk—Wirkung*, Stuttgart: Klett-Cotta 2005, 515–539, here 524.

7. See my remarks in the relevant chapter. Troeltsch's "project," which largely ground to a halt as a result of his early death, was—in addition to Durkheim—the main source of inspiration for my book *The Sacredness of the Person*.
8. Ernst Troeltsch, "Die Selbständigkeit der Religion" [1895–1896], in Ernst Troeltsch, *Schriften zur Theologie und Religionsphilosophie (1888–1902)* (= KGA, vol. 1), Berlin: De Gruyter 2009, 359–535, here 459. See Part I, ch. 2.
9. Ernst Troeltsch, "Die Zufälligkeit der Geschichtswahrheiten" [1923], in Ernst Troeltsch, *Schriften zur Politik und Kulturphilosophie (1918–1923)* (= KGA, vol. 15), Berlin: De Gruyter 2002, 551–567, here 556f.
10. For indispensable accounts on the conceptual and scholarly history of "theonomy" prior to Tillich, see Friedrich Wilhelm Graf, *Theonomie. Fallstudien zum Integrationsanspruch neuzeitlicher Theologie*, Gütersloh: Gütersloher Verlagshaus Mohn 1987. On p. 231, Graf calls this term one of the "most successful theological battle cries of the 'saddle period'" and brings out the diverse range of ways in which it was charged with meaning and deployed. See also Ernst Feil, "Zur ursprünglichen Bedeutung von 'Theonomie,'" in: *Archiv für Begriffsgeschichte* 34 (1991), 295–313.
11. In what follows I base myself chiefly on Friedrich Wilhelm Horn, "'Zur Freiheit hat uns Christus befreit.' Neutestamentliche Perspektiven," in Martin Laube (ed.), *Freiheit*, Tübingen: UTB 2014, 39–58.
12. Ibid., 51.
13. These ideas can be found in their most pronounced form in modern French political theory, in the work of Cornelius Castoriadis, Claude Lefort, and Marcel Gauchet. The latter interprets Christianity as a stage in the self-dissolution of religion, as a "religion for departing from religion." See Marcel Gauchet, *The Disenchantment of the World: A Political History of Religion*, Princeton: Princeton University Press 1997, 4. On this position, see Hans Joas, *The Power of the Sacred: An Alternative to the Narrative of Disenchantment*, New York: Oxford University Press 2021, 182–184, and the introduction to the present book.
14. Paul Tillich, "Theonomie," in *Die Religion in Geschichte und Gegenwart*, ed. Hermann Gunkel and Leopold Zscharnack, vol. 5, Tübingen: Mohr Siebeck 1931 (2nd ed.), col. 1128–1129.
15. See Hans Joas, "Respect for Indisposability," in Hans Joas, *Do We Need Religion? On the Experience of Self-Transcendence*, Boulder: Paradigm 2008, 125–132.
16. Paul Ricœur, "Theonomy and/or Autonomy," in Miroslav Volf et al. (eds.), *The Future of Theology: Essays in Honor of Jürgen Moltmann*, Grand Rapids: Eerdmans 1996, 284–298. On Ricœur, see ch. 4 in this Part.
17. See the analysis in Hans Joas (ed.), *Die Zehn Gebote. Ein widersprüchliches Erbe?*, Cologne: Böhlau 2006.
18. Ricœur, "Theonomy and/or Autonomy," 285.
19. Here Kühnlein regards Ricœur's conception as superior to Taylor's. See Michael Kühnlein, *Religion als Quelle des Selbst. Zur Vernunft- und Freiheitskritik von Charles Taylor*, Tübingen: Mohr Siebeck 2008, 238–244.
20. Huber states that a 1976 essay by Theunissen was of particularly crucial importance to him (and Heinz Eduard Tödt): Michael Theunissen, "Ho aiton lambanei. Der Gebetsglaube Jesu und die Zeitlichkeit des Christseins," in Bernhard Casper et

al. (eds.), *Jesus—Ort der Erfahrung Gottes. Festschrift für Bernhard Welte*, Freiburg: Herder 1976, 13–68. On this, see Wolfgang Huber, "Über die kommunikative Freiheit hinaus," in Heinrich Bedford-Strohm, Paul Nolte, and Rüdiger Sachau (eds.), *Kommunikative Freiheit. Interdisziplinäre Diskurse mit Wolfgang Huber*, Leipzig: Evangelische Verlagsanstalt 2014, 175–191, here 178f.
21. See the introduction to the present book, p. 8.
22. Huber's response to my concerns and questions can be found in Bedford-Strohm et al. (eds.), *Kommunikative Freiheit*, esp. 181–186.
23. Through a contrast between Fichte and William James, this was fully recognized by Michael Hampe and Felicitas Krämer. See Michael Hampe, *Erkenntnis und Praxis. Zur Philosophie des Pragmatismus*, Frankfurt am Main: Suhrkamp 2006, 283–286 (this chapter was jointly written with Felicitas Krämer); Felicitas Krämer, *Erfahrungsvielfalt und Wirklichkeit. Zu William James' Realitätsverständnis*, Göttingen: Vandenhoeck & Ruprecht 2006. For a classic pragmatist's engagement with Fichte, see also George Herbert Mead, *Movements of Thought in the Nineteenth Century*, Chicago: University of Chicago Press 1936, 85–110.
24. William James, "Human Immortality: Two Supposed Objections to the Doctrine" [1898], in William James, *Essays in Religion and Mortality* (= *Works*, vol. 9), Cambridge: Harvard University Press 1982, 75–101, here 94. On James's contribution on "immortality," see Joas, *The Sacredness of the Person*, 155–158.
25. See Horn, "Zur Freiheit hat uns Christus befreit," 43, building on the work of Samuel Vollenweider. On panpsychism, see James's sympathetic remarks on Gustav Theodor Fechner in William James, *A Pluralistic Universe* [1909], Cambridge: Harvard University Press 1977, 63–82.
26. This is also the message of the quote from Tocqueville that I have chosen as the epigraph of the present book.

III, 2

1. On the controversy itself, see the appendix to Martin Heidegger, *Kant und das Problem der Metaphysik*, Frankfurt am Main: Klostermann 1988, 247–311. The secondary literature is enormous. An outstanding contribution is Peter Eli Gordon, *Continental Divide: Heidegger, Cassirer, Davos*, Cambridge: Harvard University Press 2010. See also Thomas Meyer, *Ernst Cassirer*, Hamburg: Ellert & Richter 2006, 154–179.
2. A far-reaching argument on the relationship between analytic and Continental philosophy and on the significance of Cassirer's mediating position builds on this fact: Michael Friedman, *A Parting of the Ways: Carnap, Cassirer, and Heidegger*, Chicago: Open Court 2000.
3. Wolfgang Mommsen deals with this topic from a more political, chiefly constitutional point of view: Wolfgang Mommsen, "Die deutsche Idee der Freiheit," in Wolfgang Mommsen, *Bürgerliche Kultur und politische Ordnung. Künstler, Schriftsteller und Intellektuelle in der deutschen Geschichte 1830–1933*, Frankfurt am Main: Fischer

2000, 133–157. Additional source material in the form of letters by Troeltsch about Cassirer is now published in Ernst Troeltsch, *Briefe IV (1915–1918)* (= KGA, vol. 21), Berlin: De Gruyter 2018.

4. Ernst Troeltsch, "Naturrecht und Humanität in der Weltpolitik" [1923], in Ernst Troeltsch, *Schriften zur Politik und Kulturphilosophie (1918–23)* (= KGA, vol. 5), Berlin: De Gruyter 2002, 493–512. The "editorial report" (477–490) and the editor's introduction (by Gangolf Hübinger) to this volume (1–42) contain important information about the background to this text. For an English translation, see Ernst Troeltsch, "The Ideas of Natural Law and Humanity in World Politics," in Otto Gierke, *Natural Law and the Theory of Society 1500–1800*, vol. 1, Cambridge: Cambridge University Press 1934, appendix I, 201–222. The following passage is based on Hans Joas, "Max Weber and the Origin of Human Rights: A Study of Cultural Innovation," in Charles Camic, Philip S. Gorski, and David M. Trubek (eds.), *Max Weber's "Economy and Society": A Critical Companion*, Stanford: Stanford University Press 2005, 366–382.

5. Thomas Mann, "Naturrecht und Humanität," *Frankfurter Zeitung*, December 25, 1923, reprinted in Thomas Mann, *Aufsätze, Reden, Essays*, vol. 3, Berlin: Aufbau 1986, 428–431; Friedrich Meinecke, *Die Idee der Staatsräson* [1924], Munich: Oldenbourg 1957; Leo Strauss, *Natural Right and History*, Chicago: University of Chicago Press 1953, 1f.

6. Troeltsch, "Naturrecht und Humanität," 495; "The Ideas of Natural Law and Humanity," 203.

7. Troeltsch, "Naturrecht und Humanität," 497; "The Ideas of Natural Law and Humanity," 204.

8. Troeltsch, "Naturrecht und Humanität," 502; "The Ideas of Natural Law and Humanity," 210.

9. See Hans Joas, *The Creativity of Action*, Chicago: University of Chicago Press 1996, 75–85. It has been above all Charles Taylor who, taking up ideas from Isaiah Berlin, has forcefully drawn attention to the significance of the "expressivist" tradition.

10. Troeltsch, "Naturrecht und Humanität," 504; "The Ideas of Natural Law and Humanity," 214.

11. Troeltsch, "Naturrecht und Humanität," 510; "The Ideas of Natural Law and Humanity," 220 (my emphasis).

12. Wilhelm Ihde, *Wegscheide 1789. Darstellung und Deutung eines Kreuzweges der Europäischen Geschichte* [1941], cited in Wolfgang Schmale, *Archäologie der Grund- und Menschenrechte in der Frühen Neuzeit*, Munich: Oldenbourg 1997, 71f.

13. Alain Touraine, *Critique de la modernité*, Paris: Fayard 1992, 70–74.

14. For an intellectual biography of Cassirer that stresses this point, see David R. Lipton, *Ernst Cassirer: The Dilemma of a Liberal Intellectual in Germany 1914–33*, Toronto: University of Toronto Press 1978.

15. Ernst Cassirer, *Das Erkenntnisproblem in der Philosophie und Wissenschaft der neueren Zeit*, vol. II, Berlin: Bruno Cassirer 1907; Ernst Cassirer, *Kants Leben und Lehre*, Berlin: Bruno Cassirer 1918. As Cassirer wrote in his preface (VII) he had already finished the manuscript in the spring of 1916.

16. Ernst Cassirer, *Freiheit und Form. Studien zur deutschen Geistesgeschichte*, Berlin: Bruno Cassirer 1916.
17. Ibid., xiii.
18. Ernst Troeltsch, review of "Ernst Cassirer, Leibniz' System in seinen wissenschaftlichen Grundlagen (Marburg 1902)," in: *Theologische Literaturzeitung* 29 (1904), col. 639–643; also in Ernst Troeltsch, *Rezensionen und Kritiken (1901–1914)* (= KGA, vol. 4), Berlin: De Gruyter 2004, 354–360. The following references are to this edition.
19. Ibid., 358.
20. Ernst Troeltsch, "Leibniz und die Anfänge des Pietismus" [1902], in Ernst Troeltsch, *Gesammelte Schriften*, vol. 4, Tübingen: Mohr Siebeck 1925, 488–531.
21. Troeltsch, review of "Ernst Cassirer, Leibniz' System in seinen wissenschaftlichen Grundlagen," 359.
22. Ibid., 360.
23. Ernst Troeltsch, review of "Ernst Cassirer, Freiheit und Form," in: *Theologische Literaturzeitung* 42 (1917), col. 368–371 (reprinted in Ernst Troeltsch, *Gesammelte Schriften*, vol. 4, Tübingen: Mohr Siebeck 1925, 696–698); Ernst Troeltsch, *Humanismus und Nationalismus in unserem Bildungswesen*, Berlin: Weidmann 1917, partly reprinted in Ernst Troeltsch, *Deutscher Geist und Westeuropa*, Tübingen: Mohr Siebeck 1925, 211–243.
24. Troeltsch, *Humanismus und Nationalismus in unserem Bildungswesen*, 231.
25. Ernst Troeltsch, "Vernunft und Offenbarung bei Johann Gerhard und Melanchthon" [1891], in Ernst Troeltsch, *Schriften zur Theologie und Religionsphilosophie (1888–1902)* (= KGA, vol. 1), Berlin: De Gruyter 2009, 73–338.
26. Ernst Troeltsch, *The Social Teaching of the Christian Churches*, London: George Allen & Unwin 1931, vol. 2, 871f. and 572.
27. Troeltsch, review "Cassirer, Freiheit und Form," 332.
28. Cf. Hans-Georg Drescher, *Ernst Troeltsch. Leben und Werk*, Göttingen: Vandenhoeck & Ruprecht 1991, in particular 247, n. 42.
29. More on this above, in the "Introductory Remarks" to Part III, and in subsequent chapters.
30. Troeltsch, *Humanismus und Nationalismus in unserem Bildungswesen*, 232.
31. Troeltsch, review "Ernst Cassirer, Freiheit und Form," 333.
32. Jürgen Habermas, "The Liberating Power of Symbols: Ernst Cassirer's Humanistic Legacy and the Warburg Library," in Jürgen Habermas, *The Liberating Power of Symbols*, Cambridge: MIT Press 2001, 1–29, here 21.
33. Ernst Troeltsch, *Christian Thought: Its History and Application*, London: University of London Press 1923. Now republished avoiding the misleading title of the original German publication (*Der Historismus und seine Überwindung*) as Ernst Troeltsch, *Fünf Vorträge zu Religion und Geschichtsphilosophie für England und Schottland* (= KGA, vol. 17), Berlin: De Gruyter 2006, the English text ibid., 133–203.
34. Troeltsch, *Aufsätze zur Geistesgeschichte und Religionssoziologie*.
35. Ernst Troeltsch, review of "Ernst Cassirer, Das Erkenntnisproblem in der Philosophie und Wissenschaft der neueren Zeit, vol. 3 (Berlin 1920)," in: *Theologische Literaturzeitung* 46 (1921), col. 160–161, now in Ernst Troeltsch, *Rezensionen und Kritiken (1915–1923)* (= KGA, vol. 13), Berlin: De Gruyter 2010, 500–502, here 502.

36. Ernst Troeltsch, "Die Verösterreichung" [1922–1923], in Ernst Troeltsch, *Spectator-Briefe und Berliner Briefe (1919–1922)* (= KGA, vol. 14), Berlin: De Gruyter 2018, 569–577, here 576.
37. Ernst Cassirer, "Die Idee der republikanischen Verfassung" [1928], reprinted in Ernst Cassirer, *Aufsätze und kleine Schriften 1927–1931*, Hamburg: Felix Meiner 2004, 291–307.
38. Ibid., 293.
39. Ibid.
40. On Jellinek, Troeltsch, and later research on these questions, cf. Hans Joas, *The Sacredness of the Person: A New Genealogy of Human Rights*, Washington, DC: Georgetown University Press 2013, 9–36.
41. Cassirer, "Die Idee der republikanischen Verfassung," 296.
42. Ibid., 300.
43. Ibid., 307.
44. Ernst Cassirer, "Deutschland und Westeuropa im Spiegel der Geistesgeschichte" [1931], reprinted in Ernst Cassirer, *Aufsätze und kleine Schriften (1927–1931)*, Hamburg: Felix Meiner 2004, 207–220. Additionally, see "Vom Wesen und Werden des Naturrechts" [1932], in Ernst Cassirer, *Aufsätze und kleine Schriften (1932–1935)*, Hamburg: Felix Meiner 2001, 203–227.
45. Cassirer, "Deutschland und Westeuropa im Spiegel der Geistesgeschichte," 218.
46. Ernst Cassirer, *Die Philosophie der Aufklärung*, Tübingen: Mohr Siebeck 1932 (English translation: *The Philosophy of the Enlightenment*, Princeton: Princeton University Press 1951); Isaiah Berlin, review, in: *English Historical Review* 68 (1953), 617–619.
47. Stephen Toulmin, *Cosmopolis: The Hidden Agenda of Modernity*, New York: The Free Press 1990.
48. Ernst Cassirer, *The Myth of the State*, New Haven: Yale University Press 1946; Ernst Cassirer, "Judaism and the Modern Political Myths," in: *Contemporary Jewish Record* 7 (1944), 115–126.
49. Ernst Troeltsch, "Die Zufälligkeit der Geschichtswahrheiten" [1923], reprinted in Ernst Troeltsch, *Schriften zur Politik und Kulturphilosophie (1918–1923)*, Berlin: De Gruyter 2002, 551–567, here 556f.
50. The following quotations from Ernst Troeltsch, *Der Historismus und seine Probleme* [1922] (= KGA, vol. 16), Berlin: De Gruyter 2008, vol. 1, 185.
51. Troeltsch, "Die Zufälligkeit der Geschichtswahrheiten," 557.
52. Ibid.
53. Troeltsch, "Christian Thought," in *Fünf Vorträge*, 150.
54. Ernst Troeltsch, "Die Selbständigkeit der Religion," in: *Zeitschrift für Theologie und Kirche* 5 (1895), 361–436, and 6 (1896), 71–110 and 167–218, here 82; now in Ernst Troeltsch, *Schriften zur Theologie und Religionsphilosophie (1888–1902)* (= KGA, vol. 1), 359–536, here 459. I discuss this text in more detail above in Part I, chapter 2.
55. Ernst Troeltsch, "Die deutsche Idee von der Freiheit" [1916], reprinted in Troeltsch, *Deutscher Geist und Westeuropa*, 80–107.
56. Troeltsch, "Die Selbständigkeit der Religion," 459.
57. Ibid., 422.

58. Ernst Troeltsch, *Psychologie und Erkenntnistheorie in der Religionswissenschaft. Eine Untersuchung über die Bedeutung der Kantischen Religionslehre für die heutige Religionswissenschaft*, Tübingen: Mohr Siebeck 1905, 42, also in Ernst Troeltsch, *Schriften zur Religionswissenschaft und Ethik (1903–1912)* (= KGA, vol. 6.1), Berlin: De Gruyter 2014, 205–256, here 246. In my eyes this text is an epoch-making attempt to combine pragmatist and historicist thinking in the theory of religion. I was not familiar with it when I wrote my book *The Genesis of Values* (Chicago: University of Chicago Press 2000) and now view it as backing the argument I made there.
59. Matthias Jung, "Der Ausdruckscharakter des Religiösen. Zur Pragmatik der symbolischen Formen bei Ernst Cassirer," in Hermann Deuser and Michael Moxter (eds.), *Rationalität der Religion und Kritik der Kultur: Hermann Cohen und Ernst Cassirer*, Würzburg: Echter 2002, 119–124.
60. On this problem with Cassirer more below, in ch. 3 of this Part, 204–207, in particular 404, fn. 42.
61. Troeltsch, "Psychologie und Erkenntnistheorie in der Religionswissenschaft," 41.
62. Troeltsch, "Die Zufälligkeit der Geschichtswahrheiten," 558.
63. My sincere thanks to Thomas Meyer, who provided me with particularly helpful advice when I revised the original version of this text.

III, 3

1. On Bellah and on Tillich's importance to him, see Part III, ch. 5 in this book.
2. For an overview of Parsons's theories and their critique, see Hans Joas and Wolfgang Knöbl, *Social Theory: Twenty Introductory Lectures*, Cambridge: Cambridge University Press 2009, 20–93; on Tillich's public role in the United States, see Stuart Mews, "Paul Tillich and the Religious Situation of American Intellectuals," in: *Religion* 2, no. 2 (1972), 122–140.
3. Ernst Troeltsch, *The Social Teaching of the Christian Churches*, London: George Allen & Unwin 1931.
4. Paul Tillich, "Kairos. Ideen zur Geisteslage der Gegenwart," in Paul Tillich (ed.), *Kairos. Zur Geisteslage und Geisteswendung*, Darmstadt: Otto Reichl 1926, 1–21, here 8. This is not the place to delve into this text's complicated history.
5. For a comprehensive history-of-theology account, see Alf Christophersen, *Kairos. Protestantische Zeitdeutungskämpfe in der Weimarer Republik*, Tübingen: Mohr Siebeck 2008; for a classic treatment of parallels among right-wing intellectuals, see Christian Graf von Krockow, *Die Entscheidung. Eine Untersuchung über Ernst Jünger, Carl Schmitt und Martin Heidegger* [1958], Frankfurt am Main: Campus 1990.
6. Paul Tillich, "The Demonic: A Contribution to the Interpretation of History" [1926], in Paul Tillich, *The Interpretation of History*, New York: Scribner 1936, 77–122, here 97.
7. Hermann Heimpel, "Geschichte und Geschichtswissenschaft," in: *Vierteljahrshefte für Zeitgeschichte* 5 (1957), 1–17, here 2, which uses the phrase "antihistorical revolution"; this becomes the "antihistoricist revolution" in the work of Kurt Nowak and

Friedrich Wilhelm Graf. See Graf, *Der heilige Zeitgeist. Studien zur Ideengeschichte der protestantischen Theologie in der Weimarer Republik*, Tübingen: Mohr Siebeck 2011, 111–138.

8. For an early treatment, see Kurt Herberger, "Historismus und Kairos. Die Überwindung des Historismus bei Ernst Troeltsch und Paul Tillich," in: *Theologische Blätter* 14 (1935), col. 129–141 and col. 161–175. Hartmut Ruddies, "Ernst Troeltsch und Paul Tillich. Eine theologische Skizze," in Wilhelm-Ludwig Federlin and Edmund Weber (eds.), *Unterwegs für die Volkskirche. Festschrift für Dieter Stoodt zum 60. Geburtstag*, Frankfurt am Main: Peter Lang 1987, 409–422; John Clayton, "Paul Tillich—ein 'verjüngter Troeltsch' oder noch ein 'Apfel vom Baume Kierkegaards'?," in Horst Renz and Friedrich Wilhelm Graf (eds.), *Umstrittene Moderne. Die Zukunft der Neuzeit im Urteil der Epoche Ernst Troeltschs* (= Troeltsch-Studien, vol. 4), Gütersloh: Gütersloher Verlagshaus 1987, 259–283; Georg Neugebauer, *Tillichs frühe Christologie. Eine Untersuchung zu Offenbarung und Geschichte bei Tillich vor dem Hintergrund seiner Schellingrezeption*, Berlin: De Gruyter 2007, 318–328; Georg Pfleiderer, "Kultursynthese auf dem Katheder. Zur Revision von Troeltschs Soziallehren in Tillichs Berliner Programmvorlesung von 1919," in Christian Danz and Werner Schüßler (eds.), *Religion—Kultur—Gesellschaft. Der frühe Tillich im Spiegel neuer Texte (1919–1920)*, Vienna: LIT 2008, 119–154; Christian Danz, " 'Vom Nutzen und Nachteil der Historie für das Leben.' Nietzsche, Troeltsch und Tillich über Auswege aus der Krisis des Historismus," in: *Internationales Jahrbuch für die Tillich-Forschung* 3 (2008), 61–81.

9. Paul Tillich, "Rezension: Ernst Troeltsch, *Der Historismus und seine Probleme*," in: *Theologische Literaturzeitung* 49 (1924), col. 25–30, here col. 25.

10. Ibid.

11. Ernst Troeltsch, *Der Historismus und seine Probleme* [1922], 2 vols. (= KGA, vols. 16.1 and 16.2), Berlin: De Gruyter 2008, 1015f.

12. Ibid., fn. 370a.

13. Eduard Spranger, "Das Historismus-Problem an der Universität Berlin seit 1900," in Hans Leussink, Eduard Neumann, and Georg Kotowski (eds.), *Studium Berolinense. Aufsätze und Beiträge zu Problemen der Wissenschaft und der Geschichte der Friedrich-Wilhelms-Universität zu Berlin*, Berlin: De Gruyter 1960, 425–443, here 434. Cf. Hans Joas, *The Sacredness of the Person: A New Genealogy of Human Rights*, Washington, DC: Georgetown University Press 2013, 121–124.

14. Troeltsch, *Der Historismus und seine Probleme*, vol. 1, 382.

15. Ernst Troeltsch, *Der Historismus und seine Überwindung*, Berlin: Pan Verlag Rolf Heise 1924.

16. See Joas, *The Sacredness of the Person*, 97–139.

17. Also in Tillich, "Rezension: Ernst Troeltsch, *Der Historismus und seine Überwindung*," col. 234f.

18. Here I agree with Michael Murrmann-Kahl. See Michael Murrmann-Kahl, " 'Tillichs Trauma.' Paul Tillich liest Ernst Troeltschs Historismusband," in Ulrich Barth et al. (eds.), *Aufgeklärte Religion und ihre Probleme. Schleiermacher—Troeltsch—Tillich*, Berlin: De Gruyter 2013, 193–212, here 202.

19. Paul Tillich, "Ernst Troeltsch. Versuch einer geistesgeschichtlichen Würdigung," in: *Kant-Studien* 29 (1924), 351–358, here quoted from the reprint in Friedrich Wilhelm Graf (ed.), *Ernst Troeltsch in Nachrufen*, Gütersloh: Gütersloher Verlagshaus 2002, 646–653, here 648.
20. George Herbert Mead, *The Philosophy of the Present*, La Salle: Open Court 1932. On the interpretation of this text, see Hans Joas, *G. H. Mead: A Contemporary Reexamination of His Thought*, Cambridge: MIT Press 1985, 164–194, and Hans Joas, "Pragmatism and Historicism: Mead's Philosophy of Temporality and the Logic of Historiography," in Hans Joas and Daniel R. Huebner (eds.), *The Timeliness of George Herbert Mead*, Chicago: University of Chicago Press 2016, 62–81.
21. Robert N. Bellah, "Religious Evolution," in: *American Sociological Review* 29 (1964), 358–374; Robert N. Bellah, *Religion in Human Evolution: From the Paleolithic to the Axial Age*, Cambridge: Harvard University Press 2011.
22. On the significance of this shift within aesthetics, see Karl Heinz Bohrer, *Die Ästhetik des Schreckens. Die pessimistische Romantik und Ernst Jüngers Frühwerk*, Munich: Hanser 1978, esp. 269–357.
23. For example, Paul Tillich, "The Religious Situation" [1926] (transl. by H. Richard Niebuhr), New York: Meridian 1956, 41.
24. As Graf tells us with reference to Tillich. See Graf, *Der heilige Zeitgeist*, 350f.
25. Paul Tillich, "Geschichtsphilosophie (Vorlesungsmanuskript und Nachschrift 1929/30)," in Paul Tillich, *Vorlesungen über die Geschichtsphilosophie und Sozialpädagogik*, Berlin: De Gruyter 2007, 1–118, here 59, as quoted in Murrmann-Kahl, "Tillichs Trauma," 207.
26. Paul Tillich, "Der Protestantismus" [1929], in Paul Tillich, *Ausgewählte Texte*, 200–221, here 202.
27. Christophersen, *Kairos*, 87.
28. For a thorough account, see Wolfgang Reinhard, *Die Unterwerfung der Welt. Globalgeschichte der europäischen Expansion*, Munich: C. H. Beck 2016.
29. Paul Tillich, *Das Christentum und die Gesellschaftsprobleme der Gegenwart* [1919], quoted in Friedemann Voigt, "Historische und dogmatische Methode der Theologie. Der Absolutheitscharakter des religiösen Bewußtseins bei Troeltsch und Tillich," in Barth et al. (eds.), *Aufgeklärte Religion*, 213–228, here 223.
30. Tillich's book *The Dynamics of Faith* (New York: Harper & Brothers 1967) was translated into German as *Wesen und Wandel des Glaubens*, Frankfurt am Main: Ullstein 1975. The two versions differ substantially.
31. Tillich, "The Religious Situation," 35.
32. Paul Tillich, *The Courage to Be*, New Haven: Yale University Press 1952.
33. Troeltsch, *Der Historismus und seine Probleme*, vol. 2, 991 and 998.
34. Ernst Troeltsch, "Rezension: Auguste Sabatier, Esquisse d'une philosophie de la religion d'après la psychologie et l'histoire" [1897], originally in *Deutsche Litteraturzeitung* 19 (1898), col. 737–742; also in Ernst Troeltsch, *Rezensionen und Kritiken (1894–1900)* (= KGA, vol. 2), Berlin: De Gruyter 2007, 328–333, here 329 and 332.
35. Paul Tillich, "The Religious Symbol," in: *Daedalus* 87, no. 3 (Summer 1958), 3–21.
36. For more on Cassirer and the relationship between his philosophy and that of Troeltsch, see Part III, ch. 2.

37. Paul Tillich, "Probleme des Mythos," in: *Theologische Literaturzeitung* 49 (1924), col. 115–117; Paul Tillich, "Mythos und Mythologie" [1930], in Paul Tillich, *Gesammelte Werke*, vol. V, 187–195, Stuttgart: Evangelisches Verlagswerk 1964.
38. Tillich, "Mythos und Mythologie," 188f.
39. Ferdinand de Saussure, *Cours de linguistique générale* [1915], Paris: Payot 1969, 100.
40. Tillich, "The Religious Symbol," 3.
41. Ibid., 4.
42. Ernst Cassirer, *The Philosophy of Symbolic Forms* [1923], vol. 2, New Haven: Yale University Press 1965. A copious literature exists on the relationship between myth and religion in Cassirer's work. See the details provided in Hans Joas, "Introduction to the Special Issue on Ernst Cassirer's Philosophy of Religion," in: *Svensk Teologisk Kvartalskrift* 82 (2006), 2–4, and the contributions by Michael Bongardt and Matthias Jung in the same issue.
43. For an overview, see Robert N. Bellah and Hans Joas (eds.), *The Axial Age and Its Consequences*, Cambridge: Harvard University Press 2012; Hans Joas, *The Power of the Sacred: An Alternative to the Narrative of Disenchantment*, New York: Oxford University Press 2021, 154–194.
44. Tillich, "The Religious Symbol," 10. On the relationship between the symbol theories put forward by Tillich and Cassirer, see Christian Danz, "Der Begriff des Symbols bei Paul Tillich und Ernst Cassirer," in Dietrich Korsch and Enno Rudolph (eds.), *Die Prägnanz der Religion in der Kultur. Ernst Cassirer und die Theologie*, Tübingen: Mohr Siebeck 2000, 201–228.
45. Tillich repeatedly dismissed pragmatism as nominalism or voluntarism. See, for example, Tillich, "The Religious Situation," 76f.; Tillich, *Wesen und Wandel des Glaubens*, 48. On the overall German reception of pragmatism, see Hans Joas, "American Pragmatism and German Thought: A History of Misunderstandings," in Hans Joas, *Pragmatism and Social Theory*, Chicago: University of Chicago Press 1993, 94–121.
46. Hermann Deuser, "Gottes Poesie oder Anschauung des Unbedingten? Semiotische Religionstheorie bei C. S. Peirce und P. Tillich," in Christian Danz, Werner Schüßler, and Erdmann Sturm (eds.), *Das Symbol als Sprache der Religion*, Berlin: LIT 2007, 117–134.
47. Robert N. Bellah, *The Broken Covenant: American Civil Religion in Time of Trial*, New York: Seabury Press 1975, 4. For more on this, see Part IV, ch. 5.
48. For an informative account, see Matteo Bortolini, "Blurring the Boundary Line: The Origins and Fate of Robert Bellah's Symbolic Realism," in Christian Fleck and Andreas Hess (eds.), *Knowledge for Whom? Public Sociology in the Making*, Farnham: Routledge 2014, 205–227, here 219.
49. Robert N. Bellah, *Beyond Belief: Essays on Religion in a Post-traditional World*, New York: Harper and Row 1970, 263.
50. Talcott Parsons, "A Paradigm of the Human Condition," in Talcott Parsons, *Action Theory and the Human Condition*, New York: The Free Press 1978, 352–433, here 390.
51. For an excellent study, see Erdmann Sturm, "Tillich liest Troeltschs 'Soziallehren,'" in Barth et al. (eds.), *Aufgeklärte Religion*, 271–290.

52. Paul Tillich, "The Permanent Significance of the Catholic Church for Protestantism" [1941], in Tillich, *Ausgewählte Texte*, 277–287; the term "antisymbolism" appears on 282.
53. Werner Schüßler, "'Meine katholischen Freunde verstehen mich besser als meine protestantischen.' Wie 'katholisch' ist Paul Tillich?," in Barth et al. (eds.), *Aufgeklärte Religion*, 312–329, here 327.
54. Quoted in Thomas Franklin O'Meara, O.P., "Paul Tillich in Catholic Thought: The Past and the Future," in Raymond Bulman and Frederick Parrella (eds.), *Paul Tillich: A New Catholic Assessment*, Collegeville: Liturgical Press 1994, 9–32, here 25.
55. See Schüßler, "Wie 'katholisch' ist Paul Tillich?," 325. The expression "dynamic typology" appears in Paul Tillich, "Christianity and the Encounter of the World Religions" [1963], in Tillich, *Ausgewählte Texte*, 419–453, here 419 and 438.
56. Tillich, *Christianity and the Encounter of the World Religions*, 438.
57. Ibid., 438f.
58. Paul Tillich, "Kirche und Kultur" [1924], in Tillich, *Ausgewählte Texte*, 109–122, here 116.
59. Robert N. Bellah, "Flaws in the Protestant Code: Some Religious Sources of America's Troubles," in: *Ethical Perspectives* 7 (2000), 288–299.
60. See Bellah, "Beyond Belief," xiv–xvi and 255.
61. Robert N. Bellah, "Paul Tillich and the Challenge of Modernity" (unpublished manuscript, 2013).
62. Robert N. Bellah, *Tokugawa Religion: The Cultural Roots of Modern Japan*, New York: The Free Press 1957. The definition in Bellah's book (6) is based on Tillich. On the significance of this study to the development of sociology, see Joas and Knöbl, *Social Theory*, 330–332.
63. Robert N. Bellah, "Words for Paul Tillich," in: *Harvard Divinity School Bulletin* 30 (1966), 15f.
64. Tillich, *Dynamics of Faith*, 67.
65. For an instructive account from this perspective, see Sebastian C. H. Kim (ed.), *Christian Theology in Asia*, Cambridge: Cambridge University Press 2008.
66. Tillich, *Dynamics of Faith*, 1. The German version has "Ergriffensein von dem, was uns unbedingt angeht," *Wesen und Wandel des Glaubens*, 9.
67. Ernst Troeltsch, "The Ideas of Natural Law and Humanity in World Politics" [1923], in Otto Gierke, *Natural Law and the Theory of Society, 1500–1800*, Boston: Beacon Press 1957, 201–222.
68. Ernst Troeltsch, *Glaubenslehre*, Munich: Duncker & Humblot 1925, 201.
69. Ibid., 202.
70. Ibid.
71. Ernst Troeltsch, "Praktische christliche Ethik. Diktate zur Vorlesung im Wintersemester 1911/12," from the estate of Gertrud von le Fort, Eleonore von la Chevallerie and Friedrich Wilhelm Graf (eds.), *Mitteilungen der Ernst-Troeltsch-Gesellschaft VII*, Augsburg 1991, 129–174, here 143.
72. Tillich, "The Religious Situation," 216.

73. Paul Tillich, "On the Idea of a Theology of Culture" [1919], in Mark Kline Taylor (ed.), *Paul Tillich: Theologian of the Boundaries*, London: Collins 1987, 35–54.
74. Paul Tillich, "Theonomie," in *Die Religion in Geschichte und Gegenwart*, ed. Hermann Gunkel and Leopold Zscharnack, vol. 5, Tübingen: Mohr Siebeck 1931 (2nd ed.), col. 1128f.
75. Christian Danz, *Religion als Freiheitsbewußtsein. Eine Studie zur Theologie als Theorie der Konstitutionsbedingungen individueller Subjektivität bei Paul Tillich*, Berlin: De Gruyter 2000.
76. Such as pragmatism. Although Tillich, as I have mentioned, typically has disparaging things to say about this philosophical current, it seems to me there can be no doubt that he was influenced by William James's psychology of religion in a range of ways. Even the title of perhaps Tillich's most famous book, *The Courage to Be*, seems to echo James's famous expression "willingness to be."
77. Paul Ricœur, "Theonomy and/or Autonomy," in Miroslav Volf et al. (eds.), *The Future of Theology: Essays in Honor of Jürgen Moltmann*, Grand Rapids: Eerdmans 1996, 284–298, here 284. Tillich himself sometimes treats the term "heteronomy" as a reaction to demands for autonomy—for example, in Paul Tillich, *Systematic Theology*, vol. 1, Chicago: University of Chicago Press 1951, 84f.
78. Paul Tillich, *Systematic Theology*, vol. 3, Chicago: University of Chicago Press 1963, 251.
79. Collected in Parsons, *Action Theory and the Human Condition*. On this, see Hans Joas, "The Gift of Life: Parsons' Late Sociology of Religion," in: *Journal of Classical Sociology* 1 (2001), 127–141.
80. Robert N. Bellah et al., *Habits of the Heart: Individualism and Commitment in American Life*, Berkeley: University of California Press 1985.
81. Bellah, "Paul Tillich and the Challenge of Modernity," 16f.
82. Tillich, "The Religious Situation," 49.
83. Such as the influence of Georg Simmel, Max Weber, and Karl Mannheim on Tillich or the reception of Tillich in the work of Peter Berger and J. Milton Yinger.
84. Tillich, "The Religious Situation," 111. This assessment by no means applies to all of Tillich's intellectual comrades-in-arms who came together to advance a "religious socialism."
85. J. Milton Yinger, quoted in Mews, *Paul Tillich*, 134f. I am particularly indebted to Werner Schüßler for his crucial comments on this chapter.

III, 4

1. Stephen Toulmin, *Return to Reason*, Cambridge: Harvard University Press 2001, 143.
2. Hans Joas, *The Genesis of Values*, Chicago: University of Chicago Press 2000.
3. Alasdair MacIntyre, *After Virtue: A Study in Moral Theory*, Notre Dame: Notre Dame University Press 1981.
4. An excellent overview of Ricœur's life and work can be found in François Dosse, *Paul Ricœur. Les sens d'une vie*, Paris 1997. Of the vast and rich secondary literature,

I will mention just the following valuable study of Ricœur's philosophical development into the 1980s: Bernhard Waldenfels, *Phänomenologie in Frankreich*, Frankfurt am Main: Suhrkamp 1987, 266–335. In connection with the present book, see, for example, Maureen Junker-Kenny, *Religion and Public Reason: A Comparison of the Positions of John Rawls, Jürgen Habermas and Paul Ricœur*, Berlin: De Gruyter 2014, 184–279.

5. Paul Ricœur, *Oneself as Another*, Chicago: University of Chicago Press 1996, 170.
6. In the following remarks, I draw on my book *The Genesis of Values*, 171–175. A comparison of Ricœur and my theory of action has now appeared, though it ignores my book mentioned in the previous sentence: Paolo Furia, "Le scienze sociali e il paradigma ermeneutico in Paul Ricœur e Hans Joas. La libertà come creativitá," in Gaetano Chiurazzi and Giacomo Pezzone (eds.), *Attualità del possibile*, Milan: Mimesis 2017, 81–94.
7. Ricœur, *Oneself as Another*, 207.
8. There are obvious parallels with the ideas developed by the late Troeltsch, as set out in Part II, ch. 2. Troeltsch does not appear to have made much of an intellectual impact on Ricœur, however.
9. Ricœur, *Oneself as Another*, 24.
10. Paul Ricœur, "Experience and Language in Religious Discourse," in Dominique Janicaud et al., *Phenomenology and the "Theological Turn": The French Debate*, New York: Fordham University Press 2000, 127–146. The situation is complicated because Ricœur published a number of overlapping texts on the basis of these lectures. I will forgo discussion of the differences between these versions here.
11. Ibid., 19.
12. See, for example, Paul Ricœur and André LaCocque, *Penser la bible*, Paris: Seuil 1998.
13. William James, *The Varieties of Religious Experience*, New York: Longmans, Green and Co. 1902.
14. James M. Edie, *William James and Phenomenology*, Bloomington: Indiana University Press 1987, 49ff.
15. For a proposed expansion of perspective within Protestantism, see Wolfgang Huber, *Glaubensfragen. Eine evangelische Orientierung*, Munich: C. H. Beck 2017, 42–67 (chapter: "Quellen des Glaubens").
16. Paul Ricœur, "Manifestation and Proclamation," in Paul Ricœur, *Figuring the Sacred: Religion, Narrative, and Imagination*, Minneapolis: Fortress 1995, 48–67.
17. For an in-depth treatment of Otto, see Part I, ch. 3.
18. See Hans Joas, *The Power of the Sacred: An Alternative to the Narrative of Disenchantment*, New York: Oxford University Press 2021, 147–151.
19. See ch. 3 in this Part of the book. Ricœur built on Tillich in a number of ways, particularly his theory of symbols. See Paul Ricœur, "Préface," in Jocelyn Dunphy, *Paul Tillich et le symbole religieux*, Paris: Jean-Pierre Delarge 1977, 11–14.
20. Robert N. Bellah, "Flaws in the Protestant Code: Some Religious Sources of America's Troubles," in: *Ethical Perspectives* 7 (2000), 288–299.
21. For more detail on this, see the title essay of my book *Do We Need Religion? On the Experience of Self-Transcendence*, Boulder: Paradigm 2008, 3–19.

22. Paul Ricœur, "Theonomy and/or Autonomy," in Miroslav Volf et al. (eds.), *The Future of Theology: Essays in Honor of Jürgen Moltmann*, Grand Rapids: Eerdmans 1996, 284–298. See also my Introductory Remarks in this Part, 167–170.
23. Gabriel Marcel, *Tragic Wisdom and Beyond, Including Conversations between Paul Ricœur and Gabriel Marcel*, Evanston: Northwestern University Press 1973, 241. Jaspers and Marcel are the focus of Ricœur's first major publications in the late 1940s.

III, 5

1. Wolfgang Huber, *Von der Freiheit. Perspektiven für eine solidarische Welt*, Munich: C. H. Beck 2012. (All page references are to this volume.)
2. See esp. Part II, ch. 3 on Alfred Döblin, along with the Introductory Remarks in Part II; see also Hans Joas, *Faith as an Option: Possible Futures for Christianity*, Stanford: Stanford University Press 2014, 134.
3. Wolfgang Huber, *Kirche in der Zeitenwende. Gesellschaftlicher Wandel und Erneuerung der Kirche*, Gütersloh: Verlag Bertelsmann Stiftung 1998.
4. See Part IV, ch. 6.
5. Michael Theunissen, *Sein und Schein. Die kritische Funktion der Hegelschen Logik*, Frankfurt am Main: Suhrkamp 1978. His definition appears on 46: "Communicative freedom means that a person experiences the other not as a barrier but as a condition of possibility for his or her own self-realization." On the trigger for Huber's reception of Theunissen, see fn. 20 in the Introductory Remarks in Part III of the present book.
6. Michael Theunissen, *Der Andere. Studien zur Sozialontologie der Gegenwart* [1965], Berlin: De Gruyter ²1981.
7. Michael Theunissen, *Der Begriff Verzweiflung. Korrekturen an Kierkegaard*, Frankfurt am Main: Suhrkamp 1993.
8. Michael Theunissen, "Freiheit und Schuld—Freiheit und Sünde," in Hans-Richard Reuter et al. (eds.), *Freiheit verantworten. Festschrift für Wolfgang Huber zum 60. Geburtstag*, Gütersloh: Gütersloher Verlagshaus 2002, 343–356, here 354. The following portrait of Theunissen is well worth reading: Jürgen Habermas, "Communicative Freedom and Negative Theology: Questions for Michael Theunissen," in Jürgen Habermas, *The Liberating Power of Symbols: Philosophical Essays*, Oxford: Polity 2001, 90–111.
9. On Niebuhr and Mead, see Part IV, ch. 2.
10. Jürgen Habermas, *The Theory of Communicative Action*, 2 vols., London: Heinemann 1984, here vol. 1, 75–101.
11. Romano Guardini, *Die Macht. Versuch einer Wegweisung*, Würzburg: Werkbund 1951.
12. For a particularly vivid example, see his book on Bonhoeffer: Wolfgang Huber, *Dietrich Bonhoeffer. Auf dem Weg zur Freiheit*, Munich: C. H. Beck 2019; see esp. the chapter "Verantwortungsethik" (209–232). The other key source of Huber's conception of responsibility is H. Richard Niebuhr. See, for example, Huber, *Von der Freiheit*, 80–83, but also Wolfgang Huber, *Ethics: The Fundamental Questions of Our Lives*,

Washington, DC: Georgetown University Press 2015, 90. On H. Richard Niebuhr's conception of responsibility, see Part IV, ch. 2, as well as my remarks on differences between him and his brother Reinhold in the same Part, ch. 4.
13. On Huber's position within the landscape of Protestant theology, see Martin Laube, "Die Dialektik der Freiheit. Systematisch-theologische Perspektiven," in Martin Laube (ed.), *Freiheit*, Tübingen: UTB 2014, 174–178.
14. Thomas Hobbes, *Leviathan*, section xxi.
15. Robert N. Bellah et al., *Habits of the Heart: Individualism and Commitment in American Life*, Berkeley: University of California Press 1985. On Bellah, see Part IV, ch. 5. On this combination of both types in the same person with reference to the term "yuppie," see also Hans Joas, *The Creativity of Action*, Chicago: University of Chicago Press 1996, 256–258.
16. Important reflections on this can be found esp. in Max Scheler, *Formalism in Ethics and Non-formal Ethics of Value: A New Attempt toward the Foundation of an Ethical Personalism* [1913–16], Evanston: Northwestern University Press 1973, esp. the chapter "Value-Ethics and Ethics of Imperatives," 163–238; Franz Rosenzweig, *The Star of Redemption* [1921], Madison: University of Wisconsin Press 2005. See also Hans Joas, "Liebe, Gabe, Gerechtigkeit," in Hans Joas (ed.), *Die Zehn Gebote. Ein widersprüchliches Erbe?*, Cologne: Böhlau 2006, 175–183.
17. See my remarks on "theonomy" in the Introductory Remarks in Part III and in Part III, ch. 3 on Tillich.
18. Paul Ricœur, "Love and Justice," in Paul Ricœur, *Figuring the Sacred: Religion, Narrative, and Imagination*, Minneapolis: Fortress 1995, 315–329, here 324. On Ricœur, see ch. 3 in this Part.
19. Wolfgang Huber, *Gerechtigkeit und Recht. Grundlinien christlicher Rechtsethik*, 3rd rev. ed., Gütersloh: Gütersloher Verlagshaus 2006; on the aspect of interest here, see esp. the chapter "Gerechtigkeit und Liebe," 238–264; here (254) we find a pleasing phrase that builds on the work of Hans-Richard Reuter: "It is the Gospel that truly gilds the Golden Rule." A compressed version appears in Wolfgang Huber, "Rechtsethik," in Wolfgang Huber, Torsten Meireis, and Hans-Richard Reuter (eds.), *Handbuch der Evangelischen Ethik*, Munich: C. H. Beck 2015, 125–193. A comprehensive attempt to elaborate the consequences of a theology of communicative freedom with respect not so much to appropriate institutions as to social cohesion can be found in Heinrich Bedford-Strohm, *Gemeinschaft aus kommunikativer Freiheit. Sozialer Zusammenhalt in der modernen Gesellschaft. Ein theologischer Beitrag*, Leipzig: Evangelische Verlagsanstalt 1999.
20. Michael Sandel, *The Case against Perfection: Ethics in the Age of Genetic Engineering*, Cambridge: Harvard University Press 2007.
21. See, for example, Wolfgang Huber, *Der gemachte Mensch. Christlicher Glaube und Biotechnik*, Berlin: Wichern 2002. See also Hans Joas, *The Sacredness of the Person: A New Genealogy of Human Rights*, Washington, DC: Georgetown University Press 2013, 143–172.
22. Joas, *The Sacredness of the Person*, 158–170.

23. Axel Honneth, *Freedom's Right: The Social Foundations of Democratic Life*, New York: Columbia University Press 2014. On this, see also my remarks in the introduction to the present book.
24. Honneth, *Freedom's Right*, 337, n. 1.
25. Here and in the following sentence I draw on John Gray, *Isaiah Berlin*, Princeton: Princeton University Press 1996, 1.
26. See Hans Joas, "Combining Value Pluralism and Moral Universalism: Isaiah Berlin and Beyond," in: *The Responsive Community* 9 (1999), 17–29, as well as my obituary for Isaiah Berlin: "Der Liberalismus ist kein politisches Heilsversprechen," *Die Zeit*, November 14, 1997.
27. Since the meaning of the phrase "dignity of nature" is not self-evident, it requires explanation. See Huber, *Gerechtigkeit und Recht*, 362–381.
28. Max Weber to Adolf von Harnack, February 5, 1906, in Max Weber, *Briefe 1906–1908*, Tübingen: Mohr Siebeck 1990 (= MWGA, section II, vol. 5), 32f.
29. Wolfgang Reinhard, "Historiker, 'Modernisierung' und Modernisierung. Erfahrungen mit dem Konzept 'Modernisierung' in der neueren Geschichte," in Walter Haug and Burghart Wachinger (eds.), *Innovation und Originalität*, Tübingen: Max Niemeyer 1993, 53–69, here 68.
30. Joas, *The Sacredness of the Person*, 20–33.
31. Wolfgang Huber responded to an earlier version of my critical questions with important clarifications and remarks in Wolfgang Huber, "Über die kommunikative Freiheit hinaus," in Heinrich Bedford-Strohm, Paul Nolte, and Rüdiger Sachau (eds.), *Kommunikative Freiheit. Interdisziplinäre Diskurse mit Wolfgang Huber*, Leipzig: Evangelische Verlagsanstalt 2014, 175–191, here esp. 181–186. What emerges here is that the difference between us with respect to the status of the value of freedom in ethics seems to be more a matter of conceptual strategy than substance.

IV, 1

1. Ernst Troeltsch, review: "Hermann Süskind, *Christentum und Geschichte bei Schleiermacher*" [1913], in Ernst Troeltsch, *Rezensionen und Kritiken (1901–1914)* (= KGA, vol. 4), Berlin: De Gruyter 2004, 661–666, here 664. In a letter written after Süskind had died in the war, Troeltsch wrote that the latter had been "the most significant and most original scholar to build on my ideas"; see Ernst Troeltsch, *Briefe III (1905–1915)* (= KGA, vol. 20), Berlin: De Gruyter 2016, 724f.
2. Troeltsch, review: "Hermann Süskind, *Christentum und Geschichte bei Schleiermacher*," 664.
3. Ernst Troeltsch, *Die Absolutheit des Christentums und die Religionsgeschichte (1902–1912)* (= KGA, vol. 5), Berlin: De Gruyter 1998. English translation: *The Absoluteness of Christianity and the History of Religion*, Richmond: John Knox Press 1971.
4. Ernst Troeltsch, *Der Historismus und seine Probleme* [1922] (= KGA, vol. 16.1 and 16.2), Berlin: De Gruyter 2008. Contrary to the widely held belief that Troeltsch failed to achieve his objectives in this book and acknowledged his failure, I take

the view that he succeeded in resolving the problem he had set himself. See Hans Joas, *The Sacredness of the Person: A New Genealogy of Human Rights*, Washington, DC: Georgetown University Press 2013, 97–139.
5. Troeltsch, *Historismus*, 763.
6. For an attempt to illuminate this through a critical examination of Max Weber, see *The Power of the Sacred: An Alternative to the Narrative of Disenchantment*, New York: Oxford University Press 2021, 200–203.
7. Friedrich Wilhelm Graf, *Fachmenschenfreundschaft. Studien zu Troeltsch und Weber*, Berlin: De Gruyter 2014, 114.
8. Ernst Troeltsch, "Die Bedeutung des Protestantismus für die Entstehung der modernen Welt" [1911], in: Ernst Troeltsch, *Schriften zur Bedeutung des Protestantismus für die moderne Welt (1906–1913)* (= KGA, vol. 8), Berlin: De Gruyter 2001, 199–316, here 316. English translation: Ernst Troeltsch, *Protestantism and Progress: A Historical Study of the Relation of Protestantism to the Modern World*, London: Routledge 2017, here 116f. See also the Introductory Remarks in Part I, 34.
9. Volkhard Krech and Hartmann Tyrell, "Religionssoziologie um die Jahrhundertwende. Zu Vorgeschichte, Kontext und Beschaffenheit einer Subdisziplin der Soziologie," in Volkhard Krech and Hartmann Tyrell (eds.), *Religionssoziologie um 1900*, Würzburg: Ergon 1995, 11–78, here 14; Hartmann Tyrell, "Von der 'Soziologie statt Religion' zur Religionssoziologie," in ibid., 79–128, here 107f.
10. As far as I know, this is yet to be done on a systematic basis. An example would be the book by Louis Wallis, *Sociological Study of the Bible*, Chicago: University of Chicago Press 1912, which was reviewed by Troeltsch in 1913. The review also appears in Troeltsch, *Rezensionen und Kritiken (1901–1914)*, 721–727. On the early history of US-American sociology of religion, see William H. Swatos Jr., "Religious Sociology and the Sociology of Religion in America at the Turn of the Twentieth Century: Divergences from a Common Theme," in: *Sociological Analysis* 50 (1989), 363–375. That the inclusion of dissertations (rather than just publications) has produced a new picture is evident in Anthony J. Blasi, "Sociology of Religion in the United States," in Anthony J. Blasi and Giuseppe Giordan (eds.), *Sociologies of Religion: National Traditions*, Leiden: Brill 2015, 52–75; and in greater depth in Anthony J. Blasi, *Sociology of Religion in America: A History of a Secular Fascination with Religion*, Leiden: Brill 2014.
11. For example, in the writings of Marcel Granet and Louis Gernet. To my knowledge, such an interdisciplinary account is also yet to appear. But for a study of importance due to its strong consideration of Mauss and the work of René Girard, see Camille Tarot, *Le symbolique et le sacré. Théories de la religion*, Paris: La Découverte 2008.
12. A monograph on Honigsheim seems to me a major desideratum. See the bibliography in Alphons Silbermann and Paul Röhrig (eds.), *Kultur, Volksbildung und Gesellschaft. Paul Honigsheim zum Gedenken seines 100. Geburtstages*, Frankfurt am Main: Peter Lang 1987, 177–204, esp. the titles of his studies in the historical sociology of religion. Due to his importance to the discipline of comparative religion, more research has been done on Joachim Wach. For an overview, see Rainer Flasche, "Joachim Wach 1898–1955," in Axel Michaels (ed.), *Klassiker der Religionswissenschaft*, Munich: C. H. Beck 1997, 290–302. The same volume contains bibliographical

details of his writings and the research literature (401f.). For further information on this topic, see Hans G. Kippenberg, "Joachim Wachs Bild vom George-Kreis und seine Revision von Max Webers Soziologie religiöser Gemeinschaften," in: *Zeitschrift für Religions- und Geistesgeschichte* 61 (2009), 313–331. Also worth a look is the book by Gustav Mensching, *Soziologie der Religion*, Bonn: Röhrscheid 1947.

13. See, for example, Benjamin Nelson, *The Idea of Usury: From Tribal Brotherhood to Universal Otherhood* [1949], Chicago: University of Chicago Press 1969. See also Benjamin Nelson, *On the Roads to Modernity: Conscience, Science and Civilizations*, Totowa: Rowman & Littlefield 1981. His work is discussed in depth in Johann Arnason, *Civilizations in Dispute: Historical Questions and Theoretical Traditions*, Leiden: Brill 2003, 139–157. For an overview of his oeuvre, see Friedrich Tenbruck, "Nekrolog," in: *Kölner Zeitschrift für Soziologie und Sozialpsychologie* 30 (1978), 401–404, and Edmund Leites, "'From Tribal Brotherhood to Universal Otherhood': On Benjamin Nelson," in: *Social Research* 61 (1994), 955–965.

14. The literature is vast. The greatest services have surely been rendered by Wolfgang Schluchter. By way of contrast, it seems naive to describe the hermeneutic engagement with the classical figures as an ancestor cult and to urge its cessation. See Rodney Stark, "Putting an End to Ancestor Worship," in: *Journal for the Scientific Study of Religion* 43 (2004), 465–475.

15. We could expand our perspective further still by considering the history of the discipline of anthropology/ethnology and its key figures (such as Clifford Geertz and Victor Turner) in light of their exchange with sociology.

16. Joas, *The Power of the Sacred*, 197–199. Here I draw on a number of statements in that volume.

17. Philip Gorski, "The Return of the Repressed: Religion and the Political Unconscious of Historical Sociology," in Julia Adams, Elizabeth Clemens, and Ann Orloff (eds.), *Remaking Modernity: Politics, History, and Sociology*, Durham: Duke University Press 2005, 161–189.

18. I flesh this point out in Joas, *The Power of the Sacred*, 206–233.

19. See, for example, the contributions in Christopher Adair-Toteff (ed.), *The Anthem Companion to Ernst Troeltsch*, London: Anthem Press 2018, and Part I, ch. 1.

20. Max Weber, "Die protestantischen Sekten und der Geist des Kapitalismus," in Max Weber, *Gesammelte Aufsätze zur Religionssoziologie I*, Tübingen: Mohr Siebeck 1920, 207–236.

21. Everett Hughes, review: "H. Richard Niebuhr, *The Social Sources of Denominationalism*," in: *American Journal of Sociology* 60 (1954), 320.

22. In theology, see, for example, James M. Gustafson, *Treasure in Earthen Vessels: The Church as a Human Community* [1961], Louisville: University of Kentucky Press 1976; in sociology, see Robert Wuthnow, *The Restructuring of American Religion*, Princeton: Princeton University Press 1988.

23. See the critique in Martin Marty, *Modern American Religion*, vol. 2: *The Noise of Conflict 1919–1941*, Chicago: University of Chicago Press 1991, 318.

24. Will Herberg, *Protestant, Catholic, Jew: An Essay in American Religious Sociology*, Garden City: Doubleday & Co. 1955.

25. Dwight D. Eisenhower in the *New York Times*, December 23, 1952, here quoted in Herberg, *Protestant, Catholic, Jew*, 97.
26. Herberg, *Protestant, Catholic, Jew*, 288. On Herberg's critique of US-American secularist humanism in the form of the "common faith" inspired by John Dewey and centered on the sacralization of democracy, see ibid., 100ff. For more detail on Dewey's theory of religion, see Part III, ch. 2.
27. For a detailed account, see Hans Joas and Wolfgang Knöbl, *Social Theory: Twenty Introductory Lectures*, Cambridge: Cambridge University Press, 308–338.
28. Of Eisenstadt's voluminous oeuvre I will mention just Shmuel N. Eisenstadt, *Power, Trust, and Meaning: Essays in Sociological Theory and Analysis*, Chicago: University of Chicago Press 1995.
29. Karl Jaspers, *The Origin and Goal of History* [1949], London: Routledge 2010. For an overview of the literature, see Hans Joas, *The Power of the Sacred*, 154–194.
30. The most impressive example in my opinion is Ilana Friedrich Silber, *Virtuosity, Charisma, and Social Order: A Comparative Sociological Study of Monasticism in Theravada Buddhism and Medieval Catholicism*, Cambridge: Cambridge University Press 1995.
31. Robert N. Bellah, *Tokugawa Religion: The Cultural Roots of Modern Japan*, New York: The Free Press 1957. More details on his writings can be found in the chapter dedicated to his work in the present volume.
32. José Casanova, *Public Religions in the Modern World*, Chicago: University of Chicago Press 1994. Further details of Casanova's writings can be found in the relevant chapter.

IV, 2

1. For more detail, see Hans Joas, "Pragmatism and Historicism: Mead's Philosophy of Temporality and the Logic of Historiography," in Hans Joas and Daniel R. Huebner (eds.), *The Timeliness of George Herbert Mead*, Chicago: University of Chicago Press 2016, 62–81.
2. See the chapter "Neither Kant nor Nietzsche: What Is Affirmative Genealogy?," in Hans Joas, *The Sacredness of the Person: A New Genealogy of Human Rights*, Washington, DC: Georgetown University Press 2013, 97–139.
3. H. Richard Niebuhr, *Ernst Troeltsch's Philosophy of Religion* (Philosophical Dissertation), Yale University 1924.
4. On this term, which goes back to Hermann Heimpel, see esp. Friedrich Wilhelm Graf, "Die 'antihistoristische Revolution' in der protestantischen Theologie der zwanziger Jahre," in Friedrich Wilhelm Graf, *Der heilige Zeitgeist. Studien zur Ideengeschichte der protestantischen Theologie in der Weimarer Republik*, Tübingen: Mohr Siebeck 2011, 111–137.
5. Esp. Josiah Royce, *The Problem of Christianity* [1913], Washington, DC: Catholic University of America Press, 2001; for a recent treatment, see Joshua Daniel, *Transforming Faith: Individual and Community in H. Richard Niebuhr*, Eugene: Pickwick 2015, and

Hans Joas, *The Power of the Sacred: An Alternative to the Narrative of Disenchantment*, New York: Oxford University Press 2021, 44–57.

6. Jon Diefenthaler, *H. Richard Niebuhr: A Lifetime of Reflections on the Church and the World*, Macon: Mercer University Press 1986.
7. Walter Bodenhafer, "The Comparative Role of the Group Concept in Ward's 'Dynamic Sociology' and Contemporary American Sociology," in: *American Journal of Sociology* 26 (1920–1921), 273–314, 425–474, 582–600, and 716–743.
8. H. Richard Niebuhr, *The Meaning of Revelation*, New York: Macmillan 1941, x. Yet Niebuhr was neither a great authority on Barth nor was he ever a Barthian. For a persuasive account backed up by plenty of evidence, see James W. Fowler, *To See the Kingdom: The Theological Vision of H. Richard Niebuhr*, Nashville: Abingdon Press 1974, 32, 44, and 60f.
9. One of the most important accounts of Niebuhr's theological backgrounds concedes that justice can only be done to this thinker if "his unique, effortless interweaving of theological and sociological analyses" is acknowledged. See Hans W. Frei, "Niebuhr's Theological Background," in Paul Ramsey (ed.), *Faith and Ethics: The Theology of H. Richard Niebuhr*, New York: Harper & Bros. 1957, 9–64, here 9.
10. The great sociologist of religion Robert Bellah (for more on him, see ch. 5 in this Part) was strongly influenced by H. Richard Niebuhr. See, for example, the text of the address he held in Yale marking the one hundredth anniversary of Niebuhr's birth: Robert N. Bellah, "Religious Pluralism and Religious Truth," in Robert N. Bellah and Steven M. Tipton (eds), *The Robert Bellah Reader*, Durham: Duke University Press 2006, 474–489. He not only called him "America's foremost theologian" (in the blurb for Niebuhr's book *Faith on Earth*) but also "a good sociologist," given his emphasis on the relationality of the self. See Robert N. Bellah et al., *The Good Society*, New York: Alfred A. Knopf 1991, 283.
11. See Part I. On Mead and Dilthey, see Hans Joas, *G. H. Mead: A Contemporary Re-examination of His Thought*, Cambridge: MIT Press 1985, 18–20.
12. H. Richard Niebuhr, *Christ and Culture* [1951], New York: Harper 2001, xii.
13. José Casanova repeatedly draws attention to the great exception, namely the Polish-Lithuanian Empire. See José Casanova, *Global Religious and Secular Dynamics: The Modern System of Classification*, Leiden: Brill 2019, 21.
14. Omar M. McRoberts, "H. Richard Niebuhr Meets 'The Street,'" in Mary Jo Bane, Brent Coffin, and Richard Higgins (eds.), *Taking Faith Seriously*, Cambridge: Harvard University Press 2005, 94–112, here 94.
15. H. Richard Niebuhr, *The Social Sources of Denominationalism* [1929], New York: Meridian 1957, 135.
16. Ibid.
17. Ibid., vii.
18. Ibid., 6.
19. For an overview, see Harry S. Stout, "The Historical Legacy of H. Richard Niebuhr," in Ronald F. Thiemann (ed.), *The Legacy of H. Richard Niebuhr*, Minneapolis: Fortress 1991, 83–99 and the literature it mentions. David Martin played an important role in this shift of perspective. For more on him, see ch. 4 in this Part.
20. Niebuhr, *The Social Sources of Denominationalism*, 271f.

21. H. Richard Niebuhr, *The Kingdom of God in America* [1937], New York: Harper & Row 1959, ix–x.
22. See Joas, *The Power of the Sacred*, esp. ch. 4.
23. Niebuhr, *The Kingdom of God in America*, 164.
24. Niebuhr, *Christ and Culture*, xii.
25. Joas, *The Power of the Sacred*, 190.
26. H. Richard Niebuhr, *Radical Monotheism and Western Culture* [1943], New York: Harper & Row 1970.
27. Ibid., 18. Cf. in this respect: Justus D. Doenecke, "H. Richard Niebuhr: Critic of Political Theology," in: *Communio. International Catholic Review* 4, no. 1 (1977), 82–93.
28. For evidence of this, see Fowler, *To See the Kingdom*, 107.
29. Stanley Hauerwas and William Willimon, *Resident Aliens*, Nashville: Abingdon Press 1990, 40.
30. Niebuhr, *Christ and Culture*, 233.
31. Ibid., 241.
32. Drawing on ibid., 244.
33. Ibid., 250.
34. Niebuhr, *The Meaning of Revelation*, 1. As far as I know, this important book has gone largely unnoticed among German theologians. One exception is Heinrich Bedford-Strohm, "Radikaler Monotheismus und der Glaube an Jesus Christus," in Günter Thomas and Andreas Schüle (eds.), *Gegenwart des lebendigen Christus*, Leipzig: Evangelische Verlagsanstalt 2007, 229–245. (With thanks to Georg Kalinna for pointing this out to me.)
35. Act 5, scene 5.
36. Niebuhr, *The Meaning of Revelation*, 54.
37. It is worth mentioning that this prompted Paul Ricœur to call Niebuhr's book "the first attempt toward a narrative theology." See Paul Ricœur, *Figuring the Sacred: Religion, Narrative, and Imagination*, Minneapolis: Fortress 1995, 246. On Ricœur, see Part III, ch. 4.
38. Niebuhr, *The Meaning of Revelation*, 138.
39. Ibid., 93.
40. Ibid., 109.
41. Ibid., 80.
42. H. Richard Niebuhr, "Foreword," in Paul E. Pfuetze, *Self, Society, Existence: Human Nature and Dialogue in the Thought of G. H. Mead and Martin Buber*, New York: Harper 1961, vi; Hans Joas, "Martin Buber and the Problem of Dialogue in Contemporary Thought," in Sam Berrin Shonkoff (ed.), *Martin Buber: His Intellectual and Scholarly Legacy*, Leiden: Brill 2018, 212–215.
43. Niebuhr, *The Meaning of Revelation*, 80.
44. Ibid., 116.
45. Ibid., 126.
46. Ibid., 150.
47. Ibid.
48. H. Richard Niebuhr, "The Ego-Alter Dialectic and the Conscience," in: *Journal of Philosophy* 42 (1945), 352–359.

49. Niebuhr, "Foreword," vi. One of the few studies to examine and build on Niebuhr's reception of Mead is Konrad Raiser, *Identität und Sozialität. G. H. Meads Theorie der Interaktion und ihre Bedeutung für die theologische Anthropologie*, Munich: Kaiser / Matthias Grünewald 1971, 181–201.
50. On Cassirer, see Part III, ch. 2.
51. See fn. 5 in this chapter.
52. Niebuhr, *Radical Monotheism*, 105, fn. 1. Another reference to Mead appears in the following posthumously published text: H. Richard Niebuhr, *Faith on Earth: An Inquiry into the Structure of Human Faith*, New Haven: Yale University Press 1989, 88.
53. H. Richard Niebuhr, *The Responsible Self: An Essay in Christian Moral Philosophy* [1963], San Francisco: Harper & Row 1978, 65.
54. Ibid., 63. For more on the understanding of interpretation today, see the impressive fusion of hermeneutics and pragmatism in Johann Michel, *Homo Interpretans: Towards a Transformation of Hermeneutics* (with a Preface by Hans Joas), Lanham: Rowman & Littlefield 2019.
55. Niebuhr, *The Responsible Self*, 61.
56. Ibid., 65.
57. Developed on a broad basis in Hans Joas, *The Creativity of Action*, Chicago: University of Chicago Press 1996.
58. Niebuhr, *The Responsible Self*, 73.
59. William Schweiker puts forward an argument of this sort in his foreword to Niebuhr, *The Responsible Self*, 9–14.
60. See Hans Joas, *The Genesis of Values*, Chicago: University of Chicago Press 2000, 103–123, and, building on that book, see ch. 2 in Part II.
61. See George Herbert Mead, "The Physical Thing," in George Herbert Mead, *Philosophy of the Present*, La Salle: Open Court 1932, 119–139; George Herbert Mead, *Philosophy of the Act*, Chicago: University of Chicago Press 1938; Joas, *G. H. Mead: A Contemporary Re-examination of His Thought*, 145–166. On the assessment of Niebuhr's reception of Mead, see Joshua Daniel, "H. Richard Niebuhr's Reading of George Herbert Mead," in: *Journal of Religious Ethics* 44 (2016), 92–115. For a comprehensive treatment of Niebuhr's reception of pragmatism, though with some problematic assertions, see Joseph S. Pagano, *The Origins and Development of the Triadic Structure of Faith in H. Richard Niebuhr: A Study of the Kantian and Pragmatic Background of Niebuhr's Thought*, Lanham: University Press of America 2005.
62. See Hans Joas, *Kirche als Moralagentur?*, Munich: Kösel 2016, 73ff.
63. I am unable within the framework of this chapter to go into H. Richard Niebuhr's ethical reflections on US foreign policy, which placed him in opposition to his brother Reinhold and his justification of military interventions. I will, however, briefly comment on the latter topic in ch. 4 of this Part due to Reinhold Niebuhr's tremendous significance to David Martin.
64. Niebuhr, *The Responsible Self*, 92.
65. Ibid., 94.
66. Ibid., 109.
67. Ibid., 114.

68. See the impressive passage on "dependent freedom" in Niebuhr, *Christ and Culture*, 250–252. On Paul Tillich's comparable reflections on "indebted freedom" and on Paul Ricœur's similar conception of freedom, see Part III, chs. 3 and 4. Wolfgang Huber, whose conception of freedom I explored in Part III, ch. 5, draws in significant part on Niebuhr in addition to Bonhoeffer (see 408, fn. 12).
69. I mention this idea here only briefly and will not be pursuing it in greater depth. But see also my comments in the Introductory Remarks to Part III of this book, especially on the comparison between Troeltsch and Heidegger in fn. 6. Two younger colleagues prompted me to pursue the study embodied in this chapter. I first became seriously aware of the work of H. Richard Niebuhr thanks to one of my doctoral students at the University of Chicago, Joshua Daniel. His dissertation is available as the book mentioned in fn. 5: Daniel, *Transforming Faith*. In addition, for many years Christian Polke (Göttingen) urged me to take a closer look at this figure intermediate between Mead and Troeltsch, and between pragmatism and historicism. My thanks to both for their valuable stimulus.

IV, 3

1. A brief overview of the older Catholic-oriented sociology of religion in Germany is provided by Norbert Mette, "Religionssoziologie—katholisch. Erinnerungen an religionssoziologische Traditionen innerhalb des Katholizismus," in Karl Gabriel and Franz-Xaver Kaufmann (eds.), *Zur Soziologie des Katholizismus*, Mainz: Grünewald 1980, 39–56. Developments in France, esp. the religious sociogeography of Gabriel Le Bras, receives more attention from Hermann-Josef Große Kracht, "Von der Kirchensoziographie zu einer Sozialtheorie der 'public churches'? Ein Bilanzierungsversuch zur Soziologie des Katholizismus im 20. Jahrhundert," in Hermann-Josef Große Kracht and Christian Spieß (eds.), *Christentum und Solidarität. Bestandsaufnahmen zu Sozialethik und Religionssoziologie*, Paderborn: Schöningh 2008, 189–229. For an informative account of developments in the United States, see James C. Cavendish, "The Sociological Study of American Catholicism: Past, Present and Future," in Anthony J. Blasi (ed.), *American Sociology of Religion: Histories*, Leiden: Brill 2007, 151–176.
2. Werner Stark, *The Sociology of Religion: A Study of Christendom*, 5 vols., New York: Fordham University Press 1966–1972. I limit myself here to volumes 1 to 3, dedicated to the "macrosociology of religion." A brief summary of the entire work, in one volume, written by the author himself but without the normal scholarly accoutrements, is available in German: Werner Stark, *Grundriß der Religionssoziologie*, Freiburg: Rombach 1974.
3. For an indispensable account, see Robin R. Das and Hermann Strasser, "The Sociologist from Marienbad: Werner Stark between Catholicism and Social Science," in: *Czech Sociological Review* 51, no. 3 (2015), 417–444. For a more detailed treatment, see Robin R. Das, *The Place of Werner Stark in American Sociology: A Study in*

Marginality (PhD thesis), University of Michigan 2008. The obituary by Hermann Strasser provides biographical information: "Werner Stark—Gelehrter und Katholik, 1909–1985," in: *Zeitschrift für Soziologie* 15 (1986), 141–145.
4. On Niebuhr, see ch. 2 in this Part.
5. For a bibliography of Stark's writings, see the appendix to the festschrift dedicated to his memory: Eileen Leonard, Hermann Strasser, and Kenneth Westhues (eds.), *In Search of Community: Essays in Memory of Werner Stark, 1909–1985*, New York: Fordham University Press 1993, 245–252.
6. This information appears in Kenneth Westhues, "The Twinkling of American Catholic Sociology," in ibid., 220–244, here 228f.
7. Ibid., vii.
8. Quoting a letter from Stark's widow, Kate, to E. Doyle McCarthy of April 13, 1989, see Das and Strasser, "The Sociologist from Marienbad," 423f.
9. Drawing on Das and Strasser, "The Sociologist from Marienbad," 424f. The essay on John Henry Newman is reprinted in Werner Stark, *Social Theory and Christian Thought*, London: Routledge 1958, 106–134; the quoted passages appear on 133. The epigraph to the first volume is also from Newman; Stark refers to it again in the third volume (437).
10. See ch. 2 in this Part, esp. my remarks on denominationalism.
11. A tendency visible *in extremis* in Bryan Wilson's review: "Werner Stark, *The Sociology of Religion*, vol. 4," in: *Sociological Review* 18 (1970), 426–428. He states, for example, "Stark virtually conceives of the sociology of religion as a branch of dogmatic theology.... His volumes are, of course, a tract—certainly a learned tract—in Catholic fundamentalism.... Sociology is again pushed back into the quicksands of theology" (427).
12. Werner Stark, "The Protestant Ethic and the Spirit of Sociology," in: *Social Compass* 13 (1966), 373–377, here 376.
13. Werner Stark, "The Place of Catholicism in Max Weber's Sociology of Religion," in: *Sociological Analysis* 29 (1968), 202–211.
14. Ibid., 203.
15. Peter Brown, *The Cult of the Saints: Its Rise and Function in Latin Christianity*, Chicago: University of Chicago Press 1981; see also Hans Joas, *The Power of the Sacred: An Alternative to the Narrative of Disenchantment*, New York: Oxford University Press 2021, 19.
16. See Hans Joas, *Was ist die Achsenzeit? Eine wissenschaftliche Debatte als Diskurs über Transzendenz*, Basel: Schwabe 2014, esp. the section "Max Weber: Prophetie, Magie, Sakrament" (26–35) and the literature cited there.
17. See Werner Stark, "The Routinization of Charisma: A Consideration of Catholicism," in: *Sociological Analysis* 26 (1965), 203–211. On this, see John L. Gresham Jr., "The Collective Charisma of the Catholic Church: Werner Stark's Critique of Max Weber's Routinization Theory," in: *Catholic Social Science Review* 8 (2003), 123–139. For the comment of an orthodox Weberian on Stark, see Johannes Weiß, "Confessionalization of the Sociology of Religion? A Benevolent Critique of Werner Stark," in Leonard et al. (eds.), *In Search of Community*, 193–203. Weiß, however, does not go into Stark's

empirical arguments. A list of Stark's writings on Weber appears in the fifth volume of *Sociology of Religion*, 434f.
18. On Sohm's significance to Weber and on the relevant literature, see Martin Riesebrodt, "Charisma," in Hans G. Kippenberg and Martin Riesebrodt (eds.), *Max Webers "Religionssystematik,"* Tübingen: Mohr Siebeck 2001, 151–166.
19. Stark, *The Sociology of Religion*, vol. IV, 136ff.
20. For a more complex understanding, see Paul Ricœur, "Love and Justice," in Paul Ricœur, *Figuring the Sacred*, Minneapolis: Fortress 1995, 315–329; Wolfgang Huber, *Gerechtigkeit und Recht. Grundlinien christlicher Rechtsethik*, 3rd rev. ed., Gütersloh: Gütersloher Verlagshaus 2006.
21. Stark, *Grundriß der Religionssoziologie*, 139.
22. Ibid., 139f.
23. In his nuanced essay mentioned in fn. 18 of the present chapter, Martin Riesebrodt has shown that Weber's individualist conception of charisma criticized by Stark is not the only one in Weber's work. It also includes a collectivist counter-concept based on the notion of *mana* found in contemporary anthropology; Edward Shils and Shmuel Eisenstadt later drew inspiration from Weber's second idea. Riesebrodt says nothing at all about Stark's criticisms of Weber. But he does demonstrate how inconsistent Weber's conception was. For my own older critique of Weber's shortcomings in this regard, see Hans Joas, *The Creativity of Action*, Chicago: University of Chicago Press 1996, 44–49.
24. See ch. 2 in this Part.
25. The writings of J. Milton Yinger are useful as an overview of these developments: *Religion in the Struggle for Power: A Study in the Sociology of Religion*, Durham: Duke University Press 1946, 16–50, and *The Scientific Study of Religion*, New York: Macmillan 1970, 251–281. For a recent German attempt to construct a typology, see Volkhard Krech, Jens Schlamelcher, and Markus Hero, "Typen religiöser Sozialformen und ihre Bedeutung für die Analyse religiösen Wandels in Deutschland," in: *Kölner Zeitschrift für Soziologie und Sozialpsychologie* 65 (2013), 51–71.
26. John T. Flint, review: "Werner Stark, *The Sociology of Religion I–III*," in: *Journal of the American Academy of Religion* 40, no. 1 (1972), 110–116, here 113.
27. On this interpretation of Troeltsch, see Joas, *The Power of the Sacred*, 103–106. Vexingly, Stark always refers to a dichotomous typology in Troeltsch's work, while failing to consider that while working on the *Social Teachings* he came to embrace a tripartite schema. In an autobiographical retrospective, Stark describes his engagement with Troeltsch and mentions his plan to produce, through a collaborative effort involving around thirty specialists, a new and more complete historical account of the social philosophy of the Christian churches and sects than Troeltsch did in the *Social Teachings*. I have not yet managed to find the proposal for this. The archive of Fordham University in New York contains only a reply from Routledge of March 17, 1967, but not the project description itself. See Werner Stark, "A Survey of My Scholarly Work," in Madeline H. Engel (ed.), *The Sociological Writings of Werner Stark: Bibliography and Selected Annotations*, New York (unpublished) 1975, 2–17, here 15f.

28. Once again notably lacking in understanding: Bryan Wilson, review: "Werner Stark, *The Sociology of Religion*," in: *Sociological Review* 15, no. 3 (1968), 120–123.
29. See Stark, *The Sociology of Religion*, vol. III, 96, with reference to Ernst H. Kantorowicz, *The King's Two Bodies: A Study in Medieval Political Theology* [1957], Princeton: Princeton University Press 2016.
30. This is the argument, which I think is correct, made by two reviewers of Stark's work: Flint, review: "*Werner Stark, The Sociology of Religion IIII*," 113; Alan W. Eister, review: "Werner Stark, *The Sociology of Religion I–III*," in: *Journal for the Scientific Study of Religion* 7, no. 2 (1968), 294f.
31. Stark, *The Sociology of Religion*, vol. III, 384, with reference to David Martin, *Pacifism: An Historical and Sociological Study*, London: Routledge 1965, 4. On David Martin, see ch. 4 in this Part.
32. Max Weber, *Economy and Society* [1922], Berkeley: University of California Press 1978, 1167f. In line with this, reference is made to a "paradoxical tension" in Weber's remarks on monasticism in Otto Gerhard Oexle, "Max Weber und das Mönchtum," in Hartmut Lehmann and Jean Martin Ouedraogo (eds.), *Max Webers Religionssoziologie in interkultureller Perspektive*, Göttingen: Vandenhoeck & Ruprecht 2003, 311–334, here 328.
33. See Joas, *The Power of the Sacred*, 250–259; Robert N. Bellah, *Religion in Human Evolution: From the Paleolithic to the Axial Age*, Cambridge: Harvard University Press 2011, 117–174.
34. Stark, *The Sociology of Religion*, vol. I, 35. Henceforth, references to this work are indicated in the main text with volume and page number.
35. See Joas, *The Power of the Sacred*, 259f.
36. Marc Bloch, *The Royal Touch: Sacred Monarchy and Scrofula in England and France* [1924], London: Routledge 2020.
37. Kantorowicz, *The King's Two Bodies*.
38. It is worth noting that Stark was already familiar with and briefly addresses Jaspers's ideas about an Axial Age in world history. See Stark, *The Sociology of Religion*, vol. III, 340f.
39. Here esp. John A. Wilson, "Egypt," in Henri and H. A. Frankfort, John A. Wilson, and Thorkild Jacobsen, *The Intellectual Adventure of Ancient Man*, Chicago: University of Chicago Press 1946, 122–130.
40. David Martin, review: "Werner Stark, *The Sociology of Religion*, vols. I and II," in: *British Journal of Sociology* 18 (1967), 220–222, here 221.
41. Émile Durkheim, *The Elementary Forms of Religious Life* [1912]; on this topic and for an attempt to take stock of the critical debate, see Joas, *The Power of the Sacred*, 58–87.
42. Martin, review: "Werner Stark, *The Sociology of Religion*, vols. I and II," 221.
43. This plea might be regarded as the point of departure for David Martin's own research program and his theory of secularization. See David Martin, *A General Theory of Secularization*, Oxford: Blackwell 1978, and ch. 4 of Part IV.
44. Martin, review: "Werner Stark, *The Sociology of Religion*, vols. I and II," 222.
45. Cf. my reinterpretation of Weber's "Intermediate Reflection" in Joas, *The Power of the Sacred*, 195–233.

46. Max Weber, *The Protestant Ethic and the Spirit of Capitalism*, Los Angeles: Roxbury 1996, 175f.; Niebuhr, *The Social Sources of Denominationalism*, 70.
47. Yinger, *Religion in the Struggle for Power*, 18ff.
48. Howard Becker, *Systematic Sociology*, New York: Wiley 1932, 626.
49. Will Herberg, *Protestant, Catholic, Jew: An Essay in American Religious Sociology*, New York: Doubleday 1955. For more detail on this, see the Introductory Remarks on Part IV.
50. However, this explanation of the emergence of the system of denominationalism and the evidence that some sects became denominations should not induce us to turn the argument on its head and suggest that all denominations were originally sects. In the case of the Catholic, Orthodox, and Lutheran immigrant churches, Stark himself recognized this. In the case of the Methodists, he disputes the claim in the specialist literature that they had represented a kind of loyal opposition to the established church from their very beginnings.
51. See G. R. Dunstan, review: "Werner Stark, *The Sociology of Religion*, vol. III," in: *Religious Studies* 6 (1970), 197–199.
52. See Joas, *The Power of the Sacred*, 147–150, and the literature cited there.
53. Alois Dempf, *Sacrum Imperium. Geschichts- und Staatsphilosophie des Mittelalters und der politischen Renaissance* [1929], Darmstadt: WBG 1954, 187.
54. Reinhold Schneider, *Philipp der Zweite oder Religion und Macht* [1935], Frankfurt am Main: Suhrkamp 1987.
55. Stark, *Grundriß der Religionssoziologie*, 99.
56. Karl Rahner, "Theologische Grundinterpretation des II. Vatikanischen Konzils," in Karl Rahner, *Schriften zur Theologie*, vol. XIV, Cologne: Benziger 1980, 287–302.
57. See once again Karl Rahner, "Kirche der Sünder," and Karl Rahner, "Sündige Kirche nach den Dekreten des Zweiten Vatikanischen Konzils," in Karl Rahner, *Schriften zur Theologie*, vol. VI, Einsiedeln: Benziger 1965, 301–320 and 321–345.
58. Based on David Martin, review: "Werner Stark, *The Sociology of Religion*, vol. V," in: *Jewish Journal of Sociology* 15 (1973), 125f.
59. With thanks to Heinrich Schmidinger and Hermann Strasser for their comments on an earlier version of this chapter.

IV, 4

1. David Martin, *The Future of Christianity: Reflections on Violence and Democracy, Religion and Secularization*, Farnham: Ashgate 2011.
2. Robert W. Hefner, "Introduction: World-Building and the Rationality of Conversion," in Robert W. Hefner, (ed.), *Conversion to Christianity*, Berkeley: University of California Press 1993, 3–44, here 17.
3. Hans Joas, *Faith as an Option: Possible Futures for Christianity*, Stanford: Stanford University Press 2014, 37–49.
4. David Martin, *Secularisation, Pentecostalism and Violence: Receptions, Rediscoveries and Rebuttals in the Sociology of Religion*, London: Routledge 2017, 13.

5. As in the work of Eric Voegelin and his students. See Eric Voegelin, "The Political Religions" [1938], in Eric Voegelin, *Modernity without Restraint* (= *Collected Works*, vol. 5), Columbia: University of Missouri Press 1999, 19–74. For a critique of this and similar approaches, see Hans Joas, "Sacralization and Desacralization: Political Domination and Religious Interpretation," in: *Journal of the Society of Christian Ethics* 36, no. 2 (2016), 25–47.
6. I have developed the idea that sacralization is a universal anthropological phenomenon in Hans Joas, *The Power of the Sacred: An Alternative to the Narrative of Disenchantment*, New York: Oxford University Press 2021, 237–250.
7. Max Weber, *Economy and Society* [1922], Berkeley: University of California Press 1978, 212–301.
8. Martin, *The Future of Christianity*, 5.
9. For a detailed account, see Joas, *The Power of the Sacred*, 110–153 and 206–233. David Martin's own attempt to produce an alternative to Weber's "Intermediate Reflection" is David Martin, *Ruin and Restoration: On Violence, Liturgy and Reconciliation*, London: Routledge 2016 (with a foreword by Charles Taylor).
10. His autobiography is well worth reading: David Martin, The *Education of David Martin: The Making of an Unlikely Sociologist*, London: SPCK 2013.
11. David Martin, "The Denomination," in: *British Journal of Sociology* 13, no. 1 (1962), 1–14. One of Martin's statements in this essay has become quite famous (13): "The sociological idea of the denomination is the idea of Her Majesty's Opposition, of disagreement within consensus, except that the opposition is permanently out of office." On Niebuhr, see ch. 2 in this Part.
12. David Martin, "Towards Eliminating the Concept of Secularization," in David Martin, *The Religions and the Secular: Studies in Secularization*, London: Routledge & Kegan Paul 1969, 9–22.
13. Kevin Christiano, "Clio Goes to Church: Revisiting and Revitalizing Historical Thinking in the Sociology of Religion," in: *Sociology of Religion* 69 (2008), 1–28, here 20.
14. Ernst Troeltsch and Otto Hintze are perhaps more consistent in this respect. It is regrettable that both have been eclipsed by Weber within historical sociology.
15. David Martin, *A General Theory of Secularization*, New York: Harper 1978, 2.
16. Ibid., 3.
17. He mentions East Germany as an exception but traces its "revolution" back to military occupation by the Soviet Union (ibid., 5).
18. Ibid., 7.
19. Ibid., 129. This idea, which goes back to Max Weber, of the dependence of legitimacy within a state on the outcome of conflicts between states was elaborated in a particularly trenchant way by Randall Collins, "Imperialism and Legitimacy: Weber's Theory of Politics," in Randall Collins, *Weberian Sociological Theory*, Cambridge: Cambridge University Press 1986, 145–166. See also Hans Joas, *War and Modernity*, Oxford: Polity 2003, 48 and passim.
20. Martin, *A General Theory of Secularization*, 244–277.
21. Ibid., 311, with reference to Edward Shils, *Center and Periphery*, Chicago: University of Chicago Press 1975.

22. José Casanova, "Religions, Secularizations and Modernities," in: *European Journal of Sociology* 52 (2011), 423–445, here 436. For a classical treatment of the "path dependency" of the typewriter keyboard, see Paul A. David, "Clio and the Economics of QWERTY," in: *American Economic Review* 75 (1985), 332–337.
23. Martin, *A General Theory of Secularization*, 15.
24. Ibid., 143.
25. As argued by Paolo Costa, "The One and the Many Stories: How to Reconcile Sense-Making and Fact-Checking in the Secularization Narrative," in Hans Joas (ed.), *David Martin and the Sociology of Religion*, London: Routledge 2018, 50–66. In the United Kingdom itself, however, David Martin played a highly active role in the media as "public intellectual."
26. David Martin, *On Secularization: Towards a Revised General Theory*, Aldershot: Ashgate 2005.
27. Martin, *The Future of Christianity*, 135–164.
28. David Martin, *A Sociology of English Religion*, London: SCM 1967, esp. 50f.
29. For a critical engagement with and attempt to build on Martin's study of England, see Grace Davie, "Understanding Religion in Modern Britain: Taking the Long View," in Joas (ed.), *David Martin and the Sociology of Religion*, 67–84. Here we find the reference to Martin's self-critical statement (79); see David Martin, "Foreword," in Grace Davie, *Religion in Britain since 1945: Believing without Belonging*, Oxford: Wiley 1994, viii–ix.
30. On the figures for London, see Grace Davie, *Religion in Britain: A Persistent Paradox*, Oxford: Blackwell 2015, 107f.
31. I discuss this briefly in Joas, *Faith as an Option*, 46–49. More detailed information can be found in Hugh McLeod, *The Religious Crisis of the 1960s*, Oxford: Oxford University Press 2007. On the latter volume, see the review symposium and McLeod's reply in: *Journal of Religion in Europe* 5 (2012), 405–520. This debate has now been advanced by David Hempton and Hugh McLeod (eds.), *Secularization and Religious Innovation in the North Atlantic World*, Oxford: Oxford University Press 2017.
32. Paul Freston, "David Martin and the Growth of Protestantism in the Third World," in Andrew Walker and Martyn Percy (eds.), *Restoring the Image: Essays on Religion and Society in Honour of David Martin*, Sheffield: Sheffield Academic Press 2001, 110–124, here 113.
33. David Martin, *Forbidden Revolutions: Pentecostalism in Latin America, Catholicism in Eastern Europe*, London: SPCK 1996. This was preceded by David Martin, *Tongues of Fire: The Explosion of Protestantism in Latin America*, Oxford: Wiley 1990. Later came David Martin, "The Relevance of the European Model of Secularization in Latin America and Africa," in Hans Joas and Klaus Wiegandt (eds.), *Secularization and the World Religions*, Liverpool: Liverpool University Press 2009, 278–295.
34. See, for example, Hugh O'Shaughnessy, review: "David Martin, Tongues of Fire," *Times Literary Supplement*, August 3–9, 1990. On this reception, see Martin, *Secularisation, Pentecostalism and Violence*, 136–154.
35. Peter L. Berger, "Foreword," in Martin, *Tongues of Fire*, vii–x.
36. José Casanova, "Parallel Reformations in Latin America: A Critical Review of David Martin's Interpretation of the Pentecostal Revolution," in Joas (ed.), *David Martin and*

the Sociology of Religion, 85-106. The same argument already appears in the form of a challenge in Freston, "David Martin and the Growth of Protestantism in the Third World," 120.
37. Todd Hartch, *The Rebirth of Latin American Christianity*, Oxford: Oxford University Press 2014, 124-126 (with thanks to Raúl Zegarra for alerting me to this book).
38. David Martin, "Thinking with Your Life," in Joas (ed.), *David Martin and the Sociology of Religion*, 162-190, here esp. 165-172.
39. Ibid., 169.
40. See Martin, "The Relevance of the European Model of Secularization," esp. 288-295.
41. Martin, *Secularisation, Pentecostalism and Violence*, 170-183. For a recent account of India that advances the debate, see Sarbeswar Sahoo, *Pentecostalism and Politics of Conversion in India: With a Foreword by Hans Joas*, Cambridge: Cambridge University Press 2018.
42. An idea found in the thinking of John Wesley and Max Weber and into the present. See also ch. 3, fn. 46 in this Part.
43. See, for example, Martin, "Thinking with Your Life," 161-163.
44. Reinhold Niebuhr, "Moral Man and Immoral Society" [1932], in Reinhold Niebuhr, *Major Works on Religion and Politics*, New York: Library of America 2015, 135-350.
45. On this topic, see Richard Wightman Fox, *Reinhold Niebuhr, A Biography*, Ithaca: Cornell University Press 1996, 143-147. H. Richard Niebuhr's critique appears in letters to his brother, articulated only in this private context. An informative account based on newly analyzed sources is K. Healan Gaston, "'A Bad Kind of Magic': The Niebuhr Brothers on 'Utilitarian Christianity' and the Defense of Democracy," in: *Harvard Theological Review* 107 (2014), 1-30. On H. Richard Niebuhr, see ch. 2 in this Part.
46. For a nuanced treatment, see Richard B. Miller, "H. Richard Niebuhr's War Articles: A Transvaluation of Values," in: *Journal of Religion* 68 (1988), 242-262.
47. David Martin, *Does Christianity Cause War?*, Oxford: Clarendon Press 1997; David Martin, *Religion and Power: No Logos without Mythos*, Farnham: Ashgate 2014.
48. Andreas Hasenclever, "Taking Religion Back Out: On the Secular Dynamics of Armed Conflicts and the Potentials of Religious Peace-Making," in Joas (ed.), *David Martin and the Sociology of Religion*, 123-146.
49. David Martin, "Axial Religions and the Problem of Violence," in Robert N. Bellah and Hans Joas (eds.), *The Axial Age and Its Consequences*, Cambridge: Harvard University Press 2012, 294-316.
50. Martin, *Secularisation, Pentecostalism and Violence*, 134, fn. 1.
51. Martin, *Ruin and Restoration*, esp. 5-26.
52. Shmuel N. Eisenstadt, *Fundamentalism, Sectarianism, and Revolution*, Cambridge: Cambridge University Press 2009.
53. For a critique of Taylor in this respect, see Part II, ch. 5.
54. Martin, *Secularisation, Pentecostalism and Violence*, 14. For a similar account that goes into more depth, see Martin, *On Secularization*, 3-7.
55. After David Martin's death in 2019, two obituaries appeared that signaled moves to tap this potential: Mirjam Künkler, "David Martin in Memoriam," in: *Journal for the Scientific Study of Religion* 58 (2019), 905-912; James A. Beckford and Grace

Davie, "David Martin," in: *British Academy: Memoirs of Fellows XVIII* (2019), 387–410. German sociologist Willfried Spohn, of whom we were robbed too soon, was quick to point out the significance of Martin's work; it was he who originally made me aware of him. He made a sharper distinction than Martin between empires and nation-states and, in connection with this, between religious communities' transnational and regional ties. See Willfried Spohn, "Religion and Modernization in Comparative Perspective: David Martin's Theory of Secularization Reconsidered," in Karl-Siegbert Rehberg (ed.), *Differenz und Integration. Die Zukunft moderner Gesellschaften, Verhandlungen des 28. Kongresses der Deutschen Gesellschaft für Soziologie*, vol. 2, Frankfurt am Main: Campus 1997, 455–459; for the application of this perspective to Eastern Europe, see Willfried Spohn, "Europeanisation, Multiple Modernities and Religion: The Reconstruction of Collective Identities in Central and Eastern Europe," in Gert Pickel and Kornelia Sammet (eds.), *Transformations of Religiosity in Eastern Europe 1998-2010*, Wiesbaden: Springer VS 2012, 29–50. A posthumous publication has also appeared: David Martin, *Christianity and "the World": Secularization Narratives through the Lens of English Poetry 800 AD to the Present*, Eugene: Cascade 2020.

IV, 5

1. Robert N. Bellah, *Apache Kinship Systems: Harvard Phi Beta Kappa Prize Essay for 1950*, Cambridge: Harvard University Press, 1952.
2. Biographical information can be found in the author's introduction to Robert N. Bellah, *Beyond Belief: Essays on Religion in a Post-traditional World*, New York: Harper & Row 1970, xi–xxi, and in the comprehensive biography by Matteo Bortolini, *A Joyfully Serious Man: The Life of Robert Bellah*, Princeton: Princeton University Press 2021.
3. Robert N. Bellah, *Tokugawa Religion: The Values of Pre-industrial Japan*, New York: The Free Press 1957. In the following and in a subsequent passage (on Bellah's analysis of contemporary American society), I draw on some of the statements in Hans Joas and Wolfgang Knöbl, *Social Theory: Twenty Introductory Lectures*, Cambridge: Cambridge University Press 2009, 331f. and 492–495.
4. Robert N. Bellah, *Imagining Japan: The Japanese Tradition and Its Modern Interpretation*, Berkeley: University of California Press 2003.
5. Robert N. Bellah, "Civil Religion in America," in: *Daedalus* 96 (1967), 1–21. Following this initial appearance, the text was reprinted in numerous publications.
6. Looking back, Bellah described how the successes of the civil rights movement reconciled him with the political system, while the Vietnam War alienated him from it again: Robert N. Bellah, "God, Nation, and Self in America: Some Tensions between Parsons and Bellah," in Renée C. Fox, Victor M. Lidz, and Harold J. Bershady (eds.), *After Parsons: A Theory of Social Action for the Twenty-First Century*, New York: Russell Sage Foundation 2005, 137–147, here 137. In Germany, Rolf Schieder

engaged with Bellah's work in this respect: Rolf Schieder, *Civil Religion. Die religiöse Dimension politischer Kultur*, Gütersloh: Gütersloher Verlagshaus 1987.
7. Robert N. Bellah, *The Broken Covenant: American Civil Religion in Time of Trial*, New York: Seabury 1975.
8. In what follows I recapitulate a brief account of Tillich's theory of symbols that also appears in Part III, ch. 3. See the latter for a more in-depth treatment of Tillich, including his use of the term "symbolic realist," 204f.
9. Traces of Tillich in Bellah's thinking are unmissable in his essay collection *Beyond Belief: Essays on Religion in a Post-traditional World*, New York: Harper & Row 1970.
10. Bellah, *The Broken Covenant*, 4. For a discussion of Bellah's significance to cultural sociology, see Jeffrey Alexander and Steven Sherwood, "'Mythic Gestures': Robert N. Bellah and Cultural Sociology," in Richard Madsen et al. (eds.), *Meaning and Modernity: Religion, Polity, and Self*, Berkeley: University of California Press 2002, 1–14.
11. Robert N. Bellah and Charles Glock (eds.), *The New Religious Consciousness*, Berkeley: University of California Press 1976.
12. For example, in Talcott Parsons and Gerard Platt, *The American University*, Cambridge: Harvard University Press 1974. On this topic, see Hans Joas, "Universität und Rationalität. Über Talcott Parsons' Beitrag zur Soziologie der Universität," in Gerhard Grohs et al. (eds.), *Kulturelle Identität im Wandel*, Stuttgart: Klett-Cotta 1980, 236–250.
13. See the account by Matteo Bortolini, "The 'Bellah Affair' at Princeton: Scholarly Excellence and Academic Freedom in America in the 1970s," in: *American Sociologist* 42, no. 1 (2011), 3–33.
14. Bellah's other important sociological students (in alphabetical order) are Jeffrey Alexander, John Coleman S.J., Nina Eliasoph, Philip Gorski, Paul Lichterman, and (to some extent) Robert Wuthnow.
15. Robert N. Bellah et al., *Habits of the Heart: Individualism and Commitment in American Life*, Berkeley: University of California Press 1985.
16. Ibid., 21.
17. Ibid., 281f.
18. In a number of studies, I have sought to assess empirically the applicability of Bellah's insights to Germany. In English, see Hans Joas and Frank Adloff, "Transformations of German Civil Society: Milieu Change and Community Spirit," in John Keane (ed.), *Civil Society: Berlin Perspectives*, New York: Berghahn 2006, 103–138.
19. Robert N. Bellah et al., *The Good Society*, New York: Alfred Knopf 1991, 78.
20. Ibid., 101.
21. See Hans Joas, "Gemeinschaft und Demokratie in den USA. Die vergessene Vorgeschichte der Kommunitarismus-Diskussion," in Micha Brumlik and Hauke Brunkhorst (eds.), *Gemeinschaft und Gerechtigkeit*, Frankfurt am Main: Fischer 1993, 49–62.
22. Robert N. Bellah, "Religious Evolution," in: *American Sociological Review* 29, no. 3 (1964), 358–374.
23. An interesting early sociological exploration of these ideas in Germany can be found in Rainer Döbert, *Systemtheorie und die Entwicklung religiöser Deutungssysteme. Zur*

Logik des sozialwissenschaftlichen Funktionalismus, Frankfurt am Main: Suhrkamp 1973, 73-154. Schieder, *Civil Religion*, 83-215, also goes into Bellah's development in depth, far beyond his immediate theological topic.

24. Karl Jaspers, *The Origin and Goal of History* [1949], London: Routledge 2010. For an overview of the state of research on this thesis, see Hans Joas, *The Power of the Sacred: An Alternative to the Narrative of Disenchantment*, New York: Oxford University Press 2021, 154-194.
25. Voegelin's influence is unmistakable here. See his monumental study: Eric Voegelin, *Order and History*, 5 vols., Baton Rouge: Louisiana State University Press 1956-1987. On Bellah's relationship to Voegelin, see Peter Brickey LeQuire, "Friends in History: Eric Voegelin and Robert Bellah," in Matteo Bortolini (ed.), *The Anthem Companion to Robert Bellah*, London: Anthem 2019, 165-190.
26. Robert N. Bellah, *Religion in Human Evolution: From the Paleolithic to the Axial Age*, Cambridge: Harvard University Press 2011.
27. Under the direction of Richard Madsen and the other members of the Bellah group, these papers will be published as *Challenging Modernity*, New York: Columbia University Press 2024.
28. For an example of how other scholars have taken inspiration from this book, see Robert N. Bellah and Hans Joas (eds.), *The Axial Age and Its Consequences*, Cambridge: Harvard University Press 2012. A list of most of the important reviews can be found in Michael Stausberg, "Bellah's 'Religion in Human Evolution': A Postreview," in: *Numen* 61 (2014), 281-299.
29. Merlin Donald, *Origins of the Modern Mind: Three Stages in the Evolution of Culture and Cognition*, Cambridge: Harvard University Press, 1991.
30. Donald has responded constructively to Bellah's efforts. See Merlin Donald, "An Evolutionary Approach to Culture: Implications for the Study of the Axial Age," in Bellah and Joas (eds.), *The Axial Age and Its Consequences*, 47-76. In the same volume, see also the original attempt to develop Bellah's ideas: Matthias Jung, "Embodiment, Transcendence, and Contingency: Anthropological Features of the Axial Age," 77-101.
31. For my own account of the history of sacredness and power in this respect, which was influenced by my collaboration with Bellah, see the outline in Joas, *The Power of the Sacred*, 250-271.
32. Robert N. Bellah, "Liturgy and Experience," in James D. Shaughnessy (ed.), *The Roots of Ritual*, Grand Rapids: Eerdmans 1973, 217-234.
33. Robert N. Bellah, "Flaws in the Protestant Code: Some Religious Sources of America's Troubles," in: *Ethical Perspectives* 7 (2000), 288-299. He sometimes went so far as to describe the Reformation as a mistake: "A necessary mistake, to be sure—but one that needs to be rectified if we are to solve the crises of modernity" (Bellah, "God, Nation, and Self," 146).
34. A full listing of the writings of Robert Bellah to 2005 inclusive is provided in Robert N. Bellah and Steven M. Tipton (eds.), *The Robert Bellah Reader*, Durham: Duke University Press 2006, 523-542.

IV, 6

1. In addition to personal conversations, the biographical information provided here comes from José Casanova, "From Modernization to Secularization to Globalization: An Autobiographical Self-Reflection," in: *Religion and Society. Advances in Research* 2 (2011), 25–36.
2. On Schupp and his work, see Walter Raberger and Hanjo Sauer (eds.), *Vermittlung im Fragment. Franz Schupp als Lehrer der Theologie*, Regensburg: Friedrich Pustet 2003.
3. José Casanova, "Catholic Ethics and Social Justice: Natural Law and Beyond," in: *International Journal of Politics, Culture, and Society* 6 (1992), 322–329, here 322.
4. Benjamin Nelson, *The Idea of Usury: From Tribal Brotherhood to Universal Otherhood* [1949], Chicago: University of Chicago Press 1969. More details on Nelson can be found in the Introductory Remarks to Part IV.
5. See José Casanova, "Interpretations and Misinterpretations of Max Weber: The Problem of Rationalization," in Ronald Glassman and Vatro Murvar (eds.), *Max Weber in Political Sociology: A Pessimistic Vision of a Rationalized World*, Westport: Praeger 1984, 141–154.
6. José Casanova, "Legitimacy and the Sociology of Modernization," in Arthur Vidich and Ronald Glassman (eds.), *Conflict and Control: Challenge to Legitimacy of Modern Governments*, London: Sage 1979, 219–252, here 220.
7. To quote the title of his dissertation, though it has not been published and I have not seen it. But the same line of reasoning is evident in an array of published articles. See, for example, José Casanova, "The Opus Dei Ethics, the Technocrats and the Modernization of Spain," in: *Social Science Information* 22 (1983), 27–50.
8. As he states looking back in Casanova, "From Modernization to Secularization to Globalization," 27.
9. Robert N. Bellah, *Tokugawa Religion: The Cultural Roots of Modern Japan*, New York: The Free Press 1957. On Bellah, see ch. 5 in this Part.
10. Jürgen Habermas, *Technik und Wissenschaft als "Ideologie,"* Frankfurt am Main: Suhrkamp 1968.
11. For more on this, see the Introductory Remarks to Part IV.
12. José Casanova, *Public Religions in the Modern World*, Chicago: University of Chicago Press 1994.
13. Here I base myself on ideas presented in my book: Hans Joas, *Faith as an Option: Possible Futures for Christianity*, Stanford: Stanford University Press 2016, esp. ch. 1.
14. Max Weber, "Zur Lage der bürgerlichen Demokratie in Rußland" [1906], in Max Weber, *Gesammelte politische Schriften*, Tübingen: Mohr Siebeck 1980, 33–68, here 63f.
15. See, for example, José Casanova, "Ethno-Linguistic and Religious Pluralism and Democratic Construction in Ukraine," in Barnett Rubin and Jack Snyder (eds.), *Post-Soviet Political Order: Conflict and State-Building*, New York: Routledge 1998, 81–103.
16. José Casanova, "Civil Society and Religion: Retrospective Reflections on Catholicism and Prospective Reflections on Islam," in: *Social Research* 68 (2001), 1041–1080; José

Casanova, "Catholic and Muslim Politics in Comparative Perspective," in: *Taiwan Journal of Democracy* 1 (2005), 89–108.
17. Robert N. Bellah and Hans Joas (eds.), *The Axial Age and Its Consequences*, Cambridge: Harvard University Press 2012. (This volume includes a chapter by José Casanova, "Religion, the Axial Age, and Secular Modernity in Bellah's Theory of Religious Evolution," 191–221.)
18. Winfried Brugger, "From Hostility through Recognition to Identification: State-Church Models and Their Relationship to Freedom of Religion," in Hans Joas and Klaus Wiegandt (eds.), *Secularization and the World Religions*, Liverpool: Liverpool University Press 2009, 160–180.
19. See, for example, José Casanova, "Immigration and the New Religious Pluralism: A European Union / United States Comparison," in Thomas Banchoff (ed.), *Democracy and the New Religious Pluralism*, Oxford: Oxford University Press 2007, 59–84.
20. See his early essay: José Casanova, "Globalizing Catholicism and the Return to a 'Universal' Church," in Susanne Rudolph and James Piscatori (eds.), *Transnational Religion and Fading States*, Boulder: Westview 1997, 121–143. See also the third chapter in José Casanova, *Europas Angst vor der Religion*, Berlin: Berlin University Press 2009 (85–119), and the chapter "Religion in Modernity as Global Challenge," in Michael Reder and Matthias Rugel (eds.), *Religion und die umstrittene Moderne*, Stuttgart: Kohlhammer 2010, 1–16 (with a discussion, 17–21).
21. José Casanova, review: "Zygmunt Bauman, *Postmodern Ethics* (Oxford 1993)," in: *Contemporary Sociology* 24 (1995), 424f., here 425. A look back over his development after 1994 is provided by Casanova himself in "Public Religions Revisited," in Hent de Vries (ed.), *Religion: Beyond a Concept*, New York: Fordham University Press 2008, 101–119.
22. Talal Asad, *Formations of the Secular: Christianity, Islam, Modernity*, Stanford: Stanford University Press 2003, 181–183, and see also the detailed reply: José Casanova, "Secularization Revisited: A Reply to Talal Asad," in David Scott and Charles Hirschkind (eds.), *Powers of the Secular Modern: Talal Asad and His Interlocutors*, Stanford: Stanford University Press 2006, 12–30.
23. Asad always refers to "structural" rather than "functional" differentiation.
24. See particularly the Cadbury Lectures (cf. n. 29).
25. See chs. 2 and 4 in Part IV.
26. José Casanova, "Religion, the New Millennium, and Globalization," in: *Sociology of Religion* 62 (2001), 415–441, here 434.
27. Casanova, "Public Religions Revisited," 118.
28. Ibid., 119.
29. I am referring here to the so-called Cadbury Lectures. See José Casanova, *Global Religious and Secular Dynamics: The Modern System of Classification*, Leiden: Brill 2019.
30. Taylor, *A Secular Age*. See Part II, ch. 5.
31. José Casanova, "The Problem of Religion and Anxieties of European Secular Democracies," in Gabriel Motzkin and Yochi Fischer (eds.), *Religion and Democracy in Contemporary Europe*, London: Alliance Publishing Trust 2008, 63–74, here 64.

430 NOTES

32. Ibid., 65. Casanova's observations here could undoubtedly be enriched by greater incorporation of the insights arising from research on confessionalization, in the work of Wolfgang Reinhard and Heinz Schilling, for instance. A good example is Wolfgang Reinhard, *Ausgewählte Abhandlungen*, Berlin: Duncker & Humblot 1997, 75–147. For an overview, see Hans Joas (ed.), *Die Anthropologie von Macht und Glauben. Das Werk Wolfgang Reinhards in der Diskussion*, Göttingen: Wallstein 2008. In that volume, see especially Paolo Prodi, "Konfessionalisierungsforschung im internationalen Kontext," 63–82.
33. Peter L. Berger, *The Many Altars of Modernity: Toward a Paradigm for Religion in a Pluralist Age*, Berlin: De Gruyter 2014. This volume includes critical responses to Berger's arguments.
34. Casanova, *Global Religious and Secular Dynamics*, 17.
35. See my critique of Peter Berger's conception of pluralism in Hans Joas, *Do We Need Religion? On the Experience of Self-Transcendence*, Boulder: Paradigm 2008, 21–35.
36. Drawing on William James's distinction between living and dead options, I have distinguished between a "genuine" pluralism and mere coexistence in Hans Joas, *Kirche als Moralagentur?*, Munich: Kösel 2016, 33–35.
37. So far, the main study on this topic is a multiauthored volume, with an introduction by Casanova and his coeditor and a concluding synthesis by Casanova: Thomas Banchoff and José Casanova (eds.), *The Jesuits and Globalization: Historical Legacies and Contemporary Challenges*, Washington, DC: Georgetown University Press 2016, 1–24 and 261–285.
38. Ibid., 261.

Conclusion

1. A comprehensive account of the ideational and conceptual history of contingency can be found in Peter Vogt, *Kontingenz und Zufall*, Berlin: Akademie Verlag 2011 (with a foreword by Hans Joas, 11–16). A classic early study on the topic is Ernst Troeltsch, "Die Bedeutung des Begriffs der Kontingenz" [1910], in Ernst Troeltsch, *Gesammelte Schriften*, vol. 2, Tübingen: Mohr Siebeck 1913, 769–778.
2. John Dewey, "Progress" [1916], in John Dewey, *The Middle Works*, vol. 10, Carbondale: Southern Illinois University Press 2008, 234–243, here 234.
3. Hans Joas, "Ein Christ durch Krieg und Revolution. Alfred Döblins Erzählwerk 'November 1918,'" in: *Sinn und Form* 67 (2015), 784–799.
4. See Paul Ricœur, *Time and Narrative*, vol. 3, Chicago: University of Chicago Press 1988, 193–240.
5. After a form of words used by Jan Assmann, *Achsenzeit. Eine Archäologie der Moderne*, Munich: C. H. Beck 2018, 55.
6. A very helpful reminder of this is provided by Philip Jenkins, *The Lost History of Christianity: The Thousand-Year Golden Age of the Church in the Middle East, Africa, and Asia—and How It Died*, New York: Harper 2008.

7. Alfred Döblin, "Jenseits von Gott" [1919], in Alfred Döblin, *Kleine Schriften 1*, Olten: Walter 1985, 246–261. For more detail on this, see Hans Joas, "Auseinandersetzung mit dem Christentum," in Sabina Becker (ed.), *Döblin-Handbuch. Leben—Werk—Wirkung*, Stuttgart: Metzler 2016, 356–366, here 356–358.
8. Max Scheler, *Ressentiment* [1915], New York: Schocken 1972.
9. Ernst Troeltsch, *Der Historismus und seine Probleme* [1922] (= KGA, vols. 16.1 and 16.2), Berlin: De Gruyter 2008, 197.
10. Friedrich Nietzsche, *On the Genealogy of Morality*, Cambridge: Cambridge University Press 1994. On this, see Hans Joas, *The Genesis of Values*, Chicago: University of Chicago Press 2000. I make recourse here to some of the statements in that volume (22–25).
11. Nietzsche, "On the Genealogy of Morality," 4.
12. Ibid.
13. Ibid., 7.
14. Ibid., 7f.
15. Ibid.
16. See Joas, *The Genesis of Values*, 36–53.
17. Nietzsche, "On the Genealogy of Morality," 29.
18. Ibid., 29f.
19. This is the purpose of chapter 7 of my book *The Power of the Sacred: An Alternative to the Narrative of Disenchantment*, New York: Oxford University Press 2021, 234–273. Here I sought to bring out, as key types, the self-sacralization of collectives in tribal societies, the phenomenon of sacred kingship, the sacralization of people or nation in the history of republicanism and nationalism, the sacralization of the person in the history of human rights, and new totalitarian instances of the sacralization of leaders and race in the twentieth century.
20. Nietzsche, "On the Genealogy of Morality," 16.
21. Ibid., 17.
22. Maurice Merleau-Ponty, "Christianisme et ressentiment," in: *La vie intellectuelle* 36 (1935), 278–306.
23. Max Weber, *The Protestant Ethic and the Spirit of Capitalism*, Los Angeles: Roxbury 1996, 182.
24. As determined by Hans-Christof Kraus (University of Passau). See Hans-Christof Kraus, "Dieses Nichts von Fachmensch und Genussmensch," *Frankfurter Allgemeine Zeitung*, March 30, 2016, N3.
25. Max Weber, *Economy and Society* [1922], Berkeley: University of California Press 1978, 935.
26. Max Weber, "The Social Psychology of the World Religions," , in Hans Gerth and C. Wright Mills (eds.), *From Max Weber: Essays in Sociology*, New York: Oxford University Press 1946, 267–301, here 271.
27. Weber, *Economy and Society*, 1134.
28. Max Weber, *The Religion of India: The Sociology of Hinduism and Buddhism*, Glencoe: The Free Press 1960, 169.

29. Max Weber, "National Character and the Junkers" [1917], in *From Max Weber: Essays in Sociology*, 386–395, here 393.
30. Ernst Troeltsch, "Atheistische Ethik" [1895], in Ernst Troeltsch, *Gesammelte Schriften*, vol. 2, 525–551, here 532.
31. Ibid., 525.
32. Ibid., 546.
33. Ibid.
34. Ibid., 530.
35. Ernst Troeltsch, "Logos und Mythos in Theologie und Religionsphilosophie" [1913], in Ernst Troeltsch, *Gesammelte Schriften*, vol. 2, 805–836, here 810.
36. Troeltsch, *Der Historismus und seine Probleme*, vol. 2, 763.
37. Ibid.
38. Ernst Troeltsch, "Das Wesen des modernen Geistes" [1907], in Ernst Troeltsch, *Schriften zur Religionswissenschaft und Ethik (1903–1912)* (= KGA, vol. 6), Berlin: De Gruyter 2014, 434–473, here 435.
39. Ernst Troeltsch, *The Social Teaching of the Christian Churches*, London: George Allen & Unwin 1931, 181.
40. Ernst Troeltsch, "Glaube und Ethos der hebräischen Propheten" [1916], in Ernst Troeltsch, *Aufsätze zur Geistesgeschichte und Religionssoziologie*, Tübingen: Mohr Siebeck 1925, 34–64, here 55.
41. Troeltsch, *The Social Teaching of the Christian Churches*, 182.
42. Ibid., 245 and 35.
43. Ernst Troeltsch, "Die Sozialphilosophie des Christentums" [1911], in Troeltsch, *Schriften zur Religionswissenschaft und Ethik*, 779–808, here 781.
44. Ibid.
45. Troeltsch, *The Social Teaching of the Christian Churches*, 69.
46. Quotation from the new German edition: Ernst Troeltsch, *Die Soziallehren der christlichen Kirchen und Gruppen*, 3 vols. (= KGA, vol. 9), Berlin: De Gruyter 2021, 242f.
47. Intimations of an answer can be found in Robert N. Bellah, *Religion in Human Evolution: From the Paleolithic to the Axial Age*, Cambridge: Harvard University Press 2011, 596. On Buddhist monasticism, see the study by Eisenstadt student Ilana Friedrich Silber, *Virtuosity, Charisma, and Social Order: A Comparative Sociological Study of Monasticism in Theravada Buddhism and Medieval Catholicism*, Cambridge: Cambridge University Press 1995.
48. For a detailed account, see Hans Joas, *The Sacredness of the Person: A New Genealogy of Human Rights*, Washington, DC: Georgetown University Press, 97–139.
49. How Honneth's recourse to Kant in this regard (see the introduction to the present volume, p. 6, fn. 16) relates to my proposal would require more precise clarification.
50. On the use of this term and for a discussion of methodological issues, see Sebastian Conrad, *What is Global History?*, Princeton: Princeton University Press 2016. Jürgen Osterhammel has made particularly important methodological and substantive contributions in this field. For one of his more recent studies, see Jürgen Osterhammel,

Jacob Burckhardts "Über das Studium der Weltgeschichte" und die Weltgeschichtsschreibung der Gegenwart, Basel: Schwabe 2019.

51. In the present book, see esp. Part IV, and see also Hans Joas, *Sind die Menschenrechte westlich?*, Munich: Kösel 2015; Hans Joas, "Sakralisierung—Genealogie—Globalgeschichte. Eine Erwiderung," in Michael Kühnlein and Jean-Pierre Wils (eds.), *Der Westen und die Menschenrechte. Im interdisziplinären Gespräch mit Hans Joas*, Baden-Baden: Nomos 2019, 169–199.

Bibliography

A

Adair-Toteff, Christopher (ed.). *The Anthem Companion to Ernst Troeltsch* (London: Anthem Press, 2018).
Alexander, Jeffrey, and Steven Sherwood. "'Mythic Gestures': Robert N. Bellah and Cultural Sociology," in: Richard Madsen et al. (ed.). *Meaning and Modernity: Religion, Polity, and Self* (Berkeley: University of California Press, 2002): 1–14.
Arnason, Johann. *Civilizations in Dispute: Historical Questions and Theoretical Traditions* (Leiden: Brill 2003).
Arndt, Andreas. *Friedrich Schleiermacher als Philosoph* (Berlin: De Gruyter, 2013).
Arnett, Willard. "Critique of Dewey's Anticlerical Religious Philosophy," in: *Journal of Religion* 34 (1954): 256–266.
Asad, Talal. *Formations of the Secular: Christianity, Islam, Modernity* (Stanford: Stanford University Press, 2003).
Assmann, Jan. *Achsenzeit. Eine Archäologie der Moderne* (Munich: C. H. Beck, 2018).

B

Balthasar, Hans Urs von. *Apokalypse der deutschen Seele. Studien zu einer Lehre von letzten Haltungen*, vol. 3 (Salzburg: Pustet, 1939).
Banchoff, Thomas, and José Casanova (eds.). *The Jesuits and Globalization: Historical Legacies and Contemporary Challenges* (Washington, DC: Georgetown University Press, 2016).
Barash, Jeffrey Andrew. *Martin Heidegger and the Problem of Historical Meaning* (New York: Fordham University Press, 2003).
Barth, Karl. *Die protestantische Theologie im 19. Jahrhundert. Ihre Vorgeschichte und ihre Geschichte* (Zürich: Evangelischer Verlag, 1946).
Barth, Ulrich. "Friedrich Schleiermacher," in: Friedrich Wilhelm Graf (ed.). *Klassiker der Theologie*, vol. 2: *Von Richard Simon bis Karl Rahner* (Munich: C. H. Beck, 2005): 58–88.
Bartscherer, Christoph. *Das Ich und die Natur. Alfred Döblins literarischer Weg im Licht seiner Religionsphilosophie* (Paderborn: Igel Verlag, 1997).
Becker, Howard. *Systematic Sociology* (New York: Wiley, 1932).
Becker, Sabina (ed.). *Döblin-Handbuch. Leben—Werk—Wirkung* (Stuttgart: Metzler, 2016).
Beckford James A., and Grace Davie. "David Martin," in: *British Academy: Memoirs of Fellows XVIII* (2019): 387–410.
Bedford-Strohm, Heinrich. *Gemeinschaft aus kommunikativer Freiheit. Sozialer Zusammenhalt in der modernen Gesellschaft. Ein theologischer Beitrag* (Leipzig: Evangelische Verlagsanstalt, 1999).

Bedford-Strohm, Heinrich. "Radikaler Monotheismus und der Glaube an Jesus Christus," in: Günter Thomas and Andreas Schüle (eds.). *Gegenwart des lebendigen Christus* (Leipzig: Evangelische Verlagsanstalt, 2007): 229-245.
Bellah, Robert N. *Apache Kinship Systems: Harvard Phi Beta Kappa Prize Essay for 1950* (Cambridge: Harvard University Press, 1952).
Bellah, Robert N. *Tokugawa Religion: The Cultural Roots of Modern Japan* (New York: The Free Press, 1957).
Bellah, Robert N. *Tokugawa Religion: The Values of Pre-industrial Japan* (New York: The Free Press, 1957).
Bellah, Robert N. "Religious Evolution," in: *American Sociological Review* 29, no. 3 (1964): 358-374.
Bellah, Robert N. "Words for Paul Tillich," in: *Harvard Divinity School Bulletin* 30 (1966): 15f.
Bellah, Robert N. "Civil Religion in America," in: *Daedalus* 96 (1967): 1-21.
Bellah, Robert N. *Beyond Belief: Essays on Religion in a Post-traditional World* (New York: Harper & Row, 1970).
Bellah, Robert N. "Liturgy and Experience," in: James D. Shaughnessy (ed.). *The Roots of Ritual* (Grand Rapids: Eerdmans, 1973): 217-234.
Bellah, Robert N. *The Broken Covenant: American Civil Religion in Time of Trial* (New York: Seabury, 1975).
Bellah, Robert N., and Charles Glock (eds.). *The New Religious Consciousness* (Berkeley: University of California Press, 1976).
Bellah, Robert N., et al. *Habits of the Heart: Individualism and Commitment in American Life* (Berkeley: University of California Press, 1985).
Bellah, Robert N., et al. *The Good Society* (New York: Alfred Knopf, 1991).
Bellah, Robert N. "Flaws in the Protestant Code: Some Religious Sources of America's Troubles," in: *Ethical Perspectives* 7 (2000): 288-299.
Bellah, Robert N. *Imagining Japan: The Japanese Tradition and Its Modern Interpretation* (Berkeley: University of California Press, 2003).
Bellah, Robert N. "God, Nation, and Self in America: Some Tensions between Parsons and Bellah," in: Renée C. Fox, Victor M. Lidz, and Harold J. Bershady (eds.). *After Parsons: A Theory of Social Action for the Twenty-First Century* (New York: Russell Sage Foundation, 2005): 137-147.
Bellah, Robert N. "Religious Pluralism and Religious Truth," in: Robert N. Bellah and Steven M. Tipton (eds.). *The Robert Bellah Reader* (Durham: Duke University Press, 2006): 474-489.
Bellah, Robert N., and Steven M. Tipton (eds.). *The Robert Bellah Reader* (Durham: Duke University Press, 2006).
Bellah, Robert N. *Religion in Human Evolution: From the Paleolithic to the Axial Age* (Cambridge: Harvard University Press, 2011).
Bellah, Robert N., and Hans Joas (eds.). *The Axial Age and Its Consequences* (Cambridge: Harvard University Press, 2012).
Bellah, Robert N. *Paul Tillich and the Challenge of Modernity* (unpublished manuscript, 2013).
Berger, Peter L. *The Heretical Imperative: Contemporary Possibilities of Religious Affirmation* (Garden City: Anchor, 1979).
Berger, Peter L. "Foreword," in: David Martin, *Tongues of Fire: The Explosion of Protestantism in Latin America* (Oxford: Wiley, 1990): vii-x.

Berger, Peter L. *A Far Glory: The Quest for Faith in an Age of Credulity* (New York: The Free Press, 1992).
Berger, Peter L. (ed.). *The Desecularization of the World: Resurgent Religion and World Politics* (Grand Rapids: Eerdmans, 1999).
Berger, Peter L. *The Many Altars of Modernity: Toward a Paradigm for Religion in a Pluralist Age* (Berlin: De Gruyter, 2014).
Berlin, Isaiah. Review: "Ernst Cassirer, The Philosophy of the Enlightenment," in: *English Historical Review* 68 (1953): 617–619.
Bernstein, Richard. *John Dewey* (New York: Washington Square Press, 1967).
Bertelsmann Stiftung (ed.). *Religion Monitor 2008* (Gütersloh: Verlag Bertelsmann Stiftung, 2007).
Bertelsmann Stiftung (ed.). *What the World Believes: Analysis and Commentary on the Religion Monitor 2008* (Gütersloh: Bertelsmann, 2009).
Blaschke, Olaf. "Das Jahrhundert. Ein zweites konfessionelles Zeitalter," in: *Geschichte und Gesellschaft* 26 (2000): 38–75.
Blasi, Anthony J. *Sociology of Religion in America: A History of a Secular Fascination with Religion* (Leiden: Brill, 2014).
Blasi, Anthony J. "Sociology of Religion in the United States," in: Anthony J. Blasi and Giuseppe Giordan (eds.). *Sociologies of Religion: National Traditions* (Leiden: Brill, 2015): 52–75.
Blewett, John, S.J. "Democracy as Religion: Unity in Human Relations," in: John Blewett, S.J. (ed.). *John Dewey: His Thought and Influence* (New York: Fordham University Press, 1966): 33–58.
Bloch, Marc. *The Royal Touch: Sacred Monarchy and Scrofula in England and France* (1924) (London: Routledge, 2020).
Blumenberg, Hans. *The Legitimacy of the Modern Age* (Cambridge: MIT 1985).
Böckenförde, Ernst-Wolfgang. "The Rise of the State as a Process of Secularization" (1967), in: Ernst-Wolfgang Böckenförde, *Religion, Law, and Democracy*, ed. Mirjam Künkler and Tine Stein (Oxford: Oxford University Press, 2020): 152–167.
Bodenhafer, Walter. "The Comparative Role of the Group Concept in Ward's 'Dynamic Sociology' and Contemporary American Sociology," in: *American Journal of Sociology* 26 (1920–1921): 273–314, 425–474, 582–600, and 716–743.
Bohrer, Karl Heinz. *Die Ästhetik des Schreckens. Die pessimistische Romantik und Ernst Jüngers Frühwerk* (Munich: Hanser, 1978).
Bortolini, Matteo. "Blurring the Boundary Line: The Origins and Fate of Robert Bellah's Symbolic Realism," in: Christian Fleck and Andreas Hess (eds.). *Knowledge for Whom? Public Sociology in the Making* (Farnham: Routledge, 2014): 205–227.
Bortolini, Matteo. "The 'Bellah Affair' at Princeton: Scholarly Excellence and Academic Freedom in America in the 1970s," in: *American Sociologist* 42, no. 1 (2011): 3–33.
Bortolini, Matteo. *A Joyfully Serious Man: The Life of Robert Bellah* (Princeton: Princeton University Press, 2021).
Bremmer, Jan N. "'Religion,' 'Ritual' and the Opposition 'Sacred vs. Profane,'" in: *Ansichten griechischer Rituale. Geburtstags-Symposium für Walter Burkert*, ed. Fritz Graf (Stuttgart: Vieweg & Teubner, 1968): 9–32.
Brown, Peter. *The Cult of the Saints: Its Rise and Function in Latin Christianity* (Chicago: University of Chicago Press, 1981).
Brugger, Winfried. "From Hostility through Recognition to Identification: State-Church Models and Their Relationship to Freedom of Religion," in: Hans Joas and

Klaus Wiegandt (eds.). *Secularization and the World Religions* (Liverpool: Liverpool University Press, 2009): 160-180.

C

Caird, Edward. *The Evolution of Religion* (Glasgow: James MacLehose and Sons, 1894).
Camic, Charles. "Reputation and Predecessor Selection: Parsons and the Institutionalists," in: *American Sociological Review* 57 (1992): 421-445.
Camilleri, Sylvain. "A Historical Note on Heidegger's Relationship to Ernst Troeltsch," in: S. J. McGrath and Andrzej Wiercinski (eds.). *A Companion to Heidegger's "Phenomenology of Religious Life"* (Amsterdam: Rodopi, 2010): 115-134.
Casanova, José. "Legitimacy and the Sociology of Modernization," in: Arthur Vidich and Ronald Glassman (eds.). *Conflict and Control: Challenge to Legitimacy of Modern Governments* (London: Cambridge University Press, 1979): 219-252.
Casanova, José. "The Opus Dei Ethics, the Technocrats and the Modernization of Spain," in: *Social Science Information* 22 (1983): 27-50.
Casanova, José. "Interpretations and Misinterpretations of Max Weber: The Problem of Rationalization," in: Ronald Glassman and Vatro Murvar (eds.). *Max Weber in Political Sociology: A Pessimistic Vision of a Rationalized World* (Westport: Greenwood Press, 1984): 141-154.
Casanova, José. "Catholic Ethics and Social Justice: Natural Law and Beyond," in: *International Journal of Politics, Culture, and Society* 6 (1992): 322-329.
Casanova, José. *Public Religions in the Modern World* (Chicago: University of Chicago Press, 1994).
Casanova, José. Review: "Zygmunt Bauman, *Postmodern Ethics* (Oxford 1993)," in: *Contemporary Sociology* 24 (1995): 424f.
Casanova, José. "Globalizing Catholicism and the Return to a 'Universal' Church," in: Susanne Rudolph and James Piscatori (eds.). *Transnational Religion and Fading States* (Boulder: Routledge, 1997): 121-143.
Casanova, José. "Ethno-Linguistic and Religious Pluralism and Democratic Construction in Ukraine," in: Barnett Rubin and Jack Snyder (eds.). *Post-Soviet Political Order: Conflict and State-Building* (New York: Routledge, 1998): 81-103.
Casanova, José. "Religion, the New Millennium, and Globalization," in: *Sociology of Religion* 62 (2001): 415-441.
Casanova, José. "Civil Society and Religion: Retrospective Reflections on Catholicism and Prospective Reflections on Islam," in: *Social Research* 68 (2001): 1041-1080.
Casanova, José. "Beyond European and American Exceptionalisms: Toward a Global Perspective," in: Grace Davie et al. (eds.). *Predicting Religion. Christian, Secular and Alternative Futures* (Aldershot: Ashgate, 2003): 17-29.
Casanova, José. "Catholic and Muslim Politics in Comparative Perspective," in: *Taiwan Journal of Democracy* 1 (2005): 89-108.
Casanova, José. "Secularization Revisited: A Reply to Talal Asad," in: David Scott and Charles Hirschkind (eds.). *Powers of the Secular Modern: Talal Asad and His Interlocutors* (Stanford: Stanford University Press, 2006): 12-30.
Casanova, José. "Immigration and the New Religious Pluralism: A European Union / United States Comparison," in: Thomas Banchoff (ed.). *Democracy and the New Religious Pluralism* (Oxford: Oxford University Press, 2007): 59-84.

Casanova, José. "Public Religions Revisited," in: Hent de Vries (ed.). *Religion: Beyond a Concept* (New York: Fordham University Press, 2008): 101–119.

Casanova, José. "The Problem of Religion and Anxieties of European Secular Democracies," in: Gabriel Motzkin and Yochi Fischer (eds.). *Religion and Democracy in Contemporary Europe* (London: Alliance Publishing Trust, 2008): 63–74.

Casanova, José. *Europas Angst vor der Religion* (Berlin: Berlin University Press, 2009).

Casanova, José. "Religion in Modernity as Global Challenge," in: Michael Reder and Matthias Rugel (eds.). *Religion und die umstrittene Moderne* (Stuttgart: Kohlhammer, 2010): 1–16.

Casanova, José. "From Modernization to Secularization to Globalization: An Autobiographical Self-Reflection," in: *Religion and Society. Advances in Research* 2 (2011): 25–36.

Casanova, José. "Religions, Secularizations and Modernities," in: *European Journal of Sociology* 52 (2011): 423–445.

Casanova, José. "Religion, the Axial Age, and Secular Modernity in Bellah's Theory of Religious Evolution," in: Robert N. Bellah and Hans Joas (eds.). *The Axial Age and Its Consequences* (Cambridge: Harvard University Press, 2012): 191–221.

Casanova, José. "Parallel Reformations in Latin America: A Critical Review of David Martin's Interpretation of the Pentecostal Revolution," in: Hans Joas (ed.). *David Martin and the Sociology of Religion* (London: Routledge, 2018): 85–106.

Casanova, José. *Global Religious and Secular Dynamics: The Modern System of Classification* (Leiden: Brill, 2019).

Cassirer, Ernst. *Das Erkenntnisproblem in der Philosophie und Wissenschaft der neueren Zeit*, vol. II (Berlin: Bruno Cassirer, 1907).

Cassirer, Ernst. *Freiheit und Form. Studien zur deutschen Geistesgeschichte* (Berlin: Bruno Cassirer, 1916).

Cassirer, Ernst. *Kants Leben und Lehre* (Berlin: Bruno Cassirer, 1918).

Cassirer, Ernst. *The Philosophy of Symbolic Forms* (1923), vol. 2 (New Haven: Yale University Press, 1965).

Cassirer, Ernst. "Die Idee der republikanischen Verfassung" (1928), reprinted in: Ernst Cassirer, *Aufsätze und kleine Schriften 1927-1931* (Hamburg: Felix Meiner, 2004): 291–307.

Cassirer, Ernst. "Deutschland und Westeuropa im Spiegel der Geistesgeschichte" (1931), in: Ernst Cassirer, *Aufsätze und kleine Schriften 1927-1931* (Hamburg: Felix Meiner, 2004): 207–220.

Cassirer, Ernst. *Die Philosophie der Aufklärung* (Tübingen: Mohr Siebeck, 1932). English translation: *The Philosophy of the Enlightenment* (Princeton: Princeton University Press, 1951).

Cassirer, Ernst. "Vom Wesen und Werden des Naturrechts" (1932), in: Ernst Cassirer, *Aufsätze und kleine Schriften 1932-1935* (Hamburg: Felix Meiner, 2001): 203–227.

Cassirer, Ernst. "Judaism and the Modern Political Myths," in: *Contemporary Jewish Record* 7 (1944): 115–126.

Cassirer, Ernst. *The Myth of the State* (New Haven: Yale University Press, 1946).

Castoriadis, Cornelius. *The Imaginary Institution of Society* (Cambridge: MIT Press 1987).

Cavendish, James C. "The Sociological Study of American Catholicism: Past, Present and Future," in: Anthony J. Blasi (ed.). *American Sociology of Religion: Histories* (Leiden: Brill, 2007): 151–176.

Chappell, David L. *A Stone of Hope: Prophetic Religion and the Death of Jim Crow* (Chapel Hill: University of North Carolina Press, 2004): 297–301.

Chesterton, Gilbert Keith. *The Everlasting Man* (1925), in: Gilbert Keith Chesterton, *The Collected Works II* (San Francisco: Ignatius Press, 1986): 135–407.

Christiano, Kevin. "Clio Goes to Church: Revisiting and Revitalizing Historical Thinking in the Sociology of Religion," in: *Sociology of Religion* 69 (2008): 1–28.

Christophersen, Alf. *Kairos. Protestantische Zeitdeutungskämpfe in der Weimarer Republik* (Tübingen: Mohr Siebeck, 2008).

Clayton, John. "Paul Tillich—ein 'verjüngter Troeltsch' oder noch ein 'Apfel vom Baume Kierkegaards'?," in: Horst Renz and Friedrich Wilhelm Graf (eds.). *Umstrittene Moderne. Die Zukunft der Neuzeit im Urteil der Epoche Ernst Troeltschs* (= *Troeltsch-Studien*, vol. 4) (Gütersloh: Gütersloher Verlagshaus, 1987): 259–283.

Collins, Randall. "Imperialism and Legitimacy: Weber's Theory of Politics," in: Randall Collins, *Weberian Sociological Theory* (Cambridge: Cambridge University Press, 1986): 145–166.

Colorado, Carlos D., and Justin D. Klassen (eds.). *Aspiring to Fullness in a Secular Age: Essays on Religion and Theology in a Secular Age* (Notre Dame: Notre Dame University Press, 2014).

Colpe, Carsten. *Über das Heilige. Versuch, seiner Verkennung kritisch vorzubeugen* (Meisenheim: Anton Hain, 1990).

Conrad, Sebastian. *What Is Global History?* (Princeton: Princeton University Press, 2016).

Conze, Werner et al. "Freiheit," in: Otto Brunner, Werner Conze, and Reinhart Koselleck (eds.). *Geschichtliche Grundbegriffe. Historisches Lexikon zur politisch-sozialen Sprache in Deutschland*, vol. 2 (Stuttgart: Klett-Cotta, 1975): 425–542.

Conze, Werner, and Hermann Zabel. "Säkularisation, Säkularisierung," in: Otto Brunner, Werner Conze, and Reinhart Koselleck (eds.). *Geschichtliche Grundbegriffe. Historisches Lexikon zur politisch-sozialen Sprache in Deutschland*, vol. 5 (Stuttgart: Klett-Cotta, 1984): 789–829.

Costa, Paolo. "The One and the Many Stories: How to Reconcile Sense-Making and Fact-Checking in the Secularization Narrative," in: Hans Joas (ed.). *David Martin and the Sociology of Religion* (London: Routledge, 2018): 50–66.

Cusinato, Guido. "Werdender Gott und Wiedergeburt der Person bei Max Scheler," in: Ralf Becker and Ernst Wolfgang Orth (eds.). *Religion und Metaphysik als Dimensionen der Kultur* (Würzburg: Königshausen & Neumann, 2011): 123–134.

D

Daniel, Joshua. *Transforming Faith: Individual and Community in H. Richard Niebuhr* (Eugene: Pickwick, 2015).

Daniel, Joshua. "H. Richard Niebuhr's Reading of George Herbert Mead," in: *Journal of Religious Ethics* 44 (2016): 92–115.

Danz, Christian. "Der Begriff des Symbols bei Paul Tillich und Ernst Cassirer," in: Dietrich Korsch and Enno Rudolph (eds.). *Die Prägnanz der Religion in der Kultur. Ernst Cassirer und die Theologie* (Tübingen: Mohr Siebeck, 2000): 201–228.

Danz, Christian. *Religion als Freiheitsbewußtsein. Eine Studie zur Theologie als Theorie der Konstitutionsbedingungen individueller Subjektivität bei Paul Tillich* (Berlin: De Gruyter, 2000).

Danz, Christian. "'Vom Nutzen und Nachteil der Historie für das Leben.' Nietzsche, Troeltsch und Tillich über Auswege aus der Krisis des Historismus," in: *Internationales Jahrbuch für die Tillich-Forschung* 3 (2008): 61–81.

Das, Robin R. *The Place of Werner Stark in American Sociology: A Study in Marginality* (Ph.D. thesis) (University of Michigan, 2008).

Das, Robin R., and Hermann Strasser. "The Sociologist from Marienbad: Werner Stark between Catholicism and Social Science," in: *Czech Sociological Review* 51, no. 3 (2015): 417–444.

David, Paul A. "Clio and the Economics of QWERTY," in: *American Economic Review* 75 (1985): 332–337.

Davie, Grace. *Religion in Britain: A Persistent Paradox* (Oxford: Blackwell, 2015).

Davie, Grace. "Understanding Religion in Modern Britain: Taking the Long View," in: Hans Joas (ed.). *David Martin and the Sociology of Religion* (London: Routledge, 2018): 67–84.

Dempf, Alois. *Sacrum Imperium. Geschichts- und Staatsphilosophie des Mittelalters und der politischen Renaissance* (1929) (Darmstadt: WBG, 1954).

Deuser, Hermann. "Gottes Poesie oder Anschauung des Unbedingten? Semiotische Religionstheorie bei C. S. Peirce und P. Tillich," in: Christian Danz, Werner Schüßler, and Erdmann Sturm (eds.). *Das Symbol als Sprache der Religion* (Berlin: LIT, 2007): 117–134.

Deuser, Hermann. "'A Feeling of Objective Presence'—Rudolf Ottos 'Das Heilige' und William James' Pragmatismus im Vergleich," in: Jörg Lauster et al. (eds.). *Rudolf Otto. Theologie—Religionsphilosophie—Religionsgeschichte* (Berlin: De Gruyter, 2014): 319–333.

Dewey, John. "Self-Realization as the Moral Ideal" (1893), in: John Dewey, *Early Works*, vol. 4 (Carbondale: Southern Illinois University Press, 1971): 42–53.

Dewey, John. "Christianity and Democracy" (1893), in: John Dewey, *Early Works*, vol. 4 (Carbondale: Southern Illinois University Press, 1971): 3–10.

Dewey, John. "Religion and Our Schools," in: *Hibbert Journal* 6 (1908): 796–809, also in: John Dewey, *Middle Works*, vol. 4 (Carbondale: Southern Illinois University Press, 1977): 165–177.

Dewey, John. "Progress" (1916), in: John Dewey, *Middle Works*, vol. 10 (Carbondale: Southern Illinois University Press, 2008): 234–243.

Dewey, John. *Human Nature and Conduct: An Introduction to Social Psychology* (New York: Henry Holt and Company, 1922), also in: John Dewey, *Middle Works*, vol. 14 (Carbondale: Southern Illinois University Press, 1988).

Dewey, John. *Experience and Nature* (1925) (London: Open Court, 1958).

Dewey, John. *Art as Experience* (1934) (New York: Putnam's, 1980).

Dewey, John. *A Common Faith* (New Haven: Yale University Press, 1934).

Dewey, John. "Experience, Knowledge, and Value: A Rejoinder," in: Paul Arthur Schilpp (ed.). *The Philosophy of John Dewey* (New York: Open Court, 1939): 517–608, also in: John Dewey, *Later Works*, vol. 14 (Carbondale: Southern Illinois University Press, 1981): 3–90.

Dewey, John. *Psychology*, in: John Dewey, *Early Works*, vol. 2 (Carbondale: Southern Illinois University Press, 1967).

Diefenthaler, Jon. *H. Richard Niebuhr: A Lifetime of Reflections on the Church and the World* (Macon: Mercer University Press, 1986).

Dierken, Jörg. "Hegel und Schleiermacher. Affinitäten und Abgrenzungen," in: Thomas Hanke and Thomas M. Schmidt (eds.). *Der Frankfurter Hegel in seinem Kontext* (Frankfurt am Main: Klostermann, 2015): 251–268.

Dierken, Jörg. "'Hauskrieg' bei Kants Erben. Schleiermacher und Hegel über Religion und Christentum," in: Andreas Arndt and Tobias Rosefeldt (eds.). *Schleiermacher/Hegel* (Berlin: Duncker & Humblot, 2020): 19–36.

Dilthey, Wilhelm. "Rede zum 70. Geburtstag" (1903), in: Wilhelm Dilthey, *Die geistige Welt. Einleitung in die Philosophie des Lebens* (= *Gesammelte Schriften*, vol. 5) (Leipzig: B. G. Teubner, 1924): 7–9.

Dilthey, Wilhelm. *The Formation of the Historical World in the Human Sciences* (1910) (= *Selected Works*, vol. 3, ed. Rudolf Makkreel and Frithjof Rodi) (Princeton: Princeton University Press, 2002): 295–316.

Dilthey, Wilhelm. "The Problem of Religion" (1911), in: Wilhelm Dilthey, *Ethical and World-View Philosophy* (= *Selected Works*, vol. 6, ed. Rudolf Makkreel and Frithjof Rodi) (Princeton: Princeton University Press, 2019): 295–316.

Dilthey, Wilhelm. *Die Jugendgeschichte Hegels* (= *Gesammelte Schriften*, vol. 4) (Stuttgart/Göttingen: Teubner, 1974).

Dilthey, Wilhelm. *Introduction to the Human Sciences* (= *Selected Works*, vol. 1) (Princeton: Princeton University Press, 1989).

Dilthey, Wilhelm. *Weltanschauung und Analyse des Menschen seit Renaissance und Reformation* (= *Gesammelte Schriften*, vol. 2) (Stuttgart: Vandenhoeck & Ruprecht, 1991).

Dipper, Christof. "Die 'Geschichtlichen Grundbegriffe.' Von der Begriffsgeschichte zur Theorie der historischen Zeiten," in: *Historische Zeitschrift* 270 (2000): 281–308, also in: Hans Joas and Peter Vogt (eds.). *Begriffene Geschichte. Beiträge zum Werk Reinhart Kosellecks* (Berlin: Suhrkamp, 2011): 288–316.

Döbert, Rainer. *Systemtheorie und die Entwicklung religiöser Deutungssysteme. Zur Logik des sozialwissenschaftlichen Funktionalismus* (Frankfurt am Main: Suhrkamp, 1973): 73–154.

Döblin, Alfred. "Jenseits von Gott" (1919), in: Alfred Döblin, *Kleine Schriften I* (Olten: Walter, 1985): 246–261.

Döblin, Alfred. "Theater in Berlin (November 21, 1921)," in: Alfred Döblin, *Ein Kerl muß eine Meinung haben. Berichte und Kritiken 1921–1924* (Olten: Walter, 1976): 15–17.

Döblin, Alfred. *Journey to Poland* (1925) (New York: Paragon House, 1991).

Döblin, Alfred. *Alfred Döblin Presents the Living Thoughts of Confucius* (Toronto: Longmans, Green and Co., 1940).

Döblin, Alfred. "Brief an Wilhelm Hausenstein vom 31.1.1947," in: Alfred Döblin, *Briefe* (Olten: Walter, 1970).

Döblin, Alfred. *Briefe* (Olten: Walter, 1970).

Döblin, Alfred. *Destiny's Journey* (ed. Edgar Pässler, transl. Edna McCown) (New York: Paragon House, 1992).

Döblin, Alfred. *Der unsterbliche Mensch / Der Kampf mit dem Engel* (Frankfurt am Main: Fischer, 2016).

Doenecke, Justus D. "H. Richard Niebuhr: Critic of Political Theology," in: *Communio: International Catholic Review* 4, no. 1 (1977): 82–93.

Donald, Merlin. *Origins of the Modern Mind: Three Stages in the Evolution of Culture and Cognition* (Cambridge: Harvard University Press, 1991).

Donald, Merlin. "An Evolutionary Approach to Culture: Implications for the Study of the Axial Age," in: Robert N. Bellah and Hans Joas (eds.). *The Axial Age and Its Consequences* (Cambridge: Harvard University Press, 2012): 47–76.

Dosse, François. *Paul Ricœur. Les sens d'une vie* (Paris: La Découverte, 1997).

Dreier, Horst. "Kanonistik und Konfessionalisierung—Marksteine auf dem Weg zum Staat," in: Georg Siebeck (ed.). *Artibus ingenuis* (Tübingen: Mohr Siebeck, 2001): 133–169.

Drescher, Hans-Georg. *Ernst Troeltsch. Leben und Werk* (Göttingen: Vandenhoeck & Ruprecht, 1991).
Dunstan, G. R. Review: "Werner Stark, *The Sociology of Religion*, vol. III," in: *Religious Studies* 6 (1970): 197-199.
Durkheim, Émile. *The Elementary Forms of Religious Life* (transl. Carol Cosman) (New York: Oxford University Press, 2001).

E

Edie, James M. *William James and Phenomenology* (Bloomington: Indiana University Press, 1987).
Eisenstadt, Shmuel N. *Power, Trust, and Meaning: Essays in Sociological Theory and Analysis* (Chicago: University of Chicago Press, 1995).
Eisenstadt, Shmuel N. *Fundamentalism, Sectarianism, and Revolution* (Cambridge: Cambridge University Press, 2009).
Eister, Alan W. Review: "Werner Stark, *The Sociology of Religion I-III*," in: *Journal for the Scientific Study of Religion* 7, no. 2 (1968): 294f.
Emde, Friedrich. *Alfred Döblin. Sein Weg zum Christentum* (Tübingen: Narr, 1999).

F

Feil, Ernst. "Zur ursprünglichen Bedeutung von 'Theonomie,'" in: *Archiv für Begriffsgeschichte* 34 (1991): 295-313.
Flanagan, Kieran, and Peter C. Jupp (eds.). "Symposium on Charles Taylor with His Responses," in: *New Blackfriars* 91 (2010): 625-724.
Flasche, Rainer. "Joachim Wach 1898-1955," in: Axel Michaels (ed.). *Klassiker der Religionswissenschaft* (Munich: C. H. Beck, 1997): 290-302.
Flint, John T. Review: "Werner Stark, *The Sociology of Religion I-III*," in: *Journal of the American Academy of Religion* 40, no. 1 (1972): 110-116.
Floyd, Gregory P. "Between 'Liberale Theologie' and 'Religionsphilosophie': A New Perspective on Heidegger's 'Phenomenology of Religious Life,'" in: Gerhard Thonhauser (ed.). *Perspektiven mit Heidegger. Zugänge—Pfade—Anknüpfungen* (Freiburg: Karl Alber, 2017): 132-146.
Fowler, James W. *To See the Kingdom: The Theological Vision of H. Richard Niebuhr* (Nashville: Abingdon Press, 1974).
Fox, Richard Wightman. *Reinhold Niebuhr: A Biography* (Ithaca: Cornell University Press 1996): 143-147.
Frankopan, Peter. *The Silk Roads: A New History of the World* (London: Bloomsbury, 2015).
Frei, Hans W. "Niebuhr's Theological Background," in: Paul Ramsey (ed.). *Faith and Ethics: The Theology of H. Richard Niebuhr* (New York: Harper & Bros., 1957): 9-64.
Freston, Paul. "David Martin and the Growth of Protestantism in the Third World," in: Andrew Walker and Martyn Percy (eds.). *Restoring the Image: Essays on Religion and Society in Honour of David Martin* (Sheffield: Sheffield Academic Press, 2001): 110-124.
Friedman, Michael. *A Parting of the Ways: Carnap, Cassirer, and Heidegger* (Chicago: Open Court, 2000).

Fries, Heinrich. *Die katholische Religionsphilosophie der Gegenwart* (Heidelberg: Kerle, 1949).
Friess, Horace L. "Dewey's Philosophy of Religion," in: Jo Ann Boydston (ed.). *Guide to the Works of John Dewey* (Carbondale: Southern Illinois University Press, 1970): 200–217.
Furia, Paolo. "Le scienze sociali e il paradigma ermeneutico in Paul Ricœur e Hans Joas. La libertà come creativitá," in: Gaetano Chiurazzi and Giacomo Pezzone (eds.). *Attualità del possibile* (Milan: Mimesis, 2017): 81–94.

G

Gabel, Michael, and Hans Joas (eds.). *Von der Ursprünglichkeit der Gabe. Jean-Luc Marions Phänomenologie in der Diskussion* (Freiburg: Karl Alber, 2007).
Gantke, Wolfgang, and Vladimir Serikov (eds.). *100 Jahre "Das Heilige." Beiträge zu Rudolf Ottos Grundlagenwerk* (Frankfurt am Main: Peter Lang, 2017).
Gaston, K. Healan. "'A Bad Kind of Magic': The Niebuhr Brothers on 'Utilitarian Christianity' and the Defense of Democracy," in: *Harvard Theological Review* 107 (2014): 1–30.
Gauchet, Marcel. *The Disenchantment of the World: A Political History of Religion* (Princeton: Princeton University Press, 1997).
Gooch, Todd A. *The Numinous and Modernity: An Interpretation of Rudolf Otto's Philosophy of Religion* (Berlin: De Gruyter, 2000).
Gooch, Todd A. "The Epistemic Status of Value-Cognition in Max Scheler's Philosophy of Religion," in: *Journal for Cultural and Religious Theory* 3, no. 1 (2001), <https://www.jcrt.org/archives/03.1/gooch.shtml>, accessed January 14, 2013.
Good, Paul (ed.). *Max Scheler im Gegenwartsgeschehen der Philosophie* (Bern: Francke, 1975).
Gordon, Peter E. "The Place of the Sacred in the Absence of God: Charles Taylor's 'A Secular Age,'" in: *Journal of the History of Ideas* 69 (2008): 647–673.
Gordon, Peter E. *Continental Divide: Heidegger, Cassirer, Davos* (Cambridge: Harvard University Press, 2010).
Gorski, Philip. "The Return of the Repressed: Religion and the Political Unconscious of Historical Sociology," in: Julia Adams, Elizabeth Clemens, and Ann Orloff (eds.). *Remaking Modernity: Politics, History, and Sociology* (Durham: Duke University Press, 2005): 161–189.
Gouinlock, James. *John Dewey's Philosophy of Value* (New York: Humanities Press, 1972).
Graf, Friedrich Wilhelm. *Theonomie. Fallstudien zum Integrationsanspruch neuzeitlicher Theologie* (Gütersloh: Gütersloher Verlagshaus Mohn, 1987).
Graf, Friedrich Wilhelm (ed.). *Ernst Troeltsch in Nachrufen* (= Troeltsch-Studien, vol. 12) (Gütersloh: Gütersloher Verlagshaus, 2002).
Graf, Friedrich Wilhelm. *Der heilige Zeitgeist. Studien zur Ideengeschichte der protestantischen Theologie in der Weimarer Republik* (Tübingen: Mohr Siebeck, 2011).
Graf, Friedrich Wilhelm. "Die 'antihistoristische Revolution' in der protestantischen Theologie der zwanziger Jahre," in: Friedrich Wilhelm Graf, *Der heilige Zeitgeist. Studien zur Ideengeschichte der protestantischen Theologie in der Weimarer Republik* (Tübingen: Mohr Siebeck, 2011): 111–137.
Graf, Friedrich Wilhelm. *Fachmenschenfreundschaft. Studien zu Troeltsch und Weber* (Berlin: De Gruyter, 2014).

Gray, John. *Isaiah Berlin* (Princeton: Princeton University Press, 1996).
Greisch, Jean. *Le buisson ardent et les lumières de la raison*, vol. 2 (Paris: Cerf, 2002): 241–372.
Gresham, John L., Jr. "The Collective Charisma of the Catholic Church: Werner Stark's Critique of Max Weber's Routinization Theory," in: *Catholic Social Science Review* 8 (2003): 123–139.
Große Kracht, Hermann-Josef. "Von der Kirchensoziographie zu einer Sozialtheorie der 'public churches'? Ein Bilanzierungsversuch zur Soziologie des Katholizismus im 20. Jahrhundert," in: Hermann-Josef Große Kracht and Christian Spieß (eds.). *Christentum und Solidarität. Bestandsaufnahmen zu Sozialethik und Religionssoziologie* (Paderborn: Schöningh, 2008): 189–229.
Guardini, Romano. *Die Macht. Versuch einer Wegweisung* (Würzburg: Werkbund, 1951).
Gustafson, James M. *Treasure in Earthen Vessels: The Church as a Human Community* (1961) (Louisville: University of Kentucky Press, 1976).

H

Habermas, Jürgen. "Zur Kritik an der Geschichtsphilosophie" (1960), in: Jürgen Habermas, *Kultur und Kritik* (Frankfurt am Main: Suhrkamp, 1973): 355–364.
Habermas, Jürgen. "Verrufener Fortschritt—Verkanntes Jahrhundert," in: *Merkur* 14 (1960): 466–477.
Habermas, Jürgen. "Karl Löwith: Stoic Retreat from Historical Consciousness" (1963), in: Habermas, *Philosophical-Political Profiles* (Cambridge: MIT Press, 1983): 79–98.
Habermas, Jürgen. *Technik und Wissenschaft als "Ideologie"* (Frankfurt am Main: Suhrkamp, 1968).
Habermas, Jürgen. "Die Philosophie als Platzhalter und Interpret," in: Jürgen Habermas, *Moralbewußtsein und kommunikatives Handeln* (Frankfurt am Main: Suhrkamp, 1983): 9–28.
Habermas, Jürgen. *The Theory of Communicative Action*, 2 vols. (London: Heinemann, 1984).
Habermas, Jürgen. *The Structural Transformation of the Public Sphere: An Inquiry into a Category of Bourgeois Society* (Cambridge: MIT Press, 1991): 117–123.
Habermas, Jürgen. *The Liberating Power of Symbols: Philosophical Essays* (Oxford: Polity, 2001).
Habermas, Jürgen. "Communicative Freedom and Negative Theology: Questions for Michael Theunissen," in: Jürgen Habermas, *The Liberating Power of Symbols: Philosophical Essays* (Oxford: Polity, 2001): 90–111.
Habermas, Jürgen. "The Liberating Power of Symbols: Ernst Cassirer's Humanistic Legacy and the Warburg Library," in: Jürgen Habermas, *The Liberating Power of Symbols* (Cambridge: MIT Press, 2001): 1–29.
Habermas, Jürgen. *Glauben und Wissen* (Frankfurt am Main: Suhrkamp, 2001).
Habermas, Jürgen. *Auch eine Geschichte der Philosophie*, 2 vols. (Berlin: Suhrkamp, 2019).
Hafkesbrink, Hanna. "Das Problem des religiösen Gegenstandes bei Max Scheler," in: *Zeitschrift für systematische Theologie* 8 (1931): 145–180 and 251–292.
Hafkesbrink, Hanna. "The Meaning of Objectivism and Realism in Max Scheler's Philosophy of Religion: A Contribution to the Understanding of Max Scheler's Catholic Period," in: *Philosophy and Phenomenological Research* 2 (1942): 292–309.

Halbig, Christoph. "Hegel, Honneth und das Primat der Freiheit. Kritische Überlegungen," in: Magnus Schlette (ed.). *Ist Selbstverwirklichung institutionalisierbar? Axel Honneths Freiheitstheorie in der Diskussion* (Frankfurt am Main: Campus, 2018): 53–72.
Hampe, Michael. *Erkenntnis und Praxis. Zur Philosophie des Pragmatismus* (Frankfurt am Main: Suhrkamp, 2006): 283–286.
Harnack, Adolf von. "Rede am Sarge Ernst Troeltschs" (1923), in: Friedrich Wilhelm Graf (ed.). *Ernst Troeltsch in Nachrufen* (= *Troeltsch-Studien*, vol. 12) (Gütersloh: Gütersloher Verlagshaus, 2002): 266–271.
Hartch, Todd. *The Rebirth of Latin American Christianity* (Oxford: Oxford University Press, 2014): 124–126.
Hartmann, Nicolai. "Max Scheler (Nachruf)," in: *Kant-Studien* 33 (1928): ix–xvi.
Hartung, Gerald. "Autonomiewahnsinn? Der Preis einer Säkularisierung des Menschenbildes in der philosophischen Anthropologie Max Schelers," in: Christel Gärtner, Detlef Pollack and Monika Wohlrab-Sahr (eds.). *Atheismus und religiöse Indifferenz* (Opladen: VS, 2003): 75–92.
Hasenclever, Andreas. "Taking Religion Back Out: On the Secular Dynamics of Armed Conflicts and the Potentials of Religious Peace-Making," in: Hans Joas (ed.). *David Martin and the Sociology of Religion* (London: Routledge, 2018): 123–146.
Hatzfeld, Henri. *Les Racines de la religion. Tradition, rituel, valeurs* (Paris: Esprit/Seuil, 1993).
Hauerwas, Stanley, and William Willimon. *Resident Aliens* (Nashville: Abingdon Press, 1990).
Hausenstein, Wilhelm. "Rezension," *Süddeutsche Zeitung*, February 1, 1947, reprinted in: Ingrid Schuster and Ingrid Bode (eds.). *Alfred Döblin im Spiegel der zeitgenössischen Kritik* (Bern: Francke, 1973): 390–393.
Hefner, Robert W. "Introduction: World-Building and the Rationality of Conversion," in: Robert W. Hefner (ed.). *Conversion to Christianity* (Berkeley: University of California Press, 1993): 3–44.
Hegel, G. W. F. "Vorrede zu Hinrichs Religionsphilosophie" (1822), in: G. W. F. Hegel, *Berliner Schriften 1818–1831* (= *Werke*, vol. 11) (Frankfurt am Main: Suhrkamp, 1970): 42–67.
Hegel, G. W. F. *Enzyklopädie der philosophischen Wissenschaften III* (1830) (Frankfurt: Suhrkamp, 1986).
Hegel, G. W. F. *Vorlesungen über die Philosophie der Geschichte* (= *Werke*, vol. 12) (Frankfurt am Main: Suhrkamp, 1970). English translation: G. W. F. Hegel. *The Philosophy of History* (Kitchener: Batoche, 2001).
Hegel, G. W. F. *Vorlesungen über die Geschichte der Philosophie III* (= *Werke*, vol. 20) (Frankfurt am Main: Suhrkamp, 1970).
Heidegger, Martin. "Andenken an Max Scheler," in: Paul Good (ed.). *Max Scheler im Gegenwartsgeschehen der Philosophie* (Bern: Francke, 1975): 9.
Heidegger, Martin. *Kant und das Problem der Metaphysik* (1929) (Frankfurt am Main: Klostermann, 1988).
Heidegger, Martin. "Einleitung in die Phänomenologie der Religion," in: Martin Heidegger, *Phänomenologie des religiösen Lebens* (= *Gesamtausgabe*, vol. 60) (Frankfurt: Klostermann, 1995): 1–156.
Heimpel, Hermann. "Geschichte und Geschichtswissenschaft," in: *Vierteljahrshefte für Zeitgeschichte* 5 (1957): 1–17.

Hempton, David, and Hugh McLeod (eds.). *Secularization and Religious Innovation in the North Atlantic World* (Oxford: Oxford University Press, 2017).
Herberg, Will. *Protestant, Catholic, Jew: An Essay in American Religious Sociology* (Garden City: Doubleday, 1955).
Herberger, Kurt. "Historismus und Kairos. Die Überwindung des Historismus bei Ernst Troeltsch und Paul Tillich," in: *Theologische Blätter* 14 (1935): col. 129–141 and col. 161–175.
Hettling, Manfred, and Bernd Ulrich. "Formen der Bürgerlichkeit. Ein Gespräch mit Reinhart Koselleck," in: Manfred Hettling and Bernd Ulrich (eds.). *Bürgertum nach 1945* (Hamburg: Hamburger Edition, 2005): 40–60.
Hildebrand, Dietrich von. "Max Schelers Stellung zur katholischen Gedankenwelt," in: Dietrich von Hildebrand, *Zeitliches im Lichte des Ewigen. Gesammelte Abhandlungen und Vorträge* (Regensburg: Josef Habbel, 1932): 341–364.
Hobbes, Thomas. *Leviathan* (London: Penguin, 2017).
Honneth, Axel. "Die Unhintergehbarkeit des Fortschritts. Kants Bestimmung des Verhältnisses von Moral und Geschichte," in: Axel Honneth, *Pathologien der Vernunft. Geschichte und Gegenwart der Kritischen Theorie* (Frankfurt am Main: Suhrkamp, 2007): 9–27.
Honneth, Axel. *Freedom's Right: The Social Foundations of Democratic Life* (New York: Columbia University Press, 2014).
Honneth, Axel. "Erwiderung," in: Magnus Schlette (ed.). *Ist Selbstverwirklichung institutionalisierbar? Axel Honneths Freiheitstheorie in der Diskussion* (Frankfurt am Main: Campus, 2018): 313–337.
Horn, Friedrich Wilhelm. "'Zur Freiheit hat uns Christus befreit.' Neutestamentliche Perspektiven," in: Martin Laube (ed.). *Freiheit* (Tübingen: UTB, 2014): 39–58.
Huber, Wolfgang. *Kirche in der Zeitenwende. Gesellschaftlicher Wandel und Erneuerung der Kirche* (Gütersloh: Verlag Bertelsmann Stiftung, 1998).
Huber, Wolfgang. *Der gemachte Mensch. Christlicher Glaube und Biotechnik* (Berlin: Wichern, 2002).
Huber, Wolfgang. *Gerechtigkeit und Recht. Grundlinien christlicher Rechtsethik* (Gütersloh: Gütersloher Verlagshaus, ³2006).
Huber, Wolfgang. *Von der Freiheit. Perspektiven für eine solidarische Welt* (Munich: C. H. Beck, 2012).
Huber, Wolfgang. "Über die kommunikative Freiheit hinaus," in: Heinrich Bedford-Strohm, Paul Nolte, and Rüdiger Sachau (eds.). *Kommunikative Freiheit. Interdisziplinäre Diskurse mit Wolfgang Huber* (Leipzig: Evangelische Verlagsanstalt, 2014): 175–191.
Huber, Wolfgang. "Rechtsethik," in: Wolfgang Huber, Torsten Meireis, and Hans-Richard Reuter (eds.). *Handbuch der Evangelischen Ethik* (Munich: C. H. Beck, 2015): 125–193.
Huber, Wolfgang. *Ethics: The Fundamental Questions of Our Lives* (Washington, DC: Georgetown University Press, 2015).
Huber, Wolfgang. *Glaubensfragen. Eine evangelische Orientierung* (Munich: C. H. Beck, 2017).
Huber, Wolfgang. *Dietrich Bonhoeffer. Auf dem Weg zur Freiheit* (Munich: C. H. Beck, 2019).
Hubert, Henri, and Marcel Mauss. *A General Theory of Magic* (1904) (London: Routledge, 1972).

Hubert, Henri. "Introduction à la traduction française," in: Pierre Daniel Chantepie de la Saussaye, *Manuel d'histoire des religions* (Paris: Armand Colin, 1904): v–xlviii.
Hughes, Everett. Review: "H. Richard Niebuhr, The Social Sources of Denominationalism," in: *American Journal of Sociology* 60 (1954): 320.

I

Imbriano, Gennaro. *Der Begriff der Politik. Die Moderne als Krisenzeit im Werk von Reinhart Koselleck* (Frankfurt am Main: Campus, 2018).

J

Jaeschke, Walter (ed.). *Hegel-Handbuch. Leben—Werk—Wirkung* (Stuttgart: Metzler, 2003).
Jaeschke, Walter. "Hegels Frankfurter Schriften. Zum jüngst erschienenen Band 2 der Gesammelten Werke Hegels," in: Thomas Hanke and Thomas M. Schmidt (eds.). *Der Frankfurter Hegel in seinem Kontext* (Frankfurt am Main: Klostermann, 2015): 31–50.
James, William. "Human Immortality: Two Supposed Objections to the Doctrine" (1898), in: William James, *Essays in Religion and Mortality* (= *Works*, vol. 9) (Cambridge: Harvard University Press, 1982): 75–101.
James, William. *The Varieties of Religious Experience* (New York: Longmans, Green and Co., 1902).
James, William. "Does Consciousness Exist?" (1904), in: William James. *Essays in Radical Empiricism* (New York: Longmans, Green and Co., 1912): 1–38.
James, William. *The Will to Believe* (New York: Longmans, Green and Co., 1905).
James, William. "On Some Hegelisms," in: William James, *The Will to Believe* (New York: Longmans, Green and Co., 1905): 263–298.
James, William. *Die religiöse Erfahrung in ihrer Mannigfaltigkeit. Materialien und Studien zu einer Psychologie und Pathologie des religiösen Lebens* (transl. Georg Wobbermin) (Leipzig: J. C. Hinrichs'sche Buchhandlung, 1907).
James, William. *A Pluralistic Universe: Hibbert Lectures at Manchester College on the Present Situation in Philosophy* (1909) (Cambridge: Harvard University Press, 1977).
James, William. *The Meaning of Truth* (New York: Longmans, Green and Co., 1911).
James, William. *Essays in Radical Empiricism* (New York: Longmans, Green and Co., 1912).
Jaspers, Karl. *The Origin and Goal of History* (1949) (London: Routledge, 2010).
Jaspers, Karl. *Philosophical Faith and Revelation* (1962) (New York: Harper, 1967).
Jenkins, Philip. *The Lost History of Christianity. The Thousand-Year Golden Age of the Church in the Middle East, Africa, and Asia—and How It Died* (New York: Harper, 2008).
Joas, Hans. "Universität und Rationalität. Über Talcott Parsons' Beitrag zur Soziologie der Universität," in: Gerhard Grohs et al. (eds.). *Kulturelle Identität im Wandel* (Stuttgart: Klett-Cotta, 1980): 236–250.
Joas, Hans. "Temporality and Intersubjectivity," in: Hans Joas, *G. H. Mead: A Contemporary Re-examination of His Thought* (Cambridge: MIT Press, 1985): 167–198.
Joas, Hans. *G. H. Mead. A Contemporary Re-examination of His Thought* (Cambridge: MIT Press, 1985).

Joas, Hans. *Communitarianism: A German Perspective*, Indiana University Institute for Advanced Study. Distinguished Lecture Series, vol. 6 (Bloomington, IN, 1993).

Joas, Hans. "Gemeinschaft und Demokratie in den USA. Die vergessene Vorgeschichte der Kommunitarismus-Diskussion," in: Micha Brumlik and Hauke Brunkhorst (eds.). *Gemeinschaft und Gerechtigkeit* (Frankfurt am Main: Fischer, 1993): 49–62.

Joas, Hans. *Pragmatism and Social Theory* (Chicago: University of Chicago Press, 1993).

Joas, Hans. "American Pragmatism and German Thought: A History of Misunderstandings," in: Hans Joas, *Pragmatism and Social Theory* (Chicago: University of Chicago Press, 1993): 94–121.

Joas, Hans. "Was hält die Bundesrepublik zusammen? Alte und neue Formen sozialer Integration," in: Friedhelm Hengsbach and Matthias Möhring-Hesse (eds.). *Eure Armut kotzt uns an. Solidarität in der Krise* (Frankfurt am Main: Fischer 1995): 69–82.

Joas, Hans. *The Creativity of Action* (Chicago: University of Chicago Press, 1996).

Joas, Hans. "Ein Pragmatist wider Willen? Über Charles Taylor," in: *Deutsche Zeitschrift für Philosophie* 44 (1996): 661–670.

Joas, Hans. "Der Liberalismus ist kein politisches Heilsversprechen," *Die Zeit*, November 14, 1997.

Joas, Hans. "Combining Value Pluralism and Moral Universalism: Isaiah Berlin and Beyond," in: *The Responsive Community* 9 (1999): 17–29.

Joas, Hans. *The Genesis of Values* (Chicago: University of Chicago Press, 2000).

Joas, Hans. "Respect for Indisposability: A Contribution to the Bioethics Debate," in: Hans Joas, *Do We Need Religion? On the Experience of Self-Transcendence* (Boulder: Paradigm, 2008): 125–132.

Joas, Hans. "The Gift of Life: Parsons' Late Sociology of Religion," in: *Journal of Classical Sociology* 1 (2001): 127–141.

Joas, Hans. "Der Wert der Freiheit und die Erfahrung der Unfreiheit," in: Hans-Richard Reuter et al. (eds.). *Freiheit verantworten. Festschrift für Wolfgang Huber zum 60. Geburtstag* (Gütersloh: Gütersloher Verlagshaus, 2002): 446–455.

Joas, Hans. *War and Modernity* (Cambridge: Polity, 2003).

Joas, Hans. "Max Weber and the Origin of Human Rights: A Study of Cultural Innovation," in: Charles Camic, Philip S. Gorski, and David M. Trubek (eds.). *Max Weber's "Economy and Society": A Critical Companion* (Stanford: Stanford University Press, 2005): 366–382.

Joas, Hans. "Vorwort," in: Robert Pippin, *Die Verwirklichung der Freiheit. Der Idealismus als Diskurs der Moderne* (Frankfurt am Main: Campus, 2005): 7–13.

Joas, Hans (ed.). *Die Zehn Gebote. Ein widersprüchliches Erbe?* (Cologne: Böhlau, 2006).

Joas, Hans. "Liebe, Gabe, Gerechtigkeit," in: Hans Joas (ed.). *Die Zehn Gebote. Ein widersprüchliches Erbe?* (Cologne: Böhlau, 2006): 175–183.

Joas, Hans. "Introduction to the Special Issue on Ernst Cassirer's Philosophy of Religion," in: *Svensk Teologisk Kvartalskrift* 82 (2006): 2–4.

Joas, Hans, and Frank Adloff. "Transformations of German Civil Society: Milieu Change and Community Spirit," in: John Keane (ed.). *Civil Society: Berlin Perspectives* (New York: Berghahn, 2006): 103–138.

Joas, Hans. *Do We Need Religion? On the Experience of Self-Transcendence* (Boulder: Paradigm, 2008).

Joas, Hans, and Klaus Wiegandt (eds.). *The Cultural Values of Europe* (Liverpool: Liverpool University Press, 2008).

Joas, Hans (ed.). *Die Anthropologie von Macht und Glauben. Das Werk Wolfgang Reinhards in der Diskussion* (Göttingen: Wallstein, 2008).

Joas, Hans. "The Religious Situation in the USA," in: Bertelsmann Stiftung (ed.). *What the World Believes: Analysis and Commentary on the Religion Monitor 2008* (Gütersloh: Verlag Bertelsmann Stiftung, 2009): 317–334.

Joas, Hans. "Society, State and Religion: Their Relationship from the Perspective of the World Religions," in: Hans Joas and Klaus Wiegandt (eds.). *Secularization and the World Religions* (Liverpool: Liverpool University Press, 2009): 1–22.

Joas, Hans, and Klaus Wiegandt (eds.). *Secularization and the World Religions* (Liverpool: Liverpool University Press, 2009).

Joas, Hans, and Wolfgang Knöbl. *Social Theory: Twenty Introductory Lectures* (Cambridge: Cambridge University Press, 2009).

Joas, Hans. "Selbsttranszendenz und Wertbindung. Ernst Troeltsch als Ausgangspunkt einer modernen Religionssoziologie," in: Friedrich Wilhelm Graf and Friedemann Voigt (eds.). *Religion(en) deuten. Transformationen der Religionsforschung* (= *Troeltsch-Studien*, new series, vol. 2) (Berlin: De Gruyter, 2010): 51–64.

Joas, Hans. "Schleiermacher and the Turn to Experience in the Study of Religion," in: Dietrich Korsch and Amber L. Griffioen (eds.). *Interpreting Religion: The Significance of Friedrich Schleiermacher's "Reden über die Religion" for Religious Studies and Theology* (Tübingen: Mohr Siebeck, 2011): 147–162.

Joas, Hans, and Peter Vogt (eds.). *Begriffene Geschichte. Beiträge zum Werk Reinhart Kosellecks* (Berlin: Suhrkamp, 2011).

Joas, Hans. "Antwort auf Hermann Deuser," in: Heinrich Wilhelm Schäfer (ed.). *Hans Joas in der Diskussion. Kreativität—Selbsttranszendenz—Gewalt* (Frankfurt am Main: Campus, 2012): 49–55.

Joas, Hans, and Andreas Pettenkofer (eds.). "Introduction: Review Symposium on Hugh McLeod, *The Religious Crisis of the 1960s*," in: *Journal of Religion in Europe* 5 (2012): 425–520.

Joas, Hans. *The Sacredness of the Person: A New Genealogy of Human Rights* (Washington, DC: Georgetown University Press, 2013).

Joas, Hans. *Faith as an Option: Possible Futures for Christianity* (Stanford: Stanford University Press 2014).

Joas, Hans. *Was ist die Achsenzeit? Eine wissenschaftliche Debatte als Diskurs über Transzendenz* (Basel: Schwabe, 2014).

Joas, Hans. "Ein Christ durch Krieg und Revolution. Alfred Döblins Erzählwerk 'November 1918,'" in: *Sinn und Form* 67 (2015): 784–799.

Joas, Hans. "Situated Creativity: A Way Out of the Impasse of the Heidegger-Cassirer Debate," in: *History of European Ideas* 41 (2015): 565–570.

Joas, Hans. *Die lange Nacht der Trauer. Erzählen als Weg aus der Gewalt?* (Gießen: Psychosozial-Verlag, 2015).

Joas, Hans. *Sind die Menschenrechte westlich?* (Munich: Kösel, 2015).

Joas, Hans. "Sacralization and Desacralization: Political Domination and Religious Interpretation," in: *Journal of the Society of Christian Ethics* 36, no. 2 (2016): 25–47.

Joas, Hans. "Auseinandersetzung mit dem Christentum," in: Sabina Becker (ed.). *Döblin-Handbuch. Leben—Werk—Wirkung* (Stuttgart: Metzler, 2016): 356–366.

Joas, Hans. *Kirche als Moralagentur?* (Munich: Kösel, 2016).

Joas, Hans. "Pragmatism and Historicism: Mead's Philosophy of Temporality and the Logic of Historiography," in: Hans Joas and Daniel R. Huebner (eds.). *The Timeliness of George Herbert Mead* (Chicago: University of Chicago Press, 2016): 62–81.

Joas, Hans (ed.). *David Martin and the Sociology of Religion* (London: Routledge, 2018).
Joas, Hans. "Martin Buber and the Problem of Dialogue in Contemporary Thought," in: Sam Berrin Shonkoff (ed.). *Martin Buber: His Intellectual and Scholarly Legacy* (Leiden: Brill, 2018): 212–215.
Joas, Hans. "Sakralisierung—Genealogie—Globalgeschichte. Eine Erwiderung," in: Michael Kühnlein and Jean-Pierre Wils (eds.). *Der Westen und die Menschenrechte. Im interdisziplinären Gespräch mit Hans Joas* (Baden-Baden: Nomos, 2019): 169–199.
Joas, Hans. "Faith and Knowledge: Habermas' Alternative History of Philosophy," in: *Theory, Culture and Society* 37, no. 7/8 (2019): 47–52.
Joas, Hans, and Jörg Noller (eds.). *Geisteswissenschaft—was bleibt? Zwischen Theorie, Tradition und Transformation* (Freiburg: Karl Alber, 2019).
Joas, Hans. *The Power of the Sacred: An Alternative to the Narrative of Disenchantment* (New York: Oxford University Press, 2021).
Jung, Matthias. *Dilthey zur Einführung* (Hamburg: Junius, 1996).
Jung, Matthias. *Erfahrung und Religion. Grundzüge einer hermeneutisch-pragmatischen Religionsphilosophie* (Freiburg: Karl Alber, 1999).
Jung, Matthias, Michael Moxter, and Thomas M. Schmidt (eds.). *Religionsphilosophie. Historische Positionen und systematische Reflexionen* (Würzburg: Echter, 2000).
Jung, Matthias. "Religiöse Erfahrung. Genese und Kritik eines religionshistorischen Grundbegriffs," in: Matthias Jung et al. (eds.). *Religionsphilosophie. Historische Positionen und systematische Reflexionen* (Würzburg: Echter, 2000): 135–150.
Jung, Matthias. "Der Ausdruckscharakter des Religiösen. Zur Pragmatik der symbolischen Formen bei Ernst Cassirer," in: Hermann Deuser and Michael Moxter (eds.). *Rationalität der Religion und Kritik der Kultur: Hermann Cohen und Ernst Cassirer* (Würzburg: Echter, 2002): 119–124.
Jung, Matthias. *Der bewußte Ausdruck. Anthropologie der Artikulation* (Berlin: De Gruyter, 2009).
Jung, Matthias. "Embodiment, Transcendence, and Contingency: Anthropological Features of the Axial Age," in: Robert N. Bellah and Hans Joas (eds.). *The Axial Age and Its Consequences* (Cambridge: Harvard University Press, 2012): 77–101.
Jung, Matthias. *Gewöhnliche Erfahrung* (Tübingen: Mohr Siebeck, 2014).
Jung, Matthias. *Symbolische Verkörperung. Die Lebendigkeit des Sinns* (Tübingen: Mohr Siebeck, 2017).
Junker-Kenny, Maureen. *Religion and Public Reason: A Comparison of the Positions of John Rawls, Jürgen Habermas and Paul Ricœur* (Berlin: De Gruyter, 2014): 184–279.

K

Kaftan, Julius. "Die Selbständigkeit des Christentums," in: *Zeitschrift für Theologie und Kirche* 6 (1896): 373–394.
Kantorowicz, Ernst H. *The King's Two Bodies: A Study in Medieval Political Theology* (1957) (Princeton: Princeton University Press, 2016).
Kestenbaum, Victor. *The Grace and the Severity of the Ideal: John Dewey and the Transcendent* (Chicago: University of Chicago Press, 2002).
Kestenbaum, Victor. "Ontological Faith in Dewey's Religious Idealism," in: Hermann Deuser et al. (eds.). *The Varieties of Transcendence: Pragmatism and the Theory of Religion* (New York: Fordham University Press, 2016): 73–90.

Kiesel, Helmuth. *Literarische Trauerarbeit. Das Exil- und Spätwerk Alfred Döblins* (Tübingen: Max Niemeyer, 1986).

Kim, Sebastian C. H. (ed.). *Christian Theology in Asia* (Cambridge: Cambridge University Press, 2008).

Kippenberg, Hans G. *Die Entdeckung der Religionsgeschichte. Religionswissenschaft und Moderne* (Munich: C. H. Beck, 1997).

Kippenberg, Hans G. "Joachim Wachs Bild vom George-Kreis und seine Revision von Max Webers Soziologie religiöser Gemeinschaften," in: *Zeitschrift für Religions- und Geistesgeschichte* 61 (2009): 313–331.

Knöbl, Wolfgang. "'Das Recht der Freiheit' als Überbietung der Modernisierungstheorie," in: Magnus Schlette (ed.). *Ist Selbstverwirklichung institutionalisierbar? Axel Honneths Freiheitstheorie in der Diskussion* (Frankfurt am Main: Campus, 2018): 31–52.

Koselleck, Reinhart. "Review of Herbert Butterfield, Christianity, Diplomacy and War," in: *Archiv für Rechts- und Sozialphilosophie* 41 (1955): 591–595.

Koselleck, Reinhart. *Critique and Crisis: Enlightenment and the Pathogenesis of Modern Society* (1959) (Cambridge: MIT Press, 1988).

Koselleck, Reinhart. *Preußen zwischen Reform und Revolution. Allgemeines Landrecht, Verwaltung und soziale Bewegung von 1791 bis 1848* (Stuttgart: Klett, 1967).

Koselleck, Reinhart, and Wolf-Dieter Stempel (eds.). *Geschichte—Ereignis und Erzählung* (*Poetik und Hermeneutik* V) (Munich: Fink, 1973).

Koselleck, Reinhart. "Jaspers, die Geschichte und das Überpolitische," in: Jeanne Hersch et al. (eds.). *Karl Jaspers. Philosoph, Arzt, politischer Denker. Symposium zum 100. Geburtstag* (Munich: Piper, 1986): 291–302.

Koselleck, Reinhart. "Foreword," in: Karl Löwith, *Mein Leben in Deutschland vor und nach 1933. Ein Bericht* (Frankfurt am Main: Fischer, 1989): ix–xv.

Koselleck, Reinhart. "Aufklärung und die Grenzen ihrer Toleranz," in: Trutz Rendtorff (ed.). *Glaube und Toleranz. Das theologische Erbe der Aufklärung* (Gütersloh: Mohn, 1982): 109–124, reprinted in: Koselleck, *Begriffsgeschichten. Studien zur Semantik und Pragmatik der politischen und sozialen Sprache* (Frankfurt am Main: Suhrkamp, 2006): 340–362.

Koselleck, Reinhart. *Zur politischen Ikonologie des gewaltsamen Todes. Ein deutsch-französischer Vergleich* (Basel: Schwabe, 1998).

Koselleck, Reinhart. "Zeitverkürzung und Beschleunigung. Eine Studie zur Säkularisierung," in: Reinhart Koselleck, *Zeitschichten. Studien zur Historik* (Frankfurt am Main: Suhrkamp, 2000): 177–202.

Koselleck, Reinhart. *Futures Past: On the Semantics of Historical Time* (New York: Columbia University Press, 2004).

Koselleck, Reinhart. "Historia Magistra Vitae," in: Reinhart Koselleck, *Futures Past: On the Semantics of Historical Time* (New York: Columbia University Press, 2004): 26–42.

Koselleck, Reinhart. "History, Histories and Formal Time Structures," in: Koselleck, *Futures Past* (New York: Columbia University Press, 2004): 93–104.

Koselleck, Reinhart. *Begriffsgeschichten. Studien zur Semantik und Pragmatik der politischen und sozialen Sprache* (Frankfurt am Main: Suhrkamp, 2006).

Koselleck, Reinhart. "The Status of the Enlightenment in German History," in: Hans Joas and Klaus Wiegandt (eds.). *The Cultural Values of Europe* (Liverpool: Liverpool University Press, 2008): 253–264.

Koschorke, Albrecht. *Hegel und wir. Frankfurter Adorno-Vorlesungen 2013* (Berlin: Suhrkamp, 2015).

Krämer, Felicitas. *Erfahrungsvielfalt und Wirklichkeit. Zu William James' Realitätsverständnis* (Göttingen: Vandenhoeck & Ruprecht, 2006).
Kraus, Hans-Christof. "Dieses Nichts von Fachmensch und Genussmensch," *Frankfurter Allgemeine Zeitung*, March 30, 2016: N3.
Krech, Volkhard, and Hartmann Tyrell (eds.). *Religionssoziologie um 1900* (Würzburg: Ergon, 1995).
Krech, Volkhard, and Hartmann Tyrell. "Religionssoziologie um die Jahrhundertwende. Zu Vorgeschichte, Kontext und Beschaffenheit einer Subdisziplin der Soziologie," in: Volkhard Krech and Hartmann Tyrell (eds.). *Religionssoziologie um 1900* (Würzburg: Ergon, 1995): 11-78.
Krech, Volkhard, Jens Schlamelcher, and Markus Hero. "Typen religiöser Sozialformen und ihre Bedeutung für die Analyse religiösen Wandels in Deutschland," in: *Kölner Zeitschrift für Soziologie und Sozialpsychologie* 65 (2013): 51-71.
Krockow, Christian Graf von. *Die Entscheidung. Eine Untersuchung über Ernst Jünger, Carl Schmitt und Martin Heidegger* (1958) (Frankfurt am Main: Campus, 1990).
Kroner, Richard. *Die Selbstverwirklichung des Geistes. Prolegomena zur Kulturphilosophie* (Tübingen: Mohr Siebeck, 1928).
Kühn, Johannes. *Toleranz und Offenbarung* (Leipzig: Meiner, 1923).
Kühnlein, Michael. *Religion als Quelle des Selbst. Zur Vernunft- und Freiheitskritik von Charles Taylor* (Tübingen: Mohr Siebeck, 2008).
Kühnlein, Michael, and Matthias Lutz-Bachmann (eds.). *Unerfüllte Moderne? Neue Perspektiven auf das Werk von Charles Taylor* (Berlin: Suhrkamp, 2011).
Kühnlein, Michael (ed.). *Charles Taylor. Ein säkulares Zeitalter* (Berlin: De Gruyter, 2018).
Künkler, Mirjam, John Madeley, and Shylashri Shankar (eds.). *A Secular Age beyond the West: Religion, Law and the State in Asia, the Middle East and North Africa* (Cambridge: Cambridge University Press, 2018).
Künkler, Mirjam. "David Martin in Memoriam," in: *Journal for the Scientific Study of Religion* 58 (2019): 905-912.
Kutlu, Evrim. "Der Begriff der Person bei G. W. F. Hegel und Max Scheler," in *Hegel-Jahrbuch* 1 (2014): 276-281.

L

Lamberth, David. *William James and the Metaphysics of Experience* (Cambridge: Cambridge University Press, 1999).
Larmore, Charles. "How Much Can We Stand?," *The New Republic*, April 9, 2008: 39-44.
Laube, Martin. "Die Dialektik der Freiheit. Systematisch-theologische Perspektiven," in: Martin Laube (ed.). *Freiheit* (Tübingen: UTB, 2014): 119-191.
Laube, Martin (ed.). *Freiheit* (Tübingen: UTB, 2014).
Laube, Martin. "Tendenzen und Motive im Verständnis der Freiheit," in: Martin Laube (ed.). *Freiheit* (Tübingen: UTB, 2014): 255-267.
Laube, Martin. "Die Dialektik der Freiheit. Systematisch-theologische Perspektiven," in: Martin Laube (ed.). *Freiheit* (Tübingen: UTB, 2014): 174-178.
Lauster, Jörg et al. (eds.). *Rudolf Otto. Theologie—Religionsphilosophie—Religionsgeschichte* (Berlin: De Gruyter, 2014).
Lee, Eun-Jeung. *"Anti-Europa." Die Geschichte der Rezeption des Konfuzianismus und der konfuzianischen Gesellschaft seit der frühen Aufklärung* (Münster: LIT, 2003).

Lehmann, Hartmut. "Die Entscheidung des Jahres 1803 und das Verhältnis von Säkularisation, Säkularisierung und Säkularismus," in: Hartmut Lehmann, *Säkularisierung. Der europäische Sonderweg in Sachen Religion* (Göttingen: Wallstein, 2005): 70-85.

Leites, Edmund. "'From Tribal Brotherhood to Universal Otherhood': On Benjamin Nelson," in: *Social Research* 61 (1994): 955-965.

Leonard, Eileen, Hermann Strasser, and Kenneth Westhues (eds.). *In Search of Community: Essays in Memory of Werner Stark, 1909-1985* (New York: Fordham University Press, 1993).

LeQuire, Peter Brickey. "Friends in History: Eric Voegelin and Robert Bellah," in: Matteo Bortolini (ed.). *The Anthem Companion to Robert Bellah* (London: Anthem, 2019): 165-190.

Levinson, Henry. *Santayana, Pragmatism, and the Spiritual Life* (Chapel Hill: University of North Carolina Press, 1992).

Lipton, David R. *Ernst Cassirer: The Dilemma of a Liberal Intellectual in Germany 1914-33* (Toronto: University of Toronto Press, 1978).

Löwith, Karl. *Meaning in History: The Theological Implications of the Philosophy of History* (Chicago: University of Chicago Press, 1949).

Löwith, Karl. *Mein Leben in Deutschland vor und nach 1933. Ein Bericht* (Frankfurt am Main: Insel 1989) (Foreword by Reinhart Koselleck) (English translation: London: Athlone, 1994).

Löwith, Karl. *From Hegel to Nietzsche: The Revolution in Nineteenth-Century Thought* (New York: Columbia University Press, 1991).

Lübbe, Hermann. *Säkularisierung. Geschichte eines ideenpolitischen Begriffs* (Freiburg: Alber, 1975).

Lübbe, Hermann. *Geschichtsbegriff und Geschichtsinteresse. Analytik und Pragmatik der Historie* (Basel: Schwabe, 1977).

Lukács, Georg. *The Young Hegel: Studies in the Relations between Dialectics and Economics* (1948) (London: Merlin Press, 1975).

Lukács, Georg. *The Destruction of Reason* (1955) (London: Merlin Press, 1980).

M

MacIntyre, Alasdair. *After Virtue: A Study in Moral Theory* (Notre Dame: Notre Dame University Press, 1981).

Mann, Thomas. "Naturrecht und Humanität" (1923), *Frankfurter Zeitung*, December 25, 1923, reprinted in: Thomas Mann, *Aufsätze, Reden, Essays*, vol. 3 (Berlin: Aufbau, 1986): 428-431.

Mannheim, Karl. "Zur Problematik der Soziologie in Deutschland" (1929), in: Karl Mannheim, *Wissenssoziologie* (Neuwied: Luchterhand, 1964): 614-624.

Marcel, Gabriel. *Tragic Wisdom and Beyond, Including Conversations between Paul Ricoeur and Gabriel Marcel* (Evanston: Northwestern University Press, 1973).

Marett, Robert Ranulph. *The Threshold of Religion* (London: Methuen, 1909).

Marett, Robert Ranulph. *A Jerseyman at Oxford* (London: Oxford University Press, 1941).

Marramao, Giacomo. "Säkularisierung," in: Joachim Ritter and Karlfried Gründer (eds.). *Historisches Wörterbuch der Philosophie*, vol. VIII (Basel: Schwabe, 1992): col. 1133-1161.

Marramao, Giacomo. *Die Säkularisierung der westlichen Welt* (Frankfurt am Main: Insel, 1996).
Marsden, George. "Matteo Ricci and Prodigal Culture," in: James L. Heft (ed.). *A Catholic Modernity? Charles Taylor's Marianist Award Lecture* (New York: Oxford University Press, 1999): 83–93.
Martin, David. "The Denomination," in: *British Journal of Sociology* 13, no. 1 (1962): 1–14.
Martin, David. *Pacifism: An Historical and Sociological Study* (London: Routledge, 1965): 4.
Martin, David. Review: "Werner Stark, *The Sociology of Religion*, vols. I and II," in: *British Journal of Sociology* 18 (1967): 220–222.
Martin, David. *A Sociology of English Religion* (London: SCM, 1967).
Martin, David. "Towards Eliminating the Concept of Secularization," in: David Martin, *The Religions and the Secular: Studies in Secularization* (London: Routledge & Kegan Paul, 1969): 9–22.
Martin, David. Review: "Werner Stark, *The Sociology of Religion*, vol. V," in: *Jewish Journal of Sociology* 15 (1973): 125f.
Martin, David. *A General Theory of Secularization* (New York: Harper & Row, 1978).
Martin, David. *Tongues of Fire: The Explosion of Protestantism in Latin America* (Oxford: Wiley, 1990).
Martin, David. "Foreword," in Grace Davie, *Religion in Britain since 1945: Believing without Belonging* (Oxford: Wiley, 1994): viii–ix.
Martin, David. *Forbidden Revolutions: Pentecostalism in Latin America, Catholicism in Eastern Europe* (London: SPCK, 1996).
Martin, David. *Does Christianity Cause War?* (Oxford: Clarendon Press, 1997).
Martin, David. *On Secularization: Towards a Revised General Theory* (Aldershot: Ashgate, 2005).
Martin, David. "The Relevance of the European Model of Secularization in Latin America and Africa," in: Hans Joas and Klaus Wiegandt (eds.). *Secularization and the World Religions* (Liverpool: Liverpool University Press, 2009): 278–295.
Martin, David. *The Future of Christianity: Reflections on Violence and Democracy, Religion and Secularization* (Farnham: Ashgate, 2011).
Martin, David. "Axial Religions and the Problem of Violence," in: Robert N. Bellah and Hans Joas (eds.). *The Axial Age and Its Consequences* (Cambridge: Harvard University Press, 2012): 294–316.
Martin, David. The *Education of David Martin: The Making of an Unlikely Sociologist* (London: SPCK, 2013).
Martin, David. *Religion and Power: No Logos without Mythos* (Farnham: Ashgate, 2014).
Martin, David. *Ruin and Restoration: On Violence, Liturgy and Reconciliation* (London: Routledge, 2016) (with a foreword by Charles Taylor).
Martin, David. *Secularisation, Pentecostalism and Violence: Receptions, Rediscoveries and Rebuttals in the Sociology of Religion* (London: Routledge, 2017).
Martin, David. "Thinking with Your Life," in: Hans Joas (ed.). *David Martin and the Sociology of Religion* (London: Routledge, 2018): 162–190.
Martin, David. *Christianity and "the World": Secularization Narratives through the Lens of English Poetry 800 AD to the Present* (Eugene: Cascade, 2020).
Marty, Martin. *Modern American Religion*, vol. 2: *The Noise of Conflict 1919–1941* (Chicago: University of Chicago Press, 1991).

Marx, Karl. "A Contribution to the Critique. Introduction" (1843–44), in: Karl Marx, *Critique of Hegel's "Philosophy of Right"* (Cambridge: Cambridge University Press, 1970): 129–142.

McLeod, Hugh. *Religion and the People of Western Europe 1789–1989* (Oxford: Oxford University Press, 1981).

McLeod, Hugh. *Piety and Poverty: Working-Class Religion in Berlin, London and New York* (New York: Holmes and Meier, 1996).

McLeod, Hugh. *The Religious Crisis of the 1960s* (Oxford: Oxford University Press, 2007).

McLeod, Hugh. "Reply," in: *Journal of Religion in Europe* 5 (2012): 405–520.

McLeod, Hugh. *Secularization in Western Europe 1848–1914* (New York: St. Martin's, 2000).

McRoberts, Omar M. "H. Richard Niebuhr Meets 'The Street,'" in: Mary Jo Bane, Brent Coffin, and Richard Higgins (eds.). *Taking Faith Seriously* (Cambridge: Harvard University Press, 2005): 94–112.

Mead, George Herbert. "Review: Gustav Class, *Untersuchungen zur Phänomenologie und Ontologie des menschlichen Geistes*" (1897), in: *American Journal of Theology* 1 (1897): 789–792.

Mead, George Herbert. *The Philosophy of the Present* (La Salle: Open Court, 1932).

Mead, George Herbert. *Movements of Thought in the Nineteenth Century* (Chicago: University of Chicago Press, 1936).

Mead, George Herbert. *Philosophy of the Act* (Chicago: University of Chicago Press, 1938).

Mead, George Herbert. "The Physical Thing," in: George Herbert Mead, *Philosophy of the Present* (La Salle: Open Court, 1932): 119–139.

Mehring, Reinhard. "Heidegger und Karl Löwith," in: Dieter Thomä (ed.). *Heidegger-Handbuch* (Stuttgart: Metzler, 2003): 373–375.

Mehring, Reinhard, and Dieter Thomä, "Leben und Werk. Martin Heidegger im Kontext," in: Dieter Thomä (ed.). *Heidegger-Handbuch. Leben—Werk—Wirkung* (Stuttgart: Klett-Cotta, 2005): 515–539.

Mehring, Reinhard. "Begriffsgeschichte mit Carl Schmitt," in: Hans Joas and Peter Vogt (eds.). *Begriffene Geschichte. Beiträge zum Werk Reinhart Kosellecks* (Berlin: Suhrkamp, 2011): 138–168.

Meinecke, Friedrich. *Die Idee der Staatsräson* (1924) (Munich: Oldenbourg, 1957).

Melton, James Van Horn. "Otto Brunner and the Ideological Origins of *Begriffsgeschichte*," in: Hartmut Lehmann and Melvin Richter (eds.). *The Meaning of Historical Terms and Concepts: New Studies on Begriffsgeschichte* (Washington, DC: German Historical Institute, 1996): 21–35.

Mensching, Gustav. *Soziologie der Religion* (Bonn: Röhrscheid, 1947).

Merleau-Ponty, Maurice. "Christianisme et ressentiment," in: *La vie intellectuelle* 36 (1935): 278–306.

Mette, Norbert. "Religionssoziologie—katholisch. Erinnerungen an religionssoziologische Traditionen innerhalb des Katholizismus," in: Karl Gabriel and Franz-Xaver Kaufmann (eds.). *Zur Soziologie des Katholizismus* (Mainz: Grünewald, 1980): 39–56.

Mews, Stuart. "Paul Tillich and the Religious Situation of American Intellectuals," in: *Religion* 2, no. 2 (1972): 122–140.

Meyembergh-Boussart, Monique. *Alfred Döblin. Seine Religiosität in Persönlichkeit und Werk* (Bonn: H. Bouvier, 1970).

Meyer, Thomas. *Ernst Cassirer* (Hamburg: Ellert & Richter, 2006).

Michel, Johann. *Homo Interpretans: Towards a Transformation of Hermeneutics* (with a Preface by Hans Joas) (Lanham: Rowman & Littlefield, 2019).
Miller, Richard B. "H. Richard Niebuhr's War Articles: A Transvaluation of Values," in: *Journal of Religion* 68 (1988): 242–262.
Molendijk, Arie L. "The Notion of the Sacred," in: Arie L. Molendijk and Paul Post (eds.). *Holy Ground: Re-inventing Ritual Space in Modern Western Culture* (Leuven: Peeters, 2010): 55–89.
Mommsen, Wolfgang. "Die deutsche Idee der Freiheit," in: Wolfgang Mommsen, *Bürgerliche Kultur und politische Ordnung. Künstler, Schriftsteller und Intellektuelle in der deutschen Geschichte 1830–1933* (Frankfurt am Main: Fischer, 2000): 133–157.
Morgan, Michael. "Religion, History and Moral Discourse," in: James Tully (ed.). *Philosophy in an Age of Pluralism: The Philosophy of Charles Taylor in Question* (Cambridge: Cambridge University Press, 1994): 49–66.
Murrmann-Kahl, Michael. "'Tillichs Trauma.' Paul Tillich liest Ernst Troeltschs Historismusband," in: Ulrich Barth et al. (eds.). *Aufgeklärte Religion und ihre Probleme. Schleiermacher—Troeltsch—Tillich* (Berlin: De Gruyter, 2013): 193–212.

N

Nelson, Benjamin. *The Idea of Usury: From Tribal Brotherhood to Universal Otherhood* (1949) (Chicago: University of Chicago Press, 1969).
Nelson, Benjamin. *On the Roads to Modernity: Conscience, Science and Civilizations* (Totowa: Rowman & Littlefield, 1981).
Neugebauer, Georg. *Tillichs frühe Christologie. Eine Untersuchung zu Offenbarung und Geschichte bei Tillich vor dem Hintergrund seiner Schellingrezeption* (Berlin: De Gruyter, 2007): 318–328.
Niebuhr, H. Richard. *Ernst Troeltsch's Philosophy of Religion* (Philosophical Dissertation) (Yale University, 1924).
Niebuhr, H. Richard. *The Social Sources of Denominationalism* (1929) (New York: Meridian, 1957).
Niebuhr, H. Richard. *The Kingdom of God in America* (1937) (New York: Harper & Row, 1959).
Niebuhr, H. Richard. *The Meaning of Revelation* (New York: Macmillan, 1941).
Niebuhr, H. Richard. *Radical Monotheism and Western Culture* (1943) (New York: Harper & Row, 1970).
Niebuhr, H. Richard. "The Ego-Alter Dialectic and the Conscience," in: *Journal of Philosophy* 42 (1945): 352–359.
Niebuhr, H. Richard. *Christ and Culture* (1951) (New York: Harper, 2001).
Niebuhr, H. Richard. "Foreword," in: Paul E. Pfuetze, *Self, Society, Existence: Human Nature and Dialogue in the Thought of G. H. Mead and Martin Buber* (New York: Harper, 1961): vi.
Niebuhr, H. Richard. *The Responsible Self: An Essay in Christian Moral Philosophy* (1963) (San Francisco: Harper & Row, 1978).
Niebuhr, H. Richard. *Faith on Earth: An Inquiry into the Structure of Human Faith* (New Haven: Yale University Press, 1989).
Niebuhr, Reinhold. "Moral Man and Immoral Society" (1932), in: Reinhold Niebuhr, *Major Works on Religion and Politics* (New York: Library of America, 2015): 135–350.

Niebuhr, Reinhold. "A Footnote on Religion," in: *The Nation* 139 (1934): 358–359.
Nietzsche, Friedrich. *Werke*, vol. III (München: Hanser, 1969).
Nietzsche, Friedrich. "Jenseits von Gut und Böse" (1886), in: Friedrich Nietzsche, *Werke*, vol. III (München: Hanser, 1969): 9–205.
Nietzsche, Friedrich. *On the Genealogy of Morality* (Cambridge: Cambridge University Press, 2017).
Nippel, Wilfried. "Krieg als Erscheinungsform der Feindschaft," in: Reinhard Mehring (ed.). *Carl Schmitt. Der Begriff des Politischen: ein kooperativer Kommentar* (Berlin: Akademie, 2003): 61–70.
Nohl, Hermann. "Preface," in: Wilhelm Dilthey, *Die Jugendgeschichte Hegels* (= *Gesammelte Schriften*, vol. 4) (Stuttgart: Teubner, 1974): v–viii.
Nowak, Kurt. *Schleiermacher* (Göttingen: Vandenhoeck & Ruprecht, 2001).

O

Oexle, Otto Gerhard. "Max Weber und das Mönchtum," in: Hartmut Lehmann and Jean Martin Ouedraogo (eds.). *Max Webers Religionssoziologie in interkultureller Perspektive* (Göttingen: Vandenhoeck & Ruprecht, 2003): 311–334.
Olsen, Niklas. *History in the Plural: An Introduction to the Work of Reinhart Koselleck* (New York: Berghahn, 2012).
O'Meara, Thomas Franklin, O.P. "Paul Tillich in Catholic Thought: The Past and the Future," in: Raymond Bulman and Frederick Parrella (eds.). *Paul Tillich: A New Catholic Assessment* (Collegeville: Liturgical Press, 1994): 9–32.
O'Shaughnessy, Hugh. Review: "David Martin, Tongues of Fire," *Times Literary Supplement*, August 3, 1990: 9.
Osterhammel, Jürgen. *Unfabling the East: The Enlightenment's Encounter with Asia* (Princeton: Princeton University Press, 2018).
Osterhammel, Jürgen. *Jacob Burckhardts "Über das Studium der Weltgeschichte" und die Weltgeschichtsschreibung der Gegenwart* (Basel: Schwabe, 2019).
Osthövener, Claus-Dieter. "Ottos Auseinandersetzung mit Schleiermacher," in: Jörg Lauster et al. (eds.). *Rudolf Otto. Theologie—Religionsphilosophie—Religionsgeschichte* (Berlin: De Gruyter, 2014): 179–190.
Otto, Rudolf. Review: "Nathan Söderblom, Gudstrons uppkomst," in: *Theologische Literaturzeitung* 40 (1915): col. 1–4.
Otto, Rudolf. *The Idea of the Holy: An Inquiry into the Non-rational Factor in the Idea of the Divine and Its Relation to the Rational* (1917) (transl. John W. Harvey) (Harmondsworth: Penguin Books, 1959).
Otto, Rudolf. *Naturalistische und religiöse Weltansicht* (Tübingen: Schwabenverlag, 1929).
Otto, Rudolf. "Parallelen und Konvergenzen in der Religionsgeschichte," in: Rudolf Otto, *Das Gefühl des Überweltlichen* (Munich: Beck, 1932): 282–305.

P

Pagano, Joseph S. *The Origins and Development of the Triadic Structure of Faith in H. Richard Niebuhr: A Study of the Kantian and Pragmatic Background of Niebuhr's Thought* (Lanham: University Press of America, 2005).

Pannenberg, Wolfhart. "Weltgeschichte und Heilsgeschichte," in: Reinhart Koselleck and Wolf-Dieter Stempel (eds.). *Geschichte—Ereignis und Erzählung* (*Poetik und Hermeneutik* V) (Munich: Fink, 1973): 307-323.

Pannenberg, Wolfhart. "Erfordert die Einheit der Geschichte ein Subjekt?," in: Reinhart Koselleck and Wolf-Dieter Stempel (eds.). *Geschichte—Ereignis und Erzählung* (*Poetik und Hermeneutik* V) (Munich: Fink, 1973): 478-490.

Parsons, Talcott, and Gerard Platt. *The American University* (Cambridge: Harvard University Press, 1974).

Parsons, Talcott. "A Paradigm of the Human Condition," in: Talcott Parsons, *Action Theory and the Human Condition* (New York: The Free Press, 1978): 352-433.

Parsons, Talcott. *Action Theory and the Human Condition* (New York: The Free Press, 1978).

Patterson, Orlando. *Freedom*, vol. 1: *Freedom in the Making of Western Culture* (New York: Basic Books, 1991).

Patterson, Orlando. "Freedom, Slavery, and the Modern Construction of Rights," in: Hans Joas and Klaus Wiegandt (eds.). *The Cultural Values of Europe* (Liverpool: Liverpool University Press, 2008): 115-151.

Pfleiderer, Georg. *Theologie als Wirklichkeitswissenschaft. Studien zum Religionsbegriff bei Georg Wobbermin, Rudolf Otto, Heinrich Scholz und Max Scheler* (Tübingen: Mohr Siebeck, 1992).

Pfleiderer, Georg. "Kultursynthese auf dem Katheder. Zur Revision von Troeltschs Soziallehren in Tillichs Berliner Programmvorlesung von 1919," in: Christian Danz and Werner Schüßler (eds.). *Religion—Kultur—Gesellschaft. Der frühe Tillich im Spiegel neuer Texte (1919-1920)* (Vienna: LIT, 2008): 119-154.

Pihlström, Sami. "Dewey and Pragmatic Religious Naturalism," in: Molly Cochran (ed.). *The Cambridge Companion to Dewey* (Cambridge: Cambridge University Press, 2010): 211-241.

Pippin, Robert. *Idealism as Modernism: Hegelian Variations* (Cambridge: Cambridge University Press, 1997).

Pippin, Robert. *Die Verwirklichung der Freiheit. Der Idealismus als Diskurs der Moderne* (Frankfurt am Main: Campus, 2005).

Pippin, Robert. "Reconstructivism: On Honneth's Hegelianism," in: *Philosophy and Social Criticism* 40, no. 8 (2014): 725-741.

Pitschmann, Annette. *Religiosität als Qualität des Säkularen. Die Religionstheorie John Deweys* (Tübingen: Mohr Siebeck, 2017).

Prantl, Heribert. "Dem Einstein des Staatsrechts. Dem Juristen Ernst-Wolfgang Böckenförde zum 80. Geburtstag," *Süddeutsche Zeitung*, September 18, 2010: 5.

Prodi, Paolo. "Konfessionalisierungsforschung im internationalen Kontext," in: Hans Joas (ed.). *Die Anthropologie von Macht und Glauben. Das Werk Wolfgang Reinhards in der Diskussion* (Göttingen: Wallstein, 2008): 63-82.

Putnam, Hilary. *The Collapse of the Fact/Value Dichotomy* (Cambridge: Harvard University Press, 2002).

R

Raberger, Walter, and Hanjo Sauer (eds.). *Vermittlung im Fragment. Franz Schupp als Lehrer der Theologie* (Regensburg: Friedrich Pustet, 2003).

Rahner, Karl. "Kirche der Sünder" (1947), in: Karl Rahner, *Schriften zur Theologie*, vol. VI (Einsiedeln: Benziger, 1965): 301-320.

Rahner, Karl. "Weltgeschichte und Heilsgeschichte," in: Karl Rahner, *Schriften zur Theologie*, vol. V (Einsiedeln: Benziger, 1962): 115-135.

Rahner, Karl. "Sündige Kirche nach den Dekreten des Zweiten Vatikanischen Konzils," in: Karl Rahner, *Schriften zur Theologie*, vol. VI (Einsiedeln: Benziger, 1965): 321-345.

Rahner, Karl. "Theologische Grundinterpretation des II. Vatikanischen Konzils," in: Karl Rahner, *Schriften zur Theologie*, vol. XIV (Cologne: Benziger, 1980): 287-302.

Raiser, Konrad. *Identität und Sozialität. G. H. Meads Theorie der Interaktion und ihre Bedeutung für die theologische Anthropologie* (Munich: Kaiser / Matthias Grünewald, 1971).

Randall, John Herman, Jr. "The Religion of Shared Experience," in: Horace M. Kallen (ed.). *The Philosopher of the Common Man: Essays in Honor of John Dewey to Celebrate His Eightieth Birthday* (New York: Greenwood Press, 1940): 106-145.

Ranke, Leopold von. *Weltgeschichte*, vol. 9.2: *Über die Epochen der neueren Geschichte. Vorträge dem Könige Maximilian II. von Bayern gehalten* (Leipzig: Duncker & Humblot, 1888).

Rappaport, Roy A. *Ritual and Religion in the Making of Humanity* (Cambridge: Cambridge University Press, 1999).

Rawls, John. *A Theory of Justice* (Cambridge: Harvard University Press, 1971).

Reinhard, Wolfgang. "Historiker, 'Modernisierung' und Modernisierung. Erfahrungen mit dem Konzept 'Modernisierung' in der neueren Geschichte," in: Walter Haug and Burghart Wachinger (eds.). *Innovation und Originalität* (Tübingen: Max Niemeyer, 1993): 53-69.

Reinhard, Wolfgang. *Ausgewählte Abhandlungen* (Berlin: Duncker & Humblot, 1997).

Reinhard, Wolfgang. *Die Unterwerfung der Welt. Globalgeschichte der europäischen Expansion* (Munich: C. H. Beck, 2016).

Rendtorff, Trutz. "Geschichtstheologie," in: Joachim Ritter and Karlfried Gründer (eds.). *Historisches Wörterbuch der Philosophie*, vol. III (Darmstadt: Wissenschaftliche Buchgesellschaft, 1974): col. 439-441.

Renz, Horst, and Friedrich Wilhelm Graf (eds.). *Umstrittene Moderne. Die Zukunft der Neuzeit im Urteil der Epoche Ernst Troeltschs* (= Troeltsch-Studien, vol. 4) (Gütersloh: Gütersloher Verlagshaus, 1987).

Reuter, Hans-Richard et al. (eds.). *Freiheit verantworten. Festschrift für Wolfgang Huber zum 60. Geburtstag* (Gütersloh: Gütersloher Verlagshaus, 2002).

Richter, Melvin. *The History of Political and Social Concepts: A Critical Introduction* (Oxford: Oxford University Press, 1995).

Ricœur, Paul. "Préface," in: Jocelyn Dunphy, *Paul Tillich et le symbole religieux* (Paris: Jean-Pierre Delarge, 1977): 11-14.

Ricœur, Paul. "Le statut de la 'Vorstellung' dans la philosophie hégélienne de la religion" (1985), in: Paul Ricœur, *Lectures 3. Aux frontières de la philosophie* (Paris: Seuil, 1992): 41-62.

Ricœur, Paul. *Time and Narrative*, vol. 3 (Chicago: University of Chicago Press, 1988).

Ricœur, Paul. "Love and Justice," in: Paul Ricœur, *Figuring the Sacred: Religion, Narrative, and Imagination* (Minneapolis: Fortress, 1995): 315-329.

Ricœur, Paul. *Figuring the Sacred: Religion, Narrative, and Imagination* (Minneapolis: Fortress, 1995).

Ricœur, Paul. "Manifestation and Proclamation," in: Paul Ricœur, *Figuring the Sacred: Religion, Narrative, and Imagination* (Minneapolis: Fortress, 1995): 48–67.
Ricœur, Paul. *Oneself as Another* (Chicago: University of Chicago Press, 1996).
Ricœur, Paul. "Theonomy and/or Autonomy," in: Miroslav Volf et al. (eds.). *The Future of Theology: Essays in Honory of Jürgen Moltmann* (Grand Rapids: Eerdmans, 1996): 284–298.
Ricœur, Paul, and André LaCocque. *Penser la bible* (Paris: Seuil, 1998).
Ricœur, Paul. "Experience and Language in Religious Discourse," in: Dominique Janicaud et al., *Phenomenology and the "Theological Turn": The French Debate* (New York: Fordham University Press, 2000): 127–146.
Riesebrodt, Martin. "Charisma," in: Hans G. Kippenberg and Martin Riesebrodt (eds.). *Max Webers "Religionssystematik"* (Tübingen: Mohr Siebeck, 2001): 151–166.
Riley, Anthony W. "Nachwort des Herausgebers," in: Alfred Döblin, *Der unsterbliche Mensch / Der Kampf mit dem Engel* (Olten: Walter, 1980): 661–699.
Rockefeller, Steven. *John Dewey, Religious Faith and Democratic Humanism* (New York: Columbia University Press, 1991).
Rosa, Hartmut. *Social Acceleration: A New Theory of Modernity* (New York: Columbia University Press, 2015).
Rosenzweig, Franz. *The Star of Redemption* (1921) (Madison: University of Wisconsin Press, 2005).
Roth, John K. "William James, John Dewey and the 'Death-of-God,' " in: *Religious Studies* 7 (1971): 53–61.
Roth, Robert, S.J. *John Dewey and Self-Realization* (Englewood Cliffs: Prentice Hall, 1962).
Roth, Robert, S.J. *American Religious Philosophy* (New York: Harcourt, Brace, 1967).
Royce, Josiah. *The Problem of Christianity* (1913) (Washington, DC: Catholic University of America Press, 2001).
Ruddies, Hartmut. "Ernst Troeltsch und Paul Tillich. Eine theologische Skizze," in: Wilhelm-Ludwig Federlin and Edmund Weber (eds.). *Unterwegs für die Volkskirche. Festschrift für Dieter Stoodt zum 60. Geburtstag* (Frankfurt am Main: Peter Lang, 1987): 409–422.
Ruh, Ulrich. *Säkularisierung als Interpretationskategorie* (Freiburg: Herder, 1980).

S

Sahoo, Sarbeswar. *Pentecostalism and Politics of Conversion in India: With a Foreword by Hans Joas* (Cambridge: Cambridge University Press, 2018).
Saint-Exupéry, Antoine de. *Letter to a Hostage* (1941) (London: Pushkin Press, 1999).
Sandel, Michael. *The Case against Perfection: Ethics in the Age of Genetic Engineering* (Cambridge: Harvard University Press, 2007).
Santayana, George. "Reason in Religion," in: George Santayana, *Works*, vol. 4 (New York: Charles Scribner's Sons, 1936): 3–206.
Saussure, Ferdinand de. *Cours de linguistique générale* (1915) (Paris: Payot, 1969).
Sawilla, Jan Marco. "Geschichte und Geschichten zwischen Providenz und Machbarkeit. Überlegungen zu Reinhart Kosellecks Semantik historischer Zeiten," in: Hans Joas and Peter Vogt (eds.). *Begriffene Geschichte. Beiträge zum Werk Reinhart Kosellecks* (Berlin: Suhrkamp, 2011): 387–422.

Schaub, Edward. "Dewey's Interpretation of Religion," in: Paul Arthur Schilpp (ed.). *The Philosophy of John Dewey* (New York: Open Court, 1939): 393–416.

Scheler, Max. *Ressentiment* (1915) (New York: Schocken, 1972).

Scheler, Max. "Vorwort," in: Otto Gründler, *Elemente zu einer Religionsphilosophie auf phänomenologischer Grundlage* (Munich: Kösel, 1922): i–ii.

Scheler, Max. "Mensch und Geschichte" (1926), in: Max Scheler, *Philosophische Weltanschauung* (Munich: Lehnen, 1954): 62–88.

Scheler, Max. *Formalism in Ethics and a Non-formal Ethics of Values: A New Attempt toward the Foundation of an Ethical Personalism* (Evanston: Nortwestern University Press, 1973).

Scheler, Max. *Problems of a Sociology of Knowledge* (transl. Manfred S. Frings) (London: Routledge, 1980).

Scheler, Max. *On the Eternal in Man* (Abingdon: Routledge, 2017).

Schieder, Rolf. *Civil Religion. Die religiöse Dimension politischer Kultur* (Gütersloh: Gütersloher Verlagshaus, 1987).

Schieder, Rolf. "Der 'culte de l'individu' als Zivilreligion des Westens. Eine praktisch-theologische Relektüre von Durkheim, Foucault und Boltanski," in: Magnus Schlette (ed.). *Ist Selbstverwirklichung institutionalisierbar? Axel Honneths Freiheitstheorie in der Diskussion* (Frankfurt am Main: Campus, 2018): 287–312.

Schilpp, Paul Arthur (ed.). *The Philosophy of John Dewey* (New York: Open Court, 1939).

Schleiermacher, Friedrich. *Über die Religion: Reden an die Gebildeten unter ihren Verächtern* (1799) (Göttingen: Vandenhoeck & Ruprecht, 1899).

Schleissing, Stephan. *Das Maß des Fortschritts. Zum Verhältnis von Ethik und Geschichtsphilosophie in theologischer Perspektive* (Göttingen: Ruprecht, 2008).

Schlette, Magnus. *Die Idee der Selbstverwirklichung. Zur Grammatik des modernen Individualismus* (Frankfurt am Main: Campus, 2013).

Schmale, Wolfgang. *Archäologie der Grund- und Menschenrechte in der Frühen Neuzeit* (Munich: Oldenbourg, 1997).

Schmidt, Thomas M. "Anerkennung und absolute Religion. Gesellschaftstheorie und Religionsphilosophie in Hegels Frühschriften," in: Matthias Jung, Michael Moxter, and Thomas M. Schmidt (eds.). *Religionsphilosophie. Historische Positionen und systematische Reflexionen* (Würzburg: Echter, 2000): 101–112.

Schmitt, Carl. "Review of Koselleck, Kritik und Krise," in: *Das historisch-politische Buch* 7 (1959): 301f.

Schnädelbach, Herbert. *German Philosophy 1831–1933* (Cambridge: Cambridge University Press, 1983).

Schnädelbach, Herbert. *Zur Rehabilitierung des Animal Rationale* (Frankfurt am Main: Suhrkamp, 1990).

Schneider, Reinhold. *Philipp der Zweite oder Religion und Macht* (1935) (Frankfurt am Main: Suhrkamp, 1987).

Schoeller, Wilfried F. *Alfred Döblin* (Munich: Hanser, 2011).

Schüßler, Werner. "'Meine katholischen Freunde verstehen mich besser als meine protestantischen.' Wie 'katholisch' ist Paul Tillich?," in: Ulrich Barth et al. (eds.). *Aufgeklärte Religion und ihre Probleme. Schleiermacher—Troeltsch—Tillich* (Berlin: De Gruyter, 2013): 312–329.

Schweiker, William. "Foreword," in: H. Richard Niebuhr, *The Responsible Self: An Essay in Christian Moral Philosophy* (1963) (San Francisco: Harper & Row, 1978): 9–14.

Seel, Martin. "Die Wiederkehr der Ethik des guten Lebens," in: *Merkur* 45 (1991): 41–49.

Seibert, Christoph. "Religion aus eigenem Recht. Zur Methodologie der Religionsphilosophie bei Max Scheler und William James," in: *Neue Zeitschrift für systematische Theologie* 56, no. 1 (2014): 64–88.

Shea, William. "John Dewey: Aesthetic and Religious Experiences," in: William Shea, *The Naturalists and the Supernatural: Studies in Horizon and an American Philosophy of Religion* (Macon: Mercer University Press, 1984): 117–141.

Shils, Edward. *Center and Periphery* (Chicago: University of Chicago Press, 1975).

Siemers, Helge. "'Mein Lehrer Dilthey'? Über den Einfluß Diltheys auf den jungen Troeltsch," in: Horst Renz and Friedrich Wilhelm Graf (eds.). *Untersuchungen zur Biographie und Werkgeschichte* (= *Troeltsch-Studien*, vol. 1) (Gütersloh: Gütersloher Verlagshaus, 1982): 203–234.

Siep, Ludwig. *Der Staat als irdischer Gott* (Tübingen: Mohr Siebeck, 2015).

Silber, Ilana Friedrich. *Virtuosity, Charisma, and Social Order: A Comparative Sociological Study of Monasticism in Theravada Buddhism and Medieval Catholicism* (Cambridge: Cambridge University Press, 1995).

Silbermann, Alphons, and Paul Röhrig (eds.). *Kultur, Volksbildung und Gesellschaft. Paul Honigsheim zum Gedenken seines 100. Geburtstages* (Frankfurt am Main: Peter Lang, 1987).

Smith, Wilfred Cantwell. *The Meaning and End of Religion* (New York: Macmillan, 1963).

Söderblom, Nathan. "Das Heilige (Allgemeines und Ursprüngliches)" (1913), in: Carsten Colpe (ed.). *Die Diskussion um das "Heilige"* (Darmstadt: WBG, 1977): 76–116.

Sölle, Dorothee. *Realisation. Studien zum Verhältnis von Theologie und Dichtung nach der Aufklärung* (Darmstadt: Luchterhand, 1973).

Sorkin, David. *The Religious Enlightenment: Protestants, Jews, and Catholics from London to Vienna* (Princeton: Princeton University Press, 2008).

Spohn, Ulrike. *Den säkularen Staat neu denken. Politik und Religion bei Charles Taylor* (Frankfurt am Main: Campus, 2016).

Spohn, Willfried. "Religion and Modernization in Comparative Perspective: David Martin's Theory of Secularization Reconsidered," in: Karl-Siegbert Rehberg (ed.). *Differenz und Integration. Die Zukunft moderner Gesellschaften, Verhandlungen des 28. Kongresses der Deutschen Gesellschaft für Soziologie*, vol. 2 (Frankfurt am Main: Campus, 1997): 455–459.

Spohn, Willfried. "Europeanisation, Multiple Modernities and Religion: The Reconstruction of Collective Identities in Central and Eastern Europe," in: Gert Pickel and Kornelia Sammet (eds.). *Transformations of Religiosity in Eastern Europe 1998–2010* (Wiesbaden: Springer VS, 2012): 29–50.

Spranger, Eduard. "Das Historismus-Problem an der Universität Berlin seit 1900," in: Hans Leussink, Eduard Neumann, and Georg Kotowski (eds.). *Studium Berolinense. Aufsätze und Beiträge zu Problemen der Wissenschaft und der Geschichte der Friedrich-Wilhelms-Universität zu Berlin* (Berlin: De Gruyter, 1960): 425–443.

Stanner, William Edward Hanley. "Religion, Totemism and Symbolism," in: Ronald Berndt and Catherine Berndt (eds.). *Aboriginal Man in Australia* (Sydney: Angus & Robertson, 1965): 207–237.

Stark, Rodney. "Putting an End to Ancestor Worship," in: *Journal for the Scientific Study of Religion* 43 (2004): 465–475.

Stark, Werner. "Max Scheler," in: Werner Stark, *Social Theory and Christian Thought: A Study of Some Points of Contact* (London: Routledge, 1958): 135–174.

Stark, Werner. *Social Theory and Christian Thought* (London: Routledge, 1958).

Stark, Werner. "The Routinization of Charisma: A Consideration of Catholicism," in: *Sociological Analysis* 26 (1965): 203-211.
Stark, Werner. "The Protestant Ethic and the Spirit of Sociology," in: *Social Compass* 13 (1966): 373-377.
Stark, Werner. *The Sociology of Religion: A Study of Christendom*, 5 vols. (New York: Fordham University Press, 1966-1972). A brief summary in German: Werner Stark. *Grundriß der Religionssoziologie* (Freiburg: Rombach, 1974).
Stark, Werner. "The Place of Catholicism in Max Weber's Sociology of Religion," in: *Sociological Analysis* 29 (1968): 202-211.
Stark, Werner. "A Survey of My Scholarly Work," in: Madeline H. Engel (ed.). *The Sociological Writings of Werner Stark: Bibliography and Selected Annotations* (New York: unpublished, 1975): 2-17.
Stausberg, Michael. "Bellah's 'Religion in Human Evolution': A Post-review," in: *Numen* 61 (2014): 281-299.
Stern, Robert, and Neil W. Williams. "James and Hegel: Looking for a Home," in: Alexander Klein (ed.). *The Oxford Handbook of William James* (Oxford: Oxford University Press, 2018) (Oxford Handbooks Online).
Stikkers, Kenneth. "Technologies of the World, Technologies of the Self: A Schelerian Critique of Dewey and Hickman," in: *Journal of Speculative Philosophy* 10 (1996): 62-73.
Stockhorst, Stefanie. "Novus ordo temporum. Reinhart Kosellecks These von der Verzeitlichung des Geschichtsbewußtseins durch die Aufklärungshistoriographie in methodenkritischer Perspektive," in: Hans Joas and Peter Vogt (eds.). *Begriffene Geschichte. Beiträge zum Werk Reinhart Kosellecks* (Berlin: Suhrkamp, 2011): 359-386.
Stout, Harry S. "The Historical Legacy of H. Richard Niebuhr," in: Ronald F. Thiemann (ed.). *The Legacy of H. Richard Niebuhr* (Minneapolis: Fortress, 1991): 83-99.
Strasser, Hermann. "Werner Stark—Gelehrter und Katholik, 1909-1985," in: *Zeitschrift für Soziologie* 15 (1986): 141-145.
Stråth, Bo. "Review of R. Koselleck, Zeitschichten," in: *European Journal of Social Theory* 4 (2001): 531-535.
Strauss, Leo. "Das Heilige" (1923), in: Leo Strauss, *Philosophie und Gesetz—Frühe Schriften* (= *Gesammelte Schriften*, vol. 2) (Stuttgart: Metzler, 1997): 307-310.
Strauss, Leo. *Natural Right and History* (Chicago: University of Chicago Press, 1953).
Stroumsa, Guy G. *A New Science: The Discovery of Religion in the Age of Reason* (Cambridge: Harvard University Press, 2010).
Sturm, Erdmann. "Tillich liest Troeltschs 'Soziallehren,'" in: Ulrich Barth et al. (eds.). *Aufgeklärte Religion und ihre Probleme. Schleiermacher—Troeltsch—Tillich* (Berlin: De Gruyter, 2013): 271-290.
Swatos, William H., Jr. "Religious Sociology and the Sociology of Religion in America at the Turn of the Twentieth Century: Divergences from a Common Theme," in: *Sociological Analysis* 50 (1989): 363-375.

T

Tackett, Timothy. "The French Revolution and Religion to 1794," in Timothy Tackett and Stewart J. Brown (eds.). *Enlightenment, Reawakening and Revolution 1660-1815* (= *The Cambridge History of Christianity*, vol. VII) (Cambridge: Cambridge University Press, 2006): 536-555.

Tarot, Camille. *Le symbolique et le sacré. Théories de la religion* (Paris: La Découverte, 2008).
Taves, Ann. *Fits, Trances, and Visions: Experiencing Religion and Explaining Experience from Wesley to James* (Princeton: Princeton University Press, 1999).
Taylor, Charles. *Sources of the Self: The Making of the Modern Identity* (Cambridge: Harvard University Press, 1989).
Taylor, Charles. *Hegel* (Cambridge: Cambridge University Press, 1975).
Taylor, Charles. "What's Wrong with Negative Liberty?," in: Charles Taylor, *Philosophy and the Human Sciences: Philosophical Papers 2* (Cambridge: Cambridge University Press, 1985): 211–229.
Taylor, Charles. *Negative Freiheit? Zur Kritik des neuzeitlichen Individualismus* (Frankfurt am Main: Suhrkamp, 1988).
Taylor, Charles. "Reply and Re-articulation," in: James Tully (ed.). *Philosophy in an Age of Pluralism: The Philosophy of Charles Taylor in Question* (Cambridge: Cambridge University Press, 1994): 213–257.
Taylor, Charles. *A Secular Age* (Cambridge: Harvard University Press, 2007).
Tenbruck, Friedrich. "Nekrolog," in: *Kölner Zeitschrift für Soziologie und Sozialpsychologie* 30 (1978): 401–404.
Theunissen, Michael. *Hegels Lehre vom absoluten Geist als theologisch-politischer Traktat* (Berlin: De Gruyter, 1970).
Theunissen, Michael. "Wettersturm und Stille. Über die Weltdeutung Schelers und ihr Verhältnis zum Seinsdenken," in: Paul Good (ed.). *Max Scheler im Gegenwartsgeschehen der Philosophie* (Bern: Francke, 1975): 91–110.
Theunissen, Michael. "Ho aiton lambanei. Der Gebetsglaube Jesu und die Zeitlichkeit des Christseins," in: Bernhard Casper et al. (eds.). *Jesus—Ort der Erfahrung Gottes. Festschrift für Bernhard Welte* (Freiburg: Herder, 1976): 13–68.
Theunissen, Michael. *Sein und Schein. Die kritische Funktion der Hegelschen Logik* (Frankfurt am Main: Suhrkamp, 1978).
Theunissen, Michael. *Der Andere. Studien zur Sozialontologie der Gegenwart* (Berlin: De Gruyter, ²1981).
Theunissen, Michael. *Der Begriff Verzweiflung. Korrekturen an Kierkegaard* (Frankfurt am Main: Suhrkamp, 1993).
Theunissen, Michael. "Freiheit und Schuld—Freiheit und Sünde," in: Hans-Richard Reuter et al. (eds.). *Freiheit verantworten. Festschrift für Wolfgang Huber zum 60. Geburtstag* (Gütersloh: Gütersloher Verlagshaus, 2002): 343–356.
Tillich, Paul. "On the Idea of a Theology of Culture (1919)," in: Mark Kline Taylor (ed.). *Paul Tillich: Theologian of the Boundaries* (London: Collins, 1987): 35–54.
Tillich, Paul. *Das Christentum und die Gesellschaftsprobleme der Gegenwart* (1919), quoted in: Friedemann Voigt, "Historische und dogmatische Methode der Theologie. Der Absolutheitscharakter des religiösen Bewußtseins bei Troeltsch und Tillich," in: Ulrich Barth et al. (eds.). *Aufgeklärte Religion und ihre Probleme. Schleiermacher—Troeltsch—Tillich* (Berlin: De Gruyter, 2013): 213–228.
Tillich, Paul. "Die Kategorie des 'Heiligen' bei Rudolf Otto" (1923), in: *Begegnungen. Paul Tillich über sich selbst und andere* (= Gesammelte Werke, vol. XII) (Stuttgart: Evangelisches Verlagswerk, 1971): 184–186.
Tillich, Paul. "Rezension: Ernst Troeltsch. *Der Historismus und seine Probleme*," in: *Theologische Literaturzeitung* 49 (1924): col. 25–30.
Tillich, Paul. "Kirche und Kultur" (1924), in: Paul Tillich, *Ausgewählte Texte* (Berlin: De Gruyter, 2008): 109–122.

Tillich, Paul. "Probleme des Mythos," in: *Theologische Literaturzeitung* 49 (1924): col. 115–117.
Tillich, Paul. "Ernst Troeltsch. Versuch einer geistesgeschichtlichen Würdigung," in: *Kant-Studien* 29 (1924): 351–358, reprinted in: Friedrich Wilhelm Graf (ed.). *Ernst Troeltsch in Nachrufen* (Gütersloh: Gütersloher Verlagshaus, 2002): 646–653.
Tillich, Paul. "Rezension: Ernst Troeltsch, *Der Historismus und seine Überwindung*," in: *Theologische Literaturzeitung* 49 (1924): col. 234f.
Tillich, Paul. "Kairos. Ideen zur Geisteslage der Gegenwart," in: Paul Tillich (ed.). *Kairos. Zur Geisteslage und Geisteswendung* (Darmstadt: Evangelische Verlagsanstalt, 1926): 1–21.
Tillich, Paul. *The Religious Situation* (1926) (transl. H. Richard Niebuhr) (New York: Meridian, 1956).
Tillich, Paul. "The Demonic: A Contribution to the Interpretation of History" (1926), in: Paul Tillich, *The Interpretation of History* (New York: Scribner, 1936): 77–122.
Tillich, Paul. "Der Protestantismus" (1929), in: Paul Tillich, *Ausgewählte Texte* (Berlin: De Gruyter, 2008): 200–221.
Tillich, Paul. "Geschichtsphilosophie (Vorlesungsmanuskript und Nachschrift 1929/30)," in: Paul Tillich, *Vorlesungen über die Geschichtsphilosophie und Sozialpädagogik* (Berlin: De Gruyter, 2007): 1–118.
Paul Tillich, "Mythos und Mythologie" (1930), in: Paul Tillich, *Gesammelte Werke*, vol. V (Stuttgart: Evangelisches Verlagswerk, 1964): 187–195.
Tillich, Paul. "Theonomie," in: Hermann Gunkel and Leopold Zscharnack (eds.). *Die Religion in Geschichte und Gegenwart*, vol. 5 (Tübingen: Mohr Siebeck, ²1931): col. 1128–1129.
Tillich, Paul. "The Permanent Significance of the Catholic Church for Protestantism" (1941), in: Paul Tillich, *Ausgewählte Texte* (Berlin: De Gruyter, 2008): 277–287.
Tillich, Paul. *Systematic Theology*, vol. 1 (Chicago: University of Chicago Press, 1951).
Tillich, Paul. *The Courage to Be* (New Haven: Yale University Press, 1952).
Tillich, Paul. *Systematische Theologie*, vol. 1 (Stuttgart: Evangelisches Verlagswerk, 1956).
Tillich, Paul. "The Religious Symbol," in: *Daedalus* 87, no. 3 (Summer 1958): 3–21.
Tillich, Paul. *Systematic Theology*, vol. 3 (Chicago: University of Chicago Press, 1963).
Tillich, Paul. "Christianity and the Encounter of the World Religions" (1963), in: Paul Tillich, *Ausgewählte Texte* (Berlin: De Gruyter, 2008): 419–453.
Tillich, Paul. *The Dynamics of Faith* (New York: Harper & Brothers, 1967) (German translation: *Wesen und Wandel des Glaubens* [Frankfurt am Main: Ullstein, 1975]).
Tillich, Paul. *Ausgewählte Texte* (Berlin: De Gruyter, 2008).
Tocqueville, Alexis de. *Democracy in America* (New York: Norton, 2007).
Toulmin, Stephen. *Cosmopolis: The Hidden Agenda of Modernity* (New York: The Free Press, 1990).
Toulmin, Stephen. *Return to Reason* (Cambridge: Harvard University Press, 2001).
Touraine, Alain. *Critique de la modernité* (Paris: Fayard, 1992).
Troeltsch, Ernst. "Vernunft und Offenbarung bei Johann Gerhard und Melanchthon" (1891), in: Ernst Troeltsch, *Schriften zur Theologie und Religionsphilosophie (1888–1902)* (= KGA, vol. 1) (Berlin: De Gruyter, 2009): 73–338.
Troeltsch, Ernst. "Die Selbständigkeit der Religion," in: *Zeitschrift für Theologie und Kirche* 5 (1895): 361–436 and 6 (1896): 71–110 and 167–218, also in: Ernst Troeltsch, *Schriften zur Theologie und Religionsphilosophie (1888–1902)* (= KGA, vol.1) (Berlin: De Gruyter, 2009): 359–535.

Troeltsch, Ernst. "Atheistische Ethik" (1895), in: Ernst Troeltsch, *Gesammelte Schriften*, vol. 2 (Tübingen: Mohr Siebeck, 1913): 525–551.

Troeltsch, Ernst. "Christentum und Religionsgeschichte" (1897), in: Ernst Troeltsch, *Gesammelte Schriften*, vol. 2 (Tübingen: Mohr Siebeck, 1913): 328–363.

Troeltsch, Ernst. "Religionsphilosophie und prinzipielle Theologie," in: *Theologischer Jahresbericht* 17 (1898): 531–603, also in: Ernst Troeltsch, *Rezensionen und Kritiken (1894–1900)* (= KGA, vol. 2) (Berlin: De Gruyter, 2007): 366–484.

Troeltsch, Ernst. "Geschichte und Metaphysik" (1898), in: Ernst Troeltsch, *Schriften zur Theologie und Religionsphilosophie (1888–1902)* (= KGA, vol. 1) (Berlin: De Gruyter, 2009): 613–682.

Troeltsch, Ernst. "Rezension: Auguste Sabatier, Esquisse d'une philosophie de la religion d'après la psychologie et l'histoire" (1897), in: *Deutsche Litteraturzeitung* 19 (1898): col. 737–742, also in: Ernst Troeltsch, *Rezensionen und Kritiken (1894–1900)* (= KGA, vol. 2) (Berlin: De Gruyter, 2007): 328–333.

Troeltsch, Ernst. *Richard Rothe. Gedächtnisrede (zum 100. Geburtstag)* (Freiburg: Mohr, 1899), also in: Ernst Troeltsch, *Schriften zur Theologie und Religionsphilosophie (1888–1902)* (= KGA, vol. 1) (Berlin: De Gruyter, 2009): 732–752.

Troeltsch, Ernst. *Die Absolutheit des Christentums und die Religionsgeschichte* (1902/1912) (= KGA, vol. 5) (Berlin: De Gruyter, 1998).

Troeltsch, Ernst. *The Absoluteness of Christianity and the History of Religions* (1902/1912) (Richmond: John Knox Press, 1971).

Troeltsch, Ernst. "Leibniz und die Anfänge des Pietismus" (1902), in: Ernst Troeltsch, *Gesammelte Schriften*, vol. 4 (Tübingen: Mohr Siebeck, 1925): 488–531.

Troeltsch, Ernst. Review: "Ernst Cassirer, Leibniz' System in seinen wissenschaftlichen Grundlagen (Marburg 1902)," in: *Theologische Literaturzeitung* 29 (1904): col. 639–643, also in: Ernst Troeltsch, *Rezensionen und Kritiken (1901–1914)* (= KGA, vol. 4) (Berlin: De Gruyter, 2004): 354–360.

Troeltsch, Ernst. Review of William James, *The Varieties of Religious Experience*, in: *Deutsche Literaturzeitung* 25 (1904): col. 3021–3027, also in: Ernst Troeltsch, *Rezensionen und Kritiken (1901–1914)* (= KGA, vol. 4) (Berlin: De Gruyter, 2004): 364–371.

Troeltsch, Ernst. *Psychologie und Erkenntnistheorie in der Religionswissenschaft. Eine Untersuchung über die Bedeutung der Kantischen Religionslehre für die heutige Religionswissenschaft* (Tübingen: Mohr Siebeck, 1905), also in: Ernst Troeltsch, *Schriften zur Religionswissenschaft und Ethik (1903–1912)* (= KGA, vol. 6) (Berlin: De Gruyter, 2014): 205–256.

Troeltsch, Ernst. "Die Bedeutung des Protestantismus für die Entstehung der modernen Welt" (1911), in: Ernst Troeltsch, *Schriften zur Bedeutung des Protestantismus für die moderne Welt (1906–1913)* (= KGA, vol. 8) (Berlin: De Gruyter, 2001): 183–316.

Troeltsch, Ernst. *Protestantism and Progress: A Historical Study of the Relation of Protestantism to the Modern World* (London: Routledge, 2017).

Troeltsch, Ernst. "Das Wesen des modernen Geistes" (1907), in: Ernst Troeltsch, *Schriften zur Religionswissenschaft und Ethik (1903–1912)* (= KGA, vol. 6) (Berlin: De Gruyter, 2014): 434–473.

Troeltsch, Ernst. "Zur Frage des religiösen Apriori" (1909), in: Ernst Troeltsch, *Gesammelte Schriften*, vol. 2 (Tübingen: Mohr Siebeck, 1913): 754–768.

Troeltsch, Ernst. "Die Bedeutung des Begriffs der Kontingenz" (1910), in: Ernst Troeltsch, *Gesammelte Schriften*, vol. 2 (Tübingen: Mohr Siebeck, 1913): 769–778.

Troeltsch, Ernst. "Religiöser Individualismus und Kirche" (1911), in: Ernst Troeltsch, *Gesammelte Schriften*, vol. 2 (Tübingen: Mohr Siebeck, 1913): 109–133.

Troeltsch, Ernst. "Die Sozialphilosophie des Christentums" (1911), in: Ernst Troeltsch, *Schriften zur Religionswissenschaft und Ethik (1903–1912)* (= KGA, vol. 6) (Berlin: De Gruyter, 2014): 779–808.

Troeltsch, Ernst. "Praktische christliche Ethik. Diktate zur Vorlesung im Wintersemester 1911/12," from the estate of Gertrud von le Fort, in: Eleonore von la Chevallerie and Friedrich Wilhelm Graf (eds.). *Mitteilungen der Ernst-Troeltsch-Gesellschaft VII* (Augsburg 1991): 129–174.

Troeltsch, Ernst. "Empiricism and Platonism in the Philosophy of Religion," in: *Harvard Theological Review* 5 (1912): 401–422.

Troeltsch, Ernst. *The Social Teaching of the Christian Churches* (1912) (London: George Allen and Unwin, 1931).

Troeltsch, Ernst. *Gesammelte Schriften*, vol. 2 (Tübingen: Mohr Siebeck, 1913).

Troeltsch, Ernst. "Logos und Mythos in Theologie und Religionsphilosophie" (1913), in: Ernst Troeltsch, *Gesammelte Schriften*, vol. 2 (Tübingen: Mohr Siebeck, 1913): 805–836.

Troeltsch, Ernst. Review: "Hermann Süskind, *Christentum und Geschichte bei Schleiermacher*" (1913), in: Ernst Troeltsch, *Rezensionen und Kritiken (1901–1914)* (= KGA, vol. 4) (Berlin: De Gruyter, 2004): 661–666.

Troeltsch, Ernst. "Brief an Robert Gradmann 12.1.1915," in: Ernst Troeltsch, *Briefe III (1905–1915)* (= KGA, vol. 20) (Berlin: De Gruyter, 2016): 724f.

Troeltsch, Ernst. "Die deutsche Idee von der Freiheit" (1916), reprinted in: Ernst Troeltsch, *Deutscher Geist und Westeuropa* (Tübingen: Mohr Siebeck, 1925): 80–107.

Troeltsch, Ernst. "Rezension: Wilhelm Dilthey, Gesammelte Schriften, Bd. 2" (1916), in: Ernst Troeltsch, *Rezensionen und Kritiken (1915–1923)* (= KGA, vol. 13) (Berlin: De Gruyter, 2010): 91–94.

Troeltsch, Ernst. "Glaube und Ethos der hebräischen Propheten" (1916), in: Ernst Troeltsch, *Aufsätze zur Geistesgeschichte und Religionssoziologie* (Tübingen: Mohr Siebeck, 1925): 34–64.

Troeltsch, Ernst. *Humanismus und Nationalismus in unserem Bildungswesen* (Berlin: Weidmann, 1917), partly reprinted in: Ernst Troeltsch, *Deutscher Geist und Westeuropa* (Tübingen: Mohr Siebeck, 1925): 211–243.

Troeltsch, Ernst. Review: "Ernst Cassirer, Freiheit und Form," in: *Theologische Literaturzeitung* 42 (1917): col. 368–371, reprinted in: Ernst Troeltsch, *Gesammelte Schriften*, vol. 4 (Tübingen: Mohr Siebeck, 1925): 696–698.

Troeltsch, Ernst. "Zur Religionsphilosophie. Aus Anlaß des Buches von Rudolf Otto über 'Das Heilige,'" in: *Kant-Studien* 23 (1917): 65–76, also in: Ernst Troeltsch, *Rezensionen und Kritiken (1915–1923)* (= KGA, vol. 13) (Berlin: De Gruyter, 2010): 412–425.

Troeltsch, Ernst. Review: "Ernst Cassirer, Das Erkenntnisproblem in der Philosophie und Wissenschaft der neueren Zeit, vol. 3 (Berlin 1920)," in: *Theologische Literaturzeitung* 46 (1921): col. 160–161, also in: Ernst Troeltsch, *Rezensionen und Kritiken (1915–1923)* (= KGA, vol. 13) (Berlin: De Gruyter, 2010): 500–502.

Troeltsch, Ernst. *Der Historismus und seine Probleme* (1922), 2 vols. (= KGA, vol. 16.1 and 16.2) (Berlin: De Gruyter, 2008).

Troeltsch, Ernst. "Die Veräsüsterreichung" (1922/23), in: Ernst Troeltsch, *Spectator-Briefe und Berliner Briefe (1919–1922)* (= KGA, vol. 14) (Berlin: De Gruyter, 2018): 569–577.

Troeltsch, Ernst. "The Ideas of Natural Law and Humanity in World Politics" (1923), in: Otto Gierke, *Natural Law and the Theory of Society, 1500–1800* (Boston: Beacon Press, 1957): 201–222.
Troeltsch, Ernst. *Christian Thought: Its History and Application* (London: University of London Press, 1923).
Troeltsch, Ernst. "Naturrecht und Humanität in der Weltpolitik" (1923), in: Ernst Troeltsch, *Schriften zur Politik und Kulturphilosophie (1918-23)* (= KGA, vol. 15) (Berlin: De Gruyter, 2002): 493–512.
Troeltsch, Ernst. "Die Zufälligkeit der Geschichtswahrheiten" (1923), in: Ernst Troeltsch, *Schriften zur Politik und Kulturphilosophie (1918-1923)* (= KGA, vol. 15) (Berlin: De Gruyter, 2002): 551–567.
Troeltsch, Ernst. *Der Historismus und seine Überwindung* (Berlin: Pan Verlag Rolf Heise, 1924).
Troeltsch, Ernst. *Glaubenslehre* (Munich: Duncker & Humblot, 1925).
Troeltsch, Ernst. *Deutscher Geist und Westeuropa* (Tübingen: Mohr Siebeck, 1925).
Troeltsch, Ernst. *Aufsätze zur Geistesgeschichte und Religionssoziologie* (Tübingen: Mohr Siebeck, 1925).
Troeltsch, Ernst. *Briefe an Friedrich von Hügel 1901–1923*, ed. Karl-Ernst Apfelbacher and Peter Neuner (Paderborn: Bonifatius, 1974).
Troeltsch, Ernst. *Schriften zur Politik und Kulturphilosophie (1918-1923)* (= KGA, vol. 15) (Berlin: De Gruyter, 2002).
Troeltsch, Ernst. *Schriften zur Religionswissenschaft und Ethik (1903-1912)* (= KGA, vol. 6) (Berlin: De Gruyter, 2014).
Troeltsch, Ernst. *Rezensionen und Kritiken (1901-1914)* (= KGA, vol. 4) (Berlin: De Gruyter, 2004).
Troeltsch, Ernst. *Fünf Vorträge zu Religion und Geschichtsphilosophie für England und Schottland* (= KGA, vol. 17) (Berlin: De Gruyter, 2006).
Troeltsch, Ernst. *Rezensionen und Kritiken (1894-1900)* (= KGA, vol. 2) (Berlin: De Gruyter, 2007).
Troeltsch, Ernst. *Rezensionen und Kritiken (1915-1923)* (= KGA, vol. 13) (Berlin: De Gruyter, 2010).
Troeltsch, Ernst. *Schriften zur Theologie und Religionsphilosophie (1888-1902)* (= KGA, vol. 1) (Berlin: De Gruyter, 2009).
Troeltsch, Ernst. *Briefe III (1905-1915)* (= KGA, vol. 20) (Berlin: De Gruyter, 2016).
Troeltsch, Ernst. *Gesammelte Schriften*, vol. 1 (1912) (Darmstadt: WBG, 2016).
Troeltsch, Ernst. *Briefe IV (1915-1918)* (= KGA, vol. 21) (Berlin: De Gruyter, 2018).
Troeltsch, Ernst. *Spectator-Briefe und Berliner Briefe (1919-1922)* (= KGA, vol. 14) (Berlin: De Gruyter, 2018).
Troeltsch, Ernst. *Die Soziallehren der christlichen Kirchen und Gruppen*. 3 vols. (= KGA, vol. 9) (Berlin: De Gruyter, 2021).
Tully, James (ed.). *Philosophy in an Age of Pluralism: The Philosophy of Charles Taylor in Question* (Cambridge: Cambridge University Press, 1994).
Turner, Victor. *The Ritual Process: Structure and Anti-structure* (1969) (London: Routledge, 2017).
Tyrell, Hartmann. "Von der 'Soziologie statt Religion' zur Religionssoziologie," in: Volkhard Krech and Hartmann Tyrell (eds.). *Religionssoziologie um 1900* (Würzburg: Ergon, 1995): 79–128.

V

Van der Veer, Peter. *The Modern Spirit of Asia: The Spiritual and the Secular in China and India* (Princeton: Princeton University Press, 2014).
Voegelin, Eric. "The Political Religions" (1938), in: Eric Voegelin, *Modernity without Restraint* (= *Collected Works*, vol. 5) (Columbia: University of Missouri Press, 1999): 19–74.
Voegelin, Eric. *Order and History*, 5 vols. (Baton Rouge: Louisiana State University Press, 1956–1987).
Vogt, Peter. *Kontingenz und Zufall* (Berlin: Akademie Verlag, 2011).
Voigt, Friedemann. "Ernst Troeltsch. Leben und Werk," in: Ernst Troeltsch, *Gesammelte Schriften*, vol. 1 (1912) (Darmstadt: WBG, 2016): v–xxxiv.

W

Waldenfels, Bernhard. *Phänomenologie in Frankreich* (Frankfurt am Main: Suhrkamp, 1987).
Wallis, Louis. *Sociological Study of the Bible* (Chicago: University of Chicago Press, 1912).
Warner, Michael, Jonathan VanAntwerpen, and Craig Calhoun (eds.). *Varieties of Secularism in a Secular Age* (Cambridge: Harvard University Press, 2010).
Weber, Max. "Zur Lage der bürgerlichen Demokratie in Rußland" (1906), in: Max Weber, *Gesammelte politische Schriften* (Tübingen: Mohr, 1980): 33–68.
Weber, Max. "Letter to Adolf von Harnack, 5 February 1906," in: Max Weber, *Briefe 1906–1908* (= MWGA, section II, vol. 5) (Tübingen: Mohr Siebeck, 1990): 32f.
Weber, Max. "National Character and the Junkers" (1917), in: Hans Gerth and C. Wright Mills (eds.). *From Max Weber: Essays in Sociology* (New York: Oxford University Press, 1946): 386–395.
Weber, Max. *Gesammelte Aufsätze zur Religionssoziologie*, 3 vols. (Tübingen: Mohr Siebeck, 1920).
Weber, Max. "Die protestantischen Sekten und der Geist des Kapitalismus," in: Max Weber, *Gesammelte Aufsätze zur Religionssoziologie I* (Tübingen: Mohr Siebeck, 1920): 207–236.
Weber, Max. *Economy and Society* (1922) (Berkeley: University of California Press, 1978).
Weber, Max. "The Social Psychology of the World Religions," in: Hans Gerth and C. Wright Mills (eds.). *From Max Weber: Essays in Sociology* (New York: Oxford University Press, 1946): 267–301.
Weber, Max. *The Religion of India: The Sociology of Hinduism and Buddhism* (Glencoe: The Free Press, 1960).
Weber, Max. *Gesammelte politische Schriften* (Tübingen: Mohr, 1980).
Weber, Max. *The Protestant Ethic and the Spirit of Capitalism* (Los Angeles: Roxbury, 1996).
Weiß, Johannes. "Confessionalization of the Sociology of Religion? A Benevolent Critique of Werner Stark," in: Eileen Leonard, Hermann Strasser, and Kenneth Westhues (eds.). *In Search of Community: Essays in Memory of Werner Stark, 1909–1985* (New York: Fordham University Press, 1993): 193–203.
Westbrook, Robert. *John Dewey and American Democracy* (Ithaca: Cornell University Press, 1991).

Westhues, Kenneth. "The Twinkling of American Catholic Sociology," in: Eileen Leonard, Hermann Strasser, and Kenneth Westhues (eds.). *In Search of Community: Essays in Memory of Werner Stark, 1909–1985* (New York: Fordham University Press, 1993): 220–244.
Wichelhaus, Manfred. *Kirchengeschichtsschreibung und Soziologie im neunzehnten Jahrhundert und bei Ernst Troeltsch* (Heidelberg: Winter, 1965).
Wilson, Bryan. Review: "Werner Stark, *The Sociology of Religion*," in: *Sociological Review* 15, no. 3 (1968): 120–123.
Wilson, Bryan. Review: "Werner Stark, *The Sociology of Religion*, vol. 4," in: *Sociological Review* 18 (1970): 426–428.
Wilson, John A. "Egypt," in: Henri and H. A. Frankfort, John A. Wilson, and Thorkild Jacobsen, *The Intellectual Adventure of Ancient Man* (Chicago: University of Chicago Press, 1946): 122–130.
Winkler, Heinrich August. *Der lange Weg nach Westen. Deutsche Geschichte I und II*, 2 vols. (Munich: C. H. Beck, 2000).
Wittrock, Björn. "Cultural Crystallization and Conceptual Change," in: Jussi Kurunmäki and Kari Palonen (eds.). *Zeit, Geschichte und Politik. Zum achtzigsten Geburtstag von Reinhart Koselleck* (Jyväskylä: Jyväskylä University Press, 2002): 105–134.
Wolf, Eric R. *Europe and the People without History* (Berkeley: University of California Press, 1982).
Wuthnow, Robert. *The Restructuring of American Religion* (Princeton: Princeton University Press, 1988).

Y

Yack, Bernard. *The Fetishism of Modernities* (Notre Dame: University of Notre Dame Press, 1997).
Yamin, George J., Jr. *In the Absence of Fantasia: Troeltsch's Relation to Hegel* (Gainesville: University Press of Florida, 1993).
Yinger, J. Milton. *Religion in the Struggle for Power: A Study in the Sociology of Religion* (Durham: Duke University Press, 1946).
Yinger, J. Milton. *The Scientific Study of Religion* (New York: Macmillan, 1970).

Z

Zaccagnini, Marta. *Christentum der Endlichkeit. Heideggers Vorlesungen zur Einführung in die Phänomenologie der Religion* (Berlin: LIT, 2003).

Name Index

For the benefit of digital users, indexed terms that span two pages (e.g., 52–53) may, on occasion, appear on only one of those pages.

Adorno, Theodor W., 143
Alexander the Great, 358
Alexander, Jeffrey, 319, 426n.14
Apel, Karl-Otto, 173–74, 217–18, 386n.26
Arendt, Hannah, 180–81
Aristotle, 217, 271–72
Arndt, Andreas, 369n.53
Aron, Raymond, 56
Asad, Talal, 338–39
Augustine of Hippo, 70, 264, 283, 292

Baader, Franz von, 128
Balthasar, Hans Urs von, 379–80n.5, 380n.11
Banchoff, Thomas, 342
Barth, Karl, 7–8, 258–59, 268
Bauman, Zygmunt, 338
Beck, Ulrich, 321
Becker, Howard, 294–95
Bedford-Strohm, Heinrich, 409n.19, 415n.34
Beethoven, Ludwig van, 69–70
Bellah, Robert N., x–xi, 58–59, 112–13, 196–97, 201–2, 206–7, 210–11, 213–14, 224, 230–31, 252–54, 316–29, 332–33, 336–37, 340–41, 343, 345, 347, 361, 377n.22, 414n.10, 425–26n.6, 427n.33
Benedict of Nursia, 283, 297
Bentham, Jeremy, 279
Berger, Peter L., 133, 147–49, 311, 341–42, 406n.83
Bergson, Henri, 202
Berlin, Isaiah, 47, 186–87, 191, 235, 365n.12, 398n.9
Blackstone, William, 190
Blaschke, Olaf, 140–41
Bloch, Marc, 287–88

Blumenberg, Hans, 136–38
Böckenförde, Ernst-Wolfgang, 92–93
Bodenhafer, Walter, 258–59
Bollnow, Otto Friedrich, 175
Bonaparte, Napoleon, 12, 88, 158
Bonhoeffer, Dietrich, 27–28, 224, 417n.68
Borromeo, Carlo, 283
Brown, Peter, 281
Brugger, Winfried, 337
Brunner, Otto, 389–90n.11
Buber, Martin, 228–29, 269, 271, 273–74
Buddha, 119–20
Bultmann, Rudolf, 224, 319
Burckhardt, Jacob, 69–70, 79, 180–81
Butterfield, Herbert, 136–37

Caird, Edward, 375n.16
Calderón de la Barca, Pedro, 296–97
Calvin, John, 153–54, 236–37, 292, 295–96
Carnap, Rudolf, 175
Casanova, José, 227, 254–55, 312, 330–43, 347, 414n.13
Cassirer, Ernst, x–xi, 31–32, 165–66, 174–76, 180–95, 204–6, 271, 395n.6
Castoriadis, Cornelius, 385n.13, 396n.13
Chesterton, Gilbert Keith, 128–29
Christiano, Kevin, 302
Claß, Gustav, 46–47
Cohen, Hermann, 182–83
Coleman, John, 426n.14
Collins, Randall, 422n.19
Colpe, Carsten, 59
Confucius, 119–20
Congar, Yves, 155
Constantine the Great (Roman Emperor), 297
Cooley, Charles Horton, 65, 271

474 NAME INDEX

Costa, Paolo, 308
Cusinato, Guido, 379–80n.5

Daniel, Joshua, 417n.69
Dante Alighieri, 181–82
Danz, Christian, 212
Darwin, Charles, 42, 123, 201
Dawkins, Richard, 42
Delbrück, Hans, 176–77
Dempf, Alois, 296
Descartes, René, 180–81, 191, 256–57
Deuser, Hermann, 206, 372n.39, 378n.37, 378n.41, 379n.48
Dewey, John, 94, 99–114, 232–33, 273, 345–46, 371–72n.35, 384nn.7–8, 385nn.12–13, 385n.16, 385n.18, 385n.23, 386n.26, 386n.29, 386n.34, 386n.38, 387n.40, 413n.26
Dilthey, Wilhelm, 23–31, 35–36, 38, 46–47, 54, 82, 97–98, 150–51, 180–81, 243, 259, 345, 370n.14, 371–72n.35
Döblin, Alfred, 74–75, 94–96, 116–31, 345–46, 348
Donald, Merlin, 327–28, 377n.22
Durkheim, Émile, 43–44, 53–62, 64–65, 67, 80–81, 92–93, 100–1, 106–8, 151–52, 154–55, 213–14, 223, 241–42, 244–47, 252, 277, 289, 318, 324, 333, 373n.56, 384n.7, 385n.22
Dutschke, Rudi, 159

Ebert, Friedrich, 176–77
Edie, James M., 222–23
Edwards, Jonathan, 271
Einstein, Albert, 93, 201–2
Eisenhower, Dwight D., 249–50
Eisenstadt, Shmuel N., 252–54, 315, 336–37, 419n.23
Eister, Alan W., 420n.30
Eliade, Mircea, 223–24, 374n.64
Eliasoph, Nina, 426n.14
Epicurus, 149
Erasmus of Rotterdam, 181–82, 190

Feuerbach, Ludwig, 7, 21, 43–44, 228, 242, 356
Fichte, Johann Gottlieb, 171, 397n.23
Fink, Eugen, 175
Flint, John T., 284, 420n.30

Foucault, Michel, 338–39
Francis de Sales, 292–93
Francis of Assisi, 152, 208, 283, 297
Franco, Francisco, 330, 332–33
Frankopan, Peter, 368n.47
Frederick II (King of Prussia), 141–42
Frei, Hans W., 414n.9
Freston, Paul, 310, 423–24n.36
Freud, Sigmund, 43–44, 271
Fries, Heinrich, 70, 84
Fries, Jakob Friedrich, 34–35, 53–54, 61
Fustel de Coulanges, Numa Denis, 54–55

Gadamer, Hans-Georg, 38, 137–38
Gauchet, Marcel, 396n.13
Geertz, Clifford, 319, 412n.15
Gehlen, Arnold, 101–2
George, Stefan, 198
Gernet, Louis, 411n.11
Gibbon, Edward, 281
Girard, René, 411n.11
Goethe, Johann Wolfgang, 8–9, 181–83, 186–87, 191
Gooch, Todd A., 377–78n.24
Gordon, Peter E., 379n.46
Gorski, Philip, 426n.14
Gouinlock, James, 385n.23
Graf, Friedrich Wilhelm, 199, 244, 396n.10, 403n.24
Graham, Billy, 214
Granet, Marcel, 411n.11
Gray, John, 235
Gregory VII (Pope), 153, 296
Grotius, Hugo, 189
Guardini, Romano, 229–30

Habermas, Jürgen, 9, 15, 69–70, 94, 96–97, 133, 136, 139, 164, 170–71, 173–74, 187, 217–18, 228–29, 332–33, 346, 370n.14, 371n.27, 385n.22, 386n.26
Hafkesbrink, Hanna, 381n.21
Halbig, Christoph, 3–4
Hamann, Johann Georg, 186–87
Hampe, Michael, 397n.23
Harnack, Adolf von, 34, 236, 285
Hartch, Todd, 312
Hartmann, Nicolai, 70
Hashagen, Justus, 279

NAME INDEX 475

Hauerwas, Stanley, 266
Hausenstein, Wilhelm, 129–30
Hefner, Robert W., 299
Hegel, Georg Wilhelm Friedrich, ix, 2–18, 21–39, 44–45, 48, 87–91, 93, 97–98, 139–41, 163–66, 170–71, 181–84, 208–9, 228–29, 241–43, 254, 324–25, 344–48, 351, 353–54, 360–61, 366n.16, 366nn.21–22, 366–67nn.23–24, 367n.32, 368n.40, 370n.14, 371–72n.35
Heidegger, Martin, 38, 137–38, 165, 175–76, 182–83, 198, 225, 227–28, 274–76, 395n.6
Heimpel, Hermann, 199, 258
Hennis, Wilhelm, 354
Henry IV (Holy Roman Emperor), 296
Henry IV (King of France), 236–37
Herberg, Will, 249–51, 295
Herder, Johann Gottfried, 32, 65, 178, 186–87
Hildebrand, Dietrich von, 379–80n.5
Hintze, Otto, 422n.14
Hobbes, Thomas, 230, 232
Höffe, Otfried, 219
Hölscher, Lucian, 392n.58
Honigsheim, Paul, 244–45, 411–12n.12
Honneth, Axel, 2–7, 15, 97, 163–64, 170–71, 173–74, 233–34, 346, 366n.16, 366n.21, 370n.14, 432n.49
Horkheimer, Max, 143
Horn, Friedrich Wilhelm, 396n.11
Huber, Wolfgang, xi–xii, 170–72, 226–38, 346–47, 365n.12, 382n.11, 396–97n.20, 408–9n.12, 417n.68
Hubert, Henri, 55–56
Humboldt, Wilhelm von, 178
Hume, David, 9, 28, 57, 82, 281, 371n.27
Husserl, Edmund, 74, 227–28

Ignatius of Loyola, 208, 283, 297
Ihde, Wilhelm, 179–80

James, William, 27–32, 34–38, 41–48, 52–58, 61–67, 69–70, 73–77, 79–81, 84, 94, 99–103, 106–8, 112–13, 171–72, 193–94, 202, 222–23, 256, 258–59, 268, 345, 350–51, 367n.31, 371–72n.35, 374–75n.3, 397n.23, 406n.76

Jaspers, Karl, 50, 139, 151, 153, 205–6, 225, 253, 274, 325, 336–37, 361, 368n.40, 420n.38
Jefferson, Thomas, 321–22
Jellinek, Georg, 189–90
Jesus of Nazareth / Jesus Christ, 26, 30, 36, 77–78, 84, 89, 118–19, 123–25, 152, 168–69, 171–72, 241–42, 262–64, 270, 282, 310–11, 352, 357–59, 366–67n.24, 382n.14
Jung, Matthias, xi–xii, 64, 66, 194–95, 370n.14, 379n.48, 383–84n.4, 387n.40
Jünger, Ernst, 198

Kaftan, Julius, 375n.14
Kant, Immanuel, 9, 13, 28, 32, 37–38, 44–47, 53–54, 61, 65, 75, 97, 99–100, 139, 164–66, 169–70, 173–175, 180–83, 185–86, 188–95, 211, 217, 219, 231, 267–68, 272–73, 349, 360, 366n.16, 380n.13, 432n.49
Kantorowicz, Ernst, 285, 288
Kautsky, Karl, 358
Kestenbaum, Victor, 383–84n.4, 387n.40
Keynes, John Maynard, 279
Kierkegaard, Søren, 9, 32, 119–20, 124, 171, 183–84, 199–200, 228, 266–67, 274
Kippenberg, Hans G., 59
Klempt, Adalbert, 139–40
Knöbl, Wolfgang, xi–xii, 6
Koschorke, Albrecht, 12, 369n.52
Koselleck, Reinhart, 8–9, 96, 133–46, 225, 345–46
Krämer, Felicitas, 397n.23
Kraus, Hans-Christof, 431n.24
Krech, Volkhard, 244
Kroner, Richard, 11
Kühn, Johannes, 141–42
Kühnlein, Michael, 396n.19

Larmore, Charles, 153
Lasker-Schüler, Else, 119–20
Laube, Martin, 88, 91–92, 382nn.10–11
Leeuw, Gerardus van der, 374n.64
Lefort, Claude, 396n.13
Leibniz, Gottfried Wilhelm, 180–84, 189–90

Lenin, Vladimir Ilyich, 130–31
Lessing, Gotthold Ephraim, 116
Levinas, Emmanuel, 175, 273
Lewis, C. S., 128–29
Lichterman, Paul, 426n.14
Locke, John, 141–42
Lotze, Hermann, 46–47
Löwith, Karl, 8–9, 11, 14–15, 96, 136–40, 145–46
Lubac, Henri de, 155
Lübbe, Hermann, 133, 138–39
Lucretius, 149
Luhmann, Niklas, 78
Lukács, Georg, 367n.30, 370n.14
Luther, Martin, 54–55, 88–90, 134–35, 141–42, 181–85, 190, 229, 236–37

MacIntyre, Alasdair, 216
Madsen, Richard, 320
Mann, Thomas, 176–77
Mannheim, Karl, 70–71, 406n.83
Marcel, Gabriel, 225, 274
Marcks, Erich, 176–77
Marcuse, Herbert, 175
Marett, Robert Ranulph, 54–55, 57–58, 62
Marramao, Giacomo, 133
Marsden, George, 150
Martin, David, x–xi, 144, 157, 251–52, 285, 291–92, 298–315, 339–41, 347, 414n.19, 416n.63, 422n.9, 422n.11, 423n.25, 424–25n.55
Marx, Karl, ix, 7, 9, 87, 89–92, 140–41, 183–84, 205, 228, 230, 242, 301, 347–48, 356, 358
Mauss, Marcel, 54–60, 244–45, 277, 373n.56
Mazzini, Giuseppe, 289
Mead, George Herbert, 46–47, 65, 107–8, 201–2, 228–29, 248, 256–60, 266, 269–75, 371–72n.35, 385nn.22–23
Mehring, Reinhard, 137
Meier, Christian, 392n.58
Meinecke, Friedrich, 176–77, 181
Meireis, Torsten, xi–xii
Melanchthon, Philip, 139–40, 183–84
Mencius, ix
Merleau-Ponty, Maurice, 353
Merton, Robert, 279
Meyembergh-Boussart, Monique, 120

Meyer, Thomas, 401n.63
Mommsen, Wolfgang, 397–98n.3
Montaigne, Michel de, 181–82
Moore, Barrington, 196
Morgan, Michael, 387n.39
Moses ben Nachman, 123
Murrmann-Kahl, Michael, 402n.18

Nelson, Benjamin, 244–45, 331–32
Newman, John Henry, 279–80
Niebuhr, H. Richard, x–xi, 92–93, 229, 247–51, 254, 257–76, 278, 280, 284, 290, 293–95, 302, 314, 339, 347, 382n.14, 408–9n.12, 414nn.9–10, 415n.37, 416n.63, 417n.68
Niebuhr, Reinhold, 99, 249, 257–58, 314, 416n.63
Nietzsche, Friedrich, ix, 8–9, 17–18, 22, 31–32, 38–39, 89, 95, 124, 132–33, 165, 183–84, 202, 241–42, 291–92, 347–61, 367n.32
Nohl, Hermann, 24, 370n.14
Nowak, Kurt, 199

Oexle, Otto Gerhard, 420n.32
Origen, 128
Osterhammel, Jürgen, 16, 432–33n.50
Otto, Rudolf, x–xi, 34–38, 43–44, 52–68, 73, 75, 80–81, 198, 223, 345, 384n.6

Pannenberg, Wolfhart, 145–46
Parsons, Talcott, 196, 206–7, 213, 252–53, 316–20, 324, 327, 329
Pascal, Blaise, 128
Paul of Tarsus, 73, 88–89, 168–69, 171–72, 198, 236, 358–59
Paul, Jean, 186–87
Peirce, Charles Sanders, 206, 217–18, 256–57, 371–72n.35
Pfleiderer, Georg, 52
Philip II (King of Spain), 280, 296
Pippin, Robert, 7, 163–64, 366n.21
Pitschmann, Annette, 387n.40
Pius VI (Pope), 158
Pius X (Pope), 36
Plato, 31, 59–60, 74–75, 348–49, 359
Pohlig, Matthias, 139–40
Polke, Christian, 417n.69
Prantl, Heribert, 93

NAME INDEX

Presley, Elvis, 214
Przywara, Erich, 175

Rahner, Karl, 145–46, 298, 330
Ranke, Leopold von, 17, 33
Rawls, John, 3–4, 235
Reinhard, Wolfgang, 236–37, 430n.32
Rendtorff, Trutz, 140–41, 145–46, 382nn.10–11
Renner, Karl, 278–79
Ricœur, Paul, x–xi, 144, 170, 172, 212–13, 216–17, 219–25, 231, 276, 345–47, 368n.44, 396n.19, 407n.8, 407n.10, 415n.37, 417n.68
Riesebrodt, Martin, 419n.23
Ritter, Joachim, 175
Rockefeller, Steven, 383n.3, 385n.18, 386n.29
Rorty, Richard, 164
Rosa, Hartmut, 389n.7
Roth, Robert, 383–84n.4, 384–85n.9, 385n.12
Rothe, Richard, 366–67n.24
Rousseau, Jean-Jacques, 141–42, 189
Royce, Josiah, 63–64, 258–59, 271, 273–74

Sabatier, Auguste, 204
Saint-Exupéry, Antoine de, 66
Sandel, Michael, 231–32
Santayana, George, 103–4, 385n.13, 386n.36
Sartre, Jean-Paul, 225, 227–28
Saussure, Ferdinand de, 205
Sawilla, Jan Marco, 139–40
Scheler, Max, x–xi, 36–38, 61–62, 67, 69–84, 106–7, 291–92, 345, 347–48, 353, 379–80n.5, 380n.13, 384n.8
Schelling, Friedrich Wilhelm Joseph, 204–5
Schieder, Rolf, 6, 425–26n.6, 426–27n.23
Schiller, Friedrich, 181–82, 186–87
Schilling, Heinz, 430n.32
Schleiermacher, Friedrich, 8–9, 13–14, 17, 21–26, 32, 34–37, 43–47, 53–55, 57, 65–67, 73–75, 105, 193–94, 241–43, 267–68, 275, 371–72n.35, 380n.13
Schleissing, Stephan, 139–40, 392n.58
Schlözer, August Ludwig, 139–40
Schluchter, Wolfgang, 412n.14

Schmidinger, Heinrich, 421n.59
Schmidt, Thomas M., 7
Schmidt, Wilhelm, 81
Schmitt, Carl, 136–38, 198, 389n.9, 389–90n.11
Schmoller, Gustav von, 354
Schnädelbach, Herbert, 143, 367n.30
Schneider, Reinhold, 296
Schoeller, Wilfried F., 120
Schopenhauer, Arthur, 17, 241–42, 349, 356
Schupp, Franz, 330–31
Schüßler, Werner, 406n.85
Schweiker, William, 416n.59
Seel, Martin, 149–50
Seifert, Arno, 139–40
Shakespeare, William, 268
Shils, Edward, 307, 419n.23
Siep, Ludwig, 7
Simmel, Georg, 103, 106–7, 406n.83
Smith, Wilfred Cantwell, 21
Smith, William Robertson, 54–55
Söderblom, Nathan, 54–55, 59–63, 80–81
Sohm, Rudolph, 282
Sölle, Dorothee, 129–30
Sombart, Werner, 180–81
Spencer, Herbert, 50
Spengler, Oswald, 177
Spinoza, Baruch de, 356
Spohn, Willfried, 424–25n.55
Spranger, Eduard, 199–200
Stark, Rodney, 412n.14
Stark, Werner, 87, 250–51, 278–98, 347, 419n.23, 419n.27, 421n.50
Stockhorst, Stefanie, 139–40
Strasser, Hermann, 421n.59
Stråth, Bo, 144–45
Strauß, David Friedrich, 241–42
Strauss, Leo, 59, 175–77
Sullivan, Harry Stack, 271
Sullivan, William, 320
Süskind, Hermann, 241–42, 410n.1
Swidler, Ann, 320

Tauler, Johannes, 119–20
Taylor, Charles, x–xi, 2–3, 8, 41–42, 47, 55–56, 79, 94, 96–98, 113–15, 147–56, 160, 163–64, 186–87, 315, 341, 345–46, 379n.46, 387n.39, 394n.24, 396n.19, 398n.9

Teilhard de Chardin, Pierre, 128
Theunissen, Michael, 8, 170–71, 227–30, 346, 396–97n.20
Thomas Aquinas, 126, 271, 283
Tiele, Cornelius, 22
Tillich, Paul, x–xi, 52, 167, 169, 172, 196–214, 224–25, 276, 318–19, 327, 329, 346–47, 406nn.76–77, 417n.68
Tipton, Steven, 320
Tocqueville, Alexis de, 92–93, 320–21, 323
Tolkien, J. R. R., 128–29
Tönnies, Ferdinand, 79
Toscanini, Arturo, 214
Toulmin, Stephen, 191, 215
Touraine, Alain, 179–80
Troeltsch, Ernst, x–xi, 8–9, 17, 22–23, 26–27, 31–36, 38, 40–51, 53–54, 57, 65, 69–70, 77, 79, 83, 127, 155, 165–67, 172, 174–95, 197, 199–204, 206–8, 211–12, 214, 224–25, 241–48, 257–60, 262–69, 274–77, 280–81, 283–85, 293, 326, 331–32, 344–48, 353–59, 361, 365n.11, 366–67n.24, 380n.13, 393n.14, 395n.6, 401n.58, 407n.8, 410n.1, 410–11n.4, 419n.27, 422n.14
Turner, Victor, 151, 412n.15
Tyrell, Hartmann, 244

Voegelin, Eric, 56, 300–1, 427n.25
Vogt, Peter, 392n.58
Voltaire (François-Marie Arouet), 116

Wach, Joachim, 284, 411–12n.12
Wallis, Louis, 411n.10
Weber, Max, 34, 48, 53, 57–58, 69–71, 78, 112–13, 145–46, 150–54, 157, 173–74, 180–81, 197, 203, 209–10, 224, 231, 235–236, 241, 243–48, 251–54, 261, 265–66, 277, 280–85, 292–94, 301–3, 311, 317, 324, 326, 331–33, 335, 340–41, 348, 353–58, 361, 367n.32, 377–78n.24, 406n.83, 419n.23, 422n.9, 422n.14, 422n.19, 424n.42
Wells, H. G., 128
Wesley, John, 294, 424n.42
Williams, Roger, 237
Wilson, Bryan, 418n.11
Wilson, John A., 420n.39
Winckelmann, Johann Joachim, 186–87
Windelband, Wilhelm, 52
Winkler, Heinrich August, 165
Winthrop, John, 321–22
Wobbermin, Georg, 46–47
Wolf, Eric R., 15–16
Wolff, Christian, 190
Wundt, Wilhelm, 46–47, 52, 54
Wuthnow, Robert, 426n.14

Yack, Bernard, 143
Yamin, George J., Jr., 32
Yinger, J. Milton, 294–95, 406n.83, 406n.85

Zabel, Hermann, 133, 140–41
Zoroaster, 325–26

Subject Index

For the benefit of digital users, indexed terms that span two pages (e.g., 52–53) may, on occasion, appear on only one of those pages.

action, ix, 14, 23, 26, 30, 38–39, 47–48, 74, 77, 80–81, 83, 99, 102–9, 111–13, 126–27, 134–39, 144–46, 163–64, 166–72, 178, 180–81, 186–87, 194–95, 200–1, 212, 216–20, 235, 237, 243, 248, 256–57, 270–74, 284–85, 292, 302–3, 314, 323, 327–28, 349, 351, 360, 370n.14
Anglicanism, 210, 280, 287–88, 307, 311
anthropology, 13–14, 37–39, 56, 70–71, 97, 107–8, 122–23, 126–27, 137–38, 144, 147, 166, 168, 174, 186–87, 194–95, 204, 217, 219–20, 229, 236, 257–59, 271–72, 316, 318–19, 338, 345
articulation / expression, 2–3, 9, 11, 13–15, 21, 25, 27–30, 35, 41–42, 45–48, 56–57, 64–66, 77–78, 80, 82–83, 88–89, 95–96, 106, 110, 128–29, 160, 186–87, 195, 206–9, 222, 224, 230–32, 264, 290, 315, 319–20, 322, 327–28, 345, 352, 360
atheism, 7–8, 111–12, 141–42, 242, 244, 249, 269–70, 289, 356
autonomy, 2, 15, 79, 141–42, 154, 164, 169–70, 172, 183–87, 190, 194–95, 211–13, 224–25, 231, 338, 406n.77, *see also* heteronomy; theonomy
Axial Age, x, 35–36, 74–75, 81, 140–46, 151–54, 205–6, 209–11, 253, 281, 288, 302, 315, 325–29, 336–37, 340, 343, 347, 361, 368n.40

belief / (religious) faith, 1–2, 4–9, 11–15, 21, 26–30, 32, 34–39, 41–43, 45–51, 53, 55–60, 62, 67–68, 70–71, 73, 77–78, 80–83, 87, 89, 92–97, 99–100, 102–6, 111–27, 130–31, 139, 141–43, 147–48, 150–52, 154–55, 157–58, 160, 163–64, 168–72, 180–85, 190, 195, 201, 203, 210–11, 213–15, 221–23, 226–27, 231–32, 242, 244, 249–50, 253–54, 263–68, 270–71, 275–76, 278, 280–81, 283, 285–86, 291–93, 297–98, 300–1, 304–5, 308–13, 319, 330–31, 334–35, 340–41, 344–46, 357–58, 387n.1, 413n.26
Buddhism, 50–51, 64–65, 119–20, 207–11, 233, 253, 265, 319–20, 349, 354, 359

Calvinism / Reformed Christianity, 153–54, 210, 236–37, 251, 285–86, 295–98
charisma, 77–78, 82–83, 251, 281–85, 300–1, 310, 313
Christianity
  Catholic, 15, 36–37, 59–61, 70–71, 75, 88, 90, 94–97, 116, 119–20, 123, 128, 141–42, 145–47, 150, 153–55, 159, 177, 183–84, 197, 207–11, 224, 229–30, 236–37, 248–51, 260–61, 277–86, 288–93, 295–98, 301, 305–6, 311–14, 329–31, 333–39, 342–43, 347, 379–80n.5, 386n.34, 393n.14, 421n.50
  Evangelical, 266, 310, 312, 315
  Orthodox, 29, 249, 251, 260–61, 336, 421n.50
  post-totalitarian, 94–95, 130–31, 227, 345–46
  Protestant, xi–xii, 6–10, 15, 26, 34–36, 40, 45, 59, 69, 88–90, 96–97, 99, 112–13, 123, 127, 129, 139–42, 145–46, 159, 170–71, 176–77, 183–85, 191–92, 196–97, 199, 204, 207–11, 223–24, 226, 231–32, 236–37, 241, 244, 246–51, 253, 257–58, 260–61,

SUBJECT INDEX

Christianity (*cont.*)
277, 280–84, 296, 298, 311–14, 316–17, 329–36, 344, 347, 354, *see also individual entries*
church, 6–7, 26–27, 36, 43, 45–46, 59–60, 77–80, 84, 88, 91, 93, 110–13, 115, 123, 125, 131, 133–34, 147, 152–60, 167–69, 197, 208, 210, 226–27, 232–33, 236–37, 242, 251, 260–66, 277–78, 280–92, 294–300, 304–13, 322–23, 330–31, 333–39, 342–43, 356–59, 366–67n.24, 419n.27
colonialism, 21–22, 57, 288–89, 296–97, 310, 339–41
Confucianism, ix, 16, 58, 119–20, 210–11, 233, 265
contingency / experience of contingency, 4, 14–15, 25, 28–29, 32, 42–43, 50–51, 96, 103–4, 119, 139, 142–43, 153, 158, 170, 186–87, 194–95, 216–18, 220, 242–43, 257, 274–75, 345–46, 348–50, 356, 359–60
creativity, 2–3, 26, 28, 31, 38–39, 47–49, 79–80, 103–6, 122, 167–68, 177, 179–83, 195, 198, 209, 212–13, 218–20, 256–57, 384n.8
critical theory, 89–90, 173–74, 229–30, 330–31
Cultural Protestantism, 9–10, 45, 59, 237, 247–48

Daoism, 119–20, 210–11, 385n.18
democracy, ix, 6, 15–16, 79–80, 84, 88–89, 91, 93–94, 97, 99, 109–14, 157, 164, 172, 176–77, 213, 215, 227, 232–33, 236–37, 261, 295–96, 299–300, 320–24, 330–36, 338, 345–46, 352, 355, 386n.26, 413n.26
denomination / denominationalism, 154–55, 247–50, 254, 260–64, 284, 290–91, 294–95, 302, 305, 311–12, 318, 335, 339–42, 421n.50, 422n.11
differentiation, (functional), 78, 99–100, 247, 261, 294, 304, 337–38
disenchantment, 16, 58–59, 150–53, 157, 251, 301, 333, 355–56, 367n.32
doctrine, religious, 4–5, 22, 27, 36, 42, 45–46, 48–49, 53–54, 58–60, 63–64, 73–74, 84, 91, 110–12, 152, 207–8, 256, 261–63, 268, 277, 281–82, 290, 292–93, 299, 312–13, 319, 328, 335, 354, 358

empiricism, 28–29, 43, 46–47, 53–54
Enlightenment, 9, 12, 15–16, 56, 58, 60, 96, 113–14, 119–20, 139–40, 141–43, 145–46, 150, 156, 158, 180–81, 183–84, 190–93, 236–37, 263–64, 267, 326, 338
equality, 3–5, 16, 77–78, 163, 230–31, 233–35, 261, 270–71, 290, 299–300, 326, 328–29, 346
Eurocentrism, 1, 12–13, 15–17, 36, 253, 255, 337–38, 361
evolution, (religious), 38, 50–51, 78, 123, 201–2, 253–54, 317–18, 325–28
evolutionism, 6, 50, 96, 139, 201–2, 242, 253–54, 328, 359–60
existentialism / existential philosophy, 50–51, 137, 199–200, 225, 256–57, 274–76
experience / religious experience, 4–5, 13–14, 21–25, 27–28, 30, 34–39, 44–52, 54–59, 61–68, 72–74, 80–82, 84, 88–89, 94, 99–102, 104–9, 111–14, 118, 122, 125–27, 132, 134–35, 137–39, 144–46, 148–51, 153–54, 157, 160, 166–67, 170–72, 193–95, 199–200, 203, 206–7, 212–13, 216–17, 220–24, 228–30, 247, 256, 262, 267–68, 272–75, 280–81, 290, 292–93, 299–300, 310–11, 319, 324, 328–29, 345, 349, 351, 384–85n.9
expressivism, 11, 25, 43, 47, 77, 97, 154–55, 159, 165–66, 178, 185–89, 211, 213, 230–32, 309, 319–22, 329, 345, 398n.9

feeling / religious feeling, 11, 13–14, 24–28, 33, 36–37, 43–46, 48–50, 59–67, 71–74, 79–80, 82–83, 90–92, 95, 100–1, 104–7, 109, 111–12, 116–18, 120–22, 125, 130, 141–42, 150, 153, 164, 167–68, 171–72, 178, 193–94, 216, 218, 229, 231, 270, 272, 274–75, 319, 321, 351–53, 358, 360

SUBJECT INDEX 481

freedom / political freedom, ix, 1–6, 9–16, 18, 25, 31–32, 34, 38–39, 84, 87–93, 96–98, 116–17, 122–23, 126–27, 139, 141–42, 163–69, 172, 175–76, 179–82, 185–87, 189, 193, 211–12, 225–27, 230–37, 241, 244, 266–67, 274–76, 296, 311–12, 320–21, 330–31, 341, 344–48, 366n.21, 373–74n.63, 395n.1
- communicative freedom, 170–71, 225, 227–34, 346–47, 408n.5, 409n.19
- indebted freedom, 15, 164, 166–72, 197, 211–14, 231–32, 346–47
- moral freedom, 44–45, 97, 164, 166–67, 180–82, 185, 190–95, 211, 231

genealogy, (affirmative), 15–16, 18, 147, 149–50, 257, 269–70, 293–94, 338–39, 348, 350–51, 353–55, 357, 359–61
gift, 145–46, 213, 231–32, 267, 275
globalization, 1–2, 144, 251–52, 254–55, 298, 302, 310, 337–43, 345–47

Hegelianism, x–xi, 3–8, 11–13, 15, 17–18, 25–26, 29, 31–32, 50, 89–91, 94, 96–98, 110, 140–41, 144, 163–64, 169–71, 208–9, 212, 225, 346, 348, 350–51, 360, 369n.53, 371–72n.35, 385n.12
hermeneutics, 12, 15, 23, 46–47, 63–66, 175–76, 180–81, 183–84, 187–88, 194–95, 204, 216, 221–24, 256–59, 276, 303–4, 346, 412n.14, 416n.54
heteronomy, 4–5, 169, 184–85, 211–13, 406n.77, see also autonomy; theonomy
Hinduism, 57–58, 233, 326, 354
historicism, 47, 50–51, 53, 127, 165, 174–77, 180–81, 187–88, 199–201, 204, 248, 256–59, 263, 270–71, 275–76, 303, 401n.58
historicization, 14–15, 23–24, 42–43, 127, 166–67, 192–93, 241–42, 246, 350
human rights/dignity, ix, 2–3, 37–38, 56, 106, 117, 141–42, 149–50, 158, 163, 166, 172, 175–80, 187–90, 195, 211, 213–15, 235, 237, 242, 244, 431n.19

ideal / ideal formation, 2–4, 11, 15, 17, 26–28, 32–33, 38, 45, 47, 49–50, 61–62, 72–73, 91, 94, 103–6, 108–9, 111–14, 122–23, 125–26, 166, 169, 178–81, 183–87, 191, 199–200, 203, 224–25, 235, 237, 242, 251–53, 262–66, 274, 284–86, 315, 323, 344–45, 349–52, 357–58, 360, 366–67n.24, 385n.16
idealism, 26, 28–31, 46–47, 50–52, 97–98, 181–82, 190, 200, 206, 212
imperialism, 57, 178, 187–88, 286–89, 311, 342–43
indisposability, 91, 169–70, 231–32, 234
individualism / individualization, 22, 26, 32, 43, 49–51, 56, 79, 94, 152–55, 166, 177–79, 181–83, 185, 213, 221, 224, 230–32, 260–61, 273–74, 285–86, 309, 313, 319–22, 325, 329, 341
institution / religious institution / institutionalization, 3–4, 6–7, 22–24, 27, 43, 45–46, 48–49, 54–56, 73–74, 80, 84, 87, 90–91, 94, 99–103, 109–14, 144–46, 155, 157, 163, 176–77, 208, 210–11, 220, 226, 228–33, 244, 250–53, 261, 263–66, 277–78, 281–85, 297, 299–300, 303–6, 308–9, 311–13, 318, 320, 329–31, 339–42, 366–67n.24, 409n.19
intellectualization (of religion), 12–13, 21, 30–31, 35–37, 44–45, 87, 224, 248, 268, 283
interpretation, 21, 27–28, 44–45, 47–48, 55–56, 63–66, 72–73, 82–83, 88–89, 100–2, 106, 108, 122–23, 135, 145–46, 216–17, 220–23, 271–73, 416n.54
intersubjectivity / relationality, 15, 38–39, 82–83, 94, 107–8, 112–13, 170–71, 183, 204, 218, 227–29, 258–59, 271–73, 345–47
Islam, 42, 50–51, 57, 81, 165, 222, 233, 265, 318, 326, 336, 338, 340–41

Judaism, 8–9, 57, 59–60, 88–89, 94–95, 119, 122–23, 125, 168–72, 174, 183–84, 191–92, 206, 222, 224, 227–28, 233, 246–51, 269, 277–82, 287–88, 295–96, 298, 325–26, 341, 349–50, 352, 355, 357–60
justice, 2–6, 15, 125, 170, 219, 231, 235–36, 330–31, 349–50, 352, 355, 360

liberalism, ix, 3–4, 15, 89, 92–93, 97, 99, 119–20, 139, 156, 164, 175, 180–81, 191, 215, 227, 235, 280, 306, 335–36, 341, 356
Lutheranism, 12, 59–60, 153–54, 183–84, 236–37, 251, 282, 287–88, 304–5, 421n.50

magic, 54–55, 77–78, 127, 152–54, 205, 208–10, 223–24, 281, 356
Marxism, 5–6, 8–9, 89, 91–92, 130–31, 196, 210, 265–66, 278–79, 291–92, 301, 305, 316–17, 350, 354, 358
materialism, 29, 42, 44–45, 199–200, 344–45, 374–75n.3
metaphysics, 4, 7, 24–25, 29–30, 37–38, 44–45, 50, 73, 76, 82–83, 164, 168, 171–72, 175, 182–85, 190–91, 204–5, 244, 269–70
Methodism, 291–94, 311, 421n.50
modernity / modern, ix, 2–4, 12, 15–16, 34, 36, 52, 60, 70–72, 79, 87–93, 95–98, 111–12, 123, 127, 134–43, 147–48, 150–53, 155–56, 160, 168, 177, 180–81, 183–85, 191–92, 207–8, 210–11, 224, 227, 230, 234, 236–37, 241, 243, 246–47, 252, 257–58, 265–66, 277, 279, 286–88, 301–2, 306, 311, 313, 315, 317–18, 321–22, 324–26, 329–33, 337–38, 341–42, 344–45, 355–56
modernization / modernization theory, 6, 69, 115, 132–33, 143–45, 157–58, 179–80, 183–84, 246–47, 251–53, 287–88, 313, 317–18, 332–35, 339, 341–42, 345
mysticism, 22, 28–29, 53–54, 59–60, 63–65, 73–75, 106–7, 119–20, 141–42, 222–23, 244–45, 260, 283, 297
myth, 26–27, 42, 53–54, 58–59, 63–64, 81, 88–89, 111–12, 119–20, 122–23, 126–29, 156, 165, 191–92, 194–95, 204–7, 209–10, 223–24, 260, 300, 318–19, 327–28, 345, 352, 355

nationalism, 79, 95–96, 131, 158–59, 177, 180–81, 187–88, 216, 250, 262–63, 265–66, 280, 288–91, 296–98, 300–1, 353, 431n.19

naturalism, 9, 33–34, 36, 42, 44–45, 94, 126–27, 130–31, 269, 356, 371n.27, 373–74n.63
norms, 47, 89, 195, 200, 216–19, 248, 270–72, 274, 318–19
numinous, the, 35–36, 58–60, 63–67, 223–24

Pentecostalism, 251–52, 254–55, 302, 310–13, 315, 339
phenomenology, 24, 27–28, 36–37, 61–62, 65, 70–72, 74–75, 78, 80–83, 106–7, 122, 171–72, 203, 216, 221–24, 345, 372n.40, 374n.64
philosophy of life (*Lebensphilosophie*), 122, 126, 183–84
Pietism, 112–13, 315
pluralism, 2–5, 29–30, 144, 147–49, 157, 182–83, 187, 194–95, 215–16, 235, 247–48, 261–63, 265–66, 300, 313, 325, 336–37, 340–42
power, 27, 78, 87, 131, 138, 154–55, 163–64, 177–78, 202–3, 246, 251, 253–54, 285–86, 289–90, 296–97, 299–301, 304–5, 327–29, 335, 351, 353, 357–58
pragmatism, ix, 23, 27, 29–30, 46–48, 53–54, 69, 71, 75–76, 84, 94, 100–1, 122, 140–41, 164, 173–74, 205–6, 216–18, 248, 256–59, 270–73, 275–76, 371–72n.35, 384n.8, 401n.58, 404n.45, 406n.76, 416n.54
privatization (of religion), 147, 151, 213, 254, 334–35, 338, 341–42
progress, 25, 32, 34, 38, 42, 50–51, 78, 94, 110–13, 134–39, 150, 159, 178, 187–88, 192, 194–95, 197, 201, 235, 253–54, 256, 267, 293–94, 335, 345–48, 359–60
prophecy, 29–30, 67–68, 77–78, 127, 198–99, 202–3, 206, 208–10, 223–24, 237, 268, 282, 295–96, 329, 347, 355–58, 361
Puritanism, 263–64, 315, 321, 356

rationalism, 36, 38–39, 55, 99–100, 165–67, 175, 179–80, 182–83, 191–93, 195, 241, 243–44, 312–13 rationality, 27–28, 31, 35–38, 49–50, 52, 58–61, 65, 73–74, 88, 94, 97, 111–12, 116–17, 139–42, 144–46, 148, 169, 178, 180–81, 191–93, 195, 216–17, 228, 267, 272, 275, 293, 312–13, 317–18, 328, 344–45

rationalization, 34–36, 58–60, 67, 79, 112–13, 145–46, 157, 179–80, 244, 251, 301, 332–33, 354

reason, 2–4, 10–11, 14–15, 23, 25, 32, 36–38, 42, 49–50, 59, 73–74, 96–97, 122–27, 130–31, 138–39, 141–42, 144, 164–65, 171–72, 177, 180–81, 186–87, 190–94, 211, 235, 260, 267–69, 275, 366–67n.24

reflection / reflexivity, 15, 21, 23–25, 27–28, 38–39, 47–50, 67–68, 80, 84, 103, 106, 167–68, 169–71, 184–85, 198, 206, 212, 219–20, 264, 315, 328

Reformation, 12, 16, 88–90, 134–37, 152–53, 181–85, 237, 267, 279–80, 282, 292–93, 296–98, 304–5, 325–26, 341, 352, 366–67n.24, 427n.33

relativism, 15, 50–51, 53, 58, 148, 164, 174, 187–88, 192–93, 200, 224–25, 270, 328–29, 349

religion
    ancient, 54–55, 88–89, 119–20, 127–28, 223–24, 253, 287–88, 295–96, 324–26, 328–29, 352, 358
    "archaic," 152–53, 216, 286–89, 324–29, 336–37, 358
    extra-European, 16, 21–22, 35–36, 57–58, 62, 78–80, 91–92, 119–20, 135–36, 143, 164–65, 169, 189, 210–11, 237, 241–44, 247–55, 260–64, 280, 284, 286–87, 290–91, 295, 297–98, 305, 308–14, 317, 319–20, 330–31, 333–42, 347, 355, 361
    non-Christian, 1, 21–22, 33–36, 42–43, 48–49, 57, 87, 91, 140–41, 156, 215, 249, 336–39, *see also individual entries*
    "primitive" / tribal, 54, 57–58, 81, 152–53, 209–10, 223–24, 242, 287, 324–29, 336–37

world religion, 6, 48–50, 112–13, 241–42, 253–55, 265, 317, 326, 336–37, 339–40, 354, 358, 360

responsibility, 137, 172, 198–200, 228–30, 235, 248, 258–59, 266–67, 270–73, 275, 350

revelation, 13–15, 42–46, 73–74, 78, 80–81, 110, 141–42, 170, 198–99, 201, 203–4, 207–8, 211–12, 248, 259, 267–70

Revolution, French, 12, 88, 117, 158, 179, 188–90, 233–34, 289, 304–5, 352

ritual / religious practice, 4–5, 21–22, 41–42, 54–55, 58–60, 62, 77, 80, 95, 99–100, 132, 152, 206, 208, 216, 224, 242, 262, 281, 293–95, 300, 303, 308–9, 311–13, 328, 340–41, 345

sacralization, 14–15, 53, 59–61, 67–68, 79, 99, 110–14, 159, 213–14, 223–24, 246–47, 285–88, 292, 294–95, 300–1, 312–13, 336–37, 351, 366n.23, 413n.26
    of the people / the nation / the state, 56, 131, 246–47, 286–88, 295, 298, 431n.19, *see also* self-sacralization, (collective)
    of the person, 56, 154, 246–47, 431n.19
    of the ruler, 286–88, 292, 298, 325, 328–29, 431n.19

sacrament, 59–60, 153–54, 208–10, 224, 281, 329

sacred, the, x, 21–22, 35–36, 43–44, 52–56, 59–65, 67, 80–81, 151–52, 209, 223–24, 300–1, 345, 351

sacredness, 21–22, 35, 52–55, 57–63, 67–68, 81, 88, 110–11, 151–52, 169–70, 189, 205–6, 209–10, 213–14, 222–24, 242–44, 270–71, 288–90, 292, 300–1, 307, 318, 327–29, 336–37, 351, 379n.46

Scholasticism / neo-Scholasticism, 36–37, 70, 244–45, 296–97

sect, 208, 247, 251, 260, 262, 264, 280, 283–86, 290–95, 297, 302, 331–32, 358, 419n.27, 421n.50

"secular option," 41–42, 55–60, 67–68, 115, 147–51, 154, 160, 227, 290 secularism, 17, 21–22, 42, 47–51, 56–57, 61–62, 67, 70–71, 79, 82, 84, 96–97, 115, 128, 132–33, 142–43, 145–46, 148–49, 151, 248–50, 277, 288, 291, 300–1, 305, 308, 311–12, 320, 337, 341–42, 344, 413n.26

secularity, 1, 9, 17, 27–28, 33, 36–37, 42, 51, 56, 58, 67–68, 82–83, 92–95, 99, 109, 126, 135–36, 138–40, 142–43, 149–51, 153–54, 159–60, 164, 167–68, 205–6, 210–11, 213–14, 231–32, 264–69, 280, 286, 289, 300, 304–5, 309, 313, 317–18, 328, 335–42, 345–46, 353, 359, 387n.1

secularization / theory of secularization, 7–8, 14–15, 35, 41–42, 53, 55–56, 67–70, 79, 87, 91, 93–94, 96–98, 110, 115, 119, 131–49, 156–60, 183–84, 192–93, 208, 213–14, 227, 231–32, 246–47, 250–52, 254, 277–79, 299–300, 302–6, 308–10, 313, 317–20, 333–34, 337–39, 341–42, 345–47, 356, 379n.46

self-determination, 3, 15, 97, 163–64, 169–70, 172, 190–91, 211, 231–32, 234, 346–47

self-evidence, (sense of), 3, 13–14, 36–37, 49–50, 62, 71–76, 80–84, 148, 167, 199–200, 345, 351

self-formation, 65–66, 103–8, 113–14, 170–71, 216, 220–21, 228–29, 258, 266–67, 270–71

self-realization, 2–4, 10–12, 25, 38, 103–5, 107, 177–80, 211, 213, 228–31, 243, 322, 385n.12

self-sacralization, (collective), 131, 265–66, 286–87, 289, 295, 298, 325, 347, 431n.19

self-transcendence, 23, 27–28, 45–46, 65–68, 74–75, 94, 106–8, 126, 170, 195, 216, 221, 247, 263, 319, 324, 387n.40

sign / semiotics, 63–65, 73, 145, 166, 174, 187–88, 192–95, 197, 204–6, 208–9, 253–54, 257, 271, 319, 328

state, 7–8, 12, 14, 16, 26, 69, 79–80, 88, 92–94, 125, 131, 136–39, 141–43, 154–55, 157–59, 178–79, 183–84, 215, 227, 233, 236–37, 247, 260–61, 284–91, 295–97, 299–300, 305–8, 311–14, 320, 323–29, 334–37, 341–43, 347, 355, 358–61, 366–67nn.23–24, 422n.19, 424–25n.55

symbol / symbolization, 13–14, 22–23, 27, 47–48, 59–60, 62–65, 73, 126–27, 166, 174, 187–88, 194–95, 197, 204–11, 224, 318–19, 325, 327, 404n.44, 407n.19

teleology, ix, 4, 6, 10, 14–15, 17, 32–33, 37, 50–51, 87, 90–91, 96–100, 139, 142–43, 166–67, 178, 200–2, 217, 225, 243, 272, 275, 324–25, 346–47, 359–60

theonomy, 167, 169–70, 184–85, 211–14, 224–25, *see also* autonomy; heteronomy

tolerance, 84, 116–17, 141–43, 215, 236–37, 294–95, 341

transcendence, 32, 43, 45, 50, 57–58, 63, 81, 99–102, 106, 111–13, 132, 139–42, 145–46, 150–54, 168, 205–7, 209–10, 221, 247–48, 250, 253, 264–67, 281, 315, 319, 325–26, 329, 336–37, 358, 361, 372n.40, 379n.46, 387n.40

transcendental philosophy / (neo-) Kantianism, 26, 28, 44–47, 97, 103, 139, 164–66, 169–70, 174–76, 180–83, 185–87, 192–95, 211, 217, 231, 272, 349

truth / validity, 4, 24–27, 42–46, 49–50, 58, 72–76, 81–84, 88, 103, 106, 117–18, 127–29, 148, 178–79, 184–87, 192–93, 195, 199–200, 204–5, 219, 242, 248, 259, 266–70, 288, 325, 327–28, 335, 351, 356, 374–75n.3

universal/global history (of religion), 12–13, 15–16, 18, 57–58, 96, 139–40, 145–46, 196, 201–3, 205–6, 214, 246, 255, 316, 318, 325–27, 329, 331, 343, 347–48, 361, 368n.47

universalism, (moral), x, 2–4, 18, 26–27, 33, 50–51, 70, 81, 83, 110–11, 113–14, 125, 131, 153–54, 156, 164, 166–67, 170, 178–80, 186–88, 192–95, 215–17, 219–20, 231, 242, 245–48,

SUBJECT INDEX   485

250–55, 259, 262–67, 269–71, 274, 278, 280, 283–90, 292, 294–98, 304, 315, 318, 328–40, 343, 347–48, 351, 353–54, 358–61

utilitarianism, 43, 75–76, 177–80, 211, 213, 230–31, 319–23, 329, 360

values / value commitment / value conflict, ix, 2–5, 10, 36–38, 49–50, 61–62, 71–73, 78, 80–83, 88–89, 94, 100–9, 111–14, 116–17, 139, 147–50, 163, 166–67, 169–70, 179–81, 186–88, 192–93, 195, 199–200, 206–7, 211, 215–17, 219–21, 227, 231–37, 244, 247–48, 265–67, 269–72, 294, 316–20, 328, 345–52, 354, 356–57, 359–60, 385n.16, 387n.1

violence / history of violence, ix, 94–95, 112, 130–31, 137, 158, 195, 251–52, 265, 293–94, 302, 313–15, 346